International Management Behavior

Rigorously revised, the ninth edition of this successful, established textbook is ideal for current and future global leaders who want to lead international businesses sustainably and with impact. Combining a wealth of theoretical knowledge with real-world situations from diverse cultures, countries, and industries, the book brings key concepts to life while offering tools and strategies for putting them into practice. Reflecting global trends, this new edition features a greater focus on culture, virtual teams, leadership paradoxes, digital transformations, and a mindset-centered approach to dynamic change. All-new examples and cases contribute to bringing the book completely up to date, while reflection questions and a rich suite of online teaching resources (including suggested student exercises and classroom activities, teaching notes, further resources, and access to Aperian Globesmart) make this an essential tool for developing mindful, global leaders.

Martha L. Maznevski is Professor of Organizational Behavior and Faculty Co-Director for Executive Education at Ivey Business School, Western University, Ontario. She has 30 years of research and teaching experience in global leadership, specializing in cross-cultural effectiveness, global teams and collaboration, and leading in complex and dynamic organizations and environments. She has worked in more than 50 countries and with leaders from around the world.

Henry W. Lane is Professor Emeritus at the D'Amore-McKim School of Business, Northeastern University and at the Ivey Business School, Western University, Ontario. His research and teaching interests include executing global strategy, cross-cultural management, organizational learning, and managing change. In 2009, he received the Academy of Management, International Management Division's Outstanding Educator Award, and the 2009 Academy of Management Review Decade Award.

Vanessa C. Hasse is Assistant Professor of International Business at the Ivey Business School, Western University, Ontario. Her research focuses on organizational responses to performance signals and outlier events in international contexts, as well as the impact cultural dimensions have on managerial decision-making. As a management educator, she has authored several case studies and has been recognized for her innovations in designing transformative learning experiences.

Rikke Kristine Nielsen is Associate Professor at the Department of Communication & Psychology at Aalborg University, Denmark. Her main research areas are organizational paradox, global leadership, and engaged scholarship, and she enjoys working with practitioners in both research and teaching to enable others to make a positive difference through knowledge cocreation and exchange.

"This ninth edition is the best version yet. Tightly integrated and forward-looking, it provides insightful concepts and frameworks as well as immediately actionable guidance, while focusing on the development of global leadership skills."

Allan Bird, Rikkyo University

"Continues to stand alone in providing students a practical approach to being effective global leaders, while incorporating a foundation of relevant models and frameworks."

William Blake, Queen's University

"This is a seminal work that is thoroughly evidence-based from the research literature and is written in a manner that will catalyze the intellectual curiosity of both undergraduate and graduate students. This is a tremendous resource for the cross-cultural education community."

Mark E. Mendenhall, University of Tennessee

"A brilliant toolbox to help the reader gain valuable insights and reflect on their own experiences. The people-centric approach and concept of mindfulness underlines the importance of being able to balance 'in the moment' evaluation of a situation with the strategic goals of an organization."

Bente Toftkaer, Danish Confederation of Industry

"This book is an excellent resource for any international human resource management course, especially with its updated content and case studies that are extremely relevant for today's global context in which leaders and companies operate."

Poornima Luthra, Copenhagen Business School

International Management Behavior

Global and Sustainable Leadership

NINTH EDITION

Martha L. Maznevski
University of Western Ontario

Henry W. Lane
Northeastern University

Vanessa C. Hasse
University of Western Ontario

Rikke Kristine Nielsen
Aalborg University

CAMBRIDGE
UNIVERSITY PRESS

Shaftesbury Road, Cambridge CB2 8EA, United Kingdom

One Liberty Plaza, 20th Floor, New York, NY 10006, USA

477 Williamstown Road, Port Melbourne, VIC 3207, Australia

314–321, 3rd Floor, Plot 3, Splendor Forum, Jasola District Centre, New Delhi – 110025, India

103 Penang Road, #05-06/07, Visioncrest Commercial, Singapore 238467

Cambridge University Press is part of Cambridge University Press & Assessment,
a department of the University of Cambridge.

We share the University's mission to contribute to society through the pursuit of education, learning and research at the highest international levels of excellence.

www.cambridge.org
Information on this title: www.cambridge.org/highereducation/isbn/9781009489201

DOI: 10.1017/9781009489188

Eighth edition © Henry W. Lane and Martha L. Maznevski 2019

Ninth edition © Martha L. Maznevski, Henry W. Lane, Vanessa C. Hasse, and
Rikke Kristine Nielsen 2025

This publication is in copyright. Subject to statutory exception and to the provisions of relevant collective licensing agreements, no reproduction of any part may take place without the written permission of Cambridge University Press & Assessment.

When citing this work, please include a reference to the DOI 10.1017/9781009489188
First published 2025

Eighth edition 2019
Ninth edition 2025

A catalogue record for this publication is available from the British Library.

A Cataloging-in-Publication data record for this book is available from the Library of Congress

ISBN 978-1-009-48920-1 Hardback
ISBN 978-1-009-48921-8 Paperback

Additional resources for this publication at www.cambridge.org/maznevski

Cambridge University Press & Assessment has no responsibility for the persistence or accuracy of URLs for external or third-party internet websites referred to in this publication and does not guarantee that any content on such websites is, or will remain, accurate or appropriate.

To Julianna, Katie, Andrea, Russell, Arielle, and Alexander, to help
them inspire the next generations of dialogue and sustainability.
Martha L. Maznevski

To all the friends who have helped me learn about their cultures,
and my own.
Henry (Harry) W. Lane

To my family and friends, for instilling in me a curiosity about the world
and delight in the wonder that inhabits it.
Vanessa C. Hasse

To my children, Andreas and Dagny, who I hope will grow up to both appreciate
their heritage and at the same time take responsible, global action.
Rikke Kristine Nielsen

Contents

Preface		*page* xi
Acknowledgments		xviii
Introduction		1

Part I The New Global Context

1	Global Leaders in the 21st Century	7
2	Pathways to Mindful Global Leadership: Mindset, Competences, and Paradox Thinking	32
3	Culture: The Context of Meaning in International Management	58

Decision-Making Cases

Case I-1 McDonald's Argentina	83
Case I-2 Arla Foods and the Cartoon Crisis (A)	90
Case I-3 Tony Jamous at Oyster HR: Leadership Dilemma in a Global Virtual Organization	100

Part II Leading People across Contexts

4	Mapping Culture to Bridge and Integrate	117
5	Communicating across Cultures: Bridging and Integrating	149
6	High-Performing Global Teams	179
7	Talent Management: Selection, Preparation, and Assignment of Global Leaders	211

Decision-Making Cases

Case II-1 Charles Foster Sends an Email (A)	237
Case II-2 Diglot Capital Management: A Very Serious Ghost Story	240
Case II-3 Leadership Crisis at Steelworks' Xiamen Plant	250

Case II-4 Uwa Ode: Embracing Life and Career
across Cultures — 258

Case II-5 Selecting a Country Manager for Delta
Beverages India: Part 1 — 265

Case II-5 Selecting a Country Manager for Delta
Beverages India: Part 2 — 268

Part III Executing Strategy in a Global Context

8 Strategy and Organizational Forms — 273

9 Achieving Organizational Alignment for Performance — 310

10 Leading Change in Global Organizations — 344

Decision-Making Cases

Case III-1 Cushy Armchair — 371

Case III-2 Beiersdorf AG: Expanding Nivea's Global Reach — 373

Case III-3 Tiffany and Swatch: Lessons from an
International Strategic Alliance — 389

Case III-4 CCS Logistics: Culture Change Driving
Accountability and Responsibility — 402

Part IV Purpose, Sustainability, and Integrity

11 Toward Sustainability and Responsible Organizations — 417

12 Competing with Integrity and Ethical Decision-Making — 445

Decision-Making Cases

Case IV-1 GetYourGuide: Managing a Sudden Shock
to Business Growth — 485

Case IV-2 Ghana Investment Fund Limited: Ethical Issues — 497

Index — 506

Preface

> The real voyage of discovery consists not in seeking new landscapes, but in having new eyes
>
> Marcel Proust, French novelist (1871–1922)

Welcome to the Ninth Edition!

The international business environment has changed substantially since we published the eighth edition in 2019. Significant occurrences included global phenomena such as the COVID-19 pandemic straining health care systems worldwide and impacting millions of people, extreme weather events contributing to increased starvation and human migration, a global recession, the wars in Ukraine and the Middle East, and the rise of artificial intelligence.

To reflect these changes, we've crafted this edition with a fresh look so that instructors have the latest thinking needed to educate modern global managers and readers aspiring to be global managers in this new environment. Accordingly, we have revised and updated the content significantly to include:

- new chapters, concepts, and current examples to illuminate the complexity of today's environment;
- the addition of paradox theory to complement the thread of mindfulness – context awareness and a process orientation – that we wove through the eighth edition;
- a substantial revision of our coverage of sustainability;
- new teaching cases dealing with relevant management issues for use as a current textbook in courses on international or cross-cultural management and leadership.

Welcome to New Authors!

We are joined by two new authors in this edition, Vanessa C. Hasse (Ivey Business School, Canada) and Rikke K. Nielsen (Aalborg University, Denmark), who bring expertise that is highly relevant to understanding and navigating the current global environment. Vanessa's research centers on global strategy in uncertain and complex contexts. Rikke's work contributes to an increased understanding of sustainability challenges and examines organizational paradoxes faced by global leaders. Both are innovative and award-winning teachers.

Developing Global Leaders: A Research-Grounded, Pragmatically Tested Text

We have developed, refined, and tested the perspectives in this book for more than 40 years with undergraduates, graduate students, and practicing executives of all levels and in all types of organizations around the world. We have found this material applicable to large multinationals, small-to-medium sized enterprises (SMEs), born-global organizations, and nongovernmental organizations (NGOs). Users have also found it useful for managing domestic organizations with diverse workforces as well as for managing international companies.

The extensive supplementary material provided in the online Instructor's Manual (www.cambridge.org/maznevski) combines the conceptual knowledge with sample syllabi and assessments, contextually based skill-building class exercises, cases, PowerPoint presentations, and video links to provide an effective learning package.

In addition to drawing on the up-to-date research of experts in the business and management fields, we have conducted our own research on the issues and skills relevant to international management. Importantly, we have lived, worked, and taught internationally and bring that practicality on how best to train global managers to this text.

Objectives

The objectives in writing this text and for developing courses based on it are fourfold:

1. Individual Awareness.
   a) Help readers increase recognition of the pervasive and hidden influence of culture on behavior, particularly with respect to management practices.
   b) Help readers better understand and identify how their approaches to decision-making and problem solving are influenced by their own culture.
   c) Augment global "people skills" that may be underdeveloped as a complement to existing technical or business skills.
2. Organizational Awareness.
   a) Develop familiarity with the types of situations and issues that managers often confront when working globally.
   b) Examine, analyze, and solve actual management situations in which an appreciation of cultural differences can influence the execution of global strategy and make a difference to performance.

c) Understand the influence of culture on strategy, structure, organizational systems, and change, as well as on individual behavior.
3. Skill Development. Develop skill in using selected analytical tools (frameworks) that can guide managers working across cultures. Important examples include:
   a) The MBI (Map-Bridge-Integrate) Model for use in interpersonal and/or team situations.
   b) The Strategic Alignment Model for use in organizational diagnosis, executing strategy, and aligning the organization.
   c) The Organizational Change Framework to guide agile change programs.
4. Encouragement of Sustainability, Social Responsibility, and Ethical Behavior. We challenge readers to consider their current and future responsibilities as global leaders more broadly than from simply a financial perspective.

Orientations

Based on our research and experience, we have developed distinct orientations and perspectives that inform our approach to educating global leaders, which we elucidate below.

Management Focus

In this book we take the perspective of practicing managers and managers-to-be who are faced with situations requiring action. We therefore provide a problem-solving approach to international business. International business activities are complex situations in which both business factors and cultural factors are simultaneously embedded and need to be managed together. The skills needed to cross boundaries cannot be isolated from management realities, and appreciating various and multiple influences on behavior can make a difference in outcome and performance.

Behavioral Focus

This book emphasizes that the human element in managing effectively across cultures is just as important as, and sometimes more important than, the technical or functional elements. However, most managers develop stronger technical or business skills than the behavioral boundary-spanning interpersonal and cultural skills. They need to complement these strong business backgrounds with behavioral skills; if they don't, they may never get the opportunity to use those business or technical skills.

Process Focus

Related to the behavioral focus is the process focus: behaving, interacting, learning, and moving forward to meet objectives. This perspective is an important contributor to success in a global market. In other words, leading well in an international setting is not just about having the right characteristics or competences; it's about the dynamics of knowing how to adapt quickly and effectively, how to take a next step and then move forward. Often, good international management is less about "finding a solution or making a decision" and more about "identifying and embarking on a process."

Intercultural Focus

The focus of material in this textbook is on the interaction between people of different cultures in work settings. This intercultural orientation is distinct from a comparative approach, in which management practices of individual countries or cultures are examined and compared. Although we do often report on cultural comparisons, we focus on what happens at their intersection. This is the boundary that provides both the greatest challenges and the most interesting opportunities. We note that an intercultural focus does not necessarily mean across-country – the intercultural focus can apply equally within countries among diverse communities.

Culture-General Focus

This book is intended for a wide variety of managers and other staff who must function effectively in a global environment; therefore, we do not concentrate deeply on specific cultures, countries, or regions. A culture-general perspective provides a framework within which country-specific learning can take place more rapidly as necessary. It helps to know what questions to ask and how to interpret the answers received when conducting business globally or helping others do the same. It helps the learner become more effective at learning about and adapting to other cultures. We do provide specific examples of cultures, countries, and regional cultures: not enough to take the place of in-depth culture-specific training for people who are assigned to a particular place, but enough to enhance the impact of that training.

What, How, and When: Types of Knowledge Developed with the Ninth Edition

Bloom's Taxonomy is the most used and cited classification scheme of educational goals and objectives (Bloom et al., 1956). Over the years it has been reinterpreted numerous times to facilitate its understanding. An interpretation that we favor is that of Susan Ambrose and colleagues (2010):

- **What:** This is *declarative information* such as data, facts, concepts, and terminology.
- **How:** This is *application*, procedures, techniques, or ways to make use of the information.
- **When:** This is *judgment*, and it is highly situational. It combines an understanding of your on-the-ground context interacting with yourself, including your culture, values, and practices, to inform your decisions.

This edition addresses all three types of knowledge. Readers will find declarative information throughout the book, along with tested frameworks such as the **MBI model**, the **strategic alignment framework**, and the **leading change framework**. They will also find many examples of how the frameworks and concepts are applied and be encouraged to discover their own applications. Through further examples and reflection questions, readers will be invited to develop judgment in applying the tools in different situations.

Outline of the Book: Following the Challenges and Opportunities

The four parts of this book follow the main categories of challenges and opportunities we see international managers experiencing most frequently. Each part contains a series of teaching cases that apply the concepts of the section to management practice.

Part I examines the "New Global Context" of international business and management behavior. The first chapter, "Global Leaders in the 21st Century," looks carefully at the noteworthy changes in the business and leadership contexts of globalization. This chapter introduces the importance of mindful global leadership. Chapter 2 identifies the "Pathways to Mindful Global Leadership," including competences, mindsets, and paradox thinking. Chapter 3, "Understanding Culture," the final chapter in this section, defines culture and identifies why culture is such an important element of the international management context. The concepts and principles in these first three chapters set the foundation for the rest of the book. Part I cases offer a closer look at global leadership and situations in which cultural misinterpretation created challenges for leaders making key business decisions.

Part II consists of four chapters that look at "Leading People across Contexts." Chapter 4, "Mapping Cultural Dimensions for Effective Interaction," provides a framework for understanding differences and illustrates it with many examples.

Chapter 5, "Communicating across Cultures: Bridging and Integrating," looks at how to use the maps of cultural differences to communicate effectively, manage conflict, and generate synergies. "Designing and Leading Effective Teams," including virtual global teams, is the topic of Chapter 6. In Chapter 7, "Talent Management: Selecting and Preparing Leaders for Global Assignments," we look at how organizations select, prepare, and support people who develop expertise in global leadership. Part II cases focus on making decisions related to individuals' experiences with intercultural interactions, global teams, and selecting a global leader.

In Part III, "Executing Strategy in a Global Context," we turn to the relationship between management behavior and organizational performance. Chapter 8, "Strategy and Organizational Forms," describes a repertoire of organizational types used by firms from large, matrixed multinational enterprises to small bornglobal start-ups. Chapter 9, "Executing Strategy," discusses the principles of organizational design, drawing on a model of strategic alignment. The framework explains how aligned organizations are more likely to execute strategy effectively and perform well. Because global leaders are almost constantly involved in influencing or managing organizational change, Chapter 10 provides guidance for "Leading Organizational Change." Part III cases put readers in the position of making decisions about organizational design, strategy execution, and change management.

Part IV, "Purpose, Sustainability, and Integrity," looks at the relationship between leaders, their organizations, and society. Chapter 11, "Sustainability and Responsible Organizations," discusses the foundations of organizations' societal context, stakeholder theory, and the underlying orientations for ethical and sustainable practices. A significantly revised chapter, it examines sustainability and organizational practices. Chapter 12, "Competing with Integrity and Ethical Decision-Making," brings us back to the individual level, looking at global leaders as individual decisionmakers. This chapter also provides a conclusion for the book, with our reflections on global leadership journeys. Part IV cases highlight dilemmas and paradoxes in sustainability, responsibility, and ethical decision-making and put the reader in the position of making and implementing difficult decisions.

Each chapter includes further interactive components. Specifically:

- In-chapter activities invite the reader to pause and apply an important concept or framework to their own experience.
- End-of-chapter integrative reflection questions provide an opportunity to reflect more deeply on the application of chapter content across situations.
- A section on further resources suggests ways readers can discover more about the ideas in the chapter.

A Final Word about Our Approach to Writing

The chapters combine our own research and experience and that of many others. We do not provide a review of all the research in the field because other resources do that well. Instead, we focus on the research and frameworks that provide the most immediate practical guidance for managers and aspiring managers, and we present it in ways that have proven to be helpful for learning and practice. We provide many examples throughout the book to help readers see how others have applied the lessons and generate ideas for applying the ideas and behaviors themselves. Most of our examples come directly from the experience of managers with whom we've worked closely, and we've tried to capture the flavor, feeling, and tempo of these people and the places in which they live and work. They may not always be recognized as leaders who capture headlines in the press, but through their experiences we are able to provide more behavioral and reflective insights. We find that they are great role models.

Bibliography

Ambrose, S. A., Bridges, M. W., DiPietro, M., Lovett, M. C., & Norman, M. K. (2010). *How learning works: 7 research-based principles for smart teaching.* John Wiley and Sons.

Anderson, L. W., & Krathwohl, D. R. (eds.). (2001). *A taxonomy for learning, teaching, and assessing: A revision of Bloom's taxonomy of educational objectives.* Longman.

Bloom, B. S., Engelhart, M. D., Furst, E. J., Hill, W. H., & Krathwohl, D. R. (1956). *Taxonomy of educational objectives: The classification of educational goals* (Vol. Handbook I: Cognitive domain). David McKay Company.

Acknowledgments

The ninth edition of this book is a major revision from previous editions, owing to the magnitude and rate of change in the global context. The book has evolved significantly over its 35-year journey, shaped in every edition by the events of the world as well as the experiences of the authors in our various institutions, faculty adopting the book, students of management, and leaders with whom we work. We are very grateful for this community.

We start by acknowledging Joseph J. DiStefano's historical contribution to this book and to the field of international management development. In 1975, Professor DiStefano interviewed Professor Lane, who was a doctoral candidate at the Harvard Business School, and recruited him to Canada. He became a colleague, coauthor, and friend. Professor DiStefano started one of the first cross-cultural courses anywhere in 1974 at the Ivey Business School, which was the genesis of this book. Professor DiStefano chaired Professor Maznevski's PhD thesis committee in 1994. In January 2000, Professor DiStefano joined IMD in Lausanne, Switzerland, and recruited Professor Maznevski to IMD in 2001. They worked together developing international managers for many years before Professor DiStefano retired. In 2016, Professor Maznevski returned to the Ivey Business School where this book (and the scholarship that it is based on) has its roots and where Professors DiStefano's and Lane's influences are still very strong.

All four authors appreciate the support for our careers and our work on international business extended by our colleagues, research associates, and friends over the years at the Ivey Business School, Harvard Business School, Northeastern University, University of Virginia, IMD, University of San Francisco, Copenhagen Business School, Aalborg University, and IPADE Mexico. Some individuals' work and professional support have had a particularly important impact on the contents of this book. From Ivey, these include Professor Don Simpson, who introduced Professor Lane to Africa and doing business in developing countries; the late Professor Al Mikalachki, who developed the change model and taught us so much about change; and Professor Paul Beamish, whose international business expertise has greatly influenced our thinking. Paul supervised Vanessa Hasse's PhD dissertation and introduced us to Cambridge University Press (also referred to simply as the Press). We're also grateful for all the contributions from our current Ivey PhD student, Sabrina Goestl. At the D'Amore-McKim Business School, Professor Bert Spector influenced us greatly, this time concerning strategy and organizational change, and also introduced us to the Press. We also acknowledge our friends Professors Alan Bird and Nicholas Athanassiou, who helped in many ways. We further thank Darla and Frederick Brodsky, who sponsored the Darla and Frederick Brodsky Trustee Professorship in Global Business at the D'Amore-McKim Business School (Northeastern University), of which Professor Lane was the first holder. At the University of San Francisco, we are grateful to Professor Xiaohua Yang, whose mentorship and passion for transpacific management have influenced our thinking about global leadership. And at Copenhagen Business School, we thank Professor Emeritus Flemming Poulfelt for his unwavering support, creativity, and global outlook.

We warmly thank our good friends and colleagues at the International Organizations Network. This group has greatly facilitated and inspired our work, helping us make new friends and creating new knowledge. And they are always fun!

We have worked with many publishers and editors over the years, and our sincere thanks go to all those who helped us along the way, particularly to Rosemary Nixon at Blackwell (later Wiley). We began working with the Press with the eighth edition, and they energized our work significantly. Particular thanks go to our editor, Valerie Appleby, who has worked to integrate us into the Press's portfolio, as well as to Jane Adams (eighth edition) and Helen Shannon (ninth edition) for their wonderful partnership in writing and reviewing. We look forward to a continuing and productive relationship with them.

To this list of acknowledgments we need to add a large number of people and institutions from around the world who have broadened and informed our experience: managers in both the public and private sectors; colleagues at other universities and institutes; companies who have provided access to their operations for the purpose of writing examples and cases; colleagues who have adopted our book and have provided both appreciation and suggestions; reviewers of this and previous editions; as well as former students and research assistants who worked with us to develop material for this and previous editions. All have helped us and others learn so much. They are far too numerous to mention by name, but we trust they know how deeply grateful we are.

Last, but hardly least, we thank our families who have supported our learning and the publishing of what we have learned. This has meant time away from home, time spent alone writing, and time and energy devoted to the many visitors and friends from around the world who have shared our homes. All have been critical to our development. Our spouses have been more than patient, as have our children and grandchildren. Special thanks go to Anne Lane and Brian Maznevski, and the extended Nielsen family, whose support and commitment have been integral to the development of this edition.

Notwithstanding this list of personal acknowledgments, we close with the usual caveat that we alone remain responsible for the contents of this book.

Introduction

Welcome to *International Management Behavior: Global and Sustainable Leadership*, ninth edition!

This book is not just a book about global business. It is about *people who conduct business – and manage other types of organizations – in a global environment.* It discusses and explores typical situations that managers encounter: the problems and opportunities; the frustrations and rewards; the successes and failures; the decisions they must make and the actions they must take.

International management is not an impersonal activity, and it should not be studied solely in an impersonal way. It is important to understand trade theories, to be able to weigh the pros and cons of exporting versus licensing, or to understand the advantages of a joint venture versus a wholly owned subsidiary. But eventually theory must give way to practice; strategizing and debating alternatives must give way to action. Working globally means interacting with colleagues, customers, and suppliers from other countries to achieve a specific outcome. We focus on these interactions, on getting things done with and through other people in an international context.

Globalization means that one does not have to travel to another country to be exposed to situations of cultural diversity. For example, consider a manager in Boston who worked for Genzyme, one of the world's leading biotech companies. This company was founded in Boston in 1981 and was acquired by Sanofi SA from France in 2011. Now the American manager may travel to France frequently or interact with French managers when they come to Boston. This same manager possibly interacts with several other Boston-based companies that are also now foreign owned. They may have an account with Santander Bank (from Spain), purchase insurance from John Hancock (owned by Manulife Financial of Canada), and buy groceries from Stop & Shop (owned by Ahold Delhaize of the

Netherlands). And managers from these firms, in turn, also are likely to be experiencing working with their Canadian, Spanish, and Dutch counterparts.

In most parts of the world, even domestic organizations have substantial cultural diversity among their employees. Some countries have long histories of immigration, such as Canada, the United States, and Brazil. With recent upheavals in many parts of the world, migrants and refugees have become more common. There can be considerable diversity within domestic workforces, and many managers experience working with cultural diversity as part of their daily routine. Multicultural and diverse employee groups are now the norm, not the exception. Managers and students in all these countries will find the material in this book (mapped in Figure I.1) useful and important in these situations – without their ever having to leave their home base.

Reflect to Accelerate Learning

Throughout this book you will come across reflection questions or exercises that invite you to pause and think, digest, and put into perspective the information you have just read and apply it to your own situation. You are encouraged to use reflection to accelerate learning. These questions are general springboards to connect you personally with course material. You can find more inspiration about reflection as a vehicle for deep and critical learning in:

- Cunliffe A. L. (2004). On becoming a critically reflexive practitioner. *Journal of Management Education, 28*, 407–426.
- Cunliffe, A. L. (2016). "On becoming a critically reflexive practitioner" redux: What does it mean to be reflexive? *Journal of Management Education, 40*(6), 740–746.
- Schön, D. A. (1983). *The reflective practitioner: How professionals think in action*. Basic Books.

Focus on the Voyage

This book is based on the philosophy that learning is a lifelong, continuous process. Although the book contains many recommendations about how to interact and manage in other cultures, rather than simply provide what appear to be the "answers" about the way to act in global management situations and an illusion of mastery, we hope it stimulates and facilitates even more learning about other

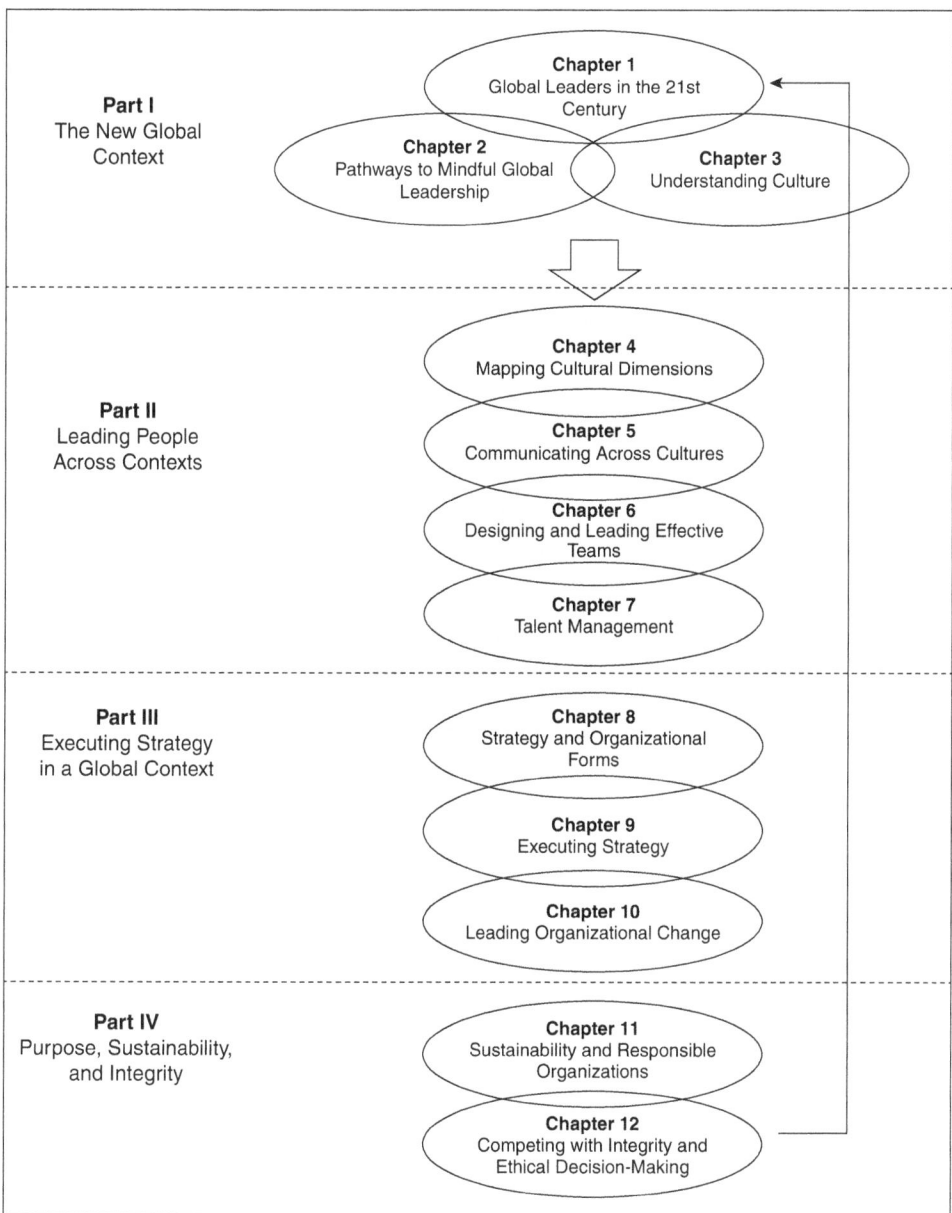

Figure I.1 Conceptual map of book contents.

cultures and how to work effectively with others. For some readers, the material in this book may represent a first encounter with different cultures. Other readers may have been exposed to different cultures through previous courses or personal experience. For those with prior exposure to other people and places, the journey continues with a new level of insight. For those without prior experiences, welcome to an interesting journey!

PART I
The New Global Context

A close examination of the current context of international management, this section illustrates why and how global leaders need to develop mindful application of a comprehensive skillset and a deep understanding of culture.

1 Global Leaders in the 21st Century

"It's a dangerous business, Frodo, going out your door. You step onto the road, and if you don't keep your feet, there's no knowing where you might be swept off to."

— J. R. R. Tolkien, *The Lord of The Rings*

Key Learning Objectives

At the end of this chapter, students will be able to:

- Describe how the economic and political contexts of business are changing.
- Recognize that managing these interdependencies is a process of managing complexity.
- Discuss the relevance of mindfulness in global leadership.
- Explain what it means to be a global company.

Globalization: That Was Then, This Is Now

The phrase "That Was Then, This Is Now" comes from the book of that title by S. E. Hinton (1971) and is a popular expression indicating that things are continuously changing. The Greek philosopher Heraclitus, 2,500 years earlier, observed simply that change is the only constant. A brief review of the globalization trajectory will provide a snapshot of the "Then" before we focus on the "Now" and implications for current managers and organizations. The word "globalization" describes "the growing interdependence of the world's economies, cultures, and populations, brought about by cross-border trade in goods and services, technology, and flows of investment, people, and information" (Peterson Institute for International Economics, 2023).

Globalization is not a recent phenomenon. The World Economic Forum (WEF) has described international trade as happening as far back as the fifth century AD with the Silk Road and Spice Routes (World Economic Forum, 2019). Global trade continued to grow during the Age of Discovery (from the 15th to the 17th centuries) with explorers sailing the oceans, discovering new lands, and finding new trade routes connecting the East and West.

The WEF article posits four phases to what we call globalization today, or the start of true global trade. Globalization 1.0 emerged in the 19th century as Great Britain ruled global commerce through its technological innovations like the steam engine and refrigerated cargo ships. The article quotes the economist, John Maynard Keynes, as saying, "The inhabitant of London could order by telephone, sipping his morning tea in bed, the various products of the whole Earth, in such quantity as he might see fit, and reasonably expect their early delivery upon his doorstep." That sounds almost like ordering from the equivalent of present-day Amazon.

After World War II, and coinciding with economic booms in the United States and the reconstruction of Europe, came Globalization 2.0. The United States sprang to the forefront of the industrialized world, and China began an open-door policy in 1978 to achieve economic growth. China attracted significant foreign investment to specialized economic zones such as open coastal cities (Kobayashi et al., 1999). American and Western European companies primarily began "going international" during that time.

Globalization 3.0 emerged during the late 1980s. The Uruguay Round of the General Agreement on Tariffs and Trade (GATT), 1986–1994, led to major reductions in tariffs and created the World Trade Organization. Countries began creating free trade agreements, and companies hastened to become global. With the fall of the Berlin Wall in 1989 and the demise of the Soviet Union two years later, optimism prevailed. In 1992, Francis Fukuyama published his book, *The End of History and the Last Man*, suggesting that the ideological contest between liberal democracy and communism had been resolved. Democracy, with its market economies, was perceived as the superior political-economic form of social organization (Fukuyama, 1992). Companies began expanding operations internationally to reduce costs and began establishing global supply chain networks.

Globalization became one of the biggest buzzwords in business and in business schools. Proponents saw it reducing poverty, improving living standards, and permitting learning about and understanding other cultures, thus drawing the world closer together. To many academics and executives, globalization simply became primarily about the production and distribution of products. Opponents, however, saw a negative side. An anti-globalization movement developed that viewed globalization as corporate colonialism and as a vehicle for continued Western or American economic and cultural domination.

Ultimately, there have been positive and negative effects of globalization. On the positive side, globalization overall has increased wealth, reduced poverty, improved living standards, and spread innovations. However, the distribution of those gains has been uneven. Detractors claim that the rich have gotten richer and the poor poorer. In addition to a distortion in the distribution of wealth, we have also witnessed the appearance of a dark side of globalization as terror organizations and criminal enterprises globalized and cyberattacks with malware such as ransomware and denial of service became a major concern. The new global interdependence had both positive and negative features.

Trade liberalization opened borders across which capital and products moved more easily. Airline travel and reliable, inexpensive communication effectively reduced distances and minimized the impact of physical boundaries so that corporations could manage far-flung operations. Alliances and networks blurred the lines of organizational boundaries. The forces of deregulation, industry consolidation, and technology significantly reshaped corporate landscapes. The optimism accompanying "the end of history" in 1992 and the fervor of corporate expansion was not destined to last indefinitely.

Twenty-five years later, *The Economist* proclaimed that the global company was in retreat, noting that "The biggest business idea of the past three decades is in deep trouble. Companies became obsessed with internationalizing their customers, production, capital and management … Such a spree could not last forever; an increasing body of evidence suggests that it has now ended" (2017). Corporate profits had declined, their cross-border investment had fallen, and their proportion of international sales had shrunk. Additionally, the social and political attitudes, particularly in Europe and the United States, had shifted.

The free movement of labor across national boundaries, in the European Union (EU) for example, had led to concern over control of national borders and the perceived influx of immigrants. **Brexit** (the withdrawal of the United Kingdom from the EU), the rise of **populism** and **economic nationalism**, concern about immigration in the United States, the 2016 election of Donald Trump as President of the United States, and the increased popularity of right-wing parties in Europe seemed to be evidence of increasing unease with some of the by-products of globalization. These developments were in progress while the eighth edition was being written. It felt like a lot of changes were taking place.

But all that was "Then"; what about "Now"? What are the dimensions of the new global context facing managers? Even more potentially far-reaching changes are taking place now.

> **Reflection Question 1.1: Globalization in Your Personal or Professional Life**
>
> In your own experience, what are the ways you, your community, or your company/industry have been affected by globalization of trade, people, and information? How has it made things better? Worse? Different?

Contrary to *The Economist*'s statement above, the WEF believes we have entered Globalization 4.0 where digital goods and services will be the primary exports. The stages of globalization are summarized in Figure 1.1.

Globalization has not ended, but its form has changed, and it continues to evolve. Corporations may slow their global growth, but they will not simply abandon their international operations and crawl back into their domestic shells. They will most likely continue to use a mix of subsidiaries, supply chain networks, franchising, and digital expansion that best suits their business. Companies with e-commerce platforms, such as Amazon or Rakuten, will continue to grow globally.

The narrow economic perspectives such as the number of markets served, the global reach of the supply chain and sources of supplies, where parts of the company's value chain are located, or alliances to source intellectual capital (knowledge) describe only a part of the reality of globalization. Countries and organizations worldwide have become more interdependent, but not just economically. There are also human, cultural, and political aspects of globalization. When the borders opened, it was not just goods that flowed across them but also people, culture, and ideas.

If you were asked what the most significant global change affecting business has been since the *Economist* article in 2017, what would you say? As we are

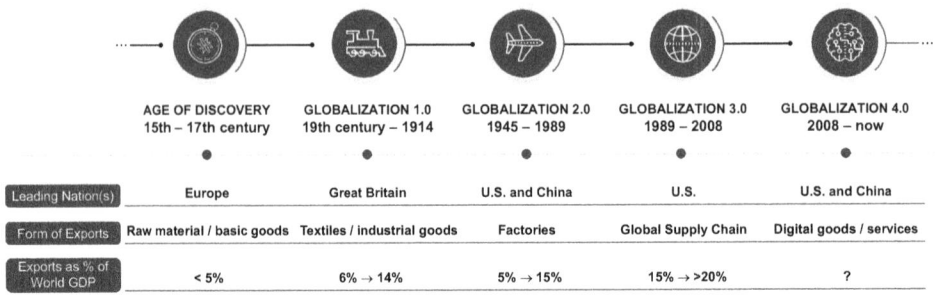

Figure 1.1 Stages of globalization.
Adapted from "A brief history of globalization", Peter Vanham, World Economic Forum, 2019.

writing this in 2023, one obvious answer might be Russia's invasion of Ukraine. This event resulted in more than 1,000 corporations from around the world curtailing their operations in Russia, whether closing them down completely, suspending them temporarily, or promising no future investments in the country (Sonnenfeld et al., 2022).

McDonald's is one high-profile example. It opened its first restaurant in Moscow's Pushkin Square in 1990. Thirty-two years later it announced that it was exiting Russia and would sell its more than 800 restaurants (McDonald's, 2022). That is a significant impact! The McDonald corporate website said:

The humanitarian crisis caused by the war in Ukraine, and the precipitating unpredictable operating environment, have led McDonald's to conclude that continued ownership of the business in Russia is no longer tenable, nor is it consistent with McDonald's values.

There have been other prominent global changes, of course, including the rise of China as an economic and political rival of the United States, the continued rise of autocracy, the fallout from Brexit in the United Kingdom, and continuing conflict and uncertainty in the Middle East. The effects of climate change have been felt worldwide, but particularly in the Global South, which has not contributed as much as the Global North to conditions exacerbating it. Those effects include forest fire disasters in Europe and North America, floods in Australia, drought and starvation in East Africa, and extreme heat, monsoon rains, and flooding in South Asia, with the accompanying human migration: All of these have affected global businesses.

The COVID-19 pandemic was a significant event that created a global social and economic crisis. Millions of people died, millions more fell into extreme poverty, and public health systems and food systems were all negatively affected. People lost jobs and the ability to feed themselves and their families. The employment and supply chain disruptions created turmoil in developed and developing countries.

A major shift began to take place in the global, political economy. The predominant system for the past three-quarters of a century beginning with the GATT was based on **neoliberalism** (Faroohar, 2022). Characterized by global economic agreements, free trade, global supply chains, and multilateral institutions, neoliberalism blossomed after the collapse of the Soviet Union and the fall of the Berlin Wall. Some observers now suggest that with the rise of China, country diplomacy may shift to **realism**, which is characterized by the primacy of national interests and security (Li et al., 2022).

An example of realism may be China's **One Belt One Road Initiative**, now referred to as the **Belt and Road Initiative** (BRI). This is a massive infrastructure project initiated by the Chinese government in 2013 connecting 150 countries from East Asia to Europe (Council on Foreign Relations, 2023). The BRI would build new roads, railroads, ports, bridges, and power stations. It would be a modern recreation of the Silk Road, one of the original thoroughfares in the process of globalization. Some analysts see this as an example of China's continuing rise to economic and political power. China is underwriting the initiative through four state-owned banks (Chatham House, 2021), and there are concerns that some countries may have taken on too much debt, making them more dependent on China and susceptible to its influence.

The United States is concerned that BRI is a vehicle for China's military expansion as well as regional economic and political development. Some observers believe that the "America First" approach is a similar political tool, reflecting a shift to realism and economic nationalism. In 2019, the United States put Huawei, China's global technology company, on a trade blacklist and later prohibited firms from selling it semiconductor chips made with US technology. Such actions and concerns suggest that the world may need a new overarching system – one that better balances national global interests. However, the features of this new system are uncertain at the moment.

Shortages of personal protective equipment (PPE) and computer chips during the COVID-19 crisis were examples of the weakness of global systems that contributed to a resurgence of interest in economic nationalism. Global supply chains became **choke points** (Farrell & Newman, 2020), developing extensive bottlenecks during the COVID-19 pandemic. There was an initial reduction in the demand for goods at the beginning of the pandemic, and then, later, as COVID-19 eased in the United States and demand quickly escalated, there were crippling labor shortages (e.g., truck drivers, dock workers) as COVID-19 lockdowns continued in China.

One example of these choke points was experienced by first responders (police, fire, and emergency medical services personnel) and health care workers in the United States who all faced severe shortages of PPE at the outbreak of COVID-19 (Cohen & Rodgers, 2020). The disruption to global supply chains was a significant reason for these shortages, as most of the PPE was sourced from and manufactured abroad. Hospitals also lacked sufficient stocks, as they were incentivized to keep costs down. The sudden overwhelming demand by hospitals along with the demand in the marketplace by consumers depleted the stocks of suppliers quickly.

Computer chips (semiconductors) were another casualty of global supply chain disruption. Increased demand from the auto industry after a period of sales decline at the start of COVID-19, the acceleration of the **Internet of Things (IoT),** and the rapid increase of 5G communication and cloud-based services were all significant contributors. Eighty-three percent of the world's chips came from Taiwan and Korea, and the producers there were not able to meet the demand (Schein, 2021). The lack of availability curtailed the manufacturing of automobiles. Peugeot and Mercedes-Benz started to ration their chips, saving them for their more expensive models. Renault installed old analog speedometers in lieu of digital ones. Porsche delayed delivery of its Macan SUV because it could not get the chip that controlled its 18-way seats (Ewing & Boudette, 2021). At one point in 2022, General Motors had about 95,000 cars in storage that it could not ship because of supply chain disruptions and semiconductor shortages.

These semiconductor shortages not only delayed the production and delivery of consumer products but also threatened the manufacture of high-tech weaponry critical for national defense and security. This was one reason behind the US Congress passing the Creating Helpful Incentives to Produce Semiconductors and Science (CHIPS) Act in 2022, providing up to $52 billion over five years for semiconductor initiatives in the United States.

As if global instability associated with a pandemic wasn't a sufficient challenge in the new global context facing managers, we can add cybersecurity risks and emerging considerations such as cryptocurrency and artificial intelligence to the picture.

What does all this mean for organizations and managers?

After all the unanticipated disruptions that have taken place in the last few years, you might best be advised to expect the unexpected and prepare yourself to manage in a global context aptly characterized by the organizational change theorist Peter Vaill's metaphor as "managing in permanent white water" – paddling to survive in your "organizational raft" in the turbulence and rocks in the changing global river (Vaill, 1996).

Global leaders in this new context should explore developing **resilience** – "the ability to prepare for and adapt to changing conditions and withstand and recover rapidly from disruptions" – rather than focusing solely on **efficiency** (Global Resilience Institute, 2023). However, there are trade-offs, as political scientist William Galston (2020) explains: "Efficiency comes through optimal adaptation to an existing environment, while resilience requires the capacity to adapt to disruptive changes in the environment." Developing resilience may mean duplicating critical systems **(redundancy)** and maintaining extra resources such as inventory and suppliers **(slack)**, which are antithetical to efficiency.

What might an outline of future global conditions look like? The National Intelligence Council publishes its Global Trends report every four years "to provide an analytic framework for policymakers early in each administration as they craft national security strategy and navigate an uncertain future. The goal is not to offer a specific prediction of the world in 2040; instead, our intent is to help policymakers and citizens see what may lie beyond the horizon and prepare for an array of possible futures" (2021). The report identifies and analyzes structural forces in demographics, economics, the environment, and technology and how they might intersect to provide five potential scenarios for 2040:

- *Renaissance of democracies* where the United States and other democracies lead a resurgence of the global economy improving the quality of life for millions around the world.
- *A world adrift.* The international system is directionless and ineffective.
- *Competitive coexistence* between China and the United States.
- *Separate silos* characterized by separate security and economic blocs of various sizes.
- *Tragedy and mobilization.* A global coalition led by the EU, China, and nongovernmental organizations address climate change, resource depletion, poverty, and global food shortages.

The need for executives who can function effectively in these scenarios or some combination thereof is going to be greater than ever. Although many changes of the last few years, such as COVID-19 and the chip shortage, could be considered "rare events," Beamish and Hasse (2022) suggest that "rare events" will occur with greater frequency and impact. Executives will need to actively monitor their organization's risk landscape and augment their risk assessment and scenario-planning capabilities to inform their market and nonmarket (political and social) strategies.

> ### Reflection Question 1.2: The World in 2040
>
> Of the five potential scenarios identified by the World Economic Forum, which do you think is most likely to occur? Why?

What Is a Global Company?

When we examine the processes of global companies, sterile statistics give way to people who create and manage the processes. The picture that emerges at the operational level is often more complicated than the one provided by macro-level descriptions. The road to globalization has been littered with the debris of ill-considered mergers, acquisitions, and new market entry attempts. In other words, globalization has been easy to talk about but difficult to do.

What exactly is a global company? Is it a company that has plants and subsidiaries in many countries? Is it a company that sells its products and services around the world? Or is it a company that derives more of its revenue from international sales than from domestic sales? Those are some of the characteristics of a global company, but we do not believe a company is truly global until the management and employees develop a **global mindset**. Jack Welch, former CEO of General Electric, said, "The real challenge is to globalize the mind of the organization ... Until you globalize intellect, you haven't really globalized the company" (Rohwer, 2000).

Just because a company operates in multiple locations around the world, sells its products in many countries, and derives revenue from international sales, it is not necessarily a global company. It simply means that it functions in a lot of countries. Global strategy is executed, and global operations are managed, by people from one country interacting with people from another. They are the managers who interface with the suppliers, alliance partners, and government officials. They are also the people who manage the plants and workforces around the world.

You do not globalize companies unless you globalize people. Think of a Japanese company that operates in many countries but whose top managers all have Japanese passports and not much direct, international experience. This is a Japanese company operating globally – but not necessarily a company that has been truly globalized. A global company has a cadre of managers who understand how to operate in the modern world of economic, political, and cultural interdependence.

C. K. Prahalad (1990, p. 30) characterized the world of global business as follows:

A world where variety, complex interaction patterns among various subunits, host governments, and customers, pressures for change and stability, and the need to re-assert individual identity in a complex web of organizational relationships are the norm. This world is one beset with ambiguity and stress. Facts, emotions, anxieties, power and dependence, competition and collaboration, individual and team efforts are all present ... Managers have to deal with these often conflicting demands simultaneously.

Although Prahalad did not use the term **complexity**, he described this characteristic of globalization accurately. Rather than considering globalization as the proportion of trade conducted across national borders, or by some other economic or social measure, we should talk about it as a manifestation of complexity that requires global companies to develop new ways of thinking and managing.

Managing Globalization = Managing Complexity

The sixth edition of this book was written just as the global economic crisis was unfolding in 2008. We fully expected that by the time we wrote the seventh edition, the crisis would have been resolved and we would be describing the opportunities and lessons from recovery. Yet, as we wrote the eighth edition (and now the ninth edition), the economic and geopolitical conditions that managers faced were becoming more demanding. Some writers described this "new normal" as VUCA – volatile, uncertain, complex, and ambiguous – a term originally used by the US military to describe the post–Cold War situation.

As part of our research for *The Blackwell Handbook of Global Management: A Guide to Managing Complexity* (Lane et al., 2004) we tried to learn from managers what globalization meant to them. Economists tended to define globalization in terms of flows of goods or money or people across borders, but there was a sense that managers experienced it differently in their day-to-day roles. We spoke with managers who were working both outside and inside their home countries, traveling a lot or a little. When we asked them, "What is the effect of globalization on your management role?" their answer surprised us. They all responded: "It's exhausting."

When we probed further, we found that whatever level of cross-border transactions a single manager dealt with, the effect of a more globalized economy and society meant increased complexity. This increased complexity, in turn, meant that the traditional way of managing – often one learned in business school – was not entirely adequate. Managers were working harder to understand complex forces in order to plan and execute with some predictability. The result was a feeling of being overwhelmed and exhausted. Our experience with managers today suggests that this trend continues. Although it may represent the "new normal," many managers have not yet developed the mindset or skills to manage effectively in it.

Interdependence: Increased Connections

What gave rise to the VUCA business environment? First, globalization of trade increased the **interdependence** between countries and people in those countries. We are all more connected than we used to be, and not just economically. Globalization has created a tightly coupled, **complex adaptive system**. The increased interactions between autonomous entities (e.g. countries, customers, suppliers, competitors) generate **feedback** to other parts of the system and may create **emergent outcomes** that can be difficult or impossible to anticipate or understand.

The fall (or at least permeability) of barriers to the cross-border flow of people, goods, and money means that events and decisions in one company or in one part of the world impact others who may be distant and seemingly unconnected to those events. In 2008, for example, a **subprime mortgage crash** in the United States triggered the global financial crisis. Subsequently, China's hunger for basic resources such as steel and wood influenced the price of those commodities globally. This impacted the environment and created social conflicts in countries where natural resources were sourced. With such high levels of interdependence around the world, so-called rare events are more likely to occur. It is impossible for a manager to predict the impact of a specific action, making effective managerial decision-making extremely difficult.

Variety and Ambiguity: Increased Variables and Options but Decreased Clarity

Executives encounter more **variety** than ever before. In many countries, the domestic workforce is becoming more diverse. For example, in metropolitan Toronto, Canada, approximately 200 languages are spoken, and in the 2021 census only 49% of the people identified English as their mother tongue (Statistics Canada, 2021). But workforce diversity is just one aspect of the increased variety that managers encounter today. With modern media and technology, businesses and consumers have become more discerning, forcing companies to better define customer segments. Competitors offer more variety in products and services. In the 2008–2013 period, companies such as Nokia and Motorola struggled to respond to challenges from Apple and Samsung, even as Skype and other voice-over-internet protocol (VOIP) software challenged traditional methods of telecommunications. Companies that operate in many countries face numerous economic, legal, and regulatory environments. Developing consistent compensation policies in a global company is almost impossible. Making decisions and taking action are much more complicated with so many variables to consider.

Along with increased variety comes more **ambiguity**, or lack of clarity. Interconnectedness and variety make it much more difficult to see **cause–effect relations**. Although there is more information available to us today than at any time in the past, the reliability of this information is not always clear or trustworthy. Financial analysts provide company ratings – but how do we know on what information they have based those ratings, and what should we do with that information? Customers complain through websites – but how representative are they of all customers? How much impact will public complaints have on potential new customers? The ambiguity of available information and news was exacerbated during and after the 2016 and 2020 US Presidential elections with the appearance of "fake news" and conspiracy theories on social media websites. Again, decision-making and action are much more challenging when information is ambiguous, when we are not sure about the cause–effect relations or the clarity of our information.

The Multiplier Effect: Dynamic Complexity and Flux

Detail complexity in a situation means that it has many parts or variables. It differs dramatically from **dynamic complexity**, which equals Variety x Interdependence x Ambiguity (Senge, 2006). Tightly linked, complex global organizations operating in a tightly coupled global environment potentially become more vulnerable as interdependence increases (Weick & Van Orden, 1990). For example, a single e-mail sent simultaneously to several locations in the world can be interpreted differently and forwarded to several other destinations, each generating varied interpretations and possible actions. The increase in complexity leads to a decrease in buffers, slack resources, and autonomy of units. There is also less time to contemplate corrective action. All this makes problem diagnosis and action planning difficult. Problems appear and must be resolved immediately. "Now" has become the primary unit of time in the world of global managers.

As if that weren't enough, the configuration of our complex environment is always shifting and changing. Even if you could take a snapshot today of the interdependence, variety, and information available and study it enough to understand and make clear decisions, tomorrow will likely be different. Decisions you made yesterday may no longer be valid. We refer to this as **flux** because it represents rapid unpredictable change in many components, not predictable change in a few.

It is no wonder that managers feel overwhelmed, whether or not they are directly involved in cross-border transactions! This environmental complexity is depicted in Figure 1.2.

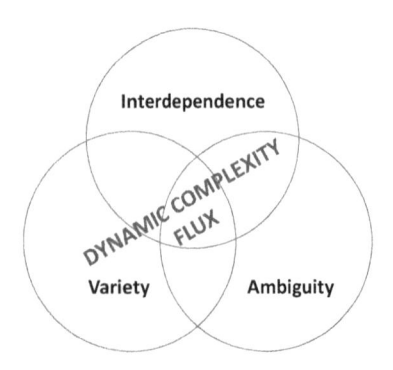

Figure 1.2 The complexity of globalization.

Global Leadership: Leading People across Boundaries

What is the role of a global (or international) manager (or leader) who must function in this complex international environment? What makes it different from someone doing the same job in a single country? We explore the tasks an international manager is responsible for and consider some basic definitions.

Formal or Informal Leadership? Manager or Leader? International or Global Company?

These three pairs of terms often create ambiguity if they are used differently or imprecisely in different contexts. In this textbook, we assume that leadership can be exercised from any position in an organization. Manager and leader are, therefore, used as complementary definitions, not maximally different roles or situations. *Global* and *international* are terms often used to differentiate organizational structures and scope of operations. However, our focus when using those words to describe leaders and managers is on their roles that require interaction across cultural and geographic boundaries, whether it is one or many boundaries.

There is also sometimes discussion about whether leadership is the purview of people who hold **formal** positions of authority, or whether leadership is the **informal** act of influencing people and can therefore be impactful from any position. We consider that processes of influencing in a positive direction are important no matter what role someone holds in the organization.

This means that everyone in the organization can and should exercise leadership: It is therefore also essential to exercise good judgment about when to follow others (whether the supervisor, a peer, a direct report, or someone else). At the same time, those with authority also have the added responsibility and accountability for decision outcomes and their impact. In this book, we often focus on the kinds of decisions that people in formal positions of authority must make, and we may refer to that person as the leader or manager (see next section), but the process of influencing toward a specific direction is referred to as leadership in general.

The debate about management versus leadership is an important one conceptually. When it was first raised by Abraham Zeleznik of the Harvard Business School in 1977, it was helpful to identify the importance of taking responsibility, setting direction, and inspiring people (**leadership**) in addition to executing organizational mandates (**management**) (Zeleznik, 2004). The debate generated an acknowledgment that those who lead businesses should include values, motivation, and other aspects of nonrational leadership into their agendas. Bennis and

Nanus (1985) put it simply: Managers do things right, leaders do the right things. However, as Mintzberg pointed out 20 years later, we cannot lose sight of the fact that even leaders need to get things done. Responsible leaders do it well, and this requires good management (Mintzberg, 2005).

In reality, the person who is responsible for mandates across international borders must both lead and manage, often at the same time. We therefore use the terms *manager* and *leader* interchangeably, and when it is important to specify which competences or perspectives are important for which aspects of the role, we do so.

The distinction between global and international has also been the subject of much conceptual debate, both in the literature and within companies. In global strategy, the terms differentiate an approach of emphasizing global integration over local responsiveness. This is often reflected in structures that are highly centralized or coordinated (global) versus ones that are more decentralized (transnational or multidomestic).

For our purposes it is more important to define *global* as *complexity*, and identify different levels of global or complexity, by the type of task and extent of global context. It is less important to distinguish global from international. The focus of this book is the perspective of the *person* in the *role* of being responsible for mandates across borders, situations involving the crossing of boundaries, and the interpersonal and organizational dynamics encountered.

Global Leaders

Although most managers' jobs have clearly become more global, some jobs are more global than others. The more global a job or mandate, the more it requires global leadership and the kinds of management competences and perspectives addressed in the following chapters.

Using the characterization of global as complexity discussed earlier, Reiche et al. (2017, p. 556) defined global leadership as

the processes and actions through which an individual influences a range of internal and external constituents from multiple national cultures and jurisdictions in a context characterized by significant levels of task and relationship complexity.

From this definition they created a typology of four global leadership roles that they termed **incremental** or **connective** based on low task complexity and either low or high relationship complexity; and **operational** or **integrative** based on high task complexity and either low or high relationship complexity. Their typology is shown in Figure 1.3.

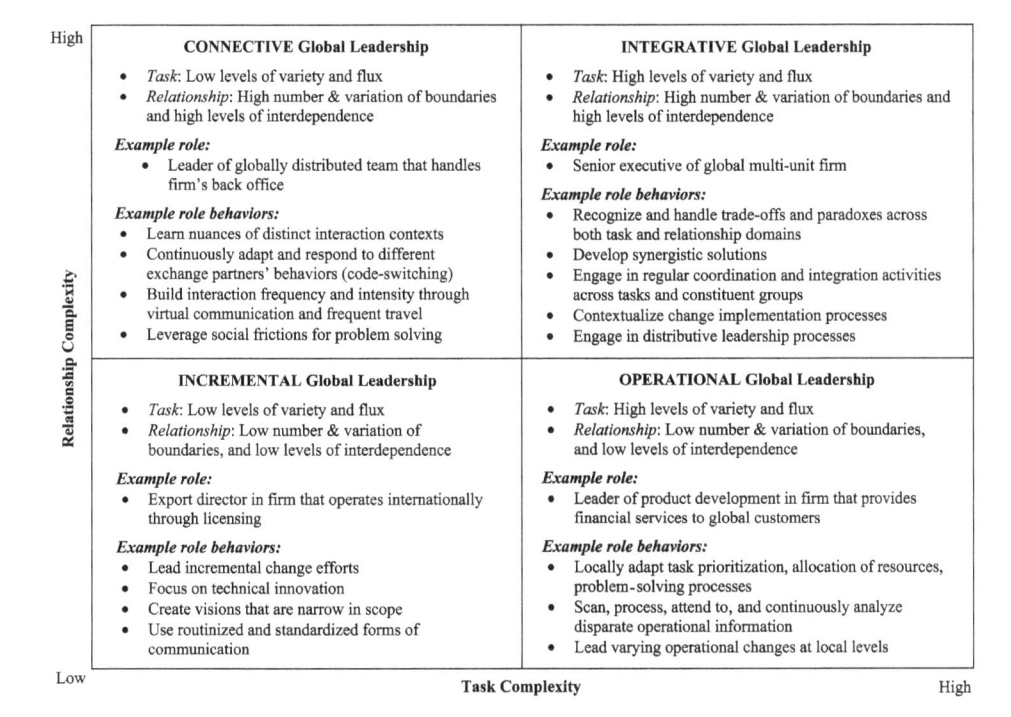

High	**CONNECTIVE Global Leadership** • *Task*: Low levels of variety and flux • *Relationship*: High number & variation of boundaries and high levels of interdependence *Example role:* • Leader of globally distributed team that handles firm's back office *Example role behaviors:* • Learn nuances of distinct interaction contexts • Continuously adapt and respond to different exchange partners' behaviors (code-switching) • Build interaction frequency and intensity through virtual communication and frequent travel • Leverage social frictions for problem solving	**INTEGRATIVE Global Leadership** • *Task*: High levels of variety and flux • *Relationship*: High number & variation of boundaries and high levels of interdependence *Example role:* • Senior executive of global multi-unit firm *Example role behaviors:* • Recognize and handle trade-offs and paradoxes across both task and relationship domains • Develop synergistic solutions • Engage in regular coordination and integration activities across tasks and constituent groups • Contextualize change implementation processes • Engage in distributive leadership processes
Relationship Complexity	**INCREMENTAL Global Leadership** • *Task*: Low levels of variety and flux • *Relationship*: Low number & variation of boundaries, and low levels of interdependence *Example role:* • Export director in firm that operates internationally through licensing *Example role behaviors:* • Lead incremental change efforts • Focus on technical innovation • Create visions that are narrow in scope • Use routinized and standardized forms of communication	**OPERATIONAL Global Leadership** • *Task*: High levels of variety and flux • *Relationship*: Low number & variation of boundaries, and low levels of interdependence *Example role:* • Leader of product development in firm that provides financial services to global customers *Example role behaviors:* • Locally adapt task prioritization, allocation of resources, problem-solving processes • Scan, process, attend to, and continuously analyze disparate operational information • Lead varying operational changes at local levels
Low	**Task Complexity**	**High**

Figure 1.3 Global leadership typology (Reiche et al., 2017).

Each role type requires a different approach to global leadership, with different skillsets and behaviors. Throughout this book, we will return to these themes of relationship and task complexity, and the related choices and requirements of leadership.

Managing Complexity

How do you manage this level of complexity in the environment? The traditional way taught in business schools encourages the use of data, comparison, measurement, categorization, analysis, planning, and maybe **stretch goals** (high-effort, high-risk goals) before taking action. However, this **command-and-control** mode may not be sufficient to respond to globalization pressures, since not everything is under our control and change is constant. The management of people in a complex setting like globalization presents much more of a challenge; however, as we have seen in our research on complexity, it is absolutely critical to the success of organizations today.

The way to manage the complexity of globalization is by using the capacity that is in people to manage it themselves, drawing on their intellectual and social capital. The most complex element of any organization is its people: human brains and human relationships. When managers simplify a few key control processes, such as the organizational structure, the company values, goals and strategy, and some key performance indicators, they can develop a **facilitative** and **collaborative** style to "let go" and empower people to manage the complexity in their own ways. This facilitative and process-oriented **mindful global leadership** style, using a flexible mode of operating, will make dealing with complexity more manageable, as will be discussed in the next section.

Mindfulness Is the Foundation of Global Leadership in Complexity Effectiveness

It should be clear by now that managers today face a complex global environment, and that their roles vary according to the task and relationship complexity they face. We will introduce many different tools and approaches in this book that help global leaders work effectively. Underlying them all is the habit of, and ability to exercise, mindfulness. So what does it really mean to be a *mindful* global leader?

Mindfulness Defined and Illustrated

In her 1989 book *Mindfulness*, Ellen Langer, a psychology professor at Harvard University, described what it means to be a mindful leader and what happens when you are not. Langer defines mindfulness as actively noticing new things, which puts you in the present and makes you more sensitive to context, perspective, and process. She starts by exploring and contrasting the opposite of mindfulness: mindlessness. She recounts the story of Napoleon Bonaparte's ill-fated attempt to conquer Russia. The outcome is well known. In June 1812, Napoleon entered Russia with 422,000 troops and in December 1812 he limped out of Russia with 10,000 – a devastating defeat. As Napoleon had rapidly advanced, the Russian army had continually retreated. Napoleon's interpretation of this rapid advance was that he was "winning" and the Russians, in retreat, were "losing." The Russian general, Mikhail Kutuzov, had a different perspective. He laid a trap, using his knowledge of the upcoming Russian winter. Kutuzov had his troops, while retreating, destroy anything Napoleon's troops could use: a method known as the scorched-earth policy. Soon Napoleon had outrun his supply lines. His troops could not be resupplied, nor were they able to forage and live off the land.

In this brief description we see why Langer described Napoleon as "mindless." First, he could not break loose from his previously created categories of events, such as "rapid advance signifies winning" and "retreat signifies losing." Second, he apparently did not question the information he was receiving about the Russian retreat. Third, he had a limited perspective, which was that conquest was capturing terrain and, eventually, Moscow. He did not consider that Kutuzov, knowing the Russian context more thoroughly, could be setting a trap for him.

Napoleon was an extremely successful general to this point. By 1812, he had conquered most of Europe and defeated his enemies through the use of firepower and maneuver. He was fixated on conquering Russia and destroying the Russian army. However, success often breeds complacency and arrogance, which can lead to "mindless" action and failure. After all, why change a formula that works so well?

Analyzing Napoleon's Russian experience illustrates the elements of mindfulness. First, Napoleon did not take *different perspectives* to assess the information he was receiving, to redefine and broaden categories. He saw actions and made assumptions about their meaning, based on his previous experience. Second, he did not pay attention to the *context* he was in: he did not consider that the context (in particular the approaching harsh winter) could affect which actions are effective and why. Finally, he was not *process oriented*, that is, he did not pay attention to the outcome of each of his troops' actions and carefully adjust his next actions based on reflecting on and interpreting these outcomes. He simply kept focused on his final objective, Moscow, and kept going the way he always had – mindlessly.

Reflection Question 1.3: Mindlessness

Can you think of an example from of a company, organization, or leader behaving mindlessly because they ignored a process or a context? It could even be yourself. What was the impact of the mindlessness? Why do you think the context or process was missed? What could have been done to increase mindfulness?

Mindfulness in Global Business

What does Napoleon's tale have to do with business today? Mindfulness is an underlying foundation for global leadership, and it becomes more and more important as the complexity of the context increases. As we have seen by teaching university and executive programs on every continent in the world, leaders' and companies' biggest mistakes moving from one country to another are often avoidable with mindfulness.

Many well-known companies that tried to enter markets outside their home countries have failed. They took business models that worked well at home into a new market and did not succeed. They tried to transfer policies and procedures that worked well in their original context only to see them fail as well. Executives gave a lot of thought to the business model and strategy, as well as the goals they wanted to achieve, but did not plan the implementation process sufficiently to reach those outcomes. They had established ways of doing business that had been successful and assumed these would work anywhere.

Consider Walmart's experience in Germany in 2006. Walmart had a successful formula it used in the United States: everyday low prices, tight inventory control, and a wide array of products in its stores. It was (and is) an exceptional and successful retailer, but in Germany it failed, and its superstores were eventually sold to a competitor. Hubris and a lack of understanding of local culture may have contributed to its failure. Germany had its own discount chains offering low prices, but Walmart must have ignored their presence and popularity or thought that its everyday low-price formula and way of operating were superior and would somehow differentiate it from the competition. It was locked into its formula, but this time it did not work. Walmart left Germany in 2006, but the company seems not to have learned the lesson about different perspectives, context, and process orientation. In 2014, its formula was giving it trouble in Brazil. Its everyday low pricing was failing to win over customers there who, unconvinced it had the lowest prices, continued their normal routine of comparison shopping and searching for the lowest prices. Its expansion plans did not sufficiently consider the impact of existing discount retailers or people with different shopping habits.

Walmart applied its formula mindlessly. It did not take different perspectives into account to see how it would be interpreted in different contexts, nor did it apply a process orientation to learning from one experience and applying it in a different context.

For a second example, we can look at different players in different contexts in the evolution of online grocery home delivery. Webvan was an early entrant into this business in the United States. It was founded in the late 1990s and became one of the textbook failures of the dot-com era, filing for bankruptcy in July 2001. Peter Relan, the founding head of technology at Webvan from 1998 to 2000, said the company made some big mistakes: its target audience segmentation and pricing model; its complex infrastructure mode; and a grow-big-fast mentality accompanied by spending too much money too fast. Webvan assumed that the business model needed big warehouses, like other delivery businesses did. Relan said, "We touted our 26-city expansion plan, signing a $1 billion Bechtel contract to build several state-of-the-art warehouses worth more than $30 million each." It cost US$50 million to start up in each city. With high start-up costs, high initial capital expenditures, and a low-margin business, the company was never profitable.

In contrast, Peapod started in the grocery delivery business in Illinois in 1989. Instead of building separate warehouses, it partnered with existing supermarket chains in its target markets. By not having such huge capital expenditures, it had a more viable business model and continues to operate on the US East Coast.

At the same time, companies in the United Kingdom such as Tesco were also exploring online grocery delivery. There was a big difference, however, between the online channel development in the United States and the United Kingdom. In the United Kingdom,

the established grocery retailers, with extensive history in the traditional store based business, were driving the development of online. In the US the start-ups entering the grocery retail industry with purely online-based business models were the active players and the traditional grocery retailers remained sceptical about the new channel. (Kivilahti, 2013)

As Tesco executives developed their **brick-and-click** model (the combination of physical retail location and e-commerce), they realized, as Peapod had done, that existing supermarkets were essentially warehouses. These executives were able to see supermarkets and warehouses as equivalents and avoid the expensive mistake that Webvan made. These two examples illustrate how leaders' mindfulness can affect businesses.

Mindfulness Elements throughout This Book

Let's review Langer's three elements of mindfulness – perspective taking, context sensitivity, and process orientation – more carefully, and look at how they will be integrated throughout this book. The three elements are shown in Figure 1.4.

Perspective taking. In the successful examples, leaders were able to take different perspectives and see their business model from different points of view. This

Figure 1.4 Dimensions of mindful leadership in a global context.

led them to increase their **category width**, an important outcome and an indicator of mindfulness. Category range or width refers to the number of different events, activities, behaviors, situations, places, and so on that one sees as equivalent. Napoleon, apparently trapped in his formula, could only see the retreat of the Russian army as losing rather than as an alternative, a trap. Bruner, Goodnow, and Austin (1956, pp. 1–2) defined categorization as "classifying a variety of stimuli as forms of the same thing." They further stated, "To categorize is to render discriminably different things equivalent, to group the objects and events and people around us into classes, and to respond to them in terms of their class membership rather than their uniqueness." When leaders are able to expand their categories mindfully, by taking different perspectives, they are better able to contextualize information and evolve it through a process orientation.

We will explore perspective taking more deeply throughout this book. In particular, in Chapter 4 on mapping culture, we will describe bridging as communicating effectively while taking differences into account. One of the key components of bridging is decentering, which is taking others' perspectives into account in communication. Perspective taking will also take the foreground in Chapters 10, 11, and 12 on leading with integrity.

Context sensitivity. Many companies that fail in their attempts to globalize also exhibit a lack of context sensitivity. Executives often do not understand the unique characteristics of the new country or the culture. They do not understand their new market or their business model from the perspective of the people in the host country. They have a limited worldview based on experience in their home countries rather than a larger, cosmopolitan worldview, or what we will call a global mindset in Chapter 2. The inability to interpret differences correctly usually results in insufficiently detailed implementation plans.

There are several different aspects of the context a mindful leader takes into account. In this book we will focus on two that are highly important. The broader context is the national one, which includes the country's institutions and the predominant culture. A leader should understand the context for how local people make sense of their structures and actions. This also includes understanding the degree of variance within the context, and the implications for that variance. In Chapter 3, we will develop a deep understanding of the cultural context. Another key contextual dimension in international management is the organizational context. Even within the same multinational firm, subsidiaries and country offices with the same basic organizational structure will have different ways of operating and interacting, and different systems and procedures for managing decisions, tasks, and processes. In Chapter 7, we will examine the organization as a context for mindful leadership.

Process orientation. The companies that fail in their international experiences tend to focus on targets and outcomes more than on the process of getting there. Leading mindfully means paying attention to the "verbs" of management, such as interact, negotiate, partner, understand, relate, train, and especially learn: the dynamics of knowing how to adapt quickly and effectively to move forward to meet objectives. Mindful leaders understand that this means interacting with colleagues, customers, suppliers, and officials from other countries to achieve the desired outcome. Success comes from getting the job done with and through other people, paying close attention to *how* it gets done. Mindful global leadership is often less about deciding and more about identifying and embarking on a process. Mindful leaders pay close attention to learning and adaptation processes in particular.

A process perspective is the "currency" of implementation. Richard Pascale, the management theorist and business advisor, contrasted the Japanese "proceeding" with a typical American "deciding" mentality. He said, "The process of 'proceeding' generates further information; you move toward your goal through a sequence of steps rather than bold-stroke actions. The distinction is between having enough data to decide and having enough data to proceed" (Pascale, 1978, p. 155). A final objective focus may obscure the need to get more or better information in order to make progress toward the desired result. Changing strategies or conducting business in other countries and cultures is an activity filled with ambiguity and uncertainty, and "proceeding" is often the appropriate mode of operation.

Several chapters in this book focus specifically on processes in global leadership while maintaining the mindfulness of perspective taking and context sensitivity. Chapters 6 and 7 on teams and talent management, respectively, look at the dynamics among people as social processes. Chapter 9 examines the process of organizational alignment, and Chapter 10 dives into the process of leading change.

Mindfulness: A Practical Approach

Mindfulness has become a popular topic in academia and practice in business, as well as other parts of society and life. The term has become conflated with many other practices. It is important to clarify how we interpret and use these concepts, not to claim that our approach is better, but rather to avoid creating confusion.

Mindfulness is an important idea across many different philosophical, spiritual, and practical spheres, and there are multiple definitions of mindfulness. Common characteristics include being fully present, having a heightened state of awareness, active attention, and not being on autopilot. Some approaches suggest that to attain mindfulness requires meditation, spiritual reflection, or other practices. Indeed, recent cognitive research on mindfulness supports the link between meditation and the brain's ability to be mindful in all three dimensions (Nadler et al., 2020; Nielsen & Minda, 2021).

Our own treatment is more pragmatic. There are many different ways leaders can develop their ability to engage in mindfulness, and we encourage individuals to explore their own. In this book, we focus on the manifestations of mindfulness and its direct impact on a global leader's impact. In this regard, Langer's orientation brings awareness and active thinking into clear relationship with the external world or "context" and action or "process." Here is Langer's full definition:

Mindfulness is ... best understood as the process of drawing novel distinctions ... Actively drawing these distinctions keeps us situated in the present ... makes us more aware of the context and perspective of our actions than if we rely upon distinctions and categories drawn in the past. Under this latter situation, rules and routines are more likely to govern our behavior, irrespective of the current circumstances, and this can be construed as "mindless" behavior. (Langer and Moldoveanu, 2000, p. 2)

Langer and Moldoveanu (2000, p. 2) enumerate the results of mindfulness over mindlessness as "a greater sensitivity to one's environment; more openness to new information; the creation of new categories for structuring perception; and enhanced awareness of multiple perspectives in problem solving." This is the foundation for the approach taken throughout this book.

Reflection Question 1.4: Cultivating Your Ability to Be Mindful

Mindfulness is an active state of mind associated with creation of new knowledge, welcoming new horizons of information, noticing new things, and being open to the possibility of new perspectives (Langer, 2014). Take a mindful moment to reflect upon your own mindfulness:

1. Can you think about a situation in which you were "mindful." What characterized that situation? Why and how did you enter a state of mindfulness?
2. What can you do to create space for mindfulness in your everyday life?
3. If you were to tell a colleague or fellow student about mindfulness, what would you say?

Conclusion

The subtitle of this volume is "Global and Sustainable Leadership." Our aim is to help develop people who lead effectively in a global environment, toward solutions and systems that are sustainable for a prosperous society and planet.

That is a complex objective, and achieving it requires great sensitivity to the context of management. Management scholars use the term *environment* routinely, usually referring to the economic, competitive, regulatory, social, and consumer behavior aspects of the marketplace. Increasingly, as suggested in this chapter and in later chapters, the wider sociopolitical and natural "environments" surrounding people and organizations are undergoing significant shifts. These shifts create enormous complexity and imperatives for global leaders, as well as enormous opportunities for them and their organizations.

Current and aspiring global leaders must embrace the challenge to recognize, monitor, and adapt their organizations to these shifts. As we state in Chapter 8, they need to acknowledge the primacy of context and to realize that "The Environment Always Wins." Neither the status quo nor the attempts to return to "the before times" will be sufficient to survive and prosper.

With such complexity, it is not practical to develop a handbook or policy manual detailing all the relevant practices for each type of context. Even if it were possible to write, the handbook would be out of date as soon as it was written. Instead, we advocate a mindful approach to global leadership. Global leaders must develop strong perspective taking, context sensitivity, and a process orientation in order to lead others across boundaries in this complex environment.

Further Resources

There are many books and articles tracing the history of globalization, and the scholarly references from this chapter point to the ones that have shaped our thinking the most. It's helpful to read about globalization as a narrative, and these are the books we think are particularly insightful, with stories told in very compelling ways.

Baldwin, R. (2016). *The great convergence: Information technology and the new globalization.* Belknap Press.

Bremmer, I. (2022). *The power of crisis: How three threats – and our response – will change the world.* Simon & Schuster.

Foroohar, R. (2022). *Homecoming: The path to prosperity in a post-global world.* Crown.

Garten, J. E. (2016). *From silk to silicon: The story of globalization through ten extraordinary lives.* Harper.

Gerstle, G. (2022). *The rise and fall of the neoliberal order: America and the world in the free market era.* Oxford University Press.

Rivoli, P. (2009). *The travels of a t-shirt in the global economy: An economist examines the markets, power and politics of the world trade* (2nd Ed). Wiley.

Stigiltz, J. (2002). *Globalization and its discontents.* W.W. Norton & Co.

Bibliography

Beamish, P. W., & Hasse, V. C. (2022). The importance of rare events and other outliers in global strategy research. *Global Strategy Journal*, 12(4), 697–713. https://doi.org/10.1002/gsj.1437

Bennis, W., & Nanus, B. (1985). *Leaders: The strategies for taking charge.* Harper & Row.

Bruner, J., Goodnow, J., & Austin, G. (1956). *A study of thinking.* Wiley.

Chatham House. (2021). What is China's Belt and Road Initiative (BRI)? Retrieved March 26, 2024, from https://www.chathamhouse.org/2021/09/what-chinas-belt-and-road-initiative-bri.

Cohen, J., & Rodgers, Y. (2020). Contributing factors to personal protective equipment shortages during the COVID-19 pandemic. *PrevMed*, 141, 106263. Retrieved August 17, 2022, from https://www.ncbi.nlm.nih.gov/pmc/articles/PMC7531934/#:~:text=Since%20early%2020

Council on Foreign Relations. (2023). *China's massive belt and road initiative.* Retrieved January 2023 from https://www.cfr.org/backgrounder/chinas-massive-belt-and-road-initiative

Ewing, J., & Boudette, N. (2021, April 23, updated October 14). *A tiny part's big ripple: Global chip shortage hobbles the auto industry.* New York Times. Retrieved August 18, 2022, from https://www.nytimes.com/2021/04/23/business/auto-semiconductors-general-motors-mercedes.html

Faroohar, R. (2022, October 17). *Globalism failed to deliver the economy we need.* New York Times. Retrieved October 27, 2022, from https://www.nytimes.com/2022/10/17/opinion/neoliberalism-economy.html

Farrell, H., & Newman, A. (2020, January–February). Choke points. *Harvard Business Review.*

Fukuyama, F. (1992). *The End of History and the Last Man.* Free Press.

Galston, W. A. (2020, March 10). *Efficiency isn't the only economic virtue.* Wall Street Journal. Retrieved January 9, 2023, from https://www.wsj.com/articles/efficiency-isnt-the-only-economic-virtue-11583873155

Global Resilience Institute. Retrieved January 9, 2023, from https://globalresilience.northeastern.edu/about/resilience

Hinton, S. E. (1998). *That was Then, this is Now.* Penguin.

Kivalahti, A. (2013, November 28). *Evolution of online groceries.* Digital Foodie. Retrieved October 2017 from http://www.digitalfoodie.com/evolution-of-online-groceries.com

Kobayashi, S., Baobo, J., & Sano, J. (1999). The "three reforms" in China: Progress and outlook. *Japan Research Institute Periodical*, 45.

Lane, H. W., Maznevski, M. L., Mendenhall, M., & McNett, J. (2004). *The Blackwell handbook of global management: A guide to managing complexity.* Blackwell Publishers.

Langer, E. J., (2014). *Mindfulness* (25th Anniversary Ed.). Da Capo Press.

Langer, E. J., & Moldoveanu, M. (2000). The construct of mindfulness. *Journal of Social Science*, 56(1), 1–9.

Li, J., Shapiro, D., Peng, M., & Ufimtseva, A. (2022). Corporate diplomacy in the age of US-China rivalry. *Academy of Management Perspectives.* Retrieved January 2023 from

https://www.cfr.org/backgrounder/chinas-massive-belt-and-road-initiative

McDonald's. Retrieved August 15, 2022, from https://corporate.mcdonalds.com/corpmcd/en-us/our2022-stories/article/ourstories.mcd-exit-russia.html

Mendenhall, M. E., Osland, J. S., Bird, A., Oddou, G. R., Maznevski, M. L., Stevens, M. J., & Stahl, G. K. (2013). *Global leadership*. Routledge.

Milanovic, B. (2016). *Global inequality: A new approach for the age of globalization*. Harvard University Press.

Mintzberg, H. (2005). *Managers not MBAs: A hard look at the soft practice of managing and management development*. Berett-Koehler Publishers.

Nadler, R., Carswell, J. J., & Minda, J. P. (2020). Online mindfulness training increases well-being, trait emotional intelligence, and workplace competency ratings: A randomized waitlist-controlled trial. *Frontiers in psychology*, *11*, 255.

National Intelligence Council. (2021, March). *Global trends 2040: A more contested world*. Retrieved September 2, 2022, from https://www.dni.gov/files/ODNI/documents/assessments/GlobalTrends_2040.pdf

Nielsen, E. G., & Minda, J. P. (2021). The mindful lawyer: Investigating the effects of two online mindfulness programs on self-reported well-being in the legal profession. *Journal of Occupational and Environmental Medicine*, *63*(12), e871–e882.

Pascale, R. T. (1978). Zen and the art of management. *Harvard Business Review*, *56*(2), 153–162.

Peterson Institute for International Economics. (2022, October 24). What is globalization. Retrieved February 15, 2023, from https://www.piie.com/microsites/globalization/what-is-globalization

Prahalad, C. K. (1990). Globalization: The intellectual and managerial challenges. *Human Resource Management*, *29*(1), 27–37.

Reiche, S. B., Bird, A., Mendenhall, M. E., & Osland, J. S. (2017, July). Conceptualizing leadership: A typology of global leadership. *Journal of International Business Studies*, *48*(5), 552–572.

Rohwer, J. (2000, October). GE digs into Asia. *Fortune*, *142*(7), 178.

Schein, E. (2021). *Global chip shortage cheat sheet*. TechRepublic. Retrieved February 17, 2023, from https://www.techrepublic.com/article/global-chip-shortage-cheat-sheet

Senge, P. M. (2006). *The fifth discipline: The art & practice of the learning organization* (Rev. Ed.). Doubleday.

Sonnenfeld, J., Tian, S., Sokolowski, F., Wyrebkowski, M., & Kasprowicz, M. (2022). Business Retreats and Sanctions Are Crippling the Russian Economy (July 19, 2022). S&P Global Market Intelligence. Available at SSRN: https://ssrn.com/abstract=4167193 or http://dx.doi.org/10.2139/ssrn.4167193. Retrieved March 26, 2024.

Statistics Canada. (2021). Retrieved August 19, 2022, from https://www.statcan.gc.ca/en/start https://www12.statcan.gc.ca/census-recensement/2021/dp-pd/prof/index.cfm?Lang=E

The Economist. (2008, September 20). A bigger world: A special report on globalization. *The Economist*, 12.

The Economist. (2017, January 28). The retreat of the global company. *The Economist*.

Vaill, P. B. (1996). *Learning as a way of being: Strategies for survival in a world of permanent white water*. Wiley.

Weick, K. E., & Van Orden, P. (1990). Organizing on a global scale: A research and teaching agenda. *Human Resource Management*, *29*(1), 49–61.

World Economic Forum. (2019, January 17). *A brief history of globalization*. Retrieved November 16, 2022, from https://www.weforum.org/agenda/2019/01/how-globalization-4-0-fits-into-the-history-of-globalization

Zeleznik, A. (2004). Managers and leaders: Are they different? *Harvard Business Review* – Reprinted in *Best of HBR*, 74–81.

2 Pathways to Mindful Global Leadership

Mindset, Competences, and Paradox Thinking

> Usually, you do not have a perfect answer. It is important that you develop good processes to assess problems that give you the best information and include different points of view.
>
> Barack Obama, former US President, from a speech on September 28, 2019, Aalborg, Denmark

Key Learning Objectives

At the end of this chapter, students will be able to:

- Define the concept of the global mindset and differentiate the four domains of the global mindset.
- Explain the three dimensions of Global Leadership Competences – perception management, relationship management, and self-management – and analyze their own strengths and development needs.
- Identify the global-local paradox in management dilemmas and describe collaborative processes for proceeding to resolve it.
- Develop mindful global leadership by practicing the three pathways as different starting points.

Mindfulness and Mindful Global Leadership

As we saw in Chapter 1, mindfulness is the process of being fully engaged in the present and actively noticing new things with increased sensitivity to context and perspective (Langer, 2014; Langer & Moldoveanu, 2000). Figure 2.1

Figure 2.1 Dimensions of mindful leadership in a global context.

shows the three elements of mindfulness: global mindfulness requires context sensitivity, perspective taking, and a process orientation. In this chapter we focus on a set of three pathways to develop and practice mindful global leadership.

We will look at the importance of a global mindset and explore how it highlights context sensitivity and hence provides a pathway into mindful global leadership. Then we will examine a framework for global leadership competences that emphasize perspective taking and show how it provides a second pathway into mindful global leadership. Finally, we will introduce a model for identifying and managing paradoxes in global leadership, one that provides a third pathway to mindful global leadership through a process orientation.

Mindful Global Leadership Starts with a Global Mindset

Global managers must learn how to function as effectively in other contexts as they do in their own country, and to build bridges between different worldviews. This requires considerable cognitive complexity. To think globally really requires an alteration of our mindset. A mindful leader must come into global interactions ready and eager to process information about different perspectives, contexts, and processes. A global mindset is the framework a global leader carries in their mind to organize this information.

Based on our previous work with global mindset development in theory and practice (e.g., Lane et al., 2004; Nielsen, 2014) as well as extant literature (e.g., Begley & Boyd, 2003; Levy et al., 2007), we define a global mindset like this:

A **global mindset** is the knowledge framework underlying the capacity to analyze situations and develop criteria for personal and business performance, independently from the assumptions of a single country, culture, or context, and to implement those criteria appropriately, taking into account different countries, cultures, and contexts.

Figure 2.2 Global mindset as a pathway to mindful global leadership.

In other words, a global mindset is a way of organizing knowledge that helps leaders separate context from other dynamics to make decisions, then to put those dynamics and context back together again to implement those decisions effectively. Figure 2.2 highlights a global mindset as a pathway to global leader mindfulness through context sensitivity.

Global Mindset Illustrated

Let's look at the effect of a global mindset in a real international management situation.

> A multinational consumer food company was implementing self-managed teams across its global plants for its new production facilities. In the dynamic global environment, the company believed it was important to have decision-making authority with the people who had the most immediate information to make the decisions, and who had to implement the decisions. These people were in the best position to have the ultimate effect on end consumers' experience of the food. The company developed a model of how self-managed teams should work, pilot-tested it in their home country, then rolled out the new structure around the world. However, it was met with resistance. In many parts of the world, the idea of teams managing themselves, without a specific boss to lead them, was completely unheard of. Some plant managers pushed through the self-managed teams program to greater and greater dissatisfaction; others gave up and just kept the more rigid and hierarchical teams. Quality and consumer satisfaction didn't decrease, but they didn't increase either.
>
> Some managers, however, did something different. They looked at the two most important criteria for identifying who should make decisions in this new manufacturing context: the people who have the information and the people who must implement it. They also realized that manufacturing would not

achieve its potential unless there was more interdependence among the various parts of the process. Then they questioned whether the only way to accomplish this was the self-managed team model that the headquarters dictated. They met with their managers and teams and developed a way to achieve the required working relationships and decision processes that fit with the local teams' preferences and context. In some cases this solution had more hierarchy, in others it had fewer specific roles and more fluidity, and still others had more individual responsibility. All of these more mindful managers achieved their ambitious performance goals. Product quality and consumer satisfaction both went up, along with market share.

The second set of managers was working with a global mindset. They were able to separate performance criteria like "people with the information make the decisions" from culturally influenced contextual preferences like "self-managed teams." Then they found a way to achieve the performance criteria in different contexts. Their global mindsets allowed them to see different perspectives, to pay attention to different aspects of the context in meaningful ways, and to develop testable ideas and implement them with a process orientation.

Components and Domains of a Global Mindset

The crux of developing a global mindset is achieving self-awareness and other awareness, including awareness of the relationship between context and characteristics of the self and others. How much of my behavior is "me" and how much of it is influenced by my context? Or, more appropriately, when and how is my behavior more or less influenced by my context? When and how is this the case for others? In business, we need this understanding both about ourselves and others as individuals, and ourselves and others in social groups, especially organizations. These orientations help develop four types of knowledge in the domains in which a global mindset operates, shown in Table 2.1.

Type 1: Knowledge about Self. A global mindset incorporates a concept of self, both as an individual and as part of an organization. We need to acknowledge and understand what it is about our mindset that has been shaped by our own context. Both national culture and organizational culture are critical parts of context that influence self. A global mindset should include sophisticated knowledge about these cultures. Becoming aware of the influence of culture on oneself can be both uncomfortable and difficult, but the ability to see and examine it is critical to developing an effective global mindset.

Table 2.1 **Domains of a Global Mindset**

	Individual	Organizational
Self	**Type 1: Myself in my own context** Understand how "who I am" is associated with my culture and the context I am in.	**Type 3: My own organization in its context** Understand my own organization and how its characteristics, organizational culture, and effectiveness are associated with the context and culture it is in.
Other	**Type 2: Others in their contexts** Understand how characteristics of people from other countries and cultures are associated with the contexts they are in.	**Type 4: Other organizations in their contexts** Understand how characteristics, cultures, and effectiveness of organizations from other countries and cultures are associated with the contexts they are in.

Type 2: Knowledge about Others. Different contexts create different assumptions and value systems. This is the more obvious part about cultural differences. It is easy to see that people from different cultures perceive the same situation differently, interpret what they notice differently, evaluate the situation differently, and take different actions. A global mindset means going beyond these superficial observations and understanding the deeper nature and impact of these differences.

Type 3: Knowledge about Own Organization. A global mindset also requires understanding how the organizations of which we are a part (families, peer groups, institutions, companies) are influenced by their context. Most companies have a particular administrative heritage or organizational culture that has evolved in their home countries. This means that a potential cultural bias may exist in their strategy, systems, and practices – the way things are done in the headquarters' home country.

Hofstede (1980) observed that "theories reflect the cultural environment in which they were written." Management concepts and practices are explained by theories regarding organization, motivation, and leadership. Therefore, theories of management systems and management practices may work well in the culture that developed them because they are based on local cultural assumptions and paradigms about the right way to manage.

Type 4: Knowledge about Other Organizations. Knowledge about other organizations and their relationship with their context allows a manager to adapt continually to business and contextual contingencies. For example, a human resource system that provides collective performance bonuses in Mexico and individual performance bonuses in the United States might fit with cultural preferences in those countries and encourage high performance today. However, a human resource system dedicated to motivating all employees to perform well, whatever their background or preferences, is needed to ensure performance across organizational contexts. Knowledge about other organizations is what helps the manager identify criteria for performance that can be universally applied, and then adapt them to different contexts.

Developing a Global Mindset through Learning

A global mindset is not something innate – it must be developed. Although some persons may be naturally talented, most managers need to dedicate themselves to developing a global mindset. The good news is that everybody can develop their mindset through active shaping and learning.

A global mindset is a specific type of mental framework, or cognitive **schema**, for organizing information. Schemas influence what we notice and what meaning we attribute to perceptions, and they shape the actions we take in the world around us. Schemas are simple at first and become more complex with greater experience. This development of more complex schemas allows a person to process enormous amounts of information and to see patterns without getting lost in the detail. There is a difference in the way that expert and novice global managers think, as shown by Bird and Osland:

When entering into a new situation [experts] notice more and different types of cues, they interpret those cues differently, they choose from a different, wider range of appropriate actions than do novices, and then they execute/implement their chosen course of action at higher levels than do novices. In the case of global managers, these differences between novices and experts are magnified ...

[As] they become more competent, experts recognize complexity and a larger set of cues. They are able to discern which cues are the most important and are able to move beyond strict adherence to rules and to think in terms of trade-offs. On attaining the expert stage, they can read situations without rational thought – they diagnose the situation unconsciously and respond intuitively because over the years they have developed the holistic recognition or mental maps that allow for effortless framing and reframing of strategies and quick adaptation. (Osland & Bird, 2004)

Once a schema exists, it changes through one of two processes – **assimilation** or **accommodation** (Furth, 1970). In assimilation, new information is perceived as consistent with the schema's organizational framework and incorporated readily. In accommodation, new information contradicts the schema to the extent that the schema itself must be changed. Good learning maximizes both processes.

Assimilation is the easier of these two processes. When perceptions are consistent with assumptions, people don't need to question those assumptions, but can simply "bolt on" new knowledge. For example, Jack, a manager at a US consumer products firm, learned that people are motivated by individual monetary incentives such as bonus schemes and commissions. He implemented incentives to influence his salespeople to focus on specific products in the portfolio – one shampoo brand this season, a shower gel product next season. The results were immediate, sales in the right categories went up, and his knowledge was reinforced through assimilation.

Accommodation is a much more difficult and uncomfortable process. When people encounter something that contradicts existing assumptions, they experience **cognitive dissonance**, a feeling of imbalance. People try to reduce the imbalance to achieve consistency again by either changing perceptions of the evidence to match the assumptions (call into question the subject of the contradiction) or by changing assumptions to match the evidence (call into question themselves). People are more inclined to invoke the first method than the second; it requires a great deal less energy, is reinforced by others who hold the same assumptions, and is less confusing. The other option, altering one's own assumptions, is unfortunately a less frequently chosen alternative considering that altering assumptions is central to changing your mindset and developing a global mindset.

James, a leader we met, moved to his company's Norwegian subsidiary after several years of success in the United States, his company's home country. But when he implemented his trusted incentive schemes and bonuses at his new location, he did not see corresponding increases in sales of the desired products. Why not? Here's how he addressed the challenge.

> At first, I thought there was something wrong with the salespeople. I knew that incentive schemes and bonuses always work, so it must have been the local salespeople that created the problem. I started to think about how to fix that – maybe I had the wrong staff? Should I fire them and hire new ones? Then I started to wonder maybe, just maybe, they motivated salespeople differently here. I began asking my Norwegian colleagues how they influenced salespeople to change their focus in their portfolios.
>
> The sales managers told me that they just talk with them, ask them questions, and then salespeople change to the right things. This sounded crazy to me, but they were getting results, so I started sitting in on the discussions to see what was going on. I saw what I thought was a very complex process

of managers discussing the market with each salesperson and combining the salesperson's advice with the manager's own expertise to kind of emerge to an agreement about what to sell. It seemed that the Norwegian salespeople – in our company at least – were motivated to change more by having their expertise valued than by financial incentives. It took me a while, but I learned to work with my salespeople in this way, and then I began to wonder if this approach would also work back in the US. I'll sure try combining it with traditional methods when I go back.

James's initial response was an assimilation one. He tried to fit the new information into his old schema. Fortunately, James eventually questioned his assumptions with an accommodation response and adjusted the schema itself. His new understanding will help him develop expertise across many other situations.

Developing Your Own Global Mindset

It is vital to recognize that developing your own global mindset requires active learning. You must engage with problems for which you must assess the situation, see options, make decisions, implement actions, and experience feedback. Second, you must pay close attention to your own reactions and to what is happening in the environment. In other words, developing our own global mindset requires mindfulness – start from being sensitive to the context, then use that sensitivity to see different perspectives engaging a process orientation.

You will become aware of how your assumptions and frameworks shape perceptions, values, and behavior as you confront the different sets of assumptions guiding the views and practices of others. If you are exposed to new experiences under the right circumstances, part of your response may include an examination of your own guiding values and theories of management – the beginning of developing a global mindset. You may find that your existing frameworks are incomplete or are disconfirmed because you did not see the whole picture or could only see it from a narrow point of view.

As you continue reading the material in this book, focus both on building awareness of yourself in your own context as well as learning about others in their contexts. This will build your mindfulness with perspective taking and context sensitivity. In line with a process orientation, question your assumptions and those of others as you test the application of your knowledge in different contexts. Ask questions of people with whom you work – questions you may not have thought of before. Pay attention to surprises, both as you read the book and as you ask questions and engage with others. Surprise is an indicator that you had hidden assumptions, and it provides an opportunity to identify them. These actions will help you build a global mindset. They will extend your repertoire of behaviors and enrich your personal experience of the world.

> ### Reflection Question 2.1: Yourself in Your Own Context
>
> Table 2.1, Domains of a Global Mindset, shows four different aspects of a global mindset. Please pause and think about the upper left quadrant, Type 1: Myself in my own context. Think about yourself: How are your behavior, preferences, values, and attitudes associated with your cultural background and the context you are in? Please think of three to five examples where your culture and context matter (for better or worse) when making new acquaintances or otherwise interacting with new people. How do you think knowledge of such impact on *you* is significant for understanding *other* individuals and organizations (lower left and right quadrants, Type 2 and 4)?

Global Leadership Competences

Competences are bundles of knowledge and skills that combine to direct behavior. What kinds of competences do you need to lead mindfully, with a global mindset, across contexts? Research on global leadership has skyrocketed, and many studies have been published identifying the skills that global leaders need. Some lists of competences include as many as 250 skills (Bird et al., 2010)! It seems that only a superhero can be a global leader.

The Pyramid Model of Global Leadership developed by Bird and Osland (2004) summarizes the key skills and knowledge and illustrates how they build on each other. It is shown in Figure 2.3. Each level of competencies presumes and builds on the level below, and the more global a job is, the more it requires sophisticated competencies in the higher levels of the pyramid.

The foundational level is **Global Business Knowledge**. This is deep knowledge about the manager's business and how that business creates value. It also includes knowledge about the political, economic, social, and technical environment. This foundational knowledge is necessary before any of the next steps.

The next level identifies **Threshold Traits**. Knowledge will lie dormant without the personal predisposition to use it. Four traits differentiate people who are effective in global settings from those who are less effective: integrity, humility,

```
                    /\
                   /System\
                  / Skills \
                 /Influencing\
                /Stakeholders \
               /Building   Leading\
              /Community    Change \
             /    Architecting      \
            / Ethical      Boundary  \
           /Decision-Making Spanning  \
          /─────Interpersonal Skills───\
         / Mindful   Building Trust & Multicultural\
        / Communication Relationships   Teaming    \
       /────────Attitudes & Orientations────────────\
      / Global Mindset  Cognitive Complexity  Cosmopolitanism\
     /──────────────Threshold Traits──────────────────────────\
    / Integrity    Humility     Inquisitiveness     Resilience \
   /──────────────Global Business Knowledge─────────────────────\
```

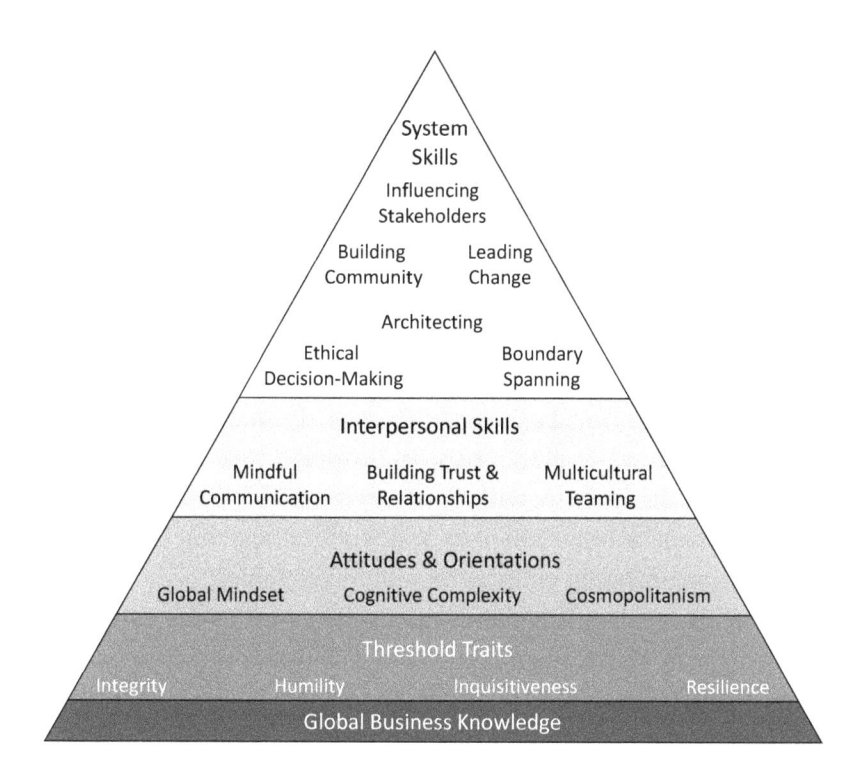

Figure 2.3 Pyramid of global leadership competencies.
Adapted from Bird and Osland (2004).

inquisitiveness, and resilience. Integrity is having a firm set of values associated with honesty and transparency and being true to those values. Humility is recognizing that knowledge and skills are widely distributed, and that others know and can do things that you, yourself, may not. Inquisitiveness, or curiosity, is the active motivation to know things one does not already know. While humility creates openness, curiosity drives action to learn more, and to experiment with different ways of creating value. Finally, resilience is the ability to persevere in the face of challenges and difficulties.

The next level of the pyramid is an important set of **Attitudes and Orientations** – ways of seeing the world and the task of international management. The basic traits suggest potential within an individual; attitudes and orientations guide that potential so the individual sees opportunities. The most important is a global mindset, or the tendency and ability to see and understand the world differently than one has been conditioned to see and understand it. In other words, it is a view from outside of one's own borders. Two attitudes and orientations contribute to developing a global mindset. Cognitive complexity is an ability to see a situation from multiple perspectives, to see connections among the perspectives, and to build new connections with existing and new information. Cosmopolitanism is having a positive attitude toward people, things, and viewpoints from other parts of the world. For example, people who are cosmopolitan are more likely to have close friends who are from countries other than their own.

The three most important **Interpersonal Skills** for global leaders are mindful communication, building trust, and multicultural teaming. Mindful communication is paying attention to how you communicate with others, especially those who are different, and adapting your communication as necessary to ensure that meaning is transmitted the way people intend. This includes both sending messages (speaking, writing, and nonverbal acts) and receiving them (listening, reading, and observing the behavior of others). Building trust is creating a relationship where all parties believe that the other will act with good intentions for the relationship and can make decisions on each other's behalf. Multicultural teaming is working effectively with people from different cultures on joint deliverables.

Armed with these skills, leaders are better equipped to work with others to develop and implement ideas. Many other interpersonal skills are of course important to global leadership effectiveness, such as negotiation and conflict resolution. However, if a manager is adept at mindful communication, building trust, and multicultural teaming, then generally these other skills will follow. The reverse is not necessarily true – one can negotiate solutions and resolve conflicts without increasing trust, for example.

Finally, a set of six **Systems Skills** are critical for global leaders: spanning boundaries, building community, leading change, architecting, influencing stakeholders, and ethical decision-making. Boundary spanning is working effectively across countries, organizations, divisions within organizations, and so on. It involves using all the skills and attitudes identified in the lower parts of the model to create insights and synergies across different perspectives. Building community is creating a sense of identity and joint commitment among a group of people distributed across different countries and units. Leading change effectively is about helping an organization through diverse ways of doing things while creating capabilities for adapting to further change. Architecting is designing and implementing organizational structures and systems that facilitate the organization. Influencing stakeholders, which is an important part of any leadership role, becomes more complex in a global role, where stakeholder variety reflects different interests in different contexts. Ethical decision-making is about making and implementing decisions that consider the long-term benefit of individuals and society.

Global Leadership Competence Dimensions

The pyramid model provides an important way to summarize the many requirements for global leadership. Researchers sought ways to consolidate the competences categories even further, so they could direct leadership development more easily. Through a rigorous program of research and practice they developed three dimensions of global leadership competences: Perception Management, Relationship Management, and Self-Management (Bird et al., 2010). The underlying theme across all the global leadership requirements is the ability to interact effectively across different perspectives, and the three-dimensional Global Leadership Competences therefore provide a key pathway to Global Mindfulness through Perspective Taking, as we illustrate in Figure 2.4.

The three dimensions are summarized in Table 2.2.

Table 2.2 Dimensions of global leadership competences, summarized from Bird et al. (2010)

Perception Management	Relationship Management	Self-Management
Sample components:	Sample components:	Sample components:
• Nonjudgmental	• Relationship interest	• Optimism
• Inquisitive	• Interpersonal engagement	• Self-identity and self-confidence
• Tolerates Ambiguity	• Emotional sensitivity	• Emotional resilience
• Cosmopolitan	• Oriented to learning	• Stress management
• High category breadth	• Social flexibility	• Interest flexibility

Note: For all components, the emphasis is on the context of interacting across international and cross-cultural boundaries with perspective taking.

Figure 2.4 Global leadership competences as a pathway to mindful global leadership.

Perception Management

This dimension concerns how people take in, analyze, and use information. It describes the processes leaders use to perceive and assess new situations and events, and their ability to deal effectively with ambiguous situations. In our discussion on mindfulness in Chapter 1, we explained how important perspective taking and context sensitivity are in global leadership. Earlier in this chapter, we identified the components of a global mindset, which is a cognitive framework. Perception management as a global leadership *competence* is about the leader's ability to use these cognitive perspectives effectively.

Leaders who are high in perception management are able to enter new situations with curiosity, even when it's hard to figure out what's going on. They withhold judgment about whether someone else's actions are good or bad; rather, they try to understand the actions in their context. They tend to be eager to learn about other cultures and their histories, and this continually expanding knowledge helps them develop hypotheses to explain people's actions.

Relationship Management

This dimension comprises a set of skills around building and maintaining strong interpersonal relationships with people who come from different cultures. In Chapter 1, we described the importance of relationships in our discussion of the process orientation in mindfulness. Simply put, leaders can get things done only through other people. This is especially true in global leadership, when the leader may not have knowledge of or access to resources needed to accomplish the task. In situations of high ambiguity and volatile change, relationships characterized by deep trust and personal commitment not only make leadership life more pleasant; they are absolutely necessary.

Leaders who are high in relationship management are curious about other people and want to build relationships. They have strong interpersonal skills, such as emotional intelligence, and are able to apply these skills to people who are quite different from themselves. They adapt their behavior according to the needs of the situation, and they have a strong orientation toward learning more about themselves and others and how we interact in different situations, grounded in an ability to see themselves as others do.

Self-Management

This final dimension addresses the fact that global leadership is very challenging, and leaders will be confronted with situations that are tough for them personally as well as difficult for the business. Effective leaders have a strong sense of stability in their self-identity and at the same time are able to learn, change, and adapt. Self-management and resilience have increasingly become part of managerial focus, especially since the start of the COVID-19 pandemic due to the fact that employees needed to work in isolation from their managers and other colleagues. But research and practice on global leadership have long recognized that one important predictor of a global leader's effectiveness is their ability to manage their sense of self in a healthy way.

Leaders who are high in self-management have a positive sense of self and are optimistic and confident. This does not suggest naïveté or arrogance – their optimism and confidence are grounded in experience and lead to an open approach rather than a superior or unquestioning one. These leaders also manage their emotions and stress effectively. Global leadership is undoubtedly emotional and stressful, so self-management is not about avoiding these dynamics. Instead, effective leaders are able to identify their emotional and stress states and have strong coping skills for managing their impact on other people as well as on themselves.

Mutually Reinforcing Dimensions

Research supports that these dimensions are separate, and each contributes independently to a global leader's effectiveness. It is also our experience that each of the dimensions supports the other two. A leader's perception management can help build relationships and manage the leader's sense of self. Good interpersonal relationships will help a leader obtain information to contribute to perception management and inform resilience and stress management. A leader's strong self-management will encourage the leader to engage perceptions with curiosity and to be open to building strong interpersonal relationships. Whichever areas of strength a leader has, they can use those strengths to build their global leadership competences further.

The Kozai Group has developed an assessment that measures these attributes of global leadership, the Global Competencies Inventory (GCI). Research with thousands of businesspeople and business students around the world has revealed eight recurring patterns shown in Figure 2.5. If you have not yet taken the GCI, you can look at the patterns below and determine which pattern likely fits you best.

Developing Your Global Leadership Competences

As the graphs show, scoring high on all three dimensions is rare. The important takeaway is to identify your strengths, then leverage them to develop in areas in which you score less highly. Are you strong on perception management? Focus

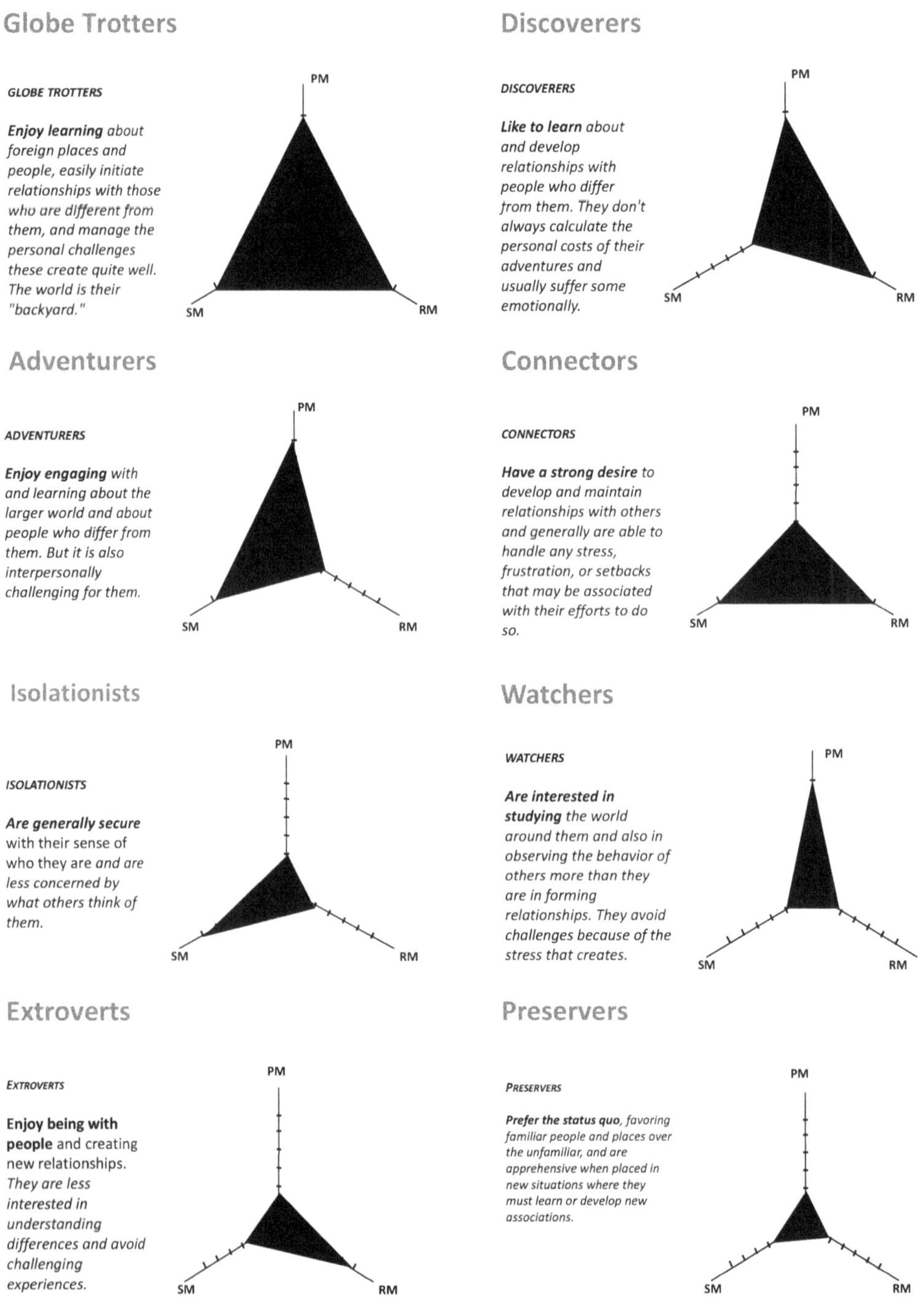

Globe Trotters

GLOBE TROTTERS

Enjoy learning about foreign places and people, easily initiate relationships with those who are different from them, and manage the personal challenges these create quite well. The world is their "backyard."

Discoverers

DISCOVERERS

Like to learn about and develop relationships with people who differ from them. They don't always calculate the personal costs of their adventures and usually suffer some emotionally.

Adventurers

ADVENTURERS

Enjoy engaging with and learning about the larger world and about people who differ from them. But it is also interpersonally challenging for them.

Connectors

CONNECTORS

Have a strong desire to develop and maintain relationships with others and generally are able to handle any stress, frustration, or setbacks that may be associated with their efforts to do so.

Isolationists

ISOLATIONISTS

Are generally secure with their sense of who they are and are less concerned by what others think of them.

Watchers

WATCHERS

Are interested in studying the world around them and also in observing the behavior of others more than they are in forming relationships. They avoid challenges because of the stress that creates.

Extroverts

EXTROVERTS

Enjoy being with people and creating new relationships. They are less interested in understanding differences and avoid challenging experiences.

Preservers

PRESERVERS

Prefer the status quo, favoring familiar people and places over the unfamiliar, and are apprehensive when placed in new situations where they must learn or develop new associations.

Figure 2.5 Global competence patterns. © Allan Bird.

on using that to learn more about people and about yourself. Are you especially strong on relationship management? Use your strong interpersonal relationships to learn more about contexts and situations, and to build your resilience. Are you especially strong on self-management? Use that positive approach and resilience to engage people and ideas in different contexts.

Because these competences are patterns of *behavior*, we encourage you also to mindfully engage in experiences that will help you directly (not just vicariously) practice perception, relationship, and self-management. These experiences do not need to involve traveling to different countries. Wherever you live, there are contexts around you that are quite different from the ones you are used to. There are also people around you who experience life quite differently from the way you do. Engaging with these people in their own contexts is a great way to practice and develop your global leadership competences.

Reflection Question 2.2: Your Global Leadership Competences

Reflect on your own global leadership competences.

1. Which of the profiles in Figure 2.5 (Global Competence Patterns) do you think fits you most closely? How did you develop that pattern?
2. What is a specific cross-boundary situation in which you drew on your strengths? How did your strengths help the situation?
3. In which area would you like to develop? Identify a situation in which you can practice this set of competences on a regular basis.

Paradox Thinking

When a context or situation is complex, filled with variety, interdependencies, and fast flux, it often presents paradoxes to managers. A **paradox** is a situation in which two mutually incompatible choices or solutions are *both* necessary for effectiveness. There is no way to resolve a paradox by making a difficult choice. One choice cannot be prioritized over the other, and they cannot be combined in a way that removes the paradox. Both solutions are necessary, but they cannot be implemented simultaneously. Instead, paradoxes must be managed using a mindful orientation and a deliberate set of dialogue processes. These processes provide a third pathway into mindful global leadership, as illustrated in Figure 2.6.

Figure 2.6 Paradox thinking as a pathway to mindful global leadership.

Paradoxes Illustrated

Let's take a look at some examples of classic paradoxes. Imagine walking through a multinational corporation's headquarters meeting spaces and overhearing this meeting.

> The product leader from a subsidiary market is attending virtually, and you can see a very different climate and cityscape in the background. "That branding just doesn't work here. The people in this country have strong traditions around this product group, and our focus groups say they find the new branding goes against those traditions. Sales will go down, and retailer groups won't give us space for it in the stores." The global brand leader patiently responds, "I understand it's not the best for your market. But we have to think of the rest of the world, too. The global retailers love the new branding, and in our biggest markets it's seen as more positive than the current brand. You'll just have to find a way to make the best of it." The subsidiary leader grumbles, "Can I get that in writing for my head of region, so it doesn't affect my bonus when revenue goes down?" The subsidiary leader grumbles because he is well aware that he will not receive any compensation for costs incurred locally as a result of delivering on global objectives.

The global brand leader is asking the subsidiary leader to balance the competing demands of local and global concerns, without making an either-or choice. The subsidiary leader must choose a both-and strategy to navigate the paradox. This is an example of the **global-local paradox**.

Further down the hall you might pass by this argument between two managers.

The marketing leader asserts, "We need to put resources into developing new solutions for customers now, or we won't have those solutions to sell next year!" The sales leader comes back with "Oh yeah? We need to put resources into our sales efforts right now or there won't BE a next year!"

This illustrates another classic paradox: the **short- and long-term paradox.** The organization needs both the short-term profits and the long-term innovation stream (both-and), but at any given moment the trade-off is challenging to resolve.

In another meeting room, there is another heated discussion.

A production director points passionately to the factory floor through the window, saying, "We need a step change in quality here to meet customer demands. We're getting too many complaints and returned products. That means retraining our production staff to work with more advanced systems and spending more time on maintenance and quality." The commercial director replies, "Our quality is good enough! We're already missing out on market demand. If we don't increase production quantities fast, we'll lose market share. It costs much more to build market share than to maintain it!"

What plays out here is actors defending the different poles of the **production-commercial paradox,** each stating the case for the superiority of their pole. The dispute, however, cannot sustainably be settled by making an either-or choice between the two. Consumers are not inclined to settle for either quality or quantity – they demand both. The production director and the commercial directors must navigate the production-commercial paradox together in an ongoing balancing act.

None of these examples can be solved by permanently choosing one side or the other. The firm needs both to be effective in a sustainable way. There is also no stable, permanent way of just combining them. This impossibility of finding a permanent solution or choice is what makes a paradox. On the one hand organizations need to differentiate their services and processes to meet local production conditions and customer needs in the different markets, but on the other hand they also want to integrate across the organization to save costs as well as to utilize unique competencies and knowledge optimally. Global organizations rarely rely on organizing principles or business strategies that are 100% local or 100% global – it is a mix and a never-ending balancing act between local/global push and pulls. Similarly, global leaders rarely operate either locally or globally, but rather both-and at the same time. Consequently, it is not a question of *either* local *or* global; organizations must be *both* local *and* global.

Exploring Paradoxes

Paradoxes are defined more specifically as "[c]ontradictory yet interrelated elements – elements that seem logical in isolation but absurd and irrational when appearing simultaneously" (Lewis, 2000, p. 760), and they "persist over time" (Smith & Lewis, 2011, p. 382).

Paradoxes are different from problems or dilemmas. A **problem** is something that prevents something else from being achieved. We think of problems as unwelcome or harmful, things that need to be dealt with and overcome through analysis. A **dilemma** is about competing choices – each with their advantages and disadvantages; you may find it difficult or harmful to decide between available options, but when you do, the dilemma dissolves.

Paradoxes are unsolvable in that they contain competing, contradictory forces "related in such a way that a choice between them is only a temporary solution, after which the tension will reappear" (Smith & Lewis, 2011, p. 387). Paradoxes are leadership challenges that persist over time, contain the other, and are interdependent. Consequently, paradox leadership is not about deciding once and for all or prioritizing tough trade-offs, but about navigating between opposing considerations. In much the same way as there is not only one particularly important direction on a compass, paradox management is an ongoing endeavor to balance competing demands in a multidimensional, multipolar, and multipurpose world.

Paradox theory and research have become an important lens for exploring many organizational topics across multiple levels of analyses, from individuals to organizations to societies (Smith & Lewis, 2011; Lewis & Smith, 2022; Smith et al., 2017; Nielsen et al., 2023). In recent years, scholars of international management and global leadership have also seen the value of an organizational and leadership paradox lens for understanding the role and work of global leaders (Nelson, 2018; Osland et al., 2020).

Paradoxes become more prevalent under the combination of three conditions:

1. The pace of change in the environment is fast, and any possible "solution" can only be temporary.
2. Interdependence in the environment is high, so complexity and ambiguity are also high. Responses to either side of the paradox are connected with so many other elements that the follow-on effects are also complex.
3. Resources are scarce, and it is practically impossible to "just do both" even if that is logically possible.

These are precisely the conditions we discussed in Chapter 1, the context for global leadership today. Today's global leaders face more and more paradoxes, and managing them is an important meta-tool for global leadership.

Paradox Thinking

Working through paradoxes requires mindfulness, with special emphasis on a process orientation. Since paradoxes cannot be "solved," they must be managed carefully and explicitly with others, toward a balance that shifts constantly according to the context. Achieving this dynamic balance requires that leaders engage in conscious perspective taking, to see both sides of the paradox.

Working effectively through paradoxes results in a firm, or an individual, being able to do both-and. Leaders seek and manage a shifting, adaptive, dynamic balance between the two poles. This does not mean having the two sides being equal all the time. In fact, there will be times and situations when it is vital to prioritize one side over the other. Even over time, one side may garner more attention. For example, in the short- and long-term example above, a leader *may* focus more attention most of the time on the short term if the organizational or national cultural context emphasizes the long term, and the leader sees a need to counter that tendency within the firm.

Nielsen and her colleagues (2023) have developed guidelines and toolboxes to help leaders evolve their ability to engage in paradox thinking. Those perspectives and tools are integrated throughout this book, as paradox thinking is one of the important skills of global leadership. They present navigation of paradox as a process consisting of five phases as illustrated in Figure 2.7.

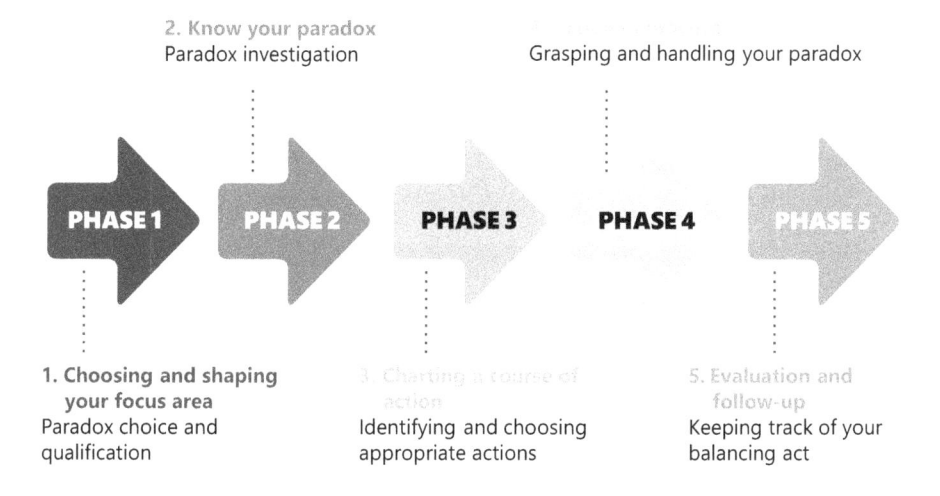

Figure 2.7 Five phases of working through paradox.
Reprinted with authors' permission from Nielsen, R. K., Bevort, F., Henriksen, T. D., Hjalager, A. M., & Lyndgaard, D. B. (*forthcoming*). *Navigating leadership paradox: Engaging paradoxical thinking in practice.* De Gruyter.

Here we outline the five phases of paradox thinking, so you can recognize the processes as you encounter them in future chapters.

Phase 1. Paradox choice and qualification – Choosing and shaping your focus area. In this phase, you identify the paradox that is most salient to the challenges and opportunities you face. You develop a rich description of it and consider why it is so important to you.

Phase 2. Paradox investigation – Know your paradox. This phase involves deeply exploring both sides of the case and articulating their inherent challenges and opportunities. This phase uses mindfulness on turbocharge – exploring different perspectives and context sensitivities through a comprehensive process orientation.

Phase 3. Identifying and choosing appropriate actions – Charting a course of action. In this phase, the leader identifies options for action and ways of thinking about how to sequence or balance actions over time. The goal here will be to propose combinations of actions that can achieve the dynamic balance.

Phase 4. Action in practice – Grasping and handling your paradox. Leaders in this phase put their plan into action, involving stakeholders actively. As they begin to actively manage their paradoxes, leaders experience the way actions can help find balance, then, when it becomes lost, renegotiate to find it again.

Phase 5. Evaluation and follow-up – Keeping track of your balancing act. This phase, of course, is never-ending. It is about developing habits to keep paradox thinking alive and to share it more widely, so other stakeholders take active and collaborative roles in shaping the paradox management.

Seeing as paradoxes persist over time, this road map of working through paradox foresees an ongoing endeavor to balance the competing demands of a paradox. The goal of the process is to develop a rich understanding of the underlying pushes and pulls of the paradox in order to be able to navigate them, not solve them. In this way, paradoxical both-and thinking is part of the process orientation presented as central to mindful global leadership.

The Local-Global Paradox Explored Further

Let's take a closer look at the local-global paradox, since it is so central to global leadership. On the one hand, organizations need to differentiate their services and processes to meet local production conditions and customer needs in the different markets. On the other hand, they also want to integrate across the organization to save costs, create alignment, and utilize unique competencies and knowledge.

This paradox has been recognized in the international management literature for many decades. Companies that operate globally are subject to pressures pushing them toward global integration (globalization) or pulling them toward local responsiveness (localization) (Bartlett & Ghoshal, 1998; Prahalad & Doz, 1987).

The objectives and actions associated with each often conflict. Similarly, managers in international subsidiaries are often caught between conflicting demands of headquarters and local operations. In the 20th century, research often recommended prioritizing *either* global integration *or* local responsiveness – that is, perceiving it as a dilemma to be solved. It was acknowledged that becoming a transnational company (one that is able to do both) was very rare and challenging, and perhaps not worth the effort.

In the third decade of the 21st century, with the complexity of the environment, most multinational companies experience global-local as a paradox, not a dilemma. Global organizations cannot ignore the importance of localization. They often experience the liability of foreignness when moving into new markets, and suffer a globalization penalty vis-à-vis local competition in different markets. At the same time, they are forced to consider that their home country competitive advantages and business models may not be transferable (see the section on context sensitivity earlier in the chapter). They may need to adjust far more than their advertising or even product offerings to be successful in new territories.

At the same time, global organizations cannot ignore the importance of global alignment. Global scale can provide enormous resources, reach, and reputation (e.g., brand). But global collaboration is more complex than local collaboration. It takes strong alignment to be able to deploy those resources across a broad reach, in a way that builds and supports a global reputation. When the company is located in many countries, it is challenging to develop alignment across languages and different ways of building relationships.

Therefore, global organizations rarely rely on organizing principles or business strategies that are 100% local or 100% global. They manage the paradox through a mix, a never-ending balancing act between local/global pushes and pulls. Similarly, global leaders rarely operate either locally or globally, but rather both, and at the same time. There is no "right" balancing point, and the balancing act differs between leaders, organizations, and situations over time. We will go into further detail regarding the global-local paradox in Chapter 8.

Developing Paradox Thinking

You may think leaders would be frustrated when faced with the reality that there is no solution to a paradox. In our experience, though, it is quite the opposite. Leaders in these highly complex environments deal daily with the frustration of not finding solutions. Learning that there is no solution is actually a relief! The process orientation of paradox thinking becomes very motivating for them, and they learn to manage the paradoxes well.

Throughout the chapters in this book, we will refer to paradoxes from time to time. We encourage you always to be thoughtful about potential paradoxes, even when they are not explicitly mentioned. As you become more aware of paradox thinking as a way of thinking about global leadership, you will also develop your global mindset and your global leadership competences.

Reflection Question 2.3: Paradox Navigation – Both-And Thinking in Action

What paradoxes do you encounter in your daily life? You may want to think about different contexts, for instance job role paradoxes (such as different managers asking you to prioritize different things), or work-life paradoxes (such as achieving high standards at work or at school and also managing your social and health needs), or organizational paradoxes (like the global-local or short-term–long-term paradoxes). Make a short list and describe the two poles briefly, then reflect on these questions:

1. Why is it important to be able to navigate these paradoxes?
2. What can you achieve by working through the paradoxes?
3. What do you risk losing by not navigating paradoxes?
4. How is your challenge a paradox and not just a problem that you can solve?

Source: Adapted with the authors' permission from Nielsen, R. K., & Lyndgaard, D. B. (2018). Grasping global leadership: Tools for next practice. Global Leadership Academy – Copenhagen Business School & Danish Confederation of Industry. Also available from www.globalledelse.dk/eng.

Conclusion

In this chapter, we introduced concepts that spell out the specifics of mindfulness when applied to a global leadership context: global mindset, global leadership competences, and paradox thinking. Ultimately, mindfulness as a habit lies at the heart of global leadership effectiveness. Figure 2.8 summarizes these three pathways to mindful global leadership.

Note that these pathways to mindful global leadership are not the only entry points, nor do they "only" enter to that place. But they do tend to help you enter the global mindfulness cycle at that place. By exercising all three of these pathways you help yourself move around and develop more mindful global leadership.

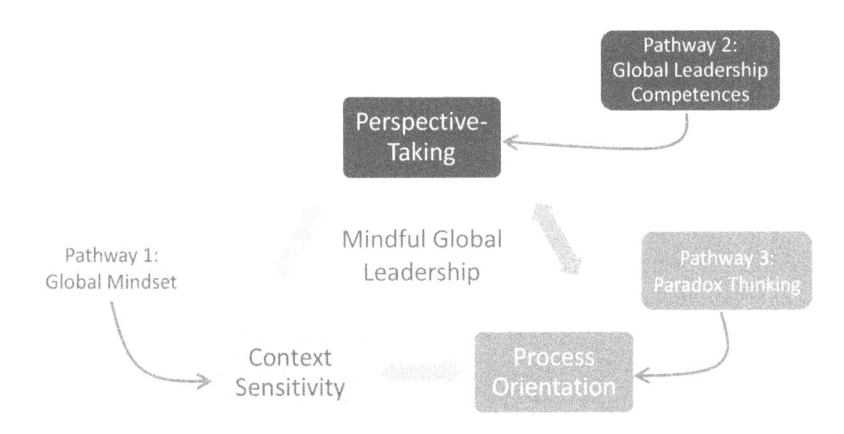

Figure 2.8 Pathways to developing global mindfulness.

These pathways will follow you through the next three parts of the book where we will apply them to central situations of organizational life and leadership.

> ### Reflection Question 2.4: Professional Beacons and Role Models
>
> Think of people you know who are strong global leaders – it could be different people with different strengths. What can you learn from these people to help your own leadership? How can you build a mentoring relationship with them?

Further Resources

This list of resources provides reviews and further insight on the themes covered in Chapter 2.

Bennett, N., & Lemoine, J. (2014). What VUCA really means for you. *Harvard Business Review*, 92(12).
Lane, H. W., Maznevski, M. L., Mendenhall, M. E., & McNett, J. (Eds.). (2004). *The Blackwell handbook of global management: A guide to managing complexity*. John Wiley & Sons.
Nielsen, R. K., & Lyndgaard, D. B. (2018). *Grasping global leadership practice*. Global Leadership Academy – Copenhagen Business School & Danish Confederation of Industry.
Osland, J. S., Mendenhall, M. E., Reiche, B. S., Szkudlarek, B., Bolden, R., Courtice, P., Vaiman, V., et al. (2020). Perspectives on global leadership and the COVID-19 crisis. *Advances in Global Leadership, 13*, 3–56.
Smith, W., & Lewis, M. (2022). *Both/And thinking: Embracing creative tensions to solve your toughest problems*. Harvard Business Review Press.
Smith, W. K., Lewis, M. W., & Tushman, M. L. (2016). Both/and leadership. *Harvard Business Review, 94*(5), 62–70.

Bibliography

Bartlett, C. A., & Ghoshal, S. (1987). Managing across borders: New strategic requirements. *Sloan Management Review*, 28(4), 7–17.

Bartlett, C. A., & Ghoshal, S. (1998). *Managing across borders: The transnational solution*. Harvard Business School Press.

Begley, T. M., & Boyd, D. P. (2003). The need for a corporate global mind-set. *MIT Sloan Management Review*, 44(2), 25–32.

Bird, A., Mendenhall, M., Stevens, M.J., & Oddou, G. (2010), Defining the content domain of intercultural competence for global leaders. *Journal of Managerial Psychology*, 25(8), 810–828.

Bird, A., & Osland, J. S. (2004). Global competencies: An introduction. In H. W. Lane, M. L. Maznevski, M. E. Mendenhall, & J. McNett (Eds.), *The Blackwell handbook of global management: A guide to managing complexity* (pp. 57–80). Blackwell.

Boyacıgiller, N., Beechler, S., Taylor, S., & Levy, O. (2004). The crucial yet illusive global mindset. In H. W. Lane, M. L. Maznevski, M. E. Mendenhall, & J. McNett (Eds.), *Blackwell handbook of global management: A guide to managing complexity* (pp. 81–93). Blackwell.

Furth, H. (1970). *Piaget for teachers*. Prentice Hall.

Hofstede, G. (1980). *Culture's consequences*. Sage.

Kozai Group. (n.d.). *Identify & develop global capabilities*. Retrieved January 10, 2023, from https://www.kozaigroup.com/global-capabilities/

Lane, H. W., Maznevski, M. L., Mendenhall, M. E., & McNett, J. (Eds.). (2009). *The Blackwell handbook of global management: A guide to managing complexity*. John Wiley & Sons.

Langer, E. (2014). Mindfulness in the age of complexity. *Harvard Business Review*, 92(3), 68–73.

Langer, E. J., & Moldoveanu, M. (2000). The construct of mindfulness. *Journal of Social Science*, 56(1), 1–9.

Levy, O., Beechler, S., Taylor, S., & Boyacıgiller, N. A. (2007). What we talk about when we talk about 'global mindset': Managerial cognition in multinational corporations. *Journal of International Business Studies*, 38(2), 231–258.

Lewis, M. W. (2000). Exploring paradox: Toward a more comprehensive guide. *Academy of Management Review*, 25(4), 760–776.

Lewis, M. W., & Smith, W. K. (2022). Reflections on the 2021 Decade Award: Navigating paradox is paradoxical. *Academy of Management Review*, 47(4), published ahead of print: https://doi.org/10.5465/amr.2022.0251

Nelson, J. A. (2018). Here be paradox: How global business leaders navigate change. In *Advances in Global Leadership (Advances in Global Leadership, Vol. 11)* (pp. 3–30). Emerald Publishing Limited.

Nielsen, R. K. (2014). *Global mindset as managerial meta-competence and organizational capability: Boundary-crossing leadership cooperation in the MNC: The case of 'group mindset' in Solar A/S*. Copenhagen Business School (CBS).

Nielsen, R. K., Bévort, F., Henriksen, T. D., Hjalager, A. M., & Lyndgaard, D. B. (2023). *Navigating leadership paradox: Engaging paradoxical thinking in practice*. De Gruyter.

Osland, J., & Bird, A. (2004). *The Blackwell handbook of global management: A guide to managing complexity*. Blackwell Publishers

Osland, J., Nielsen, R. K., Mendenhall, M., & Bird, A. (2020). The birth of a new field from CCM: Global leadership. In B. Szkudlarek, L. Romani, D. V.

Caprar, & J. S. Osland (Eds.), *SAGE handbook of contemporary cross-cultural management* (pp. 375–392). SAGE Publications.

Prahalad, C. K., & Doz, Y. L. (1987). *The multinational mission: Balancing local demands and global vision*. Simon and Schuster.

Smith, W. K., Jarzabkowski, P., Lewis, M. W., & Langley, A. (Eds.). (2017). *The Oxford handbook of organizational paradox*. Oxford University Press.

Smith, W. K., & Lewis, M. W. (2011). Toward a theory of paradox: A dynamic equilibrium model of organizing. *Academy of Management Review, 36*(2), 381–440.

3 Culture: The Context of Meaning in International Management

> Ordinarily we are unaware of the special lens through which we look at life. It would hardly be fish who discovered the existence of water.
>
> Clyde Kluckhohn, Anthropology Professor at Harvard University (1905–1960)

Key Learning Objectives

At the end of this chapter, students will be able to:

- Define culture and the important functions of culture: efficiency and identity.
- Analyze a culture's levels from surface to deep.
- Describe how culture affects individuals' ideas and behaviors.
- Observe how culture interacts dynamically with other individual and societal influences.
- Develop a mindful approach to observing culture.

Culture is to people as water is to fish. This image is so compelling that it has been invoked by many authors, from scientists and anthropologists to comedians. Water is the life-giving context for the fish, yet the fish is probably not aware of water. That is, until the fish is out of the water, or the water no longer provides the environment the fish needs. Suddenly, water is meaningful. So it is with culture for people. We are often unaware of the social environment in which we are embedded, yet this social environment provides the context through which we derive meaning in our interactions with each other. We become more aware of this context – our culture – when we leave it and enter another culture.

International management is about leading people and implementing tasks with people across cultural borders. The starting point for effective international management behavior, therefore, must be a deep understanding of culture. In this chapter, we set the foundation for culture as the context of international management. We define culture, examine its different facets, analyze its impact on people, and explore important questions about the intersection of cultures and individual characteristics. This discussion on culture will continue in Part II on "Leading People across Contexts", where frameworks will be discussed as tools that allow for comparing cultures with each other and decoding cross-cultural interactions.

Throughout this chapter we encourage you to learn from the analogy of the fish: think about your own cultures. As you develop the "my context" part of your global mindset (knowledge Type 1 and Type 2, p. 35), try to become more mindful about your "water," the contexts in which your own ideas and behaviors are meaningful.

Defining Culture

Think about the following examples of cultures: Nigerian, Japanese, Québécois, soccer (football) club fans, golfers, snowboarders, guitar players, gamers, Gen Z, engineers, artists, Unilever, and Toyota. What other examples have you come across? Try brainstorming your own list. What do they have in common? What makes each a culture?

The first thing you probably notice is that culture is a property of a group of people. No one can have a culture by themselves! Next you may recognize that members of the culture tend to share a set of norms (patterns of behavior), values (guidance for what is important or correct), and beliefs (ideas about the world). As you think further, you probably consider that cultures tend to be relatively stable – they don't change dramatically every day or even every month. When new people come in, they learn the culture from people already there. This reflection brings us to our formal definition of culture:

Culture is the set of deep beliefs and underlying values that are shared by a group of people, to guide that group of people's interactions with each other. These beliefs and values are manifested in norms and artifacts that are common in the culture and are taught to successive generations.

Culture serves two important functions for groups. First, culture makes action simpler and more **efficient** because it creates context for meaning. When people know what to prioritize and how to interact with each other, business and social interactions take place quickly and easily. There is no need to question each action.

Think about the last time you were in a new culture, for work or as a tourist. How did you feel at the end of the first day? Some people say excited or exhilarated, some say frustrated, but almost everyone says they were exhausted. This exhaustion comes from spending the day wondering what is meaningful and what is not. Should I tip the driver? How much? The receptionist didn't smile at me: Is that normal or was I rude? Or was the receptionist rude? Which side of the sidewalk should I walk on? What are others doing? Even if you have read all the guidebooks, questions like these arise. When you are interacting across cultures, you lose the efficiency that comes from shared meaning and values within a culture.

Second, culture provides an important source of **social identity** for its members. Humans have a basic need to belong to social groups. Belonging to a culture – as demonstrated by acting in accordance with the norms and values – brings safety and security from the group and separates the group from outsiders who are different and perhaps even threatening. Interestingly, most people feel this identity even more strongly when they are outside their own culture than when they are in it. For example, international students or expatriates from the same country often choose to socialize together more closely than the same people might when in their own country. You may even have experienced this yourself.

In the following sections we will explore the different elements of our definition to develop a rich set of lenses through which to view culture.

Reflection Question 3.1: Revisiting an Intercultural Experience

Reflect on experiences you've had in different cultures, whether working or on vacation, whether traveling or engaging with other cultures where you live, thinking particularly about the first few days or interactions. How did you learn the new culture? How did you become comfortable with the new norms? In what ways did you become more aware of your own culture through this process?

Groups of People: Different Types of Cultures for Different Groups

Let's look more closely at the "group of people" part of our definition. All stable groups have cultures, so there are as many types of cultures as there are types of stable groups. We're used to thinking about countries as having cultures – Malaysian culture is different from Mexican or Swedish cultures. Regions within countries, too, have distinct cultures – Americans are very conscious that the US Northeast is culturally different from the Midwest or Texas, for example. Religious groups may have cultures as well. Judaism and Islam are cultural groups that extend across countries with strong values and norms, and strong senses of identity.

Work organizations also have cultures. The culture at the technology company Alphabet (Google) is very different from the culture of energy company Shell or steel company ArcelorMittal. Some organizations value hierarchy and formal procedures, others place more emphasis on distributed decision-making and less formal adaptability. Even within the same industry, such as financial services, different companies can have very different cultures. Cutting across organizations, some professions have strong cultures. These cultures are sometimes associated with professional certifications, such as physicians, engineers, and accountants.

People belong to groups related to other elements of their lives, too. Fans of a sports team, such as football (soccer, to North Americans) clubs in the Premier Leagues, often have strong cultures. People who engage in the same hobby may form groups that have cultures, and people at similar life stages may form cultures together. Examples of these cultures include local sailing teams, online baking communities, young parents in a neighborhood, and people who play the same massively multiplayer online (MMO) game, such as *World of Warcraft.*

Cultures often have subcultures nested within them. The regions within countries referred to above are some examples. Within organizations, different functions or departments usually have different cultures – the marketing department may work quite differently from the finance department, for example. Subgenres of music each have their own culture. Families have their own cultures within their communities.

Because we all belong to many groups, from large (e.g., countries) to small (e.g., families), we are all part of many cultures. We get part of our sense of identity from each of the cultures we belong to, and it's usually easy for us to know which of our cultures is most important to guide our behavior in different situations. When we are in the situation for that culture (the marketing department, the religious center, the online community), we follow the norms for that culture. There are situations when our cultures might feel in conflict, and we will return to those situations later in the chapter after we have explored exactly how culture affects our thoughts and behaviors. For now, as we go into depth on our definition, the most important point to be mindful of is that cultures are not all singular, uniform, or mutually exclusive – they overlap and connect with each other as much as human groups interact with each other.

Guiding Interaction with Each Other: Why Do Cultures Evolve and Persist?

Now let's look at another part of our definition: *shared by a group of people, to guide that group of people's interactions with each other.* Here, it is important to explore how cultures develop and persist.

Culture arises as a group of people's collective response to a set of challenges posed by their environment. In short, people need to coordinate in order to solve challenges of survival and prosperity, and they develop a set of agreements on how they will do that. An interesting set of studies illustrates this by exploring the cultural evolution in rice-growing and wheat-growing parts of China (Talhelm et al., 2014). Rice growing is extremely labor intensive compared with wheat. Furthermore, rice almost always requires artificial irrigation, and irrigation in turn requires cooperation among neighboring farmers and villages to build and sustain the water system. Wheat growing, on the other hand, does not require as much attention and benefits from scale and inventions that save or substitute for human labor. Talhelm and colleagues hypothesized that, in order to solve these collective challenges, people living in rice-growing areas would develop cultures with more collectivism and holistic thinking, while people living in wheat-growing areas would develop cultures with lower collectivism and more analytical thinking. The researchers also hypothesized that these differences in culture would persist today, even though most people are not actually farming either rice or wheat. In a study that carefully controlled for other potential explanations such as degree of modernization, they demonstrated that people in rice-growing regions of China exhibit more holistic thinking and build social relationships with more and deeper interconnections, compared with people in wheat-growing regions. They also found that more patents per capita originated in wheat-growing regions (Talhelm et al., 2014). These differences were observed among adults, college students, and then teenagers, illustrating that these cultural norms are stable (Dong et al., 2019). The differences also extended to everyday life completely unrelated to agriculture. For example, people in wheat-growing regions were more likely to sit alone at Starbucks or to move chairs to clear their path, while people in rice-growing regions were more likely to sit in groups and adapt their path to the chairs in the way (Talhelm et al., 2018). More recently, the researchers found that people in rice-farming regions were more likely to wear masks at the onset of the COVID-19 pandemic, even after controlling for local COVID-19 exposure and other risk factors (English et al., 2022).

The norms and values of the rice-growing and wheat-growing cultures are related to survival through different types of agriculture. Religious groups develop norms and values to practice the tenets set out in their beliefs. Members of professions develop norms and values to practice their profession efficiently and to increase the profession's knowledge. Members of organizations develop norms and values to coordinate across different parts of the organization to achieve the organization's purpose.

An important corollary of our definition is this: Cultures are not inherently good or bad; they are more or less effective at solving for specific types of coordination challenges. Each culture developed in order to address a particular challenge – it is effective at addressing that challenge, and not so effective at addressing other challenges. The weakness of a particular culture's norms and values tends to become most evident when the environment changes and the challenge the culture developed for is no longer the most important one for survival or prosperity. For example, look at Kodak and Polaroid, two companies that led the film/camera industry before the rise of digital imaging. Both had cultures that valued innovation to improve a particular platform, with norms of efficiency for continuous improvement. Neither valued thinking outside the box or challenging the basic platform, and both disappeared when their platforms became less dominant in the market. The recognition that "every culture is effective at solving the coordination challenges it developed for" is key to effective cross-cultural interaction. It reminds us to be mindful around these interactions, to explore the situations each culture is adept at addressing.

Observing Culture: What Does the Surface Tell Us about the Deep?

Let's examine the final elements of our definition: *the set of deep beliefs and underlying values ... manifested in norms and artifacts that are common in the culture and are taught to successive generations.*

We see culture most easily in norms and practices, such as language and patterns of behavior. In Québec, most people speak Québécois, a dialect of French. A variety of local foods are enjoyed, including poutine, a traditional dish of French fries, cheese curds, and gravy. Football (soccer) fans often wear their team's jerseys and wave flags, sing team songs, and watch games together. Employees at many companies wear clothing with the company name, and the company values are often posted in public places and invoked in public speeches.

However, culture's meaning and influence are much deeper than these surface manifestations. Speaking French and eating poutine do not automatically make one Québécois; watching the World Cup or Premier League and wearing a team's football jersey do not automatically make one part of the football (soccer) culture. A new employee at either Unilever or Toyota becomes part of the culture slowly, not the first time they wear the logo or go to a town hall meeting. A company's explicit values – those posted on its walls – may not be entirely consistent with how people actually behave.

It is helpful to view culture as an iceberg, with only the top layer visible (Hall, 1966; Kluckhohn & Strodtbeck, 1961; Schein, 1984). In that top layer are the artifacts – the things we can see and touch that are typical of that culture – and the norms, or typical patterns of behavior. The norms include language: the vocabulary and structure of how people communicate. Just below the surface are the values that a culture talks about and encourages among its members. At the bottom of the iceberg, where they are very difficult to see and talk about but where they have enormous impact on how people think and behave, are the underlying assumptions and deeply held beliefs.

Figure 3.1 illustrates the iceberg idea using an example from a global construction company one of the authors worked with. In this culture, it was the norm to wear blue shirts. Usually the shirts were buttoned, but they could be golf shirts or sweaters. The managers at this firm didn't ever talk about shirt colors. They didn't say to each other, "We will only wear blue shirts," nor did they tell their new employees, "You must wear blue shirts." No one was fired for wearing a shirt of a different color! But whenever a group of leaders from this company got together or a picture appeared on their website, whether it was 2–3 people or 200–300 or more, blue dominated the scene. "Blue shirts" was clearly an important artifact of this company's culture. When the author asked the company leaders what values were associated with the blue shirt artifact, they knew immediately: practicality and humbleness. Blue shirts can be worn across situations, whether a construction site or a client or bank office, they don't show dirt easily, and they aren't flashy. Practical and humble were important values at the company and were explicitly talked about in meetings and leadership development. When the leaders looked below the surface, they discovered some important underlying assumptions that guided their thinking and behavior. The first was around the value of hard work: that hard work is more important than brilliant analysis or complex decision-making, and leaders should always do whatever it takes to get the job done by jumping in to help. The second was the importance of not standing out, not making yourself look better than anyone else. Through this analysis, the leaders

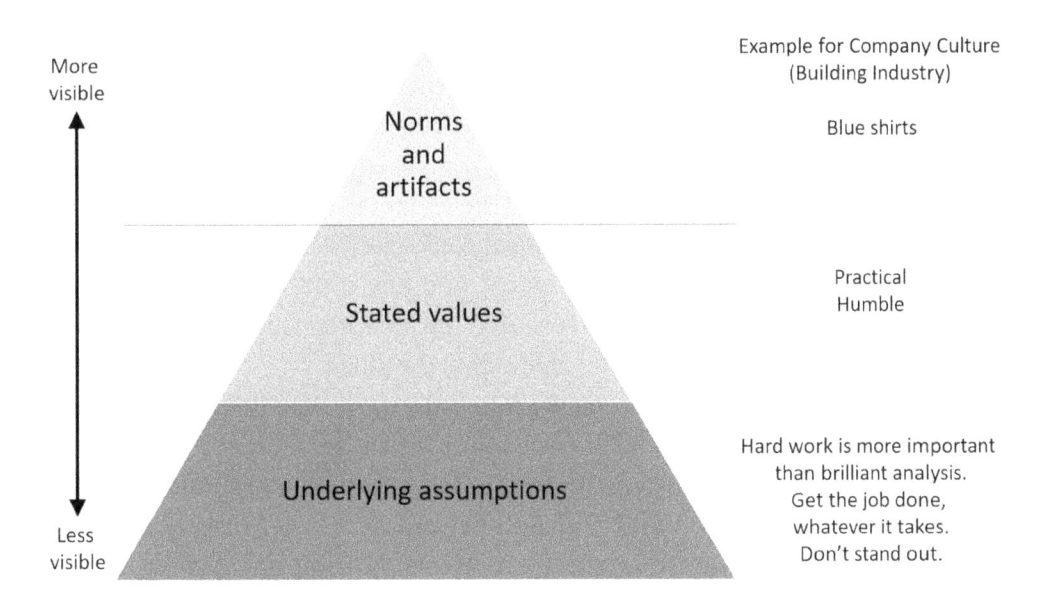

Figure 3.1 The iceberg of culture and its layers.

understood that these deep assumptions helped their firm's performance in many ways but hindered it in others.

Explore the Iceberg through Observation and Dialogue
It is only possible to understand the connection between the surface layer of artifacts and the deeper layers of values and assumptions with mindful observation and conversation. If we only look at the surface level without deeper examination, we can make the mistake of thinking we understand the culture but actually miss what is most important.

For example, many people argue that cultures around the world are converging, that business is the same everywhere. There is some truth to this at the top of the iceberg. People around the world wear t-shirts, carry European bags, eat at McDonald's, talk on Samsung phones, work on iPads, and play games on their Nintendo or Sony devices. Currencies are traded globally every moment, and there are global infrastructures and norms for conducting business. Meetings on Zoom or other video platforms have some of the same characteristics everywhere. Accounting standards are becoming more and more global. Everyone has the same basic physiological and psychological needs. From a cultural iceberg perspective, we can see that some norms and artifacts are similar globally, and the iceberg's *top levels* may sometimes look the same.

McDonald's is an interesting example to dive into more deeply. The golden arches and basic format are recognizable everywhere. Kids all over the world love the Happy Meal, and McDonald's is the world's largest toy distributor (CBS News, 2021). The Big Mac is so ubiquitous that *The Economist* has developed a **purchasing power parity** (PPP) index on its price (The Economist, 2023). They argue that the sandwich is the best example of a global consumer commodity with approximately the same sandwich in each country, and any difference in price across countries is due to differences in the cost of living. In other words, at the top layer of the iceberg McDonald's looks the same across the globe.

Now look a bit deeper: McDonald's has different menu items in different countries (McDonald's, 2023). Beer is served in Germany, a McArabia is on the menu in the Middle East, there is no beef in Indian McDonald's (but there is a Chicken Maharaja Mac), and McDonald's Singapore has a Prosperity Burger and serves lychee oolong ice cream. Look deeper still into the iceberg: watch the people, learn to see the norms about McDonald's. In the United States, about two-thirds of revenue came from drive-through business even before the COVID-19 pandemic (McDonnell, 2013). This proportion is increasing elsewhere in the world, but nowhere else does it reach the same level as in the United States (at 70% of revenue in 2022; see Glasson & Lehman, 2022). What might this indicate about the American culture? The importance of efficiency, of being on the go, of moving from one place to another? The unimportance of eating as a social event, of people sitting down for a meal together? In Pakistan and Indonesia, McDonald's offers special deals during Ramadan for the Iftar evening meal breaking the day's fast; most of these specials include multiple sandwiches, drinks, and desserts intended for a family or friends to eat together. This creates some controversy, with some appreciating McDonald's adaptation to their culture and others decrying a degeneration of Ramadan that focuses on consumerism rather than discipline and families at home.

McDonald's, one of the icons of globalization, symbolizes the layers of the cultural iceberg and illustrates how this perspective helps us become mindful of the ways in which cultures are similar and different. At the top layers, similarities help us do business together. They allow global production efficiencies to be achieved, mergers and acquisitions to be negotiated, money and goods to be traded, and employees to stay briefly in foreign countries. They allow us to work together, at least on the surface. However, deeper-level differences become apparent when people have to interact more intensively with each other on a day-to-day basis. Naïve assumptions about similarity in the deep layers can cause problems or disappointments; mindful dialogue about similarities *and* differences can create opportunities and deeper understanding.

> **Reflection Question 3.2: Explore the Iceberg Levels for a Culture You Are Part of**
>
> Identify a culture you are part of, one that is important to you. Get together with one or two other people from the culture and choose an "artifact" from the culture. It's best if you choose something tangible, something you can point to or hold during the discussion. It may be clothing, a sign on the wall, a coffee mug or a teacup, a pen – anything that people within the culture and even outside the culture recognize as being "typical" of the culture. Go through the levels of the iceberg and identify the different layers of meaning for your artifact. Tell stories and think about how the artifact is evident in different situations. What do you learn about your own culture through this exploration?

Now that we have defined culture and explored its key facets, it's important to examine exactly how culture influences people's thoughts and behaviors and therefore affects cross-cultural interactions.

Culture's Effect on Individuals and Interactions

To understand culture's influence, first we need to understand the basic role of **assumptions** and **cognitions** in influencing our thoughts and actions. This allows us to see our own culture's influence on us, and why cross-cultural encounters are both so difficult to understand and so interesting (Erez & Earley, 1993).

An assumption is an unquestioned, taken-for-granted belief about the world and how it works. Assumptions help create our worldview, or the cognitive environment in which we operate. They come in many different varieties. Some are so deeply ingrained and unquestioned that it is difficult ever to surface them; even when surfaced, they are not testable. "Human nature is essentially good" is an assumption of this type. Other assumptions are learned at various stages of our lives and, once learned, are taken for granted without further questioning. In the first few years of life, a child learns to take so much for granted: day and night follow each other; manipulating switches makes things work; things that move are either alive or powered by something; when in doubt, Google. As we develop through life, we learn more and more sets of assumptions.

Kahneman summarized the psychological research on assumption-based thinking and decision-making as System 1 thinking: fast, automatic, and powerful (Kahneman, 2011). As he notes, we rely on these assumptions to a great extent in our daily lives, even in our professional judgment. A financial analyst valuing companies takes for granted certain assumptions about efficient markets and develops analyses that affect companies' ability to obtain resources. An advertising account manager takes for granted certain assumptions about human motivations and produces advertising and social media campaigns that play to those motivations and invoke them. Although both these professionals are able to state the assumptions when asked, they tend not to think about them or question them most of the time. The assumptions work most of the time, and thinking about them consciously (System 2 thinking; Kahneman, 2011) would slow decision-making down.

Assumptions influence the process of cognition, or what we notice and how we interpret events and behaviors. The financial analyst focuses on financial ratios, earnings growth, or dividends but may not notice programs with long lead times that may enhance the company's reputation for social responsibility. If she did notice this information, she may interpret it as something admirable but nothing that should influence the company's ability to borrow money today. The advertising account manager may only notice product features that fit into his framework of assumptions about the motivations of the target audience and miss other implications of those features.

Assumptions are necessary. Without assumptions, we would be paralyzed by the constant need to inquire about the meaning of events and the motives of others. The more others share our assumptions, the more easily we can interact and communicate effectively with each other. It is not surprising that our assumptions are generally effective when we operate within our own culture.

Cognition and Social Perception: Perceive, Interpret, Evaluate

A simple way to remember this process of social perception is captured by the acronym PIE, which stands for **P**erceive, **I**nterpret, and **E**valuate. We observe something and take note of its characteristics, consciously perceiving it. What we are inclined to notice is influenced in part by our assumptions of what is important. We then interpret those facts, or give them meaning, again based on our assumptions. Finally, we evaluate the facts and take action based on our evaluation.

For example, when selecting a potential supplier for specialty chemicals, a purchasing agent may notice that different companies offer different prices for the same grade of chemical. The purchasing agent **perceives** the suppliers by building a table to compare them, including their price ranges. The purchasing agent may not notice that the suppliers offer different types of technical assistance or compound customization because their assumptions about priorities may not include this. Although price is sometimes an indicator of quality, the purchasing agent may **interpret** the chemical grade as the quality information. As long as prices are identified for the same chemical grade, the purchasing agent interprets that they are comparing them on an equal basis. Finally, the purchasing agent **evaluates** the lowest price compound as good for the company. They take action and buy this compound.

Just like the purchasing agent, we all act based on the world we know through our cognitions, the world we see through the PIE sequence. Since the sequence builds so heavily on our assumptions of the world and how it works, those assumptions end up influencing our own actions and what we think of others' actions. We tend to jump quickly to interpretation and then to evaluation before adequately "perceiving" or understanding, mainly because our quick "perceiving" tends to be based on the deepest assumptions.

Figure 3.2 shows the influence pattern of culture on assumptions, perceptions, and management behavior and demonstrates why culture and assumptions play such a large role in cross-cultural encounters.

When Cultures Meet – Do We Question the Other or Question Ourselves?

What happens when people from two or more different cultures meet or work together? Their assumptions and value systems (cultures) may direct them to perceive the same situation differently, interpret what they notice differently, evaluate the situation differently, and take different actions. Here's a very short exchange:

SUSAN (BRITISH, NEW EXPATRIATE IN CHILE): Pablo, the company has decided to transfer you to the regional headquarters in Sao Paulo!
PABLO (CHILEAN): Hmm, that will be very difficult. I'd prefer to stay here.

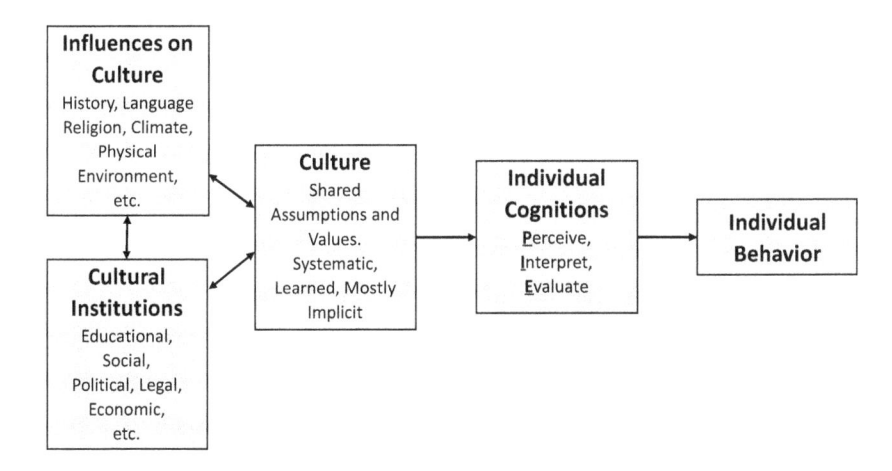

Figure 3.2 Culture's influence on individual behavior.

There is an awkward pause. What are both thinking? The same situation – transferring Pablo from Santiago to Sao Paulo – may be interpreted and evaluated differently by each of them. Susan, from a culture that emphasizes career progression and achievement over community relationships, is probably wondering whether Pablo is really interested in developing his career: "A transfer to regional headquarters is an important promotion. Very strange he would not want that." Pablo, from a culture that values these relationships over individual achievement, may wonder why Susan or the company would transfer him: "My family, my young children and elderly parents, are here. I don't even speak Portuguese. Would the company help my family move, help my children with school? When my children are older, I could go."

Cross-cultural interactions like this set up a potential conflict situation. From "my" point of view, "you" are thinking and behaving in a way that doesn't fit with my assumptions about the world (assumptions I am not conscious of holding). I experience this conflict as dissonance and I want to reduce it, to make the interpretation consistent with my assumptions.

The easiest and most common way for me to reduce dissonance is to keep my own assumptions while revising my perception of the other person. Susan could change her positive perception of Pablo's career potential and conclude he is not as ambitious as she thought; Pablo could change his positive perception of the company and conclude they don't care about him. With this interpretation, both people make assumptions about the other's motivations and values based on their own assumption set: an ethnocentric error. We all have a strong tendency to use our own group's assumptions as the benchmark when viewing other groups. Ethnocentrism is carrying that one step further and using that benchmark to evaluate "us" as better and "them" as worse (Shultz et al., 2009). Susan's thoughts may continue with "No wonder the Chilean economy is still struggling." Pablo might think, "This is just another example of Anglo values colonizing the rest of the world." Reducing dissonance by maintaining your own assumptions often leads to conflict in cross-cultural encounters.

The other way to reduce dissonance is to change assumptions. This requires active mindfulness: context sensitivity, perspective taking, and a process orientation. Susan may wonder whether managers have different typical career paths in Latin America than in the United Kingdom, and thus develop a broader understanding of motivation and leadership development in different contexts. Pablo may wonder whether UK firms look after employees differently, and thus develop a broader understanding of human capital in multinational firms. Reducing dissonance by questioning and changing your assumptions often leads to positive synergies in cross-cultural encounters.

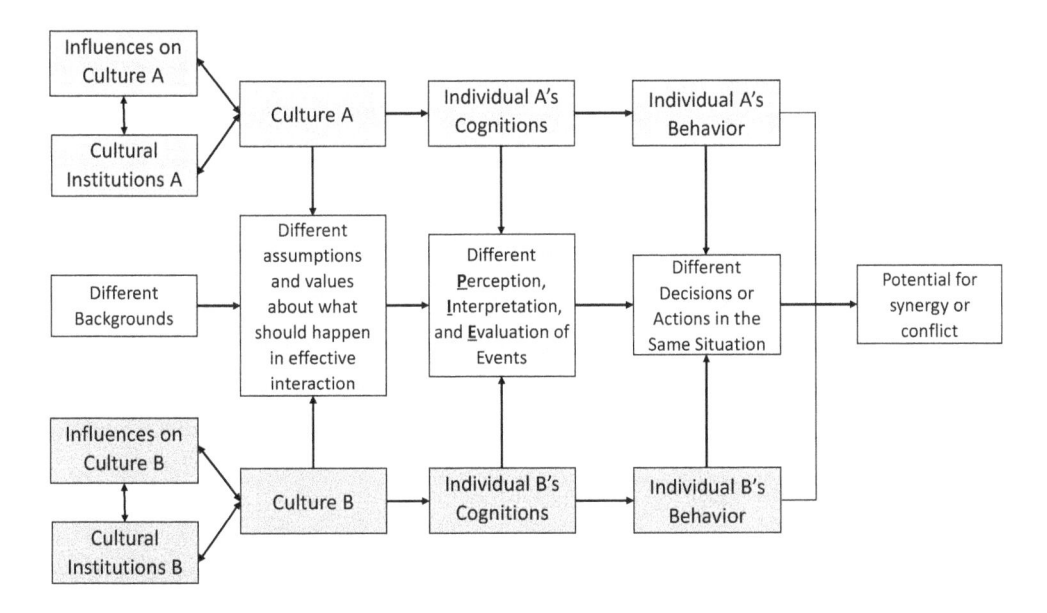

Figure 3.3 When individuals from different cultures interact.

The dynamics of what happens when individuals from different cultures meet are shown in Figure 3.3. The same perceptual process occurs as described earlier and shown in Figure 3.2, but in this case two different people are acting based on two different sets of cultural assumptions. The resulting different decisions or behaviors set up the conditions for conflict or synergy.

Mindful global leaders try to decrease negative aspects of conflict and increase potential for positive synergy. They develop greater context sensitivity through perspective taking and a process orientation. In this way, they increase the possibility to perceive, interpret, and evaluate others objectively.

Reflection Question 3.3: Observe Cross-Cultural Misunderstandings

As you go about your daily interactions, watch for situations in which two people misunderstand each other because they are viewing the same thing through different lenses. It may look like simple misunderstandings and confusion, or it may become open conflict. To what extent do you see people jumping to Interpret and Evaluate, and when do you see them pausing to reexamine their Perceptions? If you find yourself in one of these situations, try to pause and encourage both you and your interlocutor to reexamine your Perceptions. Does this lead you to a different understanding together?

Culture Often Trumps Personality, Especially Early in a Social Interaction

Of course, culture doesn't *always* affect our behavior. We can all think of times when we behaved in ways that were counter to the culture. So here is an important question to ask yourself: When do you behave according to your culture ("the expected norms of the situation") even though it is not consistent with your personality or individual strengths?

One of our authors often uses this simple illustration in class:

If you ask me on a personality survey, "What kind of clothing do you like to wear?" my answer would be "jeans, a t-shirt, and sneakers." But if you ask me on a culture survey, "What kind of clothing should business school professors wear?" my answer would be something like "business dress." Quite different!

So, which predicts my behavior? The answer is ... it depends. If I'm teaching, it's likely to be my cultural answer – business dress. But why would I "suppress" my personality for my culture?

Partly for efficiency. If I behave according to my personality – wear jeans and a t-shirt for teaching in a business school – then the students, from their own cultural lens, may wonder whether I am making some kind of statement. They'll Perceive the unexpected clothing, they will wonder how to Interpret it, and they may Evaluate it negatively or at least as odd. On the other hand, if I wear business dress, they probably won't notice or remember what I'm wearing, and we can focus on the class lessons instead.

It's also partly for identity. When I "put on the uniform" of business dress, I am also putting on an identity which is positive for me, and which is associated with a set of behaviors and norms and values.

If we're close to the end of the semester and I know the students well, I may feel comfortable bringing out more of my personality by dressing more casually. When the uncertainty of the cultural situation is decreased and the relationships and roles are strong, the culture is no longer such a powerful influence on my behavior, and my personality may be a stronger influence.

The basic definition of culture is worth repeating here: *Culture is the set of deep beliefs and underlying values that are shared by a group of people, to guide that group of people's interactions with each other.* When the context requires interactions among people, especially among a large group of people or among people who don't know each other well, the culture that is most salient in that context tends to be a strong influence on behavior. When people are working on their own, or are working with people they know extremely well, people bring in other cultural identities and their own personalities (Gibson et al., 2009).

Cultures and Their Influences Are Dynamic

We mentioned earlier in the chapter that cultures are not all singular, uniform, or mutually exclusive – they overlap and connect with each other as much as human groups interact with each other. Now that we have developed a strong foundation for understanding what culture is and how it affects people and their interactions, we turn to exploring this complexity.

Cultures Are Heterogeneous: Loose and Tight, Strong and Weak Cultures

No one exactly follows their culture all the time, across all situations. Interestingly, there is variance among cultures in the extent to which people are expected to follow the cultural rules. Gelfand and colleagues (2011) have explored this cultural looseness and tightness and discovered that country cultures differ systematically on this. They asked people how strict the behavioral norms were for a variety of situations such as job interviews, funeral ceremonies, being in one's own home, and visiting public parks. In tight cultures, such as Pakistan, Singapore, and South Korea, respondents reported strong social norms prescribing behaviors in each of the situations. In loose cultures, such as New Zealand, Hungary, and Israel, respondents reported that it was acceptable to engage in a wider variety of behaviors in these situations. Gelfand and colleagues (2011) suggest that loose and tight cultures evolved to address different coordination challenges, such as hunting for loose cultures and agriculture for tight cultures. Gelfand summarized the findings of the research stream in her 2019 book that illustrates how people in loose and tight cultures tend to approach rules differently across a wide variety of situations (Gelfand, 2019).

Moreover, in every culture there is variance among individuals. The variation comes from individual differences in personality and from the fact that people all belong to multiple groups and cultures. It is helpful to differentiate *strong* cultures from *weak* cultures. In strong cultures there is less variance among people – most people identify with and follow the norms and values of the dominant culture. In weak cultures there is more variance among people. You can probably think of examples of strong and weak cultures yourself. Company cultures like IBM and Toyota are known to have strong organizational cultures. Is it good for a culture to be strong? Certainly strong cultures are higher on both functions of culture: efficiency and identity. But they can also be closed to change – by being so efficient they may miss signals about what customers want, and by having such a strong sense of identity they may dismiss people who bring in important but challenging ideas. We mentioned Kodak and Polaroid earlier – both companies that had strong cultures and that suffered when the culture was no longer relevant to the environment. On the other hand, weak cultures may not provide enough guidance to people for coordination to be effective and may not provide enough sense of identity to bring people together and prioritize the group. Volunteer organizations sometimes have weak cultures, an effect you may have experienced yourself.

Anthropologists Kluckhohn and Strodtbeck (1961) maintained that cultures need enough variance to engage in healthy dialogue about how their culture needs to adapt to changes in the environment, without so much variance that the group cannot coordinate. Moderation seems to be important here.

Cultures Change: Responding to the Environment and Generational Shifts

It may seem obvious, but it is important to point out that cultures do change over time. Whether the culture of a family, an organization, a region, a religion, a country, a generation – the culture does evolve. The different layers of the iceberg tend to change at different rates, with the top of the iceberg changing more rapidly than the lower layers. The rice/wheat culture comparison mentioned earlier in the chapter demonstrated that the underlying cultures of rice- and wheat-growing regions are still different long after people became more urbanized.

The biggest source of cultural change is environmental change. The recent example of the COVID-19 pandemic provides a clear example of a shift in work cultures. When the pandemic struck, most knowledge workers – people whose work involves analysis and decision-making rather than manufacturing or in-person service – were forced to work from home rather than come into an office. The norms and artifacts of knowledge work changed dramatically: from in-person to virtual meetings, from fixed and bounded schedules to fluid and expanding schedules, and from business dress codes to casual dress codes. Because the environmental impact was so profound and the change in artifacts was enforced for quite a long period of time, many countries also experienced shifts in attitudes and values of the workforce. The "Great Resignation," which was first noticed in 2021, was a trend in many countries of workers quitting jobs during the pandemic because of their shift in values (Kamei, 2022; Morgan, 2022). The trend continued through the pandemic, with most observers noticing that the shift in values had been evolving slowly pre-pandemic, and the pandemic environment triggered action based on those values. With the economic slowdowns and high inflation across countries in 2023, the Great Resignation is no longer as apparent; however, employers still experience the shift in values with employees less willing to give up autonomy and work–life balance (Morgan, 2023). The return to the office has been slow in some industries and companies, making it harder for employees to enact and develop a common organizational culture.

Culture change is often evident in generational differences within a culture. Each new generation faces different challenges through their youth and early adulthood than previous generations, and develops different ways of responding to those challenges. Generational changes within countries sometimes lead to misunderstandings and are often the subject of humor and comedy. Generations are also evident in organizations, although not always associated with age. As a new firm grows, people who have been with the firm since its founding may hold values and engage in norms that are somewhat different from people who joined later, bringing outside experiences. If the culture's norms are healthy, these generational differences are noticed mindfully and discussed, and the culture continues to achieve both efficiency and identity as the environment changes.

We Are All Multicultural – Individual Complexity and Intersectionality

All individuals belong to multiple cultures, and types of cultures, simultaneously. For example, we'd like to introduce you to a good friend, Tan Sri Dr. Jemilah Mahmood.

Tan Sri Dr. Jemilah Mahmood, a prominent humanitarian, considers herself part of the Malaysian, Malay, Chinese, medical doctor, Muslim, women, mother, humanitarian aid, and global business cultures, and she articulates clearly what it means to be part of each of those cultures. Which culture she draws upon to guide her perceptions and behaviors depends on her context. She is always guided by her religious culture, covering her hair in public, observing prayers and other disciplines, and reflecting in her behavior the lessons of the Prophet and the Koran. She is proud of her Malaysian culture and a strong advocate of Malaysians worldwide. She also celebrates Chinese holidays and traditions and has close ties with her Chinese family. Earlier in her career, when delivering babies at the hospital, she behaved according to the norms and values of the medical doctor culture. When providing medical aid in an emergency situation after natural disasters in Indonesia or Myanmar or as a result of conflict in Iraq or Gaza, she may disregard some of the procedures typical of the hospital culture and behave according to the emergency (for example, doing surgery outside her area of specialization if she was the only person available to conduct the surgery), consistent with the humanitarian aid culture. When negotiating for resources with corporate sponsors for the humanitarian organization she founded, Mercy Malaysia, or when gaining access to emergency situations in her role at the International Federation of the Red Cross and Red Crescent Societies, she acted according to the global business culture, and she is well respected as a tough player. She does not always choose to act according to a single culture because she carries all these cultures in her, and often uses several at the same time to guide her behavior. For example, when trying to get emergency supplies to a conflict site, she uses both the humanitarian aid and the global business culture and leverages her identity and expertise as a doctor to establish her credibility.

Mahmood's set of cultural identities is more complex than most people's. She is one of a growing group of people in the world who are considered bicultural (or multicultural) by having two (or more) ethnic cultures. Research on biculturalism shows that people who grow up with two or more cultures, such as children of immigrants or children whose parents come from two cultures, face unique challenges in developing their identity but also can develop advantages such as flexibility and cognitive complexity (Cheng et al., 2006; Fitzsimmons, 2013; Fitzsimmons et al., 2017; Vora et al., 2019). They manage these identities in different ways: for example, they may prioritize one identity over another, they may separate them and draw on each in different situations, or they may combine them in various ways.

Mahmood's multicultural nature may be more obvious because of the different ethnic and professional cultures in which she operates, but she is not alone. We all identify with multiple cultures – ethnic, family, professional, regional, and so on. We strongly resist others who try to "label" us with only one culture because we know we are more complex than that.

Culture brings people within the group an important sense of identity, and it also signals that identity to people outside the group. As we noted earlier, cultures are not inherently good or bad; they evolved to address different collective challenges and they are effective at addressing those challenges. However, sometimes people from outside the culture do not see the value of a culture. Particularly when the sense of identity within a group is strong, members may tend to see people outside the group (culture) as "others" or "outsiders" and, subconsciously at least, as less effective, less important, or less worthy of attention. In its strongest forms, this can be associated with prejudice and discrimination against other groups and cultures. As a result, we may feel positive or negative about our *own* cultural identity based on how other people from *other* cultures see that identity.

In the next chapter we will directly address the dangers of stereotyping – assuming an individual represents their group and judging them based on that membership – and we will provide some lenses and tools for observing and combining cultural similarities and differences in positive ways. As you become more mindful about your own cultures, we encourage you to be curious about the combination of cultures and identities that other people encompass too.

Reflection Question 3.4: How Multicultural Are You?

All of us are multicultural, we all hold many cultures inside, as well as additional sources of identity. What are your main sources of identity? Think about three main categories of identity:

- individual characteristics of yourself as a person (e.g., height, coloring, personality, skill strengths, etc.)
- groups you belong to, either by your life circumstances (e.g., birth citizenship, ethnicity, religion from your family, community you grew up in) or by your own choices and actions (e.g., hobbies, graduate education, sports teams you follow, religion you chose)
- roles you hold – formal or informal positions you are in that have specific responsibilities toward other people (e.g., mother, son, boss, employee, engineer, etc.)

Don't worry about which category a particular source of identity falls into (e.g., "professor" could fit into role, group, or even individual characteristics). The categories are there to help you raise awareness about different aspects of your identity, even ones you may not think about every day.

To what extent do you integrate versus separate different elements of your identity? Do you combine them all the time, or do you separate them and draw on them in different contexts? How important are your sources of cultural identity, compared with other sources of identity, for you? What strengths do you bring to work tasks, related to your identities?

Culture as Context for International Management

The first section of this book set the frame for international management behavior. Chapter 1 introduced global leadership in a complex environment and emphasized the centrality of global mindfulness. Chapter 2 described three important paths to global mindfulness: global mindset, global leadership competences, and paradox thinking.

In this chapter, we have explored the nature of culture – what it is, what impact it has, and the complexity of acknowledging our multicultural natures. Global leaders are mindful about and sensitive to all aspects of the context, taking other's perspectives with a strong orientation to the process of engagement. Because management is about working with other people and culture guides people's expectations for interacting with each other, culture is the single most important aspect of context to be mindful about. In this chapter we have also discussed why culture is a context of which we're often unaware, so it is doubly important to be consciously mindful about our own and other's cultures: to develop a global mindset, to build global leadership competences, and to engage in the process of paradox thinking.

All these themes will be carried throughout the book. In the remaining sections we focus on analytical and behavioral skills that are key for decision-making, interacting, and leading whole organizations effectively in global contexts.

Reflection Question 3.5: What Is More Important – National Culture or Organizational Culture?

Schultz (2012) suggests four archetypical relationships between national culture/institutional setting and national culture that differ in the degree to which the two are intertwined and the strength ratio between the two. Please read:

Schultz, M. (2012). Relationships between culture and institutions: New interdependencies in a global world? *Journal of Management Inquiry*, 21(1), 102–106.

Now reflect/discuss:

- How can Schultz's framework help you in understanding global collaboration and the role of national cultures?
- Under what circumstances might we expect the influence of organizational culture to be stronger than the influence of national culture in an organization?
- How does Schultz's framework challenge frameworks and models focusing exclusively on the role of national culture? How does Schultz's framework emphasize the role of national culture?

Reflection Question 3.6: Formulating Your Global Leadership Learning Charter

Based on what you have read in Part I of this book, please take the first steps toward formulating your global leadership learning charter. Answer the questions below using "one-liners" or "tweet"-length formulations. Individual one-liners may be used as a screensaver for your laptop or similar, so you will always remember the key points:

1. I define global leadership as … .
2. For me, the biggest challenge in global leadership is … .
3. I can relate particularly to the global leadership element of …, because … .
4. In my own leadership, I think I should be more focused on …, because … .
5. I think I am most competent to handle the global leadership element of …, which I encounter when … .
6. I think I am least strong at the global leadership element of …, which I realize because … .
7. I would like to be better at … because I want to be able to … .

Please revisit your charter as you work your way through the chapters. We will invite you to update your charter at the end of the book too.

Adapted with the authors' permission from Nielsen, R. K., & Lyndgaard, D. B. (2018). *Grasping global leadership: Tools for next practice.* Global Leadership Academy – Copenhagen Business School & Danish Confederation of Industry. Also see www.globalledelse.dk/eng

Bibliography

CBS News. (2021). *McDonald's plans to "drastically" reduce plastic toys in its Happy Meals by 2025*. Retrieved March 26, 2024, from https://www.cbsnews.com/news/mcdonalds-plastic-toys-reduction-happy-meals-2025.

Cheng, C., Lee, F., & Benet-Martinez, V. (2006). Assimilation and contrast effects in cultural frame switching (CFS): Bicultural identity integration (BII) and valence of cultural cues. *Journal of Cross Cultural Psychology, 37*(6), 1–19.

Dong, X., Talhelm, T., & Ren, X. (2019). Teens in rice county are more interdependent and think more holistically than nearby wheat county. *Social Psychological and Personality Science, 10*(7), 966–976.

English, A. S., Talhelm, T., Tong, R., Li, X., & Su, Y. (2022). Historical rice farming explains faster mask use during early days of China's COVID-19 outbreak. *Current Research in Ecological and Social Psychology, 3*, 100034.

Erez, M., & Earley, P. C. (1993). *Culture, Self-Identity, and Work*. Oxford University Press.

Fitzsimmons, S. R. (2013). Multicultural employees: A framework for understanding how they contribute to organizations. *Academy of Management Review, 38*(4), 525–549.

Fitzsimmons, S. R., Liao, Y., & Thomas, D. C. (2017). From crossing cultures to straddling them: An empirical examination of outcomes for multicultural employees. *Journal of International Business Studies, 48*(1), 63–89.

Gelfand, M. J. (2019). *Rule makers, rule breakers: Tight and loose cultures and the secret signals that direct our lives*. Scribner.

Gelfand, M. J., Raver, J. L., Nishii, L., Leslie, L. M., Lun, J., Lim, B. C., Duan, L., Almaliach, A., Ang, S., Arnadottir, J., Aycan, Z., Boehnke, K., Boski, P., Cabecinhas, R., Chan, D., Chhokar, J., D'Amato, A., Ferrer, M., Fischlmayr, I. C., Fischer, R., Fülöp, M., Georgas, J., Kashima, E. S., Kashima, Y., Kim, K., Lempereur, A., Marquez, P., Othman, R., Overlaet, B., Panagiotopoulou, P., Peltzer, K., Perez-Florizno, L. R., Ponomarenko, L., Realo, A., Schei, V., Schmitt, M., Smith, P. B., Soomro, N., Szabo, E., Taveesin, N., Toyama, M., Van de Vliert, E., Vohra, N., Ward, C., & Yamaguchi, S. (2011). Differences between tight and loose cultures: A 33-nation study. *Science, 332*(6033), 1100–1104.

Gibson, B. C., Maznevski, M., & Kirkman, B. L. (2009). When does culture matter? In Bhagat, R. S., & Steers, R. M. (Eds.), *Handbook of culture, organizations, and work.* (pp. 46–68). Cambridge University Press.

Glasson, M., & Lehman, N. (2022). *What's new with fast-food drive-thrus?* QSR Magazine. Retrieved March 26, 2024, from https://www.qsrmagazine.com/operations/drive-thru/whats-new-fast-food-drive-thrus

Hall, E. T. (1966). *The hidden dimension*. Doubleday.

Kahneman, D. (2011). *Thinking, fast and slow*. Farrar, Straus and Giroux.

Kamei, A. (2022). *The post-COVID 'Great Resignation' comes to Asia: Hays CEO*. Nikkei Asia. Retrieved March 26, 2024, from https://asia.nikkei.com/Economy/The-post-COVID-Great-Resignation-comes-to-Asia-Hays-CEO

Kluckhohn, C. (1949). *Mirror for man: The relation of anthropology to modern life*. Whittlesey House, McGraw-Hill.

Kluckhohn, F. R., & Strodtbeck, F. L. (1961). *Variations in value orientations*. Row, Peterson & Company.

McDonald's. (2023). McDonald's Corporate. Retrieved March 26, 2024, from https://www.mcdonalds.com

McDonnell, S. (2013). *What percentage of sales are from drive through windows at fast food restaurants?* Chron Small Business. Retrieved March 26, 2024, from https://smallbusiness.chron.com/percentage-sales-drive-through-windows-fast-food-restaurants-75713.html

Morgan, K. (2022). *Why workers just won't stop quitting*. BBC. Retrieved March 26, 2024, from https://www.bbc.com/worklife/article/20220817-why-workers-just-wont-stop-quitting

Morgan, K. (2023). *The Great Resignation is 'over'. What does that mean?* BBC. Retrieved March 26, 2024, from https://www.bbc.com/worklife/article/20230731-the-great-resignation-is-over-what-does-that-mean

Schein, E. H. (1984). Coming to a new awareness of organizational culture. *Sloan Management Review, 25*(2), 3.

Shultz, T. R., Hartshorn, M., & Kaznatcheev, A. (2009). Why is ethnocentrism more common than humanitarianism? In *Proceedings of the 31st Annual Conference of the Cognitive Science Society* (pp. 2100–2105). Cognitive Science Society.

Talhelm, T., Zhang, X., & Oishi, S. (2018). Moving chairs in Starbucks: Observational studies find rice-wheat cultural differences in daily life in China. *Science Advances*, *4*(4), eaap8469.

Talhelm, T., Zhang, X., Oishi, S., Shimin, C., Duan, D., Lan, X., & Kitayama, S. (2014). Large-scale psychological differences within China explained by rice versus wheat agriculture. *Science*, *344*(6184), 603–608.

The Economist. (2023). *Our Big Mac index shows how burger prices are changing.* The Economist. Retrieved March 26, 2024, from https://www.economist.com/big-mac-index

Vora, D., Lee, M., Fitzsimmons, S. R., Pekerti, A. A., Lakshman, C., & Raheem, S. (2019). Multiculturalism within individuals: A review, critique, and agenda for future research. *Journal of International Business Studies*, *50*(4), 499–524.

Decision-Making Cases

CASE I-1: MCDONALD'S ARGENTINA

Professor Dominique Turpin prepared this case as a basis for class discussion rather than to illustrate either effective or ineffective handling of a business situation.

"This is just incredible ... " "How can they possibly do this?" "I cannot believe it!" Gathered in the main meeting room at their headquarters, managers of Arcos Dorados Argentina were venting their frustration and anger at what was being aired on Canal America, the fifth major TV channel in the country. At 21:00, the TV station had decided to show live the shutdown of four McDonald's stores by the local health authorities in downtown Buenos Aires. Jorge Lanata, a well-known investigative journalist and controversial television commentator, was urging all Argentines to stop visiting McDonald's stores and refrain from eating McPollo (McChicken) burgers following an official announcement that potentially harmful bacteria had been found in these chicken products.

Standing in the middle of the room, Woods Staton, CEO of Arcos Dorados S.A., tried to reduce the tension and calm people down:

"All right, all right. We all know that their information is incorrect and that our products are safe; but how are we going to fight back? Obviously, we don't like what we've just heard and seen on TV ... I doubt that the local authorities will admit their errors now. Negative stories, although unfounded, tend to travel quickly and get picked up by other media. Now, the key issues are: How do we respond? And, in fact: Should we respond? How do we regain public confidence? ... This is going to be a long and tough challenge ... Let's keep our cool and review the options!"

Copyright © 2002 by IMD – International Institute for Management Development, Lausanne, Switzerland. Not to be used or reproduced without written permission directly from IMD.

Arcos Dorados Argentina

McDonald's Argentina (also known locally under the Spanish corporate name of Arcos Dorados) had been established in 1986 by Staton, a Colombian national by birth, who had partnered with McDonald's to start a franchise operation in Argentina. Fifteen years later, McDonald's had 211 stores (70 of them in Buenos Aires) in more than 10 cities in Argentina and employed more than 11,500 people. It served an average of 300,000 meals per day and posted total annual sales of US$240 million.

Chicken products such as McPollo burgers and chicken nuggets represented between 5% and 10% of McDonald's daily sales in Argentina. For competitive reasons, Arcos Dorados imported all of its chicken meat from Brazil. On average, about 20,000 chicken meals were sold per day in McDonald's stores across Argentina. Chicken nuggets were popular with children and were usually included in the "Happy Meal Menu," which McDonald's sold for an average of US$3.70.

McDonald's major competitor in Argentina was Burger King, with 23 stores. Wendy's, another food service competitor, had withdrawn from the Argentine market one month earlier after suffering serious financial losses due to the poor economic situation in the country.

Woods Staton's Business Philosophy

Staton summarized his philosophy and his 15 years of success with the company:

> McDonald's is the largest food service retailer in Argentina. We are one of the largest employers in a country where unemployment is close to 20%. The opening of

each new McDonald's store signifies not only the creation of new jobs but also new opportunities for local industry, stimulating the growth of numerous businesses that work together with us. About 90% of McDonald's basic ingredients are purchased locally from Argentine businesses. McDonald's contributes to the growth of the agriculture and livestock sector, consuming annually a large amount of Argentine food products, including 8,000 tons of beef, 100 million bread rolls, 900 tons of tomatoes, 1,200 tons of lettuce, 4.5 million liters of ice cream, and 8,200 tons of potatoes. These facts not only confirm McDonald's involvement in our national industry but also show our deep commitment to developing the community where we conduct business.

Our commitment to this country is not limited to business and employment – we also support the Argentine community with different social contributions such as the Ronald McDonald Houses. This project is dedicated to housing families from anywhere in Argentina who have to find temporary accommodation because their children need prolonged medical treatment far from home.

Deep social and economic change have had an impact on Argentine society over recent years. McDonald's has lived through these changes and, as a result, Argentines have discovered that in McDonald's they can find meals of excellent quality, friendly and speedy service, and cleanliness – all at an accessible price. We have achieved recognition for the McDonald's brand in the country of beef and French fries.

The "Jorge Roel Problem"

On August 6, Cecilia Galasso, who worked in the customer service department at Arcos Dorados, received a call from Jorge Roel, a Buenos Aires resident who wanted to complain about food poisoning. Roel claimed that the day before, he had visited one of the main McDonald's stores in the Patio Bullrich, a shopping mall in downtown Buenos Aires, where he had eaten a McPollo burger. Roel then claimed that a few hours later he had felt sick. He now wanted to know: "What is McDonald's going to do about my problem?"

Galasso was fully trained to answer this kind of call. Typically, she received about 15 calls a day from consumers asking for information on new promotions, making suggestions, and also offering congratulations or complaints. It was not unusual for Galasso to receive calls from people like Roel, who complained about real, fake, or imagined stomach problems. McDonald's had some of the strictest – if not the strictest – sanitary standards in the country. In the past, all reported health problems were found to be linked to reasons other than McDonald's products. In Argentina, a country of 35 million inhabitants, health problems were most often linked to contaminated water or food consumed from the thousands of street vendors active in the capital. Galasso was also fully aware that in a country where one-third of the population still lived on a few dollars a day, some unscrupulous people could try their chances at extortion.

To minimize these problems, McDonald's Argentina had designed a detailed questionnaire that helped Galasso better understand consumers' health problems and their real causes. For every call related to food poisoning, Galasso asked a series of questions and entered all the answers in a computer. Then a report was e-mailed internally to the store manager concerned, the quality manager and the public relations director, and, possibly, to the legal department (depending on the nature of the case) and a doctor.

Once Galasso had completed the interview with Roel, she told him that McDonald's would immediately start an internal investigation and that she would call him back within a maximum of five working days.

Health Inspectors Move In

The following day, August 7, María José (Majo) Parodi, the public relations manager of Arcos Dorados, received a call from the McDonald's store manager at Patio Bullrich.

He told her that health inspectors from the Department of Hygiene and Food Safety (DHFS) of the city government of Buenos Aires were in the store, collecting frozen and cooked samples of chicken meat used for McPollo burgers and chicken nuggets. The inspectors told the store manager that they were acting on a call to the DHFS's toll-free line that Roel had placed the day before.

In accordance with Argentine regulations, the inspectors collected three food samples: the first was sent to the city government laboratory; the other two samples were sealed and saved, one in the DHFS fridge and the other in the store fridge. McDonald's would use its sample for a separate test by an independent private laboratory. The third sample would be saved for a potential counter-test. As a precaution, McDonald's saved a fourth sample in its store as another potential counter-test.

The first tests were conducted by the Buenos Aires city government laboratory. By law, neither McDonald's nor its legal representatives were allowed to be present during the sanitary tests. To avoid the potential for tampering with the evidence, these tests were not videoed by the city government authorities.

Unlike the city government lab, however, McDonald's insisted that the private sanitary lab should videotape all its test examinations. Within 24 hours, the second test had proved negative for any potential health problem. If the sample had shown up as "probably positive," a second test would have had to be conducted on the same sample 48 hours later.

Over the next few days, other samples were taken by Buenos Aires city government health inspectors in 27 different stores, including one at McKey, the McDonald's plant and distribution center in Garín, outside the capital. Several store managers reported concerns to their headquarters about the health inspectors' procedures. In several instances, they had not worn protective gloves, which could possibly influence the outcome of future health tests.

Tests on raw chicken lots taken from the Garín plant proved to be negative. However, to McDonald's surprise, 4 of the 27 other samples in the hands of the city government turned out to be positive: 3 raw samples and one cooked sample. All samples tested independently by McDonald's repeatedly showed up as negative. The DHFS then turned to the Malbrán Institute (a national public laboratory that was part of the national Ministry of Health) for a second opinion on the samples it had already tested. On August 13, Malbrán concluded that the four samples contained *E. coli* 0157:H7 (*Escherichia coli enterohemorrhagica*) from the same stock, or origin. In its final report, which McDonald's received directly from Malbrán, the national laboratory indicated it had not received the samples of chicken meat themselves, but a sample of *E. coli* from the DHFS for which it had been asked to confirm the type. The city government authorities never commented on this information.

At Arcos Dorados, Parodi, along with the legal director and other executives, started to become extremely concerned but also very suspicious. According to medical experts, harmless strains of *E. coli* were found as a matter of course in the intestines of healthy humans and healthy ruminant animals. However, the principal source of the harmful strain known as *E. coli* O157:H7 was cattle, especially young animals. Argentina, being a major producer and exporter of cattle meat, had one of the highest incidences of *E. coli* in the world.[1] In most instances, the source of outbreak was traceable to a cattle product, especially undercooked ground beef. Dr. Ureta, a medical expert who advised McDonald's, confirmed that *E. coli* 0157:H7 could result in serious illness ranging from simple stomach pains to diarrhea with blood and vomiting or even hemolytic umeric syndrome (HUS), and that it could be deadly in children under five years of age. The incidence of HUS in children in Argentina was 22 per 100,000 compared with rates of 0.5 to 5 per 100,000 in

---

[1] Gyles, Carlton L. "*E. coli* 0157:H7 and Other VTEC in Animals." *The Infectious Disease Review*. Vol. 1, No. 2, June 1999: 127.

Europe, the US, Canada, and other South American countries.[2] However, Dr. Ureta could not understand how Roel could have been infected within 24 hours by *E. coli*, since the bacteria needed between 3 and 10 days to strike the human body. Moreover, although *E. coli* 0157:H7 could be found in beef, this particular type of *E. coli* was not found in poultry meat.[3]

Staton explained:

> All our tests continued to be negative. We could not really understand why the authorities were coming up with different conclusions! If there is one thing McDonald's is particularly strict about, it is sanitary inspection. This is one of our core competences. Under no circumstances did we believe that our food was bad. We cook all meat for three minutes at very high temperatures (360°F/182°C) to make sure that no bacteria can survive. *E. coli* bacteria are killed at 70°C (158°F) ... We have the strictest health standards in all the industry. How could four different samples taken from four different and distant locations possibly contain the same bacteria, from the same source? This was when we seriously started to question the validity of the city government tests and thought that cross-contamination might have happened in one of their labs.
>
> Regardless of test discrepancies, food safety and our customers are absolute priorities for us, so, in consultation with the government of the City of Buenos Aires and our lawyers, we decided to recall all McPollo chicken burgers and chicken products from every store in the capital, and to extend this precautionary measure to all our stores across Argentina.
>
> Then, on August 20, we received a letter from a DHFS inspector confirming that all raw chicken products tested in the McDonald's plant in Garín were fine for human consumption. With the full approval of all the authorities concerned, we decided to resume selling chicken products the following day. Nevertheless, we found out that other health inspectors were continuing to take more samples ... and two days later, SENASA [the national sanitary services agency] asked us to stop production in our plant ...
>
> What happened was that the city government inspectors had gone out of their jurisdiction to take samples from our Garín plant, situated outside the city. The plant is in fact under the jurisdiction of the Province of Buenos Aires, for which a different health authority is responsible! These people started to get involved, too, but fortunately confirmed after two weeks that the products from our plant were safe.

Managing the Key Players

Between August 6 (when Roel made his first phone call) and August 27 (when Lanata went live with the show on TV), every Arcos Dorados executive had been mobilized to work on the case. Regular meetings presided over by Staton enabled the team to see how the situation was evolving:

- Parodi was in charge of the media, monitoring coverage of the events in the press. So far, the media had not been particularly interested in the case. For them, there was "no story."
- Germán Lemonnier, vice-president, coordinated the efforts of the legal team headed by Rivero Ayerza. Among other things, the legal team had been in regular contact with Roel. They found that Roel – who

---

[2] Gyles, Carlton L. "*E. coli* 0157:H7 and Other VTEC in Animals." *The Infectious Disease Review*. Vol. 1, No. 2, June 1999: 128.

[3] Beutin et al. found that 67% of sheep, 56% of goats, and 21% of cattle were positive, compared with 14% of dogs, 8% of cats and 0% of chickens. Source: Beutin L., D. Geier, H. Steinruck, S. Zimmermann, and F. Scheutz. "Prevalence and Some Properties of Verotoxin (Shiga-like Toxin)-Producing *Escherichia coli* in Seven Different Species of Healthy Domestic Animals." *Journal of Clinical Microbiology*, Vol. 31, Iss. 9, 1993:2483–2488.

was unemployed and lived alone with his mother – wanted to avoid any publicity and worked only by phone, even when he talked to the city government authorities. When city officials asked him to file an official complaint again McDonald's, he refused to comply, arguing that he was in direct contact with the company in order to solve the problem. The legal team also found that neither Arcos Dorados nor the city government could officially confirm that Roel had visited a McDonald's store on August 6. No doctor's report or hospital record of a visit for food poisoning was available. The legal team also discovered that Roel had recently tried to extort money from a local supermarket. Roel never asked McDonald's directly for any kind of financial compensation, but he regularly called Arcos Dorados and asked the same question: "What are you going to do for me?"

Lemonnier, together with José Fernandez (Arcos Dorados' executive vice president), had also kept close contact with the municipal and federal authorities. Fernandez, who was in charge of real estate and business development, had connections with many different officials in Buenos Aires. Lemonnier and Fernandez's objectives were to understand why the health tests had unexpectedly turned out to be positive, as well as some of the possible motivations behind something that to them did not stack up. During a meeting with some officials, one of Fernandez's contacts confidentially confirmed:

> A politician is going after you, but please don't ask me who ... With elections coming soon, don't you understand that some politicians want to look good? ... They want to show that they are caring for the health of the citizens, and that they are acting fast. They know you are an ideal target. Your company is an obvious symbol of American capitalism. You are known to be a clean company, not paying any bribes, so these people have nothing to fear from you. They owe you nothing ... and when you are down, this guy believes that his party will look great in the eyes of his supporters.

This was incomprehensible to the Arcos Dorados managers. After all, the business community and high-ranking city officials considered McDonald's to be an excellent example of good corporate citizenship. Over the years, Staton and his team had cultivated and maintained strong and good relationships with the municipal and state authorities. Staton was particularly proud of some of McDonald's Argentina's social actions. One example was a weekly program run jointly by the city government and McDonald's to take 180 kids from the slums to Buenos Aires zoo, followed by a free lunch in a nearby McDonald's store. The program was so important in the eyes of Staton and the mayor, Aníbal Ibara, that they both joined the tour on its inaugural day.

The Political Factor

Over the previous 30 years, the political situation in Argentina had been "hot." The country had experienced a military dictatorship between 1976 and 1983 during which 9,000 people had been killed or disappeared – according to official data – and up to 30,000 according to human rights groups. The country was now entering its 18th year of democracy but was still experiencing many political and socioeconomic difficulties. Both the City of Buenos Aires and the federal government were run by the "Alianza" (alliance) made up of various parties representing many different political sensitivities and factions from the far right to the far left. Down the chain of command, responsibilities within the government of Buenos Aires were split among different parties, often leading to poor implementation and/or political paralysis.

According to different sources from national and international non-governmental organizations, 20 million out of the 36 million Argentinians had recently been or were still affected by poverty. Economic growth was down. Many Argentinians were becoming increasingly nostalgic about the days, in the 1930s, when Argentina was considered one of the 10 most prosperous largest economies in the world. Many citizens attributed the decline of their country to a single major problem: political corruption. A local food exporter explained:

> We have hundreds and hundreds of politicians in this country, from the state level to the provinces and municipalities, and they are very well paid. In fact, this country has more political representatives than the United States and we are seven times smaller ... As you can imagine, these people cost us a lot of money ... and of course, they try to get money from everybody, especially from big corporations.

At Arcos Dorados, Fernandez confirmed this statement:

> When we open a new store, we have lots of papers to fill in and many kinds of approvals are needed. The legislation is vague and often obsolete, so some people can create a lot of problems for us. However, over 15 years we have been known for not paying commissions or fees for any unnecessary work or transactions ... As a US-based corporation, we are bound to abide by the "Foreign Corrupt Practices Act." The consequences of being clean are that we sometimes have to pay the price later, one way or another!

The Media Factor

Parodi commented:

> Another big challenge for us is to deal effectively with the media ... We are not always treated very fairly. I often meet journalists who have been McDonald's consumers for a long time but when they are back at their desk, they can be quite harsh on us! On August 27, the day Jorge Lanata went live on Canal America, we met in the evening with a journalist working with Lanata. He had been investigating the Jorge Roel story for about a week. We clearly explained our position to him and he privately told me that he was quite convinced of our innocence. He also confessed to me that he regularly took his children to our stores and that he would continue to do so in the future. However, he added that when city government officials called the TV network to inform him that they were going to close down four McDonald's stores this evening, this was news for any journalist and he had to do his job!
>
> He was first to tell us that our stores would be closed the same evening. His announcement was a real shock to all of us. The city government has *not* yet notified us officially and this journalist was indicating that we were going to be shut down ... That was just incredible!

Lanata Live on TV

Following the information from the journalist that within a few hours the city government was going to close down four McDonald's stores (where positive *E. coli* samples had allegedly been found), Parodi phoned Staton. He then called an emergency meeting for all senior Arcos Dorados executives. At about the same time, the lawyers had called Staton to confirm the news. Although the legal team had not yet received an official written warning, a city government agent had been called to confirm the news: The legal team now believed that the decision was for real – Rivero Ayerza was already in her car driving from one of the four stores to the next to check the legal procedures of the store closures. Staton ordered the targeted stores to switch off all their lights and neon signs to give less visibility to McDonald's on the TV screens of consumers across the country.

All key executives had rushed into the main meeting room. Parodi recalled:

> Everything went so fast, phones were ringing, people were coming in and going out, it was an incredible moment ... And a few minutes later, there he was: Jorge Lanata,

live on TV, urging Argentine consumers not to touch any McPollo burgers and making comments about McDonald's products. Cameras were now showing officials closing four stores. THIS WAS INDEED FOR REAL!

Rivero Ayerza called Staton with a major piece of information: "The health inspectors are asking us to close the stores, but they have no warrant!" With four stores nevertheless being closed by city government officials, Staton was sure that the press and TV networks would make this their headline news. Media coverage was likely to be huge and, without question, unfriendly to McDonald's. It was now 21:40. Staton and his team had to prepare a response fast. Parodi warned:

Pretty soon, the media are going to be downstairs. What are we going to tell them?

Around the table, comments and suggestions for action were flying in all directions. However, the same questions were coming back again and again:

- What position should the company take vis-à-vis Jorge Roel, the city government, their overreaction?
- Attacking the government is like attacking the people ... our clients!
- We can't attack clients, the people, the government. The consequences could be terrible.

Fernandez asked:

If we do respond, how do we do so credibly?
- ... and Lanata, how do we deal with him?!
- ... what about this guy, Jorge Roel? He created the problem in the first place.

Telephones were ringing non-stop. Parodi picked up a call from Daniel Haddad, a well-known commentator also working for Canal America. Haddad had a live TV news show at midnight and wanted to come to the Arcados Dorados headquarters for his program. Parodi wondered:

Should we let him in?

Staton was very concerned about consumers' reactions, about how to rebuild confidence with the staff, customers, and suppliers and how the city government would react. He concluded:

We are 100% committed to doing the right thing and concerned only for our customers and their faith in our product. This customer confidence is of paramount importance to us, and if there are any issues we need to address we are completely committed to doing so.

Now, we've got to be fast and have the right communication approach. We also need to think about what other actions to take. Our first moves will be critical and we must be credible!

CASE I-2: ARLA FOODS AND THE CARTOON CRISIS (A)

David Wesley wrote this case under the supervision of Professors Henry W. Lane and Mikael Sondergaard solely to provide material for class discussion. The authors do not intend to illustrate either effective or ineffective handling of a managerial situation. The authors may have disguised certain names and other identifying information to protect confidentiality.

Ivey Management Services is the exclusive representative of the copyright holder and prohibits any form of reproduction, storage, or transmittal without its written permission. Reproduction of this material is not covered under authorization by any reproduction rights organization. To order copies or request permission to reproduce materials, contact Ivey Publishing, Ivey Management Services, c/o Richard Ivey School of Business, The University of Western Ontario, London, Ontario, Canada, N6A 3K7; phone (519) 661-3208; fax (519) 661-3882; e-mail cases@ivey.uwo.ca.

Copyright © 2008, Northeastern University, College of Business Administration   Version: (A) 2010-02-26

In early February 2006, Astrid Nielsen, group communications director of Arla Foods, faced the greatest crisis of her career. Tens of thousands of Muslims in cities around the world had taken to the streets to protest the publication of caricatures of Muhammad by a Danish newspaper. The caricatures, which most Muslims viewed as blasphemous and offensive, prompted some to attack Danish embassies and businesses. In several countries, protests turned deadly.

Saudi Arabia was able to avoid much of the violence seen elsewhere. Instead, consumers protested by boycotting Danish products. For Arla Foods, which owned a large dairy in Saudi Arabia, the result was nothing short of disastrous. As other countries began to join the boycott, Nielson wondered what, if anything, her company could do to mitigate the total loss of Arla's Middle Eastern business.

Background

Arla Foods, a co-operative owned by 10,000 milk producers in Denmark and Sweden, was formed in 2000 through the merger of MD Foods of Denmark and Arla of Sweden. Arla was Europe's second largest dairy company, with 58 processing plants in Scandinavia and Britain, and annual revenues of nearly US$8 billion. It enjoyed a near-monopoly on domestic dairy products, with market shares of between 80 and 90 per cent in most categories. The United Kingdom was the company's largest market, accounting for 33 per cent of total sales, followed by Sweden and Denmark at 22 per cent and 19 per cent, respectively. The rest of Europe accounted for another 13 per cent.

Outside Europe, the Middle East was Arla's most important market (see Table 1). The company exported approximately 55,000 tons of dairy products from Denmark and Sweden to Saudi Arabia, and produced around 30,000 tons through its Danya Foods subsidiary in Riyadh. Local production was based mainly on non-perishable goods and included

Table 1 Arla Foods: Middle East Key Facts

Annual Revenues	US$550 million
Net Income	US$80 million
Danish Expatriate Workers	20
Non-Danish Workers[1]	1,200
Average Annual Growth	10–12%

[1] Most of Arla's non-Danish staff was comprised of Muslim migrant workers from less developed countries. Many entered Saudi Arabia as Hajj pilgrims and remained in the country at the end of their pilgrimage.

processed cheese, milk, and fruit drinks. In Saudi Arabia, which accounted for 70 per cent of total Middle East sales, the company's Lurpak, Puck, and Three Cows brands were market leaders in butter, cream, dairy spread, and feta categories. Other important Middle East markets included Lebanon, Kuwait, Qatar, and the United Arab Emirates.

Other overseas markets included Argentina and Brazil, where Arla produced cheese and whey products. Arla also exported significant quantities of Danish cheese to Japan, and milk powder to less developed countries in Asia and Latin America. In North America, Arla cheeses were produced under a licensing agreement.

The Muhammad Cartoons Crisis

Terrorism and Self-Censorship

In 2004, controversial Dutch filmmaker Theo van Gogh produced a short film on Islam titled "Submission."[2] The 10-minute documentary, written by Dutch Member of Parliament Hirsi Ali, featured the stories of four abused Arab women. It intentionally provoked some Muslims by showing a woman dressed in a semi-transparent burqa, under which verses from the Qur'an were projected on her skin.

After the film was shown on Dutch public television on August 29, 2004, van Gogh and Ali began to receive death threats. Then, on November 2, 2004, van Gogh was murdered while riding his bicycle in downtown Amsterdam.[3] The assailant attached a note to his body calling for Jihad against "infidel" America and Europe and threatening a similar fate for Ali.

Van Gogh's murder created broad awareness of his film, which was subsequently rebroadcast on Italian and Danish public television and widely distributed on the Internet. In Denmark, tension was already high following another well-publicized incident in which a lecturer at the University of Copenhagen was assaulted by five Muslim youths for reading the Qur'an to non-Muslims.[4] The killing of van Gogh only served to heighten the cultural distance between Muslim immigrants and native-born Danes. Although most Europeans decried the violence of radical Islamists, many publishers, authors, and artists were reluctant to participate in projects that could offend Muslims and invite the wrath of terrorists.

Fear and Self-Censorship

In the summer of 2005, Danish author Kåre Bluitgen decided to write a children's book on the life of the Prophet Muhammad. He had hoped that such a book would help Danish children learn the story of Islam and thereby bridge the growing gap between Danes and Muslim immigrants. Yet the illustrators who collaborated with Bluitgen on other books feared reprisals from extremists and, therefore, refused to participate.[5] They understood, perhaps better than Bluitgen, that graphical depictions of Muhammad were considered blasphemous by many Muslims.[6]

Bluitgen eventually found an artist willing to illustrate his book anonymously. However, when the culture editor of the Danish newspaper Jyllands-Posten heard Bluitgen's story, he was incensed. "This was the culmination of a series of disturbing instances of self-censorship," Flemming Rose later wrote:

> Three people turned down the job for fear of consequences. The person who finally

---

[2] Submission is the English translation of the word "Islam."
[3] "Gunman kills Dutch film director," *BBC News*, November 2, 2004.
[4] "Overfaldet efter Koran-læsning," *TV 2 (Denmark)*, October 9, 2004.
[5] "Allah und der Humor," *Die Zeit*, January 2, 2006.
[6] Not all Muslims agree on the interpretation of Muslim scholars who have issued *fatwas* against images of the prophet Muhammad. Some argue that Islam has a centuries-old tradition of paintings of Muhammad and other religious figures. The more famous of these continue to be displayed in palaces and museums in various Muslim countries, including Iran. Source: "Bonfire of the Pieties: Islam prohibits neither images of Muhammad nor jokes about religion," *The Wall Street Journal*, February 8, 2006.

accepted insisted on anonymity, which in my book is a form of self-censorship. European translators of a critical book about Islam also did not want their names to appear on the book cover beside the name of the author, a Somalia-born Dutch politician who has herself been in hiding.[7]

Danish Cartoons: Muhammad As You See Him

To counter what he saw as a move against free speech, Rose invited 40 artists to submit drawings of "Muhammad, as you see him." Twelve artists responded, including three members of the Jyllands-Posten staff. When the cartoons first appeared on September 30, 2005, Rose wrote in the accompanying article,

> The modern, secular society is rejected by some Muslims. They demand a special position, insisting on special consideration of their own religious feelings. It is incompatible with contemporary democracy and freedom of speech, where you must be ready to put up with insults, mockery and ridicule ... We are on our way to a slippery slope where no-one can tell how the self-censorship will end. That is why Jyllands-Posten has invited members of the Danish editorial cartoonists union to draw Muhammad as they see him.[8]

Muslim Reaction

Two weeks after the publication of the 12 cartoons, Danish imams organized a protest in downtown Copenhagen. More than 3,000 Danish Muslim immigrants gathered to show their disapproval of the cartoons. The most offensive cartoon, in their opinion, featured Muhammad wearing a turban filled with explosives. On the turban was written the *Shahādah* (Islamic creed),[9] while a lit fuse emerged from the back of his head.

Another image featured a schoolboy named Muhammad scribbling a message in Farsi[10] on a blackboard. "The editorial team of Jyllands-Posten is a bunch of reactionary provocateurs," it states. Ironically, artist Lars Refn was targeted by both sides in the ensuing quarrel. He was the first artist to receive death threats, while at the same time secular free speech advocates accused him of cowardice for not drawing the prophet. In apparent defense of Refn's decision to not draw the prophet, Rose explained in an editorial, "I wrote to members of the association of Danish cartoonists asking them 'to draw Muhammad as you see him.' We certainly did not ask them to make fun of the prophet."[11]

A few days later, eleven ambassadors from Islamic countries sought a meeting with Danish Prime Minister Anders Rasmussen to demand government action against the cartoons. The prime minister refused, noting that such a meeting would violate the principles of Danish democracy. "As prime minister I have no tool whatsoever to take actions against the media, and I don't want that kind of tool," he replied.[12]

Cartoons Circulated Abroad

Meanwhile, Danish imam Abu Laban decided to take matters into his own hands. He sent a Muslim delegation on a tour of Egypt, Lebanon, and Syria, where dignitaries, religious leaders, and journalists were shown the cartoons. The greatest stir, however, was not

---

[7] The Dutch politician refers to Hirsi Ali, who collaborated with Theo Van Gogh on the film Submission. "Why I published those cartoons," *Jyllands-Posten*, February 19, 2006.

[8] Translated from "*Muhammeds ansigt*," *Jyllands-Posten*, September 29, 2005.

[9] The *Shahādah* is the declaration of belief in the oneness of God and in Muhammad as his messenger. Recitation of the *Shahādah* is considered one of the Five Pillars of Islam by Sunni Muslims. In English the *Shahādah* reads: "There is no god but God and Muhammad is his messenger."

[10] Farsi is a Persian language spoken in Iran, Afghanistan, and several other Middle Eastern countries.

[11] "Why I published those cartoons," *Jyllands-Posten*, February 19, 2006.

[12] "The Danish cartoon crisis: The import and impact of public diplomacy," *USC Center on Public Diplomacy*, April 5, 2006.

caused by the Danish cartoons, but by three additional images that were far more graphic and offensive than those published by the newspaper.[13] While the origin of the three additional images was unknown, within days they were circulated on Islamic websites and chat rooms, causing outrage among Muslims who thought they had been published in Danish newspapers.[14]

In December, the cartoons were circulated among heads of state at a summit of the Organization of the Islamic Conference (OIC) in Saudi Arabia. The OIC later issued a statement calling on the prime minister of Denmark to apologize. When he refused, the OIC's secretary general for Islamic education and culture urged the organization's 51 member states to boycott Danish products until they received an apology.[15] Since the entire Middle East accounted for less than 1 per cent of Denmark's exports, Danes showed little concern over the threat of a boycott. Moreover, a poll conducted in late January by the Epinion Research Institute found that 79 per cent of Danes supported the prime minister's decision to not apologize for the cartoons.[16]

Outside of Denmark, the OIC found wider support. United Nations Human-Rights Commissioner Louise Arbour proclaimed her "alarm" at the "unacceptable disregard for the beliefs of others." Both the Council of Europe and the Arab League condemned the cartoons.[17]

European Media Reprint Cartoons

When the OIC called on Muslim countries to boycott Danish products (see "Arla and the OIC Boycott" below), many Europeans saw it as an attack on free speech. In protest, newspapers and magazines across Europe began reprinting the cartoons. Between the beginning of January and early February, the original cartoons appeared in more than 50 European newspapers and magazines. Prominent periodicals, such as France's *Le Monde* and Germany's *Die Welt*, displayed some of the images on their front pages.

In explaining his reason for reprinting the cartoons, the editor of *Le Monde* stated, "A Muslim may well be shocked by a picture of Mohammed, especially an ill-intentioned one. But a democracy cannot start policing people's opinions, except by trampling the rights of man underfoot."[18] Likewise, *The Economist*, which did not reprint the cartoons, stated that European newspapers had a "responsibility" to show "solidarity" with *Jyllands-Posten*.

In the Netherlands two years ago a film maker was murdered for daring to criticize Islam. Danish journalists have received death threats. In a climate in which political correctness has morphed into fear of physical attack, showing solidarity may well be the responsible thing for a free press to do. And the decision, of course, must lie with the press, not governments.[19]

For many Muslims, the reprinting of the cartoons was seen as further provocation. Some protested peacefully, while others reacted with violence. In some countries, buildings were set ablaze and shops selling European goods were vandalized. In Lebanon and Syria, the Danish and Norwegian embassies were firebombed. Elsewhere, clashes with police and security forces in Afghanistan, Pakistan, and other countries left as many as 300 people dead (see Exhibit 1). In northern Nigeria, Muslims went on a rampage, burning churches, shops, and cars belonging to the

---

[13] "Anatomy of a global crisis," *The Sunday Herald (Scotland)*, February 12, 2006.
[14] "Child's tale led to clash of cultures," *The Guardian Unlimited*, February 4, 2006.
[15] "Muslim organization calls for boycott of Denmark," *The Copenhagen Post*, December 28, 2006.
[16] "OIC demands unqualified Danish apology," *Arab News*, January 29, 2006.
[17] "Prophetic insults," *The Economist*, January 5, 2006.
[18] "France's *Le Monde* publishes front-page cartoon of Mohammed," *Agence France-Presse (AFP)*, February 2, 2006.
[19] "Cartoon wars," *The Economist*, February 9, 2006.

Christian minority. The violence left scores of dead and as many as 10,000 homeless.[20]

Arla and the OIC Boycott

At first, Arla viewed the cartoon crisis more as a security concern than an economic one. "It will be a serious blow to us if the situation becomes so grave that we are forced to withdraw our Danish workers," explained Arla Executive Director Finn Hansen.

> Our tremendous success in Saudi Arabia is thanks in large part to the fact that over the past 20 years, we've kept a number of our most talented managers constantly stationed in the country. It will hurt our credibility to pull out our Danish workers, and in the long term, it will impact sales. But I don't think things will get that bad. The Irish and Dutch dairies we compete with in Saudi Arabia are keeping their workers down there for now as well. Consumers in Saudi Arabia will continue to buy food, regardless of the terror threat. So I don't think our customer base will disappear.[21]

However, within a few weeks it became clear that Arla had underestimated the threat to its business. In Saudi Arabia, its products were featured in news stories about the boycott campaign, and religious leaders across the country called on worshipers to avoid Danish goods. By the end of January 2006, Danish products were removed from store shelves, replaced with signs stating, "Danish products were here." Egypt, Kuwait, Qatar, Bahrain, and the United Arab Emirates soon joined the boycott (see Exhibit 2 for a timeline of key events).

The boycott also aroused the anger of many local Muslims, some of whom threatened and harassed Arla employees as they went to and from work. In two separate incidents, workers were physically assaulted as they removed banned Arla products from store shelves. As a result, Arla provided employees with additional security escorts.

In early February, Iran became the first country to officially sever all economic ties with Denmark.[22] It made a further symbolic gesture by renaming domestically produced Danish pastries as "Roses of the Prophet Muhammad."[23] "The Commerce Ministry will not allow Danish brands or products which have been registered in Denmark to clear customs," announced Iranian Commerce Minister Massoud Mir-Kazemi.

> Iranian importers, including state-affiliated organs and companies, have three months to designate substitute products for Danish goods and then we will enforce the law. All on-going negotiations or contracts with Denmark which are pending will also be suspended, and all signed contracts will be reviewed. The exchange of delegations between the two countries will be suspended until further notice.[24]

The rapid deterioration in relations between Denmark and the Middle East stunned Arla Foods executives. Although they had been monitoring the situation since the cartoons were first published, the boycott "was hard to foresee," Nielsen explained.

> Some of our customers are extremely influential and powerful people. One of the retailers owns a large chain of grocery stores and he is extremely religious. Everyone else looks to see how he will react ...
> We were in constant contact with our customers, and they never suggested that they were going to boycott our products.

---

[20] Although the latest hostility was sparked by the cartoon crisis, ethnic violence has been part of an ongoing conflict that has claimed 10,000 lives in Nigeria since 1999. Source: "Nigerian religious riots continue," *BBC News*, February 24, 2006.

[21] "Terror threatens dairy exports," *The Copenhagen Post*, January 7, 2006.

[22] "EU warns Iran over boycott of Danish goods," *China Daily*, February 8, 2006.

[23] "Iran targets Danish pastries," *Aljazeera.net*, February 17, 2006.

[24] "Iran bans import of Danish products," *Islamic Republic News Agency (Iran)*, February 6, 2006.

But they had to react when the religious community told them to. Even after the boycott was announced, retailers said to us, "We want to do business with you, but we can't."

The immediate impact of the boycott was extensive. "Our business has been completely undermined," Hansen lamented. "Our products have been taken off the shelves in 50,000 stores. Without a quick solution, we will lose our business in the Middle East."[25] Meanwhile, Arla was losing sales worth US$1.5 million per day, or about 8 per cent of the company's worldwide revenues.[26]

Other companies preemptively distanced themselves from the cartoons. Switzerland-based Nestlé bought front-page advertisements in Arab newspapers to explain that its powdered milk was "neither produced in nor imported from Denmark." French supermarket giant Carrefour went further, removing Danish products from store shelves with a notice declaring "solidarity with the Islamic community." Other signs read "Carrefour doesn't carry Danish products."[27]

European Criticism: "The Right to Offend"

In Europe, some viewed attempts by European companies to show "solidarity" with Muslim protesters as cowardice. At a Berlin rally, Hirsi Ali, who rarely made public appearances in the face of the numerous threats against her life, expressed outrage. "I am here to defend the right to offend," she proclaimed.

> Shame on those European companies in the Middle East that advertised "we are not Danish" or "we don't sell Danish products". This is cowardice. Nestlé chocolates will never taste the same after this, will they? The EU member states should compensate Danish companies for the damage they have suffered from boycotts. Liberty does not come cheap. A few million Euros are worth paying for the defense of free speech.[28]

European Union President José Manuel Barroso also felt it his duty to uphold the principles of free speech. "I have spoken with the Prime Minister of Denmark and expressed [our] solidarity," he noted.

> I want to send my solidarity to the people of Denmark as well; a people who rightly enjoy the reputation as being amongst the most open and tolerant, not just in Europe, but in the world. Our European society is based on respect for the individual person's life and freedom, equality of rights between men and women, freedom of speech and a clear distinction between politics and religion. Our point of departure is that as human beings we are free, independent, equal and responsible. We must safeguard these principles. Freedom of speech is part of Europe's values and traditions. Let me be clear. Freedom of speech is not negotiable.[29]

The Crisis and Communications Group

As the seriousness of the boycott progressed, Arla CEO Peter Tuborgh decided to convene an emergency meeting with senior executives, dubbed "The Crisis and Communications Group." Earlier in his career, Tuborgh had worked in Saudi Arabia for four years as an operations manager. He understood the seriousness of the boycott, but he also felt that the company should not stray in any way from its global mission statement (see Exhibit 3). Any action taken by Arla would need to be consistent with the company's overall vision and reflect its values.

---

[25] "Muslim protest spreads to Danish butter," *The Sunday Times*, February 3, 2006.
[26] "Danish companies endure snub by Muslim consumers," *The New York Times*, February 27, 2006.
[27] "Carrefour JV with MAF in Egypt halts sale of Danish products," *AFX News Limited*, February 3, 2006.
[28] From a speech titled "The Right to Offend" given in Berlin on February 9, 2006.
[29] "EU President Barroso's statement on the issue of the cartoons of Prophet Muhammad," *Press and Public Diplomacy Delegation of the European Commission*, February 15, 2006.

Jens Refslund, director of Arla's production division, suggested that the company needed to act quickly to cut production to reduce costs. He explained,

> Once sales in the Middle East have come to a standstill, it will inevitably have consequences for production. A decision about what we do next must be taken within the next few days.[30]

Refslund estimated that the company would need to lay off as much as one-third of the staff at a Havarti cheese plant in Denmark, or approximately 50 employees. To avoid delays, negotiations with the dairy workers' union needed to begin immediately. Moreover, numerous Scandinavian dairy farmers faced a loss of some of their income if the Middle East market remained closed to Danish dairy products.

Nielsen expressed concern about the company's ability to recover from the crisis.

> One billion customers have rejected our products because it has suddenly become a synonym for the insult to the Prophet Mohammed. What can we do? We can't edit newspapers, we can't comment on government actions, we can't get involved in politics and we certainly can't address religion.

Nevertheless, Finn Hansen, who had responsibility for the Middle East, remained hopeful. He believed that in order for Arla to recover, it had to communicate with the individual consumer.

> Arla has been producing dairy products in Saudi Arabia for so long that we believe the authorities consider us a local dairy. It is not enough to persuade the supermarket chains to put our products back on the shelves. We should take our message directly to the consumer.

Exhibit 1 Selected News Headlines

Prophetic insults; Denmark and Islam, The Economist, January 7, 2006
Free speech clashes with religious sensitivity: For much of last year, various squabbles have simmered over several prominent Danes' rude comments about Islam. Now a schoolboy prank by a newspaper has landed the prime minister, Anders Fogh Rasmussen, in the biggest diplomatic dispute of his tenure in office.

Denmark Is Unlikely Front in Islam-West Culture War, The New York Times, January 8, 2006
Editorial cartoons published in a Danish newspaper have made Denmark a flashpoint in the culture wars between Islam and the West in a post–9/11 world.

After Danish Mohammed cartoon scandal, Norway follows suit, Agence France Presse, January 10, 2006
A Norwegian Christian magazine on Tuesday published a set of controversial caricatures of the prophet Mohammed following months of uproar in the Muslim world over a Danish paper's decision to print the same cartoons.

Drive to Boycott Danish, Norwegian Goods Takes Off, Gulf News, January 23, 2006
Riyadh: A vigorous campaign has been kicked off in Saudi Arabia calling for boycott of Danish and Norwegian products in response to repeated publishing of offensive cartoons of the Prophet Mohammad by some newspapers and magazines in those countries.

Threats by Militants Alarm Scandinavians; Denmark and Norway feel the backlash from cartoons, Los Angeles Times, January 31, 2006
Denmark warned its citizens Monday to avoid Saudi Arabia, and gunmen in the Gaza Strip said any Scandinavians there risked attack over newspaper cartoons of the prophet Muhammad.

Caricature of Muhammad Leads to Boycott of Danish Goods, The New York Times, January 31, 2006
A controversy over the publication of caricatures of the Muslim prophet by a Danish newspaper boiled over into a boycott.

---

[30] "Arla dairy sales crippled by Middle East boycott," *Dairy Reporter*, January 31, 2006.

Exhibit 1 (continued)

Cartoons of Prophet Met With Outrage; Depictions of Muhammad in Scandinavian Papers Provoke Anger, Protest Across Muslim World, The Washington Post, January 31, 2006
Cartoons in Danish and Norwegian newspapers ... have triggered outrage among Muslims across the Middle East, sparking protests, economic boycotts and warnings of possible retaliation against the people, companies and countries involved.

Danish Paper's Apology Fails To Calm Protests; Cartoons Trigger Muslim Outrage, The Boston Globe, February 1, 2006
An apology by Denmark's largest newspaper ... failed yesterday to calm a controversy that has ignited fiery protests across the Islamic world and provoked death threats against Scandinavians by Muslim radical groups. Muslim political and religious leaders and jihadists added their voices to the fury already thundering from mosques and blaring from television and radio stations from Morocco to Pakistan.

Bomb threat to repentant Danish paper, The Guardian, February 1, 2006
The offices of Denmark's bestselling broadsheet newspaper were evacuated last night following a bomb threat – a day after the editor-in-chief apologized for publishing cartoons of the prophet Muhammad that offended Muslims.

Anger as papers reprint cartoons of Muhammad: French, German and Spanish titles risk wrath: France Soir executive 'sacked' for defiant gesture, The Guardian, February 2, 2006
Newspapers in France, Germany, Spain and Italy yesterday reprinted caricatures of the prophet Muhammad, escalating a row over freedom of expression which has caused protest across the Middle East. France Soir and Germany's Die Welt published cartoons which first appeared in a Danish newspaper, although the French paper later apologized and apparently sacked its managing editor.

Islamic Anger Widens At Mohammed Cartoons, The Boston Globe, February 3, 2006
An extraordinary row over newspaper cartoons depicting the Prophet Mohammed intensified yesterday, with street demonstrations from North Africa to Pakistan, threats of violence against Europeans in the Middle East, and diplomatic protests by Muslim nations.

BBC shows the Islam cartoons, Daily Mail, February 3, 2006
The BBC and Channel 4 risked a Muslim backlash yesterday by showing 'blasphemous' cartoons of the prophet Mohammed that have caused outrage in the Islamic world.

Cartoons spark Islamic rage *Europe's leaders step in as controversy escalates *More newspapers publish offending images *Mideast consumer boycott hits Danish products, Financial Times, February 3, 2006
European leaders tried to contain the controversy over newspaper cartoons of the Prophet Mohammed, as the international dispute escalated into a consumer boycott and risked the gravest cultural clash with the Muslim world since the Salman Rushdie affair.

Gaza gunmen on hunt for Europeans: Aid workers, journalists, diplomats flee in fear for their lives; protests spread to Pakistan, Iraq, Ottawa Citizen, February 3, 2006
Militants threatened yesterday to kidnap or murder western citizens, in retaliation for the publication of caricatures of the Prophet Muhammad.

Broadcasters show prophet cartoons despite Muslim rage, The Herald, February 3, 2006
British broadcasters last night defied Muslim anger when they showed cartoons which have caused a storm of protest in the Islamic world.

Danes call envoys home over prophet cartoons, The Irish Times, February 3, 2006
Denmark has summoned its ambassadors back from abroad to Copenhagen for talks today about the controversial newspaper cartoons of the Prophet Muhammad that have triggered protests in the Arab world and threats by militant Muslims.

Exhibit 1 (continued)

Embassies burn in cartoon protest, BBC News, February 4, 2006
Syrians have set fire to the Norwegian and Danish embassies in Damascus in protest at the publication of newspaper cartoons of the Prophet Muhammad. Protesters scaled the Danish site amid chants of "God is great," before moving on to attack the Norwegian mission.

Danish embassy in Beirut torched, BBC News, February 5, 2006
Lebanese demonstrators have set the Danish embassy in Beirut on fire in protest at the publication of cartoons depicting the Prophet Muhammad.

Protests Over Cartoons of Muhammad Turn Deadly, The New York Times, February 6, 2006
Demonstrations against the publication of cartoons of the Prophet Muhammad by newspapers in Europe spread across Asia and the Middle East today, turning violent in Afghanistan, where at least four protesters were killed and over a dozen police officers and protesters injured.

Nigerian religious riots continue, BBC News, February 24, 2006
Violence is continuing across Nigeria where religious riots have claimed more than 100 lives this week. Some 10,000 people are still sheltering in barracks in the south-east town of Onitsha after violence there killed 80.

Exhibit 2 Timeline of Key Events

November 2, 2004	Film director Theo van Gogh is murdered in Amsterdam.
September 30, 2005	Jyllands-Posten publishes 12 cartoons portraying Muhammad.
January 20, 2006	The Saudi grand mufti calls for a boycott of Danish products.
January 24, 2006	In Saudi Arabia and Kuwait Arla's products begin to be removed from 50 grocery store shelves.
January 26, 2006	Arla products were removed from 300 stores.
January 28, 2006	Arla products were removed from 500 stores.
January 31, 2006	Arla products were removed from 50,000 stores, representing 95 per cent of the market.
February 1, 2006	Cartoons reprinted in several newspapers across Europe.
February 3, 2006	Danish and Norwegian embassies in Damascus are set on fire.
February 4, 2006	Danish embassy in Beirut is set on fire.
February 6, 2006	Iran officially bans Danish products.

Exhibit 3 Arla Mission Statement

Our Mission is:

"To offer modern consumers milk-based food products that create inspiration, confidence and well-being"

Arla Foods' primary objective is to meet consumers' wishes and requirements. Its mission underlines the company's focus on the consumer.

"Modern consumers" covers consumers of all ages who look for inspiration, variety and innovation.

"Milk-based products" means that the products must contain milk or milk components.

Arla Foods is committed to providing consumers with inspiration by offering a multitude of ways of utilizing its products.

Arla Foods creates confidence and well-being by providing tasty and healthy products that not only meet statutory quality requirements, but also satisfy consumers' demands for "soft" values. Consumers can be assured that Arla Foods consistently demonstrates its concern for the proper exploitation of resources, the environment, animal welfare, ethics, etc. throughout the entire production process.

Our Vision is:

"To be the leading Dairy Company in Europe through considerable value creation and active market leadership"

Through its vision, Arla Foods wishes to demonstrate that its activities are designed to create value for both the company and its owners.

By using the term "value creation" instead of "results," we wish to emphasize that our objectives are based on the long-term rather than short-term financial gains.

To become the world leader in value-creation within the dairy sector, Arla Foods must be:

* Northern Europe's preferred dairy group among consumers, customers and milk producers
* Northern Europe's market leader within all types of dairy products with a broad range, strong brands and a high degree of consumer confidence
* Represented in Southern Europe with a selected range of cheese and butter
* Represented in a number of markets outside Europe through a range adapted to individual markets

CASE I-3: TONY JAMOUS AT OYSTER HR: LEADERSHIP DILEMMA IN A GLOBAL VIRTUAL ORGANIZATION

Professor Martha Maznevski and Blair Tinkham wrote this case solely to provide material for class discussion. The authors do not intend to illustrate either effective or ineffective handling of a managerial situation. The authors may have disguised certain names and other identifying information to protect confidentiality.

Version: 2023–10-20

It was the afternoon of January 17, 2023, when Tony Jamous, CEO and co-founder of Oyster HR (Oyster), left home to pick up his children from school. He reflected on the decision he and his team had made to reorganize the company in the face of their new financial reality. They had created 60 new positions, but eliminated 84 others. With the mismatch between new roles and eliminated ones, Oyster would probably let go over 50 people. This was the most significant change to the company since he and colleague Jack Mardack had established it in early 2020. Jamous and his senior leadership team had explored all possible alternatives, but this was the only way to pursue Oyster's strategic priorities and protect the financial health of the company. After the evening rituals with his children were finished and they were asleep, Jamous finalized the letter communicating the difficult decision to the Oyster community. He shared it with his leadership and communication teams, then turned his thoughts to the next steps: What did this next stage mean for his own leadership? Where should his own priorities be?

Oyster was a trailblazing company in the human resources (HR) outsourcing industry. Their platform brought together employers who needed skilled knowledge workers with employees from anywhere in the world. Global and 100% virtual from its inception, Oyster lived the vision they saw of a strong employment future, especially for people from emerging economies. Throughout the company's start-up and remarkable growth, Jamous had built a cohesive and healthy organizational culture, proving that – contrary to many leaders' assumptions – global and virtual can drive engaged employees, an aligned organization, and strong business performance.

But the days of hypergrowth and generous financing in a fast-growing economic environment were over. To survive, the company had to double down on revenue growth and operational efficiency. This required a new mindset from everyone, moving quickly from a human-driven service to more of a software-driven one. Could this rapid shift in focus co-exist with the culture Jamous wanted and believed in? Jamous was also concerned about his own personal energy. The current culture required a lot of care and attention from him, and it simply wasn't possible for him to step that up while also leading on revenue and operations. It was tempting to focus on company survival now and attend to culture later. But Jamous knew that would compromise his vision, and he wasn't willing to let that go so easily.

Industry Overview: Employer of Record (EOR) Services

An employer of record (EOR) was a business that employed an individual on behalf of another organization. Usually the individual employed was located in a different country from the organization employing them. The individual legally became an employee of the EOR, but their working relationship was with the EOR's client company. The EOR handled all the legal employment requirements and managed payroll administration. The client organization retained the responsibility of managing the employee, deciding on compensation, and assigning work. Some EOR companies provided additional services such as job description development and access to employee benefits and pensions.

EORs significantly increased the available talent pool for companies. EOR services were particularly attractive to small high-growth companies, allowing them access to the talent pool while the leaders focused on other aspects of their business model.

For example, a San Francisco-based business-to-business (B2B) software company[1] wanted to hire software and data engineers to accelerate the development of their artificial intelligence (AI) products. Tasked by her Chief Technology Officer to fill five roles as soon as possible, the company's Chief People Officer, Megan Smith, was struggling to find highly skilled engineers in Silicon Valley at an affordable price. Through her peer network, she had heard that it was easier and cheaper to find such talent in Europe. She opened the roles to remote applicants from Western and Eastern Europe, and quickly identified skilled people ready to join the team remotely. She decided on five engineers based in Poland, Spain, and France. Working with an EOR, Smith's company was able to delegate all the legal, procedural, and payroll aspects of hiring and employing these engineers. Smith's company decided on the engineers' salary. Then the EOR formally hired the engineers and provided them with locally compliant contracts and benefits. The EOR paid them monthly in their local currency and took care of paying local employment taxes. The EOR, as the legal employer, assigned the engineers to work fully for the company, and the EOR's role was only in the background. The EOR invoiced the company monthly for the salaries and taxes of the five engineers plus a fee per employee per month. This San Francisco company was able to get highly skilled engineers at very reasonable costs, the engineers themselves were enthusiastic about the company's software and their role in developing it, and the company was able to fuel their growth.

Global EORs were particularly important for firms increasing their international presence. In a survey of 53 senior finance executives at internationally expanding companies, 83% of participants agreed that a global EOR is the "best practice for relieving the management and administrative burdens of overseas business expansion."[2] Eighty-five per cent agreed that "using a trusted global EOR is a best practice for addressing the enterprise risks that accompany overseas ventures."[3] Because client firms relied on a global EOR to navigate local regulations, clients particularly valued an EOR's knowledge of local laws and their ability to monitor and adapt to changes in those laws. Value for cost, accurate employee labor calculations, data security, and industry experience were also deciding factors when organizations selected a global EOR. For both the organization and the hired employee, stakeholders were looking for responsiveness and support from the global EOR.[4] Exhibit 1 shows a breakdown of the financial comparison of hiring someone abroad directly and through an EOR.

Industry Growth and COVID-19

Using global EOR services had become more and more common among multinationals as well as small- and mid-sized enterprises through the early 2000s. The demand for

---

[1] Real Oyster client use case, disguised to protect the client's anonymity. Internal company source.

[2] Schmidt, C. 2019. Hire Quickly and Compliantly Worldwide. *CFO*.

[3] Ibid.

[4] https://peoplemanagingpeople.com/tools/best-employer-of-record/

skills, especially in technology development, was not always met by supply of those skills in local markets, and firms needed to look elsewhere for talent. Post 9/11 in 2001, political dynamics increased the complexity of obtaining work visas for immigration. At the same time, availability of communications technology and internet bandwidth allowed companies to work more effectively with people virtually. Demand for global EORs continued to grow as the global economy recovered from the 2008 financial crisis and businesses looked to international expansion opportunities.[5]

By the start of the COVID-19 pandemic in early 2020, the global EOR industry was well positioned to address the dramatic increase in demand. Sudden travel restrictions, country lockdowns, and quarantines complicated international business travel, warranting the need to source employees from foreign locations.[6] Wage inflation throughout 2021 and 2022 increased the cost of hiring in-country. Firms transformed their business models to integrate new technology solutions, and needed skilled employees to support that transformation. COVID-19 also served as a catalyst for the evolution of the workplace, making work from home a new norm. Many companies enjoyed a reduction in fixed costs with the rise of remote work, and became more confident that employees would perform while working from home. Likewise, workers cited the financial benefits of remote offices and favorably viewed the options of working with flexible schedules and from any location.[7] The global EOR industry grew rapidly during this time, helping employers close their skill gaps and supporting employees in their quest to work productively from home even if their employer was in a different country.

The increase in demand for the global EOR industry was predicted to be important well beyond the end of the pandemic. Economists predicted that skill and labor shortages would impact many countries significantly. For example, the US economy was expected to decline by US$162 billion by 2030 because of skill shortages, while Germany and Canada were anticipated to experience worker shortages of 10 million and 2.3 million people, respectively, by 2030.[8,9] Globally, a talent shortage of 85.2 million people was expected by 2030, reflecting what might result in US$8.45 trillion unrealized revenue.[10] At the same time, 1.5 billion knowledge workers were expected to enter the workforce by 2033, predominantly from emerging economies.[11] In short, the demand for skilled knowledge workers in the future was predicted to be met only by supply of those skills from different countries. Global EORs would help bridge this gap.

Competitive Evolution in the 2020s

In early 2020, the combination of fast market growth with readily available start-up funding led to an influx of new entrants. These new entrants raced to build platforms to deliver global EOR services in the most efficient manner, providing scaled value for reduced prices. The dominant business model started to become software-as-a-service (SaaS). EOR firms developed software platforms that client firms could interact with directly to initiate and organize the hiring transaction. In this

---

[5] Avondet, R. (2022). Remote workers, foreign employers, and the employer of record surge. *Practical Tax Strategies*, *108*(1), 12–14.
[6] Ibid.
[7] https://www.statista.com/topics/6565/work-from-home-and-remote-work/#topicOverview
[8] https://www.kornferry.com/content/dam/kornferry/docs/pdfs/KF-Future-of-Work-Talent-Crunch-Report.pdf
[9] https://www.bcg.com/publications/2014/people-organization-human-resources-global-workforce-crisis
[10] https://www.kornferry.com/content/dam/kornferry/docs/pdfs/KF-Future-of-Work-Talent-Crunch-Report.pdf
[11] https://www.prnewswire.com/news-releases/oyster-partners-with-industry-leading-hr-service-providers-further-expanding-its-platforms-capabilities-for-distributed-companies-301332176.html

model, EOR firms delivered value to clients primarily through the breadth of their platform options – such as taxation and deductions – and scalability. The role of personal service, the expensive part of the business model, was decreased significantly in this new SaaS model.

Oyster HR

Oyster HR (Oyster) was a global EOR founded in January 2020 by Tony Jamous and Jack Mardack. At the core of its business model, Oyster provided standard EOR services for clients. By the end of 2022 it had legal entities in 50+ countries for hiring individual employees and served employer clients in 100+ countries through owned entities or a network of partners. Its 700 employees were distributed across more than 60 countries.

Oyster's value proposition to both client employers and the people those employers hired (called Team Members at Oyster) went beyond the basic employment transaction. Oyster was deeply committed to a global development mission: to bridge the gap between companies' talent needs and the location of that talent, and at the same time build greater cultural acceptance for – and competences in managing and leading – globally distributed, virtual organizations.

The business idea for Oyster came from Jamous's previous start-up experience. In 2010, Jamous founded a cloud communication platform, Nexmo, which hired employees in over 45 countries. Jamous encountered the resource-demanding and complex process of international hiring. His company spent millions of dollars to retain lawyers and set up entities in different countries. It typically took five months to hire a single employee, and Jamous lost valuable talent just through the wait times. Jamous realized the process lacked scalability and failed to deliver the best possible results to new employees or to Nexmo.

Jamous also found that inaccessibility and inequality were deeply embedded barriers to global employment. Before 2020, only 9% of employees worked from home.[12] For everyone else, employment prospects depended on their proximity to a location for a good job. This often meant being close to industry hubs in developed countries. Jamous was discouraged that this disadvantaged and limited the employment opportunities of skilled people outside of rich countries. He wanted to see a world in which skilled people from developing and emerging economies could work in global jobs while staying in their communities, building the local economies and decreasing inequalities.

Nexmo became a technology unicorn (valuation over US$1 billion), and Jamous sold to Vonage in 2016. After establishing it within the Vonage network together with Vonage's Mardack, Jamous knew what his next start-up would be. He and Mardack took on the opportunity to improve the global EOR industry while fostering accessible employment. Oyster would enable companies to hire globally through a simple, affordable, human-centric process scalable around the globe. And it would enable individuals to participate in a global workforce while living in the communities they chose.

From 2020 to 2022, the company experienced rapid growth, enjoying the effects of the remote work boom. Their business model was endorsed by venture capitalists, providing Oyster with US$224 million across seed funding and Series A, B, and C.[13] Oyster was included in Otta's annual Rocket List for 2021 and 2022 – a list that identified the 100–150 fastest-growing high-quality tech start-ups.[14] The Series C funding established Oyster's

---

[12] https://www.cipd.co.uk/about/media/press/home-working-increases#gref

[13] https://www.linkedin.com/pulse/oyster-changing-future-work-aligning-investment-mission-tony-jamous-1e/?trackingId=sEGrG9Oe2c%2BJQpW29njUPA%3D%3D

[14] https://otta.com/rocketlist/us/2021/Oyster; https://app.otta.com/companies/Oyster?_gl=1*5gp881*_gcl_au*MTQ2OTQzNDU0Ni4xNjg0NjgxMTIw&_ga=2.128484612.920287704.1685126130-165779092.1684681120

value at over US$1 billion, Jamous's second unicorn. Exhibit 2 shows their funding rounds and sources. Exhibit 3 summarizes Oyster's theory of change and outlines the company values.

Build the User Experience, Then Scale

Oyster offered full global EOR services to their company clients. Employers could use Oyster services for onboarding, payments, and care for the new employee. Oyster's start-up business plan was first to develop a valuable global EOR service with Oyster employees involved in client relationships and complex transactions, supported by software they developed. As Oyster established their network, client base, and processes, they would transform more and more of the human processes to ones conducted with sophisticated automation. This would allow the firm to gain efficiencies and scale without increasing staff.

The EOR hiring process began on the hiring company's dashboard on the Oyster website, where the company input basic information on their new Team Member. A virtual assistant, "Pearl," guided the hiring company's manager. An Oyster Hiring Success Manager (a live person) who specialized in the local region of the new Team Member ensured that all the necessary information was in place. Oyster finalized the employment agreement, the hiring company approved it, and Oyster sent an official offer letter directly to the new Team Member to collect the necessary signatures. Oyster then guided the new Team Member through an HR onboarding process, setting up the payment arrangements and any other legal or benefits arrangements.[15] Throughout the Team Member's employment, Oyster delivered payment and benefits to the Team Member in their own currency. Payment history and invoices were all available within the same platform, and hiring companies could also enroll their Team Members in Oyster's global health plan. The average time to complete the hiring process was under two weeks, but Oyster could manage the whole process in a few hours if needed. Exhibit 4 provides a graphic illustration of the Oyster process.

Companies could also access automated interactive global HR tools designed by Oyster, including an employment cost calculator, a benefits advisor, and an equity assessment tool. Through a free Oyster account, anyone could access the information tools. For clients, the Oyster team of employees could deliver specialized support through e-mail or video conferencing.

Oyster's revenue model was based on the service of hiring and managing employment logistics. In late 2022, the cost for hiring employees through the platform was US$599 per employee per month, with discounts for multiple employees and reduced prices for annual up-front payments. Exhibit 5 shows some reviews of Oyster from external sources.

Oyster's Impact

Oyster measured its impact on stakeholders extensively. Beyond providing excellent EOR services, Oyster monitored its effect on people and the planet. For example, in their Team Member impact research in late 2022, Oyster found:[16]

- 8% of Team Members said their ability to live where they would like had increased because of Oyster
- 70% said they were happy with their current job
- 74% of the women said their quality of life had improved since engaging with the Oyster platform
- 55% of women said they were able to access new employment benefits after engaging with the Oyster platform

In their April 2022 Impact Report, Oyster reported that 25% of their Team Members

---

[15] https://support.oysterhr.com/hc/en-us/articles/4405237923729-Onboarding-process

[16] https://www.oysterhr.com/library/team-member-impact-survey-remote-work

were in emerging markets, and that over US$50 million was flowing annually into emerging markets as a result of their services. After using Oyster services customers were 58% more likely to hire global talent again in the future and 57% more excited about hiring talent from emerging markets. Client companies also reported that hiring global employees through Oyster led to a positive impact on workplace culture and morale, engagement, and diversity.[17]

Inside the Oyster

Since the beginning, Oyster had been a fully remote and globally distributed company. Oysters, as Jamous described it, worked "geographically apart, but strategically very close," which enabled the team "to have a greater focus on execution, action and aims". Even Jamous had only met a few of the Oysters in person. Aside from roles that may require set hours, Oysters were in charge of their own schedules. They could clock in and out at whatever point they wanted in the day, as long as they stayed accountable for getting their work done on time.

Jamous believed that this arrangement – working remotely from anywhere an employee wanted to be – had numerous benefits, including allowing employees to be, in Jamous's words, released from the geographical shackles which have restricted people for decades. This release promoted equality, ensuring that the best jobs weren't reserved only for wealthy city dwellers. The distributed approach also delivered environmental benefits by eliminating the need to travel. Not commuting to work allowed Oysters to spend more time doing what they enjoyed, being with loved ones, and resting, while also offering a more environmentally sustainable way to work. Through Oyster's distributed work style, the company demonstrated to others, including its present and potential clients, that a distributed work style could be a successful – even a superior – way to work.

The Leader's Effect – Tony Jamous

Growing up in war-torn Beirut, Lebanon, Jamous was exposed to high unemployment rates at a young age. Corruption eroded job opportunities even among highly skilled and capable people, local companies succumbed to bankruptcy, and being hired by an overseas company proved to be onerous. Seeing such inequality first-hand was a driving reason Jamous pursued an MBA from a leading global business school in 2009. He had thought he wanted to work in and lead large companies that could offer opportunities for people facing inequality. Instead, he saw opportunities to create companies that could make a bigger difference directly. Nexmo targeted technologies that reduced inequities in access to telecom applications; now Oyster would leverage the opportunities for social impact embedded in global hiring.

By the end of 2022, Jamous had moved to Cyprus with his three children where, though busy with work, he placed utmost value on his family and being a dad. Jamous explained:

> One of the most important objectives in my life is to be present for my children, to be a good father and involved all the time. Remote and asynchronous work helps me to do this: I can be there in the morning with my children, I can spend time with them individually around their school work and other interests. I can pick my daughter up from school, and cook her Lebanese food so that she can connect with my culture and her heritage. I can go and talk with their teachers, and be there for my children when they need me. These moments are only made possible through the freedom I have to manage my own time. Providing others with the opportunity to do the same was a major motivation when launching Oyster.

---

[17] https://www.oysterhr.com/annual-impact-report-2022, https://www.oysterhr.com/resources/annual-impact-report-2023

His value and care for his family permeated to Oysters in his mission to ensure Oyster people were happy and fulfilled above all else. He believed that,

> It's not enough to pay people properly. It's not enough to help them avoid burnout. It's not enough to ask how they are. This is the bare minimum. Leaders should inspire. They should create work that is both inspirationally fulfilling and deeply human. Providing flexibility is hugely important to achieving all that.

Jamous led with a mission-oriented, inspiring, and people-first tone, which helped tremendously in his creation of the Oyster virtual culture.

Building a Strong Culture in a Global Virtual Organization

In Jamous's view, "our culture *is* our strategy. This is what we're selling to our clients and the Team Members they hire. And I firmly believe it is how we need to lead. So we *must* get it right ourselves."

At the core of Oyster's human-centric management approach was an emphasis on well-being. With flexible hours and a prioritization of rest and health, employees had the chance to care for themselves and see life as just as important as work. Jamous tried to set the example himself, communicating the importance with frequent LinkedIn posts about balancing his work–life integration and the importance of his family.

The value of care and well-being was also conveyed through various Oyster programs. For example, Oyster used Juno, a platform for employee well-being benefits, to give Oysters well-being "allowances" of Juno Points which could be spent on Juno's platform. The platform included services like therapy, childcare, healthy food delivery apps, language lessons, massages, subscriptions, etc. Oyster also used Kona, a well-being program that ran on Slack (a popular instant messaging program from technology firm Salesforce), where employees participated in mood check-ins. Managers were able to monitor burnout, morale, and the health of Oysters.

Trust was also central to Oyster's culture. Trust was helpful in any system, but was necessary for distributed working. Jamous believed that to build trust in distributed teams, you needed to be "encouraging people to work when and how suits them, offering regular opportunities for staff feedback, making changes people want to see, [using] a consistent style of management, despite working across borders and time zones, [and providing] regular opportunities for one-to-ones." Jamous spearheaded the culture of trust by sharing his own vulnerabilities with Oysters through platforms like LinkedIn and encouraging other management to share as well. He jumped on every opportunity to help people get to know each other and build bonds that facilitated trust. Exhibit 6 illustrates one tradition: the monthly one-year anniversary call with the CEO.

While Oysters didn't have chances to socialize in person or gather around a watercooler, Oyster made sure there were many ways for them to stay virtually connected. In an initiative called "oystersnaps," Oysters shared photos of the regions they worked from. Oysters socialized on Slack channels around a variety of hobbies and interests, as well as in "crew channels" for Oysters in the same region. Oysters could be matched up with other Oysters and become what they called "Loom Pals," sending virtual letters to each other and building friendships. City meet-ups for Oysters in the same area were encouraged. For all-company socialization and learning, Oyster organized retreats. For example, in November 2020, the entire team of over 650 Oysters met virtually over the course of three days to celebrate their accomplishments and work on community building.

Growth, Reorganization, and the Future of Oyster

During Oyster's hypergrowth phase, management's focus was on growth, product expansion, and scaling operations to capture the market quickly. With this rapid growth also came accelerated hiring and investment to meet Oyster's ambitious goals.

Right after Oyster's Series C fundraising in early 2022, a shift in macroeconomic conditions dampened the company's growth expectations. Unemployment and inflation both rose, and high interest rates decreased companies' investment and growth. The new scarcity of venture capital funding made it difficult for Oyster to continue to reach their growth goals. In the second half of 2022, Jamous and his team realized they had to shift their business model. They had to grow with a step change in efficiency – increasing revenue significantly without also increasing costs. This, in turn, meant automating more of the EOR process rapidly while still providing the kinds of options and services employers and employees valued. Oyster had to pivot to more of a software-as-a-service (SaaS) model while increasing the emphasis on sales.

The new structure, to be implemented by the end of February, consolidated all revenue-driving functions, including account management, under a Chief Revenue Officer, a new hire with demonstrated success from previous start-ups. There would be a significant increase in sales roles and some increase in product and engineering, coupled with small declines in roles in all other functions. Organizationally, this implied more attention to sophisticated software development and sales while decreasing the reliance on personalized expertise and service in different geographies, industries, or client relationships.

It was a hard reality to face, but Jamous and his team had all succeeded as tech entrepreneurs and knew sometimes the trade-offs were tough. Transitioning to this phase of "efficient growth" by the end of 2022, the company slowed and then froze new hiring, cancelled the promotion cycle, and reviewed department budgets and programs to apply new cost-saving measures.

Though the measures were effective initially, it soon became clear to Tony and his team that Oyster needed more action to survive the new unstable and poor macroeconomic conditions. Moving forward with a focus on the customer experience with increased automation and efficient growth, Oyster needed a change in organizational structure. The reorganization was announced on January 17, 2023. True to the culture of trust, Jamous sent the same e-mail to all employees at once. The company leaders then held one-on-one conversations with those affected. Very quickly afterward, Oyster posted the announcement on their website and Jamous posted it on LinkedIn, highlighting the importance of transparency and also reaching out to his network for jobs for those affected. Exhibit 7 shows the letter.

Jamous's Leadership Dilemma

In Jamous's mind, the hard decisions had been made and communicated, but the hard work was still to come. In particular, Jamous needed to work out a way for him and his management team to rebuild the culture of the company, remaining compassionate and human-centric, after completing a reorganization that hurt people in the Oyster community and possibly beyond.

This was crucial for Oyster as a company itself, but also for its strategy. Simply to survive as a viable business, Oyster had to be positioned for continued growth and with increased organizational efficiency. At the same time, to encourage other companies to adopt high-quality remote and distributed working, Jamous and Oyster had to demonstrate that virtual and distributed work was viable and healthy, and culture could be maintained.

How could Jamous balance the company's values and culture with the realities of the business environment? Would it be worth shifting or even sacrificing the company's culture to focus on output? Jamous was especially uncertain about what this meant for his own leadership. The financial markets and some of his team members were urging him to stop focusing on culture and turn his tech-industry expertise towards leading the operational and software development tasks more actively. But Jamous was worried that if he did that, the purpose of the organization would drift and become lost. Whatever choices he made, Team Members, clients, and other companies aspiring to transition to remote and distributed work would be watching closely as Jamous guided Oyster through this challenge.

Exhibit 1: Cost of Hiring Overseas Employees

All amounts in USD.

Average total costs for a corporation to hire an employee in a country different from their headquarters (costs vary from country to country), in addition to salary. Most costs are one-time but may need to be repeated if regulations or other conditions change.

- Entity Registration/Set-Up: $10,000
- Statutory & Labor/Employment: $5,000
- Entity Tax Compliance & Registrations: $5,000 and up
- Bank Setup & In-Country Capital Requirements: $20,000
- Legal & Financial Counsel: $10,000 and up
- Internal Staff to Manage Process & Payroll: $30,000 and up

This process can take between five and eighteen months.

Typical Employer of Record services cost $600–800 per employee per month, averaging $8,400 per year. This total does not include the employee's salary. Amount per employee decreases with the number of employees hired through the Employer of Record.

Source:

Hammell, R. (2021, 10). An Employer of Record: The Future of Global Business Expansion. *Core HR, HRIS and Payroll Excellence Essentials*, https://www.lib.uwo.ca/cgi-bin/ezpauthn.cgi?url=http://search.proquest.com/magazines/employer-record-future-global-business-expansion/docview/2645871512/se-2

Exhibit 2: Oyster HR Funding from Venture Capital

Date	Series	# of Investors	Money Raised	Lead Investor
Apr 21, 2020	Seed Round	8	US$4.2 M	Connect Ventures
Feb 2, 2021	Series A	6	US$20 M	Emergence
Jun 22, 2021	Series B	4	US$50 M	Stripes
Apr 20, 2022	Series C	13	US$150 M	Georgian

Oyster's investors include:

Salesforce Ventures, Kima Ventures, Endeavor Catalyst, Connect Ventures, Sorenson Capital, Base10 Partners, Emergence Capital Partners, Stripes, Slack Fund, Georgian Partners, PayPal Ventures, G2 Venture Partners (G2VP), Initial Capital, S16 Angel Fund, Avid Ventures, LinkedIn, Okta Ventures, PeopleTech Partners, Indeed

Sources: Company records, https://www.crunchbase.com/organization/oyster-3150/company_financials, https://otta.com/rocketlist/us/2021/Oyster

Accessed May 21, 2023

Exhibit 3: Oyster Social Impact Statement – Our Theory of Change

Status Quo	Physical proximity is required to be employed for most jobs
Stakeholders	• People Emigrating for Work • People Staying in Local Communities • Business • Local Communities • Environment
Problems	• Financial, health and family burden caused by emigration • Health, income and personal development trade-offs of staying home • Businesses are either restricted to local talent or pay high transaction costs for international recruitment • Brain drain causing stagnating local communities & economies • Increased commuter burden on the planet
Inputs/ Activities	Build a software platform which connects demand for skilled knowledge work in developed economies with the growing workforce in emerging markets simply and cheaply, enabling work to be conducted remotely
Outputs	• Number of people migrating to find work reduces • Number of people un/underemployed in local communities is reduced • Reduced costs of international recruitment, whilst accessing a wider and more diverse talent pool • Reduced number of people leaving their communities to find work • Number of global commuters reduced
Outcomes	• Financial, health and family burden caused by seeking work internationally is reduced • Health, income and personal development trade-offs of accessing employment in home community are reduced • Businesses increasingly fulfil talent needs through international hiring • Locals contribute human and financial capital to their communities • Reduced burden on the planet
Impact	• More fulfilled lives, reduced global inequality • Businesses are better able to thrive • Accelerated development of communities • Increased sustainability of the planet

https://assets-global.website-files.com/5ffc74fef1579006dc588807/6010c42acb99fbf10b9dca59_Oyster-ImpactThesis_0121_01.pdf, accessed May 21, 2023

Company Values

- **We elevate talent** – Global employment distributes opportunities equally around the world. When everyone has access to the best jobs, anyone can realize their full potential.
- **We build trust** – To build trust, we maintain an active flow of information and communication, follow through with our commitments, and provide unwavering support.
- **We thrive together** – Our team is on a shared mission to make global employment accessible to everyone. We leverage our diverse perspectives and experiences to drive this goal forward.

https://www.oysterhr.com/our-mission, accessed May 21, 2023

Exhibit 4: The Oyster HR Ecosystem

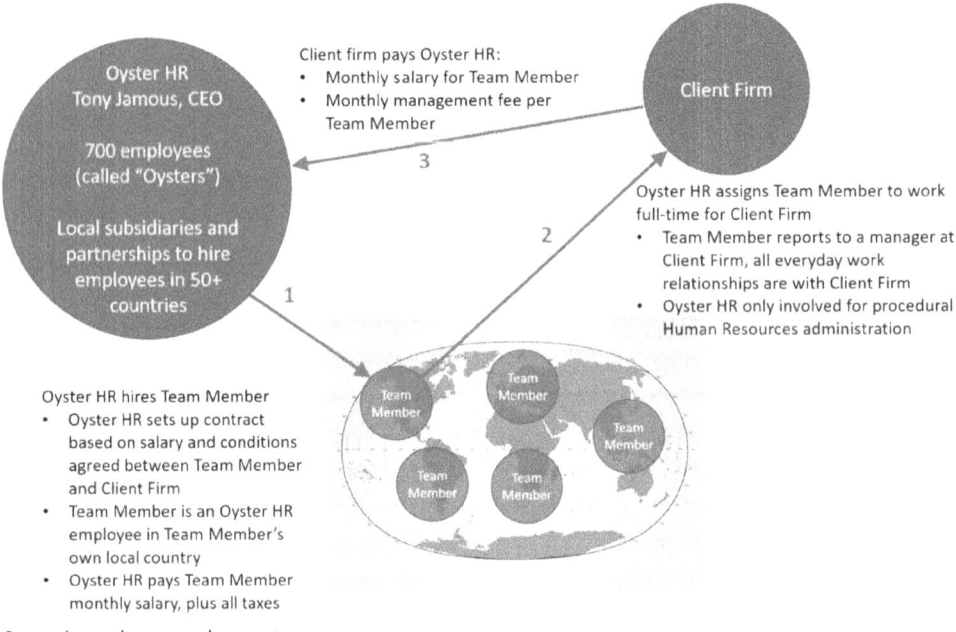

Oyster HR — Tony Jamous, CEO
- 700 employees (called "Oysters")
- Local subsidiaries and partnerships to hire employees in 50+ countries

Client firm pays Oyster HR: (arrow 3)
- Monthly salary for Team Member
- Monthly management fee per Team Member

Oyster HR assigns Team Member to work full-time for Client Firm (arrow 2)
- Team Member reports to a manager at Client Firm, all everyday work relationships are with Client Firm
- Oyster HR only involved for procedural Human Resources administration

Oyster HR hires Team Member (arrow 1)
- Oyster HR sets up contract based on salary and conditions agreed between Team Member and Client Firm
- Team Member is an Oyster HR employee in Team Member's own local country
- Oyster HR pays Team Member monthly salary, plus all taxes

Source: internal company documents

Exhibit 5: Oyster Selected Reviews

Published December 2022, FitsSmallBusiness.com gave Oyster an overall score of 4.23 / 5:

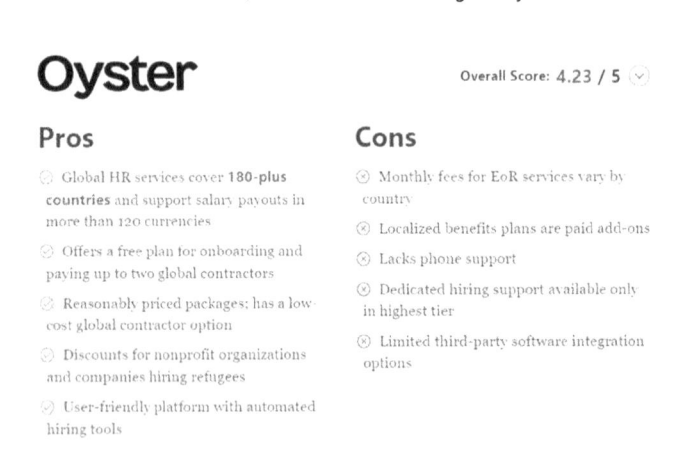

Oyster

Overall Score: 4.23 / 5

Pros
- Global HR services cover **180-plus countries** and support salary payouts in more than 120 currencies
- Offers a free plan for onboarding and paying up to two global contractors
- Reasonably priced packages; has a low-cost global contractor option
- Discounts for nonprofit organizations and companies hiring refugees
- User-friendly platform with automated hiring tools

Cons
- Monthly fees for EoR services vary by country
- Localized benefits plans are paid add-ons
- Lacks phone support
- Dedicated hiring support available only in highest tier
- Limited third-party software integration options

They awarded Oyster a perfect score for their pricing options (5) and high scores for HR features (4.75), ease of use (4.50), expertise (4.38), payroll features (4.13), but a low score for reporting (2.5) due to the limited reporting options and inability to customize the reports.

Exhibit 5 (continued)

They explained their low score for popularity:

Popularity: What Users Think About Oyster
2.50

Oyster's low score in this criteria is due mainly to the small number of user reviews on third-party review sites like G2 and Capterra. Those who left positive OysterHR reviews highlighted its responsive support team and efficient global hiring tools as its best features. Several users also like its easy-to-use platform and automated solutions that help streamline processes.

Meanwhile, there are only a handful of negative OysterHR reviews online. One user disliked having to pay the required security deposit while a few others wished for more features like additional time-off types, better health coverage, and a more robust expense claim tool.

At the time of publication, Oyster software reviews earned the following scores on popular user review sites:

- **G2:** 4.4 out of 5 based on around **70 reviews**
- **Capterra:** 3 out of 5 based on **1 review**

https://fitsmallbusiness.com/oyster-review/

Oyster Reviews

4.8 ★★★★★

- 95% Recommend to a Friend
- 98% Approve of CEO
- Tony Jamous

Source: https://www.glassdoor.ca/Overview/Working-at-Oyster-EI_IE5006547.11,17.htm, Accessed February 12, 2023

Exhibit 6: Oyster Traditions – the Anniversary Call

Tony Jamous

One of my favorite traditions here at Oyster® is my monthly one-year anniversary call.

One of the things that bring me the most joy in my job is hearing about the journeys of each of our team members.

Every month I connect live with Oysters all over the world who joined the year prior. This last week, I had the pleasure of chatting with Oysters who joined us in December 2021.

These group calls are often filled with stories, jokes, and reflections on the last year.

It's also a perfect time to show my gratitude for all their hard work and let them know they are seen and heard.

Part of human-centric leadership is learning when to put aside the need to make noise but instead, creating a space where everyone's experience is valued.

Hearing unique stories of how distributed work has changed people's lives is truly humbling.

It's what wakes me up every morning.

What a journey this year has been 💚

Exhibit 6 (continued)

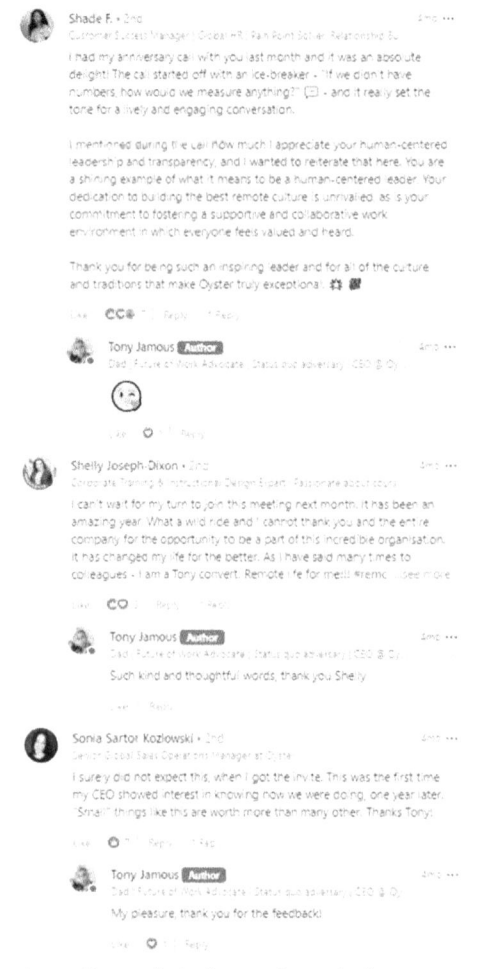

https://www.linkedin.com/posts/teljamou_one-of-my-favorite-traditions-here-at-oyster-activity-7013812837181440000-eKnG/?utm_source=share&utm_medium=member_desktop

Posted December 2022, Accessed May 21, 2023

Exhibit 7: A Letter from Oyster's CEO, Tony Jamous

Posted January 17, 2023, Accessed May 21, 2023 https://oysterhr.notion.site/oysterhr/A-letter-from-Oyster-s-CEO-Tony-Jamous-43b7218897904211bf1486e314056d4e

> Earlier today, Oyster Founder & CEO Tony Jamous sent the following letter to Oyster employees. To ensure clarity for readers outside of Oyster's internal team, this message has been lightly edited, including the removal of employee names and internal Oyster processes

Hello team,

We have weathered many storms together over the past several quarters, and we've weathered them admirably. Throughout, we have been vigilant in making necessary changes to the business in order to keep Oyster in good financial health. Today marks the most significant change we have had to make.

Today, I must confirm that we are conducting a company-wide reorganization to align our staffing with our strategic priorities and financial imperatives.

This reorganization will result in the removal of a number of roles from across Oyster and the addition of new roles in strategic areas.

Why and How We Made This Decision

Between Oyster's creation in early 2020 through our Series C fundraise in early 2022, we delivered incredible growth thanks to the powerful business you all created, buoyed by the acceleration of remote work and bullish capital markets.

Since then, the macroeconomic environment has dramatically shifted, creating headwinds for many businesses, including Oyster. These headwinds have dampened our growth expectations and radically changed the fundraising environment.

…

The hard truth is we don't know when the world will exit this phase of high inflation, high interest, and a declining employment market. As we begin the new year, the economic outlook remains uncertain. In such conditions, the responsible move for our company is to be even more vigilant about aligning the makeup of our team to a focused strategy in order to grow efficiently.

Next Steps for the Reorganization

This reorganization allows us the opportunity to laser focus on efficient growth, automation and the customer experience. As part of our 2023 planning, we identified where we would need to grow across Oyster in order to be successful this year and beyond, and we've revised our organizational structure strategy accordingly.

All Oyster staff whose roles have been impacted will have the opportunity to express interest in roles we plan to hire in the first half of this year.

We are glad to be able to offer this process and hope to fill some of our 2023 headcount with existing Oysters. However, by redesigning the Oyster workplace in such a substantial way to align with our next chapter of efficient growth, we understand that not everyone will find a new home within Oyster. In such cases, we are prepared to support our impacted teammates in the most compassionate and human-centric way possible on the next step of their journey.

How Are We Supporting Our Departing Team Members?

For a company like ours, whose mission and DNA are intimately tied to employee centricity, handling departures with empathy and generosity is especially important.

Our first priority is to make sure that those who will be departing Oyster are treated with the respect and gratitude they deserve and are supported in every way possible through this transition. The transition package we are offering includes at least twelve weeks of compensation in the form of notice, severance, or some equivalent combination thereof which meets or exceeds what they may be entitled to locally, in addition to job placement support and other benefits. We will be reviewing these packages in detail with each impacted employee and have created resource hubs in Notion containing more information about the other ways we are supporting departing employees during offboarding and in their careers beyond the Reef.

What Happens Next Oysters Whose Roles Have Been Impacted:

Within the next 30 minutes, those whose roles are impacted will receive a calendar invite from People Operations to an individual meeting with their Department Head or Director and a member of the Workplace or People Services team. During this meeting, those employees will learn more about how their role has been impacted, have the opportunity to ask questions, and explore possible opportunities for remaining at Oyster in a different role.

Oysters Whose Roles Have Not Been Impacted:

Within the next 30 minutes, those whose roles have not been impacted will receive a confirmation message. This message will also include resources we've created to support non-impacted Oysters during this transition.

What to Expect for the Rest of the Week

In light of this news, and our desire to allow each Oyster to engage with it in their own time, today's All Hands has been cancelled. Instead, later today, you will receive an invitation to a Department Town Hall that will take place between today and Friday. Your Department Head and a member of the C-level team will join the meeting to discuss this news and what it means for your team and for Oyster in general. There will be ample opportunity for Q&A in these meetings.

I understand that this announcement may trigger strong emotions for all of you, whether your role is being impacted or not. All emotions are perfectly understandable and acceptable. Personally, I feel tremendous sadness that these decisions may unexpectedly impact the lives of Oyster teammates whom we care for deeply.

To give everyone space to process and read through the materials we've curated and to be able to focus our full efforts on supporting departing employees, the rest of this week should be treated as Focus days. Please cancel all non-essential meetings. Reach out to your Department Head with any questions about how to proceed.

To all impacted Oysters, I am truly sorry. Today's outcome is not your fault. On the contrary, I'm forever grateful for what you've given to Oyster and our mission since you joined–and I hope that as many of you as possible will find new roles within Oyster this week. Regardless of the outcome, please know that your work here has mattered greatly during these formative years. Your impact still resonates today, and it will remain a meaningful chapter of our story well into the future.

With gratitude, Tony

PART II
Leading People across Contexts

Human interaction is at the center of management. This section focuses on high-quality person-to-person interactions across cultural boundaries in everyday situations and teams, and examines how organizations select and prepare people for more effective interactions.

4 Mapping Culture to Bridge and Integrate

> Organizational behavior is about effectiveness at the point of action.
>
> Dr. Peter Vaill, American business theorist (1936–2020),
> quoted by Dr. David Fearon

Key Learning Objectives

At the end of this chapter, students will be able to:

- Describe the importance of interpersonal interaction in global leadership.
- Define the three steps for effective interpersonal interaction: Map, Bridge, and Integrate.
- Identify the role of cultural Mapping tools and recognize strengths and weaknesses in different tools.
- Apply the GlobeSmart dimensions to Map different cultures.
- Analyze cross-cultural interactions by anticipating differences, similarities, and opportunities for potential conflict or synergy.
- Create a Team Map for their own team.

"Effectiveness at the point of action." We heard this phrase from Dr. David Fearon, recounting a moment when Dr. Peter Vaill, his Organizational Behavior professor, expressed the idea that profoundly influenced his academic path. Throughout their careers, Vaill and Fearon continued to explore the importance of those moments of interpersonal interaction: the moments when two or more people talking together decide to do something to which they are committed in spite of any uncertainty. These moments are very important in our own lives and societies' evolution (Vaill, 2008; Vaill & Fearon, 2022). This perspective is also reflected in our centrality of global mindfulness.

The point of action in international management usually happens when people from widely different backgrounds interact with each other. So far in the book, we've been looking at the context of international management and the context of culture. We've emphasized the importance of mindful approaches to context. All of this provides the framing for effective international management behavior. In this chapter, we turn to the basics of interaction among people. We provide a brief overview of our approach to effective interaction – Map-Bridge-Integrate – before focusing on Mapping cultures. In the next chapter, we will expand on Bridging and Integrating. Note that much of the research on cross-cultural interaction is conducted by studying teams – groups of at least two but usually more people working together toward a joint outcome. In this chapter, we will often refer to teams as the context for effective interaction, but we will focus on the interaction itself.

Effectiveness at the Point of Action: Conversations That Create Meaning and Value

Bettina (German) and Seif (Emirati from Dubai) were both senior partners in a global strategic consulting firm. Both were typical of their cultures, and both were experienced and mindful global leaders. Seif had been with the firm since graduating from his MBA program and was well respected throughout the firm. Bettina had recently joined the firm through the acquisition of a boutique firm in which she was a senior partner. The two were assigned to lead a project with a global consumer goods company. The consulting firm generally had a good relationship with the client company, but the client had been unsatisfied with the most recent project. The consulting firm now had a chance to repair the relationship with the client. Here is a sample of the conversations during Bettina and Seif's first meeting:

Beginning the Meeting	*Bettina*: Hi Seif. I'm looking forward to working with you. I know you've worked in a lot of parts of the firm, I'm sure you've got stories to tell!
	Seif: Hi Bettina. Thanks, I'm looking forward to working with you too. I know you bring a lot of industry experience, I'm sure you've got stories too.
	[they share background information and experiences for about 5 minutes]
	Seif: Well, let's talk about that more over lunch. Should we take a look at this project?
	Bettina: Sounds good.

Sharing knowledge about the client	*Seif*: As two senior partners, we'll both be responsible for an excellent outcome for the client. You may know we are a bit vulnerable now, with a fragile relationship with the client. Your industry knowledge will complement my knowledge of the firm and the client.
	Bettina: Yes, I've heard we have a bit of repair work to do. I'm sure with our combined expertise and our networks of resources we'll deliver great value. Who else from the firm should be on our project team?
Agreeing on next steps	*Bettina*: Normally I like to get started quickly – get some parallel work streams going and test some early ideas with the client before refining. What's your norm for early stages?
	Seif: I can see the benefit of efficiency in that process. I normally prefer to have some solid analysis before going to the client though. I'm also concerned about having to backtrack if the parallel streams go in different directions – I prefer to keep continuous dialogue so they can build on each other.
	Bettina: Yes, that makes sense too. How about ...
	[discussion about process]
	Seif: So, to summarize, we'll start parallel work streams, and have calls two times per week for sharing and coordination. After three weeks, we'll set up a prototyping blitz with the client, to get their input on the analysis so far and set up the next phase.

Seif and Bettina led a project that kept to all milestones and delivered on time. It was not simple to work together with their different preferences and norms, but both knew the value was worth the effort. The project deliverables exceeded the client's high expectations. Seif and Bettina ensured that everyone on the project learned a lot from the experience, and the firm was therefore better positioned to work on projects like this in the future.

Seif and Bettina were mindful global leaders in their interaction. They demonstrated global mindsets by showing awareness of each other's perspectives, even anticipating them. Rather than blindly sticking to rules and routines from the past, they adapted those appropriate for the current situation. Through mindful management at the point of action, Seif and Bettina created synergy in this cross-cultural interaction. This chapter will explore the Map-Bridge-Integrate framework, a tool for engaging in effective cross-cultural interaction. We'll examine exactly how Seif, Bettina, and many other leaders create professional value and personal growth from working across cultures.

M	B	I	High Performance
Map	**Bridge**	**Integrate**	Differences Create Value & Learning
Understand the Differences	Communicate across the Differences	Manage the Differences	

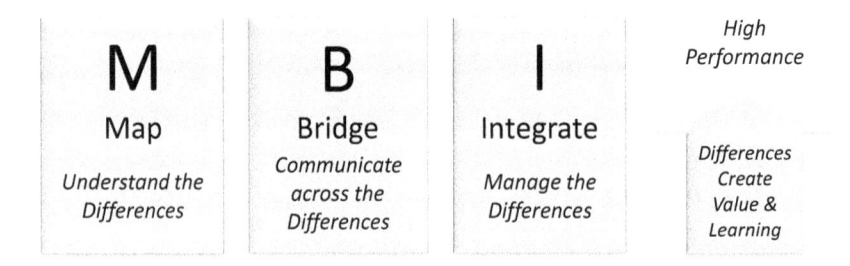

Figure 4.1 MBI in brief.

Map-Bridge-Integrate for Mindful Cross-Cultural Interactions

Our research shows that effectiveness in these multicultural moments derives from a basic set of interactions we call Map-Bridge-Integrate, or MBI (DiStefano & Maznevski, 2000; Maznevski, 1994). **Mapping** is about understanding individuals' cultural and other differences and providing context for the similarities. **Bridging** is communicating effectively taking those differences and similarities into account. **Integrating** is bringing the different perspectives together and building on them. When these three skills are executed well, interactions between individuals result in high effectiveness. The basic model is shown in Figure 4.1. Integrating leads directly to effectiveness, but our research found that Bridging is the most important process. If Bridging is done well, Integrating almost follows naturally; if Bridging is not done well, there is likely to be no Integrating. However, Bridging cannot be done without good Mapping, no matter how skilled or well intentioned the people involved are. Therefore, we focus on Mapping culture in this chapter, and Bridging together with Integrating in the next.

Mapping Cultures

In Chapter 1, we described the importance of mindful categorization, which involves having a broad range and depth of categories for understanding a set of situations. With mindful categorization, when you encounter new situations, you're able to connect and make sense of them effectively rather than pigeonhole everything into a small set of less comprehensive categories. In Chapter 2, we introduced the Global Leadership Competences, one of which is Perception Management, or actively engaging other perspectives. In this section, we build on those foundations and discuss tools for mapping cultures: frameworks for comparing cultures with each other and for developing expectations about how to work with people from different cultures. These tools are invaluable to increase mindful categorization when working across cultures, especially when the cultures are also complex and changing.

We use the metaphor of mapping quite deliberately. A map is a picture for navigating in a new territory. The map is useful to the extent that it is accurate, provides just the right level of detail and scale, and shows reference points. Features are not inherently good or bad, they must always be interpreted in context. A good map should help you develop a plan for how to get from one place to another.

Maps of social features are less common than maps of geographical ones, and mapping social features of groups is difficult because it is hard to verify the data against an objective reality. However, social maps that are carefully constructed help people enter new cultural territories mindfully as much as geographical maps help people enter new physical territories. You have probably completed surveys online or in organizational settings about your personality, then engaged in conversation with others whose scores are different about the implications of those differences. This is an example of social mapping – mapping personalities.

Choosing a Culture Map

Just as a geographer uses different types of maps for different purposes, an international manager has access to several cultural maps. Each map shows different dimensions of culture and allows different types of cultural comparisons.

Cultural mapping started in the field of anthropology. Parsons and Shills (1951) developed some of the earliest dimensions. Kluckhohn and Strodtbeck (1961b) built on their work and created the first comparative maps: the Cultural Orientations Framework. They analyzed hundreds of ethnographic descriptions of cultures from around the world and identified six problems or challenges that all societies throughout recorded history face: relation to the environment, relationships among people, mode of normal activity, orientation to time, belief about basic human nature, and use of space (Maznevski et al., 2002).

Business anthropologist Edward Hall began applying cultural maps to the activities of international business. He wrote several books and articles describing elements of culture that are relevant to business. In his classic article, "The Silent Language in Overseas Business," he described cultural differences and their impact on international behavior, relating to the five dimensions of Time, Space, Things, Friendships, and Agreements (Hall, 1960).

In the 1980s, Geert Hofstede developed an extensively researched cultural map, which contributed importantly to research and practice (Hofstede, 1984). By analyzing the satisfaction surveys of employees in a large multinational enterprise, he first identified four basic value patterns of cultures around the world: Individualism versus Collectivism, Power Distance, Uncertainty Avoidance, and Masculinity versus Femininity, linking these dimensions to management theories and practice (Hofstede, 1984). Later, with colleague Michael Bond, he identified a fifth value of Long-term Orientation versus Short-term Orientation (Hofstede & Bond, 1988). In subsequent research a sixth dimension was added: Indulgence versus Restraint (Hofstede et al., 2010).

In the ambitious GLOBE project (Global Leadership and Organizational Behavior Effectiveness), House and colleagues extended Hofstede's framework across multiple organizations and countries and linked it with leadership (House et al., 2014; Javidan et al., 2004). They included nine dimensions in their cultural map: Uncertainty Avoidance, Power Distance, Societal Collectivism, In-Group Collectivism, Gender Egalitarianism, Assertiveness, Future Orientation, Performance Orientation, and Humane Orientation. This study also examined differences and universals for leadership effectiveness. They learned that followers – no matter where they are – expect their leaders to develop a vision, inspire others, and create high-performing teams. On the other hand, cultures differ dramatically in terms of valuing leaders who are status conscious, autonomous, or face-saving (Dorfman et al., 2012; House et al., 2014).

Table 4.1 summarizes the maps that have dominated international management research and practice. All of these mapping tools have different strengths. Hofstede's, for example, provided the earliest comprehensive set of data and has been used extensively to guide interactions and research since its original publication in 1980. GLOBE's in-depth analysis of leadership values and behaviors helps guide research in these different contexts.

We find the Aperian GlobeSmart tool provides an excellent combination of validity and practical application when we map cultures for mindful international management. GlobeSmart maps five dimensions: Task vs. Relationship, Independent vs. Interdependent, Egalitarian vs. Status, Direct vs. Indirect, and Risk vs. Certainty. These dimensions are described in detail in the following subsections. Each dimension is validated with survey data from people in that country, updated on a regular basis. The five dimensions help compare cultures, and the "you are here" survey gives individuals an easy way to compare themselves with each other and with different cultural profiles.[1]

---

[1] Purchasers of this book have permission to access the Aperian GlobeSmart platform for one month. You can access the platform through the book's web page at the Cambridge University Press & Assessment website. Through this access you will be able to do the survey and receive your results, compare your results with the country database, and access all the interpretative materials for that month.

Table 4.1 Comparison of cultural mapping tools in international management research and practice

	Cultural Map					
	Kluckhohn & Strodtbeck (1961)	Hall (1966, 1973)	Hofstede (Hofstede et al., 2010)	GLOBE (House et al., 2004)	GlobeSmart (Doherty, 2016)
Logic	Each dimension separate, every culture can be high or low on each.	Bipolar dimensions, cultures are toward one end or the other.	Bipolar dimensions, cultures are toward one end or the other.	Each dimension separate, every culture can be high or low on each.	Bipolar dimensions, cultures are toward one end or the other.
Interacting with the world and people in general	**Relation to the Environment**: **Mastery** (Control the environment), **Harmony** (Work with the environment and the people in it), **Subjugation** (Be controlled by the environment)	**Time**: **Monochronic** (prioritize the task and achievement) vs **Polychronic** (prioritize relationships, do many things at once)			**Task** (Prioritize the work first) vs **Relationship** (Prioritize relationships first)
Self in relation to groups	**Relations among people**: **Individual** (Look after self), **Collective** (Look after group)	**Context in Communication**: **High context** (meaning conveyed in the context not just the words, look after relationships) vs **Low context** (meaning is all in the words, respect individual understanding)	**Individualism** (Look after self) vs **Collectivism** (Look after group)	**In-Group Collectivism**: (Prioritize cohesion in organizations and families) **Societal Collectivism**: (Distribute resources and encourage collective action across society)	**Independent** (Look after self) vs **Interdependent** (Look after relationships with group) **Direct** (Meaning is all in the words) vs **Indirect** (Meaning conveyed in the context not just words, look after relationships)

Table 4.1 (Cont.)

	Cultural Map				
	Kluckhohn & Strodtbeck (1961)	Hall (1966, 1973)	Hofstede (Hofstede et al., 2010)	GLOBE (House et al., 2004)	GlobeSmart (Doherty, 2016)
Space and ownership	Use of space: Public, Private, Mixed	Space: High territoriality (my space is mine) vs Low territoriality (space is public)			
Power distribution	Relations among people: Hierarchical (Vertical distribution of power, responsibility, and privilege)		Power Distance (Vertical distribution of power, responsibility, and privilege)	Power Distance (Vertical distribution of power, responsibility, and privilege)	Egalitarian (Flat distribution of power and responsibility) vs Status (Vertical distribution of power, responsibility, and privilege)
Approach to working together	Mode of normal activity: Doing (Taking action), Being (Focus on the moment)	Information: Slow flow (planning) vs Fast flow (frantic action)	Indulgence (Value satisfying human needs and desires) vs Restraint (Suppress emotional expression, leisure, freedom) Uncertainty Avoidance (Seek order, structure, formal processes)	Assertiveness (Be confrontational and aggressive) Performance Orientation (Prioritize performance improvement and excellence) Uncertainty Avoidance (Seek order, structure, formal processes)	Risk (Take action even without all the information) vs Uncertainty (Careful planning before taking action)

Time (if linear)	Orientation to time: Past, Present, Future	Long-term orientation vs Short-term orientation	Future Orientation (Plan, invest, delay gratification)
Gender roles			Gender Egalitarianism (Minimize gender inequality)
Nature of humanity	Belief about basic human nature: Good, Evil, Mixed	Masculinity (Emphasize heroism, assertiveness, material rewards) vs Femininity (Emphasize cooperation, caring for weak, quality of life)	Humane Orientation (Importance of being fair, altruistic, kind to others)
Strengths	Nuanced dimensions capture complex combinations of cultures.	Depth in focus on the communication process, very intuitive descriptions.	Large data set with broad source. Country scores are used in many research studies.	Large data set with broad source. Well validated at individual and country level. Multi-method validation.	Intuitive dimensions. Easy access. Excellent support materials. Continuously updated.
Limits	Complex, difficult to measure. Not updated.	Limited in scope of dimensions. Not updated.	Not well validated at individual level to explain interactions.	Complex set of dimensions. Published data not updated.	Fewer dimensions than some maps.

Mapping with GlobeSmart Dimensions

The first GlobeSmart dimension is about the primary focus of interaction. The next three compare cultures on different aspects of how people work together, while the final one is related to people's approach to the tasks they're working on. For each dimension, we provide scores from a sample of 22 countries that cross different cultural patterns and geographic regions: Argentina, Brazil, Canada, People's Republic of China, Egypt, France, Germany, India, Indonesia, Japan, Kenya, Mexico, Nigeria, Pakistan, Romania, Russia, South Korea, Sweden, Thailand, United Arab Emirates (UAE), the United Kingdom (UK), and the United States (US). The data published here were aggregated in December 2022. On the GlobeSmart platform the data are updated regularly.

The Core of the Interaction: Task versus Relationship

All groups of people need to coordinate how they get things done together. This requires taking care of both tasks (what gets done) and relationships (the connections among people who coordinate their efforts). Different cultures have different agreements or preferences, though, regarding which they prioritize in order to build the other: tasks or relationships. The 22 countries' scores are shown in Figure 4.2 from most Relationship-oriented to most Task-oriented cultures.

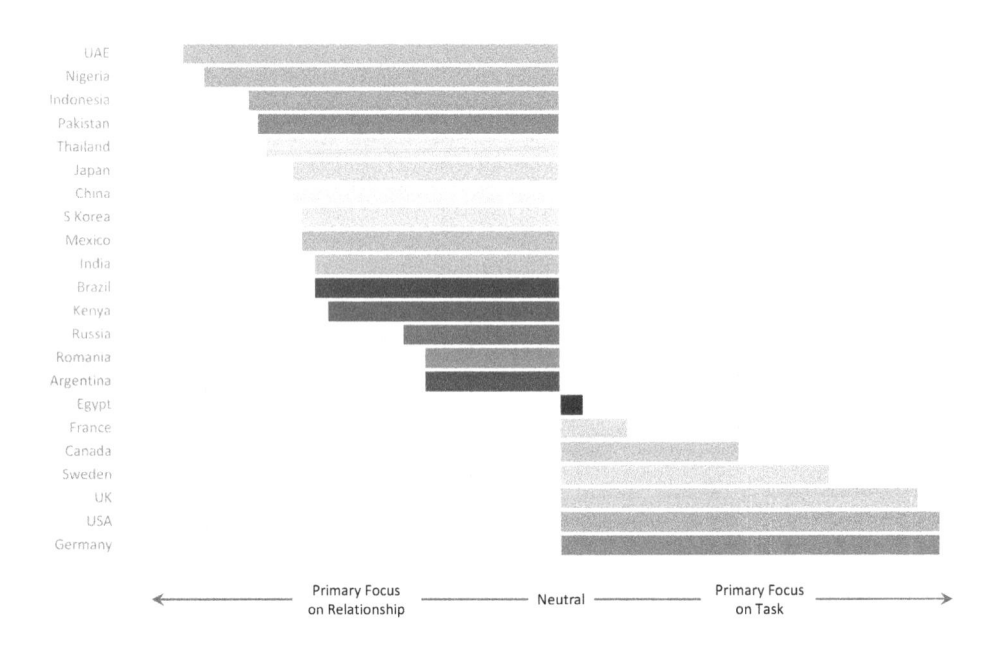

Figure 4.2 GlobeSmart profiles: Task or Relationship. Aperian GlobeSmart platform.

In Relationship-oriented cultures, people prefer to build the relationship first, then to work together. It is assumed that whatever the task, once people know and understand each other, coordination will be smoother with greater understanding and cooperation. People are valued for their ability to build relationships, and for how connected and respected they are. Most country cultures are more Relationship-focused first. Relationship-oriented cultures tend to be able to innovate and implement big initiatives well and quickly based on trust and to accomplish tasks through ambiguity by relying on the relationship. On the other hand, they may be slower to get to the task in the first place and can miss opportunities because they are focused on relationships first.

In Task-oriented cultures, people prefer to move quickly to the work to be done and then build relationships through the actual work. This is assumed to be most efficient, and the work is a common goal around which to form the relationships. People are valued and respected for what they contribute to the task, whether it's expertise, skills, or resources. This respect can build over time to deeper trust. Anglo, Nordic, and Germanic cultures tend to focus first on task. In these cultures, a new group working together likely dives straight into agreeing on a common goal and identifying a work plan. Teams measure progress by how many milestones they have achieved. They get a sense of cohesion from accomplishing parts of the task together, and this accomplishment may inspire them to get to know each other and build stronger relationships. It's quite common for colleagues from these cultures to have little or no knowledge of each other's hobbies, values, or personal lives, at least until they've worked together for a while. Task-oriented cultures tend to be efficient and productive, especially to start with. People value each other for hard work and discipline, so the work tends to be steady. On the other hand, work colleagues may be slower to build deep trust with each other, which is critical for implementing strategies and system changes in complex situations.

A Canadian executive in a global program, in a personal communication to one of the authors, reflected on the moment he deeply realized the difference between task and relationship cultures:

We had Mexicans in our class, so naturally, we discussed the Mexican culture. We spoke about their tendency to socialize first, business second, in order to build a relationship. We even saw a video of an American trying to do business when the Mexican host (obviously) wanted to speak about his family and his city. We laughed at the foolish American.

Later, we asked the Mexicans in our study team if they ever ran across people like that "for real." And one of the Mexicans put up his hand and said, "I am uncomfortable discussing these things with complete strangers. Could we introduce ourselves around the table before we continue, please? I am sorry to interrupt."

An embarrassed silence hung in the air. Here we were, discussing the concept while completely ignoring the concept. That single event had a tremendous impact on my perception of "culture." It's really there. Our culture is so ingrained, it's really hard to put it aside, even for a moment. I didn't feel a need to know more about our guests now, that would come later, at dinner, and after a few drinks. I was perfectly willing to work with someone for an hour, a day, without knowing much about them or their families. I expect Mexicans might think we are quite shallow people.

Which is better as a core focus for interaction, task or relationship? Phrased this way, the answer is obvious: Neither is inherently better or worse. As stated earlier, all cultures engage both tasks and relationships. Organizations that perform well sustainably in complex environments have systems and organizational cultures that direct people to take care of both tasks and relationships. Moreover, individuals tend to have their own personal preferences to focus on tasks or relationships first. At the same time, *cultures differ in the extent to which they prefer one or the other as the starting point for interaction.* Within a culture, whatever people's individual preferences are, they tend to work with others according to the assumptions of their own culture.

Moreover, because people tend to act most of the time according to the norms of their own culture, cross-cultural interactions offer the opportunity for synergy. For example, a team with mindful members who come from both Task and Relationship cultural norms can balance those two priorities without neglecting either. It may take more effort from the team members, but the payoffs are clear for high performance.

How We Interact with Each Other: Independent versus Interdependent

In every society, complex work tasks must be done by people working together. Different cultures have different agreements and preferences about how to coordinate work and interact with each other around work. The 22 countries' scores are shown in Figure 4.3, from most Interdependent to most Independent.

In Interdependent cultures, people are expected to work as much as possible by coordinating with and helping each other, on tasks that are related to one another. People who work well with others are highly valued, young people are taught to adapt to others, and group membership is emphasized. East Asian cultures tend to value and prefer high levels of Interdependence. In many companies from East Asian cultures, we see these assumptions in human resources practices. For example, companies in Japan, such as Mitsubishi and Dentsu, tend to hire managers based on their pre-work networks, and they rotate managers frequently

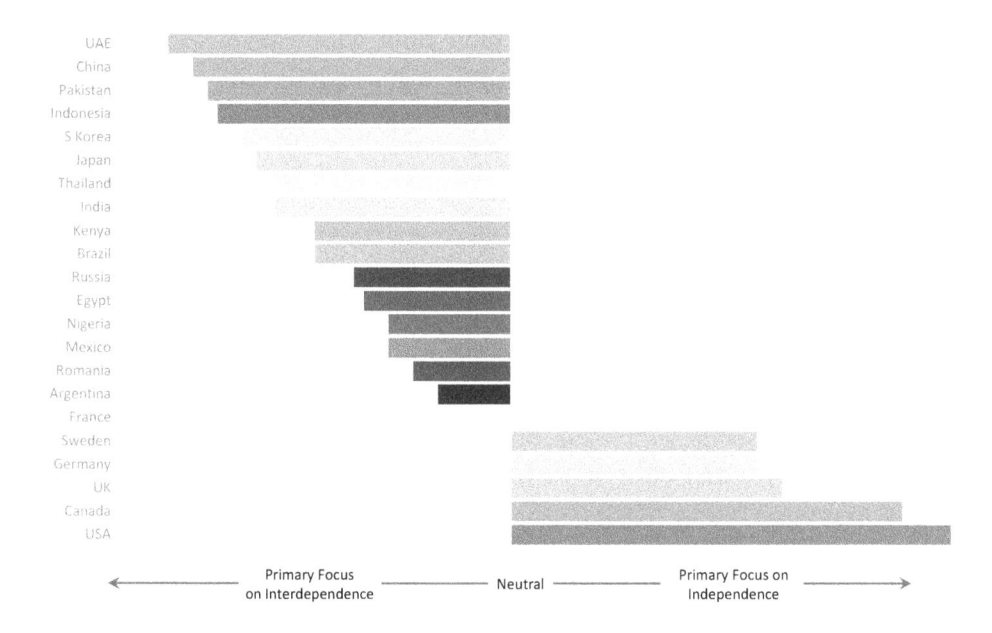

Figure 4.3 GlobeSmart profiles: Independent vs Interdependent. Aperian GlobeSmart platform.

so they develop networks and perspectives that help them see the whole company. Someone who contributes to the company wherever and however needed is considered to be a great performer.

In Independent cultures, people are expected to work as much as possible on their own, on clearly separated parts of a task. People who take individual initiative are highly valued, young people are taught to look after themselves, and individual achievements are emphasized. Anglo cultures tend to value and prefer high levels of Independence. In many companies from Anglo cultures, we see Independence assumptions in human resources practices. For example, companies in the United States such as Google, and in Canada such as Bank of Montreal (BMO), expect employees to drive their own careers and take initiative to direct their own progress. Someone who can move things ahead without relying on others is considered to be a great performer.

Independent and Interdependent cultures both value teams, but they tend to engage in teamwork differently. In Independent cultures, team members tend to work on their own (even if in the same room or virtual space) to accomplish their own part of the task. Roles must be clear so that accountability is also clear – team members must be able to track actions for milestones, praise, and blame. A good team leader coordinates the work of the team and brings the outputs together. Teams that work this way can be innovative and productive. In Interdependent cultures, team members tend to work with frequent interaction and member coordination as the task evolves. Roles are more fluid, with team members reaching out to help each other as task needs shift. Team members feel accountable for the output together and find it difficult to articulate the contribution of each member. A good team leader facilitates interaction among team members. Teams that work this way tend to be adaptable and good at implementing plans as conditions change.

Both Independent and Interdependent social interactions are important for different types of performance. In fact, all cultures interact with both Interdependence and Independence, and high-performing organizations draw on both in different situations. Individuals, personally, have different preferences for independent or interdependent work, even within the same culture. At the same time, *cultures differ in the extent to which they prefer one or the other as the starting point for interaction.* Within a culture, whatever people's individual preferences are, they tend to work according to the assumptions of their own culture. As we emphasized earlier, this provides both efficiency and identity.

If a cross-cultural interaction includes people comfortable with both Interdependent and Independent ways of working, there are opportunities for synergy. For example, a team with mindful members who were socialized through different types of cultural norms can learn to draw on both, and achieve innovation and adaptability, productivity, and the ability to implement their strategies well over time.

How We Distribute Power and Responsibility: Egalitarian versus Status

Every society must develop agreements around how power and responsibility are allocated and distributed. There seems to be a universal principle that power and responsibility ought to go hand-in-hand: Those with more power over others also have more responsibility for the performance and well-being of others. But cultures vary widely in their preferences for the extent to which power is shared. The 22 countries' scores are shown in Figure 4.4, ranging from most Egalitarian to most Status-oriented.

Egalitarian cultures tend to assume that power and responsibility should be distributed broadly and as equally as possible. Decisions should be made by consensus, and everyone has permission (and an obligation, even) to contribute to the decision process. In these cultures, a leader's role is to empower and facilitate decisions and performance, not to direct decision-making. Scandinavian cultures tend to be strongly egalitarian. In Danish and Swedish companies, such as Lego and Volvo, the hierarchy is very flat, and employees are encouraged to go directly

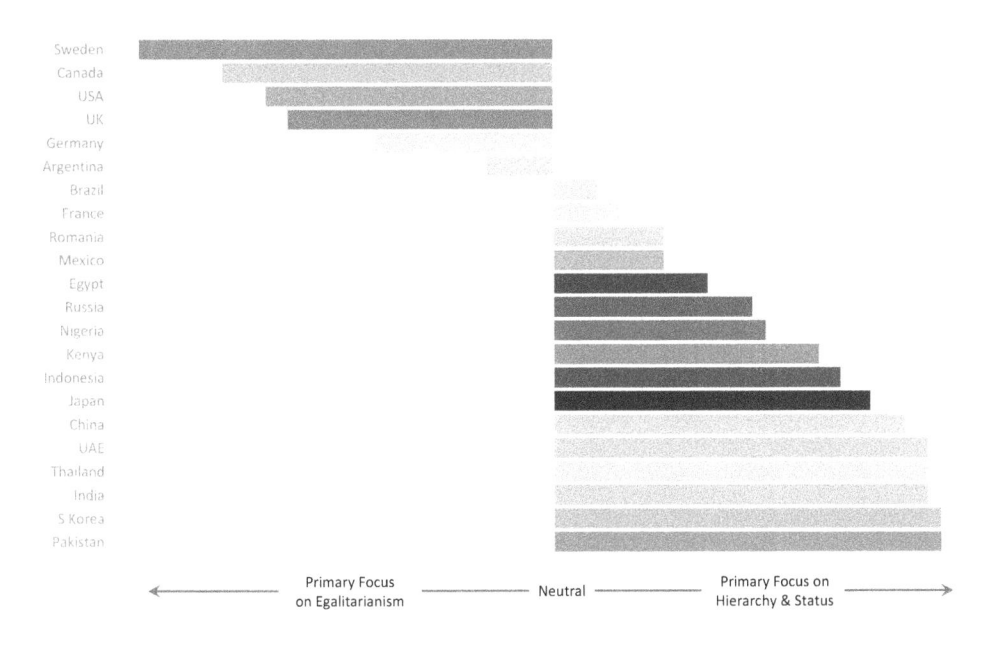

Sweden		
Canada		
USA		
UK		
Germany		
Argentina		
Brazil		
France		
Romania		
Mexico		
Egypt		
Russia		
Nigeria		
Kenya		
Indonesia		
Japan		
China		
UAE		
Thailand		
India		
S Korea		
Pakistan		

← Primary Focus on Egalitarianism —— Neutral —— Primary Focus on Hierarchy & Status →

Figure 4.4 GlobeSmart profiles: Egalitarian vs Status. Aperian GlobeSmart platform.

to people at different levels and in different parts of the organization to get information and to influence for implementation of initiatives. Volvo was the first large company to implement self-managed work teams throughout its production. These teams decide their own recruitment, performance management, compensation, and other practices, within a framework of company goals. Egalitarian cultures tend to maximize employee engagement and commitment. They tend to make high-quality decisions and creative innovation, especially in situations where different inputs are needed. On the other hand, decision-making can be slow, and ambiguity on roles can lead to either gaps or redundancies.

Status cultures tend to assume that power and responsibility should be distributed more vertically, with some people having more (even much more) power and responsibility than others. Decisions should be made by leaders at the top. Leaders may get input from others, but it's clear that the leader is responsible for making the decision and cascading it down. A good leader has a clear picture of the whole situation, is able to fit the different parts together, makes good decisions, and determines who is responsible for implementing what. A leader's role is also to take responsibility for ensuring performance and other outcomes. Whether things go well or badly, the leader is accountable. Indian culture tends to be very hierarchical, and this plays out in Indian organizations such as Tata and Reliance Industries. Roles throughout the hierarchy are clear. Information may flow in multiple directions, but authority follows a clear pattern of cascading.

Many status-oriented cultures are also very patriarchal, and this tends to also be true in India. The boss looks after his or her employees by supporting their careers, their families, and their communities. Status cultures tend to maximize efficiency in executing plans, especially when the situation is relatively clear. Employees tend to feel supported and know where to go in the organization for what they need. On the other hand, innovation and initiative can be low, and communication across different parts of the hierarchy can be slow.

Which is better, Egalitarian or Status distribution of power and responsibility? Again, the answer is obvious: Neither is inherently better or worse; the two ends of this spectrum enable different types of outcomes. It's important to realize that all cultures have mechanisms for involvement from everyone, *and* for enacting hierarchies of power. For example, Japan has a strong Status culture. The vertical hierarchy enforces direction and responsibility, while quality circles and bottom-up processes ensure that everyone contributes and has a voice for continuous improvement. In Sweden, the consensus works more efficiently over time with a boss who directs it actively and takes responsibility for the team's outcomes. Within cultures, individuals vary in their preference for Egalitarian or Status, often in ways related to family or professional background. Even though both orientations are present in all cultures, *cultures differ in the extent to which they prefer one or the other as the starting point for the distribution of power and responsibility*. Within a culture, people tend to work according to those assumptions as the default – when in doubt, go with the cultural norm – and adapt or add variations in specific situations.

For this dimension, too, cross-cultural interactions offer opportunities for synergy. A team with mindful members who come from both Egalitarian and Status cultural norms can learn to draw on both at the same time. In new product or service teams, for example, the different stages of development and implementation benefit from Egalitarian (deriving ideas from everywhere, broadening the scope) and Status (executing in an aligned way by a certain timeline for customers) modes.

How We Consider Others in Communication: Direct versus Indirect

In every culture, social interaction has norms about how to show consideration for the people you're communicating with. Effective communication is transmitting meaning from a sender to a receiver, as it was intended by the sender. This means communication requires commitment to the interaction from both the sender and the receiver. Different cultures have different social agreements about

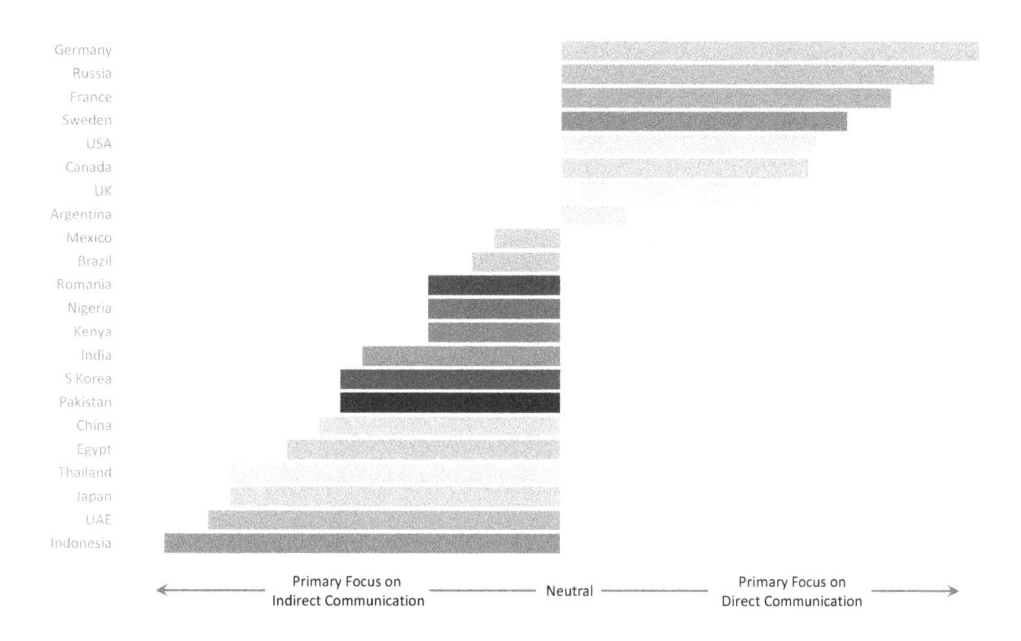

Figure 4.5 GlobeSmart profiles: Direct vs Indirect. Aperian GlobeSmart platform.

how people signal their commitment to communicating effectively together. The 22 countries' scores are shown in Figure 4.5 ranging from most Direct to most Indirect in their communication norms.

In Direct cultures, people confront difficult topics openly and value being concise, concrete, and to the point. They tend to separate the person from the message, the emotion from the facts. In Germany, for example, people often explain that it is respectful to value other's time and their need for exact understanding so they can take precise action; therefore, it is important to be clear and direct in communications. This includes saying difficult things, such as disagreement or criticism, directly. In the Netherlands, people often say that it's so important to be respectful of the other person's need for information to act on that there's no need to discuss what is good – it's more important to focus on what needs to be changed. These cultures are also sometimes referred to as **low context**: there is no need to understand anything about the context in order to understand the meaning of the words; all the meaning is in the words themselves. In cultures with a preference for Direct communication, meetings and conversations tend to be quick and to the point. Written minutes or transcripts of meetings capture all the meaning. Written communication, including e-mail or texting, can substitute fairly easily for face-to-face interactions. Direct communication styles tend to be efficient and clear, leaving little ambiguity. They provide everyone with clarity around what they should deliver, when, how, and why. On the other hand, they may miss nuances of the situation that could inform quality or adaptability, and they may miss exploring deeper reasons for current situations.

In Indirect cultures, people assume that others in the conversation may have different views or sensitivities, which should be considered or taken care of by avoiding apparent disagreement. These are often called **high context** cultures because both speakers and listeners take into account the context when they communicate, often relying on contextual cues – even pauses and silence – to deliver part of the message. In Indonesia and Thailand, a manager may provide feedback to an underperforming subordinate by pointing out that the task may have been too challenging for the employee and acknowledging that the employee has a lot of potential and could succeed with hard work. The Indonesian or Thai employee would know clearly that this is an indication they need to perform better, but the relationship has been preserved by the boss's indirect communication. When Indirect cultures are also Status cultures, which is often the case, there is a strong prohibition against disagreeing with the boss. Effective managers know how to ask the questions to save face, without the need for a direct "no." For example, an Indonesian boss may not ask "do you understand?" because a subordinate would not directly say "no." A "no" would imply that the manager has not explained correctly. Instead, a Malaysian boss may ask something like "when you explain this to your own subordinates, what questions do you think they may have?" This allows the manager's subordinate to articulate his or her own questions while contextualizing them in a situation that maintains face for both the manager and the subordinate. In Indirect cultures, communication tends to be holistic and comprehensive, exploring the situation and the contexts of the people involved in the communication. It also tends to maintain relationships among people so they are motivated and committed to reaching out to each other. On the other hand, it can be slow, and it often leaves room for ambiguity about what should happen next.

Both Direct and Indirect communication preferences have strengths and complications. In all cultures, good communicators try to look after the relationship and try to ensure the message is clearly sent and received. Even in Direct cultures, people recognize that face-to-face communication facilitates nonverbal signals about how a message is being received and ensures that the person and emotion are "looked after" even if the facts are difficult. In Indirect cultures there are many sanctioned "off the record" mechanisms, such as social interactions after work at golf courses and karaoke restaurants, that create an environment for direct messages to be delivered without disrupting work relationships. Within cultures, individuals vary in their preference for Direct or Indirect. Even though both orientations are present in all cultures, *cultures differ in the extent to which they prefer one or the other as the starting point for effective communication.* Within a culture, people tend to work according to those assumptions as the norm and compensate for its weaknesses in other ways and situations.

As for the other dimensions, cross-cultural interactions offer opportunities for synergy. For example, a team with mindful members who come from both Direct and Indirect cultural norms relies on some members to clarify ambiguity for analysis and action and on others to highlight nuances in the context for deeper understanding. Over time, all team members are likely to broaden their repertoire to be flexible in their communication norms according to the situation.

How Much Information We Need before Action: Risk versus Certainty

People in all groups must coordinate planning and action, and that means also having an implicit agreement about the relationship between planning and action: How much certainty do we need about the outcomes of an action before taking the action? Different cultures agree on different levels of certainty required, with implications for how they engage in the action itself. The 22 countries' scores are shown in Figure 4.6, ranging from most Risk oriented to most Certainty oriented.

In Risk-oriented cultures, people focus on the importance of demonstrating quick results. They tend to value flexibility and speed and make decisions to take

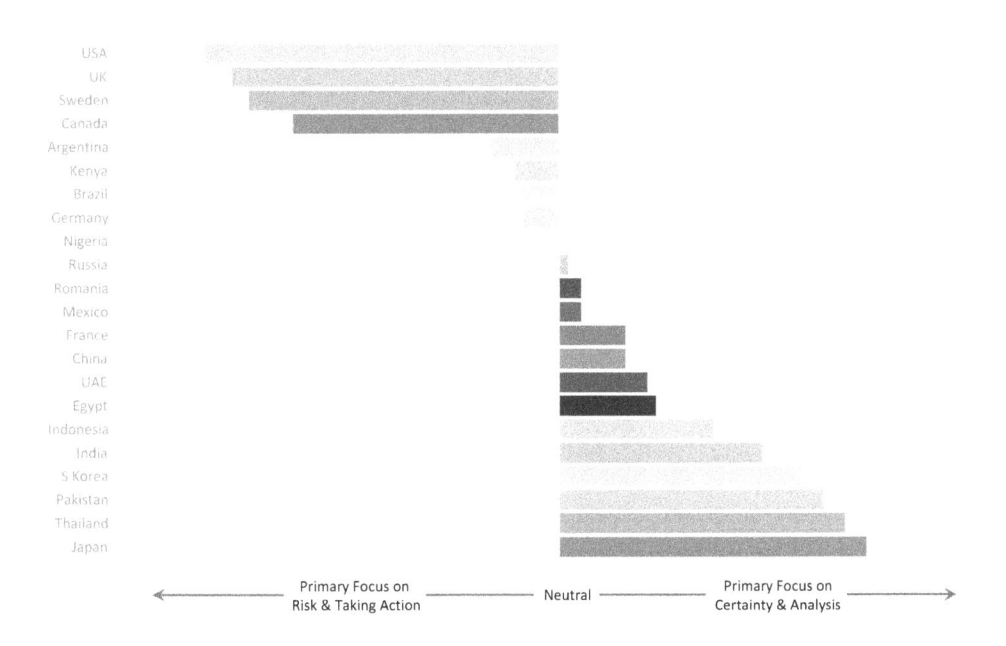

Figure 4.6 GlobeSmart profiles: Risk vs Certainty. Aperian GlobeSmart platform.

action with just enough information to indicate a direction. There's a general belief that waiting too long may risk losing an opportunity. Once people decide to go ahead with something, they tend to monitor feedback to get more information and adapt as they go along. American innovation firms, such as IDEO, are extreme examples of the US affinity toward the Risk end of this dimension. IDEO, a well-respected and award-winning design firm, is famous for their passion to "fail often to succeed sooner." Experimenting, pilot testing, fast prototyping – these are all common ways for US companies to launch new products, services, and markets. Risk cultures tend to be highly innovative and fast in taking action and adaptable in implementation. On the other hand, they can develop redundancies or miss implications for larger systems, sometimes suboptimizing quality or long-term results.

In Certainty-oriented cultures, people focus on the importance of getting it right the first time. Before committing to action, they gather extensive information and analysis and develop strong contingency plans. Once they launch action, they monitor for variation from plan and act to bring results back to the planned path. French and South Korean cultures tend to be more on the Certainty end of this dimension. In both French and South Korean companies, such as, respectively, Société Générale and Hyundai, strategic planning processes are highly structured with extensive requirements for background information and analysis. Planning across the entire company is carefully coordinated so all the pieces fit together in a logical way, with consistency and alignment built into the process. Once the plan is approved, managers expect it will be implemented with the anticipated results, and they monitor indicators for deviance. Certainty cultures tend to have strongly aligned and consistent systems, reliable results, and coordination for quality across multiple measures. On the other hand, they tend to be less innovative and find it hard to adapt to changes in the environment.

Good managers in all cultures are strong at both planning and taking action, balancing risk and certainty. In Risk cultures, various mechanisms provide a foundation for Certainty. For example, bankruptcy protection laws in the United States allow entrepreneurs and companies to take business risks without as much fear of shutting down the company in case of negative outcomes, compared with entrepreneurs and companies in many other countries. In Japan, a high Certainty culture, there is strong agreement that sometimes you need to take action without full information, and the plan becomes a series of small, specific experiments. Within cultures, individuals vary in their preference for Risk or Certainty, often from personality differences. These individual differences may translate to career choices or industry choices within the culture. Even though both orientations are present in all cultures, *cultures differ in the extent to which they prefer one or the other as the starting point for determining a course for the future.* Within a culture, people tend to prioritize those preferences and balance with the other orientation in the implementation process.

Again, cross-cultural interactions offer opportunities for synergy. For example, a team with mindful members who come from both Risk and Certainty cultural norms can draw on these different values and practices to maximize both planning and learning from action.

> ### Reflection Question 4.1: Mapping
>
> Think of someone you work with who's quite different from you. Map the ways in which you're different – culture, gender, personality, work preferences, educational or experiential background. Go beyond the surface characteristics and try to understand how those differences could add value to your work together. After you've developed some ideas, have a conversation with the person to get their own perspective.

The Discipline of Cartography: Cultural Mixes, Changes, and Other Complexities

Being able to map culture involves more than knowledge about the dimensions. It requires using the dimensions to understand, explain, and predict others' attitudes and behaviors. Mapping creates awareness and appreciation of differences and their implications in a structured and consistent way. It begins a conversation about similarities and differences using a common language and framework and allows the conversation to move quickly and constructively to individual and situational differences. Like cartographers, managers need to combine various sources of information to create their own dynamic maps and use them to navigate complex territories. Just like any other skill, managers can practice mapping and improve their ability to map.

The Limits of Maps and the Fine Line with Stereotyping

Mapping is a good first step to cross-cultural understanding, but it is important to recognize its limits.

First, as we discussed in Chapter 3, individuals do not always conform to their cultures. Variety and unpredictability are both the beauty and the complexity of human nature. We are all different, and we do not always behave as predicted!

Table 4.2 Countries categorized by within-culture variance

High Cultural Homogeneity	Moderate Cultural Homogeneity	Mixed	Moderate Cultural Diversity	High Cultural Diversity
Belgium	Austria	Australia	Greece	Brazil
Japan	Finland	Denmark	India	Canada
South Korea	France	Hong Kong	Ireland	China
Saudi Arabia	Germany	Italy	Switzerland	Philippines
Singapore		Malaysia	UK	Romania
Taiwan		Mexico	US	Russia
Thailand		Netherlands		South Africa
		New Zealand		
		Nigeria		
		Norway		
		Spain		
		Sweden		

Within cultures, some people hold more strongly to cultural norms than do others. Personality and environmental factors influence individual behavior. Even people who are strong proponents of their culture's values do not always behave in a way that is consistent with those values. This limitation is called the **ecological fallacy**: By knowing the culture (ecological level) you cannot predict every individual; by knowing an individual, you cannot automatically predict the culture. Think about yourself; are you more or less typical of the cultural group you identify yourself with?

Not surprisingly, some countries are more culturally diverse than others. Our research showed some interesting results when we looked at within-country homogeneity or diversity, as shown in Table 4.2. Countries like Brazil and Canada are diverse due to patterns of immigration, while China and Russia are diverse due to ideological shifts in the country, with younger generations preferring different ways of working than those of older generations. Anthropologists propose that within-culture diversity is important for cultural change and adaptation. Japan's cultural homogeneity was once seen as a key factor for creating initial growth through efficiency in alignment, but now may be associated with less growth from innovation.

Finally, cultures are dynamic, always changing. Cultures must change or they will stagnate and disappear, and that change is made possible by the variation of individuals within cultures and the existence of subcultures (Kluckhohn and Strodtbeck, 1961). Usually change is quite slow, but sometimes external and internal events combine to create fast change. For example, between 2005 and 2015, some country data – notably from China, India, and Russia – suggested that the cultural preference for Interdependence over Independence became much less pronounced. However, since 2018, the data for these same countries have shifted back toward more Interdependence. What are the causes and effects? It requires much deeper examination to discover, and the patterns are very complex. Our point here is that maps may show a misleadingly static picture. Those who use maps must remember that cultures shift and take care to ensure that they reflect current realities as closely as possible.

The Map Is Not the Territory

Maps are critical tools for navigation, but it is important to remember that the map is not the territory. Mapping is about describing cultures using objective, nonevaluative data to predict thinking and behavior patterns among the culture's members (Adler, 2008; Bird & Osland, 2000). As we illustrated earlier, mapping is extremely helpful when we enter new situations or try to understand unexpected events. People who go into new countries and cultures without these maps, saying, "I have no expectations, I have an open mind," are actually engaging in cognition that says, "I think they will be like me." This is due to the basic human neurological processes related to the assumptions and perceptions described earlier (Minda, 2022). When people go into a new situation with a map of expectations concerning how others may be different from oneself, they are more prepared for differences in thinking and behavior, and thus manage those differences much better.

Many people are afraid of Mapping because they worry it will lead to stereotyping. They resist being put into a box as an unthinking representative of a group and do not want to categorize others that way. This is a healthy fear and resistance, and we encourage it. And like any tool, Mapping can be misused. However, Mapping is such a powerful tool that it is worth using. Maps are objective descriptions of characteristics that are relevant to an interaction. They help people respect each other's values and perspectives and give people suggestions about how to understand and use each other's ideas better. Maps are revised whenever new data is available and are constantly tested as hypotheses rather than taken for granted as truths. Maps should be seen as windows to the complex territory of human beings, ways of entering the different perspectives and really seeing the person inside.

Stereotyping, on the other hand, is not mindful. Stereotypes are subjective descriptions of groups of people that are usually used to judge those people, often in a negative way. Stereotypes are assumed to be true and are neither tested nor changed with new information. They usually lead people to close doors – making assumptions about how people will behave – rather than open windows. The differences between Mapping and stereotyping are important (Adler, 1997; Osland & Bird, 2000). Mapping leads to healthy dynamics among individuals, with people casting aside the maps as they develop more insight into the territory.

Research shows that without explicit intervention, teams tend to spend most of their time discussing information that all team members share, and only a small portion of the time discussing information that only one or a few team members have (Stasser, 1999). This dynamic is not conducive to high performance, especially if the task is complex and multidimensional. Explicit Mapping is an excellent way to avoid this dynamic. If team members are aware of the different perspectives – the different points on the map – and of the potential contributions, they are more likely to bring them into team discussions and to create better solutions. Among individuals, such as between a leader and a subordinate or between a customer and a supplier, Mapping helps prevent conflict and aids in seeing opportunities. The more the people involved understand the nature of each other's different perspectives, the more they can use those differences to achieve high performance.

Let's Go Back to Seif and Bettina

In the opening conversation, Seif and Bettina showed they were both adept at Mapping. Their two cultures' GlobeSmart profiles are shown in Figure 4.7.

Now let's look back at the conversation with a different lens. This analysis is in Table 4.3.

Seif and Bettina, as mindful global leaders, were aware in advance of the potential for these differences. They asked each other questions and listened to each other's responses carefully to make sense within the context. This Mapping set them up for excellent Bridging in the conversation and the project.

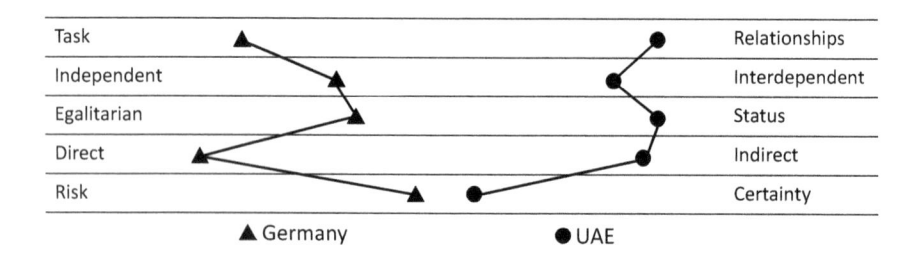

Figure 4.7 Cultural maps for Germany and UAE. Aperian GlobeSmart platform.

Table 4.3 **Mapping analysis of a cross-cultural interaction**

Beginning the Meeting	*Bettina*: Hi Seif. I'm looking forward to working with you. I know you've worked in a lot of parts of the firm, I'm sure you've got stories to tell! *Seif*: Hi Bettina. Thanks, I'm looking forward to working with you too. I know you bring a lot of industry experience, I'm sure you've got stories too. [they share background information and experiences for about 5 minutes] *Seif*: Well, let's talk about that more over lunch. Should we take a look at this project? *Bettina*: Sounds good.	*Task vs Relationship* Bettina started by building relationships with Seif, in respect of his cultural preferences. Seif reciprocated by postponing the relationship discussion until lunch, moving to task more quickly than he would have in his own culture.
Sharing knowledge about the client	*Seif*: As two senior partners, we'll both be responsible for an excellent outcome for the client. You may know we are a bit vulnerable now, with a fragile relationship with the client. Your industry knowledge will complement my knowledge of the firm and the client. *Bettina*: Yes, I've heard we have a bit of repair work to do. I'm sure with our combined expertise and our networks of resources we'll deliver great value. Who else from the firm should be on our project team?	*Status vs Egalitarian; Direct vs Indirect* Seif clarified their status as equals – demonstrating his own sensitivity to status markers while acknowledging their equal status, and he spoke of the client relationship indirectly. Bettina spoke about the client relationship directly and focused on expertise and networks, a more egalitarian approach.
Agreeing on next steps	*Bettina*: Normally I like to get started quickly – get some parallel work streams going and test some early ideas with the client before refining. What's your norm for early stages? *Seif*: I can see the benefit of efficiency in that process. I normally prefer to have some solid analysis before going to the client, though. I'm also concerned about having to backtrack if the parallel streams go in different directions – I prefer to keep continuous dialogue so they can build on each other. *Bettina*: Yes, that makes sense too. How about ... [discussion about process] *Seif*: So to summarize, we'll start parallel work streams, and have calls two times per week for sharing and coordination. After three weeks, we'll set up a prototyping blitz with the client to get their input on the analysis so far and set up the next phase.	*Risk vs Certainty; Interdependent vs Independent* Bettina expressed preferences for Independent (work in parallel) and Risk (go to the client early to test ideas) norms, while Seif expressed preferences for Interdependent (work in close collaboration) and Certainty (get it right before going to the client) norms.

Integrating Other Maps

Cultural differences are not the only ones that influence cross-cultural interaction. People differ, of course, with respect to personality, educational background, experience, gender, and many other dimensions. It's especially important to make cultural maps explicit because they are usually hidden beneath the surface and affect interactions in unintended ways. In addition to mapping culture, it's important to map some of these other dimensions as well. One helpful tool for quickly mapping some key personality and communication style preferences is the Diversity Icebreaker tool, also called the Trialogue tool (Ekelund & Langvik, 2008; Human Factors, 2023). Diversity Icebreaker uses a short survey and a specific process to get people to explore the different team roles they prefer to contribute and the implications for the team. The combination of the Mapping survey and discussion process creates a positive environment for conversations about differences and similarities, opening people up to Mapping and the entire MBI process.

Mapping in Action: A New Team

How important is it to sit down and create detailed maps, with survey data about individuals involved, or can you just know the general patterns and map from there? There is a trade-off between investment and results. Explicit Mapping takes time, but it pays off in more ideas coming into the group, more comprehensive examination and analysis of the ideas, and more possibility of building on ideas in innovative ways. The more important the task and/or the more diverse the people involved, the more critical Mapping is.

In our experience, it is best for a group to go into detailed Mapping on at least two dimensions that are important to the group's work, such as culture and personality or gender, then use those discussions to access Mapping on any other relevant dimensions. The use of an outside facilitator to help with Mapping is not necessary, but some managers prefer it, for example if the leader would rather be a neutral participant than lead the process. Some maps, such as many personality surveys, must be administered and facilitated by a certified professional, so if you want to use these maps, an outside facilitator may be necessary.

Reinhard was appointed to lead the global marketing group for a new, highly innovative medical device. The product was based on a combination of robotic, bionic, wireless, and biological technologies and had the potential to revolutionize the treatment of debilitating diseases. It could be the next big thing for the company, and everyone involved was excited about the impact. Reinhard knew he needed a diverse team of professionals to tap into different ideas and different aspects of the task and the market, so he deliberately recruited his 10 direct reports to reflect a scope of organizational veterans and newcomers, medical professionals, engineers, and social scientists, young and experienced people, and people from multiple country-cultures and with different personality types.

Shortly after the team launched, Reinhard brought the team together for a Mapping exercise. Given the importance of the product launch, the sensitivity of the product, and the diversity of the team, he decided to work with an outside facilitator, although he remained very active in the Mapping process and often took the lead. He first used the Diversity Icebreaker tool, described earlier, to look at preferences for interaction styles and roles, to help them become comfortable with Mapping and to create a positive environment for exploring differences.

Then Reinhard had the team map their personalities and cultures. For personality they used the HEXACO indicator of six personality dimensions (Lee & Ashton, 2018, 2023). For culture they used GlobeSmart, as described here. For each of these maps, the team discussed patterns associated with different dimensions and identified each individual's position on the Map. Who prefers extraversion and who prefers introversion as a personality dimension? Who prefers Task and who prefers Relationships as a cultural dimension? In this Mapping discussion, people identified specific potential contributions of individual team members. For example, the Task-oriented members will help us remember to take charge of the market and identify what we can control; the Relationship-oriented members will help us remember to keep in mind all the stakeholders and how we can work with them to cocreate solutions.

After these discussions, the team created a large grid, with team members' names down the left as rows and dimensions of diversity across the top as columns. The grid with some of the team members is shown in Figure 4.8. By the end of the process, team members were even more excited about working together, learning from each other, and using the different perspectives and some newly discovered commonalities to create a great product launch.

The team succeeded beyond the company's expectations in terms of creating new markets and value for both customers and the company. This initial Mapping set them up well, and as a team they took their interaction seriously, engaging in reflection and development frequently. Three years later the five most senior members of the team (including Reinhard) had been promoted to lead other big opportunities across the globe, and one of the more junior members was successfully leading the team to innovate and perform even more. In Reinhard's assessment, it is clear that good Mapping started the team in the right direction, and he continues to use the process with all his new teams.

	Cultural Emphasis	Trialogue	Personality (MBTI)	Gender	Country Location	Organizational function (education)	Hobbies
Reinhard	Task, Egalitarian, Certainty	Blue (red, green)	ENTJ	Male	Switzerland	Director (Sciences)	Family, sports, outdoors
Rachna	Relationships, Interdependent, Status	Red (blue)	ESTP	Female	Belgium	Purchasing and logistics (Engineering)	Family, arts
Alejandro	Relationships, Interdependent, Indirect	Red (green)	INFP	Gay Male	South Korea	Business development (Engineering)	Music, sports
Takashi	Task, Status, Risk	Blue	ESTJ	Male	Japan	Marketing & advertising (Business)	Movies, sports
John	Independent, Egalitarian, Risk	Green	ENTP	Male	USA	Technology, sales (Business)	Technology, travel
Marije	Egalitarian, Indirect, Certainty	Green (red)	ENFJ	Female	Switzerland	Post-sales technical management (Medicine)	Outdoors, travel, family
Claire	Interdependent, Direct, Certainty	Blue (green)	ISTJ	Female	Dubai	Finance (Economics)	Theatre, classical music

Figure 4.8 Example of a team's Map.

Mapping Is about Efficiency, but Don't Forget Identity

In this section on Mapping cultures, we have focused mostly on the cognitive aspect of culture: Our shared values and assumptions influence how we perceive the world and the people in it, how we make choices, and how we act. For the mechanics of doing business, this cognitive aspect is important. Furthermore, it is often misinterpreted, leading to conflict more often than synergy in intercultural interactions.

It is equally important to respect the identity that culture provides. Managers have a tendency to downplay cultural identity: "We are all part of a global business culture." But remember that identity becomes more important to the extent that it is threatened. If you disrespect identity – for example, by behaving in a way that is considered rude in the culture, by serving food that is unacceptable in the country, by not accommodating requirements of the culture – you set up a situation in which the other people become more locked into their cultural identity in order to defend it. This makes conflict more likely and makes it more difficult to achieve synergies.

> ### Reflection Question 4.2: Dual Identities and Identification in the MNE
>
> Cultural identity is a multifaceted and complex phenomenon: Different aspects of your identity surface and become salient in different contexts and situation. The supplementary article listed below discusses the dual identity of local host

country managers working in multinational enterprise (MNE) subsidiaries of a national cultural origin other than their own. This article suggests a complex relationship between host country culture, individual cultural affiliation, and organizational country of origin. Read this article and please reflect:

- What are the four dual identity profiles suggested in this article?
- How is a dual identity profile related to the level of acculturative stress of local host country managers working in an MNE?
- How would you relate your personal work life to the four suggested dual identity profiles?

Lee, K. P., Kim, M., & You, C. Y. (2023). Betwixt and between: National and organizational identification of host country managers working in MNE subsidiaries. *Academy of Management Journal*, 66(3), 744–772.

You can watch a 90-second video presenting highlights of the study at: https://www.youtube.com/watch?v=3UTJ3ZvHXKk&tab_channel=AcademyofManagement

Conclusion: Mapping Lays the Ground for Strong Bridging and Integrating

Mapping as a step in the MBI framework is summarized in Figure 4.9.

In Chapter 3, we focused on culture as the context for international management behavior. In this chapter, we provide Mapping tools for comparing international cultures with each other. Mapping helps global leaders put mindfulness into action.

M
Map
Understand the Differences
- Describe different perspectives objectively, below the surface
- Cultural dimensions
- Dimensions of Personality, Function, Gender, etc.

B
Bridge
Communicate across the Differences

I
Integrate
Manage the Differences

High Performance

Differences Create Value & Learning

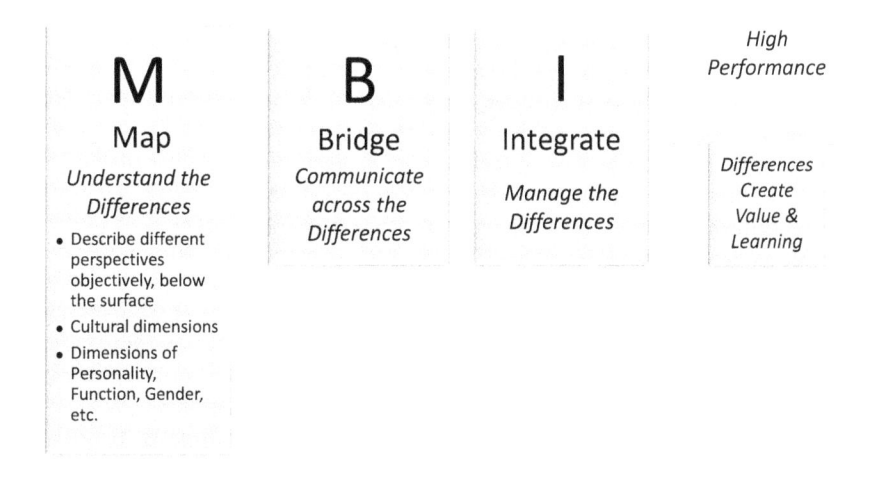

Figure 4.9 Mapping in MBI

The dimensions of the Map help a leader articulate the different elements of their global mindset. They guide perception management, relationship management, and even self-management in enacting global leader competences. They also provide a language for recognizing, analyzing, and navigating paradoxes that arise.

Knowledge about culture is one of the most important foundations of mindful global leadership, and Mapping cultures is one of the most fundamental skills. It is possible to ignore cultural differences for a short time or for basic transactions – that is, to operate without being mindful about culture – especially if you possess power or other resources. However, effectiveness and sustainable performance in a multinational business world are only possible with strong mindfulness about culture and an ability to draw on the strengths of different cultures in different situations. Moreover, all international managers we know agree that cultural differences create the most interesting, dynamic, and ever-enjoyable possible canvas on which to paint a management journey.

> **Reflection Question 4.3: How Do the Romans Feel When Visitors "Do as the Romans Do"?**
>
> An old saying goes, "When in Rome, do as the Romans do," recommending cultural accommodation when in a foreign setting. Researchers Cho, Morris, and Dow have researched cultural accommodation and highlight that "[p]ast research finds foreign visitors who accommodate their behavior to local norms to a moderate degree are appreciated more than those who accommodate little, but more extreme accommodation does not always evoke positive evaluations." To explain outcomes of an experimental study, they introduce the distinction between cultural adaptation characterized as "multiculturalism" and "polyculturalism." Please read the article below and discuss:
>
> - What is the difference between "multiculturalism" and "polyculturalism" and how are these concepts related to the degree of cultural adaptation to a foreign setting?
> - Why do you think that local nationals do not always appreciate foreigners' adaption to local norms?
> - Under what circumstances might being "foreign" be beneficial to collaborating with people from different cultures?
>
> Cho, J., Morris, M. W., & Dow, B. (2018). How do the Romans feel when visitors "Do as the Romans Do"? Diversity ideologies and trust in evaluations of cultural accommodation. *Academy of Management Discoveries*, 4(1), 11–31.

Further resources

With your one-month trial of the Aperian GlobeSmart platform, you will find many resources for mapping and bridging with other cultures. We encourage you to explore it extensively!

The cultural dimension frameworks summarized in Table 4.1 have been described and discussed in detail, and many materials are available online for them, particularly those of Hall (1966, 1973), Hofstede (Hofstede et al., 2010), and GLOBE (House et al., 2004). Two other mapping tools that many managers find useful are those of Trompenaars (1996) and Meyer (2014). We encourage you to explore many different maps and discover which are most useful for your own context.

Bibliography

Adler, N. J. (1997). *International dimensions of organizational behavior* (3rd ed.). PWS-Kent Publishers.

Adler, J. N. (2008). *International dimensions of organizational behaviour*. Thomson South-Western.

Bird, A., & Osland, J. (2000). Beyond sophisticated stereotyping: Cultural sense-making in context. *Academy of Management Executive, 14*, 65–79.

DiStefano, J. J., & Maznevski, M. L. (2000). Creating value with diverse teams in global management. *Organizational Dynamics, 29*(1), 45–63.

Doherty, W. J. (2016). Psychometric properties of the GlobeSmart profile. *Aperian Global*. Retrieved March 26, 2024, from https://docplayer.net/54432911-Psychometric-properties-of-the-globesmart-profile-william-j-doherty-ph-d.html

Dorfman, P., Javidan, M., Hanges, P., Dastmalchian, A., & House, R. (2012). GLOBE: A twenty year journey into the intriguing world of culture and leadership. *Journal of World Business, 47*(4), 504–518.

Ekelund, B. Z., & Langvik, E. (2008). *Diversity icebreaker: How to manage diversity processes*. Human Factors Publishing.

Hall, E. T. (1960). The silent language in overseas business. *Harvard Business Review, 38*(3), 87–96.

Hall, E. T. (1966). *The hidden dimension*. Doubleday.

Hall, E. T. (1973). *The silent language*. Anchor Press.

Hofstede, G. (1984). *Culture's consequences: International differences in work-related values*. Sage Publications.

Hofstede, G., & Bond, M. H. (1988). The Confucius connection: From cultural roots to economic growth. *Organizational Dynamics, 16*(4), 5–21.

Hofstede, G., Hofstede, G. J., & Minkov, M. (2010). *Culture and organizations: Software of the mind* (3rd ed.). McGraw-Hill.

House, R. J., Dorfman, P. W., Javidan, M., Hanges, P. J., & De Luque, M. F. S. (2014). *Strategic leadership across cultures: The GLOBE study of CEO leadership behavior and effectiveness in 24 countries* (2nd ed.). Sage Publications.

House, R. J., Hanges, P. J., Javidan, M., Dorfman, P. W., & Gupta, V. (2004). *Culture, leadership, and organizations: The GLOBE study of 62 societies*. Sage Publications.

Human Factors. (2023). *Diversity icebreaker* (Vol. 2023). Human Factors.

Kluckhohn, F. R., & Strodtbeck, F. L. (1961). *Variations in value orientations.* Row, Peterson & Company.

Lee, K., & Ashton, M. C. (2018). Psychometric properties of the HEXACO-100. *Assessment, 25*(5), 543-556.

Lee, K., & Ashton, M. C. (2023). *The HEXACO Personality Inventory – Revised* (Vol. 2023). University of Calgary.

Maznevski, M. (1994). Understanding our differences: Performance in decision-making groups with diverse members. *Human Relations, 47*(5), 531–552.

Maznevski, M. L., Gomez, C. B., DiStefano, J. J., Noorderhaven, N. G., & Wu, P.-C. (2002). Cultural dimensions at the individual level of analysis: The cultural orientations framework. *International Journal of Cross-Cultural Management, 2*(3), 275-295.

Meyer, E. (2014). *The culture map: Breaking through the invisible boundaries of global business.* Public Affairs.

Minda, J. P. (2022). *How to think: Understanding the way we decide, remember and make sense of the world.* Robinson.

Osland, J. S., & Bird, A. (2000). Beyond sophisticated stereotyping: Cultural sensemaking in context. *Academy of Management Perspectives, 14*(1), 65-77.

Parsons, T., & Shills, E. (1951). *Toward a general theory of action.* Harvard University Press.

Stasser, G. (1999). The uncertain role of unshared information in collective choices. In J. M. Levine, D. M. Messick, & L. L. Thompson (Eds.), *Shared cognition in organizations* (pp. 49-70). Psychology Press.

Trompenaars, F. (1996). Resolving international conflict: Culture and business strategy. *Business Strategy Review, 7*(3), 51-68.

Vaill, P. (2008). *Spirited leading and learning: Process wisdom for a new age.* Jossey-Bass.

Vaill, P., & Fearon, D. S. (2022). *On practice as a way of being.* myLibrary. Retrieved March 26, 2024, from https://www.mylibrary.world/practice

5 Communicating across Cultures: Bridging and Integrating

> Bridges are thresholds to other realities, archetypal, primal symbols of shifting consciousness. They are passageways, conduits, and connectors that connote transitioning, crossing borders, and changing perspectives. Bridges span liminal spaces between worlds, spaces I call *nepantla*, a Nahuatl word meaning *tierra entre medio*.
>
> From *Borderlands/La Frontera: The New Mestiza* by
> Gloria E. Anzaldúa, American Chicanas scholar (1942–2004)

Key Learning Objectives

At the end of this chapter, students will be able to:

- Define the three elements of Bridging: Engaging, Decentering, and Recentering.
- Analyze cross-cultural interactions and provide recommendations for improving them by applying insights from Mapping, Bridging, and Integrating.
- Identify the dangers of suppressing differences, leading to Destroying or Equalizing value in interpersonal interactions.
- Prepare to learn mindfully from mistakes in interpersonal interactions.

When one of the authors was working with an engineering and construction company, that company was involved in building some of the largest and most important bridging projects in their country locations. It was fascinating to talk with the engineers managing these projects. One from the United States told us:

The engineering part of the bridge is always interesting. Technical challenges related to the salt water and the tidal currents and potential hurricane winds. But the people part is even more interesting. On this project we're bridging two communities that have never gotten along very well, always fighting each other for resources and status. But now the bridge is bringing them together. They have to agree on a lot of the services for the bridge and flow around the entrances and exits. They realize they're going to be serving each other's communities a lot more, and they'd like that to be good for both economies. I've had to facilitate some tough conversations about different priorities, but when we find the agreement, it's amazing to think about how this will affect their future together.

Building a physical bridge needs to start with mapping the territory and all the elements in its context. Then, as construction begins, the bridge builders need to adapt to changing conditions and engage in effective problem-solving and execution processes to overcome the challenges. They need to build a bridge that is safe for transit, and that also fulfills the reasons for bringing the two sides together.

Bridging and Integrating, the second two stages of our Map-Bridge-Integrate model, look at the processes for building bridges, then crossing them and working together in interpersonal effectiveness.

Implementing IT Systems in a Global Organization

To illustrate Bridging and Integrating in the context of MBI, let's follow Canadian information technology (IT) leader Claudia as she works with her Argentinian colleague Lucas to try and get an IT system implemented.

> Claudia was a senior IT leader at a Canadian mining and minerals company. Her current priority was getting all the international subsidiaries implemented on the latest version of the enterprise resource planning (ERP) system. This version would create seamless dashboards at the corporate office to show the status of all operations and equipment, allowing for better responsiveness to problems and more timely decision-making about preventative repairs. The Argentinian subsidiary's implementation was significantly behind schedule, and she was trying to get Lucas, the Argentinian IT leader, to troubleshoot and get back on schedule.
>
> Here's how the issue showed up on Claudia's internal chat on Friday morning, with still no response from Lucas since Wednesday morning. This was so typical.
>
> <u>Claudia Tuesday 15:47</u>
> Hi Lucas, Hope you're doing well, avoiding that winter weather! Could you give me a quick update on the system implementation? I know you're behind schedule. We need to know what's holding things up so we can get you back on track. If you'd

prefer, I'm happy to chat. Just send me an invite for a time that works for us both, my calendar's up to date.

Lucas Tuesday 16:02
Hi Claudia. We've got the team from the energy alliance here these days, we're all getting to know each other's ways of operating. I understand renewable energy is a big priority for you at HQ, too? You may find this very interesting.

> **Claudia Tuesday 16:15**
> Hi Lucas, it does sound interesting, but the dashboard is behind schedule and that's holding up decisions. Let's figure out how to focus on that, then we can bring renewable energy into those decisions.

Lucas Wednesday 7:13
I will get back to you when I can. Have a great day!

> **Claudia Thursday 16:39**
> Hi again Lucas. Following up on this. Could I get a status report?

On Friday, Claudia just sighed. This had been going on for weeks. She kept asking Lucas for an update so she could help him solve the problems, and he always had something else going on, then didn't respond to her messages or meeting requests. She tried calling but he didn't pick up. Too bad she couldn't get on a plane to go see him. What else could she try?

She opened up her file with the GlobeSmart dimensions for Canada and Argentina and found the picture shown in Figure 5.1.

She had thought the cultural profiles between Canada and Argentina were remarkably similar. Both had a preference for Egalitarian power distribution, Direct communication, and taking Risks and action over uncertainty, although on all three dimensions Argentina's preference was much less strong than Canada's. She and Lucas had worked well together to get the implementation process set up. They respected each other's experience and

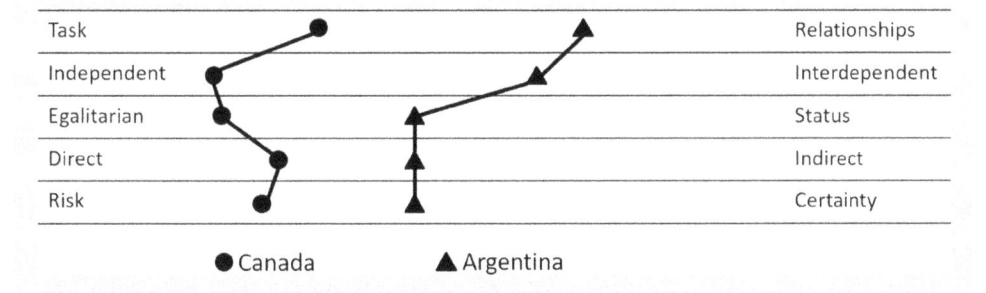

Task				Relationships
Independent				Interdependent
Egalitarian				Status
Direct				Indirect
Risk				Certainty

● Canada ▲ Argentina

Figure 5.1 Profiles for Canada and Argentina. Aperian GlobeSmart Platform.

knowledge, and they developed a good action plan together. So why was the implementation stalling?

Then Claudia took another look at the Task vs Relationships and Interdependent vs Independent dimensions and thought about how those differences might affect implementation over time. Even if Lucas was not a "typical" Argentinian, in his workplace there was probably an overall norm of preferring Relationships before Task, and Interdependence before Independence. If the local company were managing an energy alliance, the local CEO would probably expect everyone to be involved in building the relationships and would expect people to put aside their job descriptions to help build the alliance. How could she use that Mapping information to Bridge and Integrate?

Bridging Differences through Communication

As we discussed in Chapter 4, Mapping to understand the lens through which others see the world is an enormous aid to intercultural effectiveness. But this understanding provides little benefit as long as it remains latent. It must be put into use to help the flow of ideas among people in a conversation, a team, or an organization. The goal of these interpersonal flows is effective communication, or the transfer of meaning from one person to another as it was intended by the first person. Most managers recognize that effective communication within one's own culture is difficult enough. Interactions with people from different cultures are even more difficult. The challenge is to interpret correctly what a person from a different culture means by his or her words and actions. Even if interaction is aided by slowing speech, speaking more distinctly, listening more carefully, or asking more questions, there still remains the problem of interpreting the message. When your Japanese direct report says "yes," what does she mean? That she agrees, that she will undertake the action, that she accepts the importance of your input? It can make a big difference in implementing strategy!

Resolving miscommunication depends, in large part, on a manager's willingness to explain the problem rather than to blame the other person. And the quality of the explanation depends, in large part, on the manager's ability to map the other person's culture or background with respect to his or her own.

Although language is an important part of communication, communication is not simply a matter of understanding and speaking a language. Communication is broader than language alone. Someone who is able to speak five different

M — Map
Understand the Differences

B — Bridge
Communicate across the Differences
- Engage with motivation
- Decenter without blame
- Recenter to commonalities, new ideas, and norms

I — Integrate
Manage the Differences

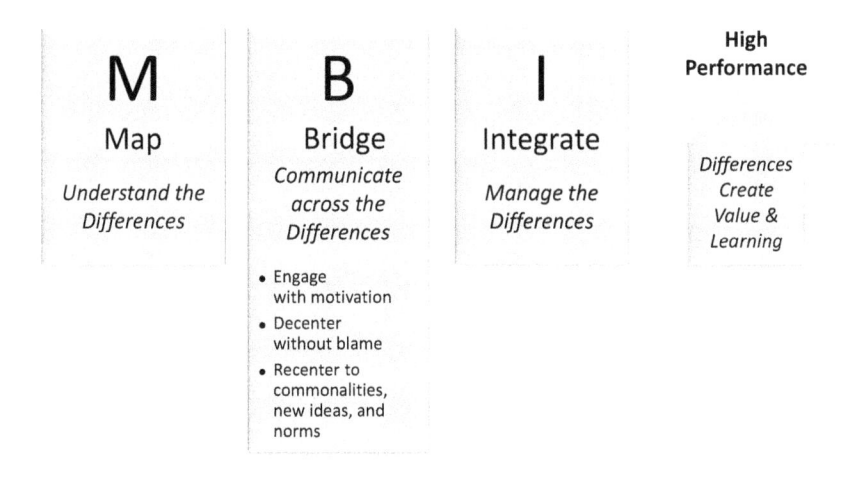

High Performance
Differences Create Value & Learning

Figure 5.2 Bridging in the context of Map-Bridge-Integrate.

languages still may not be able to understand issues from the viewpoint of those from another culture. Or, put more eloquently by an Eastern European manager to the Australians in an English-speaking group, "I can speak to you in your language, but I can't tell you what I am thinking in my own language."

There are three skills important to effective communication in a cross-cultural setting: **engaging**, **decentering**, and **recentering** (Maznevski, 1994a, 1994b). These three skills help improve all communication anywhere. In interactions within a single culture, people generally operate under the same set of background assumptions, so the steps can be conducted implicitly, often without people even being aware that they are doing them. The more culturally diverse the setting, the more difficult it is to accomplish these steps, and the more explicit they should be. But they also result in bigger payoffs.

This Bridging component of the MBI model is highlighted in Figure 5.2.

Engage to Be Open, Optimistic, and Active

Engaging is about setting the ground for communication. The most important place to set the ground is in one's own mind. Motivation is having the will to communicate across a cultural boundary both to be understood and to understand others. We are usually very good at the former but not as good at the latter. Motivation often comes with confidence from experience of effective communication, creating a virtuous cycle. People encountering important cross-cultural interactions for the first time are often worried about misunderstanding. However, with practice and even small successes, confidence increases rapidly and combines with motivation for positive engagement.

Engagement and motivation may sound simple, but actually acting this way is difficult in the rush and pressure of making decisions and getting things done. We have a tendency to assume that others are like us and forget the importance of deliberately seeing things differently. There are some simple things we can do to help ourselves, aside from just trying to remember to be motivated. For example, learning even some of the others' language signals motivation and optimism and opens windows into how the others think and what they value. Learning the language creates a positive, reinforcing cycle in cross-cultural communication, even if you do not approach fluency. Reading and studying about other countries' cultures, watching their movies, and meeting people from the culture and asking them to help you immerse in it are other ways of increasing your confidence in your cross-cultural communication ability. By mastering a cultural framework or "map," you develop the motivation and confidence to ask questions that will be especially helpful in preparing yourself for future understanding.

In Claudia's example, she thought she was engaging with motivation, but on reflection she wondered if she was really more motivated to get Lucas to accomplish *her* priority than to understand the situation.

Decenter to Transfer Meaning

Decentering is actively pushing yourself away from your own "center." It involves moving into the minds of other people to send messages in a way they will understand, and to listen in a way that allows you to understand the others from their own point of view. The fundamental idea of decentering is **empathy**: feeling and understanding as another person does. But decentering requires going beyond just having empathy, to using one's empathy in hearing and speaking. A child sees two cookies on the table and is about to take both. The mother says, "Now, if you take both cookies, how will your sister feel?" The child knows her sister will feel terrible (strong empathy) but goes ahead and takes both cookies anyway (not decentering). This interaction happens all the time in cross-cultural situations. The Canadian manager says, "I know that as a Chinese person it's hard for you to disagree openly with your boss, but I want you to know it's okay to do that with me. I don't mind when you disagree with me, in fact I expect you to." Or the Brazilian manager, "I know that in your [Scandinavian] culture it's not good to be open about feelings, but I am Brazilian and in my culture it's fine. So, when I express my anger, don't worry, it's okay." We all know people who understand exactly how we feel but nevertheless go ahead and say or do something awkward or hurtful anyway. This is practicing empathy without decentering.

There are two main elements to decentering. The first is perspective taking, which is the skill of being able to see things from the other person's point of view to the extent that you can speak and listen that way. The second is explaining without blame. When problems in communication do occur, and they inevitably will, it is critical that no one blames the other in a personal way, but that all parties seek an explanation in the situation: the differences in initial starting assumptions.

People who withhold blame and search for situation-based explanations of miscommunication interact more effectively. In our research, this emerged as the single best predictor of effective cross-cultural interaction.

Consider the sequence of events initiated when blame is suspended; this simple act leads an interaction into a positive cycle of decentering, exploring alternatives to build a shared reality, developing trust and common rules, and engaging with motivation to use different perspectives productively. This process not only resolves the present miscommunication but also prevents further ones and provides ideas for creative synergy.

Good decentering relies heavily on good Mapping. The map warns you that surprises and problems may have different explanations and provides you with some alternatives to explore. The Perceive-Interpret-Evaluate framework identified in Chapter 3 is also very helpful here. When differences are encountered, the people involved should try to come to a point where they can agree on a description of what they perceive: What are the tangible, concrete facts we are talking about? Next, they should explore their different interpretations: What do those facts mean to each person, and why? This is where the map provides a common language for sharing the analysis of interpretations. Finally, they should try to understand the different evaluations of the facts: Why do some people see something as an opportunity and others perceive the same thing as a threat? In cross-cultural situations, the greater the tendency to judge events, the greater the probability of making errors. Resisting interpretive and evaluative modes while maintaining a descriptive posture for as long as possible is the best protection against cultural blunders.

Decentering in Action: Scandinavian Managers Abroad

During our culture research studies, we developed a dialogue called "the Dark Side of Scandinavian Management." Scandinavian (the collective name that encompasses Norway, Sweden, and Denmark, sometimes Iceland, but not Finland, which is Nordic but not Scandinavian) management has often been described as unique, and several groups of Scandinavian managers asked us to help them understand the challenges they were facing when they worked with people from other cultures. Based on our own research and work done by Smith and colleagues (Smith et al., 2003; Smith, Peterson, & Schwartz, 2002), we developed a data-based picture of the Scandinavian management style (Mapping). Although all organizations and all leaders are different, and the Scandinavian country cultures differ from each other, Scandinavian managers and those from other cultures who work with Scandinavians agreed that the picture was generally accurate. We have continued to validate the perspective as cultures evolve. We mapped Scandinavian management style as:

Strongly interdependent – especially with respect to coworkers and society in general; the group is important, it is critical to get everyone aligned and on board, opinions of coworkers and subordinates are very important.

Strongly egalitarian – power and influence come not from your position but from your ideas and values and contributions to the group; considering your coworkers' and subordinates' ideas is often more important than considering your boss's ideas.

Action-oriented and pragmatic – take control of situations, influence them, get things done, focus on the task, change actions as necessary to achieve the goals.

Based on this Mapping exercise, we created a conversation that might happen between a Scandinavian manager and his or her non-Scandinavian subordinates outside Scandinavia if Bridging were not engaged. This hypothetical conversation brought tears of laughter to Scandinavian executives who recognized themselves in it.

1. *Scandinavian manager ...*
   Asks subordinates and coworkers for their opinions, tries to negotiate alignment.
2. *The non-Scandinavian employees ...*
   Don't understand why the Scandinavian boss can't just decide. May want to make decision quickly so planning phase can begin.
3. *Scandinavian manager ...*
   Responds to the requests and anxiety for decisions by asking more questions to get ideas and create alignment.
4. *The non-Scandinavian employees ...*
   Become even more frustrated with the lack of decision-making ("we'll never get to planning").
5. *Scandinavian manager ...*
   Becomes paralyzed by not wanting to act in an authoritarian way. Not sure what to do.

6. *The non-Scandinavian employees ...*
   Are frustrated with lack of speed, lose respect for the business capability of the Scandinavians.
7. *Scandinavian manager ...*
   Finally, in frustration, makes and announces a decision.
8. *The non-Scandinavian employees ...*
   Relieved, voice agreement with the boss.
9. *Scandinavian manager ...*
   Assumes agreement = alignment and signals readiness for action, shifts attention to other matters.
10. *The non-Scandinavian employees ...*
    Either wait for further directions for action or act in unaligned ways (depending on culture and situation).
11. *Scandinavian manager ...*
    Becomes frustrated by lack of action or unaligned action, waits for it to improve.
12. *The non-Scandinavian employees ...*
    Continue to wait or to act in many different directions.
13. *Scandinavian manager ...*
    Becomes frustrated with unenlightened subsidiaries.
14. *The non-Scandinavian employees ...*
    Underperform according to standards or expectations.
15. *Scandinavian manager ...*
    "Knows" (assumes) that everyone will contribute to their potential for the group and will self-correct performance. Does nothing.
16. *The non-Scandinavian employees ...*
    "Know" (assume) everything is fine because the boss has not said anything. Nothing changes.
17. *Scandinavian manager ...*
    Waits patiently for performance to self-correct; perhaps manages the environment to make it easier for people to self-correct.
18. *The non-Scandinavian employees ...*
    Start to recognize performance problem but see that boss doesn't "care" about it. Nothing changes.
19. *Scandinavian manager ...*
    Becomes frustrated with unenlightened, unempowered subsidiaries.
20. *The non-Scandinavian employees ...*
    Become convinced that Scandinavians avoid conflict and are weak managers.

This sequence shows what happens when decentering is not practiced by anyone involved. Notice the evolution to blaming that comes from not understanding each other's starting point: Scandinavian managers assuming the employees are unenlightened, the non-Scandinavian employees assuming Scandinavian managers are weak. Scandinavian managers who are effective in other cultures adapt this process through decentering in several ways. They report that they believe that in most situations getting ideas from subordinates and developing alignment is the best way to make decisions and implement change. However, when they first go to a new culture where hierarchy is stronger, they are more likely to use their position as boss to manage explicitly a process of getting ideas from others. They "command" people to take part and contribute their own ideas directly, and they use the hierarchy to dictate each part of the process. Effective Scandinavian managers abroad are also more likely to incorporate specific planning into the early discussions, recognizing others' need to make firm plans.

> Claudia thought about decentering and realized she could decenter much more explicitly on Relationships and Interdependence. She started a new chat message with Lucas. To her delight, she got immediate responses to all her messages.
>
> **Claudia Friday 9:04**
> Hi Lucas, Hope you're having a great week. I'm really curious to know more about the renewable energy alliance. How's it going?
>
> **Lucas Friday 9:13**
> Hi Claudia, thanks for asking. It's been a busy week and we'll be working all weekend too, but it's going really well. Getting the electricity from the solar and wind farms to the mine is going to be a bit complicated due to the terrain, but we're brainstorming ways to work with the different stakeholders we need on board.
>
> **Claudia Friday 9:23**
> Wow, sounds complex. We have that challenge in Western Canada too. When you figure it out, let us know!
>
> **Lucas Friday 9:31**
> We definitely will. This alliance is with an excellent partner.
>
> Okay, she was getting responses, but how to get back to the problem of the IT system implementation?

Recenter to Align and Agree

The third step to effective communication is **recentering**, or establishing a **common reality** and agreeing on common rules (Baumann Montecinos & Grünfelder, 2022). Like the other elements, this is easier said than done. For example, the implicit definition and purpose of a meeting varies from one culture to the next, with some cultures using meetings to discuss perspectives and come to a joint decision, and other cultures using meetings to publicly formalize decisions that were discussed informally among smaller subgroups of a team. A multicultural team that has not addressed even this basic definition is bound to find at least some members very frustrated with the first meeting. Good mapping helps find a common definition and give the team a point of leverage.

Members of a multi-site global R&D team differed enormously on every cultural dimension except one: virtually all preferred Certainty strongly over Risk. They were able to use their common ground of the preference to plan carefully to discuss their differences and work together. A team managing a strategic alliance in a manufacturing technology firm consisted of members from all over Europe, North America, and Asia. Like the team of R&D scientists, they had strong differences on many cultural dimensions. Coincidentally, though, all were engineers for at least some part of their career, and they shared the same focus on Task first, with a balance of Certainty and Risk. Their common reality was based on what had to be done (changed and controlled), and they used this point to launch discussions about how to divide the work and what task processes to use.

Common norms for interacting must be established. Interestingly, it is less important to agree on a single set of norms for everyone and more important to agree on a range of acceptable norms, with acceptance for some degrees of freedom for individual team members. As we showed in the opening of this chapter, it is futile to expect someone to behave in a way that is uncomfortable to them yet still expect them to participate to their full potential. Asking someone who prefers a thinking orientation to jump in and "do" because that is the dominant mode and "you'll just have to adapt" is like asking that person not to bother contributing their best ideas to the group.

The most effective interactions reflect ways of allowing different members to work within the group differently. Finding these norms is a creative process. It takes time and relies on strong relationships and trust within the group. But, like good preparing and decentering, the effort is well worth it. When the processes are not explored or discussed to find common ground, serious misunderstandings can occur, even when the cultures are not dramatically different.

Recentering in Action: A Multicultural Team

We captured a classic example of cross-cultural communication when we videoed a group of executives discussing the possibility of their company acquiring another firm.[1] The group consisted of five senior managers: two from the United States and

---

[1] This work was led by our colleague and long-time coauthor J. DiStefano. We gratefully acknowledge his insights, particularly in this section.

one each from the United Kingdom, Japan, and Uruguay. We video-recorded them at their request, to help them develop their Bridging skills. After studying various aspects of the potential deal, they had come together to make a recommendation.

The discussion was dominated by the American and British managers, who were concerned about the lack of compatible strategies and financial problems in the negotiations. In the first hour, two key incidents happened that showed the need for recentering. First, the Uruguayan manager tried three times to introduce the issue of who would constitute the top executive team should the deal be struck. Would the buying company or the acquired organization supply the key executives for the merged entity? Each time he tried to raise the issue, the four others brushed his comments aside, and he eventually became frustrated. Second, after 40 minutes of discussion, the British manager stood up, went to the flip chart, and wrote: "Do Nothing!" He added, "I don't usually entertain this option, but I really think in this situation it is our best choice. The deal is far from being ready to make." There was a moment of silence, then the Japanese manager quietly said, "Wait." The others thought that he was asking for a chance to discuss the "Do Nothing" option, but he said nothing more. The British manager crossed out "Do Nothing!" and wrote next to it, "Wait," then he proceeded with his next point.

After one hour of discussion, the group stopped and looked at their video before continuing. They analyzed the two incidents above. Regarding the Uruguayan's concerns, the group learned that for him, relationships were fundamental and related to the financial and strategic analysis of the deal. If certain members of the acquired organization were maintained, the price could be lower and returns could be more certain than if those individuals were not part of the deal. The Anglo-American managers were more focused on quantitative and product-market issues and missed the potential link. Through this discussion the group recentered around a new common objective: to identify combinations of factors that could create a positive investment outcome, then to analyze the extent to which it was possible to create those combinations of factors. This was a more complex goal, but one that the group members all agreed to and that eventually led to better value creation for the company.

The group then explored the British proposal to "Do Nothing!" vs. the Japanese suggestion to "Wait." The British executive literally meant "don't do anything more; proceed to look for other deals unless the other party indicates a change in the conditions." In contrast, the Japanese executive's "Wait" was filled with subtle actions including continuing to get to know the other parties, extending attempts to get more information about their business, and so on. Both wanted action, but in the British manager's mind, "waiting" was a passive mode and to be avoided. It was better to do nothing on this deal and move on with other things. In the Japanese manager's mind, "waiting" was a very active mode and would help create the conditions for a good deal. The group members realized that the two actions could be complementary and recentered around a more comprehensive strategy of concerted dialogue and extended research, including into alternative deals.

Finally, the group discussed some of the norms they observed, such as the dominance of three of the members. They realized that the Uruguayan had posed his ideas in the form of questions ("Don't you think we should explore from which company the top officers will be drawn?"), an indirect mode of communication. The Anglo-Americans were much more direct in their phrasing ("That's irrelevant until we get the financials and strategy agreed to!"). The team learned to recenter on norms by picking up the Uruguayan's cues about his opinions and learned to listen and take him seriously, even when he phrased his ideas as questions. It was also quite evident from the video that the Japanese manager rarely spoke unless someone asked him a question directly. All the others knew that this was a characteristic of Japanese culture, but they had not developed a set of norms that would constructively encourage the Japanese member's participation. They recentered with an agreement that in the future, at the beginning of every new stage of the discussion, they would go around the table and have each person make a two-minute statement. They would assign a facilitator (a rotating role) to ensure this happened with discipline, and that the facilitator also had the responsibility of ensuring balanced contributions afterwards.

By recentering around a common view of the task and situation, and around specific norms that facilitated participation, the team enhanced their Bridging and were able to provide much more valuable advice to the company (Integrating).

> Claudia realized she really needed to talk with Lucas to get beyond Mapping and Decentering. At the Canadian corporate office, it was common for people to just call each other or set up a meeting for a few minutes on Zoom. She thought Lucas would probably appreciate the opportunity to set up a call in advance, and to make it long enough for a conversation that included time to build the relationship. To decenter further, the agenda should be "how we can help each other" rather than "tell me about the IT project." Her efforts brought a good response for a next step.
>
> > Claudia Friday 9:42
> > I'd love to hear more about the alliance. It may help me out on a related project I'm working on here, and I may be able to connect you with someone here who has a

bit more info on it. Would you have time to talk next week? How about an hour on Tuesday afternoon or Wednesday morning?

Lucas Friday 9:51
That's a great idea. We probably have a lot to talk about. I can do Tuesday at 15:00 my time, that's 14:00 yours. Is that okay? Would you be able to send the invite? I'm working on my phone right now and it's hard to get the software right from the phone.

Claudia Friday 9:54
Perfect, I'll send the invite now.

Claudia felt like she was on her way to Integrating and she looked forward to Tuesday's call.

Reflection Question 5.1: Bridging

Observe a wide variety of interactions, paying attention to how often people jump to judgment and even blame without considering that there may simply be different perspectives. Try listening to conversations, watching documentaries and movies, or reading commentary and opinion articles. Then pay attention to your own communication. How often do you move into judgment mode without considering all the perspectives? It's impossible to eliminate this leap – it's part of what we do as human beings. But it's important to become aware of it.

Integrating to Manage and Build on the Differences

The final component of the MBI model is **Integrating** the differences (DiStefano & Maznevski, 2000). Communicating effectively (Bridging) means the people in the interaction understand each other. But they still may not be able to agree or collaborate.

Integrating is where cultural synergy actually gets created. In Chapters 3 and 4 we emphasized several times the notion that no one culture is inherently better than others. Every culture was developed by a group of people to help them be efficient and to identify each other as a group that offers mutual help. In a highly complex environment, no one culture can ever provide all the answers. Integrating is the process of drawing on the strengths of each culture for the situation at hand and combining them for synergy. With effective Bridging, the people interacting have a good understanding of what they each bring to the situation. In

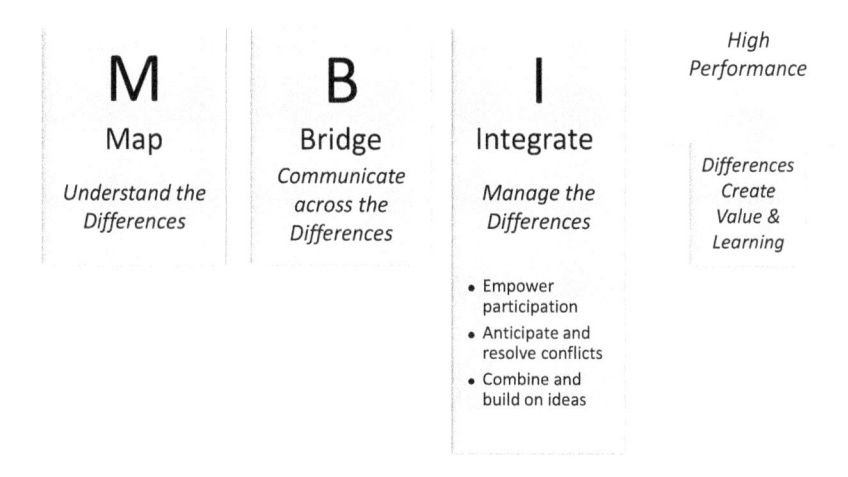

M	**B**	**I**	*High Performance*
Map	Bridge	Integrate	
Understand the Differences	*Communicate across the Differences*	*Manage the Differences*	*Differences Create Value & Learning*
		• Empower participation • Anticipate and resolve conflicts • Combine and build on ideas	

Figure 5.3 Integrating in the context of MBI.

fact, as we said earlier in this chapter, great Bridging almost automatically leads to effective Integrating, because great Bridging conversations set up all the elements for Integrating. Here we identify the three main behaviors for ensuring that great Integrating happens as well: empowering participation, resolving conflicts, and building on ideas.

Integrating in the context of MBI is highlighted in Figure 5.3.

Empowering Participation

To realize the benefits of different perspectives and ideas, it is necessary to express and listen to the ideas in the first place. Different cultures have different ways of offering information and input, and the norms of one culture often suppress participation from people of other cultures. People from cultures with a strong Status orientation, for example, are not likely to state their ideas directly in a group of which their direct superior or a higher-status person is also a member. In contrast, people from Egalitarian cultures are more likely to assert their ideas and assume that if someone has an idea, they will say it (and conversely, if they've said nothing, they have no ideas). The first Integrating challenge in a multicultural interaction, then, is to ensure that all ideas are contributed and heard.

It is especially helpful to notice whether there are systematic differences in participation rates in dialogue. Does one person speak more than others? Do people from one culture speak more than people from others? As long-time professors in multicultural settings, we know there is a strong tendency for people from Anglo cultures to dominate class and small group discussions in terms of amount of time spoken, even when they are a small minority culturally and even when the class is not taught in English. Anglo norms generally combine a first priority for Task rather than Relationships with preferences for Independent, Egalitarian, and Direct norms and Risk-taking in action. This combination of preferences is associated with a definition of meetings as a place "to discuss openly and decide," and the combinations reinforce each other to encourage and reward people speaking up freely to offer ideas, thus (inadvertently) suppressing contributions from others.

There are ways of engaging all group members and facilitating their participation. In the example given earlier, the Japanese manager hardly spoke in the first half hour; his "wait" was his lone contribution during the first 45 minutes. After the break to analyze the video and recenter, one of the Americans in the group noticed his silence and invited participation by saying, "If I recall, Sugano-san, a couple of years ago you had some experience in a merger similar to the one we are discussing. What do you think about this situation?" Notice that the invitation drew on the Japanese manager's experience, respecting this Status-orientation cue. What followed was a highly relevant discourse, fluidly expressed, which had a big impact on the shape of the group's recommendation. When his involvement was sought in a way that acknowledged his own cultural norms, this otherwise infrequent participant made an important contribution.

The most important way of **empowering participation** is to vary the modes of engaging – to broaden the definition of "meeting" to include a series of connected interactions. For example, people from some cultures – such as those preferring Status-oriented norms – may prefer to provide written input rather than to appear to be dominating or advancing their own interest by speaking in the group. Sending out written agendas well in advance of a meeting can help members prepare themselves this way and circulate responses before the meeting. In some cultures – such as those preferring Indirect norms – it's more appropriate to provide ideas outside the context of formal group meetings. A series of private, face-to-face meetings can be sequenced to gather ideas and input for broader discussion, without attributing them to individuals.

Most people find creative ways to garner everyone's input once they accept the possibility of having different norms for different people. In a situation with extensive multicultural interaction, such as a team or a negotiation, it is helpful to identify someone to play the role of facilitator to ensure that participation is genuinely empowered. This can even be a rotating role, to develop further Mapping and Bridging capabilities.

Anticipating and Resolving Disagreements

As more ideas from various viewpoints are expressed, there is an increasing likelihood that disagreements will emerge. The way these conflicts are handled becomes the next cross-cultural challenge. Even the way conflict is expressed, quite apart from how it gets resolved, varies in different cultural traditions. In Indirect cultures, it is inappropriate to express conflict openly. For a manager from a Direct culture, where open expression of disagreement is valued, the first problem becomes detecting the existence of the conflict. Moreover, in Indirect cultures, a disagreement may be expressed very subtly or indirectly through a third party. In Direct cultures, conflict is more likely to be stated bluntly, in words with little ambiguity. When these norms are not understood, frustration or anger is likely to be the result. If I am accustomed to norms of expressing conflict more directly, I may be frustrated by behavior that I read as sending "mixed signals," or I may conclude the other person is confused or cannot make up his or her mind. If I expect indirect expression of conflict, I might feel insulted by what I experience as impolite or crass comments from the other person who feels she or he is "just putting the issue on the table."

The best way to deal with these issues is to use the Mapping and Bridging components of the model noted in the previous sections. Mapping provides a way to anticipate when conflict may occur; the Bridging techniques (engage, decenter, recenter) provide tools for reaching a common understanding and shared set of rules or norms for resolving conflicts and avoiding them in the future. Remember that the single best predictor for effective cross-cultural interaction is refraining from judgment or blame and instead looking for explanations for different views. Effective communication is more than half of effective conflict resolution.

Building on Ideas

Even if the Mapping framework is well understood, communication skills are well developed, and participation and conflict issues are managed effectively, there is still a key component to realizing the potential in cross-cultural encounters, namely moving forward and building on the ideas. There are cultural barriers in this phase of activity, too. Some cultural preferences would lead a person to push their ideas (Independent), while another orientation (Status) is more likely to lead to deference to authority. If you are in a group with several cultures, there might be an agreement (common rules of interaction) to surface ideas without attributing them to individuals or using an individual's ideas as a starting point for discussion. The main idea is to encourage the exploration of ideas with the conscious attempt to invent new ideas, to build on the ideas initially surfaced. A real stimulus to innovation is to try to do more than just combine ideas and to avoid compromises. Finally, striving to find solutions to issues or problems that are acceptable to all (another rule for interaction or norm for behavior) is a further way to increasing the probability of getting synergy from the diversity in the group. Trying to invent new ideas from those available and reaching for solutions to which everyone can agree are ideals that are difficult to accomplish. But even setting them as objectives will help a multicultural team achieve its potential for high performance.

The award-winning design firm IDEO has developed and refined processes that take diverse ideas and inputs and build on them to create highly value-creating solutions (Kelley & Kelley, 2013; Kelley & Littman, 2001). Their rules and techniques for brainstorming and prototyping are especially helpful with diverse teams. The firm's founder, Tom Kelley, says this about "brainstormers":

> Hot brainstormers may generate a hundred or more ideas, ten of which may be solid leads ... People talk after brainstormers, sharing wild or practical ideas. A greater brainstormer gives you a fantastic feeling of possibility, and an hour later you walk out of the room a little richer for the experience. I think that sense of spontaneous team combustion is why we've been able to find so many unusual solutions to seemingly intractable problems. (Kelley & Littman, 2001, p. 62)

We will discuss design thinking in more detail in Chapter 10; here, we want to highlight these techniques in their Integrating role.

The complete MBI model is repeated here as a summary in Figure 5.4.

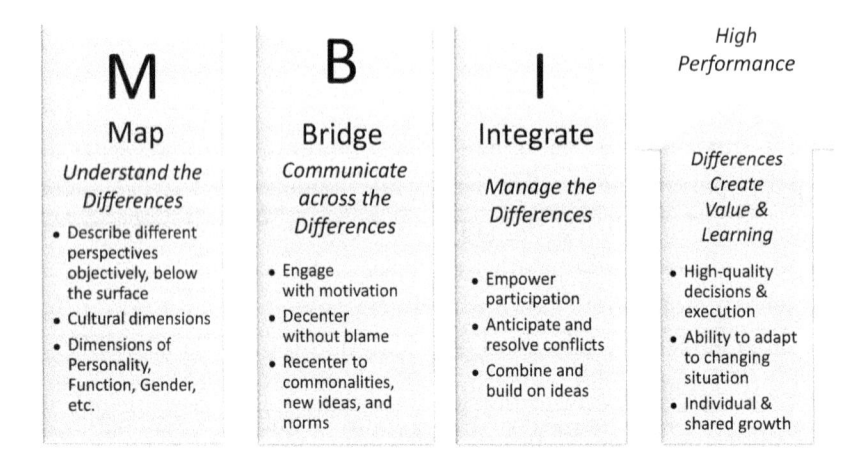

M	B	I	*High Performance*
Map	**Bridge**	**Integrate**	
Understand the Differences	*Communicate across the Differences*	*Manage the Differences*	*Differences Create Value & Learning*
• Describe different perspectives objectively, below the surface • Cultural dimensions • Dimensions of Personality, Function, Gender, etc.	• Engage with motivation • Decenter without blame • Recenter to commonalities, new ideas, and norms	• Empower participation • Anticipate and resolve conflicts • Combine and build on ideas	• High-quality decisions & execution • Ability to adapt to changing situation • Individual & shared growth

Figure 5.4 MBI full model.

Integrating in Action

Before meeting with Lucas, Claudia spent a bit of time learning some basic Spanish words and phrases so she could greet and thank Lucas in his own language. It was fun, and she enjoyed learning the different regional variations of greetings.

Her meeting with Lucas kicked off a series of effective interactions. Lucas was amused but very appreciative of Claudia's efforts to say a few words in Spanish. Claudia was careful to focus on relationships by learning more about Lucas and his family and sharing more about hers. Claudia's ethnic background was Italian, and this focus on family felt very natural to her, even if a bit out of place at work. She found she enjoyed bringing different parts of her life together. Claudia asked Lucas more about the renewable energies alliance, since it was clearly the priority Lucas was focused on. She learned that the Argentinian subsidiary was innovating with some very important transmission and storage solutions as well as further partnerships with local utilities companies. She didn't think that Corporate understood just how well the Argentinians had developed this, and she identified several Corporate colleagues who would like to know more.

Claudia was enjoying the conversation about potential innovation so much, she was a bit surprised when Lucas said at one point, "I've been thinking about how we can jump ahead with this dashboard project so we integrate the renewables information as it comes online, rather than implementing it as a separate project after. I might need a bit more help from Corporate. We've had to stop working with several of our IT subcontractors because inflation rates here made it just too expensive to keep them. But here are some ideas I've been thinking of ... ."

On later reflection, Claudia was amazed at how much progress they had made in one meeting. She thought she'd have to slow down the pace, but she could see the possibility now that they would finish in good time, especially taking the renewables implementation into account. And she'd identified some other ideas that could help the company overall. She and Lucas worked together very effectively over the next weeks and months to implement this and other projects.

> ## Reflection Question 5.2: Integrating
>
> This reflection will focus on empowering participation. Think about a meeting that you go to on a regular basis that involves at least three people. It could be a weekly sales meeting, a production review meeting, a planning and reporting meeting, a club meeting, or anything else. What are the norms for participation? For example, who speaks when, and how do you know whose turn it is? Does everyone feel comfortable with these norms? Are there people who might say more, or provide more innovation, if the norms were different? If you can, encourage different modes of participation during the meeting. For example, try having everyone write individual responses before anyone shares, or having small subgroups discuss ideas before sharing with everyone. Explicitly reinforce ideas that are different from the others. What effect does this have on the meeting? On people engaging? On you?

Troubleshooting Your Cross-Cultural Interaction: Destroying and Equalizing

Although there are many ways in which cross-cultural interaction can go wrong, they tend to fall into two basic patterns: destroying and equalizing (DiStefano & Maznevski, 2000). The two patterns have different starting points and dynamics, but both can end in suboptimal performance and repairs to be made. In this section we'll diagnose them both, compare them with the positive dynamic of Creating value described in the MBI model, and identify how to avoid them or turn them around.

Destroying Value

Here is how the conversation between Claudia and Lucas *might have looked* if they had gone down a **Destroying** path after the first chat we included, when Claudia asked for a status report and received no answer. Notice that neither is intending to be destructive; both are trying to move things forward in what they think is the most appropriate way. But neither is mindful about Mapping, Bridging, or Integrating in this cross-cultural encounter.

> <u>Claudia Friday 9:04</u>
> Hi Lucas, I know you're busy but I need that information for my status report. Could you tell me what's happening with the implementation project?

<u>Lucas Friday 11:26</u>
Claudia I will get to it when I can but I have other priorities. Corporate maybe doesn't understand what we're doing here.

> <u>Claudia Tuesday 11:41</u>
> Corporate appreciates the renewables project, Lucas. But if they can't see the operational information on the dashboard it holds up the decision-making.
> When can we talk about this?

<u>Lucas Wednesday 16:03</u>
I will ask my CEO when I can take some time to focus on this. He will understand the Corporate priorities.

This exchange is likely to spiral into conflict and more missed deadlines, with higher implementation costs and less effective implementation.

The Destroyer dynamic is common because of the efficiency of within-culture interactions. We are so used to our culture's assumptions about how things are done, we tend to jump straight to those patterns rather than question them. When two people "mindlessly" pursue two very different paths in parallel, each of which is efficient in itself but incompatible with the other, the result is conflict and inefficiency. Moreover, the Destroyer dynamic is toxic because of the nature of identity associated with culture. When someone doesn't seem to respect our norms and values, the ones we know deeply and take for granted, we experience this as an identity threat. Implicitly, below the surface, we feel we're being told that the way we do things is wrong and devalued; that we should suppress a part of who we are. This tends to make us feel defensive and closed, and therefore less likely to be open to seeing things the other person's way.

If important performance milestones are being missed or deliverable quality is below expectations, you're probably well into the Destroyer dynamic and it may be hard to turn it around. The best way to recognize the Destroyer dynamic early is to pay attention to (be mindful of) your own and others' emotional reactions and surprises. If you find yourself negatively surprised with the way someone has responded about how to work together or progress on task, pause and ask yourself if you may have different ways of working that you haven't articulated yet. Even more important, but also more difficult, is to notice (be mindful of) negative surprises that your behavior creates for others. What assumption did you just challenge for the other person? In these situations, ask questions that lead to Mapping, that show curiosity about each other. Good questions include "How would you normally … ?" or "In your experience, what would you … ?" or "What did you learn from projects like this before?"

In sum, the Destroying pattern spirals downward for two reasons. It raises conflict and interrupts efficiency and acceptance of ideas and ways of doing things; and it leads to defensive emotions and behaviors, with people less open about understanding others. The best way to avoid or turn it around is to be mindful of negative surprises, both in yourself and in others, and to ask questions that value and explicitly request other perspectives.

Equalizing Value

Most people working in cross-cultural interactions want to avoid conflict and seek the best outcome for all involved. Ironically, because of these intentions, the **Equalizing** pattern is very common. It can lead to expected performance quality in the short term, and people are caught by surprise if it suddenly turns into the Destroying dynamic. This is why it's critical to be aware of the pattern and prevent it before the turning point.

The Equalizing dynamic focuses on common ground – it sticks to what we share, the overlap of our perspectives, something we can all agree on – without *also* considering differences. The common ground is often a set of professional norms or company policies. It could also be a minimum set of norms from the dominant culture, such as the "common global business culture" (which most people see as very close to Anglo norms) or the headquarters or corporate office culture.

Here is the Claudia and Lucas conversation, after the first exchange, recast in an Equalizing mode. It draws on the norms of the IT profession.

> **Claudia Friday 9:04**
> Hi Lucas, I've been looking through your backlog list on the intranet. I see you've got a deliverables meeting scheduled for today. Can I see the visuals for that?
>
> **Lucas Friday 11:17**
> Hi Claudia. We've postponed that stand-up until next week, some other stakeholder priorities jumped the queue.
>
> **Claudia Friday 11:23**
> Okay make sure to put that info in the intranet so I can track the project. Will this change the backlog list too? If so, make sure to update that. Then let's schedule a status meeting next week to go over the queue.
>
> **Lucas Friday 16:27**
> Yes, it will mean changing some priorities, I'll update the intranet when I have a chance. Looking forward to sharing it with you next week.

In this Equalizing dialogue, both Claudia and Lucas refer to the company's internal jargon, processes, and mechanisms for managing IT projects. The conversation is very efficient, and cultural differences are almost invisible. Typically, for a relatively straightforward or short-term task or interaction, performance will meet expectations. Why is this a problem, then?

The first problem is simply about suboptimizing performance quality. The Equalizing approach doesn't take advantage of the different resources brought to the interaction and is unlikely to create extra value for the customer or the firm. It's also unlikely to lead to learning and development – the people involved won't be better prepared to take on more challenging tasks in the future, for example.

But still, it looks less risky and certainly less time- and effort-consuming than Creating, right? So why not Equalize? The deeper problem with Equalizing is that, like Destroying, it suppresses part of who people think they are, their sense of identity. This is especially true if the Equalizing norms are based on "global business culture" or the headquarters' culture.

Think about a time when you worked on a team where you felt like you couldn't be yourself. When you had to work, for a sustained period of time, in a way that was not comfortable for you. When someone's perspectives and ways of working are suppressed over time, they act through a filter. They're constantly spending energy thinking about how to present their ideas and how to participate, rather than on the act of creating and presenting ideas and reflecting on others' ideas in the first place. Most people in this situation eventually become frustrated and disengaged. They may even initiate serious conflicts or, more likely, simply leave the situation. So, what looks like a safe approach – Equalizing – very often turns into a Destroying approach over time.

It is hard to recognize the Equalizer pattern in its early stages, because it can look very positive. People are happy to talk with each other, and things are moving smoothly on the surface. The best way to avoid Equalizing in the first place is to engage in a Mapping exercise – a conversation that explicitly engages both similarities and differences in a systematic way. This creates a positive norm about bringing uniqueness to the interaction. Further down the line, be mindful of comments like "it's what we have in common that matters, we don't need to worry about differences," and "we have lots of cultures involved but we never even notice cultural differences, they certainly don't get in the way." When you notice these comments, it may be time to revisit Mapping. You may have observed that the Creating conversation that started this chapter off was longer than either the Destroying or Equalizing conversation. Avoiding Equalizing takes time and effort – if you invest in this at the beginning, it will pay off with greater effectiveness later.

In sum, the Equalizing pattern is a problem for two reasons. It suboptimizes performance by ignoring the great resource of different perspectives for innovation; and over time it almost inevitably transitions into a Destroying pattern because at least some people in the interaction must suppress an important part of their sense of identity. The best way to avoid it is to engage in Mapping at the beginning and be mindful of a focus on commonality without valuing difference.

Interaction over Technology: Virtual Communication

So much of cross-cultural communication happens over e-mail, chat, phone, video call, or other technology that it's important we address the implications. An important theme of this book is that mindful global leadership requires taking account of the context of the interaction. In this chapter, we again emphasized the importance of understanding the other in order to decenter and recenter in Bridging. We cautioned that we tend to take for granted that others' contexts and deep-level assumptions are the same as ours, so for effective interaction we need to explicitly overcome that tendency and learn more about others in a nonjudgmental way.

The main challenge with interacting through communications technology is that the context of a message is either completely stripped away (e.g., with e-mail or messaging) or it is greatly diminished (e.g., with voice or video). We therefore have an even greater tendency to ignore context and deeper understanding behind the message. We send e-mails or text messages, forgetting that the sender may not read the text with the same background assumptions and therefore may interpret it differently than intended. We don't see the context in which the sender receives the text, so we don't know the initial reaction (confusion, frustration ...). We present information in video meetings with as little "background distraction" as possible, forgetting that the "background distraction" would actually provide contextual information for the other person, to help them better understand the meaning of our messages. With virtual work so ubiquitous, it is common to work with a virtual background. It is understandable that people want privacy rather than showing their home backgrounds. But unfortunately, these virtual backgrounds completely remove any contextual information that could help in building relationships or deepening insights into the communication.

Every global leader we know – even the highly skilled ones – has had the experience of an unfortunate misinterpretation of an e-mail they've sent in a hurry. But technological communications, well used, can help cross-cultural communications enormously. For example, because e-mails and text messages are written, senders can revise them several times to make sure they have the right meaning, even check with others before sending "for real." Receivers can read the message several times over to make sure they have the right interpretation. We've seen several innovative best practices that combine different technologies for high-quality cross-cultural communication.

For example, a great sequence is e-mail or text message → voice or video call → e-mail or text message. The first message sets up the context:

Let's have a conversation about the concrete and cement accounts. I'd like to share with you some analysis from the R&D team about technical applications for a new compound and get your ideas about potential customers. The initial analysis is attached. Is tomorrow (Wednesday 17) at 18:30 your time (14:30 my time) good for a video call, using Teams?

Notice that the message doesn't make any conclusions or recommendations. It does set a clear agenda, with clear roles. It also shares information for future discussion and provides a good context for that information. It sets up a time for a call that gives the receiver enough time to read and reflect on the question and analysis, and it specifies date and time zones explicitly, using unambiguous formats (decentering). During the video call, both parties can take advantage of the synchronous communication and the ability to see facial expressions, share screens, draw pictures, and more to facilitate a rich discussion.

After the video call, a message follows quickly:

Thanks for the call today. Here is what I heard from you about potential customers ... [summary of discussion]. I also heard you say that the new compound should ideally be adjusted more for hot weather and typhoon applications. I believe we agreed that next steps for me are ... and for you are .... Would you please let me know what I might have missed in my summary? Or any other ideas you've had since?

Again, note the decentering and recentering in the message – from specifying the appointment in different time zones in the first message to summarizing the content of the meeting afterward. This message → call → message sequence is ideal for combining the cross-cultural needs for contextual understanding and careful reflection with the richness of interactive dialogue. By varying the modes of participation, it allows for different cultural preferences to play to their strengths at different times.

Another creative best practice we've seen uses easily available translation software, such as Google Translate. We know that the translations are not fluent, but they are very useful in a "reverse translation" technique. Imagine an interaction between a Japanese manager and a French manager, neither of whom speaks the other's language. The French manager writes an e-mail in French and puts it into Google Translate to translate it into Japanese. Then the French manager opens up another window of Google Translate, takes the Japanese translation, and translates it into French. Likely, the two French versions are different in some important ways. The French manager therefore goes back and clarifies the original French text, perhaps adding more sentences and context, then repeats the reverse translation process until the two French versions are similar. At that point, the French manager sends the Japanese translation. The Japanese manager would apply the same technique in responding. One interesting implication of this technique is that both managers, over time, are likely to become more precise and mindful in their native language so that the translate-retranslate cycle becomes shorter and communication more effective.

In sum, communication technologies enable cross-boundary communication, and a smart combination of these technologies can enhance interaction effectiveness. This requires mindful leadership, consciously taking into account context and explicitly Bridging across differences. The lack of context in communication over technology often leads to people forgetting the importance of context, resulting in poor interactions.

Who Should Adapt?

The MBI process assumes that at least some people involved in an interaction are adapting to the others. But who should adapt? This is a difficult question.

A number of factors influence the answer. As a general rule, the burden for adaptation usually rests with the party who is seen as the foreigner. The sheer force of numbers probably influences this. But this rule of the majority also misses significant opportunities for learning and innovating, as we saw in the example of the culturally mixed team of managers discussing the acquisition.

Power of resources is another strong factor. An American joint venture in Dhaka may choose to emphasize American cultural values and management practices in spite of the location and overwhelming majority of the Bangladeshi population, simply as a recognition of the need to acquire information. The buyer almost always expects the seller to adapt, unless the seller possesses something extremely rare for which there are many willing buyers.

Individual preference may also enter the equation. An expatriate dealing with Chinese colleagues in Shanghai may attempt to adapt to Chinese traditions, even though there is no expectation from the Shanghai staff to do so. The motives for adaptation in this situation may range from showing courtesy to a desire to learn and increase one's own repertoire of behavior. Furthermore, no matter where a company is operating, an attempt to adapt to others' customs will typically be appreciated and have a positive influence on relations.

We usually give a different but quick and easy answer to the question, "Who should adapt?": Whoever cares about the outcomes. There are a lot of contingencies that influence who *tends to* adapt and who is *expected to* adapt. But as our description of the MBI process emphasizes, the more everyone adapts mindfully, the more potential there is for outcomes to improve. If one party adapts, it is better than if no one adapts. However, if everyone adapts, outcomes are even better. Discussing "who should adapt" often becomes a negotiation of power. Discussing "How can we perform together?" becomes a dialogue of empowerment.

Conclusion: Continuous Learning for Development and Effectiveness

Managers often feel discouraged when they realize the complexity and depth of skills needed for interacting effectively across cultures. However, there is good news. A little bit of skill goes a long way. Doing a bit of Mapping will help you ask a couple of questions differently during the Bridging phase. You'll receive rich answers, which will lead you to avoid or manage a conflict differently, and you'll see yourself on the way to higher performance. This gives you and others more motivation to engage, you will ask more Mapping questions and engage in more Bridging. As a result, people will volunteer some ideas you had not heard before, and performance looks even better. And so on.

Being able to learn continuously arises from mindfulness: paying attention to your actions, selecting your behaviors carefully, concentrating on the results, managing the impact, and learning to prepare yourself for the next set of actions. Much more important than avoiding mistakes completely (because it is impossible) is learning. Ask questions about what you should have done. Ask them in a way that's appropriate to the culture. Provide "what if" scenarios and ask for people's reactions. Experiment when it feels safe. Then learn the new information and incorporate it into your Maps for next time. Experienced managers love sharing stories about these incidents with each other. All four authors and all our colleagues have experienced many of them!

If you create a negative impact you didn't intend, make sure you manage that impact. That means first of all, you must be watching for these impacts with mindfulness. Become sensitive to cues that suggest you have inadvertently created offense, such as the other person switching the type of pronoun to a more formal one or using more structured language and actions. If you see the signs, first apologize sincerely. A genuine and respectful apology goes a long way in creating the conditions for turning the matter into a learning situation. Then, being mindful, learn for next time. If you are sincere in your attempts to learn and improve, you almost always get at least one more chance and people will likely be willing to help you learn.

In the remaining chapters of the book, we look at many different contexts for international management. Sometimes we draw on the MBI model explicitly; often we incorporate other lenses to focus on other aspects of the situation. But MBI is always assumed to be a foundation underneath the other processes, to be drawn upon in all situations.

Reflection Question 5.3: Do You Speak the Language?

National cultural differences are often accompanied by language differences. Yet, we frequently speak more of cultural differences than language differences. Please discuss the impact of language differences and skills for international/global collaboration: What are the consequences of language differences (if any)? How can the impact of language differences be addressed to the advancement of international collaboration?

You may find additional inspiration for your reflection/discussion in the following articles:

- Klitmøller, A., & Lauring, J. (2013). When global virtual teams share knowledge: Media richness, cultural difference and language commonality. *Journal of World Business, 48*(3), 398–406.
- Aichhorn, N., & Puck, J. (2017). Bridging the language gap in multinational companies: Language strategies and the notion of company-speak. *Journal of World Business, 52*(3), 386–403.
- Harzing, A. W., & Pudelko, M. (2014). Hablas vielleicht un peu la mia language? A comprehensive overview of the role of language differences in headquarters–subsidiary communication. *The International Journal of Human Resource Management, 25*(5), 696–717.
- Śliwa, M., & Johansson, M. (2014). How non-native English-speaking staff are evaluated in linguistically diverse organizations: A sociolinguistic perspective. *Journal of International Business Studies, 45*, 1133–1151.
- Luo, Y., & Shenkar, O. (2017). The multinational corporation as a multilingual community: Language and organization in a global context. *Language in International Business: Developing a Field*, 59–92.
- Selmer, J., & Lauring, J. (2015). Host country language ability and expatriate adjustment: The moderating effect of language difficulty. *The International Journal of Human Resource Management, 26*(3), 401–420.

Reflection Question 5.4: Let Technology Do the Talking?

When discussing the role of language skills, particularly the asymmetry between native speakers and nonnative speakers (of whatever language is the most central to know in a situation), you may also discuss how technological progress may level the playing field (or not). Consider for instance that you can ask chatbots to write your e-mails in many languages, have Google translate your memo, dictate your word document to type itself, or use "live" subtitling of video conferences – to mention just some of the low-tech solutions that are available and can assist communication. What do you believe are the (negative/positive) consequences of these as well as more advanced technological tools for the importance of language skills in intercultural collaboration going forward?

Further Resources

To explore cross-cultural interactions further, we strongly encourage you to read literature or watch films that come from cultures other than your own. Stories about immigrants or other cross-cultural relationships are particularly insightful. When you read or watch these stories, pay attention analytically: Where do you see (or lack) Mapping, Bridging, and Integrating? What is the impact of engaging in these processes mindfully or not at all? Pay attention also to the emotions and the humanity of the stories. How do effective interactions enhance people's dignity and energy? Build new innovations?

Bibliography

Baumann Montecinos, J., & Grünfelder, T. (2022). What if we focus on developing commonalities? Results of an international and interdisciplinary Delphi study on transcultural competence. *International Journal of Intercultural Relations, 89*, 42–55.

DiStefano, J. J., & Maznevski, M. L. (2000). Creating value with diverse teams in global management. *Organizational Dynamics, 29*(1), 45–63.

Kelley, T., & Kelley, D. (2013). *Creative confidence: Unleashing the creative potential within us all*. Crown Business.

Kelley, T. A., & Littman, J. (2001). *The art of innovation: Lessons in creativity from IDEO, America's leading design firm*. Currency/Doubleday.

Maznevski, M. (1994a). Understanding our differences: Performance in decision-making groups with diverse members. *Human Relations, 47*(5), 531–552.

Maznevski, M. L. (1994b). *Synergy and Performance in Multicultural Teams*. Unpublished Dissertation, Western Business School, London, Ontario.

Smith, P. B., Andersen, J. A., Ekelund, B., Graversen, G., & Ropo, A. (2003). In search of Nordic management styles. *Scandinavian Journal of Management*, *19*(4), 491–507.

Smith, P. B., Peterson, M. F., & Schwartz, S. H. (2002). Cultural values, sources of guidance, and their relevance to managerial behavior: A 47-nation study. *Journal of Cross-Cultural Psychology*, *33*(2), 188–208.

6 High-Performing Global Teams

> Alone we can do so little, together we can do so much.
> Helen Keller, American author and deafblind disability rights activist (1880–1968), from *1920s Vaudeville Speeches*

Key Learning Objectives

At the end of this chapter, students will be able to:

- Diagnose a team's basic desired outcomes, design, operations (processes and climate), and outcomes.
- Align a team's operations (processes and climate) to achieve the desired outcomes, adapting to the team's needs as they change.
- Analyze how the team draws on the diversity brought by members and the extent to which the team creates value from the diverse composition.
- Evaluate a team's use of virtual communication tools to enhance effectiveness.

Teams Are the Basic Unit of Work and Collaboration

Most work in organizations today is done in teams: groups of people working together to accomplish something. Researchers know a lot about teams in general, including that teams in international management are highly complex. Leaders and members of international teams have to start by excelling at the basics of teamwork. In addition, they must be adept at leveraging diversity and collaborating virtually.

Formally, a team is a group of people who work together to achieve a joint outcome (Earley & Gibson, 2002). There are different kinds of teams, each with different tasks, structures, and other characteristics. Organizations typically identify at least four types of teams, as outlined in Table 6.1.

Even teams within a country have become more complex in today's fast-changing world, and there is no simple "how to" guide that fits all teams. With the

Table 6.1 **Types of teams in organizations**

Team Type	Expected Deliverables	Membership	Duration	Examples
Management teams	High-level and aggregated, e.g., combined profit margin or growth; decision-making for strategic direction	Members represent different departments or stakeholder groups	Indefinite	Global product team; Regional management team
Production / service / work teams	Production or service efficiency, quality, continuous improvement; support other teams' deliverables	Members bring specific skills or subtasks	Indefinite	Factory manufacturing team; Insurance claims processing team; Information Technology (IT) or Human Resources (HR) team for a global business unit
Long-term project teams	Solution to a specific strategic problem; implementation of a specific initiative	Core members bring specific skills and execution capabilities; temporary members bring other expertise; some members may be on team for development toward future roles	Clear start and finish date, typically several months or more	New product development team; IT system implementation team
Short-term response teams	Solution to an immediate problem, such as a crisis	Represent specific skills, stakeholder groups, and resources	Clear start and finish date, typically 2–3 months or less	Product failure response team; COVID-19 rapid response team

wide variety of tasks that groups of people work on jointly, managers must develop a sophisticated view of contingencies without forgetting the basic foundations.

Getting the Team Basics Right

When members of a global team first get together, they frequently notice the complexity: people from different cultures, working across countries and time zones. They jump straight to managing those elements with time zone calculations and translation tools. Too often do they forget to establish the basics of being a good, solid team. Researchers have been looking at teams in organizations for decades, generating a strong understanding of the basics of teamwork (e.g., Marks et al., 2001; Mathieu et al., 2008; Mathieu et al., 2017). Effective global teams start by getting these team basics right. This helps them overcome barriers raised by the inherent diversity and geographic distribution. Once they get those basics right, they can unlock opportunities – the superpowers that global teams have.

Addressing the basics starts by identifying the desired outcomes, then looking at the team's starting point or design. Next, it's about focusing attention on how the team actually operates together – the team processes and team climate. Effective teams get virtuous cycles going as they work through their early awkward stages toward productive work. The basic model is shown in Figure 6.1.

Sailing teams illustrate the team basics well. Throughout this section, we'll follow two examples of very different sailing teams: one team sails a relatively simple boat in weekly local club races and special events; the other team sails an International Monohull – Open Class Association (IMOCA) in The Ocean Race around the world over six months. We will compare how teams conducting the same basic task – sailing a boat – must focus on different goals, design their foundation differently, and manage their internal operations differently (The Ocean Race, 2023), given the different levels of complexity they are facing.

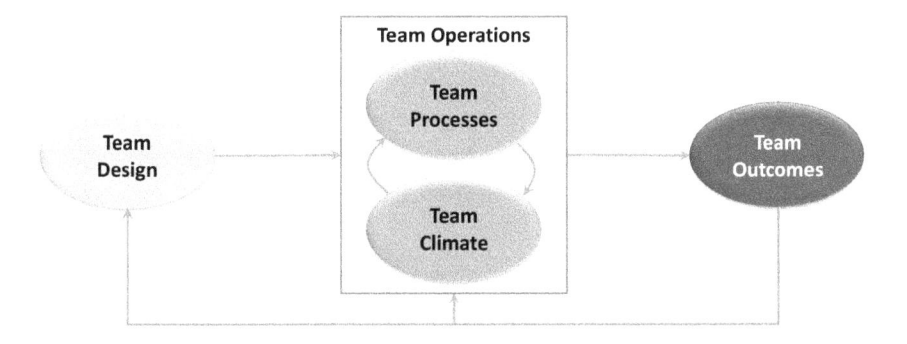

Figure 6.1 Basics of team performance: Overview

	J24 (top)	IMOCA (bottom)
Events	Local races and regattas	The Ocean Race
Hull Length	7.3 meters 24 feet	18.3 meters 60 feet
Mast Height	8.5 meters 28 feet	29 meters 95.1 feet
Draft (depth below water)	1.2 meters 4 feet	4.5 meters 14.8 feet
Crew	5 people	5 people

Figure 6.2 Comparing two types of sailboats. J24 profile drawing courtesy of J/Boats Inc. J24 photo courtesy of H. Lane. IMOCA 11th Hour Racing profile drawing and photo courtesy of 11th Hour Racing.

11th Hour Racing Team: Racing for the Health of Our Oceans

The 11th Hour Racing Team was founded by Charlie Enright and Mark Towill in 2019 with a mission to "build a high-performance ocean racing team with sustainability at the core of all team operations, inspiring positive action among sailing and coastal communities, and global sports fans, to create long-lasting change for ocean health" (11th Hour Racing, 2023a).

Charlie and Mark sailed their first ocean race together in 2007 when they were selected to participate in the documentary, *Morning Light*, produced by Roy Disney and Disney Studios, chronicling the training of the youngest crew to compete in the 2007 Transpac Race from Los Angeles to Honolulu. Charlie was a student and All-American sailor at Brown University, and Mark was a high school senior in Hawaii who later matriculated to Brown where he and Charlie were teammates.

After completing two round-the-world Volvo Ocean Races (now The Ocean Race) in 2015 and 2018, the pair set their sights on the 2023 Ocean Race. Their goal was to "win the world's premier around-the-world sailing race ... while using the team as a platform to promote the message of sustainable solutions and ocean health to millions of fans, sailors, and audiences worldwide" (1 Degree, 2023).

Philanthropist Wendy Schmidt, sailor and sailmaker Rob MacMillan, and sailor Jeremy Pochman founded the team's title sponsor, 11th Hour Racing, after sailing together in international regattas and witnessing multitudes of single-use plastic water bottles and plastic waste littering the docks and on the racecourses. They decided that the sailing world was a place that they could work to eliminate single-use plastic at regattas and then expanded their efforts by adding sponsorships, grants, and an ambassador program "to champion collaborative, systemic change across the sailing and sports communities to benefit our ocean." The name of the organization, headquartered in Newport, Rhode Island, reflects their view that "we are at the final hour in the struggle to save our ocean."

The extensive nature of the sustainability program and activities of the 11th Hour Racing Team can be found in its Campaign Report 2019–2023 (11th Hour Racing, 2023c). They align their program with the strategy of their sponsor in the areas of ocean literacy and stewardship, clean technologies and best practices, and ecosystem restoration. The scope of their program includes items directly within the control of the 35-member onshore team and racing squad, such as operations (team travel, container shipments, waste, etc.) and items they can influence that are outside their direct control such as events and stopovers, suppliers, and partners.

The 11th Hour Racing Team's accomplishments were recognized by the World Sailing Organization, who awarded them "Team of the Year" at their 2023 awards (World Sailing, 2023). Charlie Enright and his team provide an interesting example of leadership and teams, leading mindfully and responsibly in a global context.

Team Outcomes: What Do We Want from the Team?

High-performing teams not only perform well on the current task but also set themselves up for long-term success. More specifically, high-performing teams excel on three types of outcomes (Hackman, 1990). While all teams succeed in all three outcome categories, their goals within each of these categories differ in important ways, as we will illustrate with the two sailing examples. After identifying specific goals for each outcome category, leaders can move to designing their foundation to build toward those goals.

First is, of course, the **task deliverable**. Good teams deliver high quality, according to the criteria set by the manager, customer, or other stakeholders. They also deliver in a timely, efficient way, again according to criteria set by the stakeholders. A team in the local sailing club tries to win each race. Even if it does not win, a team may try to beat specific other boats competing for overall points. In The Ocean Race, the five teams aim to win each of the seven legs of the race and achieve race points, with the trophy going to the team with the most overall points at the end. Different teams set additional task deliverables for themselves. For example, 11th Hour Racing, the 2023 champion, had goals to raise awareness about ocean conservation and initiate and support actions that increase the sustainability of ocean transportation and humans' interdependence with the ocean (11th Hour Racing, 2023a).

The second outcome is **team growth**. In a high-performing team, the team gets better over time. Members work together in a way that is sustainable, and they are committed to keep working together (even if they don't always like each other). They improve their ability to work together as a team so the team can complete more challenging tasks with better quality. The local sailing club team tries to get better each week, and an effective team can handle more challenging conditions more consistently by the end of the season. The 11th Hour Racing Team developed for four years before the race. Team skipper Charlie Enright said after winning the race, "One thing we like to pride ourselves on is never getting too high, never getting too low, and just working through everything. We say if you're not winning, you're learning, and this whole race, we've just tried to improve in every single area" (11th Hour Racing, 2023b).

The third important outcome is **individual member growth**. High-performing teams enable their members to become better over time, too. They help members improve and develop new skills so they can contribute more to the team and the organization. They also work together in a way that motivates and intrinsically rewards team members so they are inspired to engage with the team and the organization as a whole. Local sailing clubs combine racing with instruction and development programs to explicitly cultivate individual skills. In The Ocean Race, individual members develop their skills significantly as they work together. For the 11th Hour Racing Team, this also meant learning more about ocean conservation and implementing sustainability practices as they raced.

The task deliverable is often the performance element the leader or the organization cares about most. However, it is at least as important to monitor and develop the other two aspects of performance: team and individual growth. For one thing, they tend to be the leading indicators of task deliverable quality. For tasks that take a long time to complete, such as a consulting engagement, new product development, or IT system implementation, quality may be difficult to measure along the way. Team and individual growth are pretty good predictors of the eventual task deliverable quality, and they can provide early diagnostics of poor quality. Moreover, team and individual growth are associated with high-performing teams over time.

When setting up a new team, it's important to carefully articulate goals around all three types of team outcomes and to communicate them so everyone understands them. Examining outcomes is also important when diagnosing the effectiveness of an ongoing team. If a team is not performing the way leaders or the organization want or expect, asking the question "What exactly do we want from this team?" is the best starting point for analysis – regardless of whether this is in the context of a sailing team or an organizational team.

Team Design: What Is Our Starting Point, The Structure of Our Team?

Once the desired outcomes are established, the team needs to build a good foundation for collaboration. Teams have a variety of structural elements they can set up to design the beginning of a team's existence and prepare it for strong dynamics and performance. The different design elements address questions about what the team will do, who is on the team, and where the team operates.

What Will the Team Accomplish?

The starting point is the "*what*" of the team: What is the task, and what are the timelines? A detailed definition of the task and timelines, with a clear understanding of the level of complexity (is this a structured task with clearly identified inputs and outputs, or is it more ambiguous with potential for change mid-task?), will be helpful. Team members must know initially their task and objectives even if they know these may change. Despite major differences in complexity, both sailing teams from our example must set specific objectives to achieve their desired outcomes. The local club team sets specific goals for each race, taking into account conditions and other boats in the race. The complexity of the task is relatively low with a short race and small boats. For The Ocean Race, the teams also set specific goals for each leg of the competition based on distance and ocean conditions. The complexity is very high given the volatile ocean and weather conditions and the long distances of each leg, as well as the added goals regarding sustainability.

It may sound obvious to set goals, but many teams in organizations do not understand their objectives well enough or do not agree on them. If a team member on a sailing team failed to understand their objective, the boat could lose speed or even capsize, whether sailing with the local club or in The Ocean Race. Sometimes, goal ambiguity is due to a lack of clear communication from the leader, who may present objectives that are clear to themselves but confusing from the team members' points of view. More often, team members have different interpretations of the task and objectives. For example, a specialty chemicals company launched a new industrial product, with a multifunctional team guiding the launch. Their mandate from the CEO was to launch the product successfully. The Vice President (VP) of Marketing on the team defined desired success as high market share, while the Finance VP defined it as high profitability. These two objectives could be conflicting, and this team did not identify their diverging views until well into the execution phase, when they had already created unaligned actions. The Marketing VP developed a marketing mix that would encourage customers to switch quickly, which meant lower prices and forecasts of high volume. The Finance VP, in contrast, built forecasts for capital expenditure and investment with assumptions about high margins and lower volume. Once they discovered the misalignment, the conflict became personal, and the team had to delay launch while they realigned.

Let's introduce another example, which we will follow through the Team Basics – this time, an example of a newly promoted leader assessing her team.

> Prisha was just promoted to lead a team of analysts for a pension plan's investment team. Before conducting any further analysis on the team and its dynamics, Prisha articulated the desired goals – the What – for each of the three outcome categories. The team's task deliverable was to identify a short list of potential investments for the senior investment leaders, who determined the final portfolio. The list needed to be updated twice a month. The team's growth goal was to develop better analytical processes, forecasting expertise, and the ability to have multiple people covering each industry over time in order to increase confidence in the quality of the short list. The individual growth goal was to develop each analyst's expertise and to keep them engaged with the firm. Once she had articulated the "What" for her team, Prisha felt ready to assess how the team's interactions contributed toward those goals.

Even though she was under pressure to perform, Prisha took the time to identify all the team's goals. This is a crucial first step toward setting a team up for success. The simple lesson here is: make sure the team has a clear mandate, and be mindful about the level and type of complexity. In complex teams such as those in international settings, you will have to revisit the goals and objectives many times.

Who's on the Team?

Next is the "*who*": Who do we need on the team and in what roles? Teams need the right combination of skills among members. The right combination depends on the task and includes technical skills, functional and geographical knowledge, skills important for managing team processes, and people who can access external resources of all types. Our local sailing team races with five people on the boat, performing Skipper, Cockpit, Foredeck, Middle, and Mast roles. This combination of roles covers leading, steering, operating the sails, and balancing the boat during changes in direction, and without any of these roles, the boat would not sail effectively. Sailors usually operate in the same role each race but can substitute in other roles if necessary – this promotes individual development even if it may compromise speed. The Ocean Race team also involves five people on the boat. Four of these roles are focused on different aspects of sailing – Skipper, Main Trimmer, Trimmer, and Navigator – with much more expertise required than for the local sailing club. In The Ocean Race, the team also includes the role of the Onboard Reporter who cannot actively sail the boat but focuses instead on communications between the boat and the external world. This extra role addresses The Ocean Race's additional goal of creating awareness of sustainability. The 11th Hour Racing Team had ten members in total – five of whom raced each leg of the competition – including two women and people from seven different countries. Each crew member was a highly experienced sailor in open ocean races, with technical expertise at a particular function. The two sailing teams are both focused on the same basic "What," and therefore their members ("Who") perform very similar roles. However, the level of difficulty and complexity of the teams' "What" is quite different, and The Ocean Race's larger, more diverse, and more expert team reflects their greater challenge.

In management, as in sailing, it is helpful to have diversity in personal characteristics among team members to boost innovation and increase the quality of decision-making. In organizations, teams are often composed based on convenience – who is available – rather than careful assignment. Sometimes the necessary skill combination is not available – for example, if there is a labor shortage or low unemployment rate. As a result, teams frequently have significant skill or knowledge gaps that should be addressed by adding members or developing the necessary knowledge or skills.

Roles are sets of specific responsibilities within a group. As with the different roles on a sailing boat, teams function best when different members take responsibility for different aspects. For most teams, task-related roles are evident. For example, people with different functional backgrounds take on analysis related to their expertise, people from different geographies take on implementation in their own markets, and someone with project management expertise will track progress and milestones. Equally important, teams should also ensure they have people fulfilling process-related roles, such as facilitator or engagement tracker.

Let's go back to Prisha and her team of analysts for the pension plan.

> Prisha's team had analysts with different types of industry expertise, and task-related roles were assigned in the typical way for such teams: Each analyst was assigned a specific industry and developed a deep expertise in assessing risk and value for that industry over time. This combination of composition and roles achieved the task deliverable objective: a good shortlist of potential investments. But in order to achieve the team and individual growth objectives, Prisha knew the members needed to learn from each other and develop their interpersonal and leadership skills. For each meeting, Prisha assigned a different team member to the role of facilitator. Prisha rotated the role so that all team members learned to lead effective meetings.

Prisha was very insightful to see that the "Who" on her team addressed one category of Outcomes (a "What") but not the others. In her situation, the best way to influence the "Who" to address team and individual growth was to develop the people themselves by coaching them toward new skills. This is likely to increase engagement in her team, and thus lead to long-term performance.

To summarize, a vital part of a team's design is the foundation of "Who" is on the team. Most leaders can list off the people or skills they need, the composition of the team. But it's important also to ensure that both task-related and process-related roles are covered. When individual team members engage in both task- and process-related roles, the team has a better chance to operate well.

Where Does the Team Work?

Finally, there is the *"where"* of the team: Where and in what environment is the team functioning? This is the most neglected part of a team's design, but it is also important. To function well, a team needs a supportive environment and access to a network of stakeholders for team resources. A good local sailing club, for example, supports the teams in their development and runs well-organized races that are safe, allowing the sailing teams to focus on managing their boats and the conditions along the route. The Ocean Race organization promotes the race and cooperates with the teams to set the rules and facilitate the teams' objectives. Within each team's organization, the sailing crew is supported by a large team of analysts, technical and strategic advisors, and other staff. Without this supportive environment, neither team would be able to achieve their outcomes even with the right people on the team.

In the case of a company, the supportive team environment could include a physical environment, such as a team room with white boards to track work and interactive spaces for discussion. Even if the team works in person, their environment should include virtual space, such as shared network drives and collaboration platforms. Perhaps even more important, though, is the organizational culture around teaming. Often, team members will work part time on this project and part time on other work. Managers must be supportive of this work arrangement, giving team members enough time and resources to focus on the team. If the organizational climate is supportive to teams, then the physical and virtual environments are more likely to be appropriate.

We can see this in Prisha's case.

At Prisha's previous employer, when she was an analyst herself, she worked with a leader who insisted that team meetings were a waste of time. Analyst "teams" were just a group of analysts supervised by someone more expert. Prisha and her peers constantly felt the pressure of not having the support of the team. Because the leader was stretched for time, too, the leader was only available to correct mistakes. The analysts lived in constant fear of making those mistakes. Prisha and her peers learned how to apply the firm's preferred analysis processes and produce reports that met expectations, but they did not understand how their work fit a larger view, nor did they develop broader expertise. Prisha was not the only team member unengaged with the firm, nor the only one who left as soon as the job market picked up. The firm's analyst teams achieved expectations on task deliverable outcomes but did not perform well on team or individual growth. Nor did they increase the task deliverable outcomes over time because they did not think about the team's environment as part of the team design.

One of the reasons Prisha selected the pension plan as her new employer was the environment for teams. Her new leader supported the approach she wanted to take and actively coached Prisha to lead the team better. Prisha felt empowered to focus on the team's dynamics, not just the individual analysts, and this led to higher performance on all the team outcomes.

Team Design: Set Up Well at the Beginning, Then Adjust as Needed

The team design is often called the structure in team research because it is usually structured by managers outside the team and the team leader, and less likely by team members themselves. These elements represent the starting conditions, and as such, they have a great influence on the team's trajectory. Of course, as the team works together, it may become apparent that some aspects of the design need to be adjusted. For example, the team may find that the task definition needs to be refined, based on new analyses about market segments or suppliers. They may find they need specific expertise that is not on the team, and they need that expertise integrated through a new team member rather than accessed through a network.

A manager who is creating a team to accomplish something should continue to pay attention to its design. Similarly, team members should be aware of the possibility of adjusting the design after they start working together and should maintain a strong dialogue with their external stakeholders regarding the structure.

Team Operations: What Team Processes Do We Need to Engage, and What Kind of Team Climate Should We Develop?

Most research on teams focuses on the processes and conditions inside the team itself, and indeed this is where team members have the most influence on their own team performance. We are sure you have experienced the power of team operations, and you have observed them with your favorite sports teams or music groups. Maybe you were on a team in which the members were all experts or stars, yet the team didn't "gel" and its performance – on all three types of outcomes – was mediocre or even terrible. Or maybe you've cheered a team that *didn't* have all the experts or stars, yet the team members worked together so well that the team excelled, and the team members couldn't wait to take on bigger challenges together. Although team design is crucial for setting up the team, team operations actually explain more variance in team outcomes. In short, team operations are even more important than team design (Mathieu et al., 2017).

This section will refer frequently to themes in Chapter 5 on interpersonal effectiveness as expressed in the Map-Bridge-Integrate framework, because interpersonal interaction is the foundation for all effective team operations.

What Do We Do? Task, Interpersonal, and Learning Processes

Team processes are the actions and behaviors that teams engage in to perform well as a team. It's helpful to identify three important categories of processes: task, interpersonal, and learning.

Task Processes: Working Directly on the Deliverable
This is often thought of as "doing the work." The three main types of task processes are planning and tracking, analyzing and deciding, and executing.

Planning and tracking are typically referred to as project management and the subject of many books, articles, guides, and software packages. Simply put, teams are more likely to achieve results if they plan clear processes with activities, milestones, and deliverables, if work and subtasks are allocated clearly to members, and if the team tracks progress compared to plan, adapting the plan when necessary. Planning and tracking are enhanced if communication and conflict management – two interpersonal processes – are effective. Without good communication and conflict management, plans are unlikely to be comprehensive, and tracking is likely to be inaccurate.

Analyzing and deciding are integral, as most teams have to make a variety of decisions and recommendations, all of which require gathering and analyzing data. They may be deciding on production parameters or maintenance processes, product attributes, candidates to hire or promote, or any other organizational issue. Again, analyzing and deciding are the subject of many books from project management to strategy. In a team, the key is to use the benefit of multiple team members to increase the scope of alternatives considered to enrich the analysis, and to debate and explore the implications of different decisions. As we will examine below, this can be particularly challenging in diverse teams.

Executing is about individual team members accomplishing their own parts of the task – whether that involves data gathering, analysis, report-writing, or other things – and the group as a whole combining the individual outputs to create a joint deliverable. This requires individual discipline – team members need to finish their own parts on time and come prepared to meetings – as well as group commitment, with team members helping each other out as unexpected challenges arise. For example, an equipment purchasing team formed after the merger of two companies was charged with identifying the best few suppliers from among the two companies' previous relationships. The team negotiated new contracts with these suppliers and worked with the suppliers and individual purchasing departments to adjust volumes and delivery conditions until new routines had been established.

Interpersonal Processes: General Interactions That Enable the Team's Work
Interpersonal processes are those that facilitate interaction, commitment, and motivation within the group. For teams, the most important interpersonal processes are communicating effectively, anticipating and resolving conflicts, and

innovating by building on ideas. Chapter 5 on Bridging and Integrating covered these interpersonal processes extensively.

Learning Processes: Getting Better Over Time

Recent research and practice on teams have focused more on this final set of processes. Learning processes are actions that review previous work, identify strengths, and enhance commitment to continuous improvement (Hajro et al., 2017; Widmann et al., 2016). Research has clearly shown that teams who engage in effective learning processes show much more improvement and better outcomes (on all three outcomes dimensions) over time (Harvey et al., 2022). Unfortunately, most teams skip these processes, especially if the next deliverable is coming up soon. Quite simply, a habit of capturing mindful team learning processes is an important predictor of sustainable team effectiveness.

Let's get back to our sailing teams. Even the sailing team in the local club needs to plan their approach to the course, decide on tactics for a particular race, and actually sail the boat together. With effective interpersonal processes, they will be better able to adapt as they need to during a race, and with good learning processes they will improve with each race. For The Ocean Race, each of these sets of processes is just as important as for the local sailing club but much more complex. The planning takes years, there are thousands of strategic and tactical decisions to be made, and during the race itself the team works together intensively to implement the strategy and adapt to extremely challenging conditions. The team must constantly communicate effectively and resolve differences. The five teams in the race are all continuously applying their learning, including enhancing their sustainability. Without this type of learning they would not be able to adapt to the different conditions. The comparison of the two sailing teams helps us see how all teams have the same fundamental process requirements, no matter what their desired outcomes or design are. At the same time, the specific processes that work most effectively and the way they unfold are quite different, depending on the desired outcomes and design. An effective leader learns to see both the similarities and differences across teams and to initiate and reinforce the appropriate processes.

Although we presented task, interpersonal, and learning processes separately here, it is important to remember that they work together. Moreover, they do not necessarily work in this order. Recall that cultures differ in their preference for prioritizing tasks or relationships. They also differ, therefore, in terms of where they prefer to begin teamwork – with the task or the interpersonal processes. What's important is for a team to monitor both sets of processes. Whenever one type seems to have stalled or to be in conflict with another, it often helps to go to the other to look for resolution and progress.

Internal Team Climate: What Does It Feel Like to Be in This Team?
Teams need to create a set of norms and a way of "being" that promotes healthy task, interpersonal, and learning processes, especially to achieve sustainable and adaptive performance (Mathieu et al., 2008; Waller et al., 2016; Woodley et al., 2019). It helps to think of this as a set of beliefs that team members have about the team as a whole, or a team climate. Certain beliefs allow the team to interact in a way that facilitates processes such as planning, analysis, deciding, executing, communicating, resolving conflict, and innovating. The climate conditions that most affect team outcomes are psychological safety, cohesion, and trustworthiness.

Psychological safety is a belief that team members look after each other's identity, or sense of self, and that people are valued for being on the team (Edmondson, 1999). When there is strong psychological safety, team members contribute ideas without fear of ridicule or pressure to conform. The team is more likely to communicate effectively, resolve conflicts constructively, and innovate well. Behaviors that reinforce psychological safety are open and active listening, showing empathy and compassion, and encouraging each other to bring unique perspectives to the team.

Cohesion is a strong sense of identity as a team (Lepine et al., 2008). It means that team members believe that the performance of the team as a whole is at least as important as their own individual contributions, and they are willing to invest a lot in helping each other achieve the team's deliverables. Cohesion is particularly important when there is conflict, or when the task or environment changes as the team works together, and roles need to be fluid and changing. With strong cohesion, individual team members are willing to put aside their individual concerns and adjust for the sake of the team.

Trustworthiness is the belief that team members will act in ways that are reliable, and that look out for each other in situations of ambiguity, risk, or vulnerability (McAllister, 1995). We often talk about two kinds of trust: cognitive and affective, or head trust and heart trust. Head trust is the belief that someone will do what they say they are going to do. Head trust comes from experience with the other person's expertise, capabilities, resources, and conscientiousness. Heart trust is the belief that someone will look after your interests as much as they can, even when you are not there. Heart trust comes from experience of the other person's values, and with the other person looking after you when you're in a state of vulnerability or taking a risk. Head trust is necessary for any kind of teamwork.

Without head trust, team members feel the need to monitor each other's work constantly, to recheck and redo. This leads to redundancies, inefficiencies, and poor performance. Heart trust is necessary for the team to engage in tasks that stretch the team's capabilities, tasks that are ambiguous or complex, and tasks that require adaptation along the way. All these latter situations require that people in the team act on behalf of the team, without everyone present or clear about the direction.

Sailing teams, like teams in a company, need a positive climate, although the implications for building and sustaining it are quite different depending on the complexity of the team. The local sailing club team needs psychological safety for responding to mistakes. They need enough cohesion to continue to be committed to the races together. Head trust is crucial – they need to rely on each other to do their jobs on the boat – but heart trust may not be vital for the team, since they are unlikely to be in a safety-threatening situation. The Ocean Race team, in contrast, needs a stronger climate in all three dimensions. Mistakes have bigger consequences, so psychological safety is crucial for asking vulnerable questions and experimenting early. The team lives in tiny, cramped conditions without privacy throughout the race, so cohesion is imperative. With extremely dangerous conditions and fast-changing information, team members need deep heart trust in each other as well as head trust. With heart trust, they don't doubt each other's actions or intentions, and they can focus on managing the challenging situations together.

All the team climate conditions develop with experience. Team members may begin with initial "trial" levels of psychological safety, cohesion, and trust, but their experiences together will determine whether the conditions increase or decrease. Full safety, cohesion, and trust can only be built with deep and challenging experiences over time. We can see an example of this with Prisha and her team.

> When Prisha first started working with her team, she was careful to make the task processes explicit. The firm had a clear template for assessing potential investments, and Prisha helped her team members apply that template rigorously, with careful attention to detail. In team meetings, she and the rotating facilitators ensured they all shared information about the potential shortlist candidates they were working on. When there was conflict, for example about selecting among a set of investments all of which fit the high potential criteria, Prisha helped the team separate the problem from the people, map and bridge the different perspectives, and resolve the conflict with a

team-generated decision. Prisha and the team then updated their internal documentation to reflect the refined criteria. Over time, Prisha's team members felt increasingly safe in bringing questions to the group, and admitting when they were not sure about how to evaluate the parameters of a potential investment. They developed commitment to help each other and learned together. Prisha worked closely with her manager in developing the team, and the circle of trust expanded. The operations in Prisha's team – both processes and climate – reinforced each other to build toward effective outcomes. It was not always smooth or easy, especially when there were tough deadlines or new, urgent requests from the investment team, but Prisha and her team developed a strong reputation for high effectiveness.

Team Processes and Climate Affect Each Other Reciprocally, Not Just Sequentially

We've presented the team operations as linear: task, interpersonal, and learning processes and team climate. In fact, as Prisha found in her team, they are and must be completely reciprocal, affecting each other constantly. Effective communication and conflict resolution lead to a strong team climate. With a strong team climate, the team has better planning, analysis, execution, and innovation and is more likely to engage in effective learning. Good task progress provides a context for extensive communication, and together these build more cohesion. When processes are effective and the climate is positive, team members pull together to solve a problem such as a failure with a customer or a sudden change in competition. This experience in turn provides a learning context for developing better processes, and creates deeper psychological safety, cohesion, and trust. The reinforcement can easily become a negative cycle, rather than a positive one, with poor processes leading to poor team conditions and the poor conditions, in turn, making it more difficult for team members to engage in good team processes. Good team leaders, team members, and those who support teams from the outside all pay attention to both the processes and the climate, working to create momentum in a positive cycle.

The full model of team basics is shown in Figure 6.3.

The basics model provides a practical checklist for leaders setting up new teams. It can also serve as an important diagnostic tool to assess an ongoing team, either to turn around negative performance or to step up the team on some important outcomes. Figure 6.4 highlights how to apply the team basics model for these two different purposes.

What?
- Task Definition (Goals) & Timelines
- Task Complexity and Interdependence

Who?
- Team Composition
- Formal Roles – task and social

Where?
- Organizational Environment
- Stakeholder network

Team Processes
Task, for example
- Planning & Tracking
- Analyzing & Deciding
- Executing

Interpersonal, for example
- Communicating
- Resolving conflict
- Negotiating

Learning, for example
- Reviewing
- Providing feedback

Team Climate
For example
- Psychological Safety
- Cohesion
- Trust

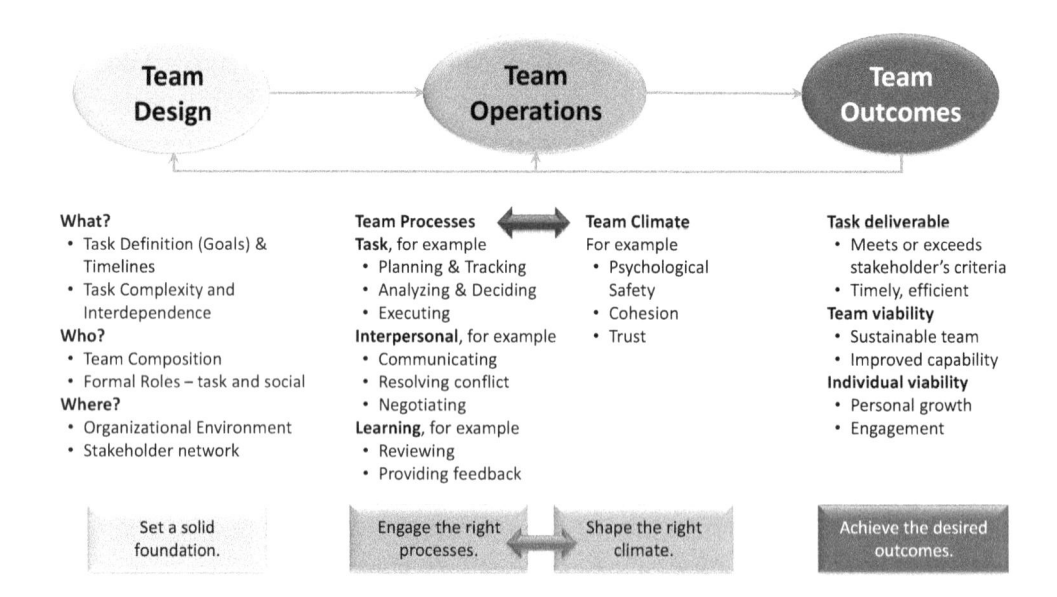

Task deliverable
- Meets or exceeds stakeholder's criteria
- Timely, efficient

Team viability
- Sustainable team
- Improved capability

Individual viability
- Personal growth
- Engagement

Set a solid foundation. | Engage the right processes. | Shape the right climate. | Achieve the desired outcomes.

Figure 6.3 Team basics: Full model.

Questions for setting up the team for a good start.
- How should we structure the team's foundation to support the Operations and achieve the desired outcomes?
- Which team processes would work best to shape the climate and achieve the desired outcomes?
- What kind of team climate do we need to support the processes and the desired outcomes?
- What do we want from the team?

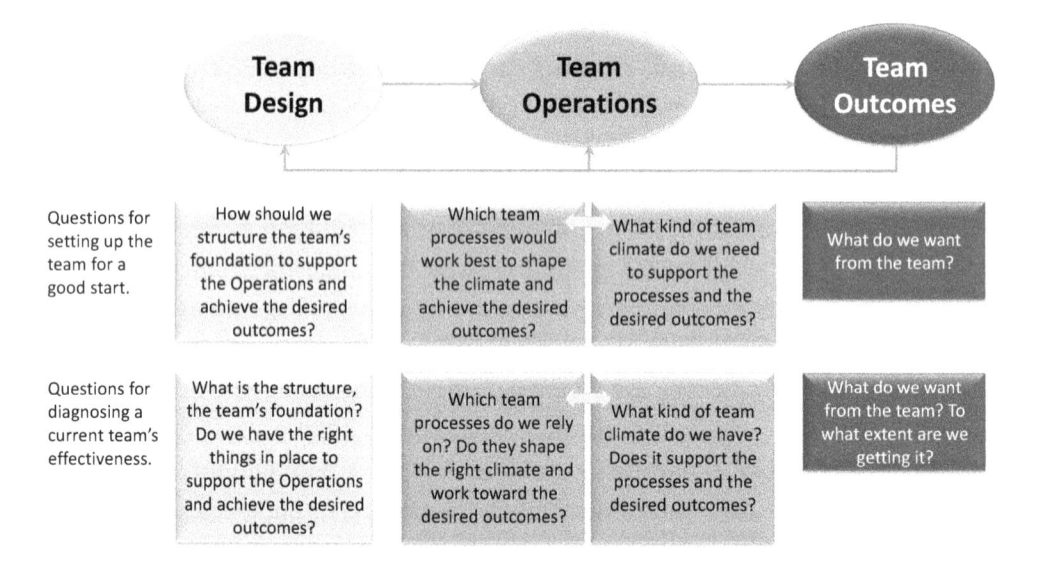

Questions for diagnosing a current team's effectiveness.
- What is the structure, the team's foundation? Do we have the right things in place to support the Operations and achieve the desired outcomes?
- Which team processes do we rely on? Do they shape the right climate and work toward the desired outcomes?
- What kind of team climate do we have? Does it support the processes and the desired outcomes?
- What do we want from the team? To what extent are we getting it?

Figure 6.4 Team basics: Start-up or ongoing diagnosis.

Now that we've covered the basics, let's add the complexity of global teams. Global teams usually have a specific team design with two elements that tend to affect their operations dramatically: **culturally diverse composition** and **geographically distributed environment**. Both those design elements raise barriers to effective operations, but they also offer opportunities. In addition, global teams tend to be formed for complex global tasks – another important design element. Good team leaders need to understand the implications of diverse composition and distributed environment, and lead in a way that overcomes the barriers while realizing the opportunities for solving complex challenges.

> ### Reflection Question 6.1: Diagnosing the Team Basics
>
> Think abo ut a team you are part of and use the team basics model and diagnostic questions to assess that team. How does your evaluation help you understand more fully what the team does well, and how can you reinforce that? In what ways could your team improve? How can you influence that, whether or not you are the formal leader?

Culturally Diverse Teams: Creating, Equalizing, or Destroying Value

Global teams tend to be much more diverse in their composition than domestic teams are. Of course, team members usually come from different country cultures. Furthermore, when the team has all the different skill sets needed for a complex task, global teams tend also to be multifunctional, and their members often come from very different parts of the organization or even different organizations (such as a customer, supplier, or expert organization).

Most people assume that highly diverse teams perform better than less diverse teams. They certainly have the potential for higher performance. They have access to more resources, from information to stakeholders, and they can therefore "cover" more of the information and analysis needs for the task. In addition, people from different cultures and backgrounds tend to ask different questions and confront assumptions differently, so highly diverse teams have more potential for innovation and more integrative ways to resolve conflicts than less diverse teams.

Unfortunately, as we foreshadowed in Chapter 4, diverse teams find it difficult to use their resources well and turn them into good performance. In a recent meta-analysis, we found that the basic relationship between cultural diversity and performance is zero; that is, there was no correlation at all between cultural diversity and performance. What we found instead is that multicultural teams, and highly diverse teams in general, tend to perform either better *or worse* than teams with low diversity, with the two patterns averaging each other out. The pattern of team results is summarized in Figure 6.5 (Adler, 1986; DiStefano & Maznevski, 2000; Maznevski, 1994; Maznevski et al., 2023; Stahl, Mäkelä, et al., 2010; Stahl & Maznevski, 2021; Stahl, Maznevski, et al., 2010).

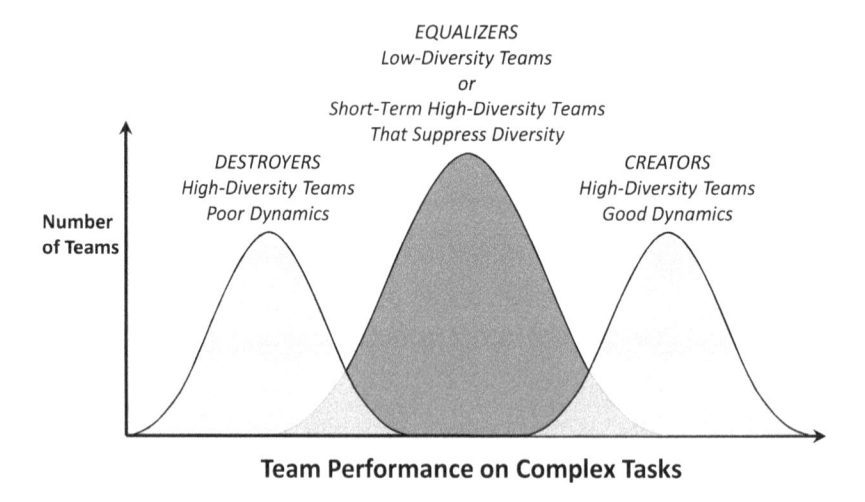

Figure 6.5 Relationship between team diversity and team performance.

Just as for interpersonal interactions, people are often worried about differences getting in the way of team performance. So most diverse teams suppress diversity by equalizing everyone to the lowest common denominator. They do this with good intentions – they believe it is the best way to have smooth processes and to build a strong team climate. But this suppression is problematic for two reasons. The obvious shortfall is that it does not realize the potential of the team. It leaves unused resources on the table and suboptimizes decision quality and implementation. "Okay," some managers respond, "but it's not worth the effort or the risk of conflict. For us, it is a good rational decision not to invest in the diversity." Maybe, in the short term.

Just as for interpersonal interactions, the equalizer approach of suppressing diversity inevitably demotivates team members whose beliefs, values, or norms are different from the dominant ones of the group. Not only do they stop contributing their knowledge; they also stop engaging with energy in the team. They may even respond with serious conflicts or, more likely, simply leave the team. This is why Figure 6.4 shows the Equalizer performance as working for highly diverse teams in the short term. In the long term, diverse teams that try to equalize end up destroying the potential value.

Managing Fault Lines: When Different Sources of Diversity Align

Global teams face yet another challenge that is less relevant for single-culture teams: managing fault lines. Fault lines are rifts in teams created by alignment of different types of diversity (Bezrukova et al., 2012; Lau & Murnighan, 1998, 2005;

Thatcher & Patel, 2012; Zellmer-Bruhn et al., 2008). For example, a global team may consist of two production engineers, two marketers, and two R&D scientists, from the United States, Japan, and Germany. If the engineers are from the United States, the marketers from Japan, and the scientists from Germany, then the functional and cultural divisions are aligned, and it is more difficult for team members to recenter and bridge across differences. On the other hand, if each of the functions is represented by people from different countries, the subgroups will be less evident, and the group will find it easier to balance their processes.

On a team that was developing a new global pricing strategy for the company's service offerings, all the finance expertise on the team came from the headquarters country. The other members of the team assumed that whatever the finance people suggested represented the headquarters' point of view, so the others on the team were unwilling to question the finance members. The company eventually took one of the headquarters people out and brought in a finance director from a moderate-sized subsidiary on a different continent, and this changed the dynamics significantly in a positive way.

Diverse Teams Do Perform Well

The good news is that highly diverse teams *can* and *do* perform extremely well. The highest performance on complex tasks in organizations is typically achieved by teams that engage their diversity well. To do this, they apply the Map-Bridge-Integrate principles with discipline to achieve the effective team operations as outlined in Chapter 4.

> ### Reflection Question 6.2: Highly Diverse Teams
>
> What is your experience with highly diverse teams? When did the diversity lead to high performance, and when were the results disappointing? How can you link the ideas from this chapter and from Chapters 4 and 5 (Map, Bridge, Integrate) to explain the performance?

Virtual Teams: Managing the Impact of Geographic Dispersion

Not only are global teams highly diverse; their processes are also hindered by the fact that they often conduct most of their interaction with members who are physically in different locations. Virtual team members are distributed widely, often around the globe. Some of the consequences are obvious. You may have experienced scheduling meetings across time zones. A Tokyo-Berlin-São Paulo conference call, for example, crosses 12 time zones. If the team wants to add a San Francisco-based customer to a meeting, another four time zones are added. Team members in at least two places will need to meet at hours that are not normally part of other people's workdays. A subtler challenge is with different infrastructures: Communicating seamlessly over different network types is often challenging.

These teams are called **virtual teams** because much of their interaction happens in the virtual space of digital information and communications technologies. Today's technologies facilitate communication and collaboration much more easily than those of even five years ago, and they are becoming more powerful and more intuitive at a fast pace. As many people experienced during the COVID-19 pandemic, we can accomplish much more virtually than most people previously imagined. Still, as human beings we have hundreds of thousands of years of experience in face-to-face teams and only a decade or two in virtual teams, so interacting virtually still presents a learning curve for us all.

Going back to the basics model helps us remember that virtual teams are teams first. They ought to achieve all three types of outcomes: task deliverable, team growth, and individual growth. With respect to team design, they likely have diverse composition and a rather complex task. The real challenge is that all the team operations need to rely on technology, and this also makes it difficult to build team climate. Research and practice suggest four important sets of recommendations for virtual teams (Gibson & Gibbs, 2006; Jarvenpaa et al., 1998; Maznevski & Chudoba, 2000; Neeley, 2015; Zander et al., 2013), discussed in the following four sections.

Organization and Discipline: A Lifeline for Virtual Teams

Face-to-face teams can get away with being disorganized and undisciplined. When members see each other, they catch up on the task, and they muddle through an agenda even without preparation or clear process. For virtual teams, lack of organization and discipline is detrimental. High-performing virtual teams set up their norms for organizing and disciplining early in the team's life and follow them with commitment. They identify clear standards for both task and interpersonal processes. Some rules may seem trivial, such as an agreement to respond to every team e-mail within one workday, even if the response is "I see it but I can't get to it right now." Although this may seem minor, it is the kind of discipline that builds trust and also keeps the task and communication going. Other norms may be more comprehensive, such as committing to conducting an action review on a regular basis, or always starting a new task phase with individual insight contributions from each member. High-performing virtual teams also understand that definitions, milestones, norms, and roles will change as the team and the task evolve. They articulate these clearly at the beginning of their work together and revisit them regularly to adapt as necessary.

Get to Know Each Other: People and Context

As we discussed in Chapter 5, virtual technology removes the context from communication. Yet, as we discussed in Chapters 3 and 4 on culture, understanding context is critical for cross-cultural effectiveness. Moreover, the lack of context in virtual communication makes it very difficult for people to build relationships, which are also vital for cross-cultural effectiveness. Throughout this book we emphasize that mindful global leaders are particularly sensitive to context, relationships, and process. Virtual teams need to be especially careful about context, because the mode of communication prevents it from being taken into account naturally.

It's important that virtual team members take extra time at the beginning of their teamwork to get to know each other, and each other's contexts. For example, we've worked with many teams whose members have a specific folder or thread on their team communication site for team building. They may begin by posting an easy phone video of themselves in their workplace, introducing their colleagues and workspaces. Some people are comfortable sharing personal information, such as family or hobbies, and of course some cultures encourage this. Other individuals are less comfortable, and some cultures discourage it. Team members should share personal information at the beginning if they're comfortable doing so but should not require it from everyone.

Each virtual interaction should try to take at least a few moments for contextual social information, and it's important to schedule this into time expectations. It would usually happen naturally in face-to-face encounters, but it must be carefully structured into virtual meetings so it's not forgotten. People in all cultures are comfortable with sharing some kind of contextual information, whether it's weather, sports scores, current events, music and theatre, or other topics. A team should start with what's comfortable for people and can move into more personal or sensitive topics (e.g., political situations) as trust builds. Each time team members interact virtually, they should also share their context with respect to the business. For example, what are the local customers like? What are the challenges and opportunities the different business units are facing, whether or not they are directly linked to the task of the team?

The Right Technology

Virtual teams are faced with a wide array of technologies and applications. However, there is no correlation between specific technologies and performance. Some good teams use mainly e-mail and phone calls, others use voice and video over internet and shared live websites with extensive use of synchronous chat. High-performing teams tend to have access to a menu of technologies and select the right one for the team process at a given time.

The one important rule of thumb is this: If you want to maximize the effectiveness of your communication – if you want to make sure your message "lands" the way you intended it – match the richness of the technology you use with the receiver's needs. Rich media are those that allow for multiple modes of communication at the same time. Video conferencing, for example, is richer than text messaging. Face-to-face is the richest communication. Figure 6.6 provides some examples of technologies along the richness spectrum and highlights some decision guidelines for applying them.

Remember that communication is about a receiver understanding the message as you intended it. Task complexity or need for explicit knowledge should be defined from the receiver's point of view, not the sender's. Even if something seems straightforward to you, if there is a chance that the receiver will not see it the same way, a richer technology is in order. In other words, it is often better to pick up the phone or send a quick video of the context than to send an e-mail or a WhatsApp message that could be misinterpreted.

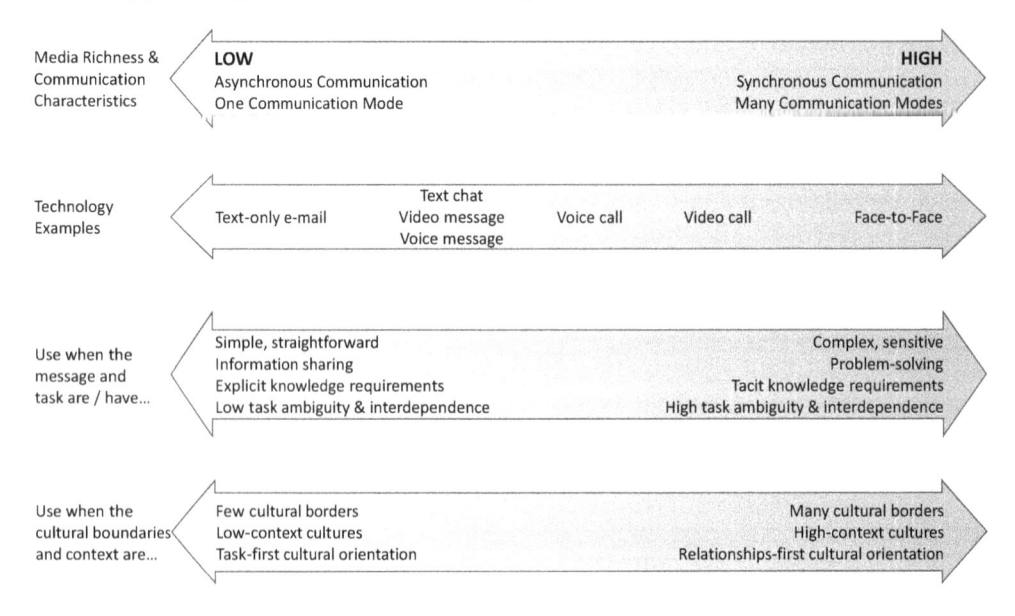

Category	LOW	HIGH
Media Richness & Communication Characteristics	Asynchronous Communication; One Communication Mode	Synchronous Communication; Many Communication Modes
Technology Examples	Text-only e-mail	Text chat; Video message; Voice message → Voice call → Video call → Face-to-Face
Use when the message and task are / have…	Simple, straightforward; Information sharing; Explicit knowledge requirements; Low task ambiguity & interdependence	Complex, sensitive; Problem-solving; Tacit knowledge requirements; High task ambiguity & interdependence
Use when the cultural boundaries and context are…	Few cultural borders; Low-context cultures; Task-first cultural orientation	Many cultural borders; High-context cultures; Relationships-first cultural orientation

Figure 6.6 Media richness and communication characteristics with example media.

The other corollary of this rule of thumb is that rich technologies should not be used for straightforward messages. Rich technologies are expensive, in terms of coordination and time, even if not in terms of financial investment. It is much more efficient to use a nonrich media, such as shared document space or e-mail, to share a routine sales report, and to save the rich media time for more complex matters such as problem-solving.

Create a Heartbeat

When should we get together in person? Leaders often assume that high-performing teams get together whenever things become complex, for example, a situation of intense conflict or when it's important to make a big step on a task. Our research and experience, however, suggest otherwise. Quite simply, high-performing virtual teams get together on a regular schedule, creating a **heartbeat** for the team (Maznevski & Chudoba, 2000).

Teams should set a schedule of regular face-to-face meetings, perhaps once a quarter or twice a year. These meetings can be planned in advance to coincide with events such as professional association meetings or larger management meetings. Heartbeat meetings should focus on progressing the team operations: task, interpersonal and learning processes, and team climate of psychological safety, cohesion, and trust. A two-day agenda of presentations sharing PowerPoint results from the last quarter will do nothing to help the team. But a two-day agenda of customer visits, site visits, and discussion of difficult cases to share knowledge and advice will pump the equivalent of highly oxygenated blood into the team's circulatory system.

The heartbeat rhythm does not need to coincide with major decision points or milestones. A high-performing team can handle intense conflict and heavy deliverables in virtual mode if it has developed strong processes and climate. Rhythm is critical. Like a human heartbeat, a team's heartbeat, the regularity of meetings, should be adjusted depending on the situation. If the team is less "fit" – for example, if there are new members or if trust has been damaged through a difficult situation – then the heart should beat faster than if the team is highly "fit." If the team's task is more difficult – which includes more ambiguity, higher strategic importance, or unexpected changes in the environment – then the heart should beat faster than if the team's task is simpler or more predictable.

Ideally, heartbeat meetings are in person, supplemented with interim virtual heartbeats. We also have seen successful teams that cannot meet face-to-face who develop strong heartbeats using virtual technologies. Like many people, you may have experienced this for the first time during the COVID-19 pandemic. These virtual-only teams consciously keep the task and interpersonal processes moving and find ways to build strong team conditions creatively. For example, members use simple phone cameras to share what is going on in their separate worlds, and they explicitly develop social relationships by sharing family and personal information as they increase their trust.

Virtual Teams Are Complex, but They Can Create Great Value

We are often asked "What's the secret?" as if there is some simple key that will unlock virtual team performance. Unfortunately, there is no such key. Collaborating across dispersion and diversity brings challenges. But it also brings opportunities that are worth the investment. Beyond their task mandate, virtual teams expand our possibilities. In today's organizations, well-managed virtual teams create development experiences with exposure to other cultures and situations. When virtual teams try to replicate their face-to-face teams, they are usually disappointed. But when they develop new skills to address the challenges discussed here, they achieve high performance and create competences that the organization as a whole can benefit from.

> ### Reflection Question 6.3: Virtual Teams
>
> Most people have worked on a team that does much of its work virtually, even if the team members are in the same geography (especially during the COVID-19 pandemic). How well have your virtual teams managed organization and discipline, getting to know people and context, and using a good portfolio of technologies? Have you developed strong rhythms? What other best practices have you observed?

Teaming to Coordinate across Global Organizations

The most determined global organizations connect global virtual teams in careful configurations to achieve ambitious goals. In our experience, global not-for-profit organizations are at the leading edge of experimenting with these networked team structures. Their mandates are highly complex and multifaceted, and they need to develop and implement solutions in close interdependence with highly complex environments. For example, they may be enforcing peace, delivering humanitarian aid in conflict zones, or alleviating climate change. They need the high interdependence of teams, and they need those teams to be connected and coordinated with each other for global decision-making and action (Gibson et al., 2019; Hajro et al., 2017).

The World Wide Fund for Nature, more commonly known as WWF and by its panda logo, has embraced a global teaming organization. WWF's global structure was historically like a federation of country organizations with a combination of fundraising and conservation project responsibilities. This structure was very effective for raising awareness and funding in different countries and sponsoring conservation projects in over 100 countries around the world. Some projects and initiatives crossed country and regional borders, but these were hard to implement with the federation-like structure. Because conservation needs are clearly global and not national, in late 2016, WWF took the bold step of reorganizing to prioritize nine global practices: forests, oceans, wildlife, food, climate and energy, freshwater, finance, markets, and governance.

Each practice is headed by a Practice Leader, who has a small management team. Each country office has one (or more, if appropriate) member of the Practice, called a Focal Point. A small team of key Focal Points – the core team – works with the Practice Leader to lead the Practice. The team is naturally highly diverse, and because of WWF's focus on conservation, virtual meetings were the norm from the 2017 kickoff onward. All the Practices partner with organizations outside WWF as well as members internally, and Focal Points are encouraged to develop those extended teams. Practice Leaders in turn work together as a team to identify synergies and reduce redundancies. Together they are accountable for delivering on the strategy of WWF globally (World Wide Fund for Nature, 2016).

WWF's Practice Leaders apply everything in this chapter, in many different ways. They identified performance goals that cover all three types of team outcomes for themselves as a team and for the Practices they lead. They began with a planning period during which they carefully designed the teams: they defined tasks and goals (What), identified the characteristics of people and the roles they needed on their leadership teams (Who), and worked closely with the WWF global organization to identify what kind of support they needed to facilitate the teams. In their operations, they pay close attention to task, social, and learning processes as well as their team climate. Because the teams are diverse, they invest considerable time and effort in understanding each other and their contexts and explicitly incorporate unique perspectives from each person. Since most of their work is virtual, they organized and became disciplined mindfully.

Even before COVID-19, they experimented with building a portfolio of technologies, including very innovative use of web-based video conferencing for multi-day conferences incorporating breakout work sessions. They carefully structured an annual rhythm of face-to-face and virtual meetings into the calendar, two to three years in advance for the major meetings. This careful application of virtual best practices helped them continue seamlessly when the pandemic halted all travel.

WWF knows that the team- and network-based structure they're implementing is challenging. Former Director General Marco Lambertini led a two-year highly inclusive planning process to help prepare the organization for implementation, and current Director General Kirsten Schuijt, who began her tenure in January 2023, continues this focus. WWF staff strongly believe this level of interdependence is the only way to achieve the collaboration needed to secure a sustainable future for all life on earth (World Wide Fund for Nature, 2023).

Managers facing complex international coordination – at WWF and other organizations – appreciate that combining teams at different levels helps them find and manage patterns in the complexity of their task. They know the task is difficult and that simple solutions and principles will only go part of the way. Even if the perspectives here are not simple to apply, they are systematic, and they provide ways of working toward performance and assessing progress.

Conclusion: Teams in International Management Start with the Basics and Add Sophistication

As work in international firms becomes more interdependent, the need for coordination increases. The most common way to coordinate is with teams. Most managers are part of multiple teams of different configurations, with at least some of those teams having members distributed across different geographies. It's important to set the team up well from the start, with the right Design. To turn the potential of the Design into reality, managers must lead and facilitate team Operations, adapting as the team works together. The team Design and Operations are part of leaders' traditional knowledge; however, managers of global teams must be able to lead them very well and in new contexts. The newer skills that are important in global organizations are managing inclusively to empower the benefits of diversity and managing virtual teams. The COVID-19 pandemic forced many people to work virtually much more than they ever had in the past, and as a result we see leaders and team members more open to experimenting with different forms of teaming. It will be exciting to see how teams evolve in this next phase of management.

Reflection Question 6.4: Fostering Collaborative Connectivity

Organizational learning researcher David A. Kolb has defined connectivity as "the mechanisms, processes, systems, and relationships that link individuals and collectives (e.g., groups, organizations, cultures, societies) by facilitating material, informational and/or social exchange. It includes geo-physical (e.g., space, time and location), technological (e.g., information technologies and their applications) as well as social interactions and artifacts" (Kolb, 2008, p. 128). Please try to think of a team or workgroup you have been part of and reflect:

How did you work with the aspects of connectivity presented in Kolb's quote (or not)? For instance, what artifacts or technological tools did you use that enabled or detracted from connectivity? What work processes did you have that enabled or detracted from connectivity?

Kolb, D. G. (2008). Exploring the metaphor of connectivity: Attributes, dimensions, and duality. *Organization Studies*, *29*(1), 127–144.

Reflection Question 6.5: Trust and Conflict in Global Collaboration

Global collaboration is characterized by complex demands for coordination across the organization, strong and varying expectations from stakeholders and constant organizational change, combined with linguistic and cultural differences and geographical distance. Many global leaders find that global collaboration raises demands for trust and that conflicts need to be prevented and addressed under different conditions than is the case in a local environment. Please think of a situation where you had to collaborate across borders or boundaries:

- What are you best at – building trust or managing conflict? And where are your weaknesses?

- Think of a difficult situation that was resolved in a good way: What did you do in that situation that worked well? What did you not do?
- What could you do more or less of in the future to build trust?
- What could you do more or less of in the future to prevent and handle conflicts?
- Who could you usefully involve in your efforts to build trust and handle conflicts?

Further Resources

In addition to the sources cited in this chapter, you can find further inspiration about the specific challenges associated with culture, language, and geographical distance, particularly in headquarters–subsidiary relations, at: https://www.globalledelse.dk/eng/chap10.html. This website, hosted by the Danish Confederation of Industry, is available free of charge and contains many other tools developed by the authors (Nielsen & Lyndgaard, 2020).

Bibliography

1 Degree. (2023). *About Us*. Retrieved October 29, 2023, from https://www.1degree.us/about

11th Hour Racing. (2023a). *The clock is ticking*. Retrieved September 15, 2023, from https://11thhourracing.org/

11th Hour Racing. (2023b). *11th Hour Racing Team wins The Ocean Race with a focus on restoring ocean health*. Retrieved September 15, 2023, from https://11thhourracing.org/11th-hour-racing-team-wins-the-ocean-race-with-a-focus-on-restoring-ocean-health/

11th Hour Racing. (2023c). *11th Hour Racing Team Campaign Report 2019–2023*. Retrieved October 29, 2023, from https://www.11thhourracingteam.org/wp-content/uploads/11th-Hour-Racing-Sustainability-Report-Sep20-FLAT.pdf

Adler, N. J. (1986). *International dimensions of organizational behavior*. PWS-Kent Publishers.

Bezrukova, K., Thatcher, S. M. B., Jehn, K. A., & Spell, C. S. (2012). The effects of alignments: Examining group faultlines, organizational cultures, and performance. *Journal of Applied Psychology, 97*(1), 77–92.

DiStefano, J. J., & Maznevski, M. L. (2000). Creating value with diverse teams in global management. *Organizational Dynamics, 29*(1), 45–63.

Earley, P. C., & Gibson, C. B. (2002). *Multinational work teams: A new perspective*. Routledge.

Edmondson, A. (1999). Psychological safety and learning behavior in work teams. *Administrative Science Quarterly, 44*(2), 350–383.

Gibson, C. B., Dunlop, P. D., & Cordery, J. L. (2019). Managing formalization to increase global team effectiveness and meaningfulness of work in multinational organizations. *Journal of International Business Studies, 50*(6), 1021–1052.

Gibson, C. B., & Gibbs, J. L. (2006). Unpacking the concept of virtuality: The effects of geographic dispersion, electronic dependence, dynamic structure, and national diversity on team innovation. *Administrative Science Quarterly*, *51*(3), 451–495.

Hackman, J. R. (1990). *Groups that work (and those that don't)*. Jossey-Bass.

Hajro, A., Gibson, C. B., & Pudelko, M. (2017). Knowledge exchange processes in multicultural teams: Linking organizational diversity climates to teams' effectiveness. *Academy of Management Journal*, *60*(1), 345.

Harvey, J.-F., Bresman, H., Edmondson, A. C., & Pisano, G. P. (2022). A strategic view of team learning in organizations. *Academy of Management Annals*, *16*(2), 476–507.

Jarvenpaa, S. L., Knoll, K., & Leidner, D. E. (1998). Is anybody out there? Antecedents of trust in global virtual teams. *Journal of Management Information Systems*, *14*(4), 29–64.

Lash, J. P. (1981). *Helen and teacher: The story of Helen Keller and Anne Sullivan Macy*. American Foundation for the Blind.

Lau, D. C., & Murnighan, J. K. (1998). Demographic diversity and faultlines: The compositional dynamics of organizational groups. *Academy of Management Review*, *23*(2), 325–340.

Lau, D. C., & Murnighan, J. K. (2005). Interactions within groups and subgroups: The effects of demographic faultlines. *Academy of Management Journal*, *48*(4), 645–659.

Lepine, J. A., Piccolo, R. F., Jackson, C. L., Mathieu, J. E., & Saul, J. R. (2008). A meta-analysis of teamwork processes: Tests of a multidimensional model and relationships with team effectiveness criteria. *Personnel Psychology*, *61*(2), 273–307.

Marks, M. A., Mathieu, J. E., & Zaccaro, S. J. (2001). A temporally based framework and taxonomy of team processes. *Academy of Management Review*, *26*(3), 356–376.

Mathieu, J., Maynard, M. T., Rapp, T., & Gilson, L. (2008). Team effectiveness 1997–2007: A review of recent advancements and a glimpse into the future. *Journal of Management*, *34*(3), 410–476.

Mathieu, J. E., Hollenbeck, J. R., van Knippenberg, D., & Ilgen, D. R. (2017). A century of work teams in the Journal of Applied Psychology. *Journal of Applied Psychology*, *102*(3), 452–467.

Maznevski, M. L. (1994). *Synergy and performance in multicultural teams*. Unpublished Dissertation, Western Business School, London, Ontario.

Maznevski, M. L., & Chudoba, K. M. (2000). Bridging space over time: Global virtual team dynamics and effectiveness. *Organization Science*, *11*(5), 473–492.

Maznevski, M. L., Steel, P., He, Y., Stahl, G. K., Chang, B., Fiscus, J., & Goestl, S. (2023). Exploring diversity sources in teams: Meta-analytic assessment of diversity taxonomies. In *Academy of Management Annual Conference*. Academy of Management.

McAllister, D. J. (1995). Affect- and cognition-based trust as foundations for interpersonal cooperation in organizations. *Academy of Management Journal*, *38*(1), 24–59.

Neeley, T. (2015). Global teams that work. *Harvard Business Review*, *93*, 75–81.

Nielsen, R. K., & Lyndgaard, D. B. (2020). *Grasping global leadership – Tools for "next practice."* Danish Confederation of Industry. Retrieved September 15, 2023, from https://www.globalledelse.dk/eng/

Stahl, G. K., Mäkelä, K., Zander, L., & Maznevski, M. L. (2010). A look at the bright side of multicultural team diversity. *Scandinavian Journal of Management*, *26*(4), 439–447.

Stahl, G. K., & Maznevski, M. L. (2021). Unraveling the effects of cultural diversity in teams: A retrospective of research on multicultural work groups and an agenda for future research. *Journal of*

Stahl, G. K., Maznevski, M. L., Voigt, A., & Jonsen, K. (2010). Unraveling the effects of cultural diversity in teams: A meta-analysis of research on multicultural work groups. *Journal of International Business Studies, 41*(4), 690–709.

Thatcher, S. M. B., & Patel, P. C. (2012). Group faultlines: A review, integration, and guide to future research. *Journal of Management, 38*(4), 969–1009.

The Ocean Race. (2023). Home page. Retrieved September 15, 2023, from https://www.theoceanrace.com

Waller, M. J., Okhuysen, G. A., & Saghafian, M. (2016). Conceptualizing emergent states: A strategy to advance the study of group dynamics. *Academy of Management Annals, 10*(1), 561–598.

Widmann, A., Messmann, G., & Mulder, R. H. (2016). The impact of team learning behaviors on team innovative work behavior: A systematic review. *Human Resource Development Review, 15*(4), 429–458.

Woodley, H. J., McLarnon, M. J., & O'Neill, T. A. (2019). The emergence of group potency and its implications for team effectiveness. *Frontiers in Psychology, 10*, 992.

World Sailing. (2023). *Team of the year awards*. Retrieved November 22, 2023, from https://www.sailing.org/awards/team-of-the-year/

World Wide Fund for Nature. (2016, August 30). *WWF launches new strategy with the appointment of eight global Practice Leaders*. Retrieved September 15, 2023, from https://wwf.panda.org/wwf_news/?276775/WWF-launches-new-strategy-with-the-appointment-of-five-global-Practice-Leaders.

World Wide Fund for Nature. (n.d.). Home page. Retrieved September 15, 2023, from https://wwf.panda.org/

Zander, L., Zettinig, P., & Mäkelä, K. (2013). Leading global virtual teams to success. *Organizational Dynamics, 42*(3), 228–237.

Zellmer-Bruhn, M. E., Maloney, M. M., Bhappu, A. D., & Salvador, R. (2008). When and how do differences matter? An exploration of perceived similarity in teams. *Organizational Behavior and Human Decision Processes, 107*(1), 41.

7 Talent Management
Selection, Preparation, and Assignment of Global Leaders

> Travel is fatal to prejudice, bigotry, and narrow-mindedness.
> Mark Twain, American writer (1835–1910)

Key Learning Objectives

At the end of this chapter, students will be able to:

- Delineate the selection, preparation, and assignment stages for global leadership postings.
- Recognize the personal challenges that international assignees face, including culture shock.
- Identify the percentage of women selected and deployed in global leadership roles.
- Define Duty of Care and an organization's responsibilities to employees.
- Identify the personal characteristics for an international assignee and conditions necessary for an effective international assignment.

Global Talent Management

Chapters 1 and 2 discussed the varied roles and characteristics of global leaders. This chapter describes the selection of global leaders and the skills they need, especially when deployed internationally.

A report by the international management consulting firm, Korn Ferry (2022) states,

A major crisis is looming over organizations and economies throughout the world. By 2030, demand for skilled workers will outstrip supply, resulting in a global talent shortage of more than 85.2 million people.

The study researched the talent–supply gap in 20 developed and developing economies in the Americas, Europe, the Middle East, and Asia Pacific. It looked at the countries as a whole and paid particular attention to three major knowledge-intensive industries: financial and business services; technology, media, and telecommunications; and manufacturing. The study classified workers as:

- Highly skilled workers who are individuals with postsecondary education (college or university) or a high-level trade college qualification.
- Mid-skilled workers who have a high school or a lower-level trade college qualification.
- Low-skilled workers who have less than a secondary education.

India is the only country projected to have a surplus of highly skilled workers by 2030. Low birth rates in Europe and Japan, baby boomers retiring and leaving the workforce, along with the "Great Resignation" resulting from the COVID-19 pandemic have all had an impact on labor supply. This talent–supply gap critically affects the search for and selection of global leaders. As the demands placed on global leaders become increasingly complex, the performance of globally operating organizations can be severely hampered. In the following sections, we briefly revisit the complexity of the global environment in which global leaders must function and use their requisite skills.

Mindful Global Leaders Are the Key to Managing Complexity

In Chapter 1, we identified several characteristics that work to increase complexity: variety, interdependence, and ambiguity. Each of these characteristics is difficult to manage, but their interconnectedness magnifies that challenge.

Globally, executives are dealing with a wider variety of organizations, governments, and employees than ever before. Globalization is not just about "more"; it is about "more and different." There are more competitors and partners, with diverse types of organizations and networks, serving customers with different needs in different markets. Companies have more operations in more locations to manage and, of course, have more governments to contend with.

Companies exist in a world of complex social, political, and economic interdependencies. Interdependence is not only a feature of the external environment. It is also something companies create themselves through offshoring, outsourcing, alliances, and network arrangements related to value chains, often to cope with competitive challenges.

If it were simply more customers, governments, interest groups, and competitors that were passive, that would represent an increase in detail complexity as explained in Chapter 1. A corporation could manage the complexity by simply adding managers and computers. However, the reality is one of dynamic complexity. The increase in interdependence and variety leads to more ambiguity. Ambiguity makes clear understanding difficult. As we have said, the whole system is in constant motion, always changing. And the rate of change seems to be accelerating.

Eliminate or Amplify?

There are two common methods for dealing with increased complexity: elimination of input variety or amplification. Elimination of input variety is the reduction of "noisy" information achieved by not being able, or willing, to see and understand the nuances in the environment; or by creating an artificial state of certainty, misleading executives into thinking they are in control. Such ostrich-like behavior usually does not bring success.

Amplification generally means increasing the number of decision-makers. Organizational structures have become more complex, with more managers and more multidimensional matrices. Increasingly complex structures, however, are at risk of becoming unwieldly. Moreover, they cannot always adapt quickly to new circumstances, since they are designed to fit a particular set of contingencies. Additional complex sets of policies may not work either. In a continually changing, dynamically complex environment, policies must be changed continually or they lose their effectiveness.

W. Ross Ashby, a pioneer in cybernetics, said, "Only variety can destroy variety" (Ashby, 1972), which became known as Ashby's Law of Requisite Variety (Ashby, 1973). In human information processing terms, this means that when there is complex, ambiguous information coming from the environment, organizational decision-makers (managers) must have the cognitive complexity to notice these inputs, decode them, process them, and possess a sufficiently varied behavioral repertoire to act on them properly.

Indeed, research has shown that for nonroutine or highly complex decisions, teams make better decisions on average than do individuals. Yet, simple amplification will not necessarily work. If, for example, executives operating out of a corporate headquarters in Norwich, Connecticut cannot generate the requisite variety in their decisions to match the variety existing in a global marketplace, simply increasing the size of the team may not work. If multiple decision-makers are highly homogeneous, with similar outlooks, a similar vested interest in the outcome, and reliance on the same selected sources for their information, they may be deceiving themselves. That is, they may think they are facing less variety than they are.

The appropriate response to complexity is the deliberate development of human requisite variety. Simply, this means that global organizations must find the right people capable of deciphering the informational content in the environment to create the appropriate responses and organizational processes to execute action plans. Weick and Van Orden stated, "Globalization requires people to make sense of turbulence in order to create processes that keep resources moving to locations of competitive advantage" (Weick & Van Orden, 1990, p. 49). Jack Welch called this the globalization of intellect: "The real challenge is to globalize the mind of the organization ... I think until you globalize intellect, you haven't really globalized the company" (Rohwer & Windham, 2000).

Today, managers face challenges that require a more complex view of the world, or they may be prone to deciding on the wrong, overly simplified solutions to their problems. To paraphrase the American journalist, H. L. Mencken, there is always a well-known solution to every problem: neat, plausible, and wrong (Mencken, 1920).

There is little doubt that dealing with the complexity of global operations requires having managers with orientations, competencies, and skill sets beyond those required in domestic organizations. Acquiring and retaining people who can function effectively in this new context becomes a critical human resource management undertaking. High-potential individuals must be carefully selected and given the necessary preparation and professional development. Their careers must be managed responsively (preparing the assignee and/or expatriate and the expatriate's family, measuring the employee's performance, and repatriating the individual) so that they remain with the organization, using their new skills to achieve strategic objectives.

Skills

A 2021 McKinsey & Company survey found that companies are increasingly focusing their skills-building efforts on softer skills and advanced cognitive skills while continuing to need technological skills as well. What are these skills?

- Higher cognitive skills: advanced literacy and writing, quantitative and statistical skills, critical thinking and complex information processing, leadership.

Doctors, accountants, research analysts, writers and editors, and global leaders/managers typically use these.
- Technological skills: basic to advanced IT skills, data analysis, engineering, and research. These are the skills that are likely to be the most highly rewarded as companies seek more software developers, engineers, robotics, and scientific experts.
- Social and emotional ("soft") skills: advanced communication and negotiation, empathy, the ability to learn continuously, to manage others, and to be adaptable. Business development, emergency response, and counseling are examples.

Dr. Joseph Aoun, President of Northeastern University, in his book *Robot-Proof: Higher Education in the Age of Artificial Intelligence* (2017), also referred to these softer skills as "human literacy" or those qualities computers cannot replicate, such as creativity, entrepreneurship, systems thinking, empathy, cultural agility, and teamwork.

International Assignments Come in Many Shapes and Sizes

International assignments have increased in importance not only for strategic reasons but also for career success. KPMG (2021) surveyed 375 global mobility professionals in 25 countries for their *2021 Global Assignment and Practices Survey*. Forty-eight percent of the companies had 50 or fewer international assignees while 39% had 51–500 assignees and 13% had over 500. According to the Society for Human Resource Management (2022), the typical reasons companies use international assignments are:

- Filling a vacancy or need in an existing operation.
- Transferring technology or knowledge to a subsidiary or a client.
- Developing an individual's career through challenging tasks in an international setting.
- Analyzing the market.
- Launching a new product or service.

Historically used in a management control role, for decades expatriate managers went abroad for long terms, usually two to three years. Very often they were accompanied by a spouse who did not have a career and was not expected to work. It was viewed as an interesting or exciting opportunity and a possible chance to make additional money or save money. Surviving the assignment was often considered to be a measure of success, and on return executives usually stayed with the company.

That scenario has changed dramatically. Today, managers are transferred to and from the parent company to learn about affiliated operations in other countries, fill skills gaps, transfer knowledge and technology, launch projects, facilitate integration of the global value chain, transfer corporate culture, and improve management development.

However, not all employees are willing to accept an international assignment and relocate to another country. The main reasons for turning down assignments are family responsibilities as well as a spouse's/partner's career and employment issues. Many potential assignees are millennials who may have elderly parents and/or small children to care for. The career impact and loss of income for spouses and partners have become important considerations as executives weigh an international assignment. Additionally, companies have had to adapt to the times and reconsider their policies on accompanied assignments with the increase in nontraditional families (e.g., same sex, unmarried). During 2020 and into 2021, COVID-19 and safety concerns were also important considerations.

> ### Reflection Question 7.1: Becoming a Global Assignee
>
> 1. Are you interested in pursuing a global assignment? Why or why not?
> 2. Different people find different kinds of conditions challenging – physical environment, social environment, distance from family and close friends, living conditions, and so on.
>   a. What types of conditions you are likely to find most challenging?
>   b. Which are so extreme for you that you would try to avoid an assignment?
>   c. Which do you think you could manage with support? What type of support would be appropriate?
> 3. How can you prepare yourself for the possibility of an international assignment in the future?

Although expatriates on long-term assignments are common and probably still the majority of international assignees, numerous surveys of multinationals have also shown an increasing use of non-standard international assignments. These assignment types take on different forms such as frequent flyer, commuter, rotations, virtual, short-term (up to 12 months), and extended business traveler (30–180 days) assignments. The *Financial Times* defines people in these new arrangements as "**flexpatriates**," or as "an employee who takes up an international assignment centered on frequent international business trips without locating abroad" (Financial Times, n.d.). The COVID-19 pandemic added a new dimension to international assignments, and many companies are anticipating what the future of work will look like. The KPMG survey states that the "work from anywhere" trend is likely to continue, particularly for professional services employees. The ability for many professionals and knowledge workers to work from any place with an internet connection has untethered them and created a cadre of digital nomads – like Sophie.

Sophie, a Digital Nomad

After graduating from university, Sophie experimented with a variety of jobs: volunteering with Teach for America, teaching at an inner-city elementary school, marketing with a small clothing accessories company, and then with a large sports clothing company, before taking a marketing position with a global fast-food restaurant. She enjoyed all these experiences, traveled, progressed in the companies, and developed her marketing skills.

She had an apartment in an historic section of the city where she had taught and a car to get out of the city on weekends with friends. She was the picture of an outgoing, personable, and successful young professional. Then COVID-19 arrived, and she transitioned to remote work. Her travel disappeared and she missed the personal contact with her colleagues and others with whom she worked. This wasn't her idea of a satisfactory situation. She wanted more in her career.

She began exploring opportunities and soon was hired by a technology equipment company for a global marketing team position. The company's headquarters was on the West Coast, her boss lived in England, and her team was spread out in the United States and Europe. Although COVID-19 had waned, the job primarily remained remote. She and her team had multiple daily Zoom meetings and met often through the year in Europe for work meetings and visiting retailers.

After a while, she wondered why she was renting an apartment and making monthly car payments. She ended her lease, sold the car, and became a digital nomad, part of the work-from-anywhere trend. Her mail is delivered to her mother's address, and she spends the year traveling to interesting locations where she visits and lives with friends and relatives, often for weeks at a time – provided they have a good Wi-Fi connection.

In 2023, the firm had a substantial layoff, but Sophie quickly secured a new position after taking a couple of weeks to tour the Nordic countries. As Director of Development for a public relations and marketing agency specializing in celebrity endorsement, social media strategy, and public relations, she remains fully remote. The headquarters, technically, is in New York City with the CEO based in London and other partners splitting their time between Boston, New York, and Los Angeles. Asked what a typical day might look like, she replied:

Time zone differences make for unique meeting times. Teams range in size from three to six people spread from Europe to California. If you have an early or late call, you may take time for personal tasks during the day, or begin your next day later or end earlier. It's no longer just 9–5 Monday through Friday. We may work nights and weekends often for events that can be fun. Colleagues quickly become friends, and time together "working" can be enjoyable.

We have an entire team morning call everyday Monday–Thursday at 9:30 EST to highlight priorities for the day and week. There are standing weekly team calls per department (Social, PR, Celebrity, etc.). I am tasked with getting new clients, so I do outreach to brands via e-mail and LinkedIn. If they are interested in learning more, I set up a call with them. Travel includes events, conferences, and networking opportunities.

There are some downsides. Working across different time zones results in not always being able to quickly solve a "fire drill" or a problem that needs a fast resolution. Personally, being a VERY social outgoing individual, I sometimes struggled being remote. Thanks to technology, I felt extremely close to some coworkers that I connected with the most. At the same time, not being able to take breaks and enjoy meals in person with most of my coworkers eliminated that element of human connection that I crave.

One downside for almost everyone now is the difficulty in separating work and home life. With no commute you can start early and work later. With work e-mails on our phones, how do we resist checking notifications and maintaining a work–life balance? Also, commitments such as children, partners, chores, etc. can interfere with productivity. I have had teams where the norm was to work during vacations, nights & weekends, and I have had others where a clear boundary was drawn and respected.

A major reason for the rise in nonstandard assignments is the expense associated with relocating expatriates and their families. The Society for Human Resource Management (SHRM) notes that the cost of a three-year assignment for an expatriate and their family can exceed US$3 million (as of 2017). Expatriates' salaries are usually higher than those of local managers, and they often receive benefits to make an overseas assignment move attractive. Benefits frequently include housing or a housing allowance, moving expenses, tax equalization, and schooling for children. Many of these benefits are not usually provided to local employees. In addition to lowering costs, having fewer expatriates thus also reduces the risk of tension between expatriate employees and local employees. Many companies that want to provide employees with more flexibility are thus actively investigating hybrid working arrangements, blending in-office, remote work, and travel as necessary.

Companies continue to try to understand and measure the cost–benefit trade-off of international assignments to gauge their effectiveness and return on investment (ROI). Some firms use specific assignments or projects that can be assessed as completed or not, while others attempt to measure more formally the successful completion at the expected cost. Companies are increasingly tracking the costs of international assignments and requiring clear statements of the assignment's objectives, as well as preapproval by business units and possibly HR. Some are doing cost–benefit analyses, but businesses that measure ROI are in the minority.

International assignments are important tools for the coordination and integration of organizational resources, which are essential activities for successful strategy implementation in geographically dispersed companies embedded in differing cultural environments. Electronic communication and data processing system options allow for the creation of sophisticated enterprise information systems to coordinate dispersed operations. However, the cultural nuances of information that provide the deepest comprehension of market-specific knowledge are not transferable electronically. Hybrid and virtual assignments also do not provide the same experiential and relationship benefits as working abroad and most likely will be used by companies as supplementary tools.

The most important nuances of operations in a particular cultural context are contained in deep-rooted **tacit knowledge**, which cannot be codified. This knowledge is acquired experientially and must be shared through face-to-face interactions. Firms gain sustainable competitive advantage from executives acquiring experiences and lessons that are held as tacit knowledge and then shared across the organization, since these are valuable, rare, and difficult to imitate by competitors.

Given the dispersed nature of multinational organizations, knowledge sharing is particularly difficult. Some solutions to this challenge include the use of short-term assignments as well as cadres of expatriates and **inpatriates** (an employee transferred from a foreign country to a corporation's home country operation or headquarters) to acquire and share tacit knowledge that exists within the organization. Short-term assignments, inpatriation, and expatriation can be used strategically to implement projects, fill positions, and, as a management development experience, provide high-potential employees with a global orientation – or all three. These employees create global relationships, inside and outside the company, and share explicit and tacit operating knowledge. The relationships and knowledge then become essential to the value creation process in global operations (Harzing, 2001).

Some of the current authors have dealt with companies that were increasing the number of inpatriates to headquarters. These inpatriate assignments were usually short-term, two to three months at headquarters for a special project. This had a double advantage of exposing the inpatriate to headquarters processes, concerns, and perspectives while allowing headquarters personnel to become acquainted with cultural orientations and views of divisions from around the world. At the same time, some of these firms were establishing formal policies that required international experience as a prerequisite for promotion to senior ranks, thereby "localizing" management and eliminating many of the perks that were formerly needed as incentives for executives to accept international assignments.

Corporations have made a number of changes in their approach to global assignments in the last few decades. Some of these trends are shown in Table 7.1.

Table 7.1 **Some trends in global assignments (Adapted from Caligiuri & Bonache, 2016).**

Some Trends in Global Assignments	Conventional Approach (1960s–early 1990s)	Modern Approach
Duration	2–4 years	Diverse: Long-term (1–4 years), short-term (< 1 year), permanent, commuter, extended business traveler (30–180 days), digital nomads
Focus	Safeguard assets including intellectual property, employee management and control	Transfer knowledge, management development, project management
Accompanied by	Assignee (generally male) accompanied by nonworking spouse (female), traditional family	Both genders, dual career partners, non-traditional relationships and families
Assignee viewpoint	Adventure, financially rewarding with benefits and tax considerations	Career development, path to C-suite
Success	Complete assignment successfully	Performance criteria such as ROI
On return	Long-term employees generally stayed with the company	May leave for better opportunities
Cross-cultural training	None	Improved

Selection

In 1973, published research showed that managers were selected for international assignments based on their proven performance in a similar, usually domestic, job (Miller, 1973). The ability to work with foreign employees was at or near the bottom of the list of important qualifications. Unfortunately, 50 years later the situation has not changed enough. SHRM (2022) states,

> Traditionally, organizations have relied on technical, job-related skills as the main criteria for selecting candidates for overseas assignments, but assessing global mindset is equally, if not more, important for successful assignments. This is especially true given that international assignments are increasingly key components of leadership and employee development.

Technical expertise and knowledge as well as previous domestic performance, although important, should not be given undue weighting in assessing a person's ability to adapt to and function in another culture. It does no good to send the most technically qualified engineers or finance managers to a foreign subsidiary if they cannot function there and must be brought home prematurely. Caligiuri (2012, p. 171) stated that,

> [S]election for international work starts where other systems stop in that only those individuals who have a demonstrated competence for the tasks and duties of the job are considered. In essence, international assignment selection attempts to take a group of "qualified individuals" and determine who can effectively deal with the challenges inherent in working with individuals, groups, and organizations that may approach work in a very different way. Not everyone with a proven record of professional success in a domestic context for a given job title will have what it takes to be successful in an international context – even doing the same job with the same job title.

Effectiveness in the International Assignment: $E = f(PAIS)$

We believe that managerial success in an international assignment comes from the ability to live and work *effectively* in the cultural setting of an assignment. A useful framework for thinking about selection in the context of overseas effectiveness was developed by Daniel Kealy in his work with the Canadian International Development Agency. It focuses on three factors: adaptation, expertise, and interaction. He asserts that for a person to be effective, they must adapt – both personally and with his/her family – to the overseas environment (both themselves personally and their family); have the technical knowledge and expertise to do the assignment well, and be able to interact effectively with people from the new culture. Effectiveness is a function of professional expertise PLUS the ability to adapt to one's host country PLUS intercultural communication skills to interact with the locals.

However, possibly one of the most overlooked and neglected factors in selection for an international assignment is **situational readiness** (Franke & Nicholson, 2002). A way to think about this is to ask the question, "Is an international assignment right for a person at this time with everything going on in their life and with their family?" Some examples include having a family that is willing, able, and probably excited to take the assignment; not having aged or sick parents to care for; or having children with special needs that cannot be accommodated in the host country.

Our shorthand notation for a candidate selection rubric following this logic is $E = f(PAIS)$, which stands for *Effectiveness is a function of (Professional expertise, Adaptation, Intercultural interaction, and Situational readiness)*.

Effectiveness on the job is the most important outcome for an international assignment. Many studies have used outcome variables such as expatriate satisfaction with an assignment as a surrogate for performance. An international assignee who is satisfied with his or her assignment is not necessarily an effective manager. Neither is a manager with previous international experience necessarily effective, although such managers are likely to be more satisfied in their assignment. Previous experience is related to increased satisfaction, ease of adjustment, and lower levels of stress, all of which are positive. However, global companies need effective managers, and an ineffective one can damage relationships in the host country. Poor performance in an international assignment can also result in high professional and personal costs to the individual and his or her family. Therefore, all the variables in $E = f(PAIS)$ are important.

> **Reflection Question 7.2: Your Personal $E = f(PAIS)$ Equation**
>
> 1. When you apply the equation $E = f(PAIS)$ to your career, on which variables are you most likely the strongest?
> 2. Which will you likely need to focus more on developing: Professional expertise, Adaptation, Intercultural interaction, or Situational readiness?
> 3. What are the implications for how you should approach your education or prepare for your next company assignment?

Women as Global Leaders

The international assignment of female executives has become an important consideration as more women have graduated from business schools and are in line for senior management and international careers. It is also a relevant concern both under employment equity guidelines and legislation in countries such as the

United States, the United Kingdom, and Canada. The overall percentage of female international assignees had been rising, with historical estimates being between 16% and 20%. In 2017, Mercer (2022) reported that 14% of the expatriate workforce were women. However, the report pointed out that there were significant differences between industries (e.g., 8–11% in the energy and tech sectors compared to 23% in the life sciences sector) and regions (e.g., lower in emerging economies than in developed economies). It stated that in developed economies the proportion of women "lingers in the 20–25 percent range."

Almost 40 years ago, Nancy Adler conducted some pioneering research on female expatriates (Adler, 1987). Her research showed that, contrary to conventional wisdom at the time, women did want careers as international managers. Another lesson learned about women expatriates was that the perception by men in the home country was more of a barrier than the behavior of men in the foreign country. Men in the company's home country tended not to select women for international assignments to protect them from imaginary difficulties in foreign countries. However, Adler learned that a foreign woman is not expected to act like a local woman, and being foreign was more noticeable than being female.

Caligiuri and Cascio state that "the four variables predicting a Western female expatriate's success [are] her individual characteristics; the support she receives from her organization; her family; [and] the host nationals with whom she works" (Caligiuri & Cascio, 1988, p. 395). To this list we add that she should be at a senior level and have significant decision-making responsibility so that executives in the foreign company will understand that she is a senior executive and the person with whom they must deal.

Our advice is to select and send the best person for the job. If a woman is the best person for an international assignment, then she should be sent. However, being a woman expatriate in some countries is undoubtedly more difficult than in others, and companies have a responsibility to prepare women well for challenging assignments in difficult countries.

Reflection Question 7.3: Potential Global Talent Biases

1. What kind of biases might you expect to see in the process of identifying and selecting international assignees? For example, how might characteristics like national culture, gender, ethnicity, profession, sexual orientation, age, or religion be viewed? (For instance: Is seniority likely to be considered a plus or a minus?)
2. What biases might play a role in assigning employees to particular countries or regions?

Assignment Destinations

According to the British CEO Magazine (2019), the demand for business leaders who have worked internationally is stronger than ever. It states,

In the high-stakes world of C-suite recruitment, leaders who can navigate international environments where local customs, cultural nuances and foreign stakeholders often impact business outcomes are in demand as businesses operate in an increasingly globalised market. Working overseas implies a leader has encountered diverse audiences with different cultural backgrounds which usually results in highly developed adaptability, listening, solution-processing and risk-mitigation skills – competencies all highly relevant in the competitive market organisations operate in.

The United States usually is the top destination for global companies, followed by Canada, Europe, and Asia/Australia/Pacific Rim locations. But where is future growth likely to come from? The World Bank's June 2022 Global Economic Prospects Report stated that global growth will decline from 5.7% in 2021 to 3% in 2023–2024. However, even with the slowdown, EMDEs (emerging markets and developing economies) will continue to grow faster than developed economies. Companies will continue to explore the CIVETS (Colombia, Indonesia, Vietnam, Egypt, Turkey, South Africa), the Next Eleven countries (Indonesia, Vietnam, Egypt, Turkey, Mexico, South Korea, Bangladesh, Iran, Pakistan, Nigeria, Philippines), and the MINT countries (Mexico, Indonesia, Turkey). It is difficult to predict which of those countries are the likely economic winners of the future, but we do know that many of them can be difficult, challenging places to work in.

It is possible that you, or someone who will be reporting to you, could be assigned to one of these countries. What is a company's responsibility when assigning an employee there? What should a company do regarding training and security for employees who work there? What is the responsibility of individuals who agree to work there?

The Fund for Peace has created an interactive Fragile States Index, which can be found on its website (https://fragilestatesindex.org/). All the countries included in the above lists fall into a "Warning" or higher category, except for South Korea, which is rated as "Stable," and Indonesia, which is close to "Warning." If these are the countries where growth is likely to come from, what are companies doing to attract and train global executives who can function effectively, and safely, there?

There are two dimensions on which to categorize countries as challenging destinations: administrative problems for international program managers (government regulations, immigration, work permits, tax issues, locating acceptable housing) and cultural difficulty for the assignee and family in adapting to a new country, including personal risks, security, and health issues.

Today, a successful assignment also means a safe assignment. Companies are formalizing programs to ensure the safety and security of their expatriates and families to minimize international assignment turndowns, attrition, early returns, and failures.

> ### Reflection Question 7.4: Choose Your International Assignment Destination
>
> Based on their research, Schotter and Beamish (2013) developed an interactive website, "The Hassle Factor" (ivey.uwo.ca/internationalbusiness/research/hasslefactor/). This dataset identifies 11 negative factors or risks for international assignees including women expatriates, as well as ones that impact foreign investment potential.
>
> 1. Choose a country in which you think you would like to live. Go to "The Hassle Factor" website. How did your chosen destination rank?
> 2. What did you learn? Do you still want to live and work there?
> 3. Compare two countries you think may be opposites. What were the differences?

Duty of Care

Someday, you or a direct report could be working internationally on your career route to the C-suite. If you fall ill, get into an accident, or are affected by dangerous events in the host country, will your organization have a plan in place to assist you? Take the example of the company Global Rescue, which provides crisis response services to corporations, governments, and individuals:

During the Arab Spring, the company ushered more than 200 people out of Egypt. Its staff spent a month evacuating clients from Haiti after the earthquake there in 2010. Last year, it helped the American snowboarder Luke Mitrani after he broke his neck in New Zealand while training for a competition. (Martin, 2014)

Do you travel internationally for your employer or with a program at your university? If so, do you know if you are covered by a Duty of Care policy? Duty of Care generally means being responsible for your students' or employees' well-being.

Collins English Dictionary defines it as "the legal obligation to safeguard others from harm while they are in your care, using your services, or are exposed to your activities."

Although security and COVID-19 have tended to be top of mind recently for many executives, there are numerous less newsworthy but serious threats that expatriates and their families may face such as air pollution, traffic accidents, and crime. The bottom line is that companies need to develop a strategy and policies for assisting employees well in advance of crises.

International SOS is another leading international health care, medical, and security assistance company that operates in more than 70 countries. It published the first comprehensive research study of duty of care responsibilities for companies that "must apply their Duty of Care responsibilities for managing different staff (business travelers, locals, expatriates, international assignees and dependents) and many different threats" (International SOS, n.d.). Their Duty of Care and Travel Risk Management Global Benchmarking Study lists the following categories and examples of threats:

- Political unrest: war, political upheaval, coup d'etat, civil unrest.
- Environmental factors: poor air quality, remoteness of work.
- Natural Disasters: earthquakes, floods, hurricanes.
- Illness, disease: infectious diseases, pandemics (COVID-19, etc.).
- Terrorism, violence, crime, kidnapping, imprisonment.
- Accidents: auto, workplace, airlines.
- Travel-related incidents: lost passport, luggage, lack of visa or other necessary documents.

This research study characterized three classes of companies on a continuum of awareness and concern for employees. The "At Risk" companies were "unaware of a duty of risk obligation or had an attitude of 'it won't happen to us'" or didn't know how to handle the issue. The "Compliance Focus" companies might have experienced an incident but were focused primarily on the legal issues. Lastly, the "Corporate Social Responsibility Focus" companies were focused on "doing the right thing for employees."

One of the authors of this book was scheduled to teach an executive education course in Saudi Arabia at a time when there were some increased tensions in the Persian Gulf area. Having recently taught about this subject, he realized he did not know if his university had a Duty of Care policy and was delighted to learn that it had quite a robust one, including a hotline for medical and security emergencies.

> **Reflection Question 7.5: Your Organization's Duty of Care Policy**
>
> Does your organization or university have a Duty of Care policy or similar policy that covers you while traveling on university or company business or events? Go to your organization's website or ask your HRM office. What did you learn?

Training and Preparation for an International Assignment

The training that a person undergoes before an international assignment should be a function of the degree of cultural exposure that they will experience. Important dimensions of cultural exposure include degree of similarity/difference with one's home culture, degree of integration into a culture, and the duration of stay. The integration dimension represents the intensity of the exposure. A person could be sent to a foreign country on a short-term, technical, troubleshooting matter and experience little significant contact with the local culture. The same person could be in another country only for a brief visit to negotiate a contract, but the cultural interaction could be very intense and might require a great deal of cultural fluency to be successful. An expatriate assigned abroad for a period of years is likely to experience a high degree of interaction with the local culture simply from living there.

The framework shown in Figure 7.1 suggests that developmental methodologies have different transformative potential that can be aligned with the nature of the international assignment. For example, for short stays with a low level of integration, an "information-giving approach" such as area and cultural briefings and basic language training will probably suffice. For longer stays with higher levels of integration, language training, role-plays, critical incidents, case studies, and possibly stress management training would be more appropriate. For people who will be living abroad for extended periods of time and/or will experience a high level of integration into the culture, extensive language training, sensitivity training, field experiences, and simulations are recommended training methodologies. Effective preparation would also include contextual understanding about the realities and difficulties of working in another culture and the importance of establishing good working relationships with the local people.

The effectiveness of educational modalities for personal development and transformation is determined by four elements present in the "degree of experiential rigor" associated with the experience. Bird (2015) refers to these by the acronym *CAIR*: the *Complexity* of the experience; whether it generates *Affect* (emotion);

Developmental methodologies

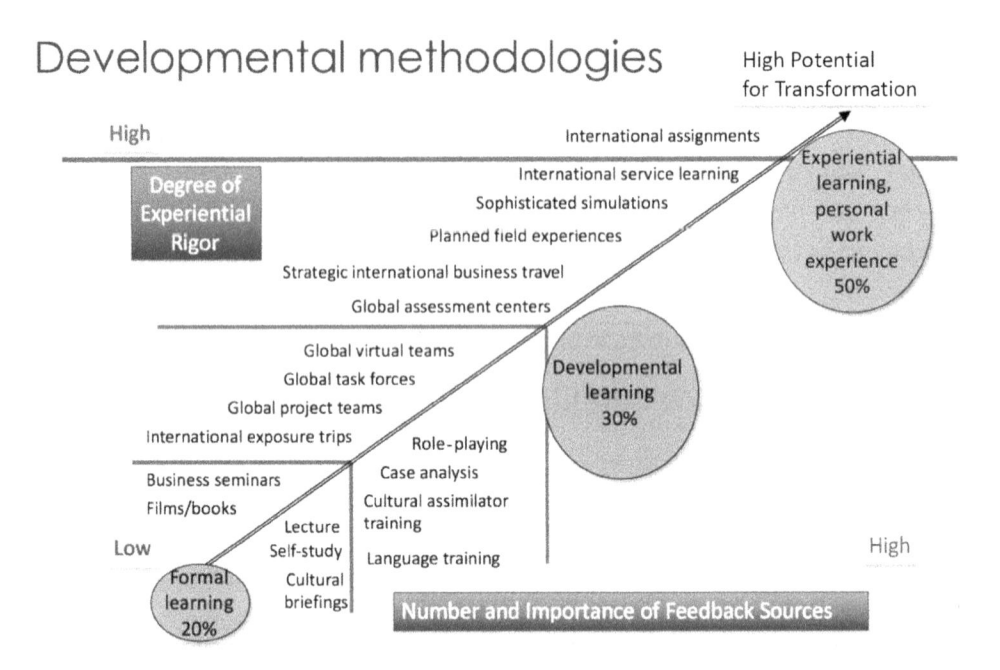

Figure 7.1 Relationship between developmental methodologies and the potential for personal transformation. (Adapted from Mendenhall et al., 2017.)

how *Intense* the experience is; and its *Relevance* to a person's career or goals. As can be seen in Figure 7.1, increases in experiential methodologies contribute to improved development outcomes.

The Canadian International Development Agency (CIDA) advanced a useful approach for augmenting assignees' training for long-term international postings requiring high levels of cultural integration. After extensive pre-departure training in Canada, expatriates were sent to the field. Shortly after they began in their new posting, more training was provided to them along with their new coworkers, thus facilitating the process of assimilation into their new post. During the expatriates' stay abroad, periodic "refreshers" or debriefing sessions were held. Finally, the expatriates were actively involved in repatriation training both prior to and after their return home. The expatriate's spouse and family were also provided with similar training and resources.

Historically, companies provided little, if any, cross-cultural training. But this is an area where some change has taken place as more companies realize the value of providing such training for assignees and family members. SHRM (2022) advises companies to invest in cross-cultural training, since it

- Prepares the individual/family mentally for the move.
- Removes some of the unknown.

- Increases self-awareness and cross-cultural understanding.
- Provides the opportunity to address questions and anxieties in a supportive environment.
- Motivates and excites.
- Reduces stress and provides coping strategies.
- Eases the settling-in process.
- Reduces the chances of relocation failure.

Adaptation and the Reality of Culture Shock

Despite a strong desire to understand and adapt to a new environment, assignees often experience some problems when entering another culture.

A condition associated with a possible failure to adapt, culture shock – or, more properly, **acculturative stress** – is rooted in our psychological processes. The normal assumptions used by managers in their home cultures to interpret perceptions and communicate intentions no longer work in the new cultural environment. International assignees may bring with them on their postings a number of implicit or explicit biases. These may range from a generalization bias ("They're all the same") to a single perspective instinct ("This is the only solution!") (Rosling, 2018). Culture shock is not a shock experienced, for example, from exposure to conditions of poverty. Culture shock is reflected in the stress and behavioral patterns associated with a loss of control and sense of mastery in a situation. Culture shock, in normal attempts to socialize or in a business context, can result in confusion and frustration. Managers who are used to being competent in such situations may find that they are unable to operate effectively.

An inability to interpret surroundings and function appropriately can lead to anxiety, frustration, and sometimes signs of depression. Most experts agree that some form of culture shock is probably unavoidable, even for experienced internationalists. People who repeatedly move to new cultures likely dampen the emotional swings they experience and probably shorten the period of adjustment, but even they do not escape it entirely. In fact, research on intercultural effectiveness has found that those who eventually become the most effective expatriates tend to report experiencing greater difficulty in their initial adjustment. This is because those who are more sensitive to different patterns of human interaction are likely to be both disrupted by changes in these patterns and become adept at adopting new patterns.

There are four typical modes of responding to a new environment (Berry, 1980):

- Going Native (assimilation): "acceptance of the new culture while rejecting one's own culture";

- Being a Participator (integration): "adaptation to the new culture while retaining one's own culture";
- Being a Tourist (separation): "maintenance of one's own culture by avoiding contact with the new culture"; and
- Being an Outcast (marginalization): "the inability to either adapt to the new culture or remain comfortable with one's own culture."

The pattern experienced by people who move into a new culture usually comes in three phases as shown in Figure 7.2: (1) the elation associated with anticipating a new environment and the early period of moving into it; (2) the distress of dealing with one's own ineffectiveness and, as the novelty erodes and reality sets in, the realization that one has to live and function in a setting perceived as strange; and (3) the adjustment to and effective coping in the new environment.

During the first and second periods, performance is usually below one's normal level. The time of adjustment back to normal or above-average performance takes from three to nine months, depending on previous experience, the degree of cultural difference being experienced, and the individual personality.

Frequently observed symptoms of culture shock are similar to most defensive or stress reactions. People reject their new environment as well as the people who live there, often with angry or negative evaluations of "strangeness." Other symptoms include fatigue; tension; anxiety; excessive concern about hygiene; hostility; an

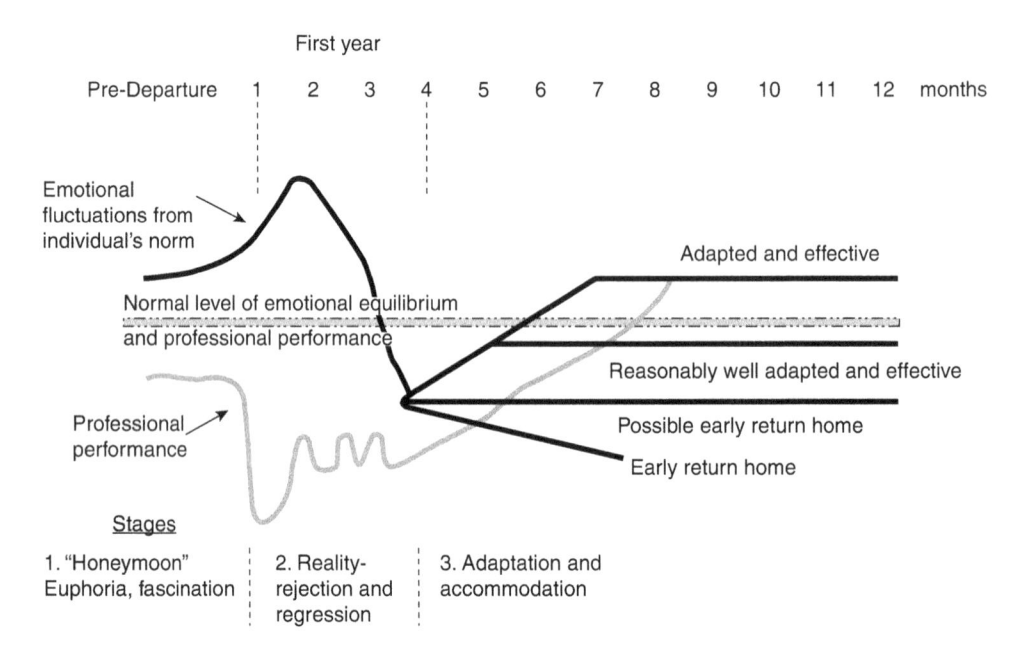

Figure 7.2 Acculturative stress. (Adapted from Sargent, 1970.)

obsession about being cheated; withdrawal into work, family, or the expatriate community; and, in extreme cases, excessive use of drugs or alcohol. The majority of people eventually begin to accept their new environment and adjust. Most emerge from the adjustment period performing adequately, and some people perform more effectively than before. A smaller percentage either "go native," which is usually not an effective strategy, or experience very severe symptoms related to an inability to adjust, such as panic attacks.

Coping with Culture Shock

Different people have different ways of coping with culture shock. Normal stress management techniques, regular exercise, rest, and a balanced diet are helpful. As noted earlier, some use work as a bridge until they adjust. Usually, the work environment does have some similarities to that of one's home culture. But for nonworking spouses or partners who are often left to cope with the new environment on their own, the effects can be more severe.

Language training is one effective way of coping and provides an entry into the host culture. Education about the local history, geography, and traditions of the new culture and then exploration of the new environment also help adjustment. Whatever methods are employed, it is wise to remember that everyone experiences culture shock. Diligent preparation can moderate the effect, not eliminate it.

Support systems are especially important during the adjustment period. One obvious source of support is the family. Doing more things together as a family is a way to cope with the pressures. Another is to realize that it is acceptable to withdraw from the new culture, temporarily, for a respite such as reading newspapers from home or enjoying familiar food from a restaurant chain from home – if not carried too far. It is important to use such temporary interruptions to one's reality as bridges to the new culture, not as permanent anchors to an old environment.

In company situations, it must be understood that the international manager in a new culture goes through these stresses. Local colleagues should not be surprised by less than perfect performance or unusual behavior and can provide crucial support for expatriate managers and their families. When one goes overseas, there are two jobs to accomplish. There is the obvious functional or technical job, such as engineering, finance, marketing, or plant management responsibilities. However, too often it is only this job that people identify, focus on, and prepare for. The other, less obvious job is cultural adaptation. If you cannot adapt successfully, you may be requested to go (or may be sent) home early – often in a matter of months. Such a manager may never get a chance to fully leverage his or her technical or functional skills during that time.

Interestingly, you do not have to leave your own country to experience culture shock. A Canadian volunteer on a project in Ghana experienced the symptoms of culture shock, even after participating in an orientation program organized by the sponsoring agency. This same person reported severe symptoms of culture shock upon returning to an urban-based MBA program in Canada. However, the ultimate culture shock came upon graduating and starting work for a manufacturer located in a small, rural community in one of Canada's Maritime Provinces. In all three experiences, the patterns were the same, and the sharpest disorientation occurred within this person's native country, perhaps because it was least expected. It is important to note that this individual also experienced a "reverse culture shock" upon the return home.

Return Shock

"Reverse culture shock," "return shock," or "reentry shock" to one's home culture is an adjustment phenomenon for which people need to be prepared. There can be a significant readjustment to one's home country, especially if a manager has been away for a long period of time.

Osland points out that there can be a high degree of uncertainty surrounding one's career upon repatriation that, combined with a loss of prestige and the autonomy of being abroad, may give an executive pause to think about his or her future career with the company (Osland, 1995). Both at work and in one's personal life, a returned international assignee may find that others lack interest in their experience. They have grown personally and changed during their assignment, but people at home only want to hear the 30-second sound bites of the experience. Their idealized image of how perfect the home country was and how well everything worked there is often shattered upon return. A person who worked for one of the current authors in Nairobi, Kenya often commented about how she could not wait to get back to North America where the copy machines worked properly. When she returned home, she discovered that the copiers there often broke down as well. On a more personal level, returned assignees often find that they miss life abroad. All these factors probably play a role in the attrition rate of returnees discussed in the next section.

Reflection Question 7.6: Your Experience with Culture Shock

Have you ever experienced culture or return shock? Where were you and what was it like?

The Return Home: Repatriation

The process of selecting the right people, training them properly, and sending them and their families on an international assignment is not the end of the story. Reintegrating expatriates into the company after the foreign assignment so that the company can continue to benefit from their experience and expertise is important and has also proven to be a challenge.

First, companies must contend with failure rates, defined as early return and attrition of assignees from the company. There are estimates in the academic literature of failure rates of anywhere from 10% to 50% for American expatriates, but these high estimates have been called into question (Harzing, 2002). A BGRS (2015) survey reported an average international assignee return rate of 6% and an attrition rate of 12%, which was the same as an average company's overall rate. However, that number is still high, especially given the investments firms make in sending employees and their families abroad.

There are many reasons for failure or early return. Various surveys have reported causes such as the inability to demonstrate a global mindset, poor leadership skills, and an aversion to change or a lack of networking skills. Others have found that the key factors of expatriate failure were partner dissatisfaction, family concerns, inability to adapt, poor candidate selection, and the job not meeting the expatriate's expectations. Usually, the number-one reason prompting early return is family-related issues such as partner/spouse dissatisfaction. Mercer's (2020) research showed that the top three reasons for assignment failure were an inability to adapt to the host country (38%), poor candidate selection (37%), and family-related issues (34%).

Expatriate attrition also is a problem. Historically, the annual average turnover rate for assignees has been about 12%. To minimize attrition, companies need to think more coherently about career-pathing for their expatriates and provide them with adequate repatriation support and a wider choice of positions after repatriation so they can use their newly acquired international experience and skills.

Regardless of the exact numbers on failure rate or attrition, it pays to get the expatriate cycle right – the right people, the right preparation, and the right repatriation. The costs associated with expatriation are significant and include moving costs, home leave, housing allowances, cost-of-living allowances, private international schooling for children, preparation, and language lessons. And these costs do not consider the personal costs to employees and their families from terminating an assignment early. If companies want to retain their internationally experienced managers, they will have to do a better job with their career management processes, including the repatriation process. Ways to improve the repatriation process include using the international experience assignees bring home with them, offering job choices upon return, recognition, repatriation career support, family repatriation support, and improving evaluations during an assignment.

An international assignment is an important vehicle for developing global managers, achieving strategic management control, coordinating and integrating the global organization, and learning about international markets and competitors, as well as about foreign social, political, and economic situations. However, the idealized goal of becoming a global, learning organization will only be reached if the right people are selected for foreign assignments, trained properly, repatriated with care, valued for their experience, and then offered assignments that draw on their unique backgrounds.

Conclusion: Ongoing Talent Development – Important for All International Companies

Advances in global talent management have been notable in some companies where they have developed sophisticated talent pipelines with effective selection and development practices (Caligiuri, 2012). Mindful global leaders are increasingly important for most companies, even those that don't consider themselves global. The more that companies approach talent selection, development, and assignments rigorously, the more they will have a strong ongoing cadre of global leaders to help them navigate in the highly complex global environment.

Further Resources

Aoun, J. (2017). *Robot-proof: Higher education in the age of artificial intelligence.* M.I.T. Press.
Caligiuri, P. (2012). *Cultural agility: Building a pipeline of successful global professionals.* Jossey-Bass.
Caligiuri, P. (2021). *Build Your Cultural Agility: The Nine Competencies of Successful Global Professionals.* Kogan Page.
Rosling, H. (2018). *Factfulness: Ten reasons we're wrong about the world – and why things are better than you think.* Flatiron Books.

To understand and keep up to date on what is happening in the corporate world regarding international assignments of executives, we recommend the annual global mobility reports published by various relocation firms such as SIRVA BGRS (formerly Brookfield Global Relocation Services), Atlas, Mercer, KPMG, Korn Ferry, and Cartus.

Bibliography

Adler, N. (1987). Pacific Basin managers: A Gaijn, not a woman. *Human Resource Management, 26*(2), 169–191.

Adler, N., & Izraeli, D. (1988). *Women in management worldwide*. ME Sharpe Inc.

Ashby, R. (1972). *Design for a brain*. Chapman Hall Ltd. and Science Paperbacks.

Ashby, R. (1973). *Introduction to cybernetics*. Chapman Hall Ltd. and University Paperbacks.

Berry, J. (1980). Acculturation as varieties of adaptation. In A. Padilla (Ed.), *Acculturation: Theory, model, and some new findings* (pp. 9–25). AAAS.

Bird, A. (2015). Introduction: Experiencing the world. In V. Taras & M. A. Gonzalez-Perez (Eds.), *The handbook of experiential learning in international business and international management* (pp. 3–11). Palgrave Handbooks.

BGRS. (2015). *Raising expatriate return rates*. SIRVA BGRS. Retrieved August 28, 2022, from https://www.bgrs.com/insights-articles/raising-expatriate-retention-rates/

Brookfield. (2015). *Mindful Mobility*. Brookfield Global Relocation Services Global Mobility Trends Survey. Retrieved April 8, 2024, from https://www.global-connection.info/hr-articles/brookfield-mindful-approach-to-mobility/

Brookfield. (2016). *Breakthrough to the Future of Global Talent Mobility*. Global Trends Mobility Survey. Retrieved April 8, 2024, from https://ivemadeit.com/pdf/Key-Findings-BGRS-2016-Global-Mobility-Trends-Survey.pdf

Caligiuri, P. (2012). *Cultural agility: Building a pipeline of successful global professionals*. Jossey-Bass.

Caligiuri, P., & Bonache, J. (2016). Evolving and enduring challenges in global mobility. *Journal of World Business, 136*, 127–141.

Caligiuri, P., & Cascio, W. (1988). Can we send her there? Maximizing the success of western women on global assignments. *Journal of World Business, 33*(4), 395.

CEO Magazine. (2019, June 12). *The importance of international experience for CEOs*. CEO Magazine. Retrieved August 27, 2022, from https://www.theceomagazine.com/business/management-leadership/the-importance-of-international-experience-for-ceos/

Financial Times. (n.d.). *Definition of Flexpatriate*. Retrieved from http://lexicon.ft.com/Term?term=flexpatriate

Franke, J., & Nicholson, N. (2002). Who shall we send? Cultural and other influences on the rating of selection criteria for expatriate assignments. *International Journal of Cross Cultural Management, 2*(1), 21–36.

Harzing, A.-W. (2001). Of bears, bumble-bees, and spiders: The role of expatriates in controlling foreign subsidiaries. *Journal of World Business, 36*(4), 366–379.

Harzing, A.-W. (2002). Are our referencing errors undermining our scholarship and credibility? The case of expatriate failure rates. *Journal of Organizational Behaviour, 23*, 127–148.

International SOS. (n.d.). Retrieved September 2022, from https://www.internationalsos.com/

Kealey, D. (1990). *Cross-cultural effectiveness: A study of Canadian technical advisors overseas*. Canadian International Development Agency.

Korn Ferry. (2022). Retrieved August 26, 2022, from https://www.kornferry.com/insights/this-week-in-leadership/talent-crunch-future-of-work

Lane, H. W., Maznevski, M. L., & Mendenhall, M. E. (2004). Globalization: Hercules meets Buddha. In H. Lane, M. Maznevski, & M. Mendenhall (Eds.),

The Blackwell handbook of global management: A guide to managing complexity (pp. 3–25). Blackwell Publishers.

Martin, C. (2014, February 15). *At the Ready, at the Sochi Games.* The New York Times. Retrieved September 2022 from https://www.nytimes.com/2014/02/16/business/at-the-ready-at-the-sochi-games.html

Matteau, M. (1993). *Towards meaningful and effective intercultural encounters.* Intercultural Training and Briefing Centre, Canadian International Development Agency.

McKinsey. (2021, April 30). *Building workforce skills at scale to thrive during – and after – the Covid-19 crisis.* McKinsey & Company. Retrieved August 26, 2022, from https://www.mckinsey.com/business-functions/people-and-organizational-performance/our-insights/building-workforce-skills-at-scale-to-thrive-during-and-after-the-covid-19-crisis#. See also https://www.weforum.org/agenda/2018/06/the-3-skill-sets-workers-need-to-develop-between-now-and-2030/.

Mencken, H. L. (2016 [1920]). *Prejudices: Second series.* CreateSpace Independent Publishing Platform.

Mendenhall, M., Dunbar, E., & Oddou, G. (1987). Expatriate selection, training, and career-pathing: A review and critique. *Human Resource Management, 26*(3), 331–345.

Mendenhall, M., Osland, J., Bird, A., Oddou, G., Stevens, M., Maznevski, M., & Stahl, G. (2017). *Global leadership: Research, practice, and development (global HRM)* (3rd ed.). Routledge.

Mercer. (2020). *Worldwide Survey of International Assignment Policies and Practices.* Retrieved August 28, 2022, from https://mobilityexchange.mercer.com/international-assignments-survey

Mercer. (2022). *The Path to Diversity: Women on Assignment, Olivier Meier.* Retrieved August 27, 2022, from https://mobilityexchange.mercer.com/insights/article/the-path-to-diversity-women-on-assignment

Miller, E. (1973). The international selection decision: A study of some dimensions of managerial behaviour in the selection decision process. *Academy of Management Journal, 16*(2), 239–252.

Osland, J. (1995). *The adventure of working abroad: Hero tales from the global frontier.* Jossey-Bass Publishers.

Pate, J., & Scullion, H. (2016). The flexpatriate psychological contract: A literature review and future research agenda. *The International Journal of Human Resource Management, 29*(8), 1402–1425.

Rohwer, J., & Windham, L., (2000, October 2). *GE digs into Asia.* Fortune. Retrieved April 6, 2024, from https://money.cnn.com/magazines/fortune/fortune_archive/2000/10/02/288447/index.htm

Sargent, C. (1970, October 23). Psychological aspects of environmental adjustment. Unpublished paper.

Schotter, A., & Beamish, P. W. (2013). The hassle factor. An explanation for managerial location shunning. *Journal of International Business, 44*, 521–544.

Society for Human Resource Management (SHRM). (2022). Retrieved August 26, 2002, from https://www.shrm.org/resourcesandtools/tools-and-samples/toolkits/pages/international-assignments.aspx

Stahl, G., Bjorkman, I., Farndale, E., Morris, S., Paauwe, J., Stiles, P., ... Wright, P. (2012). Six principles of effective global talent management. *MIT Sloan Management Review*, 25–32.

Weick, K., & Van Orden, P. (1990). Organizing on a global scale: A research and teaching agenda. *Human Resource Management, 29*(1), 49–61.

Decision-Making Cases

Northeastern UNIVERSITY

Richard Ivey School of Business
The University of Western Ontario

IVEY

CASE II-1: CHARLES FOSTER SENDS AN EMAIL (A)

Professor Henry W. Lane prepared this case solely to provide material for class discussion. The author does not intend to illustrate either effective or ineffective handling of a managerial situation. The author may have disguised certain names and other identifying information to protect confidentiality.

Ivey Management Services is the exclusive representative of the copyright holder and prohibits any form of reproduction, storage or transmittal without its written permission. Reproduction of this material is not covered under authorization by any reproduction rights organization. To order copies or request permission to reproduce materials, contact Ivey Publishing, Ivey Management Services, c/o Richard Ivey School of Business, The University of Western Ontario, London, Ontario, Canada, N6A 3K7; phone (519) 661–3208; fax (519) 661–3882; e-mail cases@ivey.uwo.ca.

Copyright © 2005, Northeastern University, College of Business Administration

Version: (A) 2009–09–28

Charles Foster was a U.S. national sales manager for a large multinational technology company headquartered in France. He was concerned about the availability of an important new disk drive that was selling better than anticipated. If he could obtain more of these drives, he was sure that they would sell. Since the product had just been launched with the company's various sales forces and distributors, Foster was worried about losing momentum. The sales force and distributors had literally thousands of products to sell and an availability problem could prove fatal to the product line, as the company's sales efforts were redirected to other products or customers chose to purchase from the competition.

The situation was complicated by the fact that the design and manufacturing of the drive had been assigned to a new Franco-Japanese joint venture (JV) located in France. Not only was the joint venture adapting to a new manufacturing system that had been introduced to produce the drive, it was also adapting to the joint venture's new organizational structure. As it tried to adapt, the joint venture encountered numerous complications, particularly those involving logistics.

Over the previous months, several attempts had been made to resolve the availability issue at lower levels but with no success. Foster decided that the problem had become serious enough to warrant the attention of his supervisor, Richard Howe, vice-president of sales for High Technology Products. Because Foster had a good, informal relationship with Howe, he decided to send him an email explaining the situation.

Howe forwarded Foster's email to Maurice LeBlanc, the head of the Strategic Business Unit (SBU) headquartered in France. In turn, LeBlanc, who previously had been head of new product development for the SBU, forwarded the email to Ahmed Hassan, president of the JV. Hassan, raised in the Middle East, had lived most of his adult life in France (see Exhibit 1).

The Phone Call

A couple of days after sending his email, Foster was in his office completing some sales reports when the phone rang. After he answered the phone, he immediately recognized the accented, emotion-laden voice that spilled out into the room.

This is Ahmed Hassan. Why are you writing such things to my boss in an email? Why are you saying so many negative things about my business? Why didn't you call me?

Foster was stunned. He did not know what Hassan was talking about or what to say. He recalled:

> Ahmed was absolutely livid. And he continued yelling at me for what seemed like an eternity.

Exhibit 1 Email String

1. Email to Richard Howe

To: Richard Howe/Techco@USHQ
Subject: Drives Availability – Further info on XD19

Dick,

I wanted to give you some further info on the XD19 stock situation.

I feel strongly that this is a precursor to what we are going to face when all of our manufacturing goes to the JV. I'm including my thoughts on what is going on and I would like your opinion on what we should do in the organization to get a handle on this before it gets too far out of hand. The issues we are facing seem to be driven by two main factors:

- Marketing is asked for forecasts on product use. Manufacturing does not believe them and makes their own forecasts based on run-rates and then ends up shipping even below that. I think that this is being driven by an inappropriately high emphasis on reducing inventory.
- The manufacturing for the XD19 is done in batches. It is often three to five months between batch runs for a specific drive. With such long lead-times, we are unable to respond to sudden swings in the market or new opportunities.

Our issues right now are magnified by a problem with the firmware[1] on the XD19. This issue is also illustrative of the types of problems that we need to prevent from happening with the JV:

- We have been using Version 07 firmware, but the JV is currently converting all of their stock to Version 08. The Version 08 firmware has a bug that does not provide true three-wire control in a keypad mode, which we consider a major safety issue.[2]
- The JV does not consider this to be a safety issue and has released this firmware for use outside of the U.S. We are going to have to live off of the remaining stock of Version 07 until the release of Version 09 next year.
- This problem is magnified by the use of masked firmware instead of flashable. When there is a mistake, as there is in this case, we are stuck with it until the next set of masks is made. (There is a cost savings in using masked units, but I would be willing to bet that we have never realized it since we are always giving customers new drives and new control boards to cover our bugs.)

---

[1] Firmware is a software program that is loaded onto a chip and cannot be modified. "Masked" firmware is etched onto the chip. "Flashable" firmware is not etched on a chip, and new versions can be downloaded onto the chip.
[2] Three-way wire control was "fail-safe" circuitry required in the United States but not required or used in the rest of the world.

Exhibit 1 (continued)

- The JV does not fully test functionality like we do, resulting in a huge list of bugs with each firmware release once we test it. We then have to live with these bugs until the next release and the next set of bugs. Since these releases are normally masked before we do our testing, the fixes can't be done on the fly.
- We are currently expediting Version 07 units from France to cover the shortfalls, but there are six catalog numbers that will need to be ordered from Japan. It is also likely that we will completely exhaust the remaining supply of Version 07 masks for all of the other sizes before production of the Version 09 firmware begins. With the batch lead times, I expect this to absolutely kill the XD19 launch and it will be a big hit on us for Core Product.

This is SCARY! If an opportunity comes along, forget about it, because we are still filling backlog. I already have OEM salespeople giving up on selling the XD19 because it is not in stock.

It is particularly frustrating being told that we are not meeting top-line objectives when we cannot even ship to the current level of sales.

Charles

2. Email to Maurice LeBlanc

To: Maurice LeBlanc/TechcoInt@HQFrance
Subject: Drives Availability – Further info on XD19

Maurice,

We are having an inventory problem with the XD19 (V07). The issue as I understand it is France does not have the inventory and we have to wait on the JV to build its next batch. In the meantime, we are losing orders due to lack of inventory.

I would like to see if you could talk with JV to expedite its manufacturing process as we need drives now. The list below contains the key part numbers that we need with Version 07.

Please see some other concerns identified by our Drives National Sales Manager – Charles Foster – in the attached email.

Thank you for any help you can provide.

Dick

3. Email to Ahmed Hassan

To: Ahmed Hassan/TechcoInt@JVFrance
Subject: Attached emails

Ahmed,

Is this correct what the emails from the U.S. say? Why aren't you following our Standard Protocol SPQ that dictates that we safety test products to the safety standards in the U.S.? I am concerned that the JV is not following our normal engineering review practice.

Maurice

CASE II-2: DIGLOT CAPITAL MANAGEMENT: A VERY SERIOUS GHOST STORY

Shreshthi Mehta and Leslie Hitch wrote this case solely to provide material for class discussion. The authors do not intend to illustrate either effective or ineffective handling of a managerial situation. The authors may have disguised certain names and other identifying information to protect confidentiality.

This publication may not be transmitted, photocopied, digitized, or otherwise reproduced in any form or by any means without the permission of the copyright holder. Reproduction of this material is not covered under authorization by any reproduction rights organization. To order copies or request permission to reproduce materials, contact Ivey Publishing, Ivey Business School, Western University, London, Ontario, Canada, N6G 0N1; (t) 519.661.3208; (e) cases@ivey.ca; www.iveycases.com.

Copyright © 2018, Indian School of Business, and Ivey Business School Foundation   Version: 2018–07-13

Please accept this letter as notice of my resignation with immediate effect from the position of Customer Service Representative. Over the past five years, Diglot Capital Management has given me numerous opportunities to grow and enhance my skills. It is a great company, and I truly enjoyed working here. However, I am scared to go in to work. I am having problems sleeping, and my family is worried about me. I hope you will understand my situation when I say that I was forced to look for other opportunities due to the unexplained sequence of events happening on the company premises over the past few weeks. Thank you.

On July 11, 2016, Sanjay Shinde, a vice-president at Diglot Capital Management (DCM), read the resignation letter with regret. The employee who had resigned was a valued worker. She had a good relationship with her manager and peers. The problem she had alluded to in her resignation letter was her belief that the workplace was haunted. This belief had led to feelings of ill omens and concerns for her safety that eventually culminated in her resignation.

Attrition was not the only problem in the DCM office in Bangalore, India; Shinde observed that there had been a spike in the number of unscheduled leaves, leading to a drop in productivity. Shinde was concerned that, at this rate, he would continue to lose staff and eventually fail to meet the annual service level agreements with the company's U.S.-based clients.

Diglot Capital Management

DCM, a consumer financial services[1] company, was headquartered in New York. DCM was a wholly owned subsidy[2] of Diglot Capital Bank, which offered credit services linked to customer accounts (see Exhibit 1). DCM's clients were e-commerce companies, retail outlets, grocery stores, airlines, and other large-scale corporations. DCM had a set of elite clients including several Fortune 500 companies. These client companies provided their customers with store credit cards. The credit cards were linked to the DCM bank and were useful

---

[1] This was the division of retail banking that dealt with lending money to consumers. It included a wide variety of loans, including credit cards, mortgage loans, and auto loans.
[2] A wholly owned subsidiary was a company that was completely owned by another company. The company that owned the subsidiary was called the parent company or holding company.

for offering rewards, cash back, store discounts, and other benefits to the consumer.

Besides credit, DCM offered loyalty programs, capital management services, and customer service. Customers of DCM's clients, the Fortune 500 companies, used the DCM store credit card and contacted DCM customer service for queries regarding sales, claims, and other membership services.

In 2016, about four-fifths of the world's 500 largest companies already outsourced customer service work to India. This was known as business process outsourcing (BPO). Outsourcing customer service work to Asia's third-largest economy—India—could typically generate cost savings for a company of between 35 and 50 per cent.[3] A large portion of the population in India and other Asian countries was well versed in English.[4] DCM had set up its offshore customer service centre in Bangalore, India, where calls were routed from the United States.

BPO Industry in India

With more than a 50 per cent share of the total global offshoring industry, India had witnessed rapid growth in demand for its BPO services. In 2012, the offshoring industry in India stood at US$23 billion. In 2014, a research firm in Pune, India, projected the Indian BPO offshoring industry to become a US$40-billion industry by 2017.[5] Seventy per cent of the revenue of India's BPO industry was from call centres, 20 per cent from data entry work, and the remaining 10 per cent from information technology-related work.[6] The voice-based processes, or call centres, offered real-time resolutions. Proficiency in English was the only hard skill required for most voice-based customer service positions as an advanced degree was not required. Since the BPO industry was growing, there was a boom in the BPO job market for young adults, both men and women (aged 18–30 years), who could speak English. The BPO customer service representative position was a lucrative option for many people who were in need of immediate financial support.[7]

In 2009, about 3.5 million people in India graduated with an undergraduate degree.[8] The BPO sector employed about 700,000 people in 2008;[9] according to a study conducted by the National Association of Software and Services Companies (NASSCOM),[10] by 2012 that number had increased to 2 million.[11]

Cosmopolitan cities in India, such as Delhi, Mumbai, Hyderabad, Bangalore, and Pune, were famous for their educational institutes

---

[3] Reuters, "India's Outsourcing Revenue to Hit $50 Billion," *Financial Express*, January 29, 2008, accessed April 14, 2017, www.financialexpress.com/archive/indias-outsourcing-revenue-to-hit-50-bn/266661/.

[4] William Greene, "Growth in Services Outsourcing to India: Propellant or Drain on the U.S. Economy?," United States International Trade Commission, January 2006, 2, www.usitc.gov/publications/332/EC200601A.pdf.

[5] VN Custom Research, "Indian BPO Industry to Prosper Due to Growth of Non-Voice Services," 2014, accessed November 28, 2016, www.valuenotes.biz/indian-bpo-industry-to-prosper-due-to-growth-of-non-voice-services/.

[6] N. Bharathi and Dr. P. Paramashivaiah, "Attrition and Retention the Real Challenge – A Study with Special Reference to IT and ITES Organizations in Bangalore," *International Journal of Innovative Research in Science, Engineering and Technology* 4, no. 2, February 2015, accessed July 13, 2018, www.ijirset.com/upload/2015/february/96_Bharathi.pdf.

[7] Sarosh Kuruvilla and Aruna Ranganathan, "Globalisation and Outsourcing: Confronting New Human Resource Challenges in India's Business Process Outsourcing Industry," *British Journal of Industrial Relations* 41, no. 2 (2010), 136–153, https://digitalcommons.ilr.cornell.edu/articles/1061/.

[8] Rama Lakshmi, "In India, Educated but Unemployable Youths," Washington Post Foreign Services, May 4, 2009, accessed November 28, 2016, www.washingtonpost.com/wp-dyn/content/article/2009/05/03/AR2009050302015.html.

[9] Reuters, op. cit.

[10] NASSCOM was a trade association of the Indian information technology and business process outsourcing industry.

[11] "Roadmap 2012 – Capitalizing on the Expanding BPO Landscape," NASSCOM–Everest India BPO Study, 2008, 4, accessed April 22, 2018, www.everestgrp.com/wp-content/uploads/2012/08/NASSCOM-Everest-Group-India-BPO-Study-2008.pdf.

that produced many English-speaking graduates. Further, these cities also had good infrastructure and a business-friendly atmosphere, making them a popular destination for BPO activities and call centres.[12]

The growth of BPOs was not without its downside. In 2015, two professors in India published a study on the attrition of employees in Indian BPOs. As per the findings of the study, the major reasons influencing employees to quit were low career prospects, better remuneration at other firms, stressful lifestyles, and unsatisfying interpersonal relationships in the workplace. Additionally, to adjust to the time zone differences between the United States and Asia, most of the working hours were from the evening through to the early morning. Sedentary lifestyles and sleep disruptions, coupled with work pressure, greatly increased the stress levels of employees. This took a toll on their health in the long run and was a major reason for the high attrition rate in the BPO industry, despite the income and freedom offered by positions in the industry.[13]

In 2014, the average rate of attrition in the BPO sector in India was 28 per cent. Due to the high turnover, there was a skill gap that increased the need for training in the sector. High investment in training, together with the high attrition rate posed a challenge for the BPO industry.[14] The average attrition rate reported by DCM in India for 2015 was about 40 per cent.[15] Like its competitors, DCM was always on the lookout for good talent, while constantly seeking ways to improve its management practices and engage people, thereby reducing attrition.

DCM in India

DCM had 1,700 employees in Bangalore. The major operating processes in the company were sales capital, collections, risk management, and the claims resolution process, besides support functions such as human resources, finance, and workforce management (see Exhibit 2). Shinde was vice-president, operations, of the sales capital process, whose major functions included telemarketing, cross-selling, managing customer accounts, and other forms of telephone customer services (see Exhibit 3). Like other call centres in India that were aligned with U.S. operations, employees at DCM India were required to work at night. Sales capital had 300 customer services representatives that worked in multiple shifts to provide appropriate coverage.

Since the parent company of operations was in the United States, many human resource policies at DCM India were adopted from the policies and practices of DCM in the United States. For instance, DCM India followed the principle of fair employment practices that was tied to the Equal Employment Opportunity principle of Title VII of the American *Civil Rights Act*.[16] As per fair employment practices, all employees of DCM India had to be treated fairly and were not to be discriminated against on the basis of race, skin colour, religion, sex, or national origin. However, to attain cultural alignment with Indian operations, policies such as the dress code policy, employee benefits, vacation, and

---

[12] Mainak Biswas, "Where to Outsource in India: The Definitive Guide," Indus Net Technologies, August 22, 2013, accessed April 14, 2017, www.indusnet.co.in/where-to-outsource-in-india-the-definitive-guide/.

[13] Dr. Sunil Kumar Dhal and Amaresh C. Nayak, "A Study on Employee Attrition in BPO Industries in India," *International Journal of Science and Research* 4, no. 1 (2015), 2242–2249, accessed July 13, 2018, https://www.ijsr.net/archive/v4i1/SUB15723.pdf.

[14] "Trends and Data Insights for the Business Process Outsourcing Industry Meeting – Gurgaon: Event Summary," WillisTowersWatson, February 3, 2015, accessed July 3, 2018, www.towerswatson.com/en/Insights/IC-Types/Ad-hoc-Point-of-View/2015/01/Trends-and-Data-Insights-for-the-Business-Process-Outsourcing-Industry-Meeting-Gurgaon.

[15] Company documents – 2015 HR Metrics, Annual Attrition Report.

[16] "Title VII of the Civil Rights Act of 1964," U.S. Equal Employment Opportunity Commission, accessed November 28, 2016, www.eeoc.gov/laws/statutes/titlevii.cfm.

paid leave, among others, often differed from the parent company in the United States.

India was the birthplace of Hinduism, Buddhism, Jainism, and Sikhism;[17] besides these religions, people in India practiced Christianity and Islam. This cultural diversity was also evident at DCM, where common Hindu rituals such as lighting a *diya*[18] and wearing a *tikka*,[19] and Christian traditions such as singing Christmas carols were observed, and work schedules were adjusted during Ramadan and other events.

Shinde's Leadership

Shinde had worked with DCM since 1999. He had joined as an operations manager and became vice-president of Operations in 2006. Shinde believed in an open-door managerial approach and regularly conducted meetings with the customer service representatives. He knew that, like any other BPO in India, attrition had been a constant challenge for DCM. Shinde used different sources to effectively detect issues that might affect productivity. The higher pay along with better management employee engagement practices, and benefits offered by other companies were among the reasons cited by employees when they quit DCM. One employee even stated in his exit interview that he was leaving because the other company had a better cafeteria. But over the past 16 years, Shinde had never encountered a situation quite like this one: employees were leaving because of the presence of ghosts in the company.

How It All Began

Shinde reflected back on the time he met the new-hire training group in early April 2016. He faintly remembered meeting Julie Rani, as she had been wearing a large necklace that said "Jesus Loves All." As the training progressed, the trainer, Madhu Das, complained that Rani was inattentive – she would look scared or suddenly start crying. Das had asked her, "What is the matter, Julie? Is everything alright?"

Rani had replied, "I see a demon there. He wants me to get up and stand near the wall." Rani pointed to a corner of the training room. Das saw nobody standing in the corner and told Rani to calm down.

The frequency of such incidents increased over time. Rani's behaviour was not only disturbing the training but also creating fear in other employees. By mid-May, Punit Gupta, an employee relations specialist, recommended Rani for the Employee Assistance Program;[20] Rani had a medical condition that caused hallucinations. By the end of June, Rani was terminated from DCM on medical grounds. However, Shinde soon realized that the employees' fear of supernatural forces lingered even after Rani had left the company.

Superstition and the Indian Workplace

After Rani left the company, other employees remained fearful of coming to work. Many employees still believed that an evil spirit was residing in the building. Shinde saw an increase in the appearance of artefacts and spiritual symbols among employees of all sects and religious groups within the company.

Shinde was disturbed by the increasing visual display of totems. He recalled reading an article. Team Lease, a staffing company in India, had surveyed 800 companies in eight metropolitan cities (New Delhi, Mumbai, Chennai, Kolkata, Bangalore, Hyderabad, Pune, and Ahmedabad) to determine the prevalence of superstition in the Indian workplace.

---

[17] Dr. Ahmed Sayeed, *Know Your India*, "Turn New Page To Write Nationalism," (New Delhi: Quills Ink Publishing, 2014), 45.

[18] This was an oil lamp that was used for temporary lighting during special and auspicious occasions.

[19] A coloured mark worn by Hindus, especially on the forehead, indicating membership in a religious sect.

[20] An Employee Assistance Program was a voluntary, work-based program that offered free and confidential assessments, short-term counselling, referrals, and follow-up services to employees who had personal and/or work-related problems.

The results of the "Superstitions at Work" survey showed that about 62 per cent of survey participants followed personal beliefs, and about 51 per cent of these participants carried these beliefs or superstitions to the workplace. Furthermore, about 48 per cent of respondents felt that practicing superstitious behaviour at the workplace had a positive effect because it boosted their confidence and improved their work performance. The management of the companies surveyed did not lend explicit support to employees who practiced superstitions, nor did the management interfere when an employee was seen to be following some superstitious belief.[21]

Most employees at DCM were full-time, whereby they worked daily eight-hour shifts, five days a week. Shinde felt that the results of the Team Lease survey could help explain the behaviour of his employees. The employees held certain values, according to which they observed certain practices. Since employees spent a considerable amount of time in the workplace, naturally the rituals they observed at home were also carried to work. Over many years, Shinde had frequently seen employees keep lucky charms, like a laughing Buddha or pictures and statues of deities, at their desks. Since these artefacts did not seem to impact work productivity in the beginning, Shinde did not mind. He believed that by accommodating employees' religious beliefs, a harmonious and inclusive workplace would evolve. During the month of Ramadan, DCM management would consider requests for leave or changes to the work shift so that employees could pray. The company accommodated employees' religious and personal preferences and tried to make modifications where possible. But the nature of these requests was seasonal or only applicable to a few employee groups. Exceptions were considered on a case-by-case basis and generally made possible by deploying a different group of people so productivity was not affected.

Shinde was concerned that ever since the incident with Rani, employees were afraid to work at night and business continuity would eventually be affected. After each call, customers had the option of rating the quality of service. DCM's goal was to get a customer satisfaction score of 100 per cent. The average satisfaction score in the months of January to April was 95–98 per cent. However, the survey scores dropped to 92 per cent in June 2016.

Growing Concerns

Fear of the evil spirit becoming active in the dark-to-dawn shift led to further unrest in the company. On July 11, 2016, Roopa Tyagi, a valued female employee, decided to resign. Tyagi explained during her exit interview that she believed it was due to the presence of the demonic entity that her family had started experiencing health and financial problems. She was scared that the evil spirit was proving to be a bad omen for her family. To avoid complications, Tyagi had started looking for other opportunities and found a role with one of DCM's competitors.

After Tyagi left, Shinde was concerned about losing more people. He observed that a few employees were even scared to use the chair that Rani had used or the computer she had accessed, for fear of being possessed by the ghost. Shinde further noticed that the number of absences during the graveyard shift[22] had starkly increased. As the call volume was low during these shifts, there were fewer employees — about 30 people — scheduled to work at that time in a facility with a capacity of 350 people, which made the working atmosphere seem one of isolation. Shinde noticed that besides an increase in the number of unscheduled absences, there was a drop

---

[21] "Are Indians 'Superstitions@Workplace'?," IIFL, November 20, 2012, accessed December 7, 2016, www.indiainfoline.com/article/print/news/are-indians-superstitionsat-the-rateworkplace-5545032108_1.html.

[22] This shift covered the early morning hours, typically the period between midnight and 8 a.m.

in customer satisfaction scores and an overall drop in productivity. He decided to meet with the customer service representatives to address the issues before they snowballed into a larger problem.

During the team meeting, Shinde reasoned,

We are here to ease your fears. I want us to be practical and factual so that we can build a high-performing team. This building was constructed 30 years ago. DCM has been operating here for the past 12 years. Never have employees even vaguely complained of such occurrences. DCM strives to maintain a safe environment. The company premises are well protected by guards and other security personnel. We even have cameras and other technological safeguards in place.

"How will the security guard help when the employees are scared of the unknown?" Shalini Mahajan, a customer service representative, replied. "I know that science and technology do not offer enough evidence. It is a matter of belief; people who believe in ghosts and spirits just cannot control their fear."

"I understand your concerns," Shinde said. "We want to make sure you are comfortable coming in to work. What can we do to help you?"

"I think we should reach out to the local church. The holy priest has been summoned before to perform exorcisms. He is well versed with situations like these," suggested Winston Roy.

"Or we could call a *pandit* [Hindu priest] and ask him to perform the *shantikaran puja*.[23] This would cleanse the work premises," suggested Mahajan.

Religions in India were divided into different castes and sub-castes, and followers developed certain beliefs based on these castes and on other factors. For instance, there were 330 million gods in Hinduism alone;[24] this was a reflection of the different ideologies held by Hindus. The number of different philosophies people in the country held was great when other religions, such as Christianity and Jainism, were considered. Shinde knew that his employees held a number of different beliefs, and that each person would have an opinion aligned with these. He did not want to favour a specific cultural group, as it would lead to other problems.

Shinde responded,

I understand and value your suggestions. But DCM is a company based on modern values and scientific principles. We must not encourage non-scientific practices. Also, as per the policies and fair employment practices of the company, we should not encourage practices that [would] show we are biased towards any specific religious group.

"I read about a scientist couple who reside in Bangalore. They explore haunted places and suggest alternatives based on research. This approach would be the best as it would be evidenced by science and not biased towards any ethnic group," suggested another employee.

Shinde felt that the discussions were leading nowhere. He realized that most of his employees were superstitious, but at the same time, he did not blame them. Shinde remembered reading an article about Mukesh Ambani, the 9th-richest man in the world.[25] Ambani, who lived in Mumbai, owned the world's most expensive home. The house, which had cost US$1 billion to build, was reportedly empty—the owner believed it would bring bad luck to move in because it did not line up correctly with the principles

---

[23] This was an auspicious Hindu religious ceremony to maintain peace and harmony.

[24] Ali Tariq Bhatti, "Reaction and Innovative Analysis on World Religions via Long Search Documentary Series and Various Scriptures," *International Journal of Research in Computer Applications and Robotics* 3, no. 7 (July 2015): 13–21, accessed July 3, 2018, www.ijrcar.com/Volume_3_Issue_7/v3i705.pdf.

[25] Adeel Halim, "India: Superstition Leaves $1B Home Empty," October 26, 2011, accessed May 31, 2017, http://abcnewsradioonline.com/world-news/tag/india?currentPage=4.

of *Vastu Shastra*.[26] Superstitions could affect real estate prices, and Shinde was afraid the company and the reputation of the office premises could be at risk.

Shinde knew he had to be careful in dealing with a sensitive issue such as this. He therefore prepared for his upcoming monthly meeting with Elizabeth Gregory in New York. Gregory was DCM's head of Operations for Asia. Besides DCM India, Gregory had stakeholders in the Philippines, Mauritius, and Malaysia.

Cultural Clashes: The United States and India

Shinde dialled into the conference line for his meeting with Gregory, who had already dialled in and was waiting for Shinde to join. "Liz here," she said. "How are things going, Sanjay?"

> "Well, not quite so well," Shinde replied honestly. "You must have observed that there is a drop in productivity compared to last month."
>
> "Yes. I am surprised to see that. What is the reason for the dip?" inquired Gregory.
>
> "We have an issue here that some employees feel the work premises are haunted. Due to this, employees are scared to come to work and in general the morale is low," Shinde replied. He explained Rani's case, the sequence of events, and how the rumours began.
>
> "This is not good. Do you know why people are behaving like this?" asked Gregory.

Shinde explained,

> India is a country deeply seeped in faiths and beliefs. Most individuals have been brought up in a socio-cultural environment where following superstitions is an accepted norm. The competitive environment seems to foster superstitious routines. Eventually, these superstitions become a source of mental and emotional reassurance.

"This is quite alarming!" Gregory exclaimed. "I am surprised to see well educated people believe in such practices."

Shine replied,

> In 2007, a survey was conducted by the Institute for the Study of Secularism in Society and Culture within Trinity College in Hartford, Connecticut. The purpose of this study was to determine [the] worldviews and opinions of scientists in India. Over 1,000 scientists were surveyed from 130 Indian institutes, of which 24 per cent admitted to believing that holy men could perform miracles, 38 per cent believed that God could perform miracles, and 49 per cent believed in the effectiveness of prayers. Most Indians do not feel there is [a] dichotomy between science and spirituality.

Shinde further explained, "It is a matter of faith. These rituals and practices are ingrained in the culture. Both educated and uneducated people go to men of God, temples, and other holy places to seek resolution to their problems." Shinde told Gregory about the meeting with his team and one employee's recommendation to perform an exorcism.

"The United States is a democracy as well. We have people from many more nationalities and religions. I haven't really seen any problems like this here," Gregory reasoned.

Shinde explained,

> India is a collectivist society. There is a high preference for belonging to a larger social framework. In such situations, the actions of the individual are influenced by various concepts such as the opinions of one's family, extended family, neighbours, work group, and other such wider social networks that one has some affiliation toward.[27]

[26] Vastu Shastra was a traditional Hindu system of architecture that literally translated to "science of architecture." These were texts found on the Indian subcontinent that described principles of design, layout, measurements, ground preparation, space arrangement, and spatial geometry.

[27] Geert Hofstede, Geert Hofstede BV, accessed May 31 2017, https://geerthofstede.com/culture-geert-hofstede-gert-jan-hofstede/6d-model-of-national-culture/.

Hence, the tradition of the joint family system and arranged marriage is seen in India even today. Due to this, the urge to abide by the norms of the society is very high, and the impact of rituals and superstitions is very strong in India. Americans, in general, are often categorized as much more independent, pragmatic, and individualistic. Because a country's collectivist or individualist culture often frames work practices, the concept of work and ethics is different in India and the United States.

Gregory inquired, "Have you discussed the situation with the legal and compliance department? Do they have any recommendations?" Shinde replied,

> There is an act in India that is basically a law[28] against superstitious practices in India. After the bill was drafted in 2003, it was severely criticized for being racist or anti-Hindu.[29] Even though the bill addressed only fraudulent practices, the law drew such a thin line between faith and blind faith that the backlash to it was severe. In short, it is legal to perform a miracle, but it would be illegal to claim to perform a miracle to cheat someone. Right now the law is only passed in the state of Maharashtra and not applicable to companies in Bangalore, which operate in the state of Karnataka. Hence, the rest of India remains without comparable protection from fraudulent healers or superstitious practices.

[28] "Section 3: Prevention and Eradication of Human Sacrifice and Other Inhuman, Evil, and Aghori Practices and Black Magic," Maharashtra Prevention and Eradication of Human Sacrifice and other Inhuman, Evil and Aghori Practices and Black Magic Act, 2013, LS, accessed July 3, 2018, www.lawyerservices.in/MAHARASHTRA-PREVENTION-AND-ERADICATION-OF-HUMAN-SACRIFICE-AND-OTHER-INHUMAN-EVIL-AND-AGHORI-PRACTICES-AND-BLACK-MAGIC-ACT-20-SECTION-3-Prevention-and-eradication-of-human-sacrifice-and-other-inhuman-evil-and-aghori-practices-and-black-magic.

[29] Justin Rowlatt, "Narendra Dabholkar: India's Maharashtra State Bans Black Magic after Killing," BBC News: India, August 21, 2013, accessed December 7, 2016, www.bbc.com/news/world-asia-india-23776406.

"I agree that this is a very sensitive situation. But this behaviour is just not acceptable. Should we do something to discourage this behaviour?" asked Gregory. Shinde replied,

I personally think that the employees cannot control their behaviour. The only way I can think of right now is to diffuse the grapevine. Hence, I was thinking of meeting [with] all the employees in small groups, to address the situation. I would be focusing on facts to ease their fear. I was also thinking of offering additional incentives to work the graveyard shift. Due to lean staffing [during that shift], we could offer more security coverage to make sure they do not feel alone and vulnerable. I also recommend working with a few rationalist groups to eradicate such superstitions.

Gregory argued,

> But did you not say it is a matter of faith and belief? People in general should be motivated to work. Based on what you said, I am not sure that their belief would change by offering more incentives. I am not sure if that would work. We need to focus on our metrics. Have you considered disciplining the employees?

"The religious backlash could be a very severe issue and could even lead to riots and other disruptions. People are already stressed. If we impose further restrictions on them, they will quit," Shinde reasoned.

"If we do not discipline them, then they will not improve. Employees may eventually start taking advantage of the situation. The sales and profits were not good in spite of the 4th of July promotion sales and discounts. I do not want my customers in the United States to feel dejected due to this issue," Gregory asserted.

Considering Alternatives

Shinde finished all of his meetings at 4 a.m. He looked back at all that had happened that day. Gregory had made a valid point about the need to fix the problem quickly. She was his client, and it was important that she was happy. He realized that Gregory was accountable for her goals, too.

However, Shinde respected the beliefs of the employees and understood their fears in working through the night, knowing they believed in superstitions. Shinde wanted both Gregory and his employees to be happy. He knew that he could not compromise the desires of one for those of the other. What was the best way to achieve a balance?

Shinde did not sleep that night as he considered various solutions and the implications of these. Before making a decision, Shinde needed to consider the pros and cons of each alternative, to finally develop a plan to achieve the business goals while respecting the concerns of all the people he worked with.

Exhibit 1: Diglot Capital Management Business Model

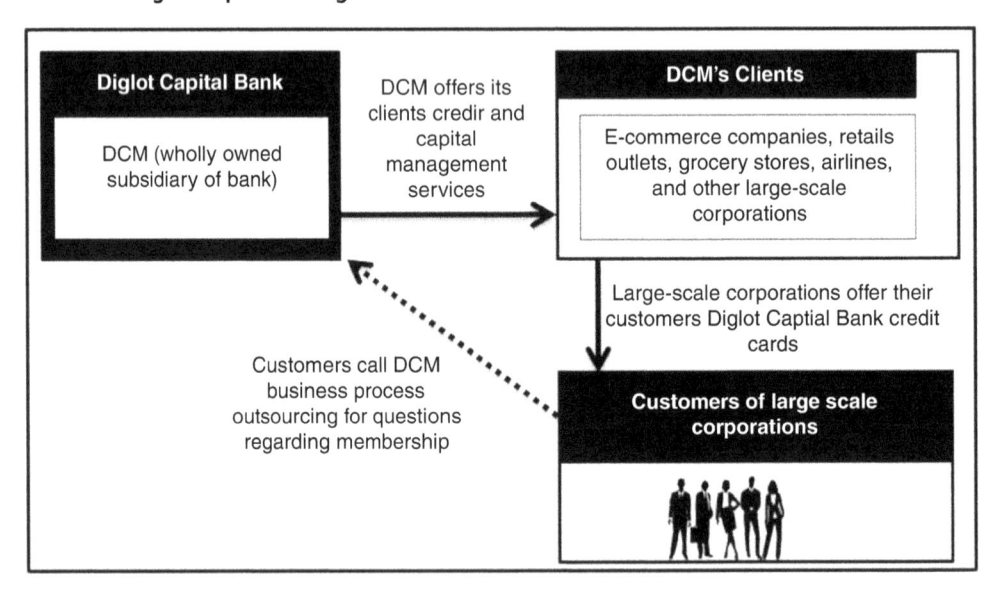

```
┌─────────────────────────────────────────────────────────────────────────┐
│  ┌──────────────────────┐                        ┌──────────────────┐   │
│  │  Diglot Capital Bank │   DCM offers its       │  DCM's Clients   │   │
│  │                      │   clients credit and   │                  │   │
│  │  DCM (wholly owned   │   capital              │ E-commerce       │   │
│  │  subsidiary of bank) │   management           │ companies,       │   │
│  │                      │   services ─────────▶  │ retails outlets, │   │
│  │                      │                        │ grocery stores,  │   │
│  │                      │                        │ airlines, and    │   │
│  │                      │                        │ other large-scale│   │
│  │                      │                        │ corporations     │   │
│  └──────────────────────┘                        └──────────────────┘   │
│              ▲                                            │             │
│              ┊         Large-scale corporations offer     │             │
│              ┊         their customers Diglot Captial     │             │
│              ┊         Bank credit cards                  ▼             │
│        Customers call DCM                        ┌──────────────────┐   │
│        business process                          │ Customers of     │   │
│        outsourcing for questions                 │ large scale      │   │
│        regarding membership                      │ corporations     │   │
│                                                  └──────────────────┘   │
└─────────────────────────────────────────────────────────────────────────┘
```

Note: DCM = Diglot Capital Management.
Source: Created by the authors based on company documents.

Exhibit 2: Organizational Structure of Diglot Capital Management, India

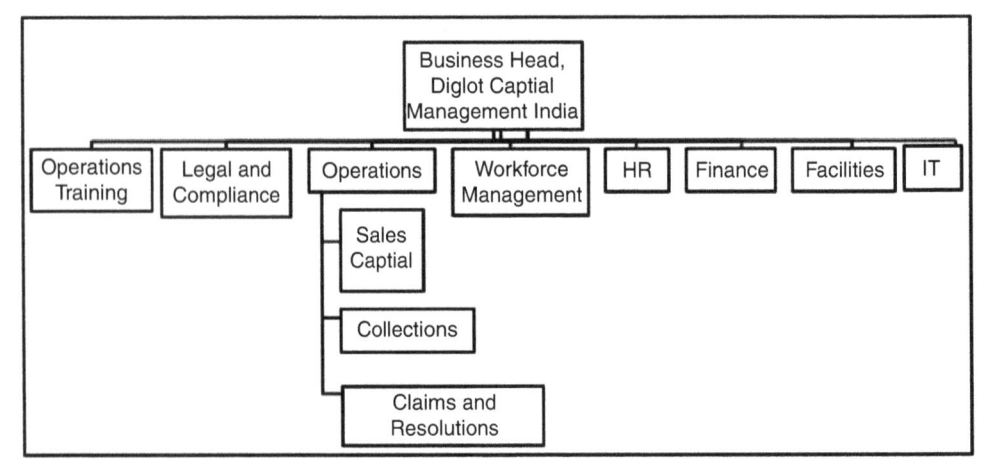

```
                    ┌──────────────────────┐
                    │ Business Head,       │
                    │ Diglot Captial       │
                    │ Management India     │
                    └──────────┬───────────┘
    ┌────────────┬─────────────┼──────────────┬──────┬────────┬────────┬─────┐
┌─────────┐ ┌──────────┐ ┌──────────┐ ┌────────────┐ ┌────┐ ┌───────┐ ┌────────┐ ┌────┐
│Operations│ │Legal and │ │Operations│ │ Workforce  │ │ HR │ │Finance│ │Facilities│ │ IT │
│ Training │ │Compliance│ │          │ │ Management │ │    │ │       │ │          │ │    │
└─────────┘ └──────────┘ └────┬─────┘ └────────────┘ └────┘ └───────┘ └────────┘ └────┘
                              │
                        ┌─────┴────────┐
                        │    Sales     │
                        │   Captial    │
                        └──────────────┘
                        ┌──────────────┐
                        │ Collections  │
                        └──────────────┘
                        ┌──────────────┐
                        │  Claims and  │
                        │  Resolutions │
                        └──────────────┘
```

Source: Company documents.
Note: HR = human resources; IT = information technology

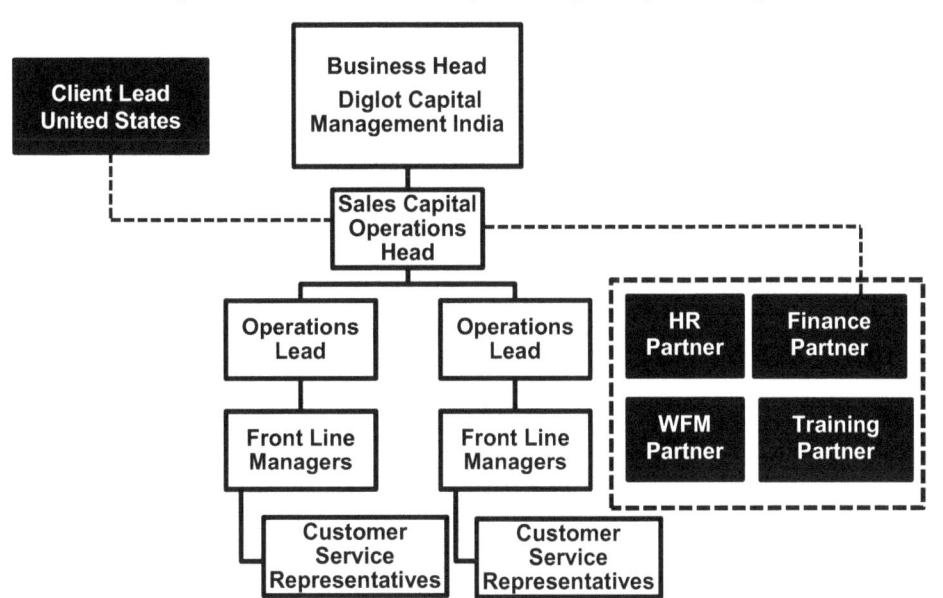

Exhibit 3: Management Structure of Sales Capital at Diglot Capital Management

```
                        ┌─────────────────┐
                        │  Business Head  │
┌──────────────┐        │ Diglot Capital  │
│ Client Lead  │        │Management India │
│United States │        └────────┬────────┘
└──────┬───────┘                 │
       │              ┌──────────┴──────────┐
       │              │   Sales Capital     │
       └--------------│    Operations       │-------------┐
                      │       Head          │             │
                      └──────────┬──────────┘             │
                 ┌───────────────┴────────────┐   ┌───────┴────────────────┐
          ┌──────┴──────┐              ┌──────┴──────┐  │ ┌─────────┐ ┌─────────┐│
          │ Operations  │              │ Operations  │  │ │   HR    │ │ Finance ││
          │    Lead     │              │    Lead     │  │ │ Partner │ │ Partner ││
          └──────┬──────┘              └──────┬──────┘  │ └─────────┘ └─────────┘│
          ┌──────┴──────┐              ┌──────┴──────┐  │ ┌─────────┐ ┌─────────┐│
          │ Front Line  │              │ Front Line  │  │ │   WFM   │ │Training ││
          │  Managers   │              │  Managers   │  │ │ Partner │ │ Partner ││
          └──────┬──────┘              └──────┬──────┘  │ └─────────┘ └─────────┘│
          ┌──────┴──────┐              ┌──────┴──────┐  └────────────────────────┘
          │  Customer   │              │  Customer   │
          │   Service   │              │   Service   │
          │Representatives│            │Representatives│
          └─────────────┘              └─────────────┘
```

Source: Company documents.
Note: HR = human resources; WFM = workforce management

CASE II-3: LEADERSHIP CRISIS AT STEELWORKS' XIAMEN PLANT

Hwee Hoon Tan and Flocy Joseph wrote this case solely to provide material for class discussion. The authors do not intend to illustrate either effective or ineffective handling of a managerial situation. The authors may have disguised certain names and other identifying information to protect confidentiality.

This publication may not be transmitted, photocopied, digitized or otherwise reproduced in any form or by any means without the permission of the copyright holder. Reproduction of this material is not covered under authorization by any reproduction rights organization. To order copies or request permission to reproduce materials, contact Ivey Publishing, Ivey Business School, Western University, London, Ontario, Canada, N6G 0N1; (t) 519.661.3208; (e) cases@ivey.ca; www.iveycases.com.

Copyright © 2016, Richard Ivey School of Business Foundation

Version: 2016-02-22

"So Chan came back and walked around the factory? He didn't say anything else?" Rajesh Kumar, chief executive officer (CEO) of Singapore's Steelworks, was baffled as he answered the phone call on a mild day in early February of 2011. C.H. Chan was the general manager (GM) of the Xiamen plant in China. Kumar thought of Chan as an efficient and hardworking man who had weathered many storms and played a key role in the China operations of Steelworks. It was unfortunate that Chan had decided to leave Steelworks.

Background

Steelworks was started in the 1960s in Singapore with a mission to provide premium metal products and solutions for the construction industries across Asia. It manufactured, traded, and exported metal products for these industries and played a key role in influencing the landscape of southern Malaysia. With operations spanning the region, the group had an annual metal production capacity of over one million tonnes as of 2011. Since 1961, Steelworks had evolved from a metal processing firm to a diversified group of companies competing in the areas of industrial gases; chemical, engineering, and technology investments; construction products; property; and trade.

In 2005, Steelworks was acquired by Southern Metals. Southern Metals was an Indian organization with a long tradition. With its position as a leading global metals company, Southern Metals was a well-respected and internationally known metals company with a footprint across the globe. Steelworks was its first acquisition outside of India.

After Southern Metals acquired Steelworks, its incumbent CEO continued to operate as the business head. Since 2005, Steelwork's management had been fully retained with only the addition of S. Venugopal and Anish Borra to the team. Following the retirement of the incumbent CEO, Southern Metals appointed Venugopal as the CEO and he served at Steelworks from 2008 to 2010. Kumar, the current CEO, took over in 2010 (see Exhibit 1). These two men brought with them different leadership styles and different mandates centring on the core Southern Metals values.

Venugopal's mandate was to align and create synergies in the partnership. He was required to infuse the Southern Metals culture in Steelworks with the core values of integrity, understanding, excellence, unity, and responsibility. Viewed as non-hierarchical, amiable, and determined, Venugopal had an interaction style that was based on discussion and letting people find solutions to problems. Collaborative and consultative, Venugopal was particularly good at bridging gaps and providing clarity of purpose to his colleagues. In 2010, Venugopal returned to Southern Metals to take on a more senior role and Kumar succeeded him at Steelworks.

The leadership qualities and attributes of Kumar varied strikingly from those of Venugopal, his predecessor. Strongly rooted in the Southern Metals culture, Kumar had a dynamic personality and strong analytical abilities, and was a quick decision maker. Decisions taken as a team were meant to be strongly adhered to and he did not appreciate individual deviations after decisions. Since he demanded immediate responses to prevent problems from growing, he regularly engaged with his colleagues on the future of Steelworks and the immediate actions to be taken. Not a person for email conversations, Kumar preferred solving problems via face-to-face conversations. This also played to one of Kumar's key strengths – his ability to quickly grasp non-verbal cues. During face-to-face discussions, Kumar could immediately sense who was disengaged and he could spot trouble ahead of time.

With the many targets that Kumar had to achieve in Singapore during his tenure as the CEO of Steelworks, he was mindful that the firm was racing against time. He thus demanded quick responses and agility from his colleagues when faced with crises. For these reasons, some employees at Steelworks felt that Kumar came across as overbearing or assertive in demanding results from the various stakeholders.

However, Kumar was also a very affable person. He had an open-door policy, where any employee – from factory workers to business heads – could walk into his office to discuss pressing matters. A strong advocate of employee engagement in the workplace, Kumar championed many initiatives within Steelworks that helped employees bond with one another, and this gave him opportunities to interact with his colleagues. Campaigns related to safety at work, sustainability, and adherence to the code of ethics of the group earned Kumar many accolades and enhanced his image as a respectable and responsive leader of a leading metals company.

Keen to accelerate the good work started by his predecessor, Kumar launched a key initiative soon after assuming his role of CEO. This was Project C3 – a massive restructuring and amalgamation of various subsidiaries in the region under the corporate umbrella of Steelworks. This exercise commenced in 2010.

Project C3

When Kumar was appointed to Steelworks in early 2010, Steelworks had business spanning Vietnam, Malaysia, Indonesia, China, and Australia in both its upstream and downstream businesses. Because Steelworks was headquartered in Singapore, the other operational units were looking to the leadership team in Singapore to make decisions. However, the fast pace of change in the external environments and the vastly different contexts in which each of the different units operated necessitated the urgent reorganization of the business and decision-making mechanisms to capitalize on opportunities in the different regions.

A study commissioned by Steelworks found that the country business units had acquired differing mindsets and had limited understanding of, and alignment with, the group's strategy and vision. The management and governance structures were also fragmented and group roles were diluted or missing (see Exhibit 2). Together with limited collaboration and varying capability levels across business units, there was difficulty in harnessing and leveraging group aspirations. Kumar therefore embarked on Project C3 by focusing on the 3Cs – collaborate (for competitive advantage), cultivate ("One Steelworks" culture), and catapult (regional growth). Key to Project C3 were the objectives to (a) create an operating model and organizational structure that balanced unique country needs with broader regional strategy, (b) focus on the common work culture attributes to drive the success of "One Steelworks," and (c) create a Steelworks leadership team to drive regional strategy and collaboration (see Exhibit 3).

As part of Project C3, a new corporate centre was created to bring together nine key areas: strategy and business development; total quality management; sales and marketing; supply chains; safety, health, and environment; human resources; information technology; finance and treasury; and legal and secretarial services. The new corporate centre functioned as the strategic business partner to the various Steelworks business units in the respective countries, akin to a shared services centre that coordinated and enabled a common strategic goal. Instead of all units taking directions from Steelworks in Singapore, a seven-person senior leadership team was constituted involving all GMs from the business units. The leadership team was tasked with one common goal – to drive business objectives for the entire Steelworks group by leveraging the competitive advantages of the various business units. Strategies, therefore, were formulated based on the goals for the group.

Project C3 created both tension and synergies. The tension arose from the new requirements for parallel reporting in many functions with the new corporate centre. The synergy came in the form of aligning business units to one common goal. Hence, while members of the business units ceded some control over their strategies and operations, they also gained involvement in the top leadership hierarchy.

Many conversations were held to help business unit GMs understand the new "One Steelworks" culture. Workshops and offsite meetings were conducted with clear articulation of the way forward. In the leadership meetings, issues were raised and ironed out. One opposing voice came from Chan, the Xiamen GM. He was of the view that local management worked better for China, and that the new corporate centre would impede the operations in China. This was especially true given the competitive environment in China and the need to build *guanxi*[1] with local stakeholders. In his view, oversight from the corporate centre would create many redundancies and would slow down the execution of many opportunities. To Chan, Project C3 was more of a temporary disruption and did not compare to the existing operational efficiencies that he had spearheaded in China.

The business case for "One Steelworks" was particularly compelling, and having addressed the issues that were raised, Kumar decided to go ahead, and the initiative gathered momentum in December 2010.

C. H. Chan

Chan, the GM of Steelworks Xiamen, was a true Steelworks man in more ways than one. With a long service record of 15 years, he had worked with almost all the members of Steelworks' senior management team. Known to be ambitious, he had been sent from Singapore to head the Xiamen operations in China at age 45. In fact, he had approached the Steelworks management for the position of GM in Xiamen. A tough taskmaster, he performed exceedingly well during his time in Xiamen and built a patriarchal image for himself and a favourable image for the company with its external stakeholders. Commenting on Chan's pursuit of leading successful operations in China, Venugopal had once commented, "Chan is one of Steelworks' best people."

As Kumar pondered over Chan, he recalled the warm and cordial relationship he had shared with Chan. Visiting the Xiamen operations was always a pleasure and he admired Chan's style of functioning. Although Kumar could use simple Mandarin phrases to interact socially with the management team in Xiamen, he was more than happy to have

---

[1] *Guanxi* is a term used in the Chinese context to denote a system of networks and relationships that facilitate business.

Chan run the factory, given the language challenges. The factory had so far been functioning with Chan as the main point of contact for the other members of the management team in the Xiamen factory. However, an issue had cropped up recently with Chan refusing to sign the audited financial statements for the Xiamen factory. "Perhaps that was the issue? The lack of transparency and a single point of communication with only Chan?" Kumar mused to himself. Kumar recalled that the consultants of Project C3 had warned him that Chan might be a potential issue. While Chan had attended most of the leadership team's C3 meetings, he had been distracted. He had walked in and out of the meetings, busy on his phone, and had not communicated much with other members of the leadership team. Other than to express his strong opposing views, Chan had been fairly disengaged. However, the current issue with the audited reports seemingly had nothing to do with Project C3. "What could have possibly gone wrong this time?" Kumar wondered, sensing that other than Chan's stellar performance in Xiamen, he had no other data points on Chan. Indeed, Chan was one-dimensional to him.

Late December 2010

As Kumar reflected on his interactions and work relationship with Chan, Kumar started unravelling some puzzles and the issues began to surface. There were latent signs of operations not going very smoothly in Xiamen. In fact, only a couple of months ago, in the third quarter of 2010, Kumar had alerted Borra, his chief financial officer, to investigate the many resignations of key personnel from the finance department in Xiamen. Borra had reached out to Ryan Ling, the deputy GM of Steelworks' recently acquired Wuxi operations in China, to investigate the resignations. In fact, all the Singaporeans seconded to the Xiamen plant had tendered their resignations within six months of starting work there!

One key observation from Ling's visit was that the operations and job descriptions in the Xiamen plant were very narrowly divided, with each person doing a small part of the work and being ignorant of the big picture. Another problem was the physical work space, where team members from the same functional team were seated away from one another. This was especially so for the finance team, where they were seated in different corners of the office with colleagues from other functional areas. When a bewildered Ling pointed this out as perhaps not an ideal state of affairs, he had been told by Chan that "this is a Steelworks practice," further confounding Ling, since he had been oblivious to the existence of such a practice. Based on his observations and experiences, Ling had proposed a reorganization of the structure and the responsibilities for the colleagues at the Xiamen plant. This proposal no doubt would have annoyed Chan, because he was fiercely possessive of his team and had an autocratic style where he only shared selected information from Steelworks Singapore. Kumar had realized that Ling's proposal was not proceeding, with Chan showing no signs of executing it. Now, to compound matters, Chan was refusing to sign off on the audited statements. Kumar wondered if there were other issues that had been hidden; had there been warning signs that the team in Singapore had overlooked? With these uneasy thoughts, he decided to let the events unfold.

The next morning, Kumar received another call from John Yang, the company's chief operating officer (COO), reporting that Chan had continued his stubborn stance in refusing to sign the documents from the auditors. Chan had put forward a new request: he wanted to speak to Kumar directly, with no middlemen involved. Kumar mulled over the various options. He concluded that a simple conversation over the phone would not yield the solution. Matters had already escalated, with Borra making a conscious effort to get Chan and the auditors to reach an amicable solution. However, Chan had refused to cooperate and had made it clear that he did not want to have any dealings with the auditors. The auditors too found themselves in a tight spot. They could not figure out what Chan was unhappy about. Chan seemed to be muted – avoiding conversation with his counterparts and peers.

"Does he want to speak with me on the phone, Yang?" Kumar asked.

"Well, that was the request, to speak with you only, but maybe if we have him back here in Singapore, we can sort this out face-to-face. He has not been cooperative with Ling as well," Yang suggested. Kumar replied, "Not a bad idea; let's have him back here in Singapore for a few days. Also, Chan has been in Xiamen for a while now, so perhaps it is also time for us to rotate him back to Singapore, or to the next position that will further his career development?" Kumar reflected on the issue, and continued, "Chan has been an asset to Steelworks; there is surely a place where he can be happy and contribute. Also, can Ling help us hold the fort for a while in Xiamen? After all, he has visited the plant and seems to know the operations somewhat."

Kumar was indeed thinking ahead. A change in the environment and job duties would probably enable the leadership team in Singapore to fix the issues with the Xiamen operations and provide a change of scenery for Chan. Indeed, Chan was Singaporean, and might appreciate a rotation back to his home country. Kumar, a career man of Steelworks, believed that employees were his real assets and was convinced that Chan was an asset to Steelworks. He thought of the day when he would go back to India, having done a commendable job in Singapore, and had a similar idea for Chan. The promise of coming home seemed to be the best solution in the current situation.

Early January 2011

"Have you spoken with Chan yet, Kumar?" Yang asked on the other end of the line. Kumar confided in Yang, "Oh, not yet, I am scheduled to meet him early this afternoon. I have yet to see him since he got back to Singapore. Did he tell you anything yet? You have known Chan for a long time, so perhaps he will tell you what is going on, as a personal friend?" Kumar then considered other people who knew Chan well. "Come to think of it, Chan has worked with almost everyone on the senior management team. In fact, Venugopal spoke very highly about him and mentioned how he has steered the China operations to our advantage. I am just not able to figure out what went wrong this time."

Kumar knew that the face-to-face meeting with Chan would not be an easy one. He had to watch his words and explain to Chan his proposal to have Chan rotated back to Singapore. In addition, the new role offered to Chan had to be exciting enough and one where Steelworks could put his potential to good use. Various scenarios flashed through Kumar's mind. Perhaps Chan should be consulted on where he would like to go next.

With all the above considerations, Kumar started the meeting in Singapore with Chan by patiently laying out his well-crafted plan for him. The conversation commenced with congratulating Chan on producing another year of stellar performance. Kumar added how the senior management at headquarters echoed the same view, and how his presence at headquarters would add the right combination of in-country exposure for the regional growth of Steelworks. Kumar then broached the subject of Chan refusing to sign the audited statements and his concerns regarding this, and checked with him if there was any information that the CEO was not privy to. This was because a refusal to sign off on the audited statements was considered a breach of duty and both Chan and Kumar would have to bear the consequences, as the seal officially bore Kumar's name. To Kumar's surprise, Chan was calm and raised no objections during the conversation. His only request was for some time to ponder over what Kumar had shared with him. It was Kumar who then proposed that Chan take the next two days to reflect and deliberate on the new assignment at the headquarters. The meeting concluded with both agreeing to meet two days later to finalize their course of action.

The Next Day

"What? Chan has gone back to Xiamen? He said he would take two days to consider my proposal and the issues I raised; he didn't talk about flying back so soon!" said a stunned Kumar.

"Chan emailed me just now that he didn't want the rotation and the new position you have offered and has flown back to Xiamen," said Yang, equally stunned. For the first time in their careers, Kumar and Yang were dealing with a situation where a senior member of the management team was behaving in a rather illogical and defiant manner.

Kumar knew he had to take matters into his own hands and deal with this before the issue escalated. "Looks like we have to make a trip to Xiamen immediately. Could you ask Fanny Ang and John Yang to come along with us? Also, please get Ling to get there ASAP. I would like Ling to assume the position of GM. We cannot wait anymore; we have to get this issue ironed out before the Chinese New Year annual holidays in February." What Kumar did not share was that just the previous evening, he had again received a call from the auditors stating that not signing the auditor's report could lead to other complications.

Late January 2011

Ling's Recollection

Ryan Ling, the deputy GM of Steelworks' Wuxi operations in China, had his own experiences with Chan, which he recounted as follows.

"I left for Xiamen immediately after receiving the call from Singapore. It was a difficult encounter with Chan. I told him that I had been instructed to take over the GM position. Chan was angry. He refused to accept me and insisted that he was the GM until he received the official notification from Kumar. What was even more worrisome was that he wanted to call a press conference to talk about what the auditors did wrong. It was becoming difficult for me to put sense into Chan. I attempted to convince him to be realistic, as he had to first work things out with us, tell us what was going on with the audit and the root cause of his unhappiness. I knew I was going there for just the interim period and Chan was certainly not happy to see me. With all the records still showing Chan as the GM, he was responsible for the entire Xiamen operations. Strangely, the auditors did not have any issues with his financials. I just could not understand why he was doing this big song and dance. Chan had decided that he did not want to talk to anyone. He even told me, 'You are not qualified to talk to me.' It was absurd!"

"Shortly after my encounter with Chan, the team from Singapore arrived. Kumar was accompanied by John Yang (COO), Fanny Ang (vice-president of human resources), and Rick Teo (legal counsel)."

"'So what is the status now?' Yang asked, as soon as he saw me."

"'No status,' I replied. 'Chan said that I am not qualified to talk to him and he has been waiting for all of you to turn up. In the meantime, you may want to know that I talked to the auditors and something unbelievable has happened. When the auditors visited the plant, Chan took them to the employee conference room and told the employees that these auditors were the reason why they were not getting their salaries for this month! The auditors were stunned. They could not make out what was eliciting such violent reactions from this man. The Chan I see now is not the Chan I knew earlier. Chan has never been so unpredictable and unreasonable. I have known him for a long time, though I will admit we are not close friends!'"

"'No worries, let's go into the factory today and since Kumar is here, let's see what Chan will tell him,' Yang assured me. I took comfort in the presence of the senior management from Singapore. With Chan refusing to sign the audited reports and publicly humiliating the auditors, the ripple effects of these actions were being felt by one and all. I hoped and prayed for a sound resolution to end all this madness."

At the Xiamen Factory

Forewarned by Ling about Chan's non-cooperation, the team from Singapore braced itself for the meeting with Chan. Upon reaching the Xiamen factory, Kumar volunteered to meet with Chan alone in his office while the rest of the team waited in the conference room. Kumar later recalled that meeting as the most painful three hours of his life – painful because questions, pleas, and requests by Kumar were met with a stony silence from Chan. Kumar was not even sure if Chan was listening to him. Three hours into his monologue, Kumar began to lose his composure, with frustration and anger mounting. Chan had wanted to talk to him and now that Kumar had made the trip to Xiamen, Chan refused to utter a single word. An exhausted Kumar finally decided to ask Yang to engage Chan in a conversation. Kumar knew that Yang and Chan went back a long way, having worked together on many projects and having been on many overseas assignments together.

"Why don't you come back to Singapore and we can take it from there? We can come up with a position for you if there are none that you want currently," Yang suggested. Chan continued his stony silence. He looked through Yang as though he did not exist. To make matters worse, Chan started giving directions to the employees around him. Sitting in his chair in his office, Chan was sending instructions to the Xiamen employees while Yang waited to get Chan's attention and response to his suggestion. "Perhaps Chan is still trying to show that he is in charge," Yang mused to himself.

The stalemate continued. By 5 p.m., and making no progress with Chan, Kumar decided it was time to make some decisions. Kumar gave Chan an ultimatum to relinquish the GM position and hand over the seals and documents to Ling. Chan responded by locking the office and leaving. The next day, Kumar received an email from Chan stating that he was sick and that he could not come to the office.

At this point, Kumar knew that legal advice was needed and he immediately contacted Steelworks' legal counsel in Beijing, who advised them to break the door to the GM's office. They also immediately drafted an eviction notice to Chan to end his employment with Steelworks. When the office was broken into, they had to break into the office safe to retrieve the seals that Kumar had authorized Chan to use in the Xiamen operations. Kumar also changed the signatories to the legal entity in the Xiamen factory and the operational power was handed over to Ling. The team left for Singapore that evening with a painful Xiamen experience that none of them would forget.

Was Project C3 the problem? C3 was taking a great deal of autonomy from the various unit heads. Chan, for one, had expressed unhappiness to the consulting team and Kumar had taken much pain to explain to the leadership team the overarching reasons for the change. What had gone wrong? Could it be the way Steelworks managed its subsidiaries? Had Chan been seconded to Xiamen for too long? What would be a good timeframe for transferred employees on overseas postings? How could a member of the senior management team who had been with Steelworks for his entire career behave this way? Could Kumar have done anything differently?

Exhibit 1: Organizational Chart of Steelworks' Head Office

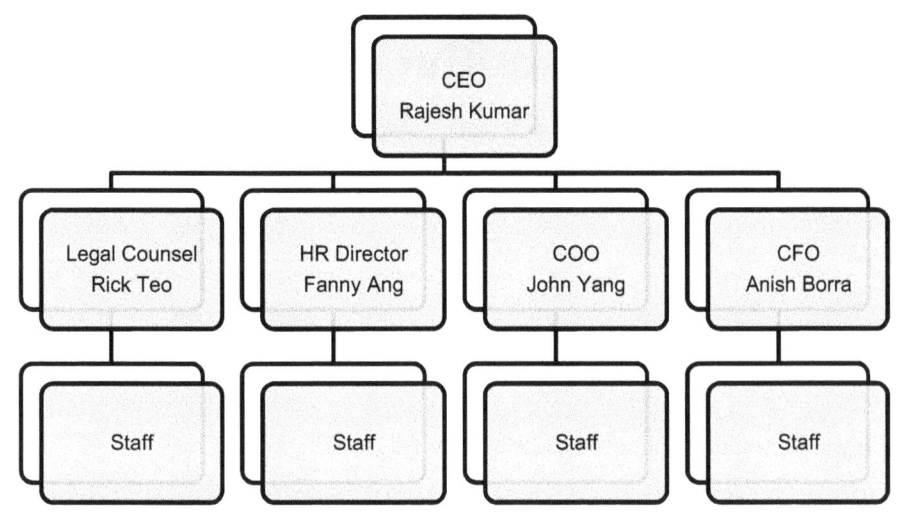

- CEO: Rajesh Kumar
  - Legal Counsel: Rick Teo
    - Staff
  - HR Director: Fanny Ang
    - Staff
  - COO: John Yang
    - Staff
  - CFO: Anish Borra
    - Staff

Source: Extracted from Steelworks' organizational chart.
CFO: chief financial officer

Exhibit 2: Organizational Chart of Steelworks' Business Units before Project C3

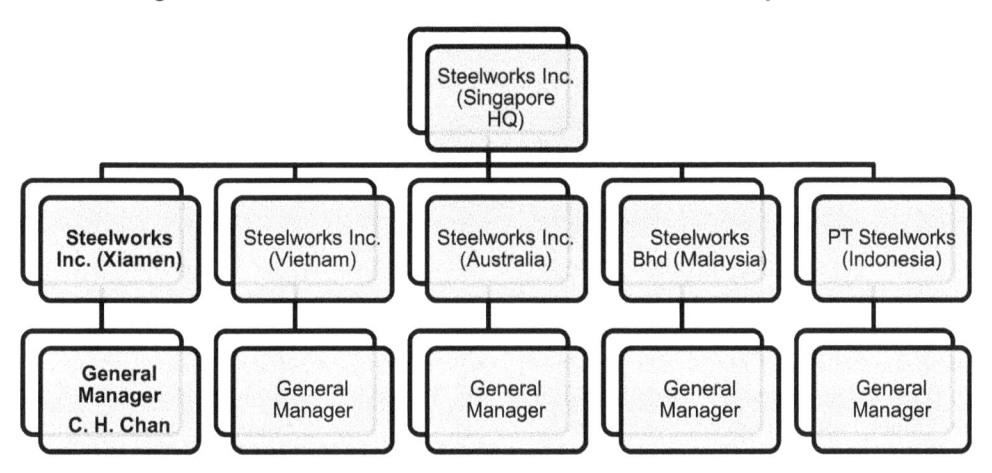

- Steelworks Inc. (Singapore HQ)
  - **Steelworks Inc. (Xiamen)** — **General Manager C. H. Chan**
  - Steelworks Inc. (Vietnam) — General Manager
  - Steelworks Inc. (Australia) — General Manager
  - Steelworks Bhd (Malaysia) — General Manager
  - PT Steelworks (Indonesia) — General Manager

Source: Extracted from Steelworks' organizational chart.

Exhibit 3: Project C3 – "One Steelworks" Work Culture

- Adapting quickly to changes in the business environment
- Continuously improving operations
- Maximizing customer satisfaction
- Encouraging teamwork
- Taking initiative
- Rewarding superior performance

Source: Extracted from Steelworks' internal records on Project C3.

CASE II-4: UWA ODE: EMBRACING LIFE AND CAREER ACROSS CULTURES

Sebastian Reiche

Yih-Teen Lee

The instrument had been there all this time, but I never quite understood how to play it. During my travels I learned all that I needed to bring MY music alive.

Uwa Ode

This case was prepared by Professors Sebastian Reiche and Yih-Teen Lee. February 2022.

This case is a variation of the case "Uwa Ode. A Cultural Chameleon or Stranded between Cultural Chairs?", DPO-281-E, from the same authors.

IESE cases are designed to promote class discussion rather than to illustrate effective or ineffective management of a given situation.

Copyright © 2022 IESE. To order copies contact IESE Publishing via www.iesepublishing.com. Alternatively, write to publishing @iese.edu or call +34 932 536 558.

No part of this publication may be reproduced, stored in a retrieval system, used in a spreadsheet, or transmitted in any form or by any means – electronic, mechanical, photocopying, recording, or otherwise – without the permission of IESE.

Last edited: 10/2/22

Uwa Ode was standing on the terrace of a Barcelona-based business school moments after graduating from a 17-month long Global Executive MBA program. It was a quiet moment before rejoining the family and fellow graduates for the graduation dinner, following the rush of accomplishment. A number of life events had taken Uwa from a childhood in Nigeria, then to England, Northern Ireland, Texas and finally, Louisiana.

With the MBA program ending, a decision had to be made: continue a career in an oilfield services company headquartered in the United States or make a professional pivot?

Uwa's current company would most likely require a relocation every two to three years from one country to the next or, alternatively, relocations within the same country. However, another option would be to make a career change and move to a place that would feel like home, and where there would be an opportunity to finally start building a more permanent life. Yet another path would be to start a company in Africa to contribute to the business landscape there and move back to the continent after being away for 17 years. Uwa felt a responsibility to Nigeria and strived to preserve its cultural heritage, after learning from many other cultures and countries. This was clearly more than just a sentimental wish, seeing that Africa offered a myriad of business opportunities and a lot of room for economic development. It would be exciting to return home and contribute to the country's development. At the same time, cultural dilemmas might arise, since Uwa was not a typical Nigerian.

A number of personal and professional decisions were looming large on the horizon. The decision was much more complex than simply weighing up the financial benefits or the opportunities to travel and see the world. This decision would be pivotal for life and the future.

A Multicultural Childhood

Uwa's parents were both from Edo State in Nigeria (See **Exhibit 1** for a geopolitical map of Nigeria). They both spoke English as their first language but because they were from the same ethnic culture they also shared a local language, which they spoke with each other. However, they left Edo State when they were teenagers and moved to Lagos State, also in Nigeria. As for their university educations, Uwa's father studied in England and Uwa's mother in France. After several years, they returned to Nigeria where the father started his career with a multinational company that relocated him every three years. That gave the family the opportunity to work and live in the Netherlands twice, in England, in the United States, in Singapore and in several different states in Nigeria. In the parents' view, some of those moves began to cause too much instability for their children, so the father began to relocate to some of the countries by himself while the rest of the family remained in Nigeria and visited him during vacations.

Uwa's father began his career in Rivers State, which had a different culture from their culture of origin. The children often wondered why, as a family, they did not eat the same food or speak the same Nigerian language as their local friends that were from Rivers State. The Ode family had one culture at home, and spoke the parents' language, but the children played, went to school and interacted with classmates in a different cultural context. Very early on, Uwa started to feel displaced, not only because the family had relocated from one state to another, but also because the parents themselves felt and acted displaced. This had a lasting impact on how cultural heritage was viewed. Today, the three siblings defined themselves differently from their parents, in spite of understanding their parents' culture and language. While they would say they were from Port Harcourt city (Rivers State), the parents would cite Benin City as their cultural origin. Aside from the relocations themselves, Uwa's father's work context also affected the way the family lived. As Uwa recalled:

> During the first 16 years of my life in Nigeria, in between the relocations, we lived in a purpose-built international, multi-racial, inter-racial and cross-cultural environment. All my friends who lived in the camp with me were also displaced from their parents' cultures. We had friends who were non-Nigerians growing up and going to school with us. Going to school we 'camp kids' were always 'odd' compared to the other kids who did not live in our 20-square-mile camp. The camp was artificially designed to remind everyone from different nationalities of their homes: there were swimming pools, tennis clubs, golf courses, a grocery store, recreational centers, a salon -you get the idea. Once you drove into the camp it was really like we did not live in Nigeria. So even though we were Nigerian, we were living in our own bubble, separated from our country.

After high school, a month after turning 16 years old, Uwa relocated to London to join an older sister, who had left two years earlier, and start A-levels. Uwa would go on to finish tertiary education in London as well. The process of adjusting to a new life in London began on the first day, as Uwa recalled:

> I realized that I didn't understand the jokes or subtle witty comments, and I sounded very different and dressed differently from the people around me. Back in Nigeria, I had graduated as head student of my school. I was very popular, I had the best grades at my high school, my mum was a

known entrepreneur in town ... Everyone knew me: the other kids, the teachers, the parents. And now, for the first time in my life the people around me wanted me to explain who I was. They didn't know my personality, my jokes, who my family was, how many siblings I had. In 16 years, I had never been unknown, undefined -and there I was. Worst of all, everyone would ask what country I was from and this immediately separated me in teenage social circles. The Nigerian teenagers were the funniest -the ones who were either born in London or who had moved there many years before me. They would identify with me but their first question was always: 'When did you move to London?' The longer you had been in London the more accepted you were because you sounded like them, understood the culture and could navigate your way around. So I would lie awake wishing for time to go by so I could say that I had been in London for three years, instead of three months.

The adjustment process involved many different steps that all happened at the same time. In the first year in London, Uwa never referred to the time spent in London in terms of months. Instead, this period was always characterized as 'almost a year.' This offered a pass to be accepted and hang out with potential friends. Changes in clothes and accent were also required during this time:

> The first weekend in London I went shopping with my mum, and my older sister and her Nigerian boyfriend, who had been going to school in London for the previous two years. That weekend I allowed the two to choose all the clothes my mum bought for me -after all I was about to start the same school they were going to and I didn't want to look different. I also realized my sister's accent had changed. That weekend I spent hours going through teenage magazines looking at how teenagers my age dressed and I watched television for countless hours trying to fine-tune my ears. I would practice the words and repeat my new-found accent over and over again. After a while, when I said that I was from Nigeria people would remark: "Wow, I never would have guessed except for your name!"

Entering the Professional World

After earning a degree in engineering, Uwa took a job at a local engineering company in London, choosing to work in the oil industry like the father. However, the fear that London would become permanent turf soon began to take hold:

> I worried that I would stop absorbing other cultures and experiences that the world has to offer. Besides, there were still days when London did not feel like "home" and I was not going to return to Nigeria – I was too different now. In a way, I was searching for what I had been used to growing up: the promise of the move.

After eight years in London, an international company offered a great opportunity. Uwa was relocated to Belfast, Northern Ireland for three years. This time in Belfast coincided with strong feelings of being uprooted and led to a pivotal decision: Uwa purchased a house in order to be able to own and go back home to something. Up to now, nothing had ever felt permanent. However, it turned out that a long-term home in Belfast was not possible, so a move to the United States with the same company came next. With this move came another dance of adaptation and assimilation.

After almost five years in Texas and one year in Louisiana, Louisiana was supposed to be the last non-permanent move. Yet no friends lived nearby. Unmarried and without children, Uwa hadn't yet put down any roots. This was the opposite of the life Uwa had aspired to have. While studying in London and with parents living in Amsterdam, Uwa remembered begging them to go home.

The parents replied: "But where do you want to go back to? We are in Amsterdam now and there is nobody in Nigeria." After relocating to Louisiana, Uwa was tired of exploring so many new places that were ultimately only temporary. Weary of building roots, making friends and establishing traditions in a place, only to leave again, Uwa had accepted life would revolve around work, an apartment and the gym.

Up to now, Uwa's moves had been linked to promotions as opposed to places where a life could be built. In those places, most people were expatriates like Uwa, all coming and going with multiple cultural experiences. Now, it was time to find out where long-term friendships could be made and a more permanent life, a home and a family could be created. In fact, an important reason for embarking on the Global Executive MBA was that the program would mean coming back to Europe. It would offer sufficient new experiences and time to explore the world, in addition to providing academic fluidity. Uwa hoped to identify where to live and find the opportunity to relocate to a place that could be called home.

Uwa realized how important this was after being offered a job back in London, an opportunity that was rejected straight away. Uwa's boss couldn't understand the refusal, because it would mean returning to a very familiar city. As tempting as it was to return to Europe, London just didn't seem like the right place. With so many cultural experiences that stretched far beyond London, it was difficult to walk away from the last six years in the United States. What's more, Uwa's British accent had given way to American English that stood out in the United Kingdom and from family members who had lived there much longer. More time was needed before choosing a final home.

The Multicultural Dividend

In contemplating future personal and professional steps, Uwa reflected on the advantages of living a multicultural life. Each culture had been like a beautifully different and unique song, and the process of living through each was the art of mastering a new dance. These experiences were treasures in a truly enriching life:

I feel like I have many personas living inside me. It is almost an exciting feeling. I know that I can change accents, the tone of my conversation, my way of thinking, my body language, my emotional intelligence, the interpretation of my surroundings, my point of view and even my jokes if I come across anyone who shares a cultural commonality with any of the places I have lived in. It means I am never afraid of change and I am never without friends. These are some of the many beautiful aspects of moving and experiencing the world the way I have.

These experiences were also beneficial from a career perspective, as they had been instrumental in leading multicultural teams successfully and bringing out the best in others. In fact, Uwa had often been selected for job promotions because of this very experience and skill. By and large, Uwa had a good understanding of how to make decisions across many cultures to create a win-win result for everyone and was often involved in client negotiations. Most of the company's clients were international, so Uwa would be selected to be part of the contract negotiations as a way of developing relationships and understanding with clients. As yet another sign that the company valued these skills, Uwa had worked with the executive board on several occasions to redefine company policy and a few times had also been selected as part of a team of 20 – out of a workforce of over 150,000 – to be the voice of the employees and help the company define effective policies across their global organization.

Further, when engaging with people who did not share the experiences of several cultures, Uwa had learned to quickly bring a new point of view into the discussion, and was always able to understand several points of view at a time. Uwa also felt privileged to have few prejudices and a high sense of tolerance and empathy. Even when not understanding another person or a cultural practice, Uwa would ask for clarification rather than making a quick judgment, because it constituted a key learning moment. Uwa also tried to instill this cultural understanding in the team:

> In the United States, when an employee is expecting a baby it is common for coworkers to plan a party called a 'baby shower'. I had one non-U.S. employee, though, who did not tell anyone that his wife was pregnant. One day he happily announced that he had just become a father. His coworkers took this badly; they felt deceived and couldn't understand how they could have worked with him for nine months without him mentioning it once. Some went as far as questioning whether they could still trust him if he would keep such a secret. When I heard about this issue, I assembled my team to explain that in some cultures there are superstitions about celebrating, naming a baby, or buying gifts before the baby's safe arrival.

They were all shocked because they had not heard of this before. But with the help of Google, everyone came to understand. I then called the employee and asked him to explain his motivations to his teammates. Needless to say, a party was planned after the baby arrived.

The Multicultural Baggage

Yet there was a flipside to a multicultural life. Because Uwa had had to say goodbyes several times, there was a permanent fear of loss – whether it was being separated from friends and loved ones or the initial rejection people may face in a new society while they are still different from the people around them. On the positive side, this meant that Uwa was very cautious about never causing other people any kind of pain or feelings of rejection. Afraid to lose another set of friends and move again, Uwa's biggest question was about belonging:

> Where is home? Where am I from? Which culture should I identify with? Is home where I work – even though it is not permanent? Or is home where my parents' house is? Because with all this moving I have not put down any roots anywhere, yet. What is the correct response to the first time someone asks: 'Where are you from?' Should I reply that I am Nigerian? But when I say so, the immediate connotations are not true and the last 17 years of my life go missing unless I respond with further detail. Should I say I am English because of my second citizenship?

But you can tell that I obviously have African heritage! Saying I am English also leaves out the first 16 years of my life. Worse yet, I have adopted an American sounding accent and have lost my British accent. Is that even a plausible response? After all, I have a U.K. passport to back up my claim, which isn't the case if I say that I am American just because I might sound it slightly, because I don't have citizenship or a green card. In fact, I'm in the United States on a visa, with the looming reality that it will expire and I will have to move again.

There was also the question of national identity and loyalty. Was it right to pick a political party in the United States or join a cause? What about voting in the English elections and contributing to charities that might benefit from Uwa's time and skills? Or was it better to focus on national loyalty to Nigeria and the African continent, which was in dire need of foreign-trained Africans?

In addition, so many experiences abroad had changed Uwa's personality. It was laughable when people remarked Uwa was quiet. How could someone think this about such a sociable and approachable person? Even the family didn't seem to recognize all of Uwa's personality anymore. While living in the United States, one sister once mentioned:

> Each time I see you it is as if another part of your personality has gone. Where is the loud laughter – people thought it was too gregarious at that time so Uwa decided to suppress it – where are the jokes – no one seemed to understand the English jokes so Uwa stopped telling them – and where is the fire and the passion in your soul – people seemed to think it was aggressive so Uwa suppressed that too?

It took a few days for the sisters to adjust. As one of them exclaimed: "It's like you are able to be multiple people depending on the situation." What had also changed was Uwa's relationship with the base culture. Experiences over the course of many moves showed that the skills Uwa's parents had taught did not always apply in every new cultural situation. This meant a whole new set of skills had to be learned in order to excel. In fact, along the way several better ways of conduct had been picked up. While Uwa's parents were hesitant to accept this deviation from some of their own cultural traditions, they also acknowledged the positive perspectives that this brought to the family's habits and activities.

The Decision

All this made the decision to move exceedingly difficult. Maybe a move to a new country, coupled with the experiences from the Global Executive MBA, would provide a fresh inspiration even if the choice was made to stay with the current employer. After all, excitement always comes with moving to a new place. Maybe a nomadic life, the thrill of discovering new cultures, and the challenge of reinventing oneself in new cultures remained enticing. While feeling rootless, there was still a fair share of restlessness, a fixation on moving and avoiding anything permanent that might take away the freedom of packing the bags and starting all over again. On the other hand, maybe the next move would turn out to be the ideal place. Uwa also still felt strangely attached to Africa, and Nigeria in particular. Uwa's parents had decided to retire in Nigeria so there was some family now. Yet one sister who had also moved back to Nigeria earlier was unhappy because she felt people did not really understand her and she did not share the views of Nigerian society. And there were not too many friends back in Nigeria.

One thing was clear. The Global Executive MBA had been undertaken in order to make a drastic career change, one that could help identify someplace to call home. Uwa had also wanted to be around likeminded people, who had colorful cultural backgrounds themselves and who were citizens of the world: people who would understand what it was like to be a citizen of many countries and to possess many different cultural experiences. Given the transience of past relationships, Uwa wanted lifelong friends who could be part of a permanent future.

Exhibit 1 Geopolitical Map of Nigeria

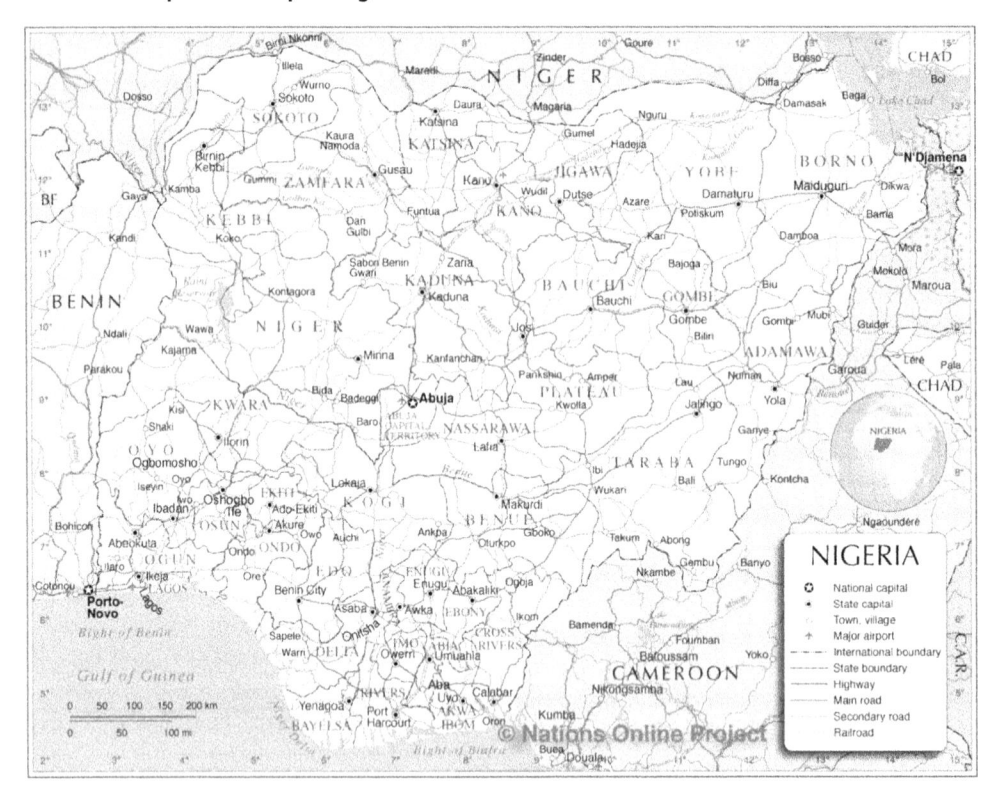

Source: Nations Online Project (www.nationsonline.org).

CASE II-5: SELECTING A COUNTRY MANAGER FOR DELTA BEVERAGES INDIA: PART 1

Professors Paula Caligiuri and Henry W. Lane wrote this case solely to provide material for class discussion. The authors do not intend to illustrate either effective or ineffective handling of a managerial situation. The authors may have disguised certain names and other identifying information to protect confidentiality.

This publication may not be transmitted, photocopied, digitized or otherwise reproduced in any form or by any means without the permission of Ivey Publishing, the exclusive representative of the copyright holder. Reproduction of this material is not covered under authorization by any reproduction rights organization. To order copies or request permission to reproduce materials, contact Ivey Publishing, Ivey Business School, Western University, London, Ontario, Canada, N6G 0N1; (t) 519.661.3208; (e) cases@ivey. ca; www.iveycases. com.

Copyright © 2015, Northeastern University, D'Amore-McKim School of Business   Version: 2018-05-22

You are the regional president, Asia, for Delta Beverages (Delta), a large U.S.-based firm headquartered in Boston. Delta is one of the world's leaders in the beverage industry, producing bottled water, carbonated beverages, teas, juice beverages and sports drinks. After having been with Delta for 10 years, you are now responsible for all of the firm's operations in Asia, including the major markets of China, India, Korea and Japan. Along with the rest of Delta's regional leadership team, you live in the Boston area and travel extensively to the subsidiaries you lead. In the two years since accepting this position, you have logged many frequent-flyer miles and, on most days, greatly enjoy the challenges of leading the company's fastest growing global region.

One of your greatest challenges is selecting your direct reports, the country managers leading each of the country-level markets within your unit. Delta's country managers are hands-on leaders who effectively direct all areas of the subsidiary's operations, including supply chain, logistics, inventory, quality control, government and customer service. Country managers need to operate with cultural agility and a deep understanding of the company's culture, values and standards of quality, safety and ethics. At the same time, country managers need to, at times, adapt to the client demands and unique challenges inherent in each of their local markets.

For large markets, such as India, Delta has traditionally promoted country managers from within — selecting leaders who have experience in the Boston-based headquarters and in running smaller and less challenging markets. Currently, most of your country managers are international assignees, with the exception of a few who are running smaller markets.

You understand, firsthand, what it takes to do this role well. Prior to this role, you had three international assignments, all as country managers. With your spouse and two children, you lived for three years in the United Kingdom, two years in Bulgaria and, most recently, two years China. You recall both joys and challenges of living and working in each of your host countries. It takes a special person — and a special family — to thrive in this type of work environment.

Today you need to make one of these critical staffing decisions. Shortly, you are scheduled for a distance communication meeting with the vice president of Human Resources for International Operations, AlUccello, and other members of your leadership team who are travelling. The meeting is to select someone for the position of country manager, India. The job will be located not far from New Delhi in the state of Haryana. This position became available a few years ahead of schedule when immediate concerns about government relations and quality control forced you to assign your strongest country leader, Canadian Xiao Zhang, the current country manager for India, to China – effective immediately.

The meeting today is important. India is among the largest and most important markets in your unit. You know that selecting the best country manager for India is critical.

Exercise 1

Before looking at the personnel files, you have decided to review what you know about selecting managers for international assignments. Attached is a list of 15 important characteristics that you believe should be considered for qualified candidates (see Exhibit 1). Ranking these characteristics may be helpful in reviewing the candidate files. Working alone, rank these characteristics in importance from high to low. Assign 1 to the most important characteristic and 15 to the least important. Although all characteristics are important, you know that some may be more important than others in terms of contributing to a successful assignment. After completing your individual ranking, go to Part 2

Exhibit 1: Ranking of Expatriate Selection Criteria (1 = most important, 15 = least important)

Item	1	2	3	4[1]	5
	Your Individual Rank	Your Team's Rank	Experts' Rank	Your Score (Difference between 1 & 3)	Team Score (Difference between 2 & 3)
Language fluency					
Prior postings					
Technical/business skills					
Availability for preparation training					
Cultural and social interests					
Low sickness record					
Spouse support					
Need for autonomy					
Interpersonal sensitivity					
Few family ties					
Vacations abroad					

[1] Your Score and Team Score are the absolute differences between columns 1 & 3 and 2 & 3.

Exhibit 1 (continued)

Item	1	2	3	4	5
	Your Individual Rank	Your Team's Rank	Experts' Rank	Your Score (Difference between 1 & 3)	Team Score (Difference between 2 & 3)
Communication skills					
No school-age children					
Extroversion					
Need for achievement					
			TOTALS		

1. Average Individual Score (Sum of individual scores, divided by number in group)
2. Team Score (From column 5 above)
3. Gain Score (Average Individual Score (#1), minus Team Score (#2))
4. Best Individual Score (Lowest Individual Score in Team)
5. Ratio (Number of individuals in group who scored lower than Team Score (#2), divided by number of individuals in the group
6. Relative Improvement (Gain score (#3), divided by average individual score (#1))

CASE II-5: SELECTING A COUNTRY MANAGER FOR DELTA BEVERAGES INDIA: PART 2

Professors Paula Caligiuri and Henry W. Lane wrote this case solely to provide material for class discussion. The authors do not intend to illustrate either effective or ineffective handling of a managerial situation. The authors may have disguised certain names and other identifying information to protect confidentiality.

This publication may not be transmitted, photocopied, digitized or otherwise reproduced in any form or by any means without the permission of Ivey Publishing, the exclusive representative of the copyright holder. Reproduction of this material is not covered under authorization by any reproduction rights organization. To order copies or request permission to reproduce materials, contact Ivey Publishing, Ivey Business School, Western University, London, Ontario, Canada, N6G 0N1; (t) 519.661.3208; (e) cases@ivey.ca; www.iveycases.com.

Copyright © 2015, Northeastern University, D'Amore-McKim School of Business   Version: 2015-06-22

Five Candidates' Notes from the Succession Planning Meeting

To prepare for today's meeting, you reviewed the materials from the past year's performance review and succession planning meetings. This activity has surfaced five possible candidates for the role of country manager, India. Your notes on these candidates are as follows.

1. Anika "Ani" Navithar
   Navithar has been with Delta for the past 15 years. She joined Delta immediately after completing her MBA at Northeastern University, joining us in the supply chain functional area. She has moved up the ranks quickly to director-level positions in both supply chain and customer service. While based in Boston, Navithar has successfully completed several short-term projects internationally, and for in the Indian subsidiary specifically. Navithar has never been a country manager. She speaks English, Hindi and Telugu. Part of Navithar's leadership development plan is an international assignment. Navithar is American.

2. Carlos Delgado
   Between his experience at Delta and with his previous employer (Delta's major competitor), Delgado has had three international assignments over the past 18 years. Delgado began his career with Delta at your Boston headquarters and is currently reporting to you as the country manager in South Korea. He is highly regarded as a global leader and, as the succession plan indicates, he was on the slate of candidates for your current role. Prior to becoming the country manager in Korea, Delgado was the Argentinean country manager for Delta and in supply chain role in Poland with his previous employer. Delgado speaks Spanish and English. He is a Mexican national.

3. Haziq Tengku
   Tengku reports directly to you and is currently the country manager for Malaysia, where he has been extremely successful. He is been serving in that role for the past six years and is ready for a promotion, according to the succession plan. With the exception of one three-month orientation at the Boston headquarters when he first

joined Delta 10 years ago, he has spent his tenure at Delta within the Malaysian subsidiary. Prior to joining Delta, Tengku worked for the Malaysian subsidiary of a U.S.-based fast-food chain. Part of Tengku's leadership development plan is to be a country manager for a larger market. He speaks Malay and English and has a degree in business from University of Malaya. Tengku is a Malaysian national.

4. Lucas Hansson

    Lucas was appointed as the vice president for Delta's Europe, Middle East and Africa (EMEA) region one year ago. In this current role, he is living and working in Delta's EMEA headquarter location of Basel, Switzerland. Prior to his current role, he was country manager in Germany (four years) and has led a variety of functional positions in the International Division from headquarters in Boston, including a two-year global quality initiative. Hansson speaks Swedish, English, French and German. He is a Swedish national.

5. Pranav Subramanium

    Subramanium is the vice president of the Indian subsidiary, reporting to Xiao Zhang, the recently re-assigned country manager of India. Subramanium joined Delta three years ago, after spending five years at a consulting firm in Delhi. The succession plan states that his performance has been exemplary, and he is considered in the top rank of the regional talent pool. Subramanium has an MBA from the Institute of Advanced Management and Research in Ghaziabad. Part of Subramanium's leadership development plan is a short-term assignment in the Boston headquarters. Subramanium speaks English, Hindi and Urdu. He is an Indian national.

Your Personal Reflections

You know all of these candidates personally, some better than others. Here are the mental notes you recall about each.

Anika "Ani" Navithar

You know Navithar well and have been extremely impressed with her. She is intelligent and authentic, rising to every leadership role in which she has been placed across multiple functional areas. Last summer at the Delta company picnic, you enjoyed meeting her family, her husband (who is a university professor in Boston) in their nine-year-old twin girls. Also, when Navithar did her short-term project in India, Xiao Zhang said she was very effective. Navithar's husband used their short-term experience in India to conduct some research and work with colleagues at Delhi University. You learned at the picnic that he now has a joint appointment at Delhi University.

Carlos Delgado

If you were hit by a bus tomorrow, Delgado would likely be asked to step into your role. He has really proven himself at Delta, with the trajectory of success. He and his family have been willing to relocate to Korea, although the demands they made regarding housing for their family, a cost-of-living allowance and education for their teenage children seemed, in your opinion, a bit excessive. Delgado would probably enjoy the expatriate community in Delhi but you wish he was more willing to integrate and acculturate and, at least, would attempt to learn the host country's national languages.

Haziq Tengku

Tengku is clearly proven himself in Malaysia and is probably ready for the next step in the Asia region. Six months ago when you were in Malaysia, Tengku was on a short leave of absence to support his wife and care for their two small children while his wife was undergoing cancer treatments. Last month, you heard that Tengku's wife is doing well.

Lucas Hansson

Hansson and his family seem to "bloom wherever they are planted," becoming part of the local community in every host country where they have lived. At the last leadership offsite, you and Hansson spoke about whether he would be interested in accepting the position as president of EMEA in the future, becoming your counterpart in EMEA. He noted that he's always looking for the next exciting opportunity – but feels as though he needs more experience running a country in emerging markets. You thought he was being exceptionally humble but appreciated his self-awareness, which probably makes him such a great international assignee. At one of the social events, Hansson also shared with you that he and his wife began to discuss whether they should retire in a few years and move back to Sweden to be with their elderly parents.

Pranav Subramanium

Subramanium is a solid performer but seems as though he needs a few more years as the second-in-command. However, this opening could be exactly the stretch challenge Subramanium needs to launch a global leadership career at Delta.

Excercise 2

Still working alone, continue to prepare for your meeting with the leadership team by considering the strengths and weaknesses of each of these five leading candidates for the job. Decide which candidate is best suited for the job.

PART III
Executing Strategy in a Global Context

Organizations achieve their strategic goals by coordinating work among people to execute the strategy. This section looks closely at the process of organizing across boundaries and leading change to achieve the desired outcomes.

8 Strategy and Organizational Forms

> Always design a thing by considering it in its next larger context – a chair in a room, a room in a house, a house in an environment, an environment in a city plan.
>
> Eliel Saarinen, Finnish-American architect (1873–1950)

Key Learning Objectives

At the end of this chapter, students will be able to:

- Recognize the primacy of context ("The Environment Always Wins!").
- Explain how the forces of global integration and local responsiveness shape organizational orientations, strategies, and forms.
- Describe major organizational forms in multinational enterprises.
- Examine the ways in which organizations grow, with a particular focus on acquisitions and strategic alliances (including joint ventures).
- Compare approaches to global business by small and medium enterprises.
- Identify two major trends in organizing related to digital transformations and lateral collaboration.

Strategy Execution Is Embedded in Context

A common thread throughout the chapters so far is the complexity and ambiguity of the context within which decision-makers devise and execute strategy. In this chapter we shine the spotlight on these notions further, by elevating our perspective to the **organizational level**. As globally operating entities, multinational enterprises (MNEs) in particular are faced with a plethora of simultaneous, multilayered, and often conflicting forces arising from their environments to which they must react swiftly and effectively. Aside from intercultural skills, this requires of the global leader an ability to discern how exactly the context will impact the company's strategy, structure, and administrative systems in light of market demands, competitors, and external constraints such as government policies.

An important part of strategy execution in that regard relates to designing effective organizational structures and collaborative processes. In a way, **organization design** is to business action and decision-making as architecture is to the design of physical spaces for living and working in. Just as the architecture of buildings and cities has evolved with our way of living, organizational forms have evolved for new requirements of doing business. In this chapter, we will identify the most common ways of organizing to execute strategy in global business, and we will highlight the alignment and leadership implications for each. We will further explore different vehicles for growth, globally operating smaller-scale companies, and current trends for organizational coordination.

We will start, however, by underscoring an essential point: Global leaders ought to acknowledge the **primacy of context** and incorporate it into their decision-making repertoire. From that the implications for strategy and organizing will follow.

The Environment Always Wins: A Tale of Two Families (and Beyond)

In 1876, **Charles A. Ropes**[1] ran a successful flour, grain, provisions, produce, and animal feed business at 222 Derby Street in Salem, Massachusetts. When he passed away, his son, Charles F. Ropes, took over the business. A few years into his role, he was one of the first to be offered an auto dealership. Believing that horseless carriages were just a flash in the pan, he turned down the opportunity. Subsequently, while car sales skyrocketed as more families were able to afford them, Ropes's business experienced a downturn and was ultimately forced to shut down.

A similar fate was experienced by **Peter Flynn** and his family, who operated a successful upscale specialty retailer and marketer of women's clothing on Tremont Street across from the Boston Common public park. In the 1930s, 1940s, and 1950s, Boston was the retail center of New England to which people would travel long distances to find a selection of clothes and other items not available locally.

---

[1] Peter Flynn was Professor Harry Lane's grandfather, and Charles A. Ropes and Charles F. Ropes were the great-grandfather and grandfather, respectively, of Professor Lane's wife.

When World War II ended in 1945, millions of soldiers returned home, married, and started families. The resulting baby boom led to the rise of suburban housing developments, and retailers began opening stores in newly emerging suburban malls rather than in downtown areas to cater to the developing middle class. This was aided by President Dwight Eisenhower's signing of the Federal-Aid Highway Act in 1956 to authorize the construction of the Interstate Highway System, which created a roadway spanning 65,000 km that enhanced the connectivity of shoppers across both rural and urban areas. In 1958, the Northshore Shopping Center opened in Peabody, Massachusetts, anchored by big-name retailers of the time such as Jordan Marsh, Filene's, Sears, and Kresge. Fifty thousand people attended opening day, crowding the expansive parking lot. Peter Flynn's son and daughter, who worked in his store, tried to convince him to open a branch in Northshore, but he did not believe malls would replace the downtown city stores. By the early 1960s, the business had declined substantially, and soon thereafter the Peter Flynn Company closed its doors.

Similar to these smaller local businesses, large companies can also struggle to consider the larger context in which they are embedded and to whose pressures they have to respond. For example, in the 1960s, Toyota, Honda, and Subaru started importing small autos into the United States. US automakers responded to this by largely downplaying the threat and concentrating on larger cars with bigger margins. This allowed the Japanese manufacturers to expand from their dominating position in the small car market to compete with their premium brands Lexus, Acura, and Infiniti within the large car market. As a result, by 2007, Toyota had surpassed General Motors's car and truck sales for the first time, and by 2020 beat Volkswagen as the world's top-selling automaker.

Other examples abound of companies failing to respond to external pressures, spanning diverse industries and including renowned brands from Digital Equipment Corporation (DEC) to Polaroid and Blockbuster. What these brands have in common is that they were all once companies with great market power that did not take the environment seriously enough to initiate a timely transformation. Ken Olsen, founder of DEC, famously commented, "There is no reason anyone would want a computer in their home": a statement that has proven to be profoundly untrue (Strohmeyer, 2008). DEC was subsequently acquired by Compaq in 1998, involving the divestment of major assets in 1998. Similarly, Polaroid missed the evolution toward digital photography, as did Blockbuster with video streaming, leading both companies to cease existing in their original form.

These anecdotes demonstrate a notion so essential that it takes on a law-like character – that context matters or, more catchy, that The Environment Always Wins! In fact, we consider this notion so fundamental that we consider it a "law."

In a global environment that has become ever more volatile, uncertain, and fast-paced (the VUCA environment we alluded to in Chapter 1), this law only grows in importance. Faced with a post-pandemic, climate-challenged, and conflict-laden reality, leaders at global companies must be able to tease out the signal from the noise amid increasing complexity and ambiguity arising from the contexts in which they are embedded.

Differentiating between a flash in the pan and a lasting shift in the environment is easy to do in hindsight but difficult while the trend is unfolding. Who can say with certainty at this point whether (and if so, how exactly) cryptocurrencies, nonfungible tokens (NFTs), blockchain, virtual reality, the metaverse, and quantum computing will prevail and impact industries, organizations, and careers?

While context by definition is complex, there are discernible patterns of broad-level forces globally operating firms face. These relate to pressures toward global integration and local responsiveness, as we detail next.

The Classic Dilemma: Global Integration versus Local Responsiveness

All companies that operate globally are subject to pressures in their environments that push them toward either an emphasis on **global integration** (globalization) or pull them toward **local responsiveness** (localization) (Bartlett & Ghoshal, 1998; Prahalad & Doz, 1987). Since the objectives and means for each emphasis can be conflicting, they create a dilemma for decision-makers with regards to the trade-offs associated with each. Global integration is about centralizing decision-making and formalizing procedures to achieve one way of doing things globally, applied the same everywhere, without redundancies. Local responsiveness is about decentralizing decision-making and having fewer formal procedures, such that each geographical region determines its own way of doing business based on what local customers want.

Pressures toward global integration include the need to align under a specific stakeholder interface, such as a global brand. Another pressure is the need to reduce costs through global efficiencies, such as leveraging scale for bulk purchasing of supplies, decreasing labor costs, or centralizing large investments such as research and development costs or large manufacturing plants. Global integration drivers require companies to control activities centrally and minimize duplication of functions in order to exploit scale. A company with high global integration can centralize decisions for aligned implementation across the globe, enabled by today's fluidity of transporting goods and information across borders. This configuration allows the company to place specific value chain activities (those that add value to a product or service) in one or several locations around the world, in particular countries with less expensive labor, specifically trained workforces, access to particular raw materials, or other resources. At the extreme, companies will locate each activity in a region from which the firm can best serve the rest of its global activities. Whatever the distribution of activities, global integration requires high levels of centralization and **standardization** in the organizational structure, with associated alignment implications for tasks, people, and systems (an important notion we will allude to throughout this chapter and unpack further in Chapter 9).

In contrast, pressures toward local responsiveness move a company to adapt its products and services, tailor its business model, or realign its administrative systems to meet the needs of a specific national market. The three main factors driving local responsiveness are differing local customer needs for the products or services, local cultural norms for effective organizing, and local regulations for business operations or products and services. Today's information and digital technologies enable localization in new ways, for example by making smaller-scale manufacturing feasible and less costly. To achieve local responsiveness, an organization adopts a structure, set of tasks, characteristics of people, and alignment systems that are consistent with the local operation. This may mean flatter or taller hierarchical structures, more or less team-based manufacturing, different professional backgrounds for salespeople and technical service, utilizing local resources, and similar approaches geared toward meeting the needs of local customers. Increasing flexibility while minimizing transport costs is an additional feature of a highly locally responsive approach.

The context within which these pressures arise is multilayered. Whole industries can be differentiated by the extent to which they are facing pressures toward global integration and local responsiveness. Within each industry, competitive pressures further set companies apart from each other in terms of where they position themselves along the two dimensions. For instance, the packaged foods industry faces much stronger pressures toward local responsiveness than the oil and gas industry. Within the packaged foods industry, in turn, some companies align their brands much more closely to local tastes than others. For instance, Mondelez International's Oreo brand of cookies encompasses more than 85 varieties, from pumpkin spice to green tea flavors. The German food company Bahlsen, in contrast, has been selling its signature cookie Leibniz Butterkeks worldwide with little variation since 1891. Global leaders must be mindful of the layers through which these environmental pressures impact their companies, and from where shifts in pressures (i.e., new trends) might arise. Figure 8.1 illustrates this notion of multilayered pressures.

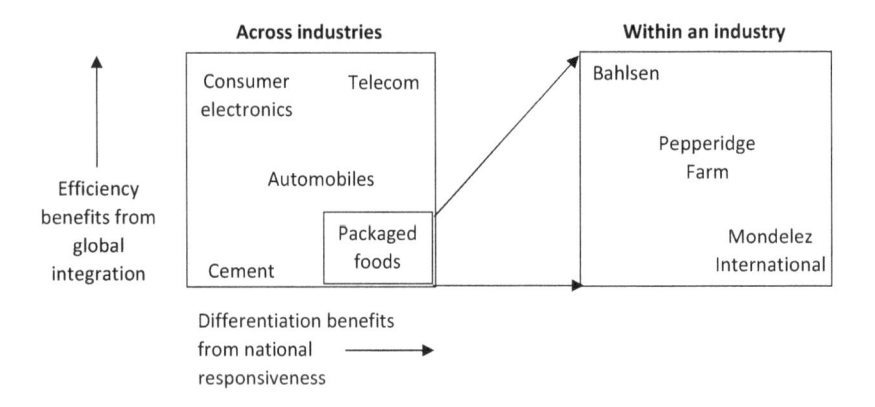

Figure 8.1 Multilayered integration–responsiveness framework.
Source: Adapted from Christopher Bartlett & Paul Beamish, *Transnational management: Text, cases, and readings in cross-border management.* McGraw-Hill Irwin, 2014, p. 210.

In addition to balancing globalization and localization, companies are faced with a third pressure toward engaging in **global learning**, that is, the transfer and sharing of new ideas and knowledge among units. A new production technology, marketing strategy, or product feature designed for one market can often be transferred to other markets. Interestingly, this has also led to the phenomenon of reverse innovation, whereby a product designed first for lower-income markets is later introduced to higher-income markets. An example is the Leveraged Freedom Chair, a wheelchair that was designed by engineers from MIT to fit the needs of people dependent on low-cost, all-terrain usability. Selling in India and other emerging markets for $100–$300, it has since been introduced to the United States and other higher-income markets with a price tag of more than $5,000 (World Design Organization, 2021). The important point to note here is that innovation can be sparked anywhere, and the applicability of the resulting design can be wide-reaching.

While learning can occur within an MNE's geographically dispersed network, it can also be nurtured through partnerships with organizations beyond the MNE's boundaries, including other firms, universities, governments, and NGOs. A growing phenomenon in that regard are environmental partnerships (EPs), which firms use to advance their sustainability agenda. For instance, a range of companies including Nestlé, Logitech, SIG, and others recently announced an EP through which they will cofund a new Chair for Sustainable Materials at the École polytechnique fédérale de Lausanne in Switzerland (Nestlé, 2020). The goal is to develop research into sustainable materials that can reduce or replace plastic waste.

Whether it occurs within MNEs or through partnerships with other organizations, the challenge of learning is to be able to identify synergistic links and transfer knowledge and skills effectively. The proper organizational structures and systems, as well as the right individuals who champion the transfer and harvesting of learning within the organization, play an important role in facilitating global learning.

Generic MNE Orientations

Companies operating within a context of competing pressures for global integration and local responsiveness typically evolve toward a particular **orientation**. One common classification scheme identifies four types of orientation, each related to a specific type of strategy and organizational form: the global, the multidomestic, the international, and the transnational. This is shown in Figure 8.2.

First, a multinational company that depends minimally on both global integration and local responsiveness exhibits an **international orientation** and is organized as a **coordinated federation**. Essentially, it replicates its home market systems in each of its foreign subsidiaries. These companies are very centralized, and their subsidiaries are simply outlets for headquarters' decisions. While this approach may have been more common pre-1980s, in today's global economy there are few industries left where such an international organization works well. The product categories most suitable to such a strategy include commodities. For example, grain businesses (ADM, Cargill) are large organizations that deal with commodity products traded around the world on the basis of price; however, even in these companies it is only a small set of operations that are conducted using international organizations. This is because they largely seek to replicate their home market systems in each of its foreign subsidiaries (i.e., little local adaptation or internationalization of systems).

	Low Pressure toward local responsiveness High	
High Pressures toward global integration **Low**	**Global orientation** *centralized hub*	**Transnational orientation** *integrated network model*
	International orientation *coordinated federation*	**Multidomestic orientation** *decentralized federation*

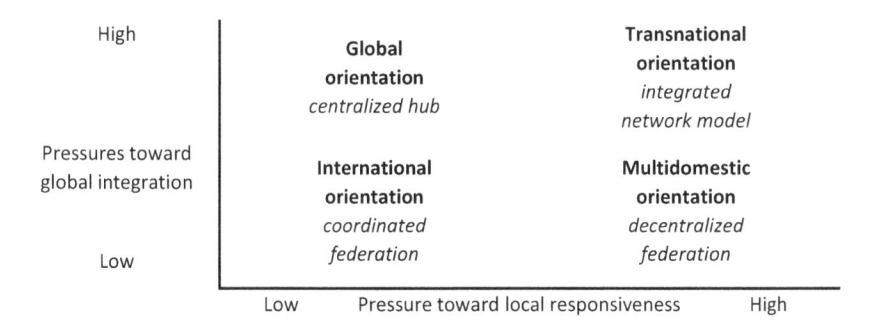

Figure 8.2 Generic international organizational orientations.
Source: Adapted from Christopher Bartlett & Paul Beamish, *Transnational management: Text, cases, and readings in cross-border management.* McGraw-Hill Irwin, 2014.

Second, a company that follows a strategy that is highly dependent on global integration for most of its value chain activities and is locally responsive for only a few of them exhibits a **global orientation** and is organized as a **centralized hub**. Such a company is usually characterized by a high number of complex interdependencies among its subsidiaries and has a governance structure that is tightly and centrally controlled. A global orientation is thus most prevalent in those companies that seek cost savings through integration and synergies. Coca-Cola has a globally standardized organization for its branding, meaning that its product and marketing strategy is centrally coordinated, and Royal Dutch Shell has a globally standardized organization for its oil production, meaning that its extraction approach is centrally devised and implemented without much adaptation at internationally dispersed sites.

Third, a company that follows a strategy that is minimally dependent on global integration but highly dependent on local responsiveness for many of its value chain activities exhibits a **multidomestic orientation** and is organized as a **decentralized federation**. These companies may experience strong pressures toward adapting their products and services to the local context and thus operate differently in each country; in an extreme case, each country or region has its own manufacturing, marketing, and research and development. They can be thought of as a confederation of loosely coupled organizations with strong local control and weak central control. The managers of multidomestic subsidiaries often function as independent "feudal lords" (i.e., individuals with much power and authority) who may or may not be expatriate managers depending on the company's administrative heritage. Traditionally, some large consumer goods companies such as Unilever and Nestlé were organized this way, although they are moving toward being transnational organizations now (see next paragraph). Companies in the building materials and construction industries, including cement and concrete firms such as Lafarge (now part of LafargeHolcim) and construction and development firms such as Vinci, also tend to be multidomestic organizations, since industries like these have to adapt to local contexts (in this case building codes, consumer preferences, local contractor networks).

Finally, a company that is simultaneously globally integrated and locally responsive exhibits a **transnational orientation** and is organized as an **integrated network model**. This organizational structure distributes the global responsibility for specific activities to the leaders who manage the subsidiary to which the activity has been assigned. Each country manager may report to different people with different worldwide activity responsibilities. The local responsiveness is achieved by managing each distributed value chain activity with enough flexibility that the local manager can make the essential compromises necessary to achieve as close a local market fit as possible. While simultaneous pressures toward both global integration and local responsiveness can drive firms toward more of a transnational orientation, executing it organizationally is a challenge. Specifically, an orientation marked by such complexity is costly to implement and requires managers who are cross-culturally and interpersonally skilled and flexible. As a result, few – if any – truly transnational corporations exist, but many are aspiring to and progressing in that direction, given the potential for superior competitive advantage. Driven by the growing popularity of customer-centric strategies (as opposed to product-centric strategies, as we will discuss in Chapter 9), and the resulting simultaneous pressures for global integration and local responsiveness, companies like Nestlé, Shell, and Panasonic have moved toward more transnational orientations.

In the sections that follow, we will see how companies with different strategies adapt these generic orientations to achieve alignment according to different needs.

> ### Reflection Question 8.1: Identifying Organizational Structure in Your Practice
>
> Think about the company you work for now, or one that you're very familiar with. Applying the categories in this chapter, how would you describe the company's organization type? Which different forms has it embodied through its history? In what ways does the organization's type reflect the complexity of the global business environment?

Global Organizing in MNEs

Identifying an organizational form that is optimized with regards to pressures toward global integration and local responsiveness and aligned with the corporate strategy is a challenging and ongoing endeavor for global leaders. The vast majority of MNEs began as companies that produced for and sold in their respective local national markets. Over time, as they grew the international portion of their operations, many added a business unit called "international," under which all international business was handled. Only after many years did these companies evolve to incorporate non-home markets into the rest of their organizational structures. Many large consumer products companies, such as Procter & Gamble, Unilever, and Nestlé, followed such a path. Across MNEs, a number of recurring patterns have emerged that represent common approaches to organizing the tension between global integration and local responsiveness, as we detail next.

Mainstay of Organizing in MNEs: Multidivisional Structures

Most MNEs are organized in many divisions, with each having responsibility for its own profits and losses. Divisional leaders can make decisions about most operations, including investments, within the parameters of global coordination from the top. Profits go to the global organization and may be redistributed to other divisions or directly to shareholders, or they may be applied to global investments. These organizations tend to prioritize either global integration or local responsiveness for each activity, although there may be units focusing on both global integration and local responsiveness across the company. Skanska, a multinational construction and development company, is based in Sweden with operations in the Nordics, Eastern Europe, the United Kingdom, and the United States. Because construction projects are essentially local, their dominant mode of organizing is multidomestic by geography: first organized by country, then by region within the country. On the other hand, Bombardier, a Canadian aircraft and transportation manufacturer, is organized by product groups: business aircraft, commercial aircraft, transportation (such as public transit and railway), and services. Because technology and global value propositions are central to their business, Bombardier's dominant mode of organizing prioritizes product groups over local markets. A generic geography-based multidivisional structure is shown in Figure 8.3.

Multidivisional structures have been the mainstay for global organizing since its inception. The separation of work into divisions allows efficiency and focus within the division on the key value proposition parameters (global integration), while the separation of different divisions allows for adaptation to different market segments (local responsiveness). Because the divisions are clear, it is possible to grow by adding a division or subdivision, or through acquisition, without affecting the whole organization. Although these organizations are large, the specialization of divisions means it is fairly straightforward to align task, structure, and

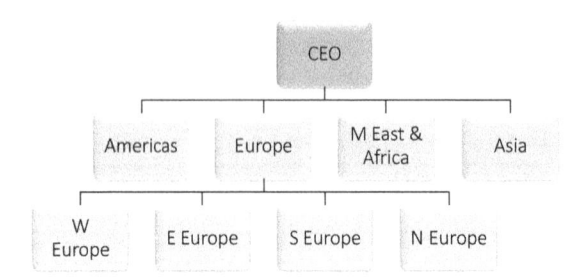

Figure 8.3 Generic multidivisional structure with geography-based business units.
(note – Americas, M East & Africa, and Asia would also have regions, not shown here)

people within a division. Headquarters is usually large enough to provide strong systems to support alignment, such as performance management, compensation, and development. Leading in a multidivisional structure requires seeing a systems view of the organization – understanding how the parts fit together to make a whole, and how one division's or subdivision's decisions affect others.

A multidivisional structure has several negative forces that must be counterbalanced. These organizations have a tendency toward internal focus and bureaucracy – they are coordinated through rules and procedures, and they can get so focused on these systems that they lose sight of either the customer and/or the larger organization. They often replicate effort and create inefficiencies without coordination – for example, several parts of the company may develop protocols for the same problems or situations, without knowing that the others are doing the same thing. Leaders at the top must constantly keep informed about what is happening in the different divisions, and enable coordination of knowledge and information transfer to "cascade" back down. Skanska, mentioned earlier, faces these challenges for developing expertise in particular kinds of projects, such as hospitals and schools, tunnels, and shopping malls. Each country organization developed its own expertise in these specialized projects, without knowing that other country organizations were doing the same. Over time, the multidivisional structure is balanced with multiple coordination mechanisms, such as centers of excellence (which are discussed under "Less Formal Collaboration" later in the chapter).

Combining Authority and Flexibility: The Quiet Return of the Matrix

An alternative way of balancing pressures for global integration and local responsiveness is to organize according to a matrix. A matrix organization has two (or more) organizing principles, such as geography and product organization, that are equal or almost equal in weight. There is a head of each geography, and also a head of each product area. Someone working on product type X in geography Y would report to two ultimate bosses, one each for product type and geography. The matrix is the structure most MNEs invoke, at least in part, to move more toward their ideal of transnational organization.

In the 1980s, most MNEs experimented with the matrix with great enthusiasm. We worked with one company that even had a six-dimensional matrix, with each person in the organization reporting equally to six bosses! Leaders found that the matrix was too complex – most people had two or more bosses with equal power, and a lot of effort was spent resolving conflicts or identifying gaps or redundancies. In status-oriented cultures, the matrix violates cultural norms of having a clear hierarchy, and it was particularly rejected in these cultures. Even in egalitarian-oriented cultures, the added coordination time and effort were deemed not worth the effort for a gain in knowledge and information distribution. By the 1990s, most companies had moved back to a multidivisional structure with some informal coordination mechanisms.

However, two trends have led to a quiet return of the matrix: the tendency toward customer-centric strategies means local responsiveness is more important to all firms; and the extreme competition and volatility of the business environment since the early 2000s mean that all firms need to focus on integrating globally for reasons of cost and efficiency. In the current situation, most companies find they *must* counter the downsides of a complex structure by giving clear authority and priority to multiple sets of organizing criteria. The main difference from the 1980s is that today's matrix organizations are usually limited to two or at most three dimensions and, importantly, they tend to clearly (if slightly) prioritize one dimension over others. These features allow for multiple perspectives and flexibility while maintaining a robust structure. Even firms from status-oriented cultures such as Tata Motors in India and Toyota Trading company in Japan are now organized with a matrix.

Figure 8.4 shows a generic version of a modern matrix organization. The solid line reporting relationships – that is, the primary ones – is geographic. But product groups are also important, and there is a clear organizational structure around product groups. This secondary organization is indicated with dotted lines. Within the organization, each person reports to both a geography leader and a product area leader. Companies tend to signal the relative priority through systems alignment – for example, compensation may be based 60% on a leader's geography

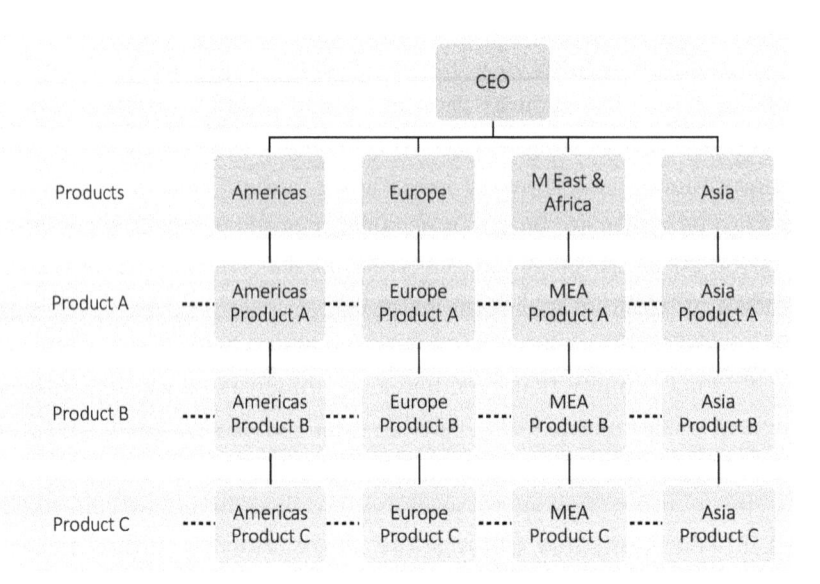

Figure 8.4 Generic matrix structure with geographies primary and products secondary.

results, and 40% on the same leader's global product results. Note that the dimensions could be any of geography, product or service, function (e.g., marketing, manufacturing, finance), customer segment (e.g., government, corporate), or other dimensions important to the firm's strategy and alignment.

It is particularly easy to see the matrix organization in consumer goods firms. For example, Nestlé is organized by geographic zones, with country and zone managers having profit and loss responsibility for their geographies. At the same time, strategic product groups are managed globally: Nutrition, Waters, Nespresso, and some brands such as Nescafé and KitKat. Unilever is organized both by geographic zones and by products groups such as Personal Care, Home Care, Foods, and Refreshment. Likewise, Procter & Gamble (P&G) is organized by geographic regions and product areas such as Baby, Family, Fabric, Grooming, and Hair.

Today's matrices are still complex; managers have accepted that some level of complexity is necessary for optimizing the effective organization of international business operations. Alignment, in particular, provides ongoing challenges. Main business units tend to be aligned according to the needs of that dimension (e.g., geography), but with adjustments made for maximizing the matrixed functions. For example, product quality may require that each plant have an expert in a particular quality process, such as Six Sigma. If the skills are not available locally, the local business unit may have to bring in an expatriate.

MNEs organized by the matrix find that they can leverage their scale strengths for global brands, innovating, and supply chain. They can develop a portfolio of expertise and have people work on projects wherever they are needed, and at the same time they can develop and execute the best plans for each market they operate in.

Central Services and Aligning MNEs: T-shaped Structures

Most MNEs, whether "simple" multidivisional or matrixed, also have some kind of business services unit that provides support for all parts of the organization. This unit could include finance and audit, human resources, technology, investor relations, and other functions that are important to support the organization as a whole. Country or product areas may have business services members assigned to them, such as a Human Resources Business Partner or a local Chief Financial Officer (CFO). Even in a simple multidivisional organization, these business services units tend to be organized as a matrix, often with the functional leader reporting first to the function (Human Resources, Finance) and second to the geography.

Especially in the context of emerging markets, where MNEs are driven to make decisions quickly and locally (local responsiveness) while cost pressures call for efficient structures (global integration), a differentiation between customer-facing and back-end operations is warranted. In a so-called **T-shaped structure**, global leaders will organize the MNE's value chain such that customer-facing processes are allowed much flexibility and autonomy. This deep integration within each country is represented by the vertical stroke of the T-shaped structure. Back-end processes, on the other hand, such as R&D, human resources, and more, are integrated across several countries, illustrated by the horizontal stroke of the T-shaped structure. General Electric, for instance, allows for localized flexibility in their geographically distributed subsidiaries, while their R&D Technology Centre located in Bangalore provides worldwide computational modeling capability (Kumar & Puranam, 2011).

Aligning the Supply Chain

An organization's strategic orientation and form may extend to its supply chain design choices as well. As a recent McKinsey study found through an analysis of more than 50 companies across Europe, Asia, and the Americas, most companies in the sample err on the side of centralized coordination of supply chain activities. This is particularly so for strategic supply chain functions, while relatively fewer companies exhibited decentralized or platform-based supply chain models.

While no particular archetype of a supply chain organization was found to be associated with superior performance, certain mechanisms were. These included "the quality of end-to-end coordination, harmonization, and clarity of decision rights; a cross-functional performance system; and employee professional support through social cohesion, mobility, and capability development." These findings underscore the notion that one of the major issues in supply chain coordination is the systematic and intentional alignment of processes and functions across a wide range of geographically dispersed units, often tied together loosely through incomplete integration efforts. Intentionally devising a strategic and operational supply chain model in line with the MNE's overall strategic orientation can thus aid in elevating efficiency and value generation (Alicke et al., 2020).

As the preceding discussion shows, developing alignment of tasks, people, structure. and systems across an MNE is a daunting challenge and an ever-moving target. The potential benefit is clear: the possibility of delivering more comprehensive and sustainable value for customers. For this reason, companies continue to aspire to these forms, adapting and adjusting as the environment changes while still maintaining stability for employees, customers, and suppliers. This discussion also makes it clear why global leadership competences are increasingly important for anyone working in an MNE. With current organizational configurations, whatever their balance of global integration and local responsiveness, leaders who are mindful of the global context will be able to coordinate better across the organization. This is especially important to consider as the MNE is growing.

> ### Reflection Question 8.2: Building a Backlog of Organizational Structure Examples
>
> The more examples and models of organizational structure you are familiar with, the better you can assess your own company's organizational options and effectiveness. We refer to "company," but we encourage you to incorporate into your repertoire not-for-profit organizations, quasi-government organizations (e.g., police forces), or any other type of organization that's of interest to you. With that in mind, list 5–10 companies you admire. You might like their products or use their services, you might appreciate their reputation for growth or innovation, you might know people who work there and enjoy their work. Try to identify companies with a range of sizes and geographic scopes. Look them up and identify the main characteristics of their organizational types.
>
> - Did they cover the range described in this chapter? Which types were most common, and why?
> - In what ways is the company's organizational design influenced by the national culture of its headquarters?
> - For the companies whose organizational forms changed over time, what was the trajectory (e.g., multidivisional to matrix)?
> - Which are the organization types you are most drawn to as a work environment? Why?

Growing the MNE's Boundaries: Acquisitions and Alliances

MNEs commonly grow internationally through organic means (growing the current operations across borders) or inorganic means (acquiring or allying with another enterprise). While organic growth adds to the organization incrementally, it does not usually require a separate form of aligning or organizing. Our focus here is thus on **inorganic growth**, which can result from contextual pressures and confront the organization's strategic and structural alignment. In this section we will consider the two common ways of executing inorganic growth that have important implications for alignment and leadership: acquisitions and strategic alliances.

International Acquisitions

Companies make **acquisitions** to fill a strategic gap in their products, people, or capabilities, to enter a new geographic market, or some combination of these reasons. This is a very common method of growth, and an enormous body of research exists on how MNEs select their acquisitions. Here, our focus is on the organizational alignment and execution issues. In this respect, the most important decision for acquisitions is how tightly to integrate. Should the newly acquired company be held at arm's length, almost as it would be by institutional investors? Or should it be integrated into the parent company? If the latter, how much, and in what ways? Most global expansion strategies integrate the acquired company at least lightly.

The Tata group has expanded internationally by acquiring big companies in many markets, including motor companies Jaguar, Land Rover, and Daewoo Commercial Vehicles, steel companies Corus, NatSteel, and Millennium Steel, hot beverage companies Tetley Tea and Eight O'Clock Coffee, and IT company Tyco Global Network. Tata follows a general practice of **light integration**. All acquired companies are required to sign onto the Tata values and some key practices, including the Business Excellence Model and the Code of Conduct. Senior Tata executives encourage collaboration around these values. However, acquired companies are left to themselves to determine strategy and run their business (Kale et al., 2009).

Most of the big technology companies, on the other hand, are more likely to engage in **tight integration**. Google, Cisco, and Amazon buy services or applications that they bring directly into the core business. At Google, for example, senior executives at the acquired company are offered roles in the parent company, along with inducements to stay. The strategy of the acquired company is integrated into the overall picture of Google, and the acquired company's products and services fold into the existing Google structure (Luckerson, 2015). Cisco's strategy execution depends so strongly on aligning and integrating the acquired organization tightly that many of the company's criteria for identifying potential acquisitions are geared toward high alignment: sharing a vision, matching corporate cultures, key people being willing to join Cisco, and being geographically close to Cisco (Bort, 2014). This is an explicit acknowledgment that international acquisitions are challenging to integrate.

Aligning and Leading International Acquisitions

Light integration makes it easier to maintain internal alignment of both the acquirer and the acquired, and is often applied when the acquirer wants to learn from the acquired company about new products or markets. Whether you are leading at the acquired or acquiring firm, it is helpful to be proactive about learning across boundaries. Asking questions and offering information in the ways outlined in the Map-Bridge-Integrate model (see Chapters 4 and 5) will provide quicker synergies for both companies.

Tight integration requires change from both the acquirer and the acquired company (see Chapter 9), and the process can be painful. Once accomplished, however, it can greatly benefit customers as well as other stakeholders, more so than light integration. For instance, tight integration can elevate efficiency by reducing redundancies, ensure brand coherence, and help in the retainment of talent. Leaders engaged in tight integration of acquisitions should aim to create synergies rather than equalize value with shared ground or just invoking the dominant way. This means leading with all cross-cultural competences and a high level of mindfulness. The main danger of tight integration is the promise of timelines to investors – these timelines are often unrealistic for integrating well across differences, and forcing the tight timelines leads to destroying value rather than creating it.

Strategic Alliances (Non-Equity Alliances and Equity Joint Ventures)

Strategic alliances refer to the umbrella of formal agreements to collaborate in order to create joint value. Most strategic alliances are structured as investment-, cost-, and/or revenue-sharing agreements, licensing, or royalty payments. If they include the deeper commitment of equity sharing, they become the special case of joint ventures. Alliances can be an efficient way of entering new markets and/or developing new products and services, and some successful alliances may become equity joint ventures or acquisitions down the line. Especially in a VUCA environment marked by high uncertainty, speed of change, and pressure toward greater specialization, alliances can allow for the flexibility needed to maintain competitiveness.

While strategic alliances appear across practically all industries, they are especially prevalent in those where it would be too costly, risky, or ineffective to rely on organic growth or acquisitions alone. In the pharmaceutical industry, for instance, conducting all research in-house or going through the complex efforts of integrating acquired companies has proven to be time consuming and costly. Instead, many new advances are developed much more quickly at university or other labs or start-ups, including gene-based therapy or new delivery mechanisms. At early stages, new drug development is a high-risk endeavor, making expensive acquisitions a risky choice. As a result, most pharmaceutical companies now engage in different types of alliances, which allow for a limited amount of capital commitment in exchange for developing new therapies while remaining flexible and promoting the innovation that comes from decentralized idea generation.

Eli Lilly (Lilly), for example, has built a strong competence in alliance management over two decades. Lilly partners with universities, start-up biotech firms, distribution companies, and firms that build technology such as analytic or simulation capabilities. They openly invite interested groups from around the world to approach them for alliances. Their alliance in India with Lupin, for example, markets and distributes oral diabetes medications. By adding a unit into their structure called the Office of Alliance Management, they are able to guide, monitor, and reap the benefits of all of the alliances the company is engaged in, thereby creating synergies and effective alliance management.

Joint ventures are alliances in which two or more parties create a new entity and share ownership equity. They are used for a number of reasons, most importantly to expand a product line or geographic market faster than organic growth would allow and at lower cost than acquisitions. Upon achieving resource complementarity, whereby one side contributes what the other needs and vice versa, partners can share financial risk, secure access to natural resources, acquire particular technical skills, gain local management knowledge and experience, obtain access to markets and distribution systems, and fulfill local regulatory requirements regarding limits to foreign ownership.

Starbucks and PepsiCo, for example, have garnered great success by partnering in a joint venture mode. In 1994, the two MNEs founded the North American Coffee Partnership, an alliance to which they both contributed equal amounts of equity. Each partner provides access to their core competencies, such that Starbucks contributes coffee expertise and PepsiCo manages the selling and distribution of products. Through the introduction of a range of ready-to-drink coffee products, the partnership has grown from a small team at foundation to a global business occupying about a 97% share of the ready-to-drink coffee market (Starbucks, 2022). An important feature of the partnership is that the two companies offer contributions that complement each other's strengths without encroaching on each other's competitive realms. It would be too costly for Starbucks to reach the same level of knowledge on bottling and distribution as PepsiCo has, and likewise, it would be unwise for PepsiCo to aim for the same depth of coffee expertise and branding as Starbucks has. As a result, each side gained more from collaborating than if they had attempted to build the business on their own.

Telecommunications companies also often engage in joint ventures to access local markets, where regulations require local ownership. MTN, a multinational telecom company headquartered in South Africa, has engaged in major joint ventures in Botswana, Swaziland, Nigeria, and Iran. They identify joint ventures and partnerships as one of their four most important keys to growth. Most of these joint ventures are for infrastructure or licensing. For example, they have partnered with IHS Towers, a Nigerian company, to provide infrastructure in several African countries. On a different path, MTN began a joint venture with financial services company MMI to provide micro-insurance products across a number of African countries. Neither MTN nor MMI could build this business on their own, and it has the potential to have a positive impact on the lives of millions of uninsured people.

Companies in the resources industries often engage in joint ventures with local companies, including Indigenous companies in countries with histories of colonization. These joint ventures are formed partly for access to the resources as well as to develop partnering relationships with local communities, with the community having adequate power in the relationship. Sometimes this is regulated by governments, but with increasing frequency it is initiated by companies as a practice that leads to sustainable, synergistic results. For example, in Canada, Indigenous communities and mining companies are increasingly developing partnerships and formal joint ventures to mine and service mines in ways that are sustainable for the social communities and more responsible to the environment.

What these examples illustrate is that each side gains from partnering, providing access to knowledge and capabilities without seeking to acquire these from their respective partners. This relates to a fundamentally important notion about joint ventures, as laid out in the access-vs-acquisition framework (see Figure 8.5).

As the framework suggests, not all joint ventures are successful. The worst position to be in is being the parent firm providing access to knowledge while the other side seeks to acquire knowledge from your company, increasing the risk of an undesired acquisition or the partner exiting and becoming a strong competitor later on. This relates to a common concern regarding joint ventures: They are growing in importance as flexibility and political risk mitigation become ever more salient, but they also exhibit inherently high failure rates. Since coordination with a joint venture partner requires an ongoing process, often across cultural, geographic, and language distances, executives need to build the personal relationships that are essential in the creation of a joint venture and to commit the time and effort necessary to make the venture successful. They need to think more clearly about joint venturing, which is a **process orientation**. There are many operational issues beyond the legal and economic ones that may not be given

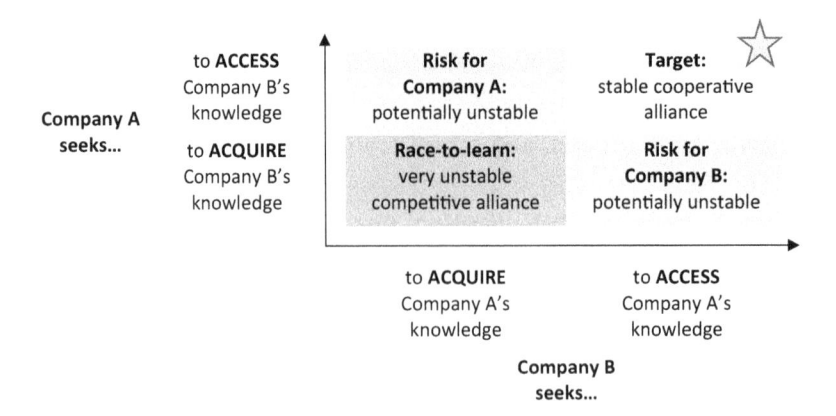

```
                                    Risk for              Target:    ☆
              to ACCESS             Company A:         stable cooperative
              Company B's        potentially unstable       alliance
 Company A    knowledge
 seeks...
              to ACQUIRE          Race-to-learn:           Risk for
              Company B's         very unstable          Company B:
              knowledge         competitive alliance   potentially unstable

                                    to ACQUIRE            to ACCESS
                                    Company A's          Company A's
                                    knowledge             knowledge
                                              Company B
                                               seeks...
```

Figure 8.5 Access-vs-acquisition framework.
Source: Adapted from Paul Beamish, *Joint Venturing*, Information Age Publishing, Charlotte, NC, 2008; and Andrew C. Inkpen & Paul W. Beamish, Knowledge, bargaining power, and the instability of joint ventures, *Academy of Management Review*, 1997, 22(1), 177–202.

enough careful forethought and thus are left to be resolved as problems arise, which typically is too late. The invisible, intangible, or non-quantifiable components of a venture, like trust, commitment, and partners' expectations, are often overlooked or ignored, especially when they are not part of a manager's prior training or mindset.

Aligning and Leading International Alliances and Joint Ventures

Perhaps the most critical decision to be made in establishing an international alliance or joint venture is the choice of a partner, as Geringer explains:

> Selecting partners with compatible skills is not necessarily synonymous with selecting compatible partners ... Although selecting a compatible partner may not always result in a successful [joint venture], the selection of an incompatible partner virtually guarantees that venture performance will be unsatisfactory. (Geringer, 1988)

How does one choose a partner? Where does one look? What characteristics should a partner have? What are one's expectations? What are the potential partner's expectations? In considering these questions and throughout the partner selection process, there are a number of criteria that should be considered, including relative power in the relationship (such as size, resources, financial capabilities, need for each other), complementarity of strategies and policies, ability to communicate, and so on.

The **role of relationships** in strategy and international joint ventures is worthy of special comment, recalling our discussion in Chapter 3 on cultures that prioritize the task or the relationship. Often in Anglosphere countries, relationships are viewed as instrumental, a means to an end, if they are thought of at all in a business context. In contrast, much of the rest of the world values relationships in and of themselves. They form a basis of trust and linkage upon which a business activity may be built. Relationships are a major determinant of strategy, if not part of the strategy themselves. Given such striking differences in perspectives on relationships, it is not surprising that partnership problems are one of the most frequently cited reasons for alliance and joint-venture failure (Beamish, 2013), and they can appear more frequently where cultural distance is high. Underappreciating the importance of such "softer" aspects of relationships can lead to serious consequences for the "harder" financial aspects of the business. In the case of Tiffany (US jewellery maker) and Swatch (Swiss watchmaker), for instance, a mismatch in decision-making approaches and organizational cultures led to a 2018 Dutch supreme court ruling that dissolved their strategic alliance and resulted in the court ordering Tiffany to pay CHF 480 million in damages.

Executing strategy through alliances and joint ventures has important implications for alignment and leadership. Both (or multiple) parties enter the alliance with their own way of leading tasks, structure, and people, aligned with organizational systems and culture. Bringing the two (or more) together means that at least one party must change. If possible, it is easiest to select a partner that is as similar as possible; however, this may defeat the purpose of learning from them or doing something new and innovative. A partner who is doing something different from you – whether it is a different business model or a different market – is very likely to be aligned differently. The goal is to seek a balance between **competences** and **comfort** with the alliance partner (Beamish, 2008), and remaining cognizant about how this balance may change over time with leadership turnover, changing environmental pressures, stages of the alliance's life cycle, and more. Most inexperienced alignment leaders underestimate the importance of realigning the alliance, so the first leadership advice is to apply the alignment tools carefully, practicing the Map-Bridge-Integrate skills, and to adjust timing expectations to allow for this. In the process of developing a new alignment for the alliance, it is important to remember that employees in the alliance also need to interface with their "home" enterprises, both to draw on them for resources and to return to after their time in the alliance. Leaders tend to focus on customers and suppliers, but they must consider the **interorganizational interfaces**, too, while maintaining organizational coherence and minimizing undue interdependence.

Also critical in leading alliances is developing a focus on learning. The Renault-Nissan Alliance, for instance, is a very complicated alliance. Both companies have shareholdings in each other, but the relationship between the companies is run with the philosophy of an alliance – neither company can compel the other to do something based on ownership. They develop common platforms and technologies, and they purchase almost all supplies through the alliance; both of these activities provide cost savings and revenue opportunities, an estimated €5 billion in annual synergies at the height of the collaboration. However, leaders at the Renault-Nissan Alliance have stated that an equally important benefit of their alliance is the ability to learn from each other (Ikegami et al., 2017; Nissan Motor Corporation, 2017). The two companies compete head-to-head in many markets around the world. The Alliance encourages this competition as experimentation, through which each company can learn quickly from their own and each other's experiences. The alliance has since experienced major disruptions, ultimately leading to the addition of Mitsubishi as a third partner and a decrease in joint equity ownership. Yet the commitment among the three companies to the alliance is still strong. As typically long-term-oriented structures, alliances require constant monitoring and assessment.

Alliances always provide opportunities for learning, but it takes mindful global leaders to make the learning happen and to harvest it for the benefit of other units within the broader MNE network. The Renault-Nissan Alliance (now Renault-Nissan-Mitsubishi Alliance) has been practicing this kind of leadership since 1999, Eli Lilly has been systematically developing alliance expertise since about the same time, MTN has developed expertise in cross-cultural interaction that allows it to enhance its alliance management, and Starbucks and PepsiCo's learning about alliance management has allowed them to grow into a market-dominating position. Developing mindful global leadership competence can take many years for an organization; the good news is that once acquired, the capabilities can be applied in so many contexts that they are well worth the investment.

The Global Business of Small Enterprises

Most of the common knowledge and research about international management relates to large MNEs, but there is a growing recognition of the importance of smaller enterprises. Normally, we think of start-ups and entrepreneurship as local, and most such companies are. But with today's globalization and technology, many small businesses are either "born global" or globalize very quickly without becoming large enough for multiple divisions and matrices, and it is important to recognize these phenomena.

Born Globals

Some small companies start global because they happen to sell a product or service internationally. **Platforms** such as eBay, Etsy, Alibaba, Tencent, and PayPal have made online transactions simple, and the global logistics industry has made the physical transfer of goods relatively straightforward. These companies may not have a global strategy – that is, they are not trying to serve specific international markets – but they do need to develop more complex alignment systems than purely domestic small companies. For example, they need access to people with foreign exchange expertise, tax jurisdiction knowledge, and international shipping insurance.

Other small companies deliberately craft their strategy to serve international needs right from their founding. Tony Jamous, for instance, a French-Lebanese telecom engineer working at a technical start-up in the United Kingdom, entered an MBA program to gain a qualification that would help him move to a larger company. However, when he graduated, he saw an important unmet need for global digitally driven businesses such as Airbnb, Uber, and Tencent. These companies needed a single technology for connecting their software with phone networks, one that would work equally well with early-generation mobile phones in emerging markets and with smartphones in developed markets. His company, Nexmo, was born in 2010 with a global strategy. Organizationally, too, it was global: it opened with headquarters in London, San Francisco, and Hong Kong, with investors from Germany, United States, and Korea. Nexmo's customers' headquarters were mainly in the United States, United Kingdom, and East Asia, but *their* customers were all over the world, working with different infrastructures and different mobile carriers. Nexmo's employee team quickly grew to include more than 50 nationalities, and they built strong relationships with more than 500 networks in different countries.

One of the most important challenges for Jamous and his team, and for any Born Global, was developing a unified company culture. The company was spread out over the globe long before the founders had a chance to establish a culture to launch and disseminate. Jamous and the other senior leaders met extensively with employees and other stakeholders in local markets, traveling to communicate in person about why and how to do things, training in everything from technical expertise to customer relations. According to Jamous, "We had to embed being global as one of our values, and live it. No time zone was *the* time zone." One important initiative for creating the culture was the requirement that every new employee, no matter how senior, must work on the customer helpdesk solving tickets until they have the highest satisfaction rating.

The company continues to leverage its Born Global character, for example by innovating to utilize new regulations and compliance requirements as competitive advantages. They were ahead of most competitors on compliance for the EU Data Privacy regulations, and they acquired telecom carrier licenses for their own platforms in some key jurisdictions. Jamous reflects that by starting off thinking and acting globally, the company has been able to create unique value. That value was reflected in the growth of the firm: its revenues grew to over US$100 million in five years. Having raised $30 million in venture capital funds to start, it was acquired by Vonage in 2016 for over $250 million with a valuation over $1 billion.

A common challenge Born Globals face is to match their globally available products with the realities of the local market. When the platform company Amazon, for instance, launched their Indian website in 2013, it encountered a market with great potential but also one that was characterized by a high percentage of the population living in rural areas, with only 35% connected to the Internet, and largely cash-based transactions. How should a platform company that relies on transactions over the Internet, use of credit cards, and a reliable distribution network enter this market? Amazon's solution was multipronged. First, it needed to build trust for its services, and it did so by recruiting sellers on their platform to personally navigate city streets with an "Amazon Chai Cart." Over a cup of tea, potential customers were able to look sellers in the eye, build trust, and address any concerns. Second, it established relationships with small family-owned businesses, which are a cornerstone of Indian economic life. Especially in rural areas, such shops are often the only place for residents to access the Internet. In exchange for a commission, these shop owners would allow residents to place their Amazon orders, handle incoming and outgoing shipments, and accept cash payments for these orders. Third, Amazon partnered with local delivery services, such as India Post, and addressed the challenge of last-mile deliveries (especially on poorly built roads in rural areas) by recruiting bicycle and motorbike couriers. All of these localized strategies helped Amazon translate their global product to the local context, and allowed it to establish a foothold in a lucrative e-commerce market early on (Govindarajan & Warren, 2016).

Born Global may be a challenging way to start an organization, and even with a good business idea, success is not guaranteed. However, with mindful global leadership, company growth and value creation for customers are achievable, as the examples of Jamous globally and Amazon in India illustrate.

Global Small- to Medium-Sized Enterprises (SMEs)

There are many well-established SMEs that offer targeted products or services globally, without developing into the scale of an MNE. In fact, the World Bank reports that 90% of businesses worldwide are SMEs (including informal ones), thus representing the majority of economic activity across industrialized and emerging markets alike (The World Bank, 2023). Many of these enterprises offer specific technologies or technical solutions. For example, the German *Mittelstand*, mid-sized companies, make up over a third of the German economy and two-thirds of its exports (Weber, 2016). Most of these companies are family owned, with 5,000 or fewer employees each, and focus on specialized niche products or services in business-to-business (B2B) relationships, such as precision manufacturing machinery, solar panels, and components. For these companies, growth is less important than excellence and ambition with a particular set of customers. Many are very global, generating far more revenue from outside Germany (or even Europe) than from inside of it.

For example, Sennheiser started in 1945 to make headphones and microphones for professionals, and has since grown to become an important manufacturer of these products globally for B2B and consumers. They now have just under 3,000 employees, about half in Germany and half abroad, with manufacturing in Germany, Ireland, and the United States. Around half of their revenue comes from Europe, the rest from outside of Europe. They are structured with two main divisions: consumer and professional. Sennheiser is now larger than the vast majority of the more than 3 million SMEs in Germany, but its roots and strategy are representative.

Aligning and Leading in Smaller Global Enterprises

The alignment of tasks, people, structure, strategy, and the environment can be simpler in a smaller enterprise than in a large MNE: there are generally fewer people and fewer tasks than in an MNE. However, because of the smaller size and fewer resources, it is more important for the fewer people in leadership to be able to cover a broad range of capabilities themselves, and to structure in a way that shares knowledge and roles fluidly. It is no coincidence that successful global SMEs focus on people development – recruiting, retaining, developing, coaching, and so on – as much as they do on strategy or business development.

Leaders in these firms must recognize the importance of their own global leadership competence for their strategy execution. As smaller players, these firms do not inherently have the power of size and resources. Their power comes from their ability to provide something very specific, and to do it well, which in turn relies on the execution of mindful global leadership practices. For instance, Alberto Bravo and Maria José Marín, cofounders of the Spain-based global e-commerce business We Are Knitters, intentionally aligned their SME for global expansion since their inception in 2011. In the early days of their company's growth, Bravo and Marín conducted or oversaw most business activities themselves, from meetings to photoshoots, human resource management, financial decisions, social media communication, and more. Over time, however, as their company grew (and experienced 240% year-over-year growth during the early stages of the pandemic), they were able to attract more funding, diversify their job specifications, hire additional people, and elevate their international exposure. By 2021, We Are Knitters had turned into a thriving SME with an international supply chain and distribution network, serving a global customer base (Hasse et al., 2022).

Emerging Ways of Organizing

Whether big or small, global companies need to consider effective ways of organizing. A number of current trends have thereby emerged from the three drivers identified elsewhere in this book: the environmental driver of high complexity and volatility (discussed throughout Chapter 1), the business driver of customer-centric strategies (described in Chapter 9), and the enabling driver of digital technology (identified in Chapter 1 and described in Chapter 6, with its effect on virtual teams). We will focus on two impactful trends: organizing for digital transformation and lateral collaboration across MNEs. All managers are likely to be exposed to these ways of organizing, and you should feel prepared to decide the extent to which you adopt them, and under what conditions. We will also identify the organizational conditions that are most conducive to executing these newer forms and trends, and describe a framework to help develop them.

Organizing for Digital Transformations

Digital transformation is the shift to business models that rely on the combination of digital technologies and the Internet of Things (IoT) to deliver more value for customers (Wade, 2017a). These technologies can transform the value proposition in three ways: **cost value** (decreasing the cost of delivery), **experience value** (increasing the quality of the customer experience), and **platform value** (providing improved cost structures or experiences by leveraging a networked platform, such as crowdsourcing or big data analytics) (Wade et al., 2015). Different industries are affected by digitization in different ways and at different rates. For example, media and entertainment, technology, telecoms, retail, and financial services industries are experiencing high levels of disruption already, with content and services rapidly moving online and traditional companies struggling. Real estate, health care and pharmaceuticals, and energy and utilities experience fewer effects, but fewer is not none: the IoT and digital data availability are affecting research and development greatly in the latter two, as well as consumer sales in real estate.

The Global Center for Digital Business Transformation, an alliance between Cisco and the IMD Business School, found three sets of organizational capabilities for thriving through the digital business transformation. **Hyperawareness** is constantly scanning both internal and external environments for opportunities and threats. **Informed decision-making** is the extensive use of data – widely available through the company – to make evidence-based decisions. **Fast execution** is the ability to move quickly, often valuing speed over perfection (Loucks et al., 2016). Combined, these capabilities can allow organizations to build agility and gain a competitive edge.

Digital Transformations: Implications for Alignment and Leadership

Organizing for digital transformation follows the same alignment principles as any other kind of strategy execution: tasks, people, and structure must be aligned to each other with systems and organizational culture, in a way that also aligns with the value proposition or strategy of the company. More specifically, though, the digital transformation compels an alignment that includes a structure of broad information-sharing and with decision-making authority as low as possible to maximize speed. A culture with preferences for independence and egalitarianism would support both information sharing and decision-making at the front lines. On the other hand, cultures with a preference for status bring a consistency of roles, which supports alignment, and interdependence-oriented cultures bring a tendency for people to share things that would help each other's decision-making.

In another study, the Center for Digital Business Transformation identified four characteristics for leaders who lead digital transformation well by embracing the notion of agility. Agile leaders are **humble** (open to feedback and ideas from others), **adaptable** (accept that changing with new information is a strength), **engaged** (have a propensity to listen, interact, and engage with interest and curiosity), and **visionary** (clear sense of long-term direction) (Neubauer et al., 2017). The first three of these characteristics are very similar to what we identified as global leadership characteristics, because the global business environment and the digital business transformation are similar in their context of volatility. The good news is that global leaders should therefore be well placed to lead digital business transformations, and vice versa (for a further discussion on agility, see Chapter 10).

Lateral Collaboration

A second important trend in global organizing is the increase in planned and facilitated collaboration across boundaries, such as collaborating across different parts of an MNE, or in association or alliance with other organizations. We referred to this trend earlier in this chapter, in the section on MNEs, and in Chapter 6 looking at networks. Here we will emphasize lateral collaboration as an organizing pattern and look at the resulting alignment and leadership dynamics.

Formal Team-Based Lateral Collaboration

Team-based lateral communication is when a group of people is formally tasked with achieving a specific joint outcome, working across different parts of the organization. The most common form of team-based lateral collaboration is the global key account team. Most firms that sell products globally identify their largest global customers and assign a global key account manager (KAM) to those accounts. In each country where the customer is present, someone is assigned to the account team. This becomes a form of matrixed relationship – a salesperson or technical service person in Vietnam reports both to the company's head of Vietnam regarding overall country sales, and to the global KAM (who could be sitting at the company headquarters or somewhere else in the world, such as the customer's headquarters city) regarding this one customer. The KAM's role is to advocate for the customer within the enterprise, communicate leading-edge innovations and even shape innovations for the customer, enable and facilitate technical service to the customer around the world, and negotiate prices with the customer for products and services. The challenge in lateral collaboration is resolving the tension that arises when local market needs are different from global customer needs, both for the customer and for the supplier – as experienced by one of our alumni, who we will call Ellen.

Ellen, a Global KAM

Ellen worked for a large MNE in the specialty chemicals industry, which we will refer to as ABChem. When Ellen first took over the account, she spent months coordinating with her team members around the world, organizing R&D projects, aligning a suite of products to cater to the next generation of needs for the customer. She met with representatives of the customer and her own company's sales and technical service staff around the world to gain a better understanding of the different local market needs. Then she worked directly with the customer's global purchasing office over a period of several weeks to negotiate a multiyear agreement.

After the agreement was completed, but before it was signed, Ellen got a phone call from a friend in another ABChem division, informing her that one of Ellen's country-based account managers had just signed a supplier contract with the local branch of the customer, for a much higher price. The people at the customer's headquarters were going to be furious with Ellen and the ABChem team for not coordinating their global purchase contract! The local customer was going to be furious with ABChem and the local supplier for not offering the global price they knew was coming! Ellen wondered what was going on. Drawing on her extensive network inside ABChem, she discovered that the ABChem operation in the local country was behind on its sales targets for the year, and the country manager was asking employees to do everything they could to hit the sales targets. He was threatening to eliminate bonuses and even fire salespeople who did not step up. To the local salesperson, the opportunity to get a sale and guarantee a job and income was more important than complying with a global headquarters agreement that had not yet been formalized.

Ellen resolved the issue by leveraging her network with ABChem country managers and at the customer's firm. She was able to implement a clause with lower prices for volume that satisfied both the country and the client. Perhaps more importantly overall, she used the opportunity to build deeper relationships with the country manager, the local account manager, and the customer. In the first year of implementing the new contract, she worked closely with the team of account managers from around the world to help them learn from each other and develop new ways of winning with the customer. Her approach with the team worked so well that her next role was to develop a new global industry segment for ABChem.

There are many other forms of lateral teams. In MNEs, they include matrixed functions, such as audit, quality control, or human resources across a company. In alliances, they may connect the formal members of the alliance with the most important stakeholders in the parent organizations. High-performing lateral teams are ones that work well across divisions of the MNE, or across different organizations as would be the case in a strategic alliance. At their best, they transfer best practices, align the organization for efficiency and better customer interfaces, and drive extensive value-creating innovation.

Less Formal Collaboration

While teams are an identifiable group of people with a joint deliverable, organizations are also developing many forms of organizing that are much less formal. Two common ones are **Centers of Excellence** (CoE) and **Communities of Practice** (CoP). CoEs are usually small groups of people within an organization who specialize in a particular type of expertise. They identify and share best practices, case studies, and recommendations with others in the organization who need the knowledge. They are often located virtually, with members embedded in different parts of the organization. CoPs are larger groups of people who are involved in similar kinds of work across the organization, and who share and develop knowledge together (Wagner, 1998). These communities are also often located virtually.

IBM was one of the pioneers of less formal collaboration, and uses both CoEs and CoPs extensively. Some of the CoEs (and many subcenters, both across and within geographies) include Software, Cyber Security, and Analytics. The core operations of each center are located in different places; for example, Cyber Security is in Haifa, Israel, and India has a strong Software Center of Excellence. They produce white papers and recommendations for people throughout IBM and externally, and they provide support to practitioners within IBM. IBM also supports CoPs for many of its software and hardware systems and applications such as Business Process Manager and Rational Application Security, for market segments like health and human services, for new innovations such as Watson (IBM's deep learning computer system), and so on. IBM supports these forms of collaboration with good alignment – participation in these communities and centers is expected, with a culture and systems of people reaching out to contribute and learn from each other. Centers and communities are aligned with the tasks that people are undertaking, and they provide a complementary structure to the main divisions within IBM.

Lateral Collaboration: Implications for Alignment and Leadership

Our research suggests that all of these forms of collaboration rely on a set of underlying social dynamics. If the social dynamics are already in place, then it is much easier to build alignment quickly and lead adaptively when needed. If the social dynamics are not in place, then alignment and adaptation are painful, and the social dynamics must be addressed before the collaboration can perform.

A useful framework for diagnosing social dynamics is the **TACK framework**: Trust, Ambition, Cohesion, and Knowledge. Each of these elements must be shared among a group of people before collaboration will yield good results. For each of these elements there are two levels: a basic level, which will provide enough collaboration to enable people to begin working well together; and an advanced level, which is important for deeper collaboration in challenging situations or adaptive collaboration in changing situations (Maznevski & Dhanaraj, 2017).

Trust is a positive belief about others that they will look after your needs when you are vulnerable or need to rely on them. Trust is the most fundamental dynamic for collaboration in any situation. The two *levels* of trust we identify are based on seminal research on two *types* of trust: cognitive and affective (McAllister, 1995). Cognitive trust is like reliability – do I believe you will do what you said you are going to do? That you are capable and will honor the commitment? Affective trust is more values-based – do I believe that you will look out for me in a situation of potential conflict? You will recall that we also referred to these as "head trust" and "heart trust" when we discussed teams in Chapter 6.

Ambition motivates collaboration. While a common goal is always necessary for a team (see Chapter 6), this common goal only gets collaboration to a basic level. Common ambition, a stretch goal with a higher purpose, motivates collaboration further. Often, to be motivating across a broad range of stakeholders, a compelling ambition is directly related to creating important value for customers or other external stakeholders such as society as a whole, rather than simply achieving organizational targets.

Cohesion is necessary at a basic level for successful collaboration. As we implied in Chapter 6, it is not necessary for people to like each other to collaborate. However, it is important that they respect each other and appreciate each other's contribution to the work, and that they are committed to helping each other out. This is the basic level of cohesion needed for collaboration. The more advanced level of cohesion is based on our social need for identity with a group (McAllister, 1995). When we identify with others as a strong and positive group identity, we are more willing to go out of our way to help each other. We define our personal success with respect to the success of the group as a whole: I can only succeed if the group succeeds. This deeper cohesion is important for more advanced collaboration.

Shared Knowledge at some level is necessary for collaboration. Collaboration in turn is necessary for organizational performance, because different collaborators have different knowledge, and it is also important to leverage that. The basic level of shared knowledge needed for collaboration is a shared idea about the reason for that collaboration. The more advanced level is shared knowledge about each other's context. This is directly related to Decentering as part of Bridging in the MBI model. Consistent with our research about interpersonal interaction, we have found that mindful contextual knowledge is critical for high-level collaboration.

The TACK model is summarized in Figure 8.6.

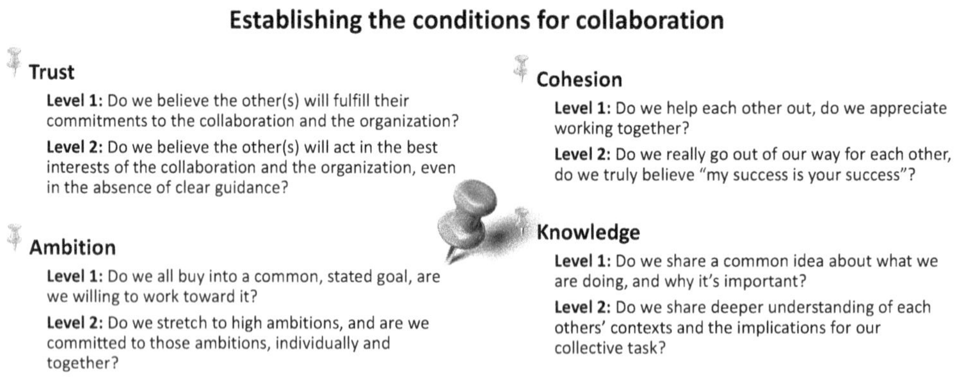

Establishing the conditions for collaboration

Trust
Level 1: Do we believe the other(s) will fulfill their commitments to the collaboration and the organization?
Level 2: Do we believe the other(s) will act in the best interests of the collaboration and the organization, even in the absence of clear guidance?

Ambition
Level 1: Do we all buy into a common, stated goal, are we willing to work toward it?
Level 2: Do we stretch to high ambitions, and are we committed to those ambitions, individually and together?

Cohesion
Level 1: Do we help each other out, do we appreciate working together?
Level 2: Do we really go out of our way for each other, do we truly believe "my success is your success"?

Knowledge
Level 1: Do we share a common idea about what we are doing, and why it's important?
Level 2: Do we share deeper understanding of each others' contexts and the implications for our collective task?

Figure 8.6 TACK: Organizational conditions for collaboration.

Reflection Question 8.3: The Future of (Global) Work

Global organizations have always had to contend with geographical dispersion and managing across distances, often relying on technological solutions to foster connectivity. After the COVID-19 pandemic, however, virtual and remote working has become a widespread arrangement within many organizations. Increasingly, the future of work is thought to be hybrid, combining physical and virtual collaboration – even when there is no geographical necessity to work together apart. Please reflect on the following questions:

- How do new forms of hybrid organization affect global collaboration?
- How might new post-pandemic ways of organizing work be different from / similar to classical global remote work experiences?
- What might newcomers to distance collaboration and management learn from experienced global collaborators?

Conclusion: The Primacy of Context in Shaping Strategy Execution and Organizational Design

In this chapter, we have argued for the importance of closely considering the environment in which globally operating firms are embedded, along with the pressures that shape organizational orientations, strategies, and forms. MNEs are the most visible form, and most large organizations today are structured in this way, with some matrixed components. Leading in MNEs requires being comfortable with the complexity of multiple types of relationship and spanning many types of boundary. However, it is important not to assume that the MNE is the only way to organize for international strategy execution. Small firms can be very global, and these forms have their own advantages, challenges, and leadership requirements. They can be nimble and focused and require leadership at the top that is both mindful and high on global leadership competences. We also looked at two major trends that affect organizing at least to some extent in every industry and geography: digital business transformation and lateral collaboration. These two trends pose challenges but also offer opportunities for effective and innovative strategy execution.

Throughout the chapter, we highlighted notions of alignment and leadership that are crucial to executing contextualized strategy. Chapter 9 will build on this by presenting a nuanced logic for organizing and a framework for analyzing organizational alignment for effective strategy execution. In Chapter 10, we further explore the foundational aspects noted in this chapter by detailing the causes, trajectories, and outcomes of organizational change.

In our work with organizations around the world, we appreciate the variety of organizational forms we see. Within the patterns of alignment and strategy execution and these basic forms, there are infinite ways of implementing them. Mindful leaders can shape the organization that best suits the needs of the enterprise and takes advantage of the different knowledge bases and experiences of different parts of the global enterprise.

Reflection Question 8.4: Stretching and Balancing the Local-Global Paradox

You have previously been introduced to paradoxical both-and thinking in Chapter 2, where we also used the competing demands of local and global to illustrate how managers need to navigate opposing organizational pulls. In this chapter, you have been introduced to the competing demands of local and global considerations seen from an organizational structure and design perspective.

- What challenges do you experience or anticipate in striking a balance between global priorities and local objectives? In which areas do you have or anticipate positive experiences of balancing local and global needs? What could you do differently to create a better balance between the local and the global?
- If you've already been exposed to the local-global paradox in your career, think of situations where you needed to display flexibility in a global leadership context. Are there situations in which your flexibility as a leader has been particularly stretched? What worked particularly well in these situations? How can you use this to inspire you in the future?

Reflection Question 8.5: Looking Back to Think Ahead – Revisiting the Matrix Organization

"The challenge is not so much to build a matrix structure as it is to create a matrix in the minds of our managers" (Senior executive reflecting upon working with matrix organizing, quoted in Bartlett & Ghoshal, 1990, p. 140).

Matrix organization is a form of organization that seeks to combine the best of both worlds of case functional specialization and cross-organizational coordination. Yet, matrix organizing comes with several challenges, among others – as indicated by the quote – that it is more complex and sometimes complicated for the people working in this structure. Please choose, read, and then reflect upon one of two of the evergreen research articles discussing classical challenges of matrix organizing listed further below:

- What are the central challenges and advantages of matrix organization discussed in the respective article?
- Given that these articles were written decades ago, are the disadvantages/ advantages of matrix organizing presented in your chosen article different from the challenges presented to you in this chapter? What (if anything) is different? Why do you think that is?
- Can you recognize the potentials and promises of matrix organizing presented in the chosen article from your work life?

Please choose one or two of the following articles:

- Barlett, C. A., & Ghoshal, S. (1989). Matrix management: Not a structure, a frame of mind. *Harvard Business Review*, 68(4), 138–145.
- Bazigos, M. & Harter, J. (2015). Revisiting the matrix organization. *McKinsey Quarterly*, 4, 8–13.
- Burton, R., Obel, B., & Haakonsson, D. (2015). How to get the matrix organization to work. *Journal of Organization Design*, 4(3), 37–45.
- Davis, S. M., & Lawrence, P. R. (1978). Problems of matrix organizations. *Harvard Business Review*, 56(3), 131–142.
- Ford, R. C., & Randolph, W. A. (1992). Cross-functional structures: A review and integration of matrix organization and project management. *Journal of Management*, 18(2), 267–294.
- Galbraith, J. R. (1971). Matrix organization designs: How to combine functional and project forms. *Business Horizons*, 14(1), 29–40.

Further Resources

For the classic work on global integration and local responsiveness, see Bartlett, C. A., & Ghoshal, S. (2002). *Managing across borders: The transnational solution*. Harvard Business Press. The organizational implications are well articulated in Prahalad, C. K., & Doz, Y. L. (1999). *The multinational mission: Balancing local demands and global vision*. Simon and Schuster.

The field's understanding of alliances and joint ventures has been developed mainly by Paul Beamish and colleagues. Beamish has published a comprehensive summary of this work in Beamish, P. (2013). *Multinational joint ventures in developing countries (RLE International Business)*. Routledge.

For more on mergers and acquisitions, see the review article by Haleblian, Devers, McNamara, Carpenter & Davison (2009). Taking stock of what we know about mergers and acquisitions: A review and research agenda. *Journal of management, 35*(3), 469–502. For a good review and study on the role of cultural differences in international mergers and acquisitions, see Stahl & Voigt (2008). Do cultural differences matter in mergers and acquisitions? A tentative model and examination. *Organization Science, 19*(1), 160–176. The annual research series *Advances in Mergers and Acquisitions*, edited by Finkelstein & Cooper (Emerald Group), provides leading-edge insights on many international topics.

IMD's Centre for Digital Business Transformation, sponsored by Cisco, is conducting a multiyear investigation into how businesses integrate the effects and opportunities of digital and internet technologies. They publish reviews, research, and recommendations with regular updates at https://www.imd.org/dbt/digital-business-transformation/.

Bibliography

Alicke, K., Dumitrescu, E., Leopoldseder, M. & Schlichter, M. (2020). *How great supply-chain organizations work*. McKinsey. Retrieved August 2023 from https://www.mckinsey.com/capabilities/operations/our-insights/how-great-supply-chain-organizations-work

Bartlett, C. A., & Ghoshal, S. (1998). *Managing across borders: The transnational solution* (2nd ed.). Harvard Business School Press.

Beamish, P. W. (2008). *Joint venturing*. Information Age Publishing.

Beamish, P. W. (2013). *Multinational joint ventures in developing countries*. Routledge.

Bort, J. (2014). *Cisco's John Chambers: What I look for before we buy a startup*. Business Insider. Retrieved December 2017 from http://www.businessinsider.com/cisco-john-chambers-acquisition-strategy-2014-7

Geringer, J. M. (1988). Partner selection criteria for developed country joint ventures. *Business Quarterly, 53*(1), 55.

Govindarajan, V., & Warren, A. (2016). *How Amazon adopted its business model to India*. Harvard Business Review. Retrieved from https://hbr.org/2016/07/how-amazon-adapted-its-business-model-to-india

Hasse, V., Kumar, M. & Hu, K. (2022). *We are knitters: Crafting a resilient digital business*. Ivey Publishing Case (W27015). Retrieved March 26, 2024, from https://www.iveypublishing.ca/s/product/

we-are-knitters-crafting-a-resilient-digital-business/01t5c00000D5BrnAAF

Ikegami, J. J., Maznevski, M., & Ota, M. (2017). Creating the asset of foreignness: Schrödinger's cat and lessons from the Nissan revival. *Cross-Cultural and Strategic Management, 24*(1), 55–77.

Kale, P., Singh, H., & Raman, A. (2009). Don't integrate your acquisitions, partner with them. *Harvard Business Review, 87*(12), 109–115.

Kumar, N. & Puranam, P. (2011). Have you restructured for global success? *Harvard Business Review, 89*, 123–128.

Loucks, J., Macaulay, J., Noronha, A., & Wade, M. (2016). *Digital vortex: How today's market leaders can beat disruptive competitors at their own game.* DBT Center Press.

Luckerson, V. (2015, April 15). *How Google perfected the Silicon Valley acquisition.* Time. Retrieved December 2017 from http://time.com/3815612/silicon-valley-acquisition/

Maznevski, M., & Dhanaraj, C. (2017). *Leading collaboration in global organizations: How to build a house without a hammer.* IMD. Retrieved from https://www.imd.org/research/insightsimd/leading-collaboration-in-global-organizations-how-to-build-a-house-without-a-hammer/

McAllister, D. J. (1995). Affect and cognition-based trust as foundations for interpersonal cooperation in organizations. *Academy of Management Journal, 38*(1), 24–59.

Nestlé. (2020). *Nestlé co-funds new professorship focusing on sustainable materials research to tackle plastic waste.* Retrieved in August 2023 from https://www.nestle.com/aboutus/research-development/news/nestle-co-funds-professorship-sustainable-materials-research

Neubauer, R., Tarlking, A., & Wade, M. (2017, March). *Redefining leadership for a digital age.* IMD Research. Retrieved December 2017 from https://www.imd.org/dbt/whitepapers/redefining-leadership/

Nissan Motor Corporation. (2017). *Making the most of cultural diversity.* Nissan-Global. Retrieved December 2017 from https://www.nissan-global.com/EN/COMPANY/DIVERSITY/CULTURE/

Prahalad, C. K., & Doz, Y. L. (1987). *The multinational mission: Balancing local demands and global vision.* The Free Press.

Starbucks. (2022). *Pepsico and Starbucks.* Starbucks. Retrieved September 2022 from https://stories.starbucks.com/wp-content/uploads/2019/01/Infographic_-_Starbucks_and_PepsiCo.pdf

Strohmeyer, R. (2008). *The 7 Worst Tech Predictions of All Time.* PC World. Retrieved September 2022 from https://www.pcworld.com/article/532605/worst_tech_predictions.html

The World Bank. (2023). *Small and Medium Enterprises (SMEs) Finance.* Retrieved August 2023 from https://www.worldbank.org/en/topic/smefinance

Wade, M. (2017a, October). *The digital vortex in 2017: It's not a question of "when".* IMD. Retrieved December 2017 from https://hbr.org/2016/08/germanys-midsize-manufacturers-outperform-its-industrial-giants

Wade, M. (2017b, December). *Standing ovation: McLaren puts the digital orchestra into action.* IMD. Retrieved December 2017 from https://www.imd.org/dbt/articles/standing-ovation-mclaren-puts-the-digital-orchestra-into-action/

Wade, M., Loucks, J., Macaulay, J., & Noronha, A. (2015, November). *New paths to customer value: Disruptive business models in the digital vortex.* IMD. Retrieved December 2017 from https://www.imd.org/dbt/whitepapers/new-paths-to-customer-value/

Wagner, E. (1998). *Communities of practice.* Cambridge University Press.

Weber, W. W. (2016, August 12). *Germany's midsize manufacturers outperform its industrial giants*. Harvard Business Review. Retrieved December 2017 from https://hbr.org/2016/08/germanys-midsize-manufacturers-outperform-its-industrial-giants

World Design Organization. (2021). *World Design Impact Prize – Leveraged Freedom Chair*. Retrieved August 2023 from https://wdo.org/site-project/leveraged-freedom-chair/

9 Achieving Organizational Alignment for Performance

> Vision without execution is just hallucination.
>
> Thomas Edison, American inventor and businessman (1847–1931)

Key Learning Objectives

At the end of this chapter, students will be able to:

- Conceptualize organizational alignment as a process involving context, strategy, tasks, people, structure, systems, and culture.
- Understand how organizations must align with their respective contexts.
- Describe alignment with different strategic orientations and business models.
- Recognize the importance of and interplay between tasks, people, and structure, as well as the systems that aid in creating alignment.
- Consider how culture suffuses the process of organizational alignment.

Aligning the Organizational System for Performance

A core theme in Chapter 8 was the primacy of context – or as we like to say, "The Environment Always Wins!" In this chapter, we build on this theme with an example and elaboration on how organizations must align themselves with the context they are embedded in to maximize performance. The cultural context of a host country in particular can affect a company's strategy, structure, administrative systems, and operations. The formulation and implementation of strategy depends on this nuanced understanding of context and impacts the selection of a fitting business model. Within the business model, the tasks, people, and structure must be aligned, typically reinforced by appropriate systems. Culture, the "shoulds" and "oughts" of life and business that people often have difficulty articulating, thereby suffuses an organization's strategy, structure, systems, and practices through largely implicit knowledge or assumptions.

These considerations funnel into a compact **organizational alignment framework** that highlights the organizational elements to be aligned – the people, work tasks, coordination structures, and administrative systems (Lane, 1980). Organizations are thereby conceptualized as **socio-technical systems**, meaning that they have both social and technical components, and need to be understood as such. In practical terms this means that what happens in one part of the organization impacts other parts. The "socio" component represents the human element, the people and groups, with their skills, needs, feelings, expectations, experience, and beliefs, who carry out the tasks and operations. The "technical" component represents the numerous technical and/or functional tasks of the business. These include acquiring inputs such as capital and raw materials, as well as using specific technology and work processes to create finished products or services. Each of the major functional areas of an organization – such as production, marketing, sales, or finance – also is a system within the larger "technical" organizational system. Each has a set of tasks and operations necessary to the effective functioning of the entire organization.

Through the use of structures and systems, managers connect and align the interdependent social and technical elements of a company to achieve the organization's goals. In this chapter, we draw from these notions to develop an organizational alignment model – its full form is shown below (Figure 9.1), but we will

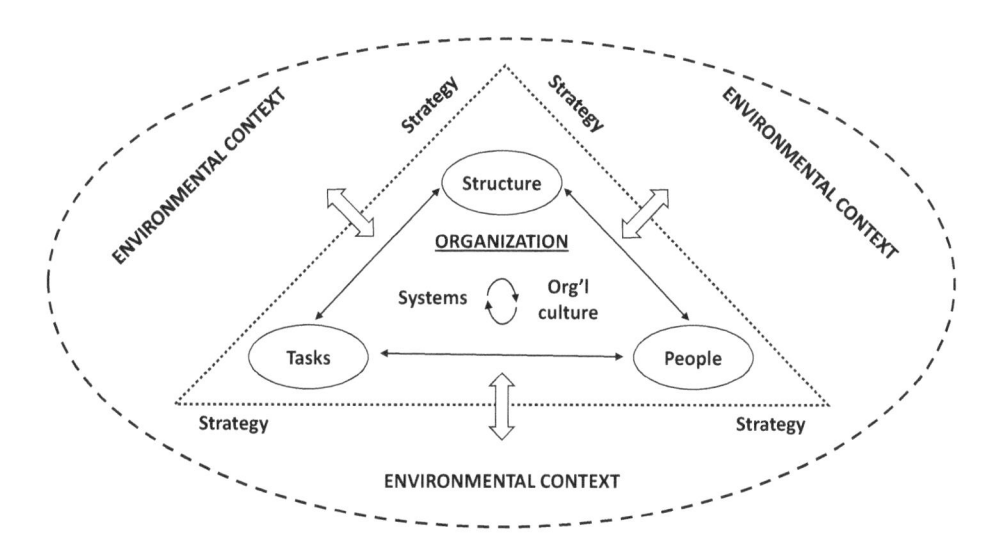

Figure 9.1 Organizational alignment model: Complete alignment.

develop each of its parts and their alignment within the organization in turn, starting with an example that is set in a global company operating in Chile.

The Case of Global Multi-Products Chile

An international example of organizational and strategic alignment and change is the experience of "Global Multi-Products" (GMP) in Chile (see Lane & Campbell, 2007; although this is a disguised case, the company is a real Fortune 100 company).

The Case of Global Multi-Products Chile (GMP)

GMP's corporate strategy was the continuous introduction of new, innovative products based on proprietary technology that had high margins. Approximately 30% of its sales came from products introduced in the previous few years. Historically, its value proposition for the customer was: buy our products because they are the best quality, are based on the latest technology, and are reliable.

To deliver on this strategy, GMP excelled in R&D, where the new products originated, and it had a formal program of R&D with multiple technology platforms that were the seedbeds of the company's new products. It distributed its products through separate product-related strategic business units (SBUs). We could characterize the company's business model as investing in R&D; developing proprietary technology and high-margin products; manufacturing them efficiently; and continually introducing these new products.

Over time, the competitive **environmental context** in Chile that GMP had been operating in successfully thus far changed. Small sole proprietorships were largely replaced by prominent American retailers and local retailers developing similar superstore models. Previously, the superstore segment (local and international) represented approximately 60% of retail sales, but it grew quickly to represent more than 90% of the company's business, resulting in a power shift from the manufacturer to the large retailers. Moreover, the level of sophistication among customers' purchasing managers increased. They were concerned with return on investment (ROI) and demanded more from their suppliers, such as increased advertising and lower prices. Products that traditionally had margins averaging around 80% for GMP now had margins not very different from competitor products. Finally, customers wanted to reduce the number of GMP's sales representatives with whom they were dealing, instead preferring one person to represent the manufacturer.

At the time that one of the authors was involved with GMP in Chile, it was in the process of transitioning from a best product strategy to a customer solutions strategy, which had been forced on it by the shift in power to large retail customers. The new **strategy** was to sell "solutions" to its customers by understanding in detail their processes where GMP's offerings were, or could be, used. GMP would make money by helping customers decrease costs while selling more products at lower margins.

Internally, this change meant that more integration was required among business units and that employees had to work in teams horizontally across the **organization** to analyze customer operations in order to provide solutions and recommend products for them. This program sought to reorient the sales and marketing effort around the needs of customers instead of the company's product groups. GMP also developed a program of strategic relationships with customers to conduct joint R&D to develop new products that could benefit the customer and be turned into products for their wider market. The company was now competing on the basis of its total organization, as well as its technology, to provide solutions for its customers.

Many of the companies we have worked with have also wanted to follow the customer solutions strategy. What is often underappreciated is that the shift in strategy also needed to be accompanied by a thorough reassessment and realignment of **tasks**, **structures**, and **people**, embedded in and empowered by the organization's **systems** and **culture**. To compete on the basis of creating value to the customer by providing "solutions," companies have to learn to leverage all of their capabilities more effectively by working horizontally across the organization. For GMP Chile, it was not a simple change to implement. There were a number of barriers, or misfits, in the way of necessary changes. These barriers can be organized using the alignment framework in the following categories:

- *Organizational structure*: SBUs, product groups, hierarchy, and functional "silos" worked against cooperation. Teams had to work laterally across them.
- *Organizational culture*: Heads of functions had a great deal of autonomy, leading to the semblance of a "feudal" system.
- *Top management team*: Executives often did not have sophisticated skills with regards to group/team processes. Many of them were also concerned with their potential loss of authority, and there was resistance to change.
- *Society/national culture*: Status was important to executives, reflecting Chile's status-conscious culture.
- *Political history*: Although the Pinochet era was long in the past, a legacy of distrust and not speaking out continued to exist. There was little trust among the executives.

- *People*: The sales representatives' status, lack of required new skills, title, education, and age/seniority all worked against their success in the new environment. Their job title was not associated with high status, and they often lacked the necessary skills and training to interact with the new, sophisticated purchasing executives of the "big box" stores. The company had to find new sales representatives, provide them with new titles, and improve training.
- *Rewards:* The reward system did not encourage selling other SBUs' products or working together in teams. The behavior required of sales representatives at the Chilean office was to continually introduce new products and not simply push the old ones, which the local reward system did not encourage.

It took the managing director a number of years to implement the organizational changes necessary to realign the Chilean organization with its new business model.

GMP provides an example of changes in the entire strategic and organizational alignment model. The change in strategy created a need to calibrate the management systems that were aligned with the old strategy. For best performance, there should thus be a fit, or *alignment*, between the people and their new job demands. The organizational alignment framework can thereby serve as a diagnostic tool to detect fits and misfits that require either enforcement or correcting. While the GMP example provides a high-level introduction to the managerial challenges of alignment, we will next consider in much greater detail the different parts of the framework, starting with environmental context.

Aligning Organizations within the Environmental Context

Global organizations like GMP are embedded in environmental contexts that shape whether and how they are able to conduct their business. Understanding context thus marks the first step in analyzing organizational alignment (see Figure 9.2). As architect and design theorist Christopher Alexander, in writing about the process of designing physical objects such as buildings or transportation systems, put it,

Every design problem begins with an effort to achieve fitness between two entities: the form in question and its context. The form is the solution to the problem; the context defines the problem. In other words, when we speak of design, the real object of discussion is not the form alone, but the ensemble comprising the form and its context. (Alexander, 1964)

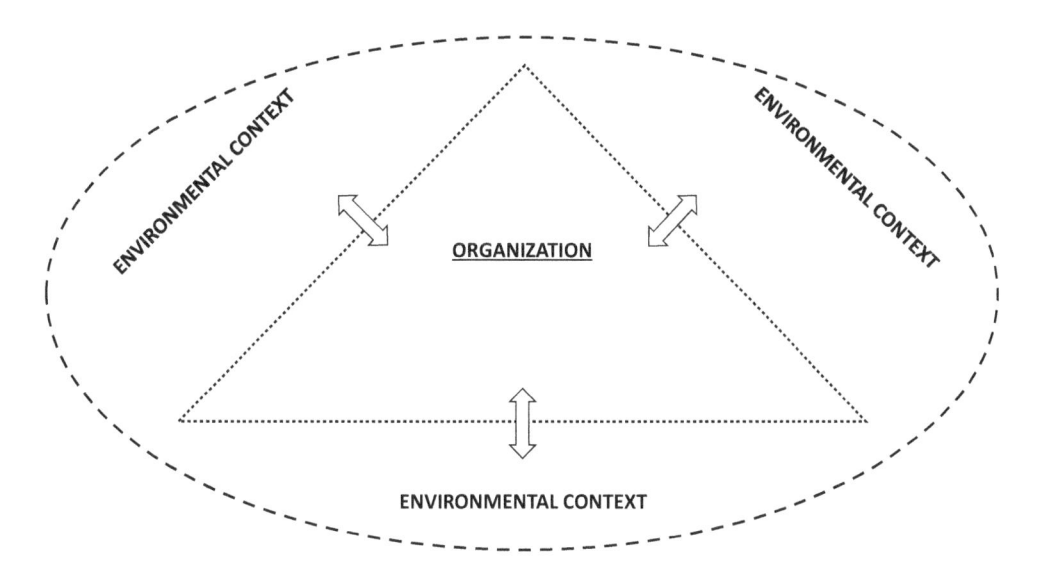

Figure 9.2 Organizational alignment model: Aligning within context.

The contexts in which global organizations are situated encompass complex and multilayered political, economic, social, technological, environmental, and legal influences (PESTEL). Taken together, they determine the rules and norms that guide and limit behavior within the organization's competitive environment – what are known as **institutions**. Some of these institutions are formal and explicit (e.g., laws), while others are more informal and tacit (e.g., ideologies and culture). Although often enduring, many of these formal and informal institutions are evolving at an ever-faster pace, given the forces toward digitalization, economic and political uncertainty, and environmental disruptions described in Chapter 1.

Global leaders must function effectively within these complex systems to maximize performance and ensure their organizations are perceived as sincere participants in the local market environment. People at the highest levels generally are more concerned with forces outside of the organization and linking the organization to its external environment, while those reporting to them are more concerned with internal operations. The consideration of complex and interconnected institutions, however, suffuses decision-making across hierarchies.

Informal institutions are especially difficult to navigate for foreign firms, since it takes time and immersion before the respective nuances about "how things should be done" or the "right way to manage" are absorbed and understood. We thus focus our attention especially on **culture** in this chapter, and the way it shapes assumptions about management systems and practices. Although there is some debate about the ways that cultures around the world are converging or diverging, there is no doubt that, in the realm of systems and practices favored in a given country, culture influences preferred behavioral styles and the management systems that are acceptable or even desirable. For instance, many North American companies exhibit a set of shared viewpoints that favor rational, economic cost–benefit analyses when devising strategies, structures, and systems.

The cultural assumptions underlying administrative systems may not be immediately obvious. When problems arise at an international location, it might be easier to conclude that workers are the problem instead of examining the assumptions underlying a reward or evaluation system, for instance. Types of questions one could ask in such a situation include: What would be the effect of a highly individualistic or independent compensation system in an interdependent culture? What are the cultural assumptions underlying practices such as empowerment, self-directed work teams, and 360-degree feedback? How would they work in status-oriented versus egalitarian cultures?

Moreover, the difficulties in transferring assumptions to another context are of central concern to international management. As the Dutch social psychologist Geert Hofstede put it, "Theories reflect the cultural environment in which they were written. [...] To what extent do theories developed in one country and reflecting the cultural boundaries of that country apply to other countries?" (Hofstede, 1980, p. 50). In particular, many management theories and resulting practices were developed in North America and work well within that context's paradigms – but encounter limitations when applied elsewhere.

Earlier chapters, especially Chapters 3 and 4, provided numerous examples of how culture has influenced management systems and processes. The alignment model can be used by any executive formulating and implementing strategy in his or her home market. Unless they are operating in a very multicultural domestic context, decision-makers do not necessarily give much thought to cultural influences in their domestic operations. They must learn to do so when crossing cultural borders both within and between nation states. When firms start operating in different cultural environments, creating alignment can suddenly become rather challenging – often dramatically so.

Administrative systems should be adaptable to changing conditions and workforces and not be ends in themselves. Furthermore, the fit that they create needs to be dynamic. This means that as strategies, competitive environments, or geographic locations change, structures, systems, and policies also need to be reevaluated and modified.

Counterexamples exist of managerial systems that are successful despite their lack of alignment with the local culture. It is important to remember that cultures are not monolithic and that there is a distribution of values, beliefs, and ways of doing things in each one as we discussed in Chapter 3. Executives must decide whether existing practices, systems, and management styles can be transferred from one culture to another, or whether they must be changed and adapted when they appear to conflict with the norms of another culture.

Aligning Strategy in Global Organizations

Recalling the observation by Christopher Alexander referred to earlier that, "Every design problem begins with an effort to achieve fitness between two entities: the form in question and its context," we now turn to a brief discussion of strategy.

Strategy ("form" in Alexander's quote) defines the way an organization chooses to position itself in its competitive environment ("context" in Alexander's quote), as represented by the permeable triangular shape shown in Figure 9.3. It encompasses such notions as the firm's segment in its industry and the control of critical factors for competing successfully in such a segment.

To be successful in a business or industry, there are certain activities that an organization must do well. For example, if you are producing a commodity product, it can be critical to have a secure source of supply and efficient production or processing operations so you can be the low-cost producer. If you are producing highly differentiated products, advertising, marketing, and product development are likely the critical activities. If you are in the aerospace industry, your R&D capability and the ability to manage contracts to produce on time and within budgets may be key success factors.

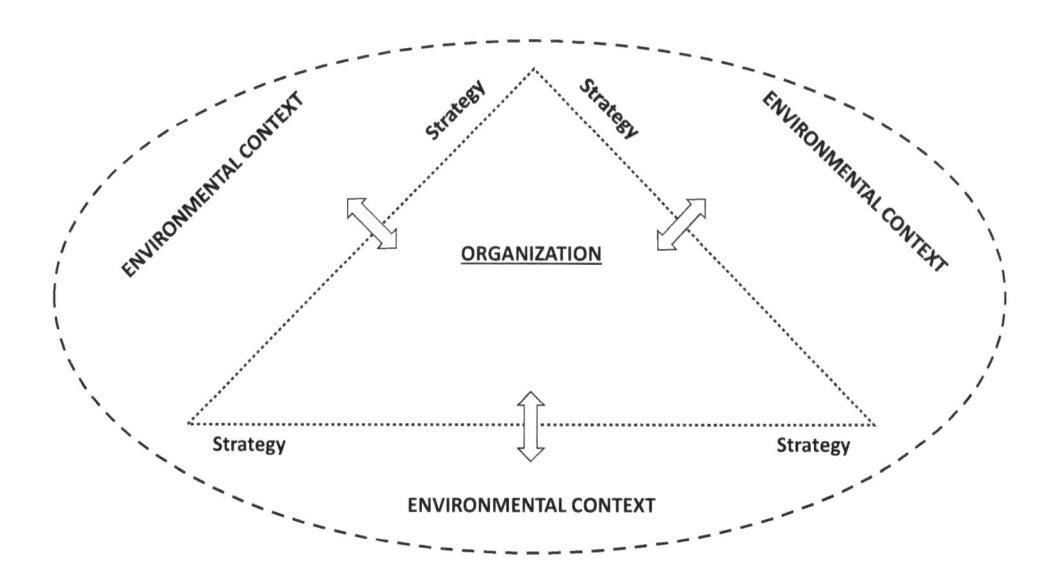

Figure 9.3 Organizational alignment model: Aligning with strategy.

All firms need finance, production, marketing, sales, and human resource capabilities, but the relative emphasis or importance of each is determined by the nature of the business and specific competitive situation within an industry. Once you understand how you have to compete in your business, you can translate this into the tasks to be performed within the organization, which in turn determine the structure and set of administrative systems that need to be implemented to get the jobs done properly.

Business Strategy: The Most Fundamental Business Decisions

Although this chapter is not about formulating strategy but executing it, a basic understanding of a firm's strategy (or any planned changes to a strategy) is needed to evaluate its alignment, or misalignment, with the internal structure and systems, and with the skills and abilities of employees.

There are multiple levels and types of strategy, with corporate and business strategy as the main categories. Corporate strategy, in a diversified company, is about deciding what businesses the company engages in, where in the world it should operate, and how these businesses should be managed to create value. Both business and corporate strategy tell you what the company does and, just as importantly, what it does not do. It also tells executives where to allocate resources. Management expert Peter Drucker asserted that strategic management combines formulation – from analytical thinking – with execution, or a commitment of resources to action (Drucker, 1974).

We will focus here mostly on business strategy. In a stand-alone business or within a business unit of a diversified company, business (or competitive) strategy refers to a company's way of creating a competitive advantage by offering better customer value than competitors. Three questions to ask about strategy are *who*, *what*, and *how*: Who are our customers, what is our product or service, and how is it delivered? In the following sections, we present three frameworks for devising business strategies we have found particularly useful in our work with managers.

Porter's Generic Competitive Strategies for Product Focus

Probably the best-known and most widely used competitive strategy framework is that by Michael Porter (Porter, 1980). He identified three generic strategies: cost leadership, differentiation, and focus. **Cost leadership** requires keeping costs (and, therefore, prices) low through a combination of tight cost control, efficient operations, low overheads, and leveraging the benefits of a well-managed supply chain. Industries that produce goods such as sugar, microchips, or other commodity-like offerings usually fit into this category. In retailing, companies like Walmart and IKEA come to mind.

Differentiation means creating distinct products or services for which customers are willing to pay a premium. This can be achieved in multiple ways, such as through prestige or brand image, proprietary technology or state-of-the-art product features, or outstanding service networks. For instance, in the automobile industry, Mercedes stands for quality engineering, BMW for the driving experience, and Volvo for safety.

Focus, or market segmentation, refers to choosing a niche within an industry and tailoring a strategy to serve clients in this niche (Dess et al., 2005). This strategy is thus narrower in competitive scope but still requires a choice between cost leadership and differentiation. Southwest Airlines and Ryanair are examples of companies that focus on a niche approach emphasizing cost leadership, while Ferrari focuses on a niche approach aimed at differentiation.

While these strategic emphases remain relevant, additional trends have emerged over the years. An important one is that companies must move beyond simply offering products and instead compete on the basis of customer solutions, as was the case with GMP from our introductory example. In some cases, companies work closely with customers to develop the solutions together – this is referred to as cocreation. The following two perspectives thus complement and expand Porter's framework, starting with an emphasis on the rise of the **customer dimension**.

Galbraith's Rise of the Customer Dimension

According to the first perspective, there are five factors that have given rise to the customer dimension in most industries (Galbraith, 2001):

1. Globalization of customers
2. Customers' preference for partnerships or relationships
3. Customers' desire for solutions
4. The rise of e-commerce
5. The continuing increase in the power of buyers

The influence of these factors has caused many companies to create customer-facing organizational units, while also experiencing implementation challenges because their structures remained oriented toward SBUs, countries, and functions; and internal alignments favored business as usual. Fundamentally, Galbraith found, product-centric and customer-centric companies exhibit different characteristics, especially with regards to mindsets and organizational cultures (see Table 9.1).

Table 9.1 Comparison of product- and customer-centric organizations

The Product-Centric Company	The Customer-Centric Company
Best product for customer	Best solution for customer
Creates value through cutting-edge products, useful features, new applications	Creates value through customizing for best total solution
Divergent thinking: How many possible uses of product?	Convergent thinking: What combination of products is best for this customer?
Manage through product profit centers, product reviews, product teams	Organized by customer segments, customer teams, customer P&Ls
Most important process: New Product Development	Most important process: Customer Relationship Management
Measures • Number of New Products • % revenue from products less than two years old • Market share	Measures • Customer share of most valuable customers • Customer satisfaction • Lifetime value of a customer • Customer retention
New product culture – open to new ideas, experimentation	Co-creation culture – open to new ideas, experimentation, together with customer
Most important customer is advanced customer	Most important customer is most profitable, loyal customer
Priority setting around portfolio of products	Priority setting around portfolio of customers, customer profitability
Highest reward is working on next most challenging product	Power to people with in-depth knowledge of customer's business
Manage creative people through challenges with a deadline	Manage creative people through exposure to customer insight and customer problem-solving challenges
Power to people who develop products	Personalized packages of service, support, education, consulting
On the side of the seller in a transaction	On the side of the buyer in a transaction
Price according to market	Price according to value and risk share

'Building Organizations Around the Global Customer', J. Galbraith, *Ivey Business Journal*, September/October 2001; 20–21.

Hax and Wilde's Delta Model

The second perspective expands Porter's framework by more explicitly considering all the ways in which companies compete in a dynamic, networked economy (Hax & Wilde, 2001). While this framework includes Porter's emphasis on product characteristics, it goes beyond a product orientation to focus heavily on creating customer value. Companies must shift their thinking from "developing, making and distributing standardized goods and services to [creating] a bundle of competencies that can be packaged into a well-integrated portfolio of products and services" to provide exceptional and unique value for their customers. The resulting so-called Delta Model is summarized in Figure 9.4.

The basic premise of the model is that in a networked economy, companies ought to not only focus on competitive advantage but also aim to achieve **customer bonding,** which creates a beneficial relationship for the company and its customers. They propose three strategic options: best product, total customer solutions, and system lock-in. The first two are relatively straightforward. **Best product (BP)** competition is essentially low cost or differentiation based on product economics, while **total customer solutions (TCS)** competition is based on customer economics; the challenge is to reduce customer costs or increase their profits.

System lock-in (SLI) competition, on the other hand, is based on system economics or network effects and economies. This means that companies may bundle products and services and customize them to the needs of their customers or conduct joint product development. Key strategies in this regard include: lock in "complementors," lock out competitors, or develop proprietary standards. Complementors are thereby companies that, due to their involvement and products, contribute to the value of the total system. For instance, companies that develop applications for Windows are complementors to Microsoft's value proposition. K-Cups used in the Keurig brewing systems for coffee, tea, and hot cocoa similarly provide

Systems Lock-In
Competition based on total system economics, network effects based on market dominance through "complementor" lock-in, competitor lock-out, or proprietary standards.

SLI

Total Customer Solutions (TCS)
Competition based on providing a customized solution to problems and/or reducing customers costs or increasing their profits.

Best Product (BP)
Competition based on characteristics of a superior product such as low cost or differentiation.

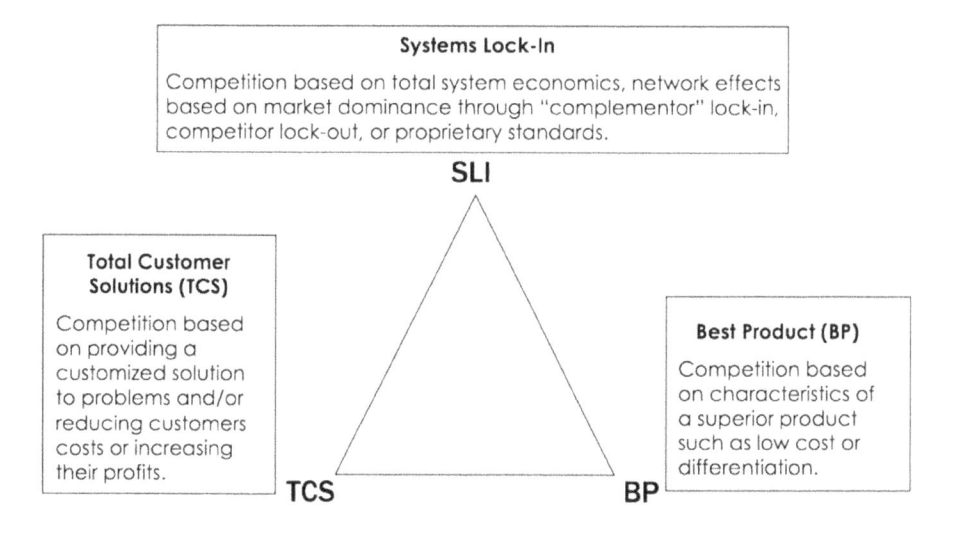

TCS   BP

Figure 9.4 Hax and Wilde's Delta Model for customer-centric strategy.
Reprinted with permission of Palgrave. Adapted from Arnoldo C. Hax and Dean L. Wilde, *The Delta Project,* p. 31, 2001 and *The Delta Model: Reinventing Your Business Strategy,* Arnoldo Hax, Springer, 2010.

complementary value. Well-known brands such as Starbucks, Celestial Seasonings, Wolfgang Puck, Caribou Coffee, Gloria Jean's, Swiss Miss, Twinings of London, and Dunkin' Donuts all use K-Cups to package their products. The more name brands that package their products in this format, the greater the value the system creates for Keurig and the more difficult it becomes for competitors to gain market share.

To achieve system lock-in, companies must therefore consider all the meaningful players in a system that contribute to the creation of economic value. Customers, suppliers, and complementors are all important contributors to thinking about strategy.

Many models for making strategic choices exist, and their applicability depends on the company's industry, competitive context, and degree of change in the environment. What these models have in common, however, is that they focus on the choices companies need to make to compete in their respective marketplaces. An important component of such choices is determining *how* to compete, that is, what the logic of the firm ought to be. This is what is captured in a company's business model, to which we turn next.

Business Models: Making the "How" Choices

A business model describes how a firm creates and captures value and earns a profit in a competitive environment. Simply stated, it is how a firm delivers its value proposition to customers and how it makes money. Consider the following example from the book retail industry.

Barnes & Noble Booksellers was founded in New York in 1917 and had become a national chain in the United States by 1987. In the late 1980s and early 1990s, it evolved the concept of the suburban superstore, which generated 96% of its retail sales. The company offered a comprehensive selection of books and music (the *what*), using experienced staff in spacious stores, complete with cafés that sold Starbucks coffee (the *how*). It became a destination for people, a sort of town meeting place, but its business model was to deliver products and services to its customers in brick-and-mortar stores that could only be accessed during opening hours. Although Barnes & Noble opened its first online book superstore on America Online in 1997, it was Amazon.com that became known for developing this new industry business model.

Founded in 1994, Amazon.com went public in 1997 and generated over US$1.6 billion in sales by 1999. Amazon.com turned the retail bookselling industry upside down. Its business model was to sell books to customers anytime and anyplace using the Internet. It shaped an online community of customers by allowing people to write their own book reviews and share them. This created a network effect typical of platform companies, as opposed to Barnes & Noble's more conventional pipeline approach. This example shows how companies in the same industry, selling the same products, can have vastly different business models to deliver their products and services, with people, skills, and systems aligned vastly differently between them. Eventually, Amazon's business model turned out to be the more commercially successful, with 2022 revenue about 300-fold above that of Barnes & Noble's – in part owed to the advantages that e-commerce platforms had over brick-and-mortar stores during the COVID-19 pandemic.

Another example is the movie rental business. Blockbuster was founded in 1985 when the market was dominated by small local shops. These outlets required a deposit for bulky VHS or Betamax tapes. Blockbuster introduced a membership model and opened stores across the United States, allowing members to rent videos from any of its locations. By 1999 it was the largest video rental company in the world, crowding out the local shops with its scalable business model.

Soon after, the introduction of DVDs in the mid-1990s made videotape technology obsolete and forced Blockbuster to reconsider their inventory. Competitors emerged with innovative business models, which further eroded Blockbuster's market share. For instance, Redbox, which offered extremely cheap video rentals from automated retail kiosks in convenient, high-volume traffic locations such as supermarkets, had captured 25% of the rental market by 2010. Similarly, Netflix emerged in 1998 with a mail-order DVD service, completely eliminating the need for physical locations. Netflix in turn faced competition when video streaming took hold, and is now competing against services like Amazon Prime Video on Demand, Hulu, Disney+, and Apple TV. As a result of these rapid and profound business model innovations, Blockbuster lost the competitive game and filed for bankruptcy in 2010, and in 2011 it was bought by DISH Network. Netflix ceased its mail-order DVD service in 2023 and is now focused on offering streaming content, including both licensed TV shows/movies and original productions.

Although it is not always necessary to have a technologically sophisticated business model like Amazon or Netflix to displace existing companies and be successful, technology has become a critical tool and asset in disruption. Ride-sharing services like Uber and Lyft, for example, used technology to disrupt the taxi industry, and Airbnb has done the same with hotel accommodations. In fact, many of the most successful business model innovations in the last two decades have been those that leverage the network effect through a platform approach. While the top 10 most valuable companies (by market value) in 2008 were all conventional pipeline companies (those that add value along a value chain), just 10 years later 7 of the top 10 most valuable companies – by a significant margin – were platform companies.

Companies Are Becoming More Customer Focused

It is easy to talk about globalization, being customer centric, and business model innovation, but it is not easy to put these ideas into practice. It has been the authors' experience over the years working with a number of companies in various industries such as defense, financial printing, telecommunications, financial services, fast-moving consumer goods, construction and development, and even law enforcement that they all were experiencing the need to provide "solutions" and to develop organizations that were customer centric. We also see this in the way company slogans have evolved. The coffee brand Folgers, for instance, changed its slogan from "Mountain grown, the richest kind of coffee" to "The best part of waking up is Folgers in your cup." Similarly, BMW in the United Kingdom and the United States made the adjustment from "The ultimate driving machine" to "Sheer driving pleasure," and McDonald's switched from "Look for the Golden Arches" to "You deserve a break today" and "I'm loving it." What these changes have in common is that they shift emphasis away from the product's attributes and instead focus on the value and experience provided for customers.

In all cases the authors were involved in, the need to operate and communicate differently was driven by changes in the organizations' external environment. For some, it was the appearance of new competitors with new products and business models that sparked the need to coordinate across functional or business areas. For others, firms in financial services like accounting, for example, the consolidation of the global players into the Big Four and increased regulation (Sarbanes-Oxley and other changes) affected their customer orientation. For law enforcement agencies, it was the appearance of new criminal or terrorist network organizations posing new threats that drove the change.

However, the characteristic that they all had in common was that to become customer centric and provide solutions, they had to work horizontally across the organization to coordinate information and activities in order to improve performance in the new environments that they faced. Although they understood that a change in strategy was necessary, many struggled to realize which realignments would be most beneficial for their future growth.

Culture's Influence on Strategy

It takes a deep understanding of a company's strategy and management systems and an understanding of the history and culture of the host country to execute a global strategy properly. And it takes time.

What happens when a company takes its strategy "on the road," so to speak – when it begins implementing it in another country and context? What appears to be obvious and straightforward in a firm's home market or in another international location may not work in a new country. What executives take for granted at home may not apply abroad. Thus, the context-dependent tension between global integration and local adaptation discussed in Chapter 8 matters greatly for the success of the strategy.

Consider TJX Companies, the world's leading off-price retailer of apparel and home fashions, operating multiple businesses through five divisions: The Marmaxx Group (T.J. Maxx and Marshalls), Sierra Trading Post, and HomeGoods in the United States; TJX Canada (Winners, HomeSense, and Marshalls); and TJX Europe (T.K. Maxx and HomeSense). At the end of its 2017 fiscal year, it operated more than 3,800 stores in nine countries and three e-commerce sites. Its revenue exceeded US$33 billion, and it employed approximately 235,000 employees ("Associates"). We learned about the company's globalization journey in a conversation with Ted English, the CEO at the time the company entered Europe.

TJX's value proposition was to deliver a rapidly changing assortment of fashionable, quality, brand name merchandise at 20% to 60% below regular department and specialty store prices. It was able to do this because it relied on opportunistic buying, disciplined inventory management, and a low expense structure. Stores are located in community shopping centers and are flexible spaces with no permanent, fixed store features. TJX's target market consists of value-conscious customers across a wide range of income levels and demographics.

Customers entering the T.J. Maxx & HomeGoods Store in Newport, Rhode Island, for example, encounter this business model by driving to a shopping mall, parking their car in a spacious parking lot, and taking a shopping cart as they enter the store, which they push to hold all the merchandise they select in their "exciting treasure-hunt shopping experience." This is a straightforward, common experience in the United States in this type of retail store. However, this mode of operating has several built-in, culturally influenced assumptions, which include:

- Customers can and will drive to the mall where there is plenty of parking.
- Customers will need and use a shopping cart in order to purchase many items.
- Customers can identify the value inherent in their purchases because they recognize the brand name and its reduced selling price in the store.

When TJX opened its first European stores in the United Kingdom and the Netherlands, it discovered that many of its customers only bought one or two items. Also, the idea of using a shopping cart was foreign to them, and they initially refused to use them. In the Netherlands, there were even more obstacles to overcome than in the United Kingdom, including language and culture. TJX was not able to replicate the brand/value proposition in the Netherlands, as customers did not easily recognize the value offering (the brand-vs.-price trade-off). The business model did not work there as it did in the United States.

The Importance of Mindful Leadership and Adaptation in Executing Global Strategy

Three basic premises of adaptation that apply domestically or globally are important to consider when executing global strategy, as we will illustrate using the following examples from the retail industry.

1. *The environment is always changing.*
   We introduced the importance of this notion in Chapter 8, and it remains relevant for organizational alignment as well. The retail industry has gone through what some observers refer to as "Retail Darwinism," meaning survival of the fittest (or more accurately, survival of the best adapted to the environment). The US retail landscape largely consisted of small family stores ("mom and pop" stores) in the 1800s and into the 1900s. In the 1900s, chains that had coexisted with the family stores in major city centers expanded regionally, aided by the development of suburbs, an increase in automobile ownership, and shopping malls. Also, around the mid-1900s many of the chains located in the malls and center cities declined in importance for the retail trade. Then came the "big box" stores like we saw in the GMP case. More recently, e-commerce platform companies like Amazon created another inflection point, while traditional retailers are struggling to remain competitive.

2. *Strategies need to change, or firms need to find market niches to remain in alignment with their environment.*
   A classic example of failure to adapt successfully is Sears (formerly Sears, Roebuck and Company), which at one time was the largest retailer in the United States. It has been called the Amazon of the early 20th century because it was a very innovative company for its time, starting as a distance retailer with its famous mail-order Sears Catalog in the late 1800s. However, the company failed to update its retail model to remain in sync with the changing tastes, fashions, and industry competitors such as Wal-Mart, Home Depot, and Amazon. Consequently, it was displaced by Wal-Mart as the largest retailer in 1990. Speculation continued about its ability to survive after it filed for bankruptcy in 2018, following years of declining revenues. By May 2023, it was a shadow of its former self with only 16 stores left. Amazon, on the other

hand, has continued to modify its business model and morphed into more of a technology company than a bookseller. Although it owns companies outside the retail industry, it most visibly continues its disruption of retail industry segments such as shoes, with the purchase of Zappos, and grocery, by buying Whole Foods.

3. *Execution is key.*

Sears entered businesses that it had no experience with, such as real estate and financial services. It developed many well-known product brands that it no longer owns and had to sell off in order to remain in business. These products could have contributed to its success in the 21st century if they had been managed well, but the company was unable to capitalize on them. Sears was even an early mover in using the Internet. Along with CBS and IBM, it created Prodigy, which ultimately was sold to SBC Communications (which later became AT&T) and the Mexican telecommunications provider Telmex. In short, the company was not able to turn innovative ideas into sustainable businesses.

> ### Reflection Question 9.1: Global Strategy
>
> Please think of a global/international company you know well and consider: What is the company's current strategy? In what way does this strategy reflect that the company is doing business across borders and boundaries?

Aligning Internally: The Tasks-People-Structure Triangle

Following the consideration of strategic alignment within the organization's context, our attention now shifts to the interdependent challenges of aligning internally. The three key components to consider are tasks, people, and structure, which we depict as a triangle in Figure 9.5. We start with tasks, since these constitute the building blocks of an organization's operations and are often overlooked, as decision-makers jump straight from strategy to structure and people without analyzing the requirements of the tasks that will be organized and executed.

Tasks Are the Building Blocks

Global organizations employ many people for distinct jobs or tasks that contribute to overall organizational performance. Tasks and their coordination are the foundation for creating organizational structure. These tasks have different characteristics,

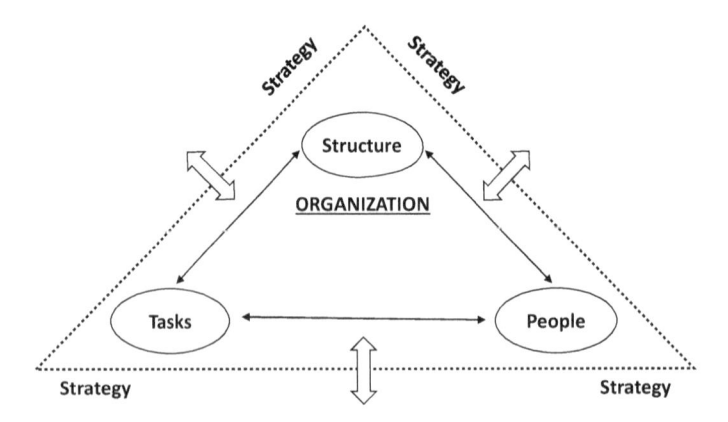

Figure 9.5 Organizational alignment model: Aligning organization with strategy.

requiring different skills, which means employing people with various educational backgrounds, knowledge bases, and competences. There are, for instance, patterns of systematic variance between people in such functions as accounting, marketing, R&D, or manufacturing. Functions within a company are organized for specific tasks, and some people seem more drawn to certain jobs than others based on education, experience, attitude, and preference. This is the concept of differentiation or the "difference in cognitive and emotional orientation among managers in different functional departments" (Lawrence & Lorsch, 1969, p. 11). This concept encompasses the specialized technical knowledge required for the tasks ("hard skills"), as well as the differences in attitude and behavior of the people in the jobs ("soft skills"). As complexity in organization increases, differentiation likely expands as well. As this happens, the potential for departments to pursue their own particular goals increases, as does the likelihood for potential conflict. Therefore, it is important to coordinate these functional areas effectively, which is not always an easy feat in large corporations, since people may be separated both physically and attitudinally by their personal predispositions and orientations. Integration is needed, which encompasses the complex coordination of tasks and interrelationships, including conflict resolution, and depends on the level of task interdependence.

What Is the Level of Task Interdependence?

To ensure proper coordination, managers must be aware of how each area is dependent on the others to achieve its goals. There are three basic types of internal interdependence in organizations, and the most complex organizations exhibit all three (Thompson, 1967). The simplest type is **pooled** or **simple interdependence**. This means that each part of an organization can pursue the achievement of its goals relatively independently from other parts and still contribute to the overall

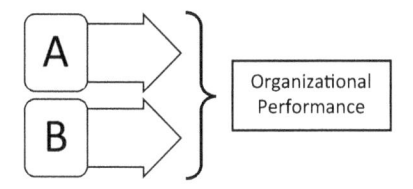

Figure 9.6 Task interdependence: Pooled or simple.

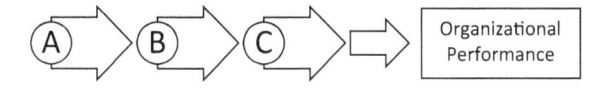

Figure 9.7 Task interdependence: Sequential.

objectives of the organization, as shown in Figure 9.6. This is a situation in which each part contributes to the whole and is supported by the whole. For example, in a department store, personnel from the furniture department do not necessarily have to interact with people from the sporting goods department for each to fulfill their objectives. They can contribute, independently, to the goals of the store. Each, however, is supported by, for instance, the human resource department and the accounting department. Similarly, a McDonald's restaurant in Seattle does not need to interact with a McDonald's in Boston for the corporation to succeed.

Higher up on the complexity scale is **sequential interdependence**, meaning that there is a predetermined and ordered progression by which tasks must proceed. As the name implies, one group must accomplish its task before the next one can begin. In the manufacture of a relatively standard product, one can see a progression from the design department to engineering to purchasing to production scheduling and then to manufacturing. On the assembly line of an automobile, for example, the car's frame and axles must be assembled before the engine and the body can be attached. This notion of completing task A before task B can begin is depicted in Figure 9.7.

A situation of **reciprocal** or **complex interdependence** between tasks means that "the output of each becomes the input for the others." Rather than having discrete linear relationships between groups and tasks, the relationships are continuous and almost circular in nature. For example, in creating sophisticated technology systems, production must understand what the researchers have developed, and the development engineers must understand the constraints on manufacturing. Similarly, both the researchers and the engineers must understand the customers' needs in order to accurately forecast delivery dates. As can be inferred from

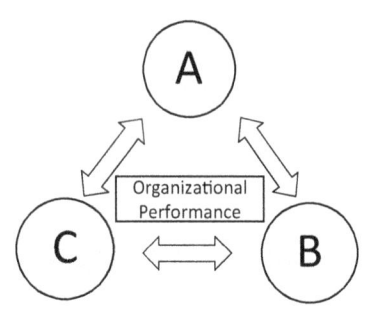

Figure 9.8 Task interdependence: Reciprocal.

this simple example, reciprocal interdependence creates an iterative process in which the required level of intergroup communication is high and the potential for conflict increases dramatically. Think of an advertising agency working on a new account. Copywriting, photography, art, production, finance, and the account executive constantly meet to decide on the latest iteration of an advertising campaign. Each has to understand the constraints on the others. And if, upon the customer seeing the advertisement, changes are required, the interactive process starts all over again. Reciprocal interdependence is depicted in Figure 9.8.

Coordination Mechanisms and Conflict Resolution

In reality, companies are complex webs combining all three types of task interdependencies. As the complexity of organizations increases, the need to coordinate and control the activities of diverse groups of individuals also increases, and formal control mechanisms, such as accounting, auditing, and management information systems, are important. Most organizations systematically collect, analyze, and disseminate information on production, finances, and personnel. Budgets are developed, refined, and monitored. Like other mechanisms, these provide messages about what is required or valued.

For example, requiring the manufacturing department to concentrate on costs and the sales department to prioritize customer satisfaction could in some circumstances produce high levels of dysfunctional conflict. Manufacturing would want long production runs to minimize downtime and retooling costs, while sales might want runs stopped to meet a valued customer's urgent need for another product. Both need to understand the other and act in a coordinated fashion if either is to satisfy their objectives.

The managerial issue is how best to coordinate interdependence (see Table 9.2). At the simplest level – for example, with pooled interdependence – standardization by rules and budgets can be used. A department is given a budget, a set of

Table 9.2 Summary: Interdependence, coordination, and task alignment

Interdependence	Coordination	Task Environment Characteristics
Pooled (simple)	Standardization: rules, regulations	Relatively simple, static, certain, predictable, unchanging (stability)
Sequential	Plans: schedules, budgets, milestones	Multiple interrelated components, frequent but manageable changes (complexity)
Reciprocal (complex)	Mutual adjustment: constant communication; often face-to-face	Multiple interrelated components, rapidly changing, unpredictable, multiple interpretations, cause-and-effect uncertainty (dynamic complexity)

operating procedures, hours of operation, and a set of well-defined tasks, while being measured on its results against set objectives. With sequential interdependence, coordination is usually accomplished by also adding plans and schedules.

However, at the level of reciprocal interdependence, special structural integrating roles such as project teams or product managers may be necessary, and coordinating mechanisms such as task forces are often used. Direct, face-to-face communication or coordination through mutual adjustment usually is required as well. For instance, in the case of GMP discussed earlier in the chapter, the shift in strategy away from product-focused selling within strategic business units to team-based selling across SBUs increased the interdependence among units that previously had little, if any, interdependence.

Particularly in situations of reciprocal interdependence where there is a lot of interpersonal engagement, the potential for conflict arises. This is an area where intercultural skills are important.

People in different cultures tend to prefer different ways of solving this interdependence conflict. Stella Ting-Toomey's research, for instance, shows that cultural variability (individualism vs. collectivism, power distance, and high vs. low context communication patterns) provides "lenses" through which conflict is viewed: individualists tend to use an outcome-oriented model while collectivists follow a process-oriented model (Ting-Toomey, 1999). Whereas members from an individualistic, low-context culture may embrace conflict as potentially beneficial, members from a collectivistic, high-context culture often seek to avoid open conflict and may prefer hierarchical structures with clearer responsibilities. As Ting-Toomey (1999, p. 211) states,

For individualists, effective conflict negotiation means settling the conflict problem openly and working out a set of functional conflict solutions conjointly. Effective conflict resolution behavior (e.g., emphasizing the importance of addressing incompatible goals/outcomes) is relatively more important for individualists than is appropriate facework behavior. For collectivists, on the other hand, appropriate conflict management means the subtle negotiation of in-group/out-group face-related issues – pride, honor, dignity, insult, shame, disgrace, humility, trust, mistrust, respect, and prestige – in a given conflict episode. Appropriate facework moves and countermoves are critical for collectivists before tangible conflict outcomes or goals can be addressed.

The nature of interdependence required is thus the most fundamental characteristic of tasks that affects decisions around organizing and executing, situated within a cultural context. Next, tasks must be aligned with the skills of the people who perform them. While Chapter 7 focused on selecting, preparing, and moving people, we will now specifically concentrate on people-related decisions and actions as part of aligning for execution.

The Right People: Selection and Development

The people brought into an organization through its recruitment and selection systems affect organizational alignment. The most obvious effect is on the pool of knowledge, skills, and attitudes. Selection is the mechanism by which a pool of candidates is narrowed to the number of job vacancies. Several sources of assessment biases can enter these decisions. The one most frequently described is the "just like me" bias, whereby the successful candidate is the one who is closest in skills and personality to those making the decision. Although it might augur well for the fit between the person and his or her supervisor, this type of decision might not provide the required congruence between person and task. Selection, like recruitment, involves a careful analysis of both the job and the organization to determine the most fitting type of employee.

Rarely does a selection decision alone provide a perfect person–task (P–T) or person–organization (P–O) fit. P–T fit is the traditional focus of employee selection, the skills and abilities to do the job; while P–O fit is concerned with a person's compatibility with broader characteristics of the organization, such as culture, values, and colleagues. Most employees need some form of training or development to enable them to become effective performers. So even if the fit is perfect, continual development is still needed as conditions change.

In the case of GMP, the existing sales representatives in Chile did not have the requisite skills for the new sales task. They were accustomed to relationship selling with customers with whom they had dealt over the years. Now they had to contend with purchasing agents who cared about ROI and expected professional presentations. New sales representatives were needed and some existing ones required training and developmental experiences to perform the new task.

Structure

The people and tasks they are working on are organized using various divisions of labor and structures to achieve coordination, efficiency, and effectiveness. Structure is the set of formal relationships between people in an organization and is one mechanism that communicates to organization members what behavior is expected of them, what tasks to work on, what not to do, what goals to work toward, with whom to work, whom to obey, and whom to direct. As noted in Chapter 8, this includes structural options such as hierarchy, teams, and rules and procedures. Structures also are used as integrating mechanisms. These may include taskforces, teams, liaison people, product or project managers, product management departments, and matrix organization designs.

Organizational structures are not free from the influence of culture. Each structure contains identifiable assumptions about the legitimacy of certain practices and relationships and defines the locus of authority, responsibility, and bases of power differently. Each legitimizes a different pattern of communication and interaction. In addition to "fitting" better with certain competitive situations or product characteristics, some structures may be more acceptable than others in a given culture. For example, the matrix organization, a structure in which a person has two supervisors, has cultural assumptions built into it. It violates the principle of unity of command that can be commonplace in some hierarchical cultures, and because of the existence of potentially competing interests, it can force conflict into the open, which ought to be avoided in some cultures.

Aligning the Organization: The Critical Role of Systems

Organizations should be designed to elicit the behavior needed by their strategy. All too often, procedures are imposed without due consideration of the task at hand, simply because, de facto, they just "have become company policy." In such situations, the administrative heritage of the company may become the controlling factor, with jobs and people forced into existing systems, when it should be the other way around.

Managers use administrative systems to create alignment between people and tasks. Systems are social-relational tools that channel the activities of employees, thereby implying what is expected of them. Care must be taken not to mix messages, which can happen when a strategy changes. Managers may expect that employees will automatically adjust their behavior, but the systems may tell them to continue as before. Different systems send different messages or signals.

Ineffectiveness often results when individuals cannot reconcile those different messages, instead paying attention to the messages of one system to the exclusion of messages coming from another.

Encouraging Performance: Performance Appraisal and Rewards

Two of the most studied management systems are **performance appraisals** and **rewards**. Appraisal processes are seen in many forms and administered in many ways. However, at the core, there are several common purposes:

- communicate expectations or standards of performance;
- provide feedback on how well one is doing against expectations or standards;
- identify areas of developmental need and develop a plan of remedy;
- provide information and documentation for decisions about salary, promotion, or discipline.

Rewards come in a variety of forms. One person's reasons for working are different from another's. Basically, rewards fall into one of two categories: **intrinsic**, those that come from doing the job itself or being directly part of the work environment; and **extrinsic**, those that are often more tangible and externally oriented. More job autonomy is an example of the former, while getting a raise or winning an award is an example of the latter.

The meaning of rewards may also differ between people. Some rewards (particularly financial ones) have instrumental value, helping us obtain other things of importance such as food and shelter. Rewards also often serve as a signal that one's contribution or presence is valued: a form of recognition. They can serve as a signal to others of one's value, thereby enhancing self-esteem. Individual needs determine which of these meanings are most important at any one time and which reward will have the desired effect.

In designing and administering reward systems from the employee's perspective, several issues are important. From the organization's perspective, it is helpful to ask the following questions about rewards:

1. Are they competitive? Can the organization attract the people it wants vis-à-vis its competitors? Are the rewards commensurate with what the employee brings to the job in terms of skill, knowledge, and aptitude?
2. Are they sufficient? Do employees get enough of the right things to satisfy their needs? Is the sum of both intrinsic and extrinsic rewards enough to motivate and retain employees?
3. Are they equitable? Is the internal distribution of rewards fair? Are they commensurate with the required attitude and effort?

4. Do they motivate the right task-related behaviors, or do they create a disincentive? Do they motivate for a sustained period of time?

Evaluation and reward systems help create alignment with the strategy. In the case of GMP, the compensation system was changed to reflect not only the sales representatives' individual goals but also the performance of their team and the company. The evaluation and reward systems further changed from primarily individualistic to a combination of individualistic and collectivistic components.

As another example, let's look at a firm with which we worked that we will call ABC Financial Printing. ABC had long provided transaction services for companies' initial public offerings (IPOs), mergers, and acquisitions, such as completing and filing required documents with government regulators. This highly customized service was based on relationship selling by a sales force and exhibited very high margins. The sales representatives who were hired to sell transaction services were aggressive self-starters who liked the substantial salary, bonuses, and reputation that came from being successful in the high-margin, relationship-oriented transaction business.

In 2002, the Sarbanes-Oxley Act required firms to file numerous routine standardized periodic reports that were time consuming to prepare. As a result, companies like ABC, pushed by competitors that were offering low-cost "do it yourself" computer programs and Internet products, introduced a compliance service for their customers to meet the requirements of Sarbanes-Oxley. This service was a lower-margin offering than the transaction service. As a portion of company revenue, however, it was growing to become a very important part of the firm's business.

ABC developed a range of products, including computer programs, to address this market. However, it had difficulty motivating sales representatives to sell compliance products. They did not have the technical skills to sell the new products, nor was there a fit between the characteristics of the salespeople and the reward and evaluation systems associated with the new products. Because of this, ABC subsequently struggled to meet the demands of the new market and the needs of compliance customers, which ultimately led to it being acquired.

Responsibility Centers and Evaluation

Earlier in the chapter, we referred to the practice of using budget systems to manage task interdependencies. Identifiable parts of an organization, such as departments, divisions, or subsidiaries, usually are established as responsibility centers to manage financial resources and account for revenue and expenses. The three basic types of responsibility centers are cost, profit, and investment. The heads of these centers have differing responsibilities and accountabilities. **Cost center** managers are responsible for managing expenses within the budgets that they are allocated. **Profit center** managers in turn are responsible for the expenses of their units and the revenue that they generate. Finally, **investment center** managers control expenses, revenue, and assets.

These managers have the authority to run their operations in a manner that they deem best to achieve their goals, and they are evaluated on their results. For our purposes, the important point to note is that the responsibility systems of a firm directly influence the behavior of executives and contribute significantly to alignment. A change in strategy may create conflict with existing control systems and responsibility centers, necessitating realignment.

Fostering Organizational Cultures That Support Performance

Organizational cultures may facilitate or hinder the work of the company, and management is responsible for fostering the culture of the organization. A philosophy and set of values will develop in every organization, whether created explicitly with careful forethought or emerging without specific guidance. The result may be positive or negative. Management's values can encourage a culture of trust, problem solving, and adaptation, or they can create mistrust, blind obedience, and domination.

Many books have been written about the notion of organizational culture, and numerous consulting companies offer tools for assessing the same. Our intention is not to replicate that material, but to make the point that organizational culture is an important element in the success of a company. When it is well aligned with the company's context, strategy, and purpose, it can be a valuable asset in achieving performance, as the example of Zappos demonstrates.

Zappos is reputed to be a company with a positive culture. It regularly shows up in rankings of top corporate cultures. It is known for terrific customer service and a unique culture where everyone is a brand ambassador and enjoys working there. Robert Richman is the former culture strategist at Zappos and author of *The Culture Blueprint* (Richman, 2015). Two of his principles of culture are that it is cocreated and that it is comprised of systems. No single person is in charge of creating a company culture, but rather it is the outcome of the continuing daily interactions of the people in the organization and the feelings that they create at work (Richman, 2015). Regardless of what a company says about its culture and values it prints on the posters, it is the behavior of the employees, the systems, and the tone set by top management that becomes the culture.

Organizational culture is a variable that needs to be taken seriously in creating alignment, which is why it is included in the model. "Culture eats strategy for breakfast," a compelling quotation widely attributed to Peter Drucker, highlights the importance of culture in the hierarchy of organizational ingredients needed for success. Similarly, Lou Gerstner, in a 2002 Harvard Business School speech about the renewal effort he led at IBM, said, "The thing I have learned at IBM is that culture is everything" (Lagace, 2002).

Aligning the Organization with Systems: Each Part Affects the Whole

In summary, people are selected for certain skills and attitudes they possess, trained and educated (developed) to improve these skills, evaluated on how they do their jobs, and subsequently rewarded. Evaluation and reward systems, development, budgets, and control systems are also used to motivate people. To make sure that the tasks of the organization are coordinated and carried out in the best possible way, companies use various structures. Too often decisions about the administrative systems are made as a result of unexamined assumptions about motivation rather than an understanding of the organization in its context.

Managers must anticipate that if they make a change in either the task or the people, their action may impact other parts of the system, with potentially unintended implications for overall results. This is one of the properties of a system; a change in one part affects other parts. Therefore, a systemic and integrated perspective of organizations is essential in diagnosing problems and considering courses of action. The organization's systems and culture thus are the dynamic motors at the core of the completed organizational alignment framework, as depicted in Figure 9.9.

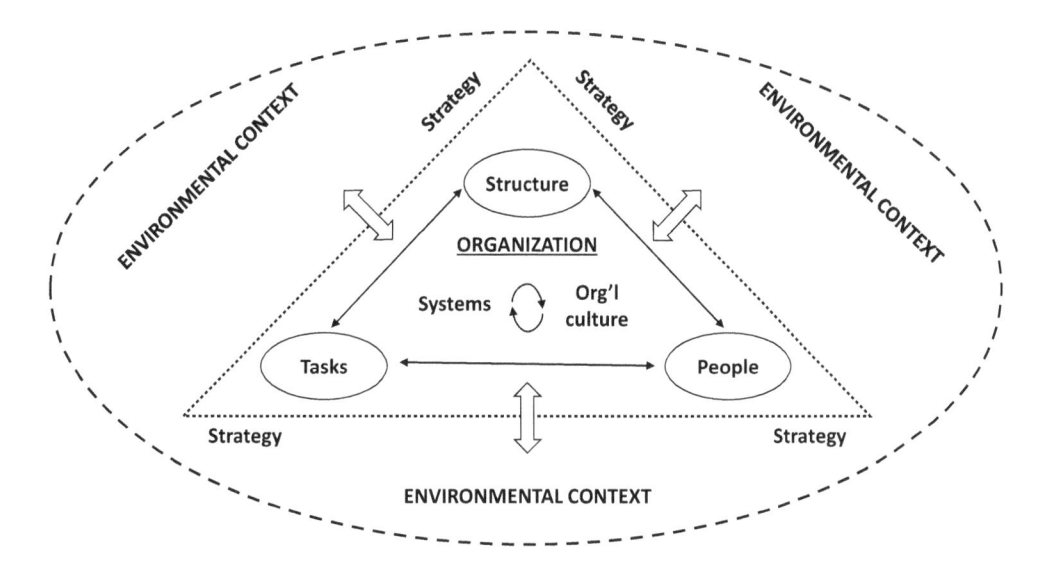

Figure 9.9 Organizational alignment: Systems to shape internal alignment.

Can You Transfer Practices Directly? Should You Adapt to the Culture or Not?

Once organizational alignment is approximated, companies often encounter the question of whether existing practices, systems, and management styles can be transferred or adapted to other contexts. The answer is: It all depends. It is not necessary to always change the system, even if it is different from the host country. When in Rome, you do not always have to do as the Romans do! Sometimes people in another culture simply need to be trained to use a system (remembering, of course, that the format of training may be influenced by the respective culture). However, to assume that training is all that is required is also usually a mistake. Each response has a proper time and place.

The decision regarding transferring, adapting, or possibly creating a new hybrid practice should be the result of careful, informed judgment based on understanding the cultural biases of management systems and the cultural norms of the country in which the operations are located. Are there rules? Not really, but careful analysis can help sort out the issues and help managers solve the problem. First, one must remember that cultures are not monolithic or deterministic. Also, if certain cultural values or practices are a critical part of an organization's model for success, then managers can use their selection system to find employees who display these characteristics.

Questions such as "How important is it that we do it identically to the way it's done at home?" can guide your decisions. Following procedures the same way may not be as important as achieving results. Just because headquarters does it one way does not mean that it will be effective in a different cultural environment.

What Does the Business Need?

The first important questions are around the business imperatives: tasks that must be done well for the firm to create value. For example, a customer-centric strategy requires a lot of interfaces with the customer. If the customer is in a dynamic industry, customer-facing employees will need to make decisions on their own about how to adapt to the customer's needs. These business imperatives suggest a more egalitarian rather than a status-oriented decision-making structure, no matter what the national culture prefers. A company that relies on deep technology development must put a lot of resources into research and development. Rather than scattering those around the world, they may need to centralize with some sizeable capital purchases. This implies a less egalitarian way of managing R&D resources, even in an otherwise egalitarian country culture.

Professor Paula Caligiuri's (2012) concept of **cultural agility** describes a characteristic of professionals who "succeed in contexts where the successful outcome of their jobs, roles, positions or tasks depends on dealing with unfamiliar sets of cultural norms or multiple sets of them" (p. 5). They achieve success by being able to draw on three different behavioral responses: cultural minimization, cultural adaptation, or cultural integration. These three responses also describe the spectrum of adaptation responses for strategy execution. We describe each in turn below.

Keep Your Own Practices (Cultural Minimization)

Take the experience of a Canadian bank, the Bank of Nova Scotia, in Mexico. When the Mexican banking system was about to collapse after the economic crisis in 1994, the Mexican government put most of the Mexican banks up for sale. The Bank of Nova Scotia bought Inverlat. In 1982, Mexico's banks had been nationalized, and they remained essentially government institutions for many years. Mexican banks stagnated, despite substantial innovations in the global banking industry. Many Inverlat managers claimed that their bank had generally deteriorated more than the rest of the banking sector in Mexico, and overall had failed to create a new generation of bankers who understood and reflected the changed conditions and times. The bank had been lending primarily to the government, and managers were unfamiliar with the challenges of lending to the private sector, and therefore failed to collateralize their loans properly or to ensure that covenants were being maintained. The existing managers did not have the knowledge or the capacity to manage the critical credit assessment function.

Whose practices should be followed? Banks make money by lending money, and the credit function is critical, or what we think of as a business imperative. The Canadians were the experts in this situation, and their practices should dominate.

Adapt to Your Partner (Cultural Adaptation)

A different situation faced a US auto parts company that entered into a joint venture in North America with a Japanese company to learn about just-in-time manufacturing, a technique in which the Japanese company was a leader. The US company had a short-term orientation to cost control, and as the joint venture progressed, it became uncomfortable with the Japanese partner's longer-term orientation and wanted to institute tighter controls, which, however, interfered with its original objective for the joint venture – learning. In this situation, whose way should be followed? The Americans wanted to learn from the Japanese, who were the clear experts. The Japanese way should take precedence.

Create a New Way (Cultural Integration)

An example of cultural integration is that of Hisense and Hitachi, who entered a joint venture in 2003 to sell commercial air conditioners in China. While Hisense provided local knowledge of the Chinese market, its Japanese partner contributed technological expertise and a global network. Although the scope of the joint venture initially covered only the region of China, emerging trust allowed for international expansion to Africa, Russia, and later the broader Southeast Asian region. With each expansion, both parties learned together and about each other, leading to the integration of their organizational cultures within the scope of the joint venture, creating new, combined ways of conducting business (Liu & Beamish, 2017).

Conclusion: The Strategic Alignment Model in Practice

In this chapter, we identified key elements that managers should keep in mind as they implement strategy. We shared a model of internal alignment within the organization, including the task, the people, structure, and administrative systems. We examined the relationship between organizational alignment and the environment, including the role of strategic choices and business models.

We encourage you to use the alignment model as an analytic tool, remembering that organizations and their environments are dynamic. The model provides an initial analytic tool to help global leaders adapt their organizations. There is no simple formula for choosing effective structures and systems. Use judgment in assessing the likely impact of systems on employees and in adjusting the systems to support job achievement and organizational results. Successful and mindful implementation means finding the right combination of strategy, structure, and systems that motivates people to strive for high performance.

Reflection Question 9.2: Applying the Alignment Framework to Your Own Business

Applying the alignment framework to your own business (or one that you are familiar with) increases your mindfulness about how your own organizational system works, allowing you to compare it with others you encounter. We will refer to your "business," but you can adapt the questions to a not-for-profit organization, to a business unit or department within a larger business, or any other organizational unit.

1. Internal alignment
   - Structure: What are the key elements of your structure? How much hierarchy is there? How centralized is decision-making? Who has power (which positions or roles)?
   - Tasks / Work Systems: What is the main set of tasks or work system? How is this work organized? For example, what kind of interdependence is required, and how complex are the tasks? What professional skills and knowledge do they require?
   - People: What are the main skill sets and areas of expertise that people currently have? What are some patterns of personal values? Think about the key people in power and decision-making roles – what are their likely motivations and priorities?
   - Culture and systems: How would you characterize the organizational culture? What are some dominant guiding values? How strong is the organizational culture? On what basis is performance measured and rewarded? What other systems are particularly important in guiding decision-making and action?
   - Alignment: How well aligned are the elements of the organization? Where are the strongest alignments, where are there gaps? What's the cause of the gaps (e.g., labor shortage, new regulations for tasks, organizational restructuring, new business planning system for the company)?
2. External alignment
   - Environment: What are the key characteristics of the external environment that affect your business? This could be a long list, but try to prioritize the main effects of customer demands, competitive pressures, and your industry's business model.
   - Strategy: How would you describe your business's strategy and business model? Who are your customers, what do you deliver to them, and how do you do it? Again, this could be a long and comprehensive exercise. For these purposes focus on the key elements that most affect your decision-making and how you and others work together.
   - Alignment: How well aligned is the strategy with the external environment for your business? Does your strategy consider changes happening now in the environment?
3. Total alignment
   - Alignment is a moving target, and often the internal alignment of an organization is aligned with a *past* business environment and strategy but less with the *current* business environment and strategy. How would you assess the match between internal and external alignment in your

company? Does the alignment among structure, task / work systems, and people match the alignment between strategy and the environment?
- How does this alignment explain patterns of performance? Your areas of lower performance are likely related to areas of misalignment. What could be changed to increase alignment?
- To what extent do you think your business's alignment choices might be affected by the culture you're embedded in? The culture of the headquarters? In what ways does this enable or hinder performance in your current environment?

Reflection Question 9.3: Strategy Execution

There is often quite a gap between the formulated business strategy and the implemented business strategy. Indeed, lack of execution of strategy is thought to be one of the primary reasons for strategic failure. Please reflect upon possible reasons for this gap.

Further Resources

The organizational design framework and analytic model have been adapted from a number of writers on the contingency theory of organizations, including Daft, R. *Organization Theory and Design* (South-Western College Pub, 2020), Joly, H. and Lambert, C. *The Heart of Business: Leadership Principles for the Next Era of Capitalism* (especially Chapter 9; Harvard Business Review Press, 2021), and Stanford, N. *Organization Design: The Practitioner's Guide* (Routledge, 2018). Some classic sources that still provide important perspectives today include: Lawrence, P. R., & Lorsch, J. W. *Organization and Environment* (Homewood, IL: Richard D. Irwin, 1969) and Galbraith, J. R. *Organization Design* (Reading, MA: Addison-Wesley, 1977).

Two excellent resources on modern organizations are Galbraith's *Designing Matrix Organizations That Actually Work*, 2009, Jossey-Bass; and Kates & Galbraith's *Designing Your Organization*, 2007, Jossey-Bass.

The Delta Model is described in a summary article, "The Delta Model: Adaptive Management for a Changing World," Sloan Management Review (Winter 1999), 11–28. An updated and extended version of the original book is Arnoldo Hax, *The Delta Model: Reinventing Your Business Strategy*, Springer, 2010.

Some of the better-known corporate culture assessments are the following:

- Competing Values Framework (Quinn & Rohrbaugh, 1983), https://www.ocai-online.com/about-the-Organizational-Culture-Assessment-Instrument-OCAI

- Dennison Culture Model (Dennison Consulting), https://www.denisonconsulting.com/
- Organizational Culture Inventory (Human Synergistics), https://www.humansynergistics.com/
- CultureIQ Survey, https://cultureiq.com/

Bibliography

Alexander, C. (1964). *Notes on the synthesis of form*. Harvard University Press.

Caligiuri, P. (2012). *Cultural agility: Building a pipeline of successful global professionals*. Jossey-Bass.

Dess, G., Lumpkin, G., & Taylor, M. (2005). *Strategic management*. McGraw-Hill Irwin.

Drucker, P. (1974). *Management: Tasks, responsibilities, practices*. Harper.

Galbraith, J. (2001, September/October). *Building organizations around the global customer*. Ivey Business Journal. Retrieved April 8, 2024, from https://www.iveypublishing.ca/s/product/building-organizations-around-the-global-customer/01t5c00000CwZxhAAF

Hax, A. (2010). *The Delta Model: Reinventing your business strategy*. Springer.

Hax, A., & Wilde, D. (2001). *The Delta Project*. Palgrave.

Hofstede, G. (1980). Motivation, leadership, and organization: Do American theories apply abroad? *Organizational Dynamics*, *8*(2), 50.

Lane, H. (1980). Systems, values, and action: An analytic framework for intercultural management research. *Management International Review*, *20*(3), 61–70.

Lane, H. W., & Campbell, D. D. (2007). *Global Multi-Products Chile*. Ivey Publishing Case (9A98C007). Retrieved April 8, 2024, from https://www.iveypublishing.ca/s/product/global-multiproducts-chile/01t5c00000CwYmWAAV

Lagace, M. (2002). *Gerstner: Changing culture at IBM – Lou Gerstner discusses changing the culture at IBM*. HBS Working Knowledge, Retrieved April 8, 2024, from https://hbswk.hbs.edu/archive/gerstner-changing-culture-at-ibm-lou-gerstner-discusses-changing-the-culture-at-ibm

Lawrence, P., & Lorsch, J. (1969). *Organization and environment*. Richard D. Irwin.

Liu, S., & Beamish, P. W. (2017). *Hisense-Hitachi joint venture: Expanding internationally*. Ivey Publishing.

Nonaka, I., & Takeuchi, H. (1995). *The knowledge creating company*. Oxford University Press.

Porter, M. (1980). *Competitive strategy*. Hill.

Quinn, R., & Rohrbaug, J. (1983). A spatial model of effectiveness criteria: Towards a competing values approach to organizational analysis. *Management Science*, *29*(3), 363–377.

Richman, R. (2015). The culture blueprint. *Culture Hackers*, *1*(5), 31, 35.

Thompson, J. (1967). *Organizations in action*. McGraw Hill.

Ting-Toomey, S. (1999). Constructive intercultural conflict management. In S. Ting-Toomey (Ed.), *Communicating across cultures* (pp. 194–233). The Guilford Press.

10 Leading Change in Global Organizations

> I never stopped getting ready. Just in case.
>
> Chris Hadfield, retired Canadian astronaut and commander of the International Space Station (1959–), quoted from Hadfield (2013), p. 44.

Key Learning Objectives

At the end of this chapter, students will be able to:

- Identify the need for change in a constantly evolving environment.
- Recognize the importance of culture in the effective implementation of organizational change.
- Embrace a mindset-centered approach to change in the Age of Agile.
- Describe three types of change scenarios in relation to a firm's current performance.
- Consider the process of change, including appraising readiness for change, initiating change and adopting new behavior, and reinforcing change – facilitated by design thinking.
- Discuss the dilemma of excessive persistence and premature abandonment.

As we described in Chapter 9, strategic alignment is a continuing process that involves people, tasks, processes, and systems. Change – small or large, anticipated or surprising – is the norm and not the exception in most industries. This chapter zooms in on **global organizational change**, which we define as strategically aligned alterations in patterns of employee behavior within organizations operating across national borders. In particular, we highlight how the dynamics of a volatile, uncertain, complex, and ambiguous (VUCA) world (see Chapter 1) challenge preexisting mindsets and move us into the "Age of Agile." We delineate three types of change scenarios in relation to a firm's current performance and describe how the process of change unfolds, facilitated by a design thinking approach. We juxtapose the notions of excessive persistence and premature abandonment, which suggest that the trade-offs of staying on or leaving a course of action must be carefully considered. As an entry into these themes, we start this chapter by tracing IBM's change trajectory, which fundamentally altered the company for decades to come.

IBM: A Model of Successful Strategic Change

In the 1960s and 1970s, the computer technology industry was vertically integrated. IBM's core business was manufacturing and selling mainframe computers, including the software that ran on them. The software was primarily for transaction processing applications like accounting and payroll, or word processing and e-mail.

In the decades that followed, IBM experienced a "perfect storm" of disruption. Technology, competitors, and customers all changed. Mini-computers reduced the size and cost of computers, making them affordable for more companies. The PC revolution decentralized computing and ushered in the client-server computing model where mainframes were often repurposed as servers. Large companies, IBM's target market, adopted client-server systems while no longer demanding mainframes and bundled software. As a result, they started buying hardware from multiple vendors and third-party software from companies like Oracle and SAP.

Around the same time, a new breed of chief information officers appeared. They were "web-focused, e-business aware, and did not demonstrate the vendor loyalty that characterized their predecessors – the 'career customers' who would buy equipment and software only from IBM" (Meyer, 2007, p. 14). Over time, customers became disenchanted with what IBM referred to as "piece-part technologies" or purchasing different pieces of software and hardware from various vendors and integrating these components themselves. They again wanted comprehensive integrated solutions that worked across their organizations, regardless of size or geographic location (Palmisano, 2003). When Lou Gerstner became CEO of IBM in April 1993, the company's annual net losses were US$8 billion and there were calls to break up the company. IBM had been organized to sell products (mainframes) developed on the basis of strong research and development. Gerstner decided to offer customers integrated business solutions focused on solving problems rather than just selling products – a key IBM strength that combined the company's expertise in solutions, services, products, and technologies (Cortada, 2018). Gerstner subsequently aligned the resources of the company behind the Internet as a medium for real business, and in 1997, IBM announced its new *e-business* strategy (Gerstner, 2002).

There were a plethora of changes that had to take place to implement this new strategy. Aligning the complex organizational structure – 20 separate business units with independent and different systems – presented a challenge. IBM's "religion of decentralization" had led to autonomous country general managers who reported to powerful regional executives and grew their business based on local responsiveness, but at the cost of collaboration and cost-effective global integration.

IBM's global customers complained about interacting with what seemed like separate mini-IBMs in each country. They wanted to see one face for IBM globally. Gerstner believed that customer-focused, global teams that transcended national borders would allow a unified responsiveness to global customers. To do this, he had to integrate IBM's US and overseas operations.

A new structure of 12 customer groups (e.g., banking, government, and insurance) and 1 small and medium-sized company group would take over all IBM accounts, including responsibility for budgets and personnel. Most employees in non-US operations were reassigned to industry groups under the global leaders of their group instead of their respective country-level general managers.

The reaction from country-level general managers was overwhelmingly negative, claiming that the reassignment would not work and would instead destroy the company. Some ignored the new structure, and one reportedly blocked all communications with Gerstner. It took clear messaging from Gerstner to motivate change, including an emphasis that employees do not belong to any particular executives – but to IBM (Wharton, 2002).

Company units were internally focused and competed with each other. Gerstner changed the compensation system from one based on individual performance to one based on the overall performance of IBM, without reference to division, unit, or geography. He also increased the amount of executive compensation given as stock and options, set quotas for how many customer calls each executive had to make, and relentlessly pushed coordination among IBM's many divisions. At a talk at the Harvard Business School in 2002, he said, "We needed to integrate as a team inside the company so that we could integrate for the customers on their premises" (Lagace, 2002).

He also had to contend with IBM's strong company culture. There was a dynamic, highly motivated, and successful sales culture. Employees shared a belief in hard work and ethical behavior. There was also the famously strict dress code (dark suits and white shirts), an exemplar of the Organization Man ethos

(Whyte, 1956, 2002). Gerstner came to see the culture as the "company's DNA" – which was then marked by notions such as paternalism, a stingy stock option program, no-drinking policy at corporate gatherings, and a preference for employees to be married (Gerstner, 2002).

He felt that many of the values on which IBM had been founded had ossified into hard-and-fast rules that, in fact, failed to represent the founders' real views. At a meeting with IBM's top 400 executives, Gerstner told them that they would all need to become change agents within the company:

> We don't execute, because, again, we don't have the perspective that what counts outside [the company] is more important than what happens inside. Too many IBM'ers fight change if it's not in their personal interest. (Gerstner, 2002, p. 205)

He continued, "Those of you who are uncomfortable with it, you should think about doing something else. Those of you who are excited about it, I welcome you to the team, because I sure can't do it alone."

It took three years of a "painful and sometimes tumultuous process" to implement Gerstner's changes. Only after shifts in resources and changes to systems and processes, as well as the removal and replacement of numerous country managers who could not or would not make the transition, did the new structure take hold. Gerstner said:

> Changing the attitude and behavior of thousands of people is very, very hard to accomplish. You can't simply give a couple of speeches or write a new credo for the company and declare that a new culture has taken hold. You can't mandate it, can't engineer it. What you can do is create the conditions for transformation, provide incentives. (Wharton, 2002)

This leads to a number of lessons learned with regards to change, which we detail next.

Lessons about Implementing Strategic Change

IBM's example highlights a number of important insights or "lessons learned" about strategic change and our orientation to the topic.

1. Adapting to changes in the environment is essential to remaining competitive and successful – as we noted in Chapters 8 and 9, "The environment always wins!"
2. All change is behavioral. A new strategy may require employees to assume new roles, develop new skills (technical and interpersonal), assume new responsibilities, or build new relationships.
3. Employees need to understand that the old way of doing business is no longer sustainable and see the benefits of the new way.
4. Change often brings discomfort and possibly resistance.

5. Effective communication is essential. "Telling" is not effective communicating or executing. Employees may "see" and interpret the same situation differently. Executives need to understand what others "see" and work to create a shared frame of reference or common understanding.
6. Organizations don't change; people do. The final result of a successful change effort may look like and act like a changed organization.
7. Strategic change is a process and not just an outcome. It may take a long time to complete.
8. Executives need not only to work with people (individuals and groups) but also to realign the organization. Existing systems, structures, practices, and/or cultures may need to change in order to reinforce and support the new required behaviors and tasks.

Many of these insights underscore the importance of culture and mindsets when enacting a change process. In the following sections, we highlight this notion further, before presenting different types of change scenarios and a three-phase framework for strategic change that managers can use as a guide – a checklist before starting off on the journey.

> ## Reflection Question 10.1: Why Do Organizations Change?
>
> Please try to think of companies that you know from (social) media, personal experience, or your network that have gone through significant organization changes. Why did that change come about? What needed to change and why?

> ## Reflection Question 10.2: Cultural Change
>
> *"Company cultures are like country cultures. Never try to change one. Try, instead, to work with what you've got."* (Drucker, 2004)
>
> When implementation of change proceeds too differently than expected, one specific factor is often pointed to: the organizational culture. Both when it is more difficult to change behavior and values to more constructive approaches than expected and when an otherwise difficult turnaround succeeds against all odds, organizational culture is often identified as an/the explanatory factor. Please reflect: Why is (organizational) culture important for organizational change? Can you think of examples of the positive or negative effect of organizational culture on organizational change processes?

The Age of Agile: A Mindset-Centered Approach to Change

Perhaps the most important point the IBM example demonstrates is that change is most effective when it focuses on mindsets first and strategies/structures second (Bartlett & Beamish, 2018). If the prioritization followed the opposite direction, any strategic initiatives or structural adjustments would be futile – they would be resisted (openly or covertly) by those expected to implement them. Even if such a mindset-centered approach involves a more time-consuming and complex process, any change efforts should account for communicating change in such a way that it allows for a shift in mindsets. In the IBM example, managers needed to first buy into the necessity for change from a product-focused model to a consumer-focused model (and not just on the surface level) before true and long-lasting change was possible.

Importantly, for such an approach to work, the mindsets of those who initiate and enact the change must be receptive to it as well. The notion of an **agile mindset** can be particularly conducive to this objective. Originated in software development, the concept has since entered management mainstream and is characterized by a focus on creating customer value through iterative processes, self-organizing teams, and collaborative networks. The resulting **adhocracy** model of corporate organizing allows for rapid and innovative adjustments to quickly changing environments and is vastly different from the more conventional models focused on bureaucracy. In the latter, rules, routines, and top-down hierarchies prevail, with a predominant emphasis on creating shareholder value (Denning, 2019). In many industries, a bureaucratic mindset leads to organizations that change too slowly to keep up with their more agile competition.

We now live in the **Age of Agile** (Denning, 2018). Given the accelerating rate with which we are moving within a VUCA world, change will no longer be the punctuation in an otherwise stable environment, but instead become the modus operandi. This brings about difficult challenges, since many characteristics of a VUCA world are at odds with how we are wired as humans. For instance, many of today's grand challenges are the result of exponentially growing developments, including climate change, artificial intelligence, or the global pandemic. These phenomena are deceptive because they often remain under the radar for much of their early emergence – until doubling rates reach a threshold beyond which reining them in becomes a tremendous effort. A simple exercise demonstrates this point.

Folding Papers

Evolution has not prepared us well for anticipating or estimating big numbers or nonlinear trajectories. To illustrate, take (or imagine) a standard piece of office printing paper (letter sized, DIN A4, or otherwise). What is the world record for the number of times such a paper has been folded in half? Frequently, the guesses we hear in our management courses range from 10 to 200 times! The real answer is that it is impossible to fold a piece of paper with these dimensions more than seven times[1] (Matthews, n.d.). With each fold, the thickness of the layers doubles (i.e., an exponential function), and if it were possible to fold it 42 times, the stack of paper would be so tall that it could reach the moon.

If it is nonintuitive to imagine a simple exponential function such as this one, anticipating and predicting a nonlinear trajectory in business contexts become even more challenging. However, in today's business context marked by high levels of unpredictability and rates of change with complex dynamics, having an agile mindset will be a critical source of competitive advantage. In the next section, we will unpack three types of change scenarios and describe how the notion of a mindset-centered approach suffuses each of them.

Three Types of Change Scenarios

There are at least three change scenarios companies may face, depending on their current performance: anticipatory, reactive, and crisis, as shown in Figure 10.1.

Ideally, companies continuously monitor environmental shifts during the **anticipatory stage** and make changes through a process of learning geared toward organizational renewal. This is not always easy to do when performance is still meeting or exceeding expectations and there are no real indicators that there is trouble ahead. Not everyone in the company will be looking into the future or be attuned to important environmental shifts. The management challenge at this stage is education – educating people about the potential dangers or threats that could arise. Approaching the anticipatory stage with an agile mindset thereby facilitates a holistic perspective, such that the status quo is not taken for granted but regularly reviewed. The resulting anticipatory change generally proceeds at a slow pace.

---

[1] There is a Guinness world record for the most times to fold a piece of paper in half, established by Britney Gallivan in 2002 – the total number of folds was 12. However, this was only possible with a piece of paper that was narrow and 4,000 ft (0.75 miles [1.2 km]) long.

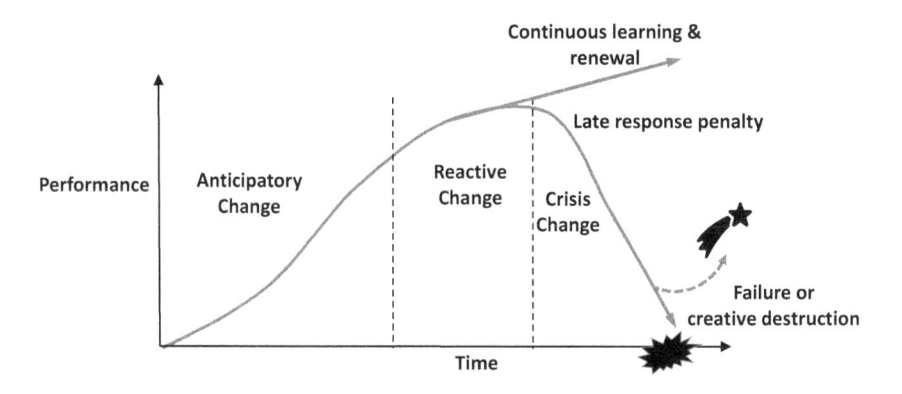

Figure 10.1 Strategic change and renewal.
Adapted from our colleagues Peter Killing, Nick Fry, Rod White, and Mary Crossan at the Ivey Business School and at IMD.

Once shifts in internal or external conditions lead to a performance shortfall, companies enter the **reactive stage.** Managers across all levels start to see the warning signs, but they very likely interpret them differently, depending on their roles or functional perspectives. Change initiatives may move faster now as more people acknowledge the potential threats. The management challenge at this stage is to paint a cohesive picture of the future and achieve agreement on it by facilitating the mindset shift needed to embark on this path of organizational renewal.

In the **crisis stage**, the problems are clear for everyone to see. Crises generally encourage and permit rapid change – indeed, organizations may require it to survive. However, while most will agree that change is needed at this stage, opinions often differ with regards to the best strategy with which to move forward, especially when strategy and structure are prioritized over shifts in mindsets. The organization is unlikely to have access to the resources needed to make the change.

Examples abound of companies that resisted change or that did not respond fast enough to major changes in their industries, leading to further downturn or eventual demise. Polaroid, for instance, missed the shift to digital photography. About the same time, the Boston area was the center of the mini-computer industry that included companies like Digital Equipment, Wang, Prime, and Data General; none of these survived the personal computer revolution. In the US automobile industry, General Motors, in particular, is a good example of the late response penalty, brought upon them by their failure to innovate and adapt to changes in consumer preferences. It took the US government to bail out General Motors. Moreover, the CEO was fired, the Pontiac division was shut down, the brands Hummer, Saturn, and Saab were sold, and about 35% of the executives in the United States were let go. Critics had warned for years that GM needed to change, and by the time it was unavoidable, it was too late.

More recently, we witnessed the decline of numerous retailers in the face of online competitors (e.g., Macy's, Sears, and JCPenney), a trend accelerated by the COVID-19 pandemic but not started then. The taxi industry is another business model that is struggling to adapt in the face of dramatic disruption by companies like Uber and Lyft, as well as the prospect of driverless cars.

Organizational change and renewal should thus be on the corporate agenda at all levels of performance, in order for the company to remain vigilant in light of ever-frequent shifts in the environment. In a VUCA world, firms may find themselves moving from good performance to crisis mode much more rapidly than in previous times, so an agile mindset will be required in many industries. In the following section, we go into further detail about the process of change, starting with the design thinking approach underlying this process perspective.

Design Thinking and the Process of Change

Mindful global leaders are process oriented, not simply goal and outcome fixated. There are many "noisy" signals and much extraneous information coming from the complex global environment, and decision-makers need a way of determining what is, or is not, important. Engineers use filters to remove unwanted noise from signals. Similarly, the change model presented in this section can act as a filter to block out noise and focus the attention of change agents on mission-critical variables, as well as to serve as a guide and a checklist for implementing successful change.

Underlying our conceptualization of change as a process is the idea of **design thinking**. We were first introduced to the notion when some of us authors attended a conference at the Stanford Design School and took a field trip to IDEO, one of the preeminent design firms in the world. The firm has used its process to design services, spaces, and even school systems in addition to consumer products. They emphasized to us that thinking like a designer can transform the way organizations develop products, services, processes, and strategy. Then-CEO Tim Brown further noted that "design thinking is a human-centered approach to innovation that draws from the designer's toolkit to integrate the needs of people, the possibilities of technology, and the requirements for business success" (Brown, 2017). In thinking about implementing strategic organizational change and requiring employees to behave differently, one realizes that it is a human-centered activity focused on designing new processes or systems for accomplishing organizational goals. As such, design thinking is closely related to the concept of agile: both focus on frequent iterations and a customer-focused orientation (Denning, 2016).

We quickly realized the potential of the design thinking process to inform our understanding of, and approach to, managing strategic change.

The design thinking process as defined by IDEO and the Stanford Design School consists of five steps: empathize, define, ideate, prototype, and test (Platner, 2017). For the purpose of this chapter, we translate and expand these steps to understand the specific activities to be undertaken.

1. **Empathize.** Observe and understand the situation or problem from the end user's point of view. In line with Alfred Korzybski's remark, "the map is not the territory," aim to gather a firsthand understanding of the situation as it exists on the ground and in reality, not merely in theory.
2. **Define.** Remember that the presenting problem or the initial assessment of a situation may not be the problem, but only a symptom of the same. It is thus important to take care in defining the real problem.
3. **Ideate.** Develop potential solutions, get user feedback, and repeat. The goal is to seek validation of ideas and possible acceptance of solutions. Jointly explore and formulate possible options, as well as build allies and coalitions that will support the change.
4. **Prototype.** Experiment with various solutions, or what designers refer to as rapid prototyping. Develop some alternatives, then evaluate and refine them.
5. **Test.** Create pilot projects that allow for short-term wins (Kotter, 2012). Implement these in a strategically selected location or locations with personnel who are supportive of the change.

The model that follows recognizes that change occurs in a larger organizational context. New strategies or changes to strategies usually are devised at headquarters by executives who often pay attention to only half the challenge that they face, which is strategy formulation. They focus on the big picture – the new product, service, or business model. However, they tend to not spend as much time or effort on the process of change – how the actual implementation will take place on the ground. Think back to the insight of Jesús Sotomayor: "Nobody ever lost money on a spreadsheet." It is easy to overestimate benefits and underestimate costs when planning change in the abstract. In the following, we thus delineate three phases in the actual unfolding of change initiatives, by exploring how to appraise the need for change, as well as commence and reinforce resulting initiatives. This provides managers with a checklist of things to consider, much like a pilot going through a before-takeoff checklist procedure.

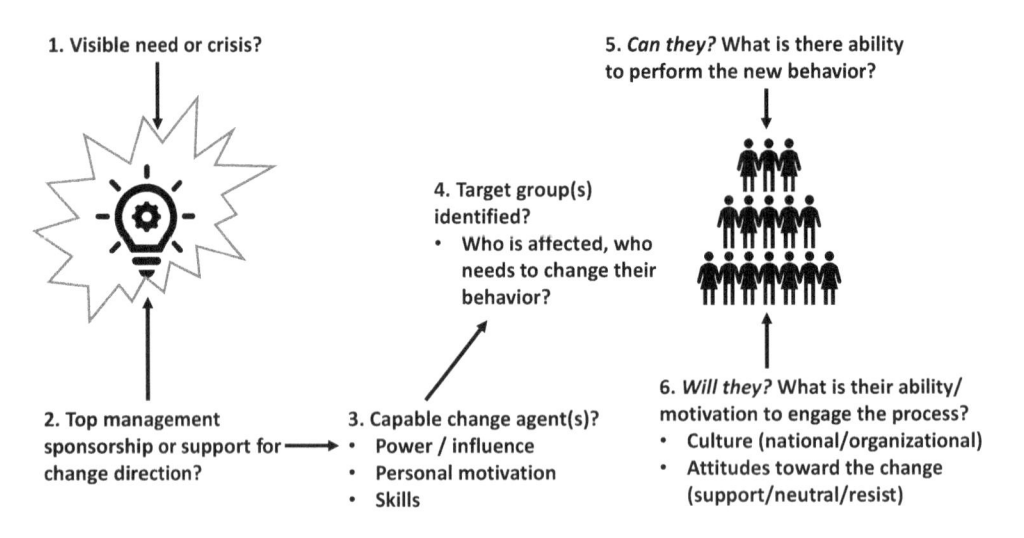

Figure 10.2 Phase 1: Appraising readiness for change.

Phase 1: Appraising Readiness for Change

An organization's readiness for change can be determined by analyzing several factors that affect the support of, or resistance to, a change initiative. It contains a number of elements, which are summarized in Figure 10.2 and described in further detail below.

Visible Need or Crisis?

Importantly, the need for change must be visible to decision-makers and employees for it to lead to engagement in change behavior. When an organization is doing well and engages in anticipatory change, managers and employees will not necessarily see the need for change. "If it ain't broke, don't fix it," or "Why should we change something that works well?" are common comments that can be heard in organizations. If, however, the environment has already shifted and the organization engages in reactive change, managers and employees will more easily recognize why the organization's strategy and employees' behaviors have to change.

> ### Reflection Question 10.3: The Stability–Change Paradox
>
> Organizational change involves embracing the paradox that changes coexist with a certain level of stability. Stability and change can be seen as mutually interdependent: stability enables change by supplying psychological safety and consistency, preserving existing knowledge pools/talent, fostering

engagement, and facilitating the availability of the necessary resources to work through changes. Change, on the other hand, enables the organization to move to a new state of (relative) stability by introducing innovation, experimentation, and new knowledge. Please think of an example of organizational change (perhaps from your answers to reflection question 10.1) and reflect: What remained the same, while the changes were implemented? In what way was doing "business as usual" enabling or hampering efforts to change the organization?

Diagnosing the visibility of the need for change is important because (1) employees will not embrace the change unless they see the need for it, and (2) the more the need for change is visible to employees, the faster managers can accelerate the change process. Once the need for change has become visible, change efforts are impacted by a number of factors:

- **Organizational management style.** Employees may be used to a management style that differs from the management style needed to lead the change effort. Many change practitioners in the West in countries like Canada and the United States advise a participatory approach to managing change that involves the employees. In many cultures, however, employees may be used to an authoritarian management style and might be confused if they were given a say in the change process.
- **History of change processes.** If change processes have gone awry in the past, employees may mistrust new change efforts. In the foreign subsidiaries of global organizations, expatriates often come in for limited-term assignments, unleash a major change effort, and then leave after a couple of years, independent of the completion status of the change process. This leaves local employees distinctly uncomfortable with the next change initiative.
- **Timing of the change effort.** If the resources of the organization are already stretched to the limit, it does not make sense to launch an anticipatory change effort that will further stretch resources. Such situations can arise during recessions, peak seasons, or when changes occur concurrently with other change efforts (e.g., a product launch).

The notion of timing is especially relevant when it comes to change in reaction to subpar performance, confronting managers with the dilemma of whether to persist or abandon a particular course of action. Management lore is full of stories where situations looked dire and no one believed in the cause anymore – except for the lone leader, who goes on to devote everything to the cause. Upon overcoming struggles and resistance, they eventually emerge as the vindicated hero, as turnaround is achieved.

For instance, when Apple was just weeks away from bankruptcy in 1997, Bill Gates famously stepped in to save Steve Jobs's company with a US$150-million investment from Microsoft. When the deal was announced at the Macworld Boston conference, the audience booed – but the subsequent meteoric rise of Apple (from a US$3.3-billion market capitalization in 1997 to $3 trillion in 2023, surpassing Microsoft) showed that the decision had been serendipitous after all (Markoff, 1997). Similarly, Tesla was on the verge of bankruptcy on Christmas Eve in 2008, and CEO Elon Musk had invested all of his personal money into the business. When no one seemed to believe in a turnaround anymore, he persisted – and in the last hour of the last possible day, the company was saved by an investment from the German automaker Daimler (Thompson, 2015).

What anecdotes such as this one do not capture, however, is the fact that they usually only make sense in hindsight, once we know that success was achieved and the leader was right to persist. What we don't hear about are all the other tales of leaders who persisted but failed even worse than if they had course-corrected earlier.

The phenomenon of investing more into failing ventures is called **escalation of commitment**, and discerning it from its counterpart, **premature abandonment**, is very difficult to do in practice. In 1961, for instance, British Petroleum and the American entrepreneur Bunker Nelson Hunt had been searching lucklessly for oil in the Libyan desert for seven years. When they were finally called home, they decided to drill one last time, three meters deeper into the ground than they had before. Thus they discovered "Hunt's Ace," one of the largest oil fields in the world (Drummond, 2014). What had looked like escalation of commitment for several years would in fact have been premature abandonment if they had left the site without that final drill (see Figure 10.3 for an illustration of the excessive persistence – premature abandonment dilemma).

Managers thus ought to be aware of the forces that elevate their proclivity toward either persistence (e.g., overconfidence, perceived need for self-justification, denial, social costs of admitting failure) or abandonment (e.g., loss aversion, perceived risk of persistence, intolerance of failure; Drummond, 2014). Importantly, cultural notions may play a role here, such that in those contexts where single-hero-narratives prevail, undue persistence can be more common. In contexts where uncertainty avoidance is valued, on the other hand, premature abandonment can occur more frequently.

EXCESSIVE PERSISTENCE   PREMATURE ABANDONMENT

Figure 10.3 Excessive persistence vs. premature abandonment.

Top Management Sponsorship or Support?

Once the need for change has been identified, change agents need to ensure top management support for the proposed changes or build support for it as necessary. Top management can provide both direction and resources (e.g., funds) and has the power to remove obstacles. More importantly, top management support signals the importance of the change effort. An important way for top management to support the change is to be visibly involved and, in conjunction with the change agent, be the initial communicators of the change effort.

Employees evaluate the sincerity of a change effort in large part vis-à-vis top management support and commitment. Hence, the visibility of top management support is critical for implementing change successfully, especially in the early stages of the change process. Employees will be more likely to engage in the change process enthusiastically if top managers make the effort to explain the goals and reasons underlying the decision. In addition, top management signals the importance of an organizational change through the allocation of resources.

Thus, while top management support alone will not elicit a change in employee behaviors, the absence of top management support can result in resistance or indifference among employees.

> ### Reflection Question 10.4: Resistance ... to Resistance to Change?
>
> If employees are not immediately onboard when presented with a change process, this is not necessarily the same as resistance to change. Employee complaints in connection with change processes may very well be real and should only be dismissed after careful consideration – constructive criticism and skepticism from employees should not be confused with resistance to change. Please reflect (and discuss):
>
> - How can constructive criticism be distinguished from resistance to change?
> - And what can managers and other change agents do to appreciate and respond to employees' reactions or otherwise include employee perspectives in (and before) a change process?

Capable Change Agent(s) Selected?

In selecting a change agent, managers need to ask three questions:

- **Does the change agent possess the power to implement the change?** Power can be derived from position, expertise, or personal connections, all relating to the credibility of the change agent. But note that different cultures emphasize different aspects of such bases of power. If employees do not have confidence or trust in the change agent, it will be difficult to motivate them to change.
- **What are the change agent's personal motivations?** The change agent must support the change and act as a positive example.
- **What are the change management knowledge, skills, and abilities of the change agent?** The change agent should have the communication, management, and conflict resolution skills needed to carry out the change effort. The more cultural boundaries that the change crosses, the greater the need for cross-cultural skills.

Depending on the size and global scale of a company and the magnitude of its change program, implementing a strategic change in multiple countries will likely require a whole team of change agents. The three questions above still need to be asked of team members.

Target Group(s) for the Change?

The key players in a change process include the obvious, immediately involved employees who will have to engage in new behaviors. However, less obvious stakeholders such as unions, suppliers, or customers whose business, systems, or behavior that may be affected need to be considered as well. Managers need to think about the organization as a social system and the target group(s) in the broadest possible terms by considering interdependencies between the immediate target group and others with whom they may interact.

If a global organization embarks on an organization-wide change effort, both headquarters and foreign subsidiaries are affected. Subsidiaries may differ regarding effective change processes, depending on local cultural differences, proximity to headquarters, and the relationship between headquarters and subsidiaries. Hence, managers of global change must understand local differences to determine the processes needed to motivate the expected change in employee behaviors.

Ability and Motivation to Perform the New Behavior?

In assessing the readiness of employees to change, two questions are critical. First is the **ability** question: *Can* they do it? What knowledge, skills, abilities, and resources do employees need to perform the new behaviors? Even if they are supportive, they may not be able to behave appropriately. Worry about an inability to perform the new behaviors often leads to anxiety and can undermine support for a change. If employees cannot perform the new behaviors, the change process will have to include education and/or training. Provision of other resources (e.g., computers or equipment) may be needed as well. A lack of resources will lead to frustration.

Second is the **motivation** question: *Will* they do it? What is the predisposition of employees toward the change? Will they support or resist it? This is an important question to assess the organization's readiness for change, because high motivation leads people to acquire the needed skills and to exert the extra effort that contributes to success. Managers need to identify opponents as well as supporters and analyze the reasons for the resistance or support. This analysis provides information about how opposition may be turned into support. If employees resist because, for example, they do not see the need for change, managers need to explain the links between the new strategy, the new behaviors, and the resulting improvements for the organization and the employees.

Are there preemptive problems like previous failed change efforts and a lack of trust that will discourage employees from engaging with the change effort? If so, then these issues need to be addressed before moving forward.

Here is where cultural differences potentially are important and managers need to understand employees' expectations about the appropriate role for managers in the change process and their expected role. Knowledge of local ways of expressing agreement and disagreement is very important.

Phase 1 can be viewed as a gap analysis and a checklist to assess an organization's and its employees' readiness to enact a new strategy. Our advice is that if any of the answers to the questions asked in Figure 10.2 are "no," then it is important to stop and work to turn those answers into "yes." The gap analysis can help managers create an initial change plan, but how do they really get the answers to the questions?

This is a time in the process when we believe design thinking can be a useful tool in a manager's toolbox, given the principles presented earlier in the chapter. Following the design thinking process might unfold as follows:

1. Get out of your office and visit subsidiaries to observe and understand firsthand what is going on there ("*empathize*").
2. Based on step 1, you may consider redefining your initial analysis and change plan ("*define*").
3. Meet the people who will be involved in the change ("*ideate*"). This can be beneficial in multiple ways:
   - It can give you an understanding of capabilities and possible resource needs.
   - The visits may generate ideas that you had not considered.
   - It can provide insight into personal motivations.
4. You can do a preliminary test of your initial solutions; assess who might be allies in the change program; and identify possible locations for pilot programs ("*prototype and test*").

Phase 2: Initiating Change and Adopting New Behavior

Leading strategic change is a full-time effort and requires intimate knowledge of the organization, which is why in most cases the change agent is a capable and respected insider. A capable change agent is one who has the requisite power, motivation, and change management skills. These skills include analysis, communication, conflict resolution, and, in global organizations, cultural intelligence. Once chosen, he or she needs to initiate the change by making sure the right people are in place for the new tasks and by building support for the change effort. This process might unfold as depicted in Figure 10.4.

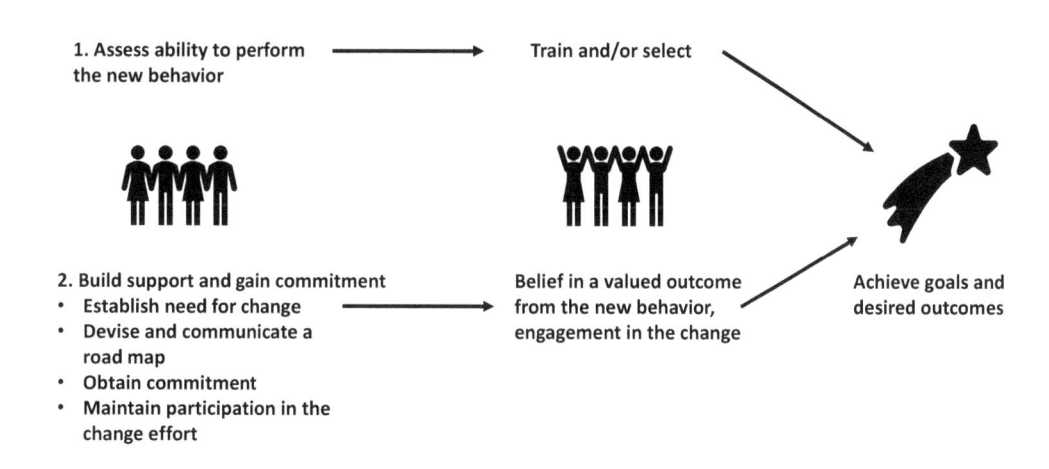

Figure 10.4 Phase 2: Initiating the change.

Ability to Perform New Behavior

When the change calls for behaviors that current employees do not have the skillset to perform, managers must either provide training or select new employees. Any training and/or selection should occur early because any inability to perform the new behaviors will cause employees to be frustrated, leading to resistance or lowered efforts.

We want to be clear about our use of the terms *selection* or its opposite *deselection*. We do not necessarily mean laying off a person. They may be transferred to another job or department, for example. It is important to have alignment between employees and tasks that need to be done. If new abilities to perform tasks are a necessary part of the strategic change, then it is important to have in place people who can do these tasks.

Building Support and Gaining Commitment

Change agents need to establish the need for change; build commitment and a winning coalition to support the change; and devise and communicate a road map to all stakeholders. Parts of this chapter focus on anticipatory change and early-stage reactive change in which educating employees is critical to the success of the change effort. It is important to recognize also that every change situation is different. If your change involves working with a union, negotiations will typically be required. If it is a crisis, then rapid top-down decision-making may be appropriate.

Establish the need for change. This is an educational process. In anticipatory change and even reactive change, resistance is most likely a result of different interpretations of the company's situation. The challenge is to establish the most accurate interpretation and to educate employees. It is essential to convince the target group that the change and associated new behaviors will lead to benefits, such as improved performance for their organization, recognition for them, or, possibly, monetary rewards. Some companies we have worked with have used the "burning platform" metaphor for this activity, which describes an explosion on an oil-drilling platform that causes a survivor to face a dire decision: jump into a sea of burning oil or face certain death on the platform. The metaphor is intended to convey a sense of immediate urgency and thus convince employees of an impending discontinuity, significant change, or potential crisis – and emphasize the insight that *not* changing can be the worst decision of all.

Learning new behaviors can be stressful and at first glance seems costlier than sticking with old habits. It is imperative that managers convincingly show that, after a suitable adjustment period, survival and success will follow. Since change is a complex undertaking that involves many different people and possibly different cultures and many different interpretations of the situation, it is usually difficult to convince people of the need to change with just words, a memo, or an e-mail. In addition to being on the lookout for the "If it ain't broken, why fix it?" attitude, change agents need to also be alert to the "What's in it for us?" attitude.

In such situations, it can be useful to make use of as many different media and types of data as possible. Personal visits by senior executives, video recordings, financial and market data, comparisons with competitors, and firsthand customer or supplier data all can help make the case for change.

The initiators of the change and the target groups may have different cultural backgrounds. Thus, the change agent must consider the perspectives of various groups of employees with regard to their knowledge of the change and their preferred mode of communication. Remember, this is the Bridging (B) part of the MBI model described in Chapter 5.

Devise and communicate a road map. A good road map shows the destination and a route to get there. These are the new strategy, objectives, task behaviors, and possible new organizational structures and systems that appear necessary. The road map describes the path toward these goals to include education, skills training to learn the new behaviors, and resources to be provided. It serves as a starting point, and the change agents update it through the application of the design thinking process.

The communication strategy should include feedback opportunities such as meetings (town hall and small group), surveys, or suggestion boxes. Depending on the cultural background, employees will react differently to the feedback modes. For example, indirect feedback through a trusted third party may be the local way of disagreeing upward while simultaneously seeming to agree publicly with a superior. This can be confusing to a manager from a culture where disagreement is openly and directly expressed regardless of different status levels.

Establishing effective dialogue takes time, something that managers do not have during crisis change. Instead, they must act quickly. It may be tempting to push through with a change process by creating crises. We do not recommend the use of such a tactic, as employees may lose confidence in the manager's objectives, or the organization might be exposed to unnecessary risks.

Obtain commitment. A clearly communicated and data-driven new strategy will build commitment, as will a diligent assessment of the readiness for change. However, it is of utmost importance that the target group is involved in the change process. The application of the design thinking process is helpful in this regard. Involvement breeds ownership of and commitment to the solution and to the change process. Involvement requires skillful leadership, as people may initially resist a change effort. It also takes time and, hence, is hardly feasible in crisis-driven change management.

Maintain participation in the change effort. The change agent must ensure that the target group stays involved throughout the change process. An effective change process typically includes joint discussions between the target group, the change agent, and top management. If the change yields negative outcomes for employees, such as job loss, outside facilitators may join the discussions to assist handling potential hostility.

The benefits of involving the target group are obvious. Employees will know more about the change process, and their task-related knowledge is relevant, in particular for determining new behaviors. As mentioned earlier, the most important benefit is a sense of ownership. It also becomes easier for this group to convince their peers to join in the change effort.

In obtaining commitment and gaining participation of employees in the change effort, the mode of involvement needs to be appropriate to the cultural norms of the situation. But it is equally important that the assessment of the appropriate mode is not based on stereotypes or assumptions based on partial or inaccurate information.

Phase 3: Reinforcing the Change

A change and the associated new behaviors are sustainable only if the organization supports and rewards them. We have seen many companies that have sent executives to management programs to develop general management skills and learn new techniques but have failed to reinforce the new lessons and ideas when they return. To facilitate the performance of the new behaviors, we recommend that senior executives do two things: plan for and showcase the small wins, and adjust the alignment model as necessary. Figure 10.5 summarizes these key aspects of Phase 3.

Small Wins

Our first recommendation is to make sure that outcomes the change agents told the target group to expect actually do occur. Many writers on the subject of change would argue in favor of the "theory of the small win." It is the small, incremental changes that stand the best chances of success (Quinn, 1980). Unless forced by a crisis into making major, system-wide changes, you may be wise to start small and let the change mature and grow. The diffusion of change beyond its initiation depends in large measure on perceived success – continuation of change is fueled by such success, and if early success is not apparent, the chances of realizing your goals are slim.

Recognizing that it is not feasible to control all variables in a change process or that trying to change an entire global company at once may not be feasible, we suggest eating the elephant one bite at a time. This is where the theory of the small win plays an important part. If you design your change plan to incorporate small wins, then you have some control over positive reinforcement that supports the

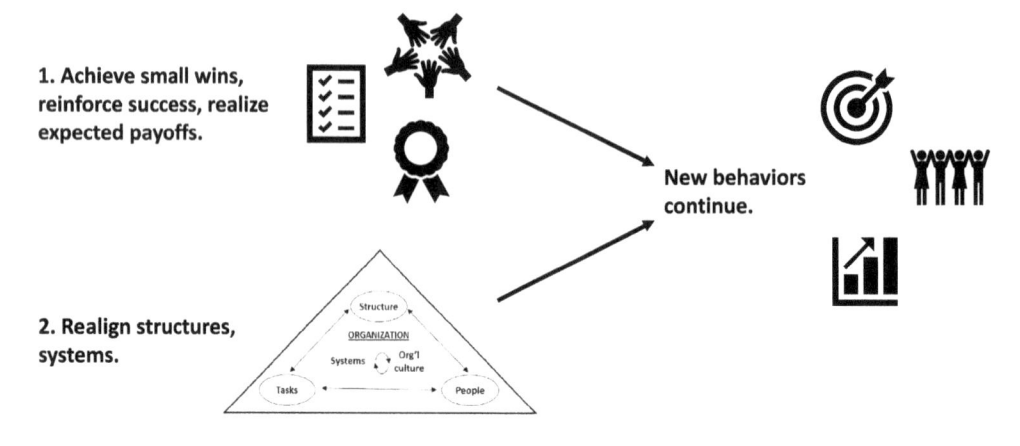

Figure 10.5 Phase 3: Reinforcing the change.

change. Employees will continue to engage in the new behaviors if the rewards (both tangible and intangible) match their expectations. They must see that their behaviors advance the organization's goals and serve their self-interests.

Small wins often are intermediate steps on the road to a larger strategic change. They build credibility, commitment, and allies and reduce the power of critics. Our recommendation in planning a change effort is to make sure to deliberately design in some small wins. Showcasing or celebrating successes is vital, because employees appreciate being part of a winning team, which in turn increases commitment and breeds confidence. At the same time, as important as it is to showcase small wins, it is equally important not to confuse achieving interim goals with final success – in other words, not declaring victory too soon (Kotter, 2012).

Realignment

If the existing systems, structures, and culture are not aligned with the new required behaviors, managers must adjust them. A potential new alignment model should be a part of the change plan, but modifications may be necessary based on insights gained during the design thinking process. This step is critical. Many employees respond to signals sent by reward and evaluation systems, for example. It does no good to train employees in new behaviors and then put them back in an organizational system that inhibits these new behaviors.

Conclusion: Organization Renewal

Organizational change efforts are not one-time events. They are continuous processes that require discipline and communication. Skipping a part of the change process can result in failure of the change initiative. The change model focuses on issues that managers should consider in change efforts and suggests actions that they can take. The model, in particular, centers on enabling and motivating employees to engage in the new behaviors.

Although the change model suggests a process for completing one change, the reality in a VUCA world is that it is often more meaningful to think about change as a continuous process that can be broken into actionable phases. In many industries, companies will need to engage in continuous business model innovation to stay competitive, which brings about substantive strategic alignment efforts.

In such an environment, organizations should ideally try to build a culture for change that becomes part of the organizational mindset – organizational cultures that create "nimbleness," allowing for agility, flexibility, and adaptation to changing environmental conditions on the one hand while fulfilling the traditional task of creating stability and predictability on the other (Worley & Lawler, 2006).

As discussed in earlier chapters, organizational structures and management systems have generally been viewed as means of reducing the variability and increasing the stability of human behavior and programs like total quality management or Six Sigma, for example, do that. Global corporations, however, do not operate in stable and predictable environments. Trying to manage a global company with models and processes designed to reduce variation in an environment that is characterized by dynamic complexity will probably be ineffective or possibly work only in the short term, if at all. Responding to dynamic complexity means that organizations must find the right people and to manage the complexity and execute action plans.

Change can be a challenge in any culture, but when trying to make changes in a global company in multiple countries, the challenge can be compounded by different cultural understandings. The MBI framework (Chapters 4 and 5), organizational alignment framework (Chapter 9), and design thinking and change model are all tools that will help provide mindful global leaders with the confidence and skills to negotiate the challenge.

Reflection Question 10.5: Ongoing Change

Please reflect on a change going on in your organization right now, or on a required change, perhaps as the result of the implementation of a new strategy (cf. Chapter 9):

1. Appraise the readiness for change. Is there a visible need? Does the change have top management support and commitment? Is there a ready and engaged change agent (maybe this is you!)? Is there a good understanding of the target group for the change?
2. In initiating the change and influencing people to adopt the new behavior, how well defined are the implementation mechanisms, especially regarding the following?
   a. Select people with particular skills and attitudes
   b. Train for new skills and knowledge
   c. Communicate to establish the need for change
   d. Build a road map with a clear process
   e. Develop commitment from stakeholders
   f. Ensure continuous participation from target group

Which could be improved? How?
3. What is being done to reinforce the change?
   a. How are small wins acknowledged, celebrated, and communicated?
   b. How are realignment needs monitored and responded to?
   c. How is the company supporting the need for continuous change and organizational renewal?

Reflection Question 10.6: Thinking about Design Thinking

Please form a group of three or four persons. Please each choose one of the 10 inspirational articles on design thinking listed below. Read your selected article and be prepared to share the main findings of the article with your group (or class). Please highlight in your presentation how your chosen article adds new or different perspectives to design thinking in connection with organizational change as outlined in this chapter.

- Cousins, B. (2018). Design thinking: Organizational learning in VUCA environments. *Academy of Strategic Management Journal, 17*(2), 1–18.
- Dorst, K. (2011). The core of "design thinking" and its application. *Design Studies, 32*(6), 521–532.
- Oster, G. W. (2008). Practitioners corner: Derailing design thinking. *International Journal of Leadership Studies, 4*(1), 107–115.
- Wrigley, C., Nusem, E., & Straker, K. (2020). Implementing design thinking: Understanding organizational conditions. *California Management Review, 62*(2), 125–143.
- Brenner, W., Uebernickel, F., & Abrell, T. (2016). Design thinking as mindset, process, and toolbox: Experiences from research and teaching at the University of St. Gallen. In W. Brenner & F. Uebernickel (Eds.), *Design thinking for innovation. Research and practice* (pp. 3–21). Springer.
- Ejsing-Duun, S., & Skovbjerg, H. M. (2019). Design as a mode of inquiry in design pedagogy and design thinking. *International Journal of Art & Design Education, 38*(2), 445–460.
- Felder, M., Kleinhout-Vliek, T., Stevens, M., & de Bont, A. (2023). From "if only" to "what if": An ethnographic study into design thinking and organizational change. *Design Studies, 86*, 101178.
- Liedtka, J. (2014). Innovative ways companies are using design thinking. *Strategy & Leadership, 42*(2), 40–45.

- Lee, K. (2021). Critique of design thinking in organizations: Strongholds and shortcomings of the making paradigm. *She Ji: The Journal of Design, Economics, and Innovation, 7*(4), 497–515.
- Dell'Era, C., Magistretti, S., Cautela, C., Verganti, R., & Zurlo, F. (2020). Four kinds of design thinking: From ideating to making, engaging, and criticizing. *Creativity and Innovation Management, 29*(2), 324–344.

Further Resources

To learn more about agile change, we recommend reading Rigby D., Elk, S., & Berez, S. (2020). *Doing agile right: Transformation without chaos*. Harvard Business Review Press, and McChrystal, G. S., Collins, T., Silverman, D., & Fussell, C. (2015). *Team of teams: New rules of engagement for a complex world*. Portfolio.

Two excellent books on change management are Brown's 2009 book *Change by design* (HarperCollins) and Spector's 2013 book *Implementing organizational change* (3rd ed) (Pearson). Another good source is Cawsey, T. F., Deszca, G., et al. (2015). *Organizational change: An action-oriented toolkit* (3rd ed) (Sage Publications).

For more on IBM's change story, the most comprehensive explanation is still Louis Gerstner Jr's 2002 book, *Who says elephants can't dance? Inside IBM's historic turnaround* (Harper Business).

If you would like to know more about the burning platform metaphor and where it originated, here is some background on the story: http://gardner.utah.edu/_documents/outreach/articles/pp-burning-platform.pdf

Bibliography

Bartlett, C. A., & Beamish, P. W. (2018). *Transnational management: Text and Cases in Cross-Border Management*. Cambridge University Press.

Brown, T. (2017). *Design thinking is a process for creative problem solving*. Ideou. Retrieved November 2017 from https://www.ideou.com/pages/design-thinking

Denning, S. (2018). *The age of agile: How smart companies are transforming the way work gets done*. Amacom.

Denning, S. (2019). *Understanding the agile mindset*. Retrieved June 2023 from https://www.forbes.com/sites/stevedenning/2019/08/13/understanding-the-agile-mindset/?sh=21c2ef485c17

Denning, S. (2016). *The Age of Agile: What every CEO needs to know*. Retrieved June 2023 from https://www.forbes.com/sites/stevedenning/2016/12/09/the-age-of-agile-what-every-ceo-needs-to-know/?sh=5d5f13d561ab

Drucker, P. (2004). *The daily Drucker: 366 days of insight and motivation for getting the right things done*. Harper Business.

Drummond, H. (2014). Escalation of commitment: When to stay the course? *Academy of Management Perspectives, 28*(4), 430–446.

Gerstner, Jr., L. V. (2002). *Who says elephants can't dance? Inside IBM's historic turnaround*. Harper Business.

Hadfield, C. (2013). *An astronaut's guide to life on earth*. Pan Macmillan.

Kotter, J. (2012). *Leading change*. Harvard Business Review Press.

Lagace, M. (2002). *Gerstner: Changing Culture at IBM – Lou Gerstner Discusses Changing the Culture at IBM*. HBS Working Knowledge, 12, https://hbswk.hbs.edu/archive/gerstner-changing-culture-at-ibm-lou-gerstner-discusses-changing-the-culture-at-ibm

Markoff, J. (1997). *Microsoft comes to the aid of a struggling Apple*. The New York Times. Retrieved July 2023 from https://www.nytimes.com/1997/08/07/business/microsoft-comes-to-the-aid-of-a-struggling-apple.html

Matthews, R. (n.d.). *What's the maximum number of times that you can fold a piece of paper?* Retrieved March 28, 2024, from https://www.sciencefocus.com/science/whats-the-maximum-number-of-times-that-you-can-fold-a-piece-of-paper

Meyer, M. (2007). *The fast path to corporate growth*. Oxford University Press.

Palmisano, S. (2003, July). *Our values at work: On being an IBMer*. IBM. Retrieved July 2017 from https://www.zurich.ibm.com/pdf/hr/Our_Values_at_Work.pdf

Platner, H. (2017). *An introduction to design thinking: Process guide*. Institute of Design at Stanford. Retrieved November 2017 from https://dschool-old.stanford.edu/sandbox/groups/designresources/wiki/36873/attachments/74b3d/ModeGuideBOOTCAMP2010L.pdf

Quinn, J. (1980, Summer). Managing strategic change. *MIT Sloan Management Review, 21*(4), 3–20.

Sernovitz, G. (2016, December 29). *What the organization man can tell us about inequality today*. The New Yorker. Retrieved July 2017 from https://www.newyorker.com/business/currency/what-the-organization-man-can-tell-us-about-inequality-today

Swatch Group. (n.d.). *Swatch Group History: The Swatch Group Yesterday*. Retrieved March 28, 2024, from https://www.swatchgroup.com/en/swatch-group/swatch-group-history

Thompson, C. (2015). *The Christmas Miracle that saved Tesla*. Business Insider. Retrieved June 2023 from https://www.businessinsider.com/elon-musk-shares-the-miracle-that-saved-tesla-2015-12

Wharton. (2002). *Lou Gerstner's turnaround tales at IBM*. Retrieved September 2023 from https://knowledge.wharton.upenn.edu/podcast/knowledge-at-wharton-podcast/lou-gerstners-turnaround-tales-at-IBM/

Whyte, W. (1956). *The organization man*. Doubleday Anchor Books.

Whyte, W. (2002). *The organization man*. Simon and Schuster Inc.; University of Pennsylvania Press.

Worley, C., & Lawler, E. (2006). Designing organizations that are built to change. *MIT Sloan Management Review, 48*(1), 19–23.

Decision-Making Cases

CASE III-1: CUSHY ARMCHAIR

Professor Brian Golden prepared this case solely to provide material for class discussion. The author does not intend to illustrate either effective or ineffective handling of a managerial situation. The author may have disguised certain names and other identifying information to protect confidentiality.

This publication may not be transmitted, photocopied, digitized or otherwise reproduced in any form or by any means without the permission of the copyright holder. Reproduction of this material is not covered under authorization by any reproduction rights organization. To order copies or request permission to reproduce materials, contact Ivey Publishing, Ivey Business School, Western University, London, Ontario, Canada, N6G 0N1; (t) 519.661.3208; (e) cases@ivey.ca; www.iveycases.com.

Copyright © 2001, Richard Ivey School of Business Foundation

Version: 2013-08-08

Cabletronica U.S. is a large, prosperous cable and wireless company based in upstate New York. In order to expand the scope of operations, it has recently targeted several strategically related industries in which to take a greater stake. Specifically, its research on changing demographic and cable viewing patterns concluded that reclining armchairs would be a growth business over the next 20 years. Cabletronica thus moved their minority investment position in Cushy Armchair (CA), based in Hong Kong, to a position of total equity and operating control. Cabletronica had just completed the acquisition of WorldFurniture, also based in New York.

Cushy Armchair is a recognized leader in the global reclining chair business, with fully autonomous business groups in 17 countries. This decentralized model evolved as a result of the substantial communication and logistics challenges facing multinationals in 1962, the year it was founded. And since economies of scale had been inconsequential while national market differences were substantial, this model had been sensible and had paid off handsomely. National differences could be seen, for example, in the U.S. division's recent introduction of reclining chairs that offered drink-holders and coolers built into the chair armrests. The Scandinavian market had introduced a "tingling fingers" massage chair, and although successful in that market, it was shown to have minimal attractiveness elsewhere. Other differences across the world included fabric preferences as well as size requirements (to accommodate varying torso characteristics as well as differing housing space constraints). Although historically a sleepy industry, the recliner industry is expected to heat up as a result of consolidation, new materials and technology, and shortening design cycles. In addition, competitors founded in the past few years have built global (centralized) rather than multidomestic (decentralized) businesses. This further enhances their potential cost and cycle-time advantages.

As part of Cabletronica's attempts to breathe new life into Cushy Armchair, the company dispatched Alison Sampson to take the helm of CA in Hong Kong, replacing the well-regarded founder, Frances Wong. Cabletronica's chief operating officer announced this appointment like all Cabletronica senior personnel changes, through a global e-mail message. Sampson's appointment was to begin March 14, the busiest time of year as most of the businesses ramped up design and manufacturing for strong end-of-year holiday sales. Sampson's immediate goals were to reduce costs, speed product design, and improve technology transfer. Specifically, production, design (fabric and style), sales and distribution (advertising), and procurement would be her focus in the short term. Sampson came to this with a successful background integrating numerous acquisitions for Cabletronica, mainly in the cable industry. She had risen through the finance ranks and was looking forward to the challenge of moving into a manufacturing setting and working for the first time with line managers. Wong would serve as a consultant to Sampson for the next six months in an effort to ensure a smooth transfer of control. Sampson, after careful examination of industry trends and competitor analysis, was keen to hit the ground running. After two weeks on the job, she drafted the following e-mail memorandum to the executives responsible for purchasing, sales, and design in each of the 17 countries.

To: National Purchasing, Marketing, and Design managers
From: Alison Sampson, C.A., M.B.A.
Date: April 1

As you know, our industry is changing dramatically, and although virtually all of our national business have been very successful these past years, that is going to change unless we change. I know you share my observations and concerns for the future of Cushy Armchair, and I trust that you will welcome these changes as I move to consolidate operations. We will begin with some small steps, all involving greater centralization in order to achieve economies of scale and scope. Specifically, from the first of next month onwards, I would like to request the following of all purchasing, marketing and design managers:

1. All purchasing managers should ensure that all chair glide-mechanisms, as well as fabric orders in excess of HK$1 million be contracted through WorldFurniture's procurement division in New York.
2. Advertising campaigns will in the future be co-ordinated through New York, where we have an expert group of advertising specialists. Therefore, all interest in launching new advertising campaigns should be cleared by our New York staff.
3. The New York staff should approve any substantial design and feature changes.

Though I haven't yet had the opportunity to meet with most of you, I look forward to doing so over the next three months to discuss the impact of these policy changes and the changes ahead.

A. Sampson, C.A., M.B.A.

Before sending this e-mail, Sampson asked Wong for his reaction. Wong suggested that e-mail was perhaps not the most effective way to deliver this message. While Sampson appreciated the advice, she felt e-mail was most expedient, given the urgency to change in time for next season's rush.

Two months later, in a casual conversation with the head of procurement for WorldFurniture, Sampson learned that no orders from any of Cushy Armchair's divisions had yet been received. It didn't take long for Sampson to learn that either all of her policy changes had been ignored *or* that no actions or decisions by purchasing, design or marketing had yet met the criteria set out by Sampson in her e-mail memo of April 1.

CASE III-2: BEIERSDORF AG: EXPANDING NIVEA'S GLOBAL REACH[1]

Vanessa C. Hasse wrote this case under the supervision of Professor Paul W. Beamish solely to provide material for class discussion. The authors do not intend to illustrate either effective or ineffective handling of a managerial situation. The authors may have disguised certain names and other identifying information to protect confidentiality.

This publication may not be transmitted, photocopied, digitized, or otherwise reproduced in any form or by any means without the permission of the copyright holder. Reproduction of this material is not covered under authorization by any reproduction rights organization. To order copies or request permission to reproduce materials, contact Ivey Publishing, Ivey Business School, Western University, London, Ontario, Canada, N6G 0N1; (t) 519.661.3208; (e) cases@ivey.ca; www.iveycases.com.

Copyright © 2013, Richard Ivey School of Business Foundation

Version: 2017-12-04

On April 26, 2012, Stefan F. Heidenreich walked into the conference center in Hamburg, Germany, for Beiersdorf's annual stockholder meeting. There he would officially be introduced as the new chief executive of the NIVEA producer and take the reins in a time of transition and complex challenges. His predecessor, Thomas-Bernd Quaas, was to give his farewell speech in front of 800 shareholders. Quaas had been the CEO for the past seven years and had led the company's international expansion. The company's flagship brand, NIVEA, had turned 100 years old last year, and consumers around the world were familiar with the cream in a signature blue tin. The expansion was not only geographical but also categorical: a number of innovations had resulted in a broad product range under the NIVEA brand.

However, this expansion was hurting profitability. While competitors like Henkel, Unilever, and Procter & Gamble had recovered from the economic recession and were expanding rapidly, Beiersdorf's revenues were still lagging expectations. As a consequence, the company had announced a major restructuring project costing €270 million in March 2010. Under the slogan "Focus on skin care. Closer to markets," Beiersdorf aimed at reorganizing its consumer division to boost revenues again. The objective was to increase profitability by downsizing structures and streamlining the expansive product range while remaining responsive to local tastes by granting foreign subsidiaries more responsibility.

As Quaas spoke about the progress of the restructuring project, it became clear that it was far from complete. Although most measures were on target, operating margins were still not satisfactory.[2] Just a few months earlier, Beiersdorf had announced a plan to cut up to 1,000 jobs worldwide. The progress of restructuring had been slower than planned because the challenges had been bigger than expected.[3] In fact, the last quarter of 2011 had ended with a loss. Thus, an investor at the annual stockholder meeting voiced his opinion: "The management has been asleep for the past few years instead of setting the course

---

[1] This case has been written on the basis of published sources only. The interpretation and perspectives presented in this case are not necessarily those of Beiersdorf or any of its employees.

[2] Daniela Stürmlinger, "Hamburger Nivea-Hersteller: Aktionäre kritisieren Beiersdorf-Vorstand," *Hamburger Abendblatt*, www.abendblatt.de/hamburg/article2259390/Aktionaere-kritisieren-Beiersdorf-Vorstand.html, accessed September 15, 2012.

[3] "Gewinnrueckgang: Konzernumbau lastet schwer auf Beiersdorf," *Financial Times Deutschland*, www.ftd.de/unternehmen/industrie/:gewinnrueckgang-konzernumbau-lastet-schwer-auf-beiersdorf/60159302.html, accessed September 21, 2012.

for the company's future!"[4] This outcry raised numerous questions: Was Beiersdorf's restructuring approach the right way to get back on track? Would the company be able to compete against the big players in the industry again? And was downsizing really the right path to international growth? Heidenreich had certainly taken on a major task.

Background

In 1882, Paul C. Beiersdorf, owner of a pharmacy in Hamburg, Germany, filed a patent for the manufacturing process of medical sticking plasters, which he had developed in collaboration with leading dermatologists. Through academic publications, the company acquired popularity among doctors and pharmacists, which helped increase revenues. In 1890, the associated laboratory was sold to the pharmacist Dr. Oscar Troplowitz, who turned the small enterprise into a rapidly growing consumer products manufacturer with a consumer care and a sticking plasters/adhesives division. In accordance with the company's medical and academic background, Dr. Troplowitz continued to focus on a highly scientific research and development process.

Around 1900, a chemist at Beiersdorf discovered the emulsifying agent *Eucerit*, which allowed for a stable combination of oil and water. This discovery laid the foundation for the unique skin-moisturizing formula of the NIVEA cream. The first NIVEA cream tin was sold in 1911. It provided good results at low cost and quickly became popular among a broad range of consumers. Beiersdorf was quick to continue to deliver innovations such as Labello, a creamy colorless lipstick, and other care products. The sticking plasters segment grew as well, with innovations such as Hansaplast and Leukoplast.

In 1922, Beiersdorf was turned into a public company. The success of the young company's brands, especially NIVEA, gave it the opportunity to expand internationally. By the beginning of World War II, Beiersdorf had 34 representative offices abroad (in countries including the United States, Mexico, Brazil, and Thailand) and subsidiaries in England and Austria. As a result of the war, the trademark rights for NIVEA in these international locations were confiscated by the respective countries. It took years for Beiersdorf to regain all the rights, a process that ended in 1997 with the repurchase of the rights in Poland.

These setbacks, however, did not stop Beiersdorf from expanding internationally again after the war. By the end of the fiscal year 2011, the company employed 17,666 people, owned more than 150 subsidiaries worldwide, and earned 85 percent of its total revenues (€4.75 out of €5.6 billion) outside of Germany.

Throughout its 130-year history, Beiersdorf repeatedly emphasized traditional values such as trust, reliability, and quality. This was in accordance with the tradition of the "Hanseatic merchant" – in the old trading town of Hamburg, businessmen took pride in the fact that they concluded reliable contracts with a simple handshake. Thus, the company built on its traditional foundations and continuous innovations to attain its vision: "To become the best skin care company in the world."

Company Structure

Divisions/Regions

Due to its origins, Beiersdorf was divided into two rather unrelated divisions. The main division, *consumer*, generated the lion's share of the company's revenues at 84 percent, or €4.73 billion, in 2011. In this division, about 13,870 employees worked to serve three segments: the mass market; the dermo-cosmetic segment, which offered medical care products; and the premium segment. Each segment had very successful brands: the leading global brands were NIVEA for the mass market, Eucerin for the dermo-cosmetic segment, and La Prairie for the premium segment.

The other division, *tesa*, was named after its main brand and became a legally independent subsidiary in 2001. About 3,795

[4] See note 2.

employees developed adhesives for industrial and consumer clients. In 2011, the tesa division contributed 16 percent of Beiersdorf's total revenue. After major restructuring efforts, which ended in 2010, as well as the recovery of the auto industry, which was one of the main buyers of adhesives, the tesa division outperformed the consumer division in terms of growth rates: while the consumer division grew by 1.1 percent in 2011, tesa reported growth of 7.9 percent.

In 2011, the consumer division generated 59 percent of its revenue in Europe (of which 15 percent came from Germany), 12 percent in Latin America, 7 percent in North America, and 22 percent in Africa, Asia, and Australia combined. A network of more than 150 subsidiaries ensured that these markets were served reliably (see Exhibit 1). Moreover, Beiersdorf exported to 200 countries, making it a company with a truly global reach.

In an earlier effort to reduce costs and become more profitable, Beiersdorf closed many of its 20 European facilities between 2006 and 2008.[5] By 2012, Beiersdorf owned 16 production facilities including locations in Germany, Spain, Poland, Argentina, Chile, Brazil, Mexico, Indonesia, India, China, Thailand, and Kenya. Throughout Beiersdorf's current restructuring project, even more production facilities were either closed (e.g., in Germany and the United States) or put up for sale (e.g., in Switzerland).

For years, much of Beiersdorf's internationalization strategy focused on securing profits in mature markets such as Europe. Among these, Germany continued to be one of Beiersdorf's most important. In 2011, sales within the consumer division were €717 million, which accounted for 34 percent of all sales in the European market. At the same time, Beiersdorf invested in exploring new opportunities for growth in some of the BRIC nations (Brazil, Russia, India, and China). In fact, between 2010 and 2011, consumer sales in Latin America and Eastern Europe (including Russia) grew by 15.2 percent and 5.2 percent, respectively – as opposed to a 3.7 percent decrease in Western European sales (excluding Germany, which decreased by 3.2 percent).

However, not all of the internationalization strategy worked as smoothly as Beiersdorf had hoped. Despite its long experience with international expansion, Beiersdorf faced difficulties, especially with regards to entering new emerging countries. In 2007, the company acquired 85 percent of the shares of C-Bons, China's third-largest hair care producer, for €269 million. The objective was to enhance awareness of the NIVEA brand in the Chinese market by benefiting from C-Bons's distribution and sales network. However, the returns on this investment were slow in coming. In 2011, the investment resulted in a €50 million loss because the Chinese brand could not prevail over international competitors who had entered the Chinese market. As a result, unsold products filled C-Bons's warehouses. Moreover, the distribution and sales network turned out to be heavily focused on non-target areas, whereas Beiersdorf's initial intention was to use C-Bons's network to distribute the NIVEA brand throughout the large Chinese market, mostly to metropolises. As a consequence of this unsuccessful acquisition, Beiersdorf had to lay off about 4,000 Chinese workers and report massive write-offs, and the newly appointed executive board member James C. Wei left the company by the end of 2011.[6]

The U.S. market was identified as another area with major potential for growth. Despite intensive marketing efforts, profits remained sluggish[7] and revenues increased by a meager 2.1 percent in 2011. After pursuing a strategy of deemphasizing non-focus brands, a

---

[5] "Beiersdorf strafft seine Produktion," *Financial Times Deutschland*, www.ftd.de/unternehmen/industrie/: beiersdorf-strafft-die-produktion/31664.html, accessed September 17, 2012.

[6] Christoph Kapalschinski, "Beiersdorf und sein Ringen um den Klassenerhalt," *Handelsblatt*, www.handelsblatt.com/unternehmen/industrie/hauptversammlung-beiersdorf-und-sein-ringen-um-den-klassenerhalt/6555266.html, accessed September 16, 2012.

[7] Ibid.

process which had started in 2007, Beiersdorf remained present in the U.S. market with its core skin care brands like Eucerin and NIVEA. Since then, Beiersdorf outperformed its closest category competitors in terms of sales growth by at least 5.2 percentage points.[8] In total, however, the North American market accounted for only 6 per cent (€300 million) of Beiersdorf's total revenues.[9]

Management and Ownership

In accordance with German corporate governance law, the management of Beiersdorf was divided into two distinct committees. While the executive board was in charge of developing a company strategy and putting it into action, the supervisory board's task was to assist the executive board in developing the strategy while taking the interests of various stakeholders (e.g. employees, investors) into consideration.

Until April 26, 2012, the *executive board* (composed of Peter Feld, Ralph Gusko, Dr. Ulrich Schmidt, and Ümit Subaşi) was chaired by the CEO Thomas-Bernd Quaas. Quaas was born in 1952 and entered the company in 1979 as a trainee. He worked his way up through a sales/marketing career until he ascended to the CEO position in 2005. He was described as a manager who was so enthusiastic about Beiersdorf's brands that he preferred them over any other brands, even in his personal life.[10] When Quaas became the CEO, subordinates and employee representatives described him as "smart and very warm in interaction." "He is a very open, team-minded, communicative person. And he is one of us."[11]

Heidenreich's appointment as CEO came as a surprise to shareholders and employees[12] and marked a major change from the company's previous tradition of appointing CEOs from within the company. Heidenreich came from the food producer Hero as a replacement for Quaas. There had been an internal heir apparent for the CEO position for years, the former board member Markus Pinger (responsible for brands and supply chain), but he surprisingly announced he would leave the company by June 30, 2011 in the midst of the restructuring process. Pinger knew the company inside out, and Quaas had been hopeful that Pinger would put it back on track and lead it to its former success. Pinger's departure thus left Beiersdorf in a state of shock and uncertainty. Rumor had it that disagreements about the strategic direction of the repositioning were the reason for the sudden falling out.[13]

Stefan F. Heidenreich, born in 1962, became a member of the executive board on January 1, 2012, before his official appointment as CEO of Beiersdorf on April 26, 2012. In his previous position at Hero, where he had been the CEO for seven years, Heidenreich convinced many investors of his ability to generate continuous profits and grow share prices. Employees at Beiersdorf, however, were skeptical of the company outsider,

---

[8] "Kalender & Präsentationen – Investorenkonferenz German Investment Seminar (New York)," *Beiersdorf AG*, www.beiersdorf.de/Investoren/Kalender_Pr%C3%A4sentationen/2010.html, accessed September 29, 2012.

[9] Birger Nicolai, "Beiersdorf steht in China vor einem Scherbenhaufen," *Die Welt*, www.welt.de/wirtschaft/article13898137/Beiersdorf-steht-in-China-vor-einem-Scherbenhaufen.html, accessed September 29, 2012.

[10] Thiemo Heeg, "Porträt: Der Nivea-Mann," *Frankfurter Allgemeine Zeitung*, www.faz.net/aktuell/wirtschaft/portraet-der-nivea-mann-1233868.html, accessed October 1, 2012.

[11] Translation. "Beiersdorf: 'Mr Nivea' geht – Quaas übernimmt," *Hamburger Morgenpost*, www.mopo.de/news/beiersdorf-mr-nivea-geht-quaas-uebernimmt,5066732,5792958.html, accessed October 1, 2012.

[12] Daniela Stürmlinger, "Nivea-Hersteller Beiersdorf: Thomas B. Quaas: 'Endlich mehr Zeit für die Familie,'" *Hamburger Abendblatt*, www.abendblatt.de/wirtschaft/article2081992/Thomas-B-Quaas-Endlich-mehr-Zeit-fuer-die-Familie.html, accessed October 1, 2012.

[13] "Wechsel im Topmanagement: Beiersdorf beruft Ersatz für Kronprinzen," *Financial Times Deutschland*, www.ftd.de/karriere/management/:wechsel-im-topmanagement-beiersdorf-beruft-ersatz-fuer-kronprinzen/60068592.html, accessed October 1, 2012.

especially during a time of economic and cultural turmoil.[14] Heidenreich had strong supporters, though, including the head of the supervisory board, Dr. Reinhard Pöllath, who had met Heidenreich during an investor meeting and who was the driving force behind convincing him to join Beiersdorf.[15] Like Beiersdorf, Heidenreich's former employer Hero had undergone major restructuring efforts and was controlled in part by a major blockholder. Heidenreich had been especially efficient in managing the blockholder's influence and leading Hero to continuous growth and increased share prices.[16]

Heidenreich was described as strong-willed and dynamic but also risk-seeking and aggressive.[17] He held the title of Vice European Champion in windsurfing[18] and sometimes participated in races with his cross-country motorcycles.[19] In the company's newsletter to employees, he gave a glimpse of what to expect from him: "I know what I want .... You have to act – not just react."[20]

The *supervisory board* of Beiersdorf, on the other hand, was composed of twelve members and chaired by Pöllath. Three of the twelve board members represented Beiersdorf's work council, whereas another three members were associated with the investment firm Maxinvest AG, including Pöllath. Maxinvest AG was owned by the Herz family and owned a total of 50.89 percent of Beiersdorf's shares. This gave the family, and Michael Herz as the CEO of Maxinvest AG especially, major voting right privileges and influence over the executive board members' decisions.

After Quaas's resignation as a member of the executive board, he would be appointed a new member of the supervisory board. This was an uncommon procedure, and some felt that it would have been better corporate governance to allow for the usual two-year cooling-off period. Such a period was usually imposed on CEOs after resignation to make sure that they did not hinder the correction of mistakes they had made during their time as executive board members.[21]

Apart from the 50.89 percent held by the Herz family, Beiersdorf itself owned 9.99 percent of its shares and had 39.12 percent in free float. It was listed in the Deutscher Aktien Index (DAX), a German stock exchange index of the country's 30 biggest public companies in terms of market capitalization and order volume.

Research and Development (R&D)

Beiersdorf's commitment to rigorous skin research became apparent when it opened its extended Hamburg-based Global Research Center in 2004. In the 16,000-square-meter (172,222 square foot) building complex, researchers from all over the world collaborated with universities and dermatological institutes to not only work on product innovations but also advance basic skin research. The center was considered one of the biggest and most modern skin research facilities in Europe, and one of its highlights was the auditorium: a room with the architectonic shape of a cell. Researchers at Beiersdorf called it the "philosopher's stone" because it housed research efforts that aimed at discovering

---

[14] Sven Oliver Clausen, "Kopf des Tages: Stefan Heidenreich – Blaue Hoffnung," *Financial Times Deutschland*, www.ftd.de/unternehmen/industrie/:kopf-des-tages-stefan-heidenreich-blaue-hoffnung/60176444.html, accessed October 1, 2012.

[15] Johannes Ritter and Jürgen Dunsch, "Heidenreich neuer Vorstandsvorsitzender: Ein Frühstücksdirektor für Beiersdorf," *Frankfurter Allgemeine Zeitung*, www.faz.net/aktuell/wirtschaft/unternehmen/heidenreich-neuer-vorstandsvorsitzender-ein-fruehstuecksdirektor-fuer-beiersdorf-11484569.html, accessed September 30, 2012.

[16] See note 14.

[17] Mario Brück, "Das neue Gesicht des Nivea-Konzerns," *Wirtschaftswoche*, www.wiwo.de/unternehmen/industrie/beiersdorf-heidenreich-im-profil/5965848-2.html, accessed September 30, 2012.

[18] See note 14.

[19] See note 17.

[20] See note 14.

[21] Sven Oliver Clausen, "Neuer Vorstandschef. Beiersdorf holt Schwartau-Chef," *Financial Times Deutschland*, www.ftd.de/unternehmen/industrie/:neuer-vorstandschef-beiersdorf-holt-schwartau-chef/60112470.html, accessed September 30, 2012.

ingredients that had rejuvenating effects on the skin.

Another feature of the center was its capacity to simulate the climatic conditions of other regions such as Asia or Latin America. Thus, the majority of consumer tests were conducted there, with an annual total of about 1,500 tests with 21,000 test persons to ensure that products met quality standards as well as consumer needs. About 1,000 studies were carried out in countries other than Germany to respond to local consumer preferences. For this purpose of local adaptation, Beiersdorf collaborated with approximately 50 institutes from around the world. This was in accordance with an important part of Beiersdorf's innovation philosophy, especially with regards to NIVEA: "to offer the best skin care for every age, skin type, culture, and location."[22]

For example, in 2008 Beiersdorf launched a product called "Whitening Oil Control" – a whitening cream specifically designed for male Indian consumers with oily skin. A similar product line, NIVEA Body Natural Tone, was popular in Latin America, where it helped consumers even their skin tone as a response to sun damage. The local adaptation strategy was so pervasive that many of Beiersdorf's international customers considered NIVEA a local brand.

As a result of this heavy emphasis on innovation and local adaptation, the NIVEA brand had proliferated from its humble beginnings to become the largest skin care brand in the world, incorporating more than 500 products and a variety of product lines (see Exhibit 2). This innovation intensity was also reflected in the fact that about 30 percent of Beiersdorf's revenue was generated with products that were less than five years old.[23] In 2011 alone, Beiersdorf filed for 81 new product-related patents. R&D expenses were €163 million in 2011 (as opposed to €152 million in 2010), and 967 employees worldwide worked in this area (out of which 564 were in the consumer division and 403 were in the tesa division).

In 2011, Beiersdorf intensified its innovation efforts by launching a web-based open innovation platform called Pearlfinder. It enabled external researchers from all over the world to collaborate with Beiersdorf on creative ideas and research proposals with regards to products and packaging. The purpose of this platform was to generate innovative concepts early on in the research process.

Despite this vast research effort and emphasis on innovation, there were some trends that Beiersdorf addressed relatively late. For instance, the first product that responded to consumer preferences towards more natural products was introduced in 2011 – many years after competitors had already established themselves in the natural cosmetics realm.[24]

Brands

Beiersdorf's portfolio encompassed a total of nine brand families: NIVEA, Eucerin, La Prairie, Labello, Florena, 8&4, Hansaplast, SLEK, and tesa. Of these, the first three were Beiersdorf's global brands.

NIVEA

NIVEA was Beiersdorf's most important brand by revenue and brand awareness. The first NIVEA tin was sold in 1911, which made it almost as time-honored a brand as Campbell's Soup or Coca-Cola. The brand's name was derived from the Latin word for snow (*nix, nivis*) because of the cream's pure white color. NIVEA soon became a household brand for many families in booming post-war economies, and the ritual of using the cream was passed down from parents to children. Many consumers had childhood memories that involved the NIVEA brand – for instance, when families started to have disposable income again after World War II, they went

---

[22] Translation. "Verschiedene Hauttypen: Verschiedene Bedürfnisse," *NIVEA*, www.nivea.de/Unser-Unternehmen/beiersdorf/NIVEAHistory#!stories/story02, accessed October 1, 2012.

[23] Thomas Schönen (Beiersdorf AG), "NIVEA," www.beiersdorf.de/GetFile.ashx?id=3061, accessed October 9, 2012.

[24] "Nivea: Beiersdorf liftet seine Kultmarke," *Wirtschaftswoche*, www.wiwo.de/unternehmen/nivea-beiersdorf-liftet-seine-kultmarke/5262218.html, accessed September 25, 2012.

on vacation, and the preferred choice for sunscreen was NIVEA. Beiersdorf fostered the connection between its products and the beach by releasing the now-famous inflatable NIVEA beach ball – a marketing strategy so successful that NIVEA distributed about 20 million of these balls due to popular demand within the past 40 years alone. The profoundness of such a generation-spanning product might be reflected in the fact that consumers associated the brand with core values like trust, honesty, reliability, family, and quality, even in 2011.

Over the decades, a variety of categories evolved under the NIVEA brand umbrella, including products for babies, body hygiene, body care, deodorants, facial care, hair care & styling, care for men, moisturizers (NIVEA soft), sunscreen, and makeup. All of these categories again had specific product types subsumed underneath them; for instance, the *deodorants* category was divided into spray, roll-on, diffuser, stick, and cream. However, not only did the products themselves change, but also their design. While the original NIVEA cream was sold in a tin with a simple white and blue design, the new products were now packaged in fashionable designs like curvy bottles with a color palette ranging from white to beige, light blue, dark blue, and purple.

In 2011, the brand celebrated its 100th birthday with a major worldwide marketing campaign "NIVEA – 100 Years Skin Care for Life." In an effort to bridge the historical origins of the brand with modern consumer tastes, Beiersdorf initiated a massive social network campaign with American singer Rihanna as the voice of the anniversary campaign. By the end of 2011, the brand's Facebook page had 2.7 million fans.

Eucerin

Eucerin was based on the same chemical innovation as NIVEA, the emulsifier *Eucerit*. While NIVEA's main focus was on personal care, the Eucerin product line was intended for medical use. Thus, the first products of the line were soap, cream, and powder for the treatment of wounds, and were often recommended by dermatologists. Beiersdorf's main focus with the Eucerin brand was on providing the basic ingredients for ointments to pharmacies. This changed in 1950, when Beiersdorf launched yet another innovation based on scientific research: the ointment Eucerin-ph5, which protected the natural acid mantle of the skin. This was significant because it marked Beiersdorf's entry into selling ready-made products to consumers through pharmacies as the preferred distribution channel.

During the 1960s, the Eucerin product line evolved from a brand with predominantly medical use to one that could also be applied to more common issues such as rough skin on hands or feet. Like NIVEA, the Eucerin brand incorporated a wide range of innovations, from products for extra dry skin or atopic eczema to sun protection and anti-aging. That it was recommended by dermatologists and sold in pharmacies gave it a considerable amount of credibility.

In 2011, Eucerin celebrated its 111th birthday with a global marketing campaign that aimed at direct interaction with the consumer at the point of sale. By that time, the brand included eight product lines, which covered medically relevant skin issues from head to toe. It was available in 41 countries on four continents and generated 4.8 percent growth in 2011 compared to the previous year.

La Prairie

In 1991, Beiersdorf acquired the Laboratoires La Prairie, a Swiss research company that had evolved from the renowned Clinique La Prairie in Montreux. Laboratoires La Prairie was focused on developing high-end anti-aging skin care products with ingredients such as caviar and a substance called Exclusive Cellular Complex. Soon after the acquisition, Beiersdorf integrated other high-end brands into the La Prairie group, including Juvena and Marlies Möller beauty hair care. By the end of 2011, the La Prairie brand was available in 17 countries on three continents and reported growth of 3.4 percent in 2011.

Financial Situation

At the beginning of the global financial crisis in 2008, Beiersdorf reported the best results in its history with €5,971 million in revenues (an 8.4 percent increase compared to 2007) and earnings before interest and taxes (EBIT) of €797 million (including special items) (see Exhibits 3-4). The consumer division contributed €5,125 million (85.83 percent) to the company's revenues, while the tesa division reported €846 million (14.17 percent). This success culminated in Beiersdorf's inclusion in the DAX, Germany's index of the country's top 30 companies in terms of book value and market capitalization, on December 22, 2008.

Just a year later, Quaas started his *Letter to Investors* in the annual report with the statement that "2009 was a difficult year."[25] Although revenues were still at a relatively high level at €5,748 million, the company's growth rates had declined to −0.7 percent.

By 2012, Beiersdorf had still not returned to its previous strength. At the annual stockholder meeting, the company reported €5,633 million in revenues, less than in 2008. Unlike in previous years, the tesa division was the main driver of growth. Another reason for the delayed recovery was identified in the massive write-downs in the context of the acquisition of C-Bons. These impairment losses accumulated to €213 million between 2010 and 2011. Moreover, the restructuring project not only increased one-time costs by €213 million in 2011 alone but also led to a decrease in sales in affected countries.

Despite these sobering figures, Beiersdorf was not a poor company by any means. In fact, it enjoyed a comfortable cushion of reserves worth about €2.2 billion.[26] The continuous flow of profits from the NIVEA brand kept the company liquid.

Market Environment and Competition

Beiersdorf was operating in an industry with very strong global competitors, the closest of which were Procter & Gamble, Unilever, L'Oreal, Henkel, and Johnson & Johnson (see Exhibits 5-7). The effects of such strong competition were especially apparent in the Western European market, where market saturation was high. Here, Beiersdorf competed for limited shelf space in an economic environment of decreasing market size. In many cases, innovations such as stain-free deodorants were merely designed as a substitute for a competitor's product on the shelves. Thus, Quaas identified "maintaining the current position" as a priority.[27]

The European Union's economic downturn, with Greece announcing its bankruptcy and other countries being on the verge of it, did not help matters. The inflation rate in the European Union grew by 2.7 percent while consumer spending practically stagnated at 0.5 percent in 2011. This economic environment was especially distressing because the European market was where Beiersdorf earned most of its profits. Here, Beiersdorf earned 92 percent of its EBIT, with 59 percent of its revenue in the consumer division. Thus, any losses in European market share were especially painful.

At the same time, Beiersdorf was still able to defend the NIVEA product family's position as the biggest skin care brand in the world,[28] with 166 category leadership positions worldwide.[29] Clearly, the value of the NIVEA brand did not go unnoticed by Beiersdorf's competitors. Procter & Gamble expressed its continued interest in the company. In 2003, a takeover by the U.S.-based company was prevented with the help of the Herz family and the Hanseatic City of Hamburg. In 2010, Procter & Gamble's CEO Robert McDonald renewed interest in an acquisition.[30]

The Restructuring Project

The overarching vision for the restructuring process was for Beiersdorf to get closer to becoming the world's best skin care company. The slogan "Focus on Skin Care. Closer to Markets" was the means through which this vision was to be attained.

---

[25] Translation. "Finanzberichte – Geschäftsbericht 2009," *BeiersdorfAG*, www.beiersdorf.de/Investoren/Finanzberichte/Gesch%C3%A4ftsberichte.html, accessed September 15, 2012.

[26] See note 6.

[27] See note 9.

[28] Jens Bergmann, "Die Vernuenftige," *Brand Eins Online*, www.brandeins.de/magazin/qualitaet-ist-was-geht/die-vernuenftige.html, accessed September 30, 2012.

[29] See note 8.

[30] Birger Nicolai, "Nivea macht Sorgenfalten," *Die Welt*, www.welt.de/print/die_welt/wirtschaft/article12101352/Nivea-macht-Sorgenfalten.html, accessed October 2, 2012.

Focus on Skin Care

A core element of the restructuring strategy was for Beiersdorf to remember its core competence – excellence in skin and body care – and refocus its resources accordingly. This entailed an emphasis on core product lines. For instance, the NIVEA brand was heavily advertised with a new marketing platform of integrated 360-degree channels (including radio, TV, and cruise ships). Moreover, non-core product lines were deemphasized. In Europe alone, Beiersdorf removed about 1,000 products from shelves (19 percent of the European assortment). Beiersdorf not only sold regionally distributed brands like Juvena and Marlies Möeller but also exited the makeup category.

Closer to Markets

One of the first measures after the restructuring project was announced in 2010 was the rearrangement of responsibilities in the top management team. In 2009, members of the executive board were associated with corporate functions such as finance, law, logistics, sustainability, communication, and marketing. In March 2010, Beiersdorf announced the introduction of two functional (finance/HR and brands / supply chain) and three regional areas of responsibility (Europe / North America, Asia/Australia, and emerging markets). Each member of the board was responsible for either a function or a region.

Since the beginning of this rearrangement within the top management team in 2010, all of the members of the executive board had left the company. Quaas's resignation marked the departure of the last member who had also been on the board in 2009, before the rearrangement. Thus, in 2012 the functions and regional responsibilities were divided such that Peter Feld was responsible for Europe / North America, Ralph Gusko for brands and supply chain (as a replacement for Markus Pinger), and Dr. Ulrich Schmidt for finance/HR. Ümit Subaşi was appointed a new member of the board in March 2011 and given the responsibility to develop the emerging markets area.

Beiersdorf also realigned its corporate structures in an effort to grant regional subsidiaries more decision-making authority. Only the broad corporate strategy was to be provided by the headquarters. This led to an overall thinning of structures with an accompanying cost savings of an estimated €90 million per year, predicted to be in full effect by 2014. In 2011, Beiersdorf cut about 1,000 jobs in the consumer division worldwide (almost 7 percent of the division's workforce),[31] with most of them at the German headquarters.

Challenges

On April 26, 2012, all of these measures were still very fresh in the minds of many of Beiersdorf's shareholders and employees. Just a year ago, at the 2011 annual shareholder meeting, employees were standing outside of the conference center, protesting against the job cuts.[32] The company, founded on traditional values like trust and consistency, was deeply shaken to the core of its cultural identity. Within just a few years, Beiersdorf had evolved from a company with stable management and solid profitability to one with high volatility in the top management team and sobering year-end accounts, as well as ever-growing competitors. Employees were confused and anxious; shareholders were starting to become impatient.

Had Beiersdorf taken too big a bite of the world's consumer market? Was Beiersdorf big enough to take on its major competitors? Had it made the right choice of strategy and was it the right timing for its implementation? And how could it balance profitability while maintaining local responsiveness? On April 27, 2012, Heidenreich's first day as the new CEO, he would have to be ready to deliver.

---

[31] Daniela Stürmlinger, "Nivea-Konzern: Beiersdorf baut 1000 Arbeitsplätze ab," *Hamburger Abendblatt*, www.abendblatt.de/wirtschaft/article2111611/Beiersdorf-baut-1000-Arbeitsplaetze-ab.html, accessed September 15, 2012.

[32] Daniela Stuermlinger, "Angst vor Arbeitslosigkeit: Beiersdorf schminkt sich ab – Protest auf Hauptversammlung," *Hamburger Abendblatt*, www.abendblatt.de/wirtschaft/article1865982/Beiersdorf-schminkt-sich-ab-Protest-auf-Hauptversammlung.html, accessed October 8, 2012.

Exhibit 1: Beiersdorf Subsidiaries

Region	Countries with subsidiaries
North America	United States, Canada
Latin America	Argentina, Bolivia, Brazil, British Virgin Islands, Chile, Costa Rica, Dominican Republic, Ecuador, El Salvador, Guatemala, Colombia, Mexico, Panama, Paraguay, Peru, Uruguay, Venezuela
Europe	Belgium, Bulgaria, Denmark, Germany, Estonia, Finland, France, Greece, United Kingdom, Ireland, Iceland, Italy, Croatia, Latvia, Lithuania, Macedonia, Netherlands, Norway, Austria, Poland, Portugal, Serbia, Romania, Russia, Sweden, Slovakia, Slovenia, Spain, Czech Republic, Turkey, Ukraine, Hungary
Africa	Ghana, Kenya, Morocco, South Africa
Asia	China, India, Indonesia, Japan, Kazakhstan, South Korea, Malaysia, Singapore, Thailand, United Arab Emirates, Vietnam
Australia	Australia, New Zealand

Source: www.beiersdorf.de.

Exhibit 2: Major Innovations under the NIVEA Brand Umbrella

Date of introduction	Product
Dec. 1911	Original NIVEA cream
1919	NIVEA soap
1920	NIVEA hair milk (hair care product line)
1922	NIVEA shaving soap for men
1927	NIVEA bleaching cream
1960	NIVEA baby line
1986	NIVEA for men
1991	NIVEA hair care, NIVEA deodorant
1992	NIVEA body
1993	NIVEA sun, NIVEA visage
1994	NIVEA vital for mature skin
1996	NIVEA bath care
1997	NIVEA beauté
1998	NIVEA visage anti-wrinkle cream Q10, NIVEA hand
...	...
by 2012	More than 500 products in various product lines

Sources: NIVEA, http://www.nivea.de/Unser-Unternehmen/beiersdorf/NIVEAHistory#!stories/story02, accessed September 17, 2012; Thomas Schönen (Beiersdorf AG), "NIVEA," www.beiersdorf.de/GetFile.ashx?id=3061, accessed October 9, 2012.

Exhibit 3: Beiersdorf Balance Sheet 2008–2011

[in million €]	2008	2009	2010	2011
ASSETS				
Intangible assets	398	382	306	172
Property, plant, and equipment	727	725	716	635
Non-current financial assets/securities	11	10	438	686
Other non-current assets	4	2	2	3
Deferred tax assets	36	58	76	87
Non-current assets	**1,176**	**1,177**	**1,538**	**1,583**
Inventories	634	561	632	699
Trade receivables	894	906	1,001	1,019
Other current financial assets	128	91	72	113
Income tax receivables	45	41	63	73
Other current assets	81	96	112	115
Securities	897	955	704	712
Cash and cash equivalents	613	767	973	941
Non-current assets and disposal groups held for sale	-	-	-	20
Current assets	**3,292**	**3,417**	**3,557**	**3,692**
	4,468	4,594	5,095	5,275
LIABILITIES				
Share capital	252	252	252	252
Additional paid-in capital	47	47	47	47
Retained earnings	2,280	2,450	2,609	2,700
Accumulated other consolidated income	−129	−123	−1	3
Equity attributable to equity holders of Beiersdorf AG	**2,450**	**2,626**	**2,907**	**3,002**
Non-controlling interests	10	10	13	14
Equity	**2,460**	**2,636**	**2,920**	**3,016**
Provisions for pensions and other post-employment benefits	235	221	209	190
Other non-current provisions	131	138	117	107
Non-current financial liabilities	72	7	8	5
Other non-current liabilities	6	5	5	4
Deferred tax liabilities	164	161	155	148
Non-current liabilities	**608**	**532**	**494**	**454**

Exhibit 3 (continued)

[in million €]	2008	2009	2010	2011
Other current provisions	363	391	486	527
Income tax liabilities	99	107	126	82
Trade payables	690	699	863	946
Other current financial liabilities	174	158	135	172
Other current liabilities	74	71	71	78
Current liabilities	**1,400**	**1,426**	**1,681**	**1,805**
	4,468	4,594	5,095	5,275

Sources: "Finanzberichte – Geschäftsberichte – Ausgewählte Kennzahlen 2009," Beiersdorf AG, www.beiersdorf.de/Investoren/Finanzberichte/Gesch%C3%A4ftsberichte.html, accessed October 20, 2012; "Finanzberichte – Geschäftsberichte – Ausgewählte Kennzahlen 2011," Beiersdorf AG, www.beiersdorf.de/Investoren/Finanzberichte/Aktuelle_Finanzberichte.html, accessed September 30, 2012.

Exhibit 4: Beiersdorf Income Statement and Additional Financials 2008–2011

[in million €]	2008	2009	2010	2011
INCOME STATEMENT*				
Sales	**5,971**	**5,748**	**5,571**	**5,633**
Change against prior year (in %)	8.4	–3.7	7.8	1.1
Consumer	5,125	5,011	4,698	4,696
Tesa	846	737	873	937
Europe	4,090	3,767	3,450	3,414
America	832	851	932	993
Africa/Asia/Australia	1,049	1,130	1,189	1,226
Cost of goods sold	–1,979	–1,882	–2,016	–2,077
Gross profit	**3,992**	**3,866**	**3,555**	**3,556**
Marketing and selling expenses	–2,874	–2,766	–2,336	–2,454
Research and development expenses	–149	–149	–152	–163
General and administrative expenses	–292	–283	–278	–291
Other operating income	108	94	86	158
Other operating expenses	–89	–175	–292	–375
Special factors relating to divestments	96	-	-	-
Special factors relating to the realignment of the consumer supply chain	5	-	-	-
Operating result (EBIT)	**797**	**587**	**583**	**431**
Interest income	47	21	19	31

Exhibit 4 (continued)

[in million €]	2008	2009	2010	2011
Interest expense	−14	−15	−13	−19
Net pension result	8	−2	−6	−2
Other financial result	−16	−8	−30	−1
Financial result	25	−4	−30	9
Profit before tax	822	583	553	440
Taxes on income	−255	−203	−227	−181
Profit after tax	567	380	326	259
Profit attributable to equity holders at Beiersdorf AG	562	374	318	250
Profit attributable to non-controlling interests	5	6	8	9
ADDITIONAL FINANCIALS				
Cost of materials**	1,453	1,199	1,370	1,437
Personnel expenses**	922	947	974	1,000
Basic/diluted earnings per share (in €)	2.48	1.65	1.40	1.10
Dividend per share (in €)	0.90	0.70	0.70	0.70
Beiersdorf's shares—year-end closing price	42.00	45.93	41.53	43.82
Market capitalization as of Dec. 31	10,584	11,574	10,466	11,043
Employees as of Dec. 31	21,766	20,346	19,128	17,666

*The income statement was prepared according to the cost of sales approach.

**The cost of materials and personnel expenses are included but not explicated in the income calculation and are therefore listed here for transparency purposes.

Sources: "Finanzberichte – Geschäftsberichte – Ausgewählte Kennzahlen 2009," Beiersdorf AG, op. cit.; "Finanzberichte – Geschäftsberichte – Ausgewählte Kennzahlen 2011," Beiersdorf AG, op. cit.

Exhibit 5: Biggest Global Competitors (Overview)

	Location of HQ	Employees	Revenue [in million US $]	Revenue growth to previous year [%]	Net profit [in million US $]	Most similar product to NIVEA
Beiersdorf	Hamburg, Germany	17,666 (in 2011)	7,843.4 (FY* 2011)	1.1	348.1	-
Unilever	London, U.K.	171,000 (in 2011)	64,700.7 (FY 2011)	5.0	5,920.5	Dove, Vaseline, St. Ives
Procter & Gamble	Cincinnati, U.S.A.	126,000 (in 2012)	83,680 (FY 2012)	3.2	10,756	Olay
Johnson & Johnson	New Brunswick, U.S.A.	117,900 (in 2012)	65,030 (FY 2011)	5.6	9,672	Aveeno, Clean & Clear

Exhibit 5 (continued)

	Location of HQ	Employees	Revenue [in million US $]	Revenue growth to previous year [%]	Net profit [in million US $]	Most similar product to NIVEA
L'Oreal S.A.	Clichy, France	68,900 (in 2011)	28,325.7 (FY 2011)	4.3	3,395.2	L'Oreal Paris, Garnier
Henkel AG & Co KGaA	Düsseldorf, Germany	47,265	21,728.4 (FY 2011)	3.4	1,744.7	Aok, Schwarzkopf, Diadermine
Avon Products, Inc.	New York City, U.S.A.	40,600 (in 2011)	11,291.6 (FY 2011)	3.9	513.6	Avon
Estee Lauder Companies	New York City, U.S.A.	32,300 (in 2011)	8,810 (FY 2011)	13.0	700.8	Estee Lauder, Clinique, Aveda
Clarins S.A.	Neuilly-sur-Seine, France	6,100	Not published			Clarins

* FY: Fiscal Year

Note: In order to allow for better comparability, all figures were converted into U.S. dollars.

Source: Marketline Database, Company Reports 2011–2012.

Exhibit 6: Global Market Segmentation

		Regional share [%]			
Industry	Global market value [in million $, 2010]	Asia-Pacific	Europe	Americas	Middle East & Africa
Global facial care	50,891.9	51.0	30.1	17.1	1.7
Global sun care	7,326.1	29.5	39.8	28.9	1.8
Global hand & body care	18,049.7	41.1	31.2	25.8	1.8
Global hair care	49,515.7	30.8	35.0	30.9	3.3

Source: Marketline Database, Industry Reports 2011.

Exhibit 7: Competitors (Overview of Selected Market Shares)

	Market value in 2010	Market growth in 2010	1st position		2nd position		3rd position		Rest
	[million US $]	[%]		[%]		[%]		[%]	[%]
FACIAL CARE INDUSTRY									
Global	50,891.9	4.6	L'Oreal S.A.	13.6	Unilever	7.8	**Beiersdorf AG**	7.5	71.0
Europe	15,335.3	3.6	L'Oreal S.A.	23.8	**Beiersdorf AG**	16.3	Estée Lauder	6.1	53.8
Germany	2,229.2	2.1	**Beiersdorf AG**	22.5	L'Oreal S.A.	20.6	Reckitt Benckiser PLC	8.0	48.9
Asia-Pac.	25,953.1	5.4	Kao Corporation	10.1	Unilever	10.1	Shiseido	9.1	70.7
China	7,703.4	10	L'Oreal S.A.	16.6	Procter & Gamble	12.5	Cheng Ming Ming	12.0	58.9
U.S.	5,012.5	3.3	Procter & Gamble	20.9	Johnson & Johnson	14.2	Unilever	12.4	52.5
Canada	821.5	3.3	Unilever	35.8	Johnson & Johnson	18.2	**Beiersdorf AG**	11.2	34.8
SUN CARE INDUSTRY									
Global	7,326.1	5.1	L'Oreal S.A.	14.0	**Beiersdorf AG**	13.5	Johnson & Johnson	9.8	62.7
Europe	2,919.0	3.4	L'Oreal S.A.	26.0	**Beiersdorf AG**	23.0	Johnson & Johnson	6.3	44.7
Germany	200.6	0.8	**Beiersdorf AG**	29.8	L'Oreal S.A.	20.0	Coty Inc	12.3	38.0
Asia-Pac.	2,161.2	5.4	Kao Corporation	14.3	**Beiersdorf AG**	7.9	Shiseido	6.4	71.5
China	762.7	5.8	Kao Corporation	29.9	Procter & Gamble	9.3	Johnson & Johnson	8.3	52.6
U.S.	1,155.6	4.3	Merck & Co., Inc.	23.8	Johnson & Johnson	18.2	Energizer Holdings	18.1	39.9
Canada	172.6	3.6	L'Oreal S.A.	17.5	Schering-Plough	12.2	Johnson & Johnson	9.4	60.8

Exhibit 7 (continued)

	Market value in 2010	Market growth in 2010	1st position		2nd position		3rd position		Rest
	[million US $]	[%]		[%]		[%]		[%]	[%]
HAND & BODY CARE INDUSTRY									
Global	18,049.7	3.8	Beiersdorf AG	13.0	Unilever	9.5	L'Oreal S.A.	7.3	70.2
Europe	5,632.3	2.5	Beiersdorf AG	24.0	L'Oreal S.A.	11.8	Unilever	10.6	53.5
Germany	1,216.7	0.7	Beiersdorf AG	39.6	Unilever	12.9	L'Oreal S.A.	6.9	40.6
Asia-Pac.	7,420.1	3.7	Shiseido	16.0	Kao Corporation	10.7	Beiersdorf AG	5.8	67.5
China	no data								
U.S.	2,374.1	3.3	Unilever	13.0	Kao Corporation	11.4	Avon Products	8.7	66.8
Canada	no data								
HAIR CARE INDUSTRY									
Global	49,515.7	3.1	Procter & Gamble	24.1	L'Oreal S.A.	16.7	Unilever	11.7	47.4
Europe	17,326.0	2.0	Procter & Gamble	32.5	Henkel KGaA	17.0	-	-	50.5
Germany	2,473.9	0.3	Henkel KGaA	31.5	L'Oreal S.A.	26.6	P&G	18.7	23.2
Asia-Pac.	15,266.1	4.5	Procter & Gamble	22.0	Unilever	15.2	Kao Corporation	11.4	51.4
China	3,767.1	5.4	Procter & Gamble	39.4	Unilever	14.1	Beiersdorf AG	7.9	38.6
U.S.	7,232.3	−1.6	Procter & Gamble	28.2	L'Oreal S.A.	20.1	Unilever	9.6	42.1
Canada	1,116.0	2.3	Procter & Gamble	30.4	Unilever	15.7	L'Oreal S.A.	13.7	40.2

Source: Marketline Database, Industry Reports 2011.

CASE III-3: TIFFANY AND SWATCH: LESSONS FROM AN INTERNATIONAL STRATEGIC ALLIANCE[1]

Vanessa C. Hasse wrote this case solely to provide material for class discussion. The author does not intend to illustrate either effective or ineffective handling of a managerial situation. The author may have disguised certain names and other identifying information to protect confidentiality.

This publication may not be transmitted, photocopied, digitized, or otherwise reproduced in any form or by any means without the permission of the copyright holder. Reproduction of this material is not covered under authorization by any reproduction rights organization. To order copies or request permission to reproduce materials, contact Ivey Publishing, Ivey Business School, Western University, London, Ontario, Canada, N6G 0N1; (t) 519.661.3208; (e) cases@ivey.ca; www.iveycases.com. Our goal is to publish materials of the highest quality; submit any errata to publishcases@ivey.ca. i1v2e5y5pubs

Copyright © 2020, Ivey Business School Foundation   Version: 2020–11-25

On November 23, 2018, the US jewelry maker Tiffany & Co. (Tiffany) received notice from the Supreme Court of the Netherlands. It was the final decision after a years-long legal battle with the Swiss watchmaker The Swatch Group Ltd. (Swatch) regarding a strategic alliance the two companies had formed in 2007. The decision stated that an earlier verdict that had required Tiffany to pay Swatch about CHF480 million[2] in damages (plus additional legal fees) was upheld, and with this, all rights of appeal had been exhausted.

This final outcome was a far cry from the excitement and hope for a successful future that were apparent when the two companies announced the formation of their strategic alliance on December 2, 2007. The goal of the alliance had been to design, manufacture, market, and distribute luxury watches under Tiffany's brand name, utilizing Swatch's watchmaking capabilities and vast distribution network.

In the announcement, Michael (Mike) J. Kowalski, Tiffany's chairman and CEO, had stated: "I am delighted that these discussions have led to this historic agreement. Swatch Group is the best conceivable strategic partner for Tiffany's long-planned re-entry into watch distribution. It is the leader in the high-end watch business with unparalleled distribution capabilities and experience in the luxury segment of the watch business." Similarly, Nicolas G. Hayek, Swatch's chairman and co-founder, had noted: "This agreement is a pathbreaking strategic move …. It allows without any financial capital transaction the maximum utilization of manufacturing and distribution resources of both partners."[3]

It thus came as a surprise to many that less than four years later, the optimism was all but

---

[1] This case has been written on the basis of published sources only. Consequently, the interpretation and perspectives presented in this case are not necessarily those of Tiffany & Co, The Swatch Group Ltd., Tiffany Watch Co. Ltd., or any of their employees. Please also note that cross-referenced footnotes are from the original publication.

[2] CHF = Swiss franc; all currency is in CHF unless specified otherwise; average annual conversion rates (CHF/USD) relevant to the time frames in this case, CHF1 equals: US$1.200 (2007), US$1.083 (2008), US$1.088 (2009), US$1.043 (2010), US$0.888 (2011), US$0.938 (2012), US$0.978 (2018). Source: OECD Data, "Exchange Rates," https://data.oecd.org/conversion/exchange-rates.htm, accessed January 20, 2020.

[3] The Swatch Group Ltd., "The Swatch Group and Tiffany Announce Strategic Alliance," December 2, 2007, www.swatchgroup.com/en/services/archive/2007/swatch-group-and-tiffany-announce-strategic-alliance, accessed January 1, 2020.

gone. On September 12, 2011, Swatch released the following statement:

> Today Swatch Group terminated its cooperation contracts with Tiffany & Co. This action became necessary following Tiffany & Co's systematic efforts to block and delay development of the business .... [The strategic alliance] will be permitted to wind down current business over the course of two years following effective termination of the cooperation contracts. Swatch Group and [the strategic alliance] will press claims for damages against Tiffany ... in compensation for the loss of planned long-term future business.[4]

Tiffany's response was swift. The same day, a press release was published, stating:

> It has become increasingly clear that Swatch is unwilling to honor the terms of our agreement, make the necessary commitments and work cooperatively to develop the business for TIFFANY & CO. watches in the luxury space. Despite assurances to the contrary made in 2007, Swatch has failed to provide appropriate distribution for TIFFANY & CO. brand watches, with the result that our current business forecasts do not include any meaningful increase in watch sales or royalty income. Tiffany has honored its obligations under the agreement, and insisted that Swatch honor its own obligations, particularly its obligation to respect Tiffany's rights regarding brand-management and product design. Tiffany & Co. is confident that its position will be vindicated in the pending arbitral proceedings in relation to this matter and Swatch's misconduct.[5]

How could this "historic agreement" and "pathbreaking strategic move" have turned into such bitter statements, followed by a prolonged legal battle and substantial financial consequences? What had gone wrong, and was there any way in which Kowalski or Hayek could have foreseen or even prevented this outcome? Most importantly, reflecting in 2018, what lessons were learned that could benefit either company in the formation and operation of future strategic alliances?

Tiffany & Co (Tiffany)

In 1837, during an era of high economic growth in the United States, 25-year-old jewelers Charles Lewis Tiffany and John B. Young opened the first Tiffany store in New York City. At the time, much of the competition was in Europe, where the focus was on opulent and ceremonial designs. To distinguish its brand, Tiffany focused on simple and harmonic designs inspired by nature. In 1845, Tiffany first published its annual catalog, the Tiffany Blue Book, which by 1878 had started featuring the signature blue color that eventually became the company's trademark and most recognizable marketing feature.[6]

Soon, Tiffany had built a reputation for excellence in craftsmanship, demonstrated by being the first American company to receive the grand prize for silver craftsmanship at the 1867 world's fair in Paris. In 1878, Tiffany presented the Tiffany Yellow Diamond, one of the largest yellow diamonds ever discovered. It was cut into 82 facets by Tiffany's gemmologist Dr. George Frederick Kunz, making it particularly reflective of light. Another milestone was the introduction of the solitaire

---

[4] The Swatch Group Ltd., "End of Partnership with Tiffany & Co.," September 12, 2011, www.swatchgroup.com/en/services/archive/2011/end-partnership-tiffany-co, accessed January 1, 2020.

[5] Tiffany & Co., "Tiffany Responds to Swatch Termination Claim," September 12, 2011, https://investor.tiffany.com/news-releases/news-release-details/tiffany-responds-swatch-termination-claim, accessed January 1, 2020.

[6] "About Tiffany & Co.," *Tiffany & Co., For the Press*, http://press.tiffany.com/ViewBackgrounder.aspx?backgrounderId=33, accessed January 3, 2020; Bethany Biron, "Tiffany & Co. Was Just Acquired by LVMH in a Massive, $16.2 Billion Deal. Here's How the Iconic Jewelry Chain Became one of America's Most Beloved Luxury Brands," *Business Insider*, November 26, 2019, www.businessinsider.com/tiffany-and-co-history-iconic-luxury-brand-2019-11, accessed January 3, 2020.

six-prong setting for engagement rings in 1886 (trademarked as the "Tiffany Setting"), at a time when diamond rings were typically set in bezels. This laid the foundation for the company's dominant reputation in the engagement ring business.[7]

The company's growing reputation had earned it an appointment as the Royal Jeweller to European monarchs, the Ottoman Emperor, and the Czar of Russia. It counted US presidents and other prominent members of American and international society as its customers, and it designed and manufactured historic artefacts such as the Great Seal of the United States (depicted on the US dollar bill), the Congressional Medal of Honor (the United States' highest military award), and the Vince Lombardi Trophy for the NFL's Super Bowl championship.[8]

Tiffany had been active in the watch business since the middle of the nineteenth century and was one of the first foreign companies to establish a manufacturing base in Geneva, as early as the 1860s and 1870s. This continued until World War II, after which other products were prioritized.[9] By the late 1980s, watches were contributing about 9–10 percent of sales, when the strategic decision was made to largely abandon the complex and costly manufacturing of watches and focus on the jewelry business (particularly engagement rings) instead.[10] This led to the arrangement that Tiffany's brand watches were sourced from various third-party Swiss manufacturers,[11] contributing only about 2 percent of Tiffany's net sales by 2007. In contrast, although Tiffany had sold its first watch 30 years before Cartier and 130 years before Bulgari, competitors such as these now had a much larger watch business (about 30–35 percent of sales[12]). This evident gap eventually led the company to consider wholesale distribution as an opportunity for rekindling its watch business, as Tiffany's James (Jim) Fernandez, executive vice-president and chief financial officer, described:

> We have been very successful in design grade watches. But with 200 store distributions in only our stores, it's just never going to add up to the big part of our business.... If you look at some of our luxury competitors, their watch businesses can represent anywhere from 30 per cent to 50 per cent of their business. So there is definitely an opportunity here for us.[13]

At the time the strategic alliance with Swatch was announced, Tiffany was a thriving multinational enterprise (MNE) (see Exhibit 1). By a large margin, jewelry constituted Tiffany's main business segment at about 86 percent of net sales, while tableware, timepieces (including wrist watches), and other products contributed the remaining amount. The company's shares were mostly held by a range of institutional owners (for a total of at least 87 percent).[14]

Tiffany was headed in 2007 by Wharton- and Harvard-educated Kowalski, who had joined the company in 1983 as director of planning and became CEO in 1999, and then chairman in 2003. An avid environmentalist, Kowalski

---

[7] Ibid.
[8] Ibid.
[9] Thomson Reuters StreetEvents, "Tiffany & Co. at Deutsche dbAccess Global Consumer Conference," June 11, 2015, p. 10, Mergent Investext, accessed January 2, 2020.
[10] Thomson Reuters StreetEvents, "Tiffany & Co. at William Blair Growth Stock Conference," June 12, 2013, p. 6, Mergent Investext, accessed January 2, 2020.
[11] Tiffany & Co., "Year-End Report 2010," K-14, https://investor.tiffany.com/static-files/39cee6c0-5e2a-4a27-81cb-3bca87eefcf6, accessed January 2, 2020.
[12] Thomson Reuters StreetEvents, "Tiffany & Co. at Deutsche Bank Securities Global Consumer, Food Retail and Luxury Goods Conference," June 17, 2010, p. 7, Mergent Investext, accessed January 2, 2020.
[13] Thomson Reuters StreetEvents, "Tiffany & Co. at Goldman Sachs Global Retailing Conference," September 3, 2008, p. 9, Mergent Investext, accessed January 2, 2020.
[14] Tiffany & Co., *Yahoo! Finance*, https://finance.yahoo.com/quote/tif/holders?ltr=1, accessed January 3, 2020.

emphasized the importance of embracing a bigger perspective – a notion that was reflective of Tiffany's organizational culture overall: "You find a lot of humility here – this management team, although we have been here over 20 years together, we know we were dealt a good hand. It is not about us." This was mirrored by Tiffany's president, James (Jim) Quinn: "There is only one star in this company, and it is Tiffany. It is not about me or Mike or us, it is about the brand. ... We have married the product into our culture – the pursuit of excellence through the quality, value, and integrity of the product without elitism, but with Tiffany being part of our people and part of our customers' lives."[15]

The Swatch Group Ltd. (Swatch)

Swatch was the result of a merger between Swiss watchmaking companies ASUAG and SSIH, initiated by Hayek in 1983. ASUAG was founded in 1931 and possessed strong watch movement manufacturing capabilities along with brands such as Rado and Longines, while SSIH originated in 1930 and produced high-quality watches under brand names such as Omega and Tissot. Both companies, however, experienced severe financial difficulties due to a lack of strategy,[16] the repercussions of a recession, the "quartz crisis" in the Swiss watch industry (i.e., the replacement of mechanical watches by digital watches), and increasing competition from Asia. Hayek, at the time CEO of Hayek Engineering, was tasked with developing a strategy for turning the two companies around, and his recommendations ultimately led to the merger (with the resulting company being called SMH Group) as well as his nomination as CEO. Five years later, the company was the most valuable watchmaker in the world (Swatch Group, n.d., last paragraph)

Several distinguishing features contributed to this success story. First, Swatch emphasized the importance of keeping production in high-wage Switzerland and being vertically integrated throughout the watchmaking value chain. This differentiated Swatch from many of its peers and allowed it to maintain control, create synergies, and gather extensive knowledge. Another key aspect was the then recent development of injection-molding machines for the automation of plastic watch manufacturing, which allowed for significantly reduced production costs. The first watch made with this technique was launched by the SMH Group in March 1983 under the newly created Swatch brand name. The name Swatch stood for "second watch" and resembled the idea that watches could be replaceable fashion accessories at an affordable price point (CHF50 for the first several years). The colorful designs led customers to pick different Swatch watches for different outfits ("watch wardrobing") and collectors to invest in special editions. Notable designs included a transparent watch (the "Jellyfish"), watches with furry straps (e.g., "Fury" or "Frozen Tears"), a watch with scented straps ("Granita di Frutta"), and watches designed to look like vegetables, which were sold at farmer's markets ("Swatchetables").[17] However, the company aimed to offer more than just a fashion style, as Hayek explained:

> We are offering [people] ... a strong, exciting, distinct, authentic message that tells people who you are and why you do what you do. There are many elements that make up the Swatch message. High quality. Low cost. Provocative. Joy of life. But the most important element ... is the hardest for others to copy. Ultimately, we are not just offering watches. We are offering our personal culture.[18]

---

[15] Edward D. Hess, *Smart Growth: Building an Enduring Business by Managing the Risks of Growth* (New York: Columbia University Press, 2010), p. 24.

[16] William Taylor, "Message and Muscle: An Interview with Swatch Titan Nicolas Hayek," *Harvard Business Review*, March–April 1993, 98–110, p. 101. Available from Ivey Publishing, product no. 93205.

[17] Rohit Deshpandé, Karol Misztal, and Daniela Beyersdorfer, *The Swatch Group* (Boston, MA: Harvard Business School Publishing, January 15, 2014 (revised)), p. 5. Available from Ivey Publishing, product no. 512052.

[18] See note 16, p. 103.

As a result of these features, demand for Swatch watches soared quickly (from US$3 million in 1984 to US$105 million in 1985). In 1998, SMH Group was renamed The Swatch Group Ltd., after its most prominent brand. Over time, the company expanded its portfolio and categorized brands into different ranges, whereby Swatch and Flik Flak made up the foundation in the basic range. Brands such as Tissot, ck watch & jewelry, Balmain, Hamilton, Certina, and Mido made up the middle range, while Longines, Rado, and Union Glashütte constituted the high range, and Breguet, Blancpain, Glashütte Original, Jaquet Droz, Léon Hatot, and Omega were brands in the prestige/luxury range. Brands largely maintained sovereignty, keeping management, buildings, and brand development separate from each other.[19]

At the time the strategic alliance with Tiffany was announced, Swatch was a successful MNE (see Exhibit 2). Swatch's main business was in the watches and jewelry category, followed by the production of watch parts sold to original equipment manufacturer brands, and electronic systems. Over time, several of Hayek's family members had become involved in the company through top management team positions and equity stakes. His daughter Nayla Hayek had been a board member since 1995 and became chairwoman in 2010, while his son Nick Hayek Jr. had been the CEO since 2003 and became a board member in 2010. Hayek's grandson, Marc A. Hayek, became a member of the Executive Group Management Board in 2005. The "Hayek Pool," a conglomeration of companies, institutions, and individuals (including family members) connected to Hayek, controlled 39.1 percent of the shares in 2007.[20]

In 2007, Swatch was still headed by co-founder and chairman Hayek, who had by then earned honorary doctorates and other distinctions for his achievements in the watchmaking industry, such as the "Grosses Ehrenzeichen mit Stern" from the government of Austria, the "Officier de la Légion d'honneur" from the government of France, and the Swiss Lifetime Award.[21] Hayek described himself as "a provocateur, [trying] to initiate change through provocation, irony or violent criticism, and also, if necessary, through logical explanation,"[22] and the statement "modesty is hypocrisy for the successful" was cited as his belief.[23] His daughter Nayla Hayek portrayed her father as "someone who went against the tide and loved freedom; a man of very strong character who liked to assert himself, sometimes very bluntly; a person with inexhaustible curiosity and energy."[24]

The Global Luxury Watch Industry in 2007

On the production side, the global watchmaking industry was centralized in three areas: Switzerland, Japan, and Hong Kong. Watch movements (micromechanical and electronic components) were only built in Switzerland and Japan.[25] Switzerland in particular possessed a country-specific advantage in the watchmaking industry, with a tradition dating back to the sixteenth century and generations of families working in the industry's factories. Several innovations (such as the balance spring, self-winding mechanisms, chronographs, and perpetual calendars) had led to the country's renown for high-quality watchmaking "made in Switzerland." By

---

[19] See note 18, p. 7.
[20] The Swatch Group, *Annual Report 2007*, p. 130, www.swatchgroup.com/sites/default/files/media-files/2007_annual_report_complete_en.pdf, accessed January 2, 2020.
[21] The Swatch Group, *Annual Report 2008*, p. 137, www.swatchgroup.com/sites/default/files/media-files/2008_annual_report_complete_en.pdf, accessed January 2, 2020.
[22] The Swatch Group, *Annual Report 2010*, p. 4, www.swatchgroup.com/sites/default/files/media-files/2010_annual_report_complete_en.pdf, accessed January 2, 2020.
[23] Christophe Roulet, "Time Runs out for Nicolas Hayek," *FHH Journal*, June 29, 2010, https://journal.hautehorlogerie.org/en/time-runs-out-for-nicolas-hayek, accessed January 2, 2020.
[24] See note 23, p. 4.
[25] See note 16, p. 7.

1945, Swiss watchmakers controlled 87.2 percent of the world's watch production,[26] and 90 percent of the 2,500 companies were small, with fewer than 50 employees.[27] This changed with the influx of inexpensive watches from Asia, and by the late 1960s, the Swiss watch industry's global market share had fallen to 41 percent. When Japanese watchmakers started becoming successful with quartz watches in the 1970s, Swiss watchmakers reacted by retreating towards the high end, adding more gold and diamonds and increasing prices but failing to introduce any significant innovations.[28]

The result was a significant contraction of export volume by 1983, from 83 million to 30 million watches. Employment plummeted from 90,000 to 34,000 jobs, and almost two-thirds of the Swiss watchmaking companies had to close down.[29] The formation of the SMH Group in 1983 with its focus on the basic range of the market was thus a much-needed reinvigoration of Swiss horology.

By 2007, the global luxury goods industry was booming. Among the largest companies in the hard luxury business (watches, jewelry, stationary[30]) were Richemont, Swatch, Tiffany, and LVMH. Largely driven by expansion into emerging markets like China, the industry had experienced a compound annual growth rate (CAGR[31]) of 8 percent since 2004 (compared to a CAGR of 3 percent with regards to the worldwide real gross domestic product in the same time frame) and was valued at €170 billion[32] by the end of 2007.[33] Nick Hayek Jr. reported: "At this moment, our business is fantastic. [November 2007 sales have been the] best ever."[34] It was in this context that the strategic alliance between Tiffany and Swatch had been conceived.

The Strategic Alliance: Strategic Rationale

Tiffany and Swatch had explored collaboration possibilities for more than a year prior to the announcement in December 2007.[35] Each partner had a clear strategic rationale for allying with the other. Swatch was looking to expand its prestige/luxury range with an operational mode that did not require as much capital investment as buying a brand through mergers or acquisitions. As Nick Hayek Jr. noted, "We have no need to invest ... in buying another brand. But what we are doing is pushing Tiffany forward."[36] Moreover, Swatch was interested in expanding into the jewelry business. The strategic alliance with Tiffany would allow for this by opening its own stores to sell watches, along with a significant Tiffany jewelry collection (30–40 percent of products), boosting Swatch's revenue. As Nick Hayek Jr. noted, "This is an additional possibility to enter the jewelry market with a very, very strong and professional partner."[37]

---

[26] See note 18, p. 2.
[27] Allen Morrison and Cyril Bouquet, *Swatch and the Global Watch Industry* (London, ON: Ivey Publishing, May 23, 2017 (revised)), p. 3. Available from Ivey Publishing, product no. 9A99M023.
[28] Jake Rossen, "A Timeless History of the Swatch Watch," *Mental Floss*, July 4, 2019, https://www.mentalfloss.com/article/581875/swatch-watch-history, accessed January 2, 2020.
[29] See note 18, p. 2.
[30] As opposed to "soft" luxury, which includes personal care and fashion.
[31] CAGR is calculated as $\left(\dfrac{final\,value}{beginning\,value}\right)^{1/years} - 1$.
[32] € = euro = EUR; €1 = CHF 1.677 on December 31, 2007.
[33] Bain & Company, "Luxury Goods Worldwide Market Study," October 19, 2009, slide 3, www.bain.com/contentassets/5cf5c5b034724c629f74b6d286c6fe48/bain20studie_trends20und20entwicklungen20im20luxusgc3bctermarktt_2009.pdf, accessed January 3, 2020.
[34] Aarthi Sivaraman, "Tiffany, Swatch Execs Upbeat on Holiday Sales," *Reuters*, December 5, 2007, www.reuters.com/article/tiffany-sales/tiffany-swatch-execs-upbeat-on-holiday-sales-idUSN0562780720071205, accessed January 2, 2020.
[35] See note 3.
[36] Thomson Reuters StreetEvents, "Interim 2008 Swatch Group Ltd Earnings Conference Call," August 15, 2008, p. 5, Mergent Investext, accessed January 2, 2020.
[37] Ibid, p. 6.

Tiffany, on the other hand, had a strong need for improving its wholesale distribution. Kowalski explained:

> We did reach the conclusion actually several years ago that at some point wholesale distribution was essential so that we clearly wanted to look for a partner who could provide us with that. ... Swatch can do that. We also felt that if we were to be a major player in the watch business, we needed a degree of vertical integration much like we've achieved in diamond sourcing and jewelry. Since we were not willing to become a major primary watch manufacturer or component manufacturer we thought that the most logical partner was the most significant movement and ... quality watch manufacturer in the world. So it kind of let us very naturally to Swatch.[38]

Moreover, Fernandez echoed Swatch's preference for allying over organic growth or acquisitions, saying, "For us to establish a wholesale distribution network around the world and try to do that competitively, we didn't think was a real possibility ... within a 10 year period. It would just be too expensive and the sales would come too slow."[39] Indeed, Tiffany's strategy was not to build a watch business as large as competing brands, but to focus on being a jeweler first and effectively outsourcing the watch business to a trusted industry partner.[40] Thus, it saw benefits in gaining profits at lower costs through the strategic alliance's profit-sharing arrangement, as well as additional marketing support.[41] Moreover, the alliance allowed Tiffany to gain access to Swatch's expertise and dominant position in the Swiss network of watch manufacturing.[42]

The Strategic Alliance: Operational Design

Legally, the alliance was designed as a wholly owned subsidiary of Swatch, which would then enter a 20-year license and distribution agreement with Tiffany. The license agreement allowed Swatch to use selected Tiffany trademarks as well as carry the Tiffany name in the subsidiary's title.[43] The capital invested in the subsidiary was CHF20 million.[44]

The revenue model was such that retailers and watch distributors would purchase watches from the alliance and both partners would partake in profit sharing (according to an undisclosed percentage distribution schedule).[45] The resulting operating earnings, essentially a royalty revenue, would be recorded by Tiffany as sales with no cost. Tiffany stores would be able to purchase watches directly from the alliance without an intermediate distributor[46] at lower margins (wholesale prices).[47]

As for the performance goals of the strategic alliance, Fernandez stated, "If we could get to 5 per cent to 10 per cent [of Tiffany's sales coming from watch sales], I'd be happy. And if worldwide distribution ... became a total of US$300 million or US$400 million, I think we'd all be thrilled with it because that means the marketing impact would be dramatic."[48]

The board of directors was comprised of four people representing the Swatch group and Fernandez representing Tiffany, with a focus on performance oversight. Nayla Hayek assumed operational leadership as the president of the new venture. The headquarters of this new venture was in Biel, Switzerland, where Swatch had acquired a prestigious villa in a historic part of the city.[49]

The strategic alliance was tasked with the design, manufacturing, marketing, distribution,

---

[38] Thomson Reuters StreetEvents, "Tiffany & Co. at Oppenheimer & Co. Consumer Growth Conference," July 9, 2008, p. 6, Mergent Investext, accessed January 2, 2020.
[39] See note 13, p. 9.
[40] See note 12, p. 6.
[41] See note 13, p. 9.
[42] Thomson Reuters StreetEvents, "Tiffany & Co. at Thomson Reuters Global Luxury and Retail Summit – New York," June 10, 2009, p. 17, Mergent Investext, accessed January 2, 2020.

[43] See note 11.
[44] See note 22, 202.
[45] See note 39, p. 3.
[46] Ibid.
[47] See note 13, p. 9.
[48] See note 12, p. 7.
[49] See note 12, p. 47.

and service of Tiffany watches.[50] The design committee was staffed with two Swatch representatives and two Tiffany representatives (senior vice-president of merchandising and senior vice-president of marketing).[51] Swatch then was to contribute its expertise in watch design to propose extensions of the already successful Tiffany watch collections (Mark, Atlas, and Grand), as well as introduce new designs.[52] The representatives from Tiffany in turn ensured that the designs were in line with the brand's identity.[53] The manufacturing of the watches was done through Swatch's production capacities in Switzerland.

The two Tiffany representatives on the design committee also represented the company on the marketing committee, joined by two Swatch representatives. Besides approving advertising plans and campaigns to advance watch sales, the committee also ensured that the advertising supported the global recognition of the Tiffany brand as a whole. The marketing budget was about 10 percent of sales. Tiffany's responsibility was further to promote the watches by displaying them prominently in its stores.[54]

A core part of the deal, and a novelty for Tiffany, was the focus on wholesale distribution. As Nick Hayek Jr. emphasized, the distribution network was crucially important: "You can have nice brands, but if you don't have ... control over the distribution, how your product is presented to the final consumer, it's not very helpful."[55] Swatch's distribution network dated back to the early 1990s, when Hayek lessened the company's dependence on local distributors by setting up wholesale subsidiaries in each major market. While each of those subsidiaries was led by a country manager and housed their own sales and marketing organization for each major brand, they also shared back-office tasks across other brands. This setting ensured the ability to be both locally responsive through country-level strategies and globally integrated through a coherent design and marketing approach.[56] From this global network, the watches could then also be handed over to third-party distributors, often in connection with an advertisement commitment made by the respective retailer. Tiffany would be able to buy its watches from the strategic alliance directly, without an intermediate distributor,[57] and Swatch would also distribute the watches in its high-end stores, such as the Tourbillon Boutique.[58]

On January 22, 2008, the companies officially incorporated their strategic alliance under the name Tiffany Watch Co. Ltd. With the establishment of this alliance, Tiffany significantly reduced its existing in-house watch business, resulting in a pre-tax charge of US$19,212,000 within cost of sales.[59]

The Strategic Alliance: Performance

The year 2008 was considered a transition and set-up period. As Tiffany's Mark Aaron, vice-president of investor relations, reported, "We are making excellent progress in [the] partnership with The Swatch Group to develop a global Tiffany & Co. watch business."[60]

Sales were soft that year,[61] but clear signs of progress were expected to show by 2009.[62] The first widely visible outcome from the strategic alliance was a collection of luxury timepieces

---

[50] See note 3.
[51] See note 12, p. 6.
[52] See note 39, p. 3.
[53] See note 12, p. 6.
[54] See note 12, p. 6.; Ariel Adams, "Why Tiffany & Co. Was Ordered to Pay Almost Half a Billion Dollars to the Swatch Group," *Forbes*, December 23, 2013, www.forbes.com/sites/arieladams/2013/12/23/why-tiffany-co-was-ordered-to-pay-almost-half-a-billion-dollars-to-the-swatch-group/#24c977425001, accessed January 4, 2020.
[55] See note 37, p 5.
[56] See note 18, p. 4.
[57] See note 12, p. 6.
[58] See note 55.
[59] See note 22.
[60] Thomson Reuters StreetEvents, "Q1 2008 Tiffany & Co. Earnings Conference Call," May 30, 2008, p. 3, Mergent Investext, accessed January 2, 2020.
[61] Thomson Reuters StreetEvents, "Q3 2008 Tiffany & Co. Earnings Conference Call," November 26, 2008, p. 3, Mergent Investext, accessed January 2, 2020.
[62] See note 61.

that extended existing Tiffany watch designs. Most notable were designs that were part of the heritage-rich Atlas collection, inspired by the Atlas clock above Tiffany's New York flagship store entrance on 5th Avenue, made up of a round dial and large Roman numerals.[63] Moreover, the strategic alliance introduced, among other models, a chronograph made of stainless steel (Tiffany Mark), a classic design (Tiffany Grand), a watch targeted at women (Tiffany Tesoro), and an oval diamond-studded timepiece (the Cocktail Oval). These collections were debuted at Baselworld 2009,[64] the industry's most important trade show. The products hit the shelves around the holidays,[65] and the first markets to receive them were the United States, the Middle East, and Asia (China, Hong Kong, and Japan).[66]

Interest from the media and industry experts was significant, and global orders were in line with expectations.[67] However, although Swatch considered the new designs a success[68] and Tiffany also deemed the watches "beautiful,"[69] not all observers agreed. As one industry expert, Ariel Adams, put it, "Tiffany & Co. Watches were not as elegant and classy as they should have been. ... [Swatch] did not produce the watches Tiffany ... envisioned for itself, and they were not similar enough to the previous generation of ... watches that existed before the Swatch Group relationship."[70] Overall, watch sales fluctuated in 2009, but the alliance introduced new designs in their U.S. stores and ran marketing campaigns, including advertisements in *The New York Times* and *The Wall Street Journal* for the Atlas Dome watch, targeted at male customers.[71]

By then, the global financial crisis was in full force and the luxury watch industry was hit particularly hard: CAGR between 2007 and 2009 was −9 percent. As the global economy contracted and market uncertainty increased, consumers stayed away from purchasing luxury goods, especially in the hard luxury sector. "Luxury shame" manifested, whereby visible luxury goods (such as watches or jewels) became less socially acceptable during times of economic crises.[72] Despite these external circumstances, the strategic alliance continued its launch. In February 2010, Nick Hayek Jr. reviewed how the process had gone thus far:

We told this already in March that 2009 will be – it's not a very good year to launch full-fledged. So we didn't launch in many countries. We launched in our own network. Of course, Tiffany launched in their stores, but not in all countries. Mainly in the United States, and the United States is a little bit weak. So the first results of the sell out of Tiffany are very good. It's mainly female, and female[s] are buying much more than men we have discovered in these times, even in crisis times. And yes, we stick to it that in a range of three to five years we should be able to achieve CHF300 million to CHF500 million. But it will not be 2010.[73]

New models were added in 2010, including the Tiffany Gemea and 5th Avenue (5AV) models, the Grand Collection, and an expansion of

---

[63] See note 22, p. 46.
[64] The Swatch Group, "Tiffany Watch Co. Ltd Debuts at Baselworld 2009," March 31, 2009, www.swatchgroup.com/en/services/archive/2009/tiffany-watch-co-ltd-debuts-baselworld-2009, accessed January 2, 2020.
[65] See note 12, p. 7.
[66] The Swatch Group, *Annual Report 2009*, p. 45, www.swatchgroup.com/sites/default/files/media-files/2009_annual_report_complete_en.pdf, accessed January 2, 2020.
[67] Ibid., p. 46.
[68] See note 23, p. 51.
[69] Thomson Reuters StreetEvents, "Tiffany and Co at Deutsche Bank Securities Inc. Global Consumer Conference," June 16, 2011, p. 8, Mergent Investext, accessed January 2, 2020.
[70] See note 55.
[71] Thomson Reuters StreetEvents, "Q3 2009 Tiffany & Co. Earnings Conference Call," November 25, 2009, p. 3, Mergent Investext, accessed January 2, 2020.
[72] See note 34.
[73] Thomson Reuters StreetEvents, "Full Year 2009 Swatch Group Ltd Sales Conference Call," February 9, 2010, p. 14, Mergent Investext, accessed January 2, 2020.

the Atlas collection. These watches were presented at Baselworld 2010, where the alliance set up a "Breakfast at Tiffany's"-themed coffee shop to welcome customers.[74] Fernandez commented in June 2010:

> We introduced the new Grand Collection in Basel this year, had very good reception. That product will probably hit the shelves in September. But it's going to be a few years before we build up a large collection. ... But we're all pleased with it, with the progress. Sales in our stores are about 2 per cent of sales. So I think they can only go up. We'd like it to be a more meaningful business.[75]

On June 28, 2010, Swatch experienced a shock when its co-founder and chairman Hayek passed away from heart failure at age 82 while working in his office. Newspapers around the world reported on his legacy, calling him a "savior of the Swiss watch industry"[76] and the king in "the court of watchmaking."[77] Nayla Hayek was elected by unanimous vote as chairwoman on June 30, 2010.[78]

Watch sales for the alliance increased in 2010, though mainly in Tiffany's own stores (by about 30 percent). Fernandez commented in August 2010, "We are pleased with customer response to new watches in our stores, and we look forward to a significant expansion of wholesale distribution."[79] The alliance ramped up its marketing efforts in the second half of 2010, with VIP cocktail receptions for retailers at several locations worldwide, a new advertising campaign, and an expansion to the retail network.[80] Products were also introduced to several new locations, such as Belgium, Spain, Italy, Canada, Colombia, Mexico, South Africa, and other countries, where they were received well. Also, by the end of 2010, the worldwide luxury industry had started to show signs of recovery.

By March 2011, however, it became apparent that the performance of the alliance was not developing as expected and there were signs of an ongoing conflict. As Kowalski reported, "While sales in Tiffany's-owned stores have been strong, we have been disappointed with the slower than expected rollout of wholesale watch distribution. ... We are also hopeful that our differences with our watch partner can be resolved collaboratively and professionally."[81] Watch sales had contributed only about 1 percent of Tiffany's worldwide sales in 2009 and 2010 (from 2 percent in 2008), and royalty revenue had been insignificant (less than 1 percent of Tiffany's net sales). Despite this, the alliance continued to showcase at Baselworld 2011, where it introduced the Art Deco–inspired Tiffany Gallery watch and further expansions to the Atlas collection.[82] Other marketing efforts continued as well, such as editorial breakfasts in locations worldwide. On June 16, 2011, Fernandez suggested,

> The one thing I think that we probably would like to see expand more rapidly is that wholesale distribution piece, which is a key part of our agreement. So, we're still working on that with [Swatch]. We both have different opinions, maybe, on how quick that pace should go, but we'll work

---

[74] See note 23, p. 53.
[75] See note 12, p. 7.
[76] Goran Mijuk, "Swatch Group Founder and Chairman Nicolas Hayek Dies," June 29, 2010, www.wsj.com/articles/SB10001424052748703964104575335003183982666, accessed January 5, 2020.
[77] See note 24.
[78] Joe Thompson, "Nayla Hayek Named Swatch Group Chairwoman," WatchTime, July 10, 2010, www.watchtime.com/wristwatch-industry-news/industry/nayla-hayek-named-swatch-group-chairwoman, accessed January 3, 2020.
[79] Thomson Reuters StreetEvents, "Q2 2010 Tiffany & Co. Earnings Conference Call," August 27, 2010, p. 5, Mergent Investext, accessed January 2, 2020.
[80] See note 23, 53.
[81] Thomson Reuters StreetEvents, "Q4 2010 Tiffany & Co. Earnings Conference Call," March 21, 2011, p. 8, Mergent Investext, accessed January 2, 2020.
[82] The Swatch Group, *Annual Report 2011*, p. 44, www.swatchgroup.com/sites/default/files/media-files/2011_annual_report_complete_en.pdf, accessed January 2, 2020.

through it. It's a long-term agreement, and Tiffany, as being the license holder, obviously we have certain points of control that we want to make sure that we keep in place in this agreement. And for Swatch, I think it's a new type of relationship. They're not used to having a license arrangement where they can't make 100 per cent of the decisions without possibly stopping for approval along the way.[83]

Just a few days later, on June 24, 2011, Swatch (and the alliance, as its wholly owned subsidiary) started arbitration proceedings against Tiffany, alleging that Tiffany had exhibited "systematic efforts to block and delay development of the business."[84]

The Strategic Alliance: Arbitration and Termination

The arbitration was held confidentially in front of a three-member arbitral panel at the Netherlands Arbitration Institute in the Netherlands. With the press releases on September 12, 2011, the matter became public. Swatch stated that any attempts at solving the dispute amicably had remained fruitless, noting that it sought full compensation for all losses accrued due to Tiffany's alleged breach of contract, including a claim for lost profits valued at CHF3.8 billion.[85]

Tiffany responded by filing a Statement of Defence and Counterclaim on March 9, 2012, declaring that Swatch's claim was without merit. Instead, Tiffany asserted counterclaims, alleging that Swatch had "failed to provide appropriate management, distribution, marketing and other resources for [Tiffany's] brand watches and to honor their contractual obligations to the Tiffany Parties regarding brand management," seeking compensation for damages in the range of CHF120 million–540 million. The counterclaim also referred to Swatch's breach by making the notice of termination public on September 12, 2011.[86]

Swatch's reaction to Tiffany's counterclaim was that it had "no factual or legal basis and will be vigorously contested by Swatch."[87] An arbitration hearing was held in October 2012 before a three-member panel, and the report was completed by mid-February 2013. The terms of the arbitration award considered the partnership terminated as of March 1, 2013, and while Tiffany was found to not have acted in bad faith, it was deemed to have breached its contractual terms (one of the panel members issued a dissenting opinion on this ruling).[88] Tiffany was ordered to pay damages of about CHF403 million plus interest, legal fees, and associated costs, for a total of about CHF480 million. Tiffany had deemed such an outcome improbable and had thus not established any accrual in its financial statements.[89]

Although Tiffany had paid the amount in full by January 2014, it filed a petition on March 31, 2014, in the District Court of Amsterdam to have the arbitration award annulled. This was made possible by a provision in Dutch law allowing for the possibility to set arbitration awards aside (normally, arbitration awards are final). The claim was heard by a three-judge panel on January 19, 2015, which arrived at a decision in favor of Tiffany by March 4, 2015.

Swatch swiftly appealed the decision to set the arbitration award aside. On June 29, 2016, a three-judge panel at the Appellate Court of Amsterdam heard the appeal and issued a decision on April 25, 2017, in favor of Swatch,

---

[83] See note 70, p. 9.
[84] The Swatch Group, *Annual Report 2012*, p. 195, www.swatchgroup.com/sites/default/files/media-files/2012_annual_report_complete_en.pdf, accessed January 2, 2020.
[85] Ibid.
[86] Tiffany & Co., *Annual Report 2013*, K-20–K-22, https://investor.tiffany.com/static-files/ffcf0031-67be-464c-aaf0-73b2430561c4, accessed January 2, 2020.
[87] See note 85, p. 195.
[88] See note 87, PS-26.
[89] Raphael Minder, "Swatch Wins Case Against Tiffany Over Failed Partnership," *New York Times*, December 23, 2013, www.nytimes.com/2013/12/24/business/swatch-wins-case-against-tiffany-over-failed-partnership.html?auth=login-email&login=email, accessed January 3, 2020.

including an order for Tiffany to reimburse Swatch's additional legal costs (€6,340).

In response, Tiffany appealed this decision by the Appellate Court of Amsterdam and took the matter to the Supreme Court of the Netherlands. On November 23, 2018, the court dismissed the appeal, and Tiffany had to once again reimburse Swatch for its additional legal costs. After this, all rights of appeal had been exhausted and the arbitration award was considered final.[90]

After a long and dramatic legal battle, this final decision thus marked the formal end of the strategic alliance, which Tiffany and Swatch had once called a "historic agreement" and a "pathbreaking strategic move." What was left to do now, in 2018, was to reflect on what had caused this unfortunate chain of events and how it could have been predicted or even prevented. What were the lessons learned, so that future alliance endeavors could be more successful?

[90] Onno Hennis, "Dutch Supreme Court Upholds CHF402 Million Arbitral Award in Proceeding Between Tiffany & Co. and Swatch," *AMS Advocaten*, December 12, 2018, www.amsadvocaten.com/blog/litigation/dutch-supreme-court-upholds-chf-402-million-arbitral-award-in-proceedings-between-tiffany-co-and-swatch, accessed January 3, 2020.

Exhibit 1: Tiffany Key Indicators

Fiscal year	2007	2008	2009	2010	2011
KEY INDICATORS					
Net sales (in US$ millions)	2,939	2,860	2,710	3,085	3,643
Operating profit (in US$ millions)	370	232	266	368	439
Number of employees	8,800	9,000	8,400	9,200	9,800
SALES BY PRODUCT SEGMENT (percentage of net sales)					
Jewelry (gemstone jewelry, diamond rings, wedding bands, gold or platinum jewelry, sterling silver jewelry)	86.3	86.7	90.2	91.0	91.3
Tableware, timepieces, and other (timepieces, sterling silver merchandise, trophies, key holders, picture frames and desk accessories, stainless steel flatware, crystal, glassware, china and other tableware, custom engraved stationery, writing instruments, eyewear and fashion accessories, wholesale of diamonds)	13.7	13.3	9.8	9.0	8.8
Proportion contributed by watches	~2	~2	~1	<1	~1
SALES BY GEOGRAPHY [percentage of net sales]					
Americas	59.9	55.5	52.1	51.0	49.6
Asia-Pacific	29.1	32.2	35.3	35.5	37.5
Europe	8.3	10.0	11.5	11.7	11.6
Other	2.8	2.3	1.1	1.8	1.4

Source: Created by the authors using data from company annual reports 2007–2011.

Exhibit 2: Swatch Key Indicators

Fiscal year	2007	2008	2009	2010	2011
KEY INDICATORS					
Net sales (in CHF millions)	5,646	5,677	5,142	6,108	6,764
Operating profit (in CHF millions)	1,236	1,202	903	1,436	1,614
Number of employees	23,577	24,270	23,562	25,197	28,028
SALES BY PRODUCT SEGMENT (percentage of net sales)					
Watches & jewelry	79	80	82	85	88
Proportion contributed by prestige and luxury watches (Breguet, Blancpain, Glashütte Original, Jaquet Droz, Léon Hatot, Omega, Tiffany & Co)	Estimate for Omega:* CHF1.5 billion	Estimate for Omega: CHF1.8 billion	Estimate for Omega: CHF1.5 billion	Estimate for Omega: CHF2.0 billion	Estimate not available
Production (ETA Manufacture Horlogère Suisse, Frédéric Piguet Valdar, Nivarox-FAR, Comadur, Rubattel & Weyermann, MOM Le Prélet, Deutsche Zifferblatt Manufaktur GmbH, Universo, Favre et Perret, Manufacture Ruedin, Lascor, Meco, Swatch Group Assembly)	11	11	11	8	7
Electronic systems (EM Microelectronic, Micro Crystal, Renata, Microcomponents, Michel Präzisionstechnik, Sokymat Automotive, Oscilloquartz, Lasag, Swiss Timing)	10	9	7	7	5
SALES BY GEOGRAPHY [percentage of net sales]					
Europe	47.9	47.4	45.2	39.5	36.4
Asia	39.2	40.9	44.2	50.7	54.0
America	10.7	9.6	8.3	7.8	7.9
Oceania	1.4	1.3	1.4	1.2	1.1
Africa	0.8	0.9	0.9	0.8	0.6

* Rohit Deshpandé, Karol Misztal, and Daniela Beyersdorfer, *The Swatch Group*, (Boston, MA: Harvard Business School Publishing, January 15, 2014 (revised)), p. 13. Available from Ivey Publishing, product no. 512052.

Source: Created by the authors using data from company annual reports 2007–2011.

CASE III-4: CCS LOGISTICS: CULTURE CHANGE DRIVING ACCOUNTABILITY AND RESPONSIBILITY

Amy Moore, Maxine Jaffit, and Tanya Stevens wrote this case solely to provide material for class discussion. The authors do not intend to illustrate either effective or ineffective handling of a managerial situation. The authors may have disguised certain names and other identifying information to protect confidentiality.

This publication may not be transmitted, photocopied, digitized, or otherwise reproduced in any form or by any means without the permission of the copyright holder. Reproduction of this material is not covered under authorization by any reproduction rights organization. To order copies or request permission to reproduce materials, contact Ivey Publishing, Ivey Business School, Western University, London, Ontario, Canada, N6G 0N1; (t) 519.661.3208; (e) cases@ivey.ca; www.iveypublishing.ca. Our goal is to publish materials of the highest quality; submit any errata to publishcases@ivey.ca. i1v2e5y5pubs

Copyright © 2023, Ivey Business School Foundation   Version: 2023–04-24

On March 1, 2022, Ina Botha, executive director[1] of Commercial Cold Storage and Logistics (CCS Logistics), part of the Oceana Group Ltd., sat at her desk in the company's Cape Town office contemplating the year's plans. A significant element of her work over the previous three and a half years had been to create a high-level strategy underpinned by an enabling culture to help drive greater accountability and improve results. Having stabilized CCS Logistics' strategy and operations and with a strong leadership team in place, Botha was preparing to move into a new role with Oceana. She reflected on whether the new culture had been embedded within CCS Logistics and what recommendations she could make to the organization's incoming joint executive directors in terms of what to continue doing or do differently to ensure the new culture supported the business in achieving its strategic objectives. What other elements should she consider to further embed this new culture?[2]

CCS Logistics: Part of the Global Oceana Group

CCS Logistics was founded in 1971 and was part of the Oceana Group, a global diversified fishing group, which itself was founded in 1918. The group's business focused on harvesting and processing fish through its sea and land production facilities. Oceana's products, which ranged from fish oil and fish meal to tinned fish and food products,[3] were sold to consumers in 41 countries.[4] In 2021, Oceana reported R7.6 billion[5] in revenue, with an operating profit of R1.2 billion.[6] Oceana's operations were split into four business units: canned fish and fish meal (Africa); fish meal and fish oil (USA); Blue Continent Products

---

[1] The executive director position's responsibilities were similar to those of the managing director.
[2] Ina Botha (Executive Director), in discussion with the case authors, February 14, 2022.
[3] Approximately 800,000 cans of Oceana's product Lucky Star (a canned fish and fish meal product) were sold every day. Around 54 percent of Oceana's revenue in 2021 was attributed to Lucky Star; Oceana Group, *Integrated Report for the Year Ended 30 September 2021*, p. 6, https://oceana.co.za/pdf/Oceana_Group_Limited_Integrated_Annual_Report_2021.pdf, accessed February 6, 2023.
[4] Ibid.
[5] R = ZAR = South African rand; R15.95 = US$1 as of December 2021.
[6] See note 127, p. 14.

(Pty) Ltd (Africa);[7] and CCS Logistics. In the same year, CCS Logistics represented 6 percent of the group's revenue.[8]

CCS Logistics provided cold-storage solutions to customers based in South Africa and Namibia. Over 94,000 tons of temperature-controlled storage (with temperatures ranging from chilled to frozen) was available through seven warehousing facilities in South Africa (in Cape Town and in Johannesburg's Midrand and City Deep locations) and Namibia (Walvis Bay). Services ranged from cold storage and blast freezing to pallet picking, container transport, and vessel loading.[9] Customers were internal to Oceana (for example, storing frozen fish for Lucky Star) as well as external.

The First Few Months: Putting the Right Leadership Team into Place

Botha had an undergraduate degree in commerce and a long career in supply chain management and logistics; since 2001, she had worked in retail, wholesale, and the restaurant industry. As a woman in a traditionally male-dominated industry, she had reflected during her career development on how her leadership style might differentiate her from others. Over the years she had realized that her core values were authenticity, integrity, courage, and inclusion. She believed her leadership represented collaboration and psychological safety, and in her various roles she had been deliberately intentional in creating an environment where people knew what was expected of them and felt safe to take accountability, try new things, and admit when mistakes had been made.

Botha took on the role of executive director for CCS Logistics in December 2018 because she saw an opportunity to lead authentically and make a difference. She had been working within the company for the previous 18 months as the supply chain executive, focusing on collaboration between customer service and operations. A substantial project that had occupied her time was the new enterprise resource planning implementation project. Therefore, when starting her executive director role, she had a good understanding of the organization and knew that the first things to accomplish were to be clear about the strategy and to create the right leadership team to focus on the behaviors that would drive greater clarity and results.

She developed a customer-oriented strategy, focusing on creating a responsible and accountable community that also drove efficiency and compliance. Creating and stabilizing the executive committee (exco) was another important building block following vacancies created when colleagues retired or moved into other roles. In a short period, she confirmed two key appointments: Adam Firfirey as finance director – a 12-year Oceana veteran and chartered accountant – and Lundi Sishi as supply chain director. Sishi's background included senior executive experience in supply chain management in distribution centers, with a focus on operations and procurement at South African Breweries and PEP Africa. He had a reputation for being very people-oriented and had extensive experience in industrial relations and wage negotiations. With these new executives, herself, and four existing colleagues – Namibia General Manager Willie Venter, Customer Manager Juan Swanepoel, Human Resources (HR) Business Partner Melanie Samuels, who joined in July 2018, and Commercial Manager Ganeefah Dawood, who joined in August 2018 – the relatively new exco created an opportunity to drive change and form a new culture (see Exhibit 1). Additionally, the exco now represented CCS Logistics' commitment to transformation by having senior leaders of differing genders and racial backgrounds in place, which was important for internal and external stakeholders.

---

[7] Blue Continent Products was Oceana's horse mackerel, hake, lobster, and squid fishing business.
[8] See note 127, p. 6.
[9] "Home page," *CCS Logistics*, www.ccslogistics.co.za, accessed February 6, 2023.

Botha's first months were also spent trying to diagnose a variety of issues across the business that were broader than those she had encountered in her previous supply chain role. There were safety incidents to be resolved, including a rack (a framework used for storing inventory in the warehouse that could be several metres high) collapse in Gauteng, and a long list of litigation matters linked to other customers' claims. Internally, concerns had also been raised that senior management teams reporting into exco might be unmotivated and with low levels of commitment. Combined, these factors created doubt in her mind, as well as in the minds of others, particularly Oceana's exco, around the company's processes, procedures, and staff's capabilities. Was this a business with good people that had become complacent, a problem with competency levels, or something else?[10]

Creating Visibility within Oceana Group

At Botha's first Oceana exco meeting, she realized that CCS Logistics' internal brand within the larger business entity needed to be raised. Given that CCS Logistics only generated a small proportion of Oceana's overall revenue, limited time was given to discussing what was happening in the organization. The time allocated to CCS Logistics in Oceana's exco meetings was usually focused on reporting problems that were seen as high risk for the company, such as litigation matters and safety incidents, and overall revenue forecasts. There had also been questions surrounding the previous financial director's accounts reporting, so the focus of any additional board time was on CCS Logistics' numbers and occupancy levels and the accuracy and reliability of information.

Botha also found that while CCS Logistics serviced Oceana in terms of access to temperature-controlled warehouses, booking needs for this space by the group's internal customers were varied and erratic: at times larger portions of storage were needed for several months of the year, and at others little storage space was required. Yet regardless of internal group usage, the same level of profit and occupancy levels were expected, which created competing demands for warehouses to maintain capacity and bookings. Botha believed that this tension in booking cycles and what it meant for external customers (if no space was available, for instance) was not fully understood by the Oceana exco. As exco members did not have an in-depth understanding of how the business operated, they could not understand the impact that a lack of space could have on external customers and, in turn, on CCS Logistics' reputation.

One way to address this visibility was to move the CCS Logistics' head office from Paarden Eiland, Cape Town, closer to Oceana's headquarters in the city, Oceana House – a move Botha completed in January 2018. She hoped such a move might enable more informal contact between colleagues, which could in turn foster greater collaboration within Oceana's shared services and a better general understanding of how CCS Logistics operated. She also tried to create opportunities to speak informally with Oceana exco colleagues around what was going well within CCS Logistics: Botha did not want them to assume a negative issue was going to be raised every time they engaged in conversation, since that had often been the focus of exco discussions. With Oceana's exco also making many decisions and influencing CCS Logistics' strategy and budgets, Botha wanted to ensure that it had a balanced perspective on the whole business.

Engaging Visibly with All Employees

Perception was important not only in terms of how CCS Logistics was viewed by the group but by how the company's exco was perceived and seen by its staff, something Botha believed was important. She and other CCS Logistics exco members created a quarterly road show rotation, where they visited each logistics center, presenting and speaking to all employees on topics ranging from strategy to financial results

---

[10] Ina Botha (Executive Director), e-mail correspondence with the case authors, December 2021.

and the role that each center and employee played in creating overall value. These focused engagements were scheduled across all work shifts to engage with all individuals and hear their questions and suggestions.

The first round of road shows focused on creating clarity on the company strategy and around general expectations. The message of creating an accountable and responsible community focused on customer service, efficiency, and daily compliance was shared for the first time.[11] In the second round of road shows, Botha perceived a level of discomfort from warehouse employees around what she and her executive team were trying to achieve; she did not think this was unexpected, since she had been told by one warehouse employee that hers was the first executive director visit in eight years. The discomfort was manifested through "finger pointing" and minimal engagement in conversations. Where engagement did occur at the end of presentations, it was typically around administrative matters, with questions often related to vacation time or uniform issues. Where possible, Botha and her team would quickly address and resolve employee concerns, working with the senior management in each warehouse.

To support the content shared with staff through the road shows, Botha also screened a video that she had commissioned. It had clips featuring staff from different warehouses conducting varying operational roles, with the narrative focusing on accountability and client relationships. It was the exco's hope that seeing colleagues would inspire staff and emphasize the one-team approach the exco was looking to embody.

Additionally, opportunities for the Oceana exco to visit different warehouse sites were encouraged and created. Botha's objective for this was twofold: to show all staff that there was interest from Oceana's senior leadership in what teams were doing, and to create greater understanding of the workings of CCS Logistics for Oceana's exco and board members. From her perspective, they were equally important. She hoped the staff would feel valued and recognized if they saw other senior Oceana managers spending time in their area. And she hoped her Oceana exco colleagues might have a greater understanding and appreciation for CCS Logistics' work.

Finding Other Opportunities to Drive Culture

Following the initial road shows and after engaging with employees on the shop floor, Botha was able to get a better understanding of what needed to change. Patrick Kerspuy, warehouse manager for Paarden Eiland who had been involved with CCS Logistics for 27 years, shared with her and the new CCS Logistics exco what the prevailing culture had been before they had joined: while there were experienced and competent employees in the company, little emphasis had been put on staff development – individuals had found themselves pigeonholed into roles and required to only perform duties related to their job description.[12] There was a clear hierarchy and a general lack of opportunity for staff to voice their ideas. Employees were encouraged to focus on their tasks rather than on personal connections and teamwork. As business competition increased with new cold stores and technology being provided by other organizations, morale declined internally, evidenced through greater staff turnover and absenteeism.

During the third round of road shows, Botha felt that a shift had occurred. There was a higher level of employee engagement across all warehouses, observed through the level

---

[11] The community represented employees from different grade levels from Grades A-E: Grade A (semi-skilled workers, 22 percent of the workforce); Grade B (skilled employees, 54 percent of the workforce); Grade C (middle management, 15 percent of the workforce); Grade D (senior management, 8 percent of the workforce); and Grade E (executive management, 1 percent of the workforce). Grades C-E were considered leadership positions, and the total workforce in 2022 comprised 279 people.

[12] Patrick Kerspuy (Warehouse Manager, Paarden Eiland), in discussion with the case authors, April 1, 2022.

and number of questions asked. One forklift driver shared with the HR business partner that in his 30 years of service no one had ever asked him what he thought.[13] The exco team believed that the questions and sharing of ideas reflected engagement, which was a core building block for successful team performance. The questions asked following the exco presentation had shifted from grievances to ways of co-creating value: How could the warehouse increase occupancy, for example, or get more customers? That was the level of engagement the exco wanted to foster and experience among site leadership teams and employees.

A Company-Wide Culture Program: "Keeping It Cool"

Botha believed that the first building block of an organization's journey was to put the right leadership team into place and the second was exco visibility and engagement with staff through road shows. However, the road shows identified that the strategy could only be implemented effectively if the right culture was in place. Botha and the rest of the exco team discussed what else could be done to create clarity, direction, and alignment while also getting buy-in from CCS Logistics' general community.

To help refine the ideas that the team had, Botha engaged the ONE Agency, a creative advertising firm based in Cape Town.[14] From her time working in operations, she understood the importance of having the right language that everyone could understand, relate to, and remember. She shared the vision of the culture journey the exco wanted to achieve, and ONE Agency created the "Keeping It Cool" campaign, including messaging and visual materials.

In May 2019, the third building block was launched: the Keeping It Cool company-wide cultural program, focused on creating cohesion, compliance, and accountability. Botha believed it was important to reinforce the message that staff should follow the correct and agreed processes and procedures to ensure good results, and to stop creating situations that could lead to poor service or even litigation. She did not want a policing system driven by fear and instructions, but rather an accountable and responsible community that took ownership for the performance of the business, where people adhered to processes and procedures because they understood the underpinning rationale and importance and who wanted to contribute to the company's future (see Exhibit 2). The exco team believed that a shift was needed from the current state of staff following instructions to one of collaboration and thinking on their own.

Exco road shows, now referred to as engagement sessions, were held at all sites and were attended by all employees, staff, and contractors at all levels. The concept of a responsible community was explored, with simple objectives stated: to create a positive customer experience, drive compliance, and have fit-for-purpose solutions. Suitable behaviors were identified for each area: what should be kept, avoided, and started. Posters were created by the ONE Agency in line with the Keeping It Cool campaign messaging (see Exhibit 3). Some posters specifically featured photographs of employees from different sites. A communications plan was also given to the senior leadership team that reinforced this message. The objectives were also included in the annual employee performance indicators to ensure clear alignment with strategy.

Self-Awareness and the Leadership Integration Program

Simultaneously, the Leadership Integration Program (LIP) was created for managers, developed, and implemented with the boutique leadership consultancy firm BeClear.[15]

---

[13] Melanie Samuels (HR Director), in discussion with the case authors, April 13, 2022.
[14] One Agency, "Home page," www.oneagency.one, accessed February 6, 2023.
[15] Be Clear, "Home page," www.beclear.co.za, accessed February 6, 2023.

Botha wanted to supplement the road shows by creating a level of self-awareness among managers about the behaviors needed to drive responsibility and accountability. Targeting managerial levels was intentional, since Botha hoped managers could influence their senior managers as well as their teams. Launched in June 2019, 12 people representing a range of CCS Logistics' divisions were selected from different warehouses. The first cohort included individuals in roles ranging across compliance, finance, and operations. Botha wrote a personalized e-mail to each participant:

> Congratulations on being part of our first Leadership Integration Program. As a leadership team, we embarked on a journey to change and influence behaviour to cultivate a culture that creates an accountable and responsible CCS community. We want to foster a safe environment where we can question what we do, share ideas, and contribute to the future of the organization and the growth of our people. This is an opportunity to think and explore why you do what you do as a leader. And to build the ability to influence the people around you with personal mastery as a starting point. The impact of this journey is now in your hands. You will grow and flourish in direct relation to the magnitude you give of yourself and contribute to discussions and opportunities. Leadership is a lifelong commitment, and it will never be perfect. And that's okay. As long as our intentions are rooted in our values and principles, be assured that you have my support. And then I'm excited about the opportunity presented to you and your experiences during this journey – keeping it cool and inspired in a word.[16]

The program was structured to include eight in-person sessions over the course of a year. Content was focused on a journey of self-awareness, equipping the participants to lead themselves as well as others. There was a deliberate overlap between leadership concepts from the BeClear content and two other programs that CCS Logistics exco staff were attending, run by a South African business school. Midway through the LIP, participants were asked to present to each other and Botha about what it meant to motivate others. BeClear believed that this allowed participants to explore important questions about their own authentic leadership style, what ownership looked like, and what it meant to be a responsible individual and team member.

At the end of the program participants also presented to the CCS Logistics exco about their learning journey and what they would commit to in future. At the final presentation, CCS Logistics exco staff gave feedback to each participant about what they had heard and observed from the individual's development. Six months after completion of a program – four subsequent programs were run – Botha and line managers also had one-to-one sessions with each participant, asking them what they had carried forward and implemented. Botha could see from these debriefs that there was a much higher level of employee engagement, better team cohesion, and an understanding of the impact of employees on the business and on each other. Eventually, five groups completed the program, involving 67 people in total.[17]

Measuring Progress

The exco team carefully tracked and measured warehouse performance and the impact of the overall culture change program. Some indicators had been part of the management team's regular conversations, such as debtors' days, occupancy levels, and litigation matters. New areas were introduced by the exco, such as customer surveys, which had not been measured systematically, and

---

[16] Ina Botha (executive director), in correspondence with the case authors, April 25, 2022.

[17] This represented everyone in a leadership position at Grade C and D levels.

customer complaints. By early 2020, the exco could see that some indicators were improving: customer survey satisfaction levels had increased, and the total number of incidents had started declining (see Exhibit 4). Relevant data were shared with staff, asking them for ideas on enhancements. But not all indicators had moved to where Botha and the exco team would have liked, especially in relation to claims and debtors' days. More engagement and conversations were planned with the broader team within the distribution centers to tackle this.

While performance indicators were important, shifts in accountability and teamwork could also be observed in subtler ways. Samuels could see that staff were taking ownership for safety by the way in which they would approach her if she was not wearing the correct safety shoes when visiting a site or if she was walking at incorrect crossing. From an HR perspective, Samuels was interested in how people's families were doing, and when she first started in post, she would ask staff about them. Colleagues from all levels would later greet her and share this information without waiting to be asked. Sishi, who took the lead on wage negotiations, could see a shift in overall tone from staff demands to requests.[18]

The Impact of COVID-19 on the Culture Change Program and Staff Engagement

The COVID-19 pandemic affected plans for further group sessions, especially when lockdown was enforced in South Africa in March 2020. Since CCS Logistics was considered an essential service, operational shifts continued while those in administrative positions worked from home. Any external or non-operational group sessions were moved online. Road shows continued in a virtual format using the Teams software program: big screens were purchased and used, and there was a learning curve in how to facilitate sessions and elicit questions and feedback in a way in which everyone's voice could be heard. The first few sessions were difficult, but the process slowly improved through trying to drive engagement with more interactive online technology tools, such as breakout rooms, a virtual whiteboard, and Mentimeter – a tool that used quizzes, polls, and word clouds to engage individuals and facilitate discussions.

Botha was aware that the team needed to connect with staff in a much more personal way – anxiety levels were high within the team, especially in the first few months following lockdown measures being imposed, and knowing about their staffs' home life and context was an important part of the company's COVID-19 operational plan. Exco and the senior management team practiced cold-calling scenarios with employees who were sick or who had a sick family member (for example, how to support them if someone needed to go to hospital), and then consciously approached each conversation with empathy. Colleagues who lived alone were contacted more frequently to provide emotional support.

Company-Wide Conversations on Accountability: "Cooler Together"

The COVID-19 pandemic also highlighted the need to work together and build on the culture change journey; as such, from October 2020 to April 2021, a customized one-day customer training program was rolled out and attended by every employee from sales and finance to debtors and operations. Additionally, in October 2020, a new campaign was launched across CCS Logistics called "Cooler Together." The full workforce was divided into smaller functional teams of six to eight people with a team host. Most of the team hosts had been through LIP. All team hosts received training from BeClear on how to facilitate small-group conversations aimed at driving collaboration across six specific themes, spaced over a year.

---

[18] Over 60 percent of CCS Logistics staff were part of a labor union.

Every second month, team hosts received a three-hour training and debriefing session on the themes for the next two sessions and how to conduct small-group conversations. To support the overall campaign, posters and banners were created (see Exhibit 3) which were installed in each site.

The theme of the first session focused on "Why Am I Keeping It Cool?" Conversations were encouraged to focus on the purpose of CCS Logistics and the importance of providing safe food to customers within South Africa and the wider region. The second theme focused on "Creating a Cooler Space," getting to know colleagues and what was needed for everyone to support each other personally and professionally. The third theme, "Cooler and Connected," involved brainstorming around team communication and how feedback could be provided on requests, problems, and opportunities for improvement. "Cooler Customer Experience" was the fourth theme, which evaluated recent progress on customer experience post-training and gave additional suggestions for better service. The fifth theme, "Cooler or Not," focused on the teams' progress and status of the business for the 2021 financial period. Finally, following an exco road show that communicated the objectives for 2022, the "Cool Commitment" theme was about encouraging each team to provide SMART (specific, measurable, actionable, realistic, and timebound) goals that would help achieve national and site objectives and which would be reflected in individual staff members' performance reviews.

Sishi helped lead on the creation of standard operating procedures (SOPs) to ensure everyone in their respective roles understood what was expected of them and had been trained properly. Over 2021, following input from colleagues, the SOPs were revised and communicated to staff, after which colleagues' knowledge was tested through the "Cooler Games." Workstations were set up within the warehouses, and teams of five were formed. Scenarios were provided, such as broken glass in the middle of the warehouse, and teams were judged by their colleagues acting as adjudicators and using the SOPs to assess performance and provide feedback. Sishi thought it was a fun and enriching experience to check learning and adherence to standards and to build up the team.

To help support the Cooler Together campaign, the executive team identified areas in which to drive efficiency and measure progress. Once indicators were identified focusing on common targets across sites and departments, the executives got together with their operational teams and developed detailed indicator dashboards. Initially developed in Excel and displayed using PowerPoint on televisions in the canteens and office staff screen savers, it was hoped that the dashboards could be automated in the future. In the meantime, the display of specific indicators was viewed as creating a healthy competitive environment focused on improvement across all distribution centers (see Exhibit 5).

Not all elements of the overall campaign ran as expected. Site and department leaders soon found that they needed support in handling the issues and ideas raised. This partly stemmed from the fact that they were used to commanding and telling, and now needed to shift to creating a psychologically safe space where listening and collaboration were paramount. It was also important to have a way to address the ideas raised by staff; how to do this later became an internal phrase of "How do we close the loop?" encouraging accountability and action where appropriate. Handouts for facilitating conversations and sharing with colleagues were viewed as too detailed and had to be revised. When team hosts gave feedback that the pace of the campaign was too intensive, an additional debriefing team host session was scheduled by an alternative team host to debrief learnings and hear what opportunities and challenges there were for implementing the program intentions, as well as to ensure that initiatives were implemented to improve operations.

Learning from the Past and Looking to the Future

As Botha reflected on the last few years, she thought about the many lessons learned through the culture change journey. The process had helped in a variety of ways. There was a shift in that ideas began to be generated from all levels, creating more distributed responsibility. Greater trust was forged through increased collaboration across different team members. Bottlenecks were identified, with practical solutions recommended and implemented, such as improving the turn-around times of trucks entering and leaving the warehouse and improving efficiency and productivity, resulting in improved customer service. With the increased trust and creation of a safe space in which to share ideas, more problems were raised as staff identified risks and felt comfortable raising them. Employees also had a more in-depth understanding of their impact and contribution.

Botha also thought there had been numerous lessons specifically around teamwork. The teams did not grow at the same pace, and it was important to be patient to allow everyone to get comfortable with the process. Some departments or sites needed more engagement than others. She specifically did not restrain the faster-moving areas from making progress, since their success stories assisted in getting buy-in from some of the slower adapters. And not everyone practiced accountability: several employees in 2021 were terminated for safety and misconduct misdemeanors. But the exco was satisfied that a new understanding had been created about the importance of teamwork and that a foundation on which to build had been established.

The overall culture change strategy had not been shared with Oceana colleagues – Botha wanted them to hear from others and to experience and see the results for themselves. She had been criticized before for such an approach and counseled to be more deliberate in sharing within the group and to lead from the front rather than from behind. Botha thought differently: she wanted the results to speak for themselves and for them to reflect a team approach, one in which she led from among others.

The strategic objectives for 2022 had been deliberately created by the extended leadership team and included a focus on driving customer satisfaction and adding value. Botha believed this was a step change from the previous focus on service and operational efficiencies, and necessary with the increased competition that had come into the market and the difficult post-COVID-19 economic environment. Botha was confident that the right leadership was in place to take the strategy forward, underpinned by the solid platform of accountability that had been created through the culture change journey. As she planned her next career move, she wondered what else could be done to enhance these culture changes.

Exhibit 1: Old and New Executive Committee Members

Exco (before November 2018)			Exco (post November 2018)		
Position	Name	Date of Relevance	Position	Name	Date of Relevance
Managing director	Naude Rademan	Left November 2018	Replaced by executive director	Ina Botha	Joined October 2018
Financial director	Mirella Mcgowan	Left November 2018	Financial director	Adam Firfirey	December 2018 (joined Oceana February 2006)

Exhibit 1 (continued)

Exco (before November 2018)			Exco (post November 2018)		
Operations manager	Peter Bristow	Retired January 2020	Replaced by supply chain executive	Lundi Sishi	May 2019
Namibia general manager	Willie Venter	Still in post. Started at CCS Logistics February 2001	Namibia general manager	Willie Venter	Still in post
Customer manager	Juan Swanepoel	Still in post. Started at CCS Logistics August 2012	Customer manager	Juan Swanepoel	Still in post
Human resources business partner	Shane Welby Solomon	Left June 2018	Human resources business partner	Melanie Samuels	Started at CCS Logistics July 2018 (joined Oceana April 2012)
Commercial manager	Feroza Mowzer	Left July 2018	Commercial manager	Ganeefah Dawood	Started at Oceana and CCS Logistics August 2018

Source: Adapted by the case authors from company files.

Exhibit 2: Keeping It Cool Campaign

Team value	Keep, avoid, start behaviors	CCS Logistics leadership team	
		Current objectives	Future objectives
Keeping It Cool and Accountable	KEEP Responsibility AVOID Waiting on somebody else to start START Understanding compliance	Step change Customer experience	Market leader
Keeping It Cool and Connected	KEEP Engagement AVOID Passing the buck START Prioritizing customer experience	Brilliance in compliance	Trust and revenue
Keeping It Cool and Proud	KEEP Work ethic AVOID Excuses START Brand building	Do things differently	Adding value

Source: Adapted by the case authors from company files.

Exhibit 3: Keeping it Cool and Cooler Together Campaign Poster Examples

Focus of conversation (theme)	Detail
Why am I Keeping Cooler?	It is not only our farmers and fishers that keep the nation's food secure.
	It is also CCS Logistics that keeps our nation's food secure, by keeping our customers' food safe, uncompromised, and in peak condition.
	We play a critical role in the handling, storing, and distribution of the essential foods that feed us and connect our local producers to foreign markets.
	Even during lockdown our jobs were secure because of the critical role we play in people's lives across the country, and we are grateful for that.
Cooler Together	During 2019 we started Keeping It Cool at CCS Logistics.
	It stands for building an accountable and responsible community where every person understands their contribution to Keeping CCS Logistics Cool. We focused on creating clarity and alignment through engagement.
	We are part of a bigger purpose to provide safe food to our nation, and we need to understand our role in this important matter. Over the next year, we will be introducing themes that will challenge our thinking and the way we do things—individually and as a company.
	We look forward to taking this journey together.
Creating a Cooler Space	At CCS Logistics we believe in empowering and advancing our people.
	In terms of their work, their attitude, and their roles as future leaders.
	We believe in our people and the potential to create an environment of growth, advancement, and excellence.
	This all starts with us and those around us: how we treat each other, how we improve each other, and how we co-operate for mutual benefit and progress.
Cooler and Connected	"Communication is merely an exchange of information, but connection is an exchange of our humanity." Sean Stephenson
	CCS Logistics values relationships and teamwork where people are respected and valued. To build an accountable and responsible community, it is important to have clarity and a good understanding of what is expected. There is a need to understand how each person contributes and connects to their duties and to each other.
	Together, a safe work environment is cultivated where people can collaborate, share, and listen for better understanding. This environment holds the keys to successful debates and discussions in the quest for continuous improvement.

Source: Adapted by the case authors from company files.

Exhibit 4: Tracking Progress

Indicator	Financial year 2018 (end Sep 2018)	Financial year 2019 (Oct 2018 to Sep 2019)	Financial year 2020 (end Sep 2020)	Financial year 2021 (end Sep 2021)
Claims, bad debts, and credits (R)	15.2 million	6.2 million	4.3 million	1.8 million
Compliance	Compliance focused on closing out non-conformances in time for an audit	Driving focus of daily compliance, upgrading documentation, and educating management teams	Daily compliance becoming a way we do business 80% of the time. Replaced compliance clerks with compliance officers and provided them with a voice at all site management meetings	Upgraded compliance to daily compliance with implementation of FSSC* standard, testing scenarios on emergencies and improved reporting and trending
Cost per pallet (R)	63.59	62.44	68.31	61.33
Credit notes (R)	-	4,686	1,477	710
Customer complaints	Not tracked	Not tracked by all sites	Started tracking and improved by 15%	Tracked and showed a 30% improvement based on limited information and an online portal implemented for financial year 2022
Customer satisfaction surveys	Not measured	Average of 76%	Average of 83%	Average of 92%
Debtors' days	42	High: 85 Average: 60 Close: 39	High: 75 Average: 58 Close: 45	High: 75 Average: 58 Close: 49
Engagements	Limited visibility of leadership team	Visibility of leadership team with minimal engagement from CCS Logistics teams	Visibility of leadership team with partial engagement from teams down to supervisor level Minimum engagement at Grade A level	Visibility of leadership team with full engagement from teams at all levels
Incidents	1.86	1.91	1.87	1.33 (Met the DFIR† target of 1.5)
Litigation matters	6	4	2	-
No. of staff	608 (330 permanent)	479 (324 permanent)	458 (312 permanent)	358 (255 permanent)

Exhibit 4 (continued)

Indicator	Financial year 2018 (end Sep 2018)	Financial year 2019 (Oct 2018 to Sep 2019)	Financial year 2020 (end Sep 2020)	Financial year 2021 (end Sep 2021)
Store occupancy levels (%)	78.04	81.39	89.98	83.28
Margin (%) per store	14.4	14	17	22

Note: * FSSC = food safety system certification; † DFIR = disabling injury frequency rate examines the ration between actual disabling injuries per 200,000 hours and is expressed as a percentage. The figure 200,000 used in the standard formula is based on the assumption that one employee works approximately 2000 hours per year, therefore 1000 employees work 200,000 per year. Disabling injuries refers to incidents in the workplace that result in a disability or an employee missing work due to an injury.

Source: Adapted by the case authors from company files.

Exhibit 5: Examples of Dashboards

Focus areas across all distribution centres	Description	Target
Carbon footprint	Measured carbon footprint	2% reduction
DFIR*	Measured the frequency of injuries in the workplace and the drive behavior of reporting on incidents and near-miss incidents	1.5
Electricity	Measured electricity consumption	2% reduction
Truck turnaround time	Measured time to offload: the shorter the time to offload, receive, and conclude a load, the more loads could be accommodated during a shift, which would result in customer savings on transport costs and standing time	30% improvement
Water consumption	Measured water consumption	2% reduction

Detailed dashboard – truck turnaround time financial years 2021–2022

CCS Logistics depot	Financial year 2021 (time)	Financial year 2022 (time)	Targeted improvement (%)†
Epping	01:29:00	01:05:41	35
Duncan Dock	01:26:33	01:09:50	24
Midrand	02:19:32	01:55:59	20
Walvis Bay	01:52:56	02:05:08	−10
Paarden Eiland	00:18:24	00:26:01	−29
City Deep	01:37:19	02:30:09	−35

* DFIR = disabling injury frequency rate; † improvement target of 30%.

Source: Adapted by the case authors from company files.

PART IV
Purpose, Sustainability, and Integrity

Organizations and their leaders play a vital role in addressing sustainability of societies and our planet. This section addresses the purpose of business, social and environmental sustainability, and ethical decision-making in the complex context of working across boundaries.

11 Toward Sustainability and Responsible Organizations

> The future is not something we enter. The future is something we create.
> Leonard I. Sweet, American author and theologian (1961–)

Key Learning Objectives

At the end of this chapter, students will be able to:

- Compare state capitalism, shareholder capitalism, and stakeholder capitalism.
- Explain stakeholder theory and stakeholder capitalism.
- Summarize the chronological development of the concepts of sustainability and corporate responsibility.
- Identify the major corporate sustainability frameworks.
- Recognize the paradoxical tensions that exist in sustainability management.

Overview: The Purpose of Business

There are three major concepts and theories related to the responsibility of business to society and to sustainability. The three contrasting models are: **shareholder capitalism**, **state capitalism**, and **stakeholder theory**, also referred to as **stakeholder capitalism**. This chapter is not intended as a complete treatise on the topics of sustainability and corporations' responsibilities to society, as there are entire books devoted to those topics. The intent is to offer ways of thinking about the role of business in society and management's responsibility regarding sustainability.

Table 11.1 Global mindset framework applied to ethics, corporate social responsibility, and sustainability

	Individual/Personal	Organizational
Self	Clarify and understand my beliefs about ethical behavior.	Clarify and understand my organization's approach to corporate social responsibility and sustainability.
Other	Clarify and understand other beliefs about ethical behavior in the context of other cultures and principal theories of moral philosophy.	Clarify and understand other corporate approaches to social responsibility and sustainability in the context of other industries, other cultures, and principal codes of conduct.
Choice	Belief in and commitment to a set of ethical principles.	Belief in and commitment to an approach to social responsibility and corporate sustainability.

There are hundreds of definitions of "sustainability" and "sustainable development" (Johnston et al., 2007). Some writers and companies include ethics in their definitions of corporate sustainability, but we have separated out that discussion. To be sure, there may be ethical issues associated with some business decisions or a product that will impact the environment or a community. Our reasoning for the separation is that legal and ethical behavior, as will be discussed in Chapter 12, should be expected by managers in all activities. Ethical behavior also deserves focused attention. Even though corporations may have codes of conduct specifying standards of behavior for their employees, the decision to act legally and ethically is, in the final analysis, a personal decision.

As we continue to address the domains of global mindset, we focus in this chapter on the organizational level as shown in Table 11.1, raising awareness of sustainable decision-making for your own and other organizations, and Chapter 12 focuses on individual and personal ethics as shown in the table.

The Evolution of Corporate Social Responsibility and Sustainability

As recounted by Spector (2008), the history and ideology of Western corporations having social responsibility as an explicit management theme can be traced back to 1927. At that time Wallace Donham, Dean of the Harvard Business School, advocated for greater corporate social responsibility as a way of "aligning business interests with the defense of free-market capitalism against what was depicted as the clear and present danger of Soviet Communism."

Serious discussion of corporate social responsibility in North America increased in 1953 with the publication of Bowen's *Social Responsibilities of the Businessman* (Bowen, 1953; Carroll, 1979). The discussion became a debate with strong disagreement from Harvard Business School professor Theodore Levitt, who in 1958 published a critique in *Harvard Business Review* on "the dangers of social responsibility" (Levitt, 1958).

1960–1970

Even in the face of Levitt's concern, the perceived role of business in society was changing. Starting in the 1960s, Rachel Carson and Ralph Nader initiated a new dialogue. Carson's book *Silent Spring* spoke to the dramatic impact of pesticides on humans and the environment, and Nader's book *Unsafe at Any Speed* alerted the public to the importance of paying attention to product safety (Carson, 2002; Nader, 1966). These authors sparked movements that gained momentum over the next decades, beginning a trend of public outcry forcing corporate accountability in terms of what companies were expected to do and mobilizing the ability of stakeholders to enforce many of those expectations. Using the courts, the internet, their wallets, and social media, stakeholders now can exert a lot of power.

However, in 1970, the best-known, and most widely cited, proponent of free-market or **shareholder capitalism**, Milton Friedman, asserted that a company's only social responsibility was to make a profit for its shareholders:

[T]here is one and only one social responsibility of business – to use its resources and engage in activities designed to increase its profits so long as it stays within the rules of the game, which is to say, engages in open and free competition without deception or fraud. (Friedman, 1970, p. 17)

Friedman argued that in a free-enterprise, private-property system, executives were employees of the organizations' owners and that management's responsibility was to the owners. They should run the business according to the owners' desires if these were legal. He clearly saw business and society as separate, independent entities. He even believed that people who advocated that business had a social responsibility were "preaching pure and unadulterated socialism" (Friedman, 1970, p. 17) and "were unwitting puppets of the intellectual forces that have been undermining the basis of a free society these past decades" (Friedman, 1970, p. 17).

Governments, Friedman believed, only had three functions: national defense, personal and property protection, and enforcement of contracts. Regarding the government's role in the economy, he believed a government "should be a referee, not an active player" (reported in Blackwell, 2014).

Friedman's viewpoint on the role of government in the economy distinguishes **shareholder capitalism** from **state capitalism**, the latter being "a broad concept meant to explain mixed economies in which the state retains a dominant role amidst the presence of markets and private firms" (Pearson et al., 2021, p. 207). Governments may direct markets and may own the organizations managing the production activities. Governments can intervene in this system as they see fit for state interests and for political reasons as well as for economic outcomes. State capitalist systems exist in authoritarian countries like China and Russia as well as in democratic countries like India, Brazil, and Norway.

Although Friedman's view that what was good for shareholders was good for society was controversial in 1970, it took root in many business schools' finance departments. It undoubtedly is more controversial today. The world, and business's place in it, are more complex than in 1970.

Into the 2000s

As society's expectations of business changed over time, as summarized in Figure 11.1, concerns that were once primarily seen to be the responsibility of the government became areas in which businesses were expected to show leadership.

Although the expectations of the 2010s remain, Gen Zs and Millennials have become the most engaged generations on the issue of climate change (PEW Research Center, 2021). Creating a sustainable environment is a top priority for

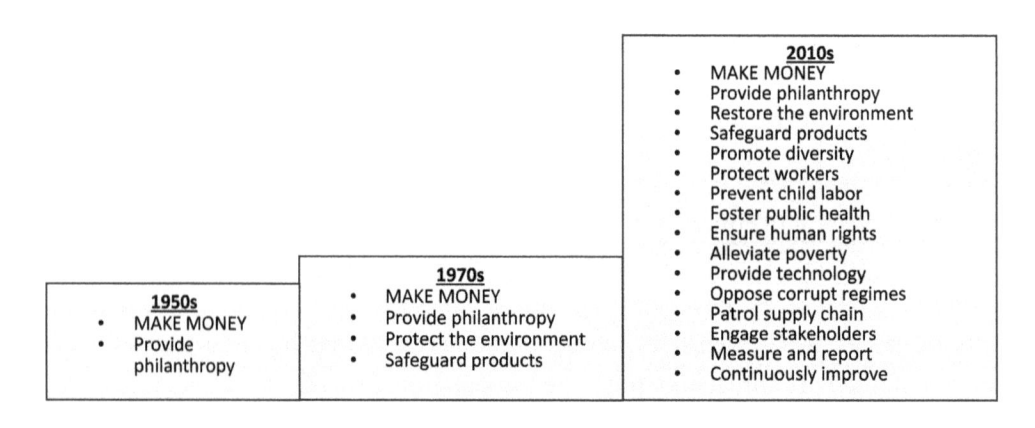

1950s
- MAKE MONEY
- Provide philanthropy

1970s
- MAKE MONEY
- Provide philanthropy
- Protect the environment
- Safeguard products

2010s
- MAKE MONEY
- Provide philanthropy
- Restore the environment
- Safeguard products
- Promote diversity
- Protect workers
- Prevent child labor
- Foster public health
- Ensure human rights
- Alleviate poverty
- Provide technology
- Oppose corrupt regimes
- Patrol supply chain
- Engage stakeholders
- Measure and report
- Continuously improve

Figure 11.1 The rise of corporate accountability.
From Andrew Savitz & Karl Weber, *Talent, Transformation, and the Triple Bottom Line: How Companies Can Leverage Human Resources for Sustainable Growth*, Jossey-Bass, 2013. Used with permission of the authors.

many members of these generations. Their interests include addressing climate change, building support for sustainable causes, developing sustainable brands and retail, advancing sustainable product development and packaging, and advocating for sustainable investments.

The concept of "sustainable development" came into common usage when the UN General Assembly's World Commission on Environment and Development issued its 1987 report on "Our Common Future." The report defined sustainable development as "development which meets the needs of current generations without compromising the ability of future generations to meet their own needs" (World Commission on Environment and Development, 1987). To many people this concept became synonymous with simply protecting the environment or being "green." However, it encompassed more than a focus on the physical ecosystem, including also a concern for economic and social development.

John Elkington (1997) coined the concept and term "triple bottom line" in his book, *Cannibals with Forks*. Sustainability was about performance and progress on the three pillars of sustainability – people, planet, and profits – and the triple bottom line was a way of measuring and reporting this performance (Savitz, 2006).

American science fiction writer William Gibson (1999) said in many interviews, "The future is already here – it's just not evenly distributed." If he is correct, what will the global future look like? Is it the one with flying automobiles, cancer cures, and artificial intelligence solving society's problems? Or is it the one of continued economic disparity and unequal distributions of power and wealth, devastating weather episodes, disappearing ice shelves, sinking countries, and artificial intelligence replacing workers and creating global chaos? Or will it be both, with the continuing uneven distribution? And what are the responsibilities of corporations in contributing to these possible futures?

Over the years and in earlier editions of this book, numerous terms have been used to capture business's responsibility to society and to evaluate business performance: corporate citizenship, corporate social responsibility (CSR), the triple bottom line, and most recently ESG (environmental, social, and governance) initiatives, including an increased emphasis on responsible governance. Figure 11.2 provides a graphical view of the chronological development of these concepts.

Stakeholder Theory

In 1984, R. Edward Freeman began delineating stakeholder theory, which addresses the issue of corporate social responsibility and sustainable development (Freeman, 2010). It promulgates the view that corporate social responsibility encompasses continued strong economic performance, a broad concept of social

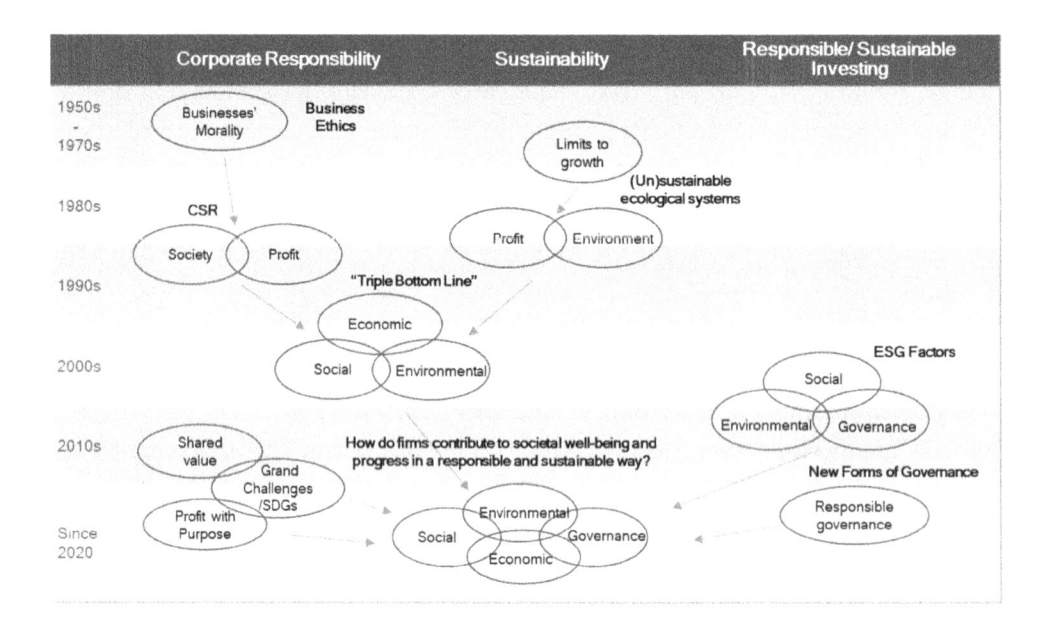

Figure 11.2 Development of sustainability and corporate responsibility concepts.
From Stahl, G. K., Miska, C., & Sully de Luque, M. *Encyclopedia of International Strategic Management.* Asmussen et al. (Eds.). Edward Elgar, forthcoming.

justice, a concern for environmental quality, and recognition of the interdependence between the three areas. Unlike Friedman's view that businesses and society were independent, stakeholder theory and stakeholder capitalism reject the idea that shareholders and stakeholders are unrelated, and that one group has more rights than the other. Shareholders are just one class of stakeholders.

Stakeholder theory and stakeholder capitalism hold that companies should create long-term value not only for its shareholders but for all its stakeholders including employees, customers, suppliers, investors, and the communities in which they operate. Management should be concerned with the health and welfare of societies, the planet, and future generations. Nations today are more closely linked than ever before, which means that the planet's health is a systemic, global issue that cannot be resolved by independent actors but requires partnerships at all levels.

Proponents of stakeholder theory also believe that values are explicitly part of what management entails. The approach that managers choose will most likely depend on the senior executives' and board of directors' values and their view of the relationship between business and society. If they believe that society's moral or social values and business objectives are inherently in conflict, or at best totally separate domains of activity, they may favor a stance that resists doing more than the minimum. A paradigm in which business objectives and societal values are in harmony or are complementary will more likely lead to actions deemed today as progressive or as leading the way.

Stakeholder theory asks two questions that executives need to answer (Freeman et al., 2004):

1. What is the purpose of the firm?
2. What responsibility do managers have to stakeholders?

The Business Roundtable (2019), an association of more than 200 CEOs of America's leading companies, has periodically issued its *Statement on the Purpose of a Corporation*. From 1997 to 2018, it supported the principle that corporations existed primarily to serve shareholders. In 2019, it issued a new statement, superseding the previous ones, that defined a new, contemporary standard for corporate responsibility. The member companies committed to:

- Delivering value to our customers.
- Investing in our employees.
- Fostering diversity and inclusion.
- Dealing fairly and ethically with our suppliers.
- Supporting the communities in which we work.
- Protecting the environment by embracing sustainable practices across our businesses.
- Generating long-term value for shareholders.

It also stated that "Each of our stakeholders is essential. We commit to deliver value to all of them, for the future success of our companies, our communities and our country."

Reflection Exercise 11.1: The Business of Business Is…?

1. Which view of capitalism do you find most compelling: shareholder capitalism, stakeholder capitalism, or state capitalism?
2. Why did you choose it? What problems do you see with the others?

How should company executives think about their organization's purpose in relation to private ownership interests versus society's interests? There is no simple answer to that question other than that they need to actively address the question in a responsible manner. The answer is not simple because the factors to be considered are complex. The answer must come from a combination of value judgments and financial analyses that executives of individual corporations will have to take for themselves. What is clear is that top management must set its desired course for corporate sustainability initiatives. One company that did this is Unilever.

Unilever: A Net Positive Company

What is a **net positive company**? A net positive company is "A company giving more than it takes [and does] not focus on profits with a side of philanthropy" (Polman & Winston, 2021, p. 11). Paul Polman, former CEO of Unilever (2009–2019), and Andrew Winston, a leading thinker and author on business sustainability, wrote *Net Positive: How Courageous Companies Thrive by Giving More Than They Take*. The book was selected to be on the *Financial Times/McKinsey* longlist of the best business books of 2021. Polman is credited with leading a major turnaround of Unilever between 2009 and 2019. He was also named a "standout CEO of the past decade" by the *Financial Times* in 2018 (Skapinker, 2018).

The authors define net positive firms as ones that "improve well-being for everyone [they] impact and at all scales – every product, every operation, every region and country, and for every stakeholder, including employees, suppliers, communities, customers, and even future generations and the planet itself" (Polman & Winston, 2021, p. 7). In 2010, Polman instituted the Unilever Sustainable Living Plan (USLP) that was the vehicle for the turnaround. More detail on the USLP, the challenges of implementation, and its impact on business can be found in this section.

The authors see two existential crises facing society today that businesses can contribute to addressing: climate and inequality. "Climate" is their shorthand for environmental problems affecting planetary health, and "inequality" is their shorthand for the problems impacting society's health.

The five core principles of net positive companies are:

1. Ownership of all impacts and consequences, intended or not.
2. Operating for the long-term benefit of business and society.
3. Creating positive returns for all stakeholders.
4. Driving shareholder wealth as a result, not a goal.
5. Partnering to drive systemic change.

How did Unilever perform during Polman's 10 years as CEO? It doubled its revenues, achieved a 300% shareholder return and a 19% return on invested capital, *and* reduced its environmental impact by 50% (Le, 2022). How did Polman achieve this? He began by thinking long term (e.g., ending quarterly earnings reports) and working on *purpose* – individual employees' purpose for working as well as his own purpose in leading the company; and then working collectively with employees to define the company's purpose. The result was Unilever's Sustainable Living Plan (USLP) that refocused company efforts and guided the company's success. The USLP's three big goals could be considered what Collins and Porras (1994) called big, hairy, audacious goals (BHAGs). These were to "help a billion people improve their health and well-being, halve the environmental footprint while doubling sales, and enhance the livelihoods of hundreds of thousands of people" (Polman & Winston, 2021, p. 101).

In 2013, the United Nations began working on the Sustainable Development Goals (SDGs, described in the next section). The working group initially did not have a representative from the private, business sector, since "representatives from national governments and the UN did not trust multinationals" (Polman & Winston, 2021, p. 135). However, Polman and Unilever had built credibility with the Dutch and UK governments, which were confident that Unilever would not put its self-interests ahead of the world's interests. Those two governments nominated Polman, and he became the sole private-sector representative in the SDG working group.

Corporate Sustainability Frameworks

Just as there are numerous definitions of sustainability, similarly there are many organizations, public and private, focusing on sustainability. Numerous international accords and sets of principles have been formulated, adopted, and endorsed in the latter half of the 20th century that provide a base for the development of a transcultural standard of how corporations should behave in the global economy. These documents include: The United Nations Universal Declaration of Human Rights (1948), The European Convention on Human Rights (1950), The Helsinki Final Act (1975), The OECD Guidelines for Multinational Enterprises (1976), The International Labor Office Tripartite Declaration of Principles Concerning Multinational Enterprises and Social Policy (1977), The United Nations Code of Conduct for Transnational Corporations (1983), and The United Nations Global Compact (2000). These accords and principles address the following issues:

- **Employment practices and policies.** For example, multinationals should develop nondiscriminatory employment practices, provide equal pay for equal work, observe the right of employees to join unions and to bargain collectively,

give advance notice of plant closings and mitigate their adverse effects, respect local host country job standards, provide favorable work conditions and limited working hours, adopt adequate health and safety standards, and inform employees about health hazards. They should not permit unacceptable practices such as the exploitation of children, physical punishment, gender-based abuse, or involuntary servitude.
- **Consumer protection.** MNCs should respect host country laws regarding consumer protection; safeguard the health and safety of consumers through proper labeling, disclosures, and advertising; and provide safe products and packaging.
- **Environmental protection.** MNCs should preserve ecological balance, protect the environment, rehabilitate environments damaged by them, and respect host country laws, goals, and priorities regarding protection of the environment.
- **Political payments and involvement.** MNCs should not pay bribes to public officials and should avoid illegal involvement or interference in internal politics.
- **Basic human rights and fundamental freedoms.** Multinationals should respect the rights of people to life, liberty, security of person, and privacy; and freedom of religion, peaceful assembly, and opinion.
- **Community responsibility.** MNCs should work with the governments and communities in which they do business to improve the quality of life in those communities.

The UN Global Compact, the Global Reporting Initiative (GRI), and the Dow Jones Sustainability Indices (DJSI) are three global organizations that currently focus on different aspects of corporate sustainability and have established frameworks and programs. Together, they provide a set of lenses for diagnosing and discussing corporate sustainability. The UN Global Compact is a quasi-governmental international organization and links corporate practices with human rights and international law. GRI is a nonprofit, network-based organization that develops standards for reporting, monitoring and comparing sustainability initiatives. DJSI is a private company that develops indices of sustainability performance for the use of the financial industry, for creating sustainable funds and other financial instruments. We will describe each of them next.

The UN Global Compact

The Global Compact was formally launched in July 2000. It is a voluntary program and the world's largest corporate sustainability initiative, with 18,000 companies and 3,800 nonbusiness signatories from over 160 countries (United Nations, 2023). Its focus is not regulatory but rather on transparency and disclosure for public accountability. Companies sign on to the Global Compact, and in doing so commit to adhering to the UN's 10 principles on human rights, labor, environment, and anti-corruption.

The 10 Global Compact Principles are as follows (United Nations, 2023):

Human Rights

- Principle 1: Businesses should support and respect the protection of internationally proclaimed human rights; and
- Principle 2: make sure they are not complicit in human rights abuses.

Labor
- Principle 3: Businesses should uphold the freedom of association and the effective recognition of the right to collective bargaining;
- Principle 4: the elimination of all forms of forced and compulsory labor;
- Principle 5: the effective abolition of child labor; and
- Principle 6: the elimination of discrimination in respect of employment and occupation.

Environment
- Principle 7: Businesses should support a precautionary approach to environmental challenges;
- Principle 8: undertake initiatives to promote greater environmental responsibility; and
- Principle 9: encourage the development and diffusion of environmentally friendly technologies.

Anti-Corruption
- Principle 10: Businesses should work against corruption in all its forms, including extortion and bribery.

Starting in 2016, after the establishment of the 17 Sustainable Development Goals (SDGs, listed in Figure 11.3), companies in the Global Compact also committed to advance the goals of the UN's 2030 Agenda for Sustainable Development. The SDGs are

a universal call to action to end poverty, protect the planet and improve the lives and prospects of everyone, everywhere ... The 17 Goals are interconnected, apply to all countries, and need to be carried out by all stakeholders – governments, the private sector, civil society, the United Nations system and others – in a collaborative partnership. (UN.org, n.d.)

The *UN Global Compact Progress Report* provides annual updates of the extent to which goals are being addressed or met (United Nations, 2023). The Global

Figure 11.3 The 17 Sustainable Goals of the agenda for 2030. (United Nations, Department of Economic and Social Affairs.)

Compact organization facilitates collaboration and best practice sharing among members and facilitates innovation through research and encouragement of new company initiatives.

Have the SDGs had an impact? The 2023 SDG Progress Report (UN Statistics Division, 2023) presented a sobering view that the world is falling short of meeting most of the goals by 2030. The impacts from COVID-19, the war in Ukraine, extreme climate events, and the resultant global economic weakness all contributed to slowing progress everywhere. The report also pointed out that the poorest countries are the most vulnerable and will suffer the most without increased effort toward meeting the goals.

A study based on publicly available information from Fortune 500 corporations (Song et al., 2022) found that 304 (60.8%) of the 500 reported information directly relevant to the SDGs. Of these 304 only 0.2% developed methods and tools to evaluate progress; 32.6% simply matched their normal business practice to relevant SDGs but reported no new initiatives; 22.8% planned strategies and actions for specific SDGs; and 5.2% briefly mentioned the SDGs. The remainder of the 500 (39%) were uninvolved or no information could be found.

Companies appeared to be focusing on the goal areas related most closely to their existing operations and brands, which is understandable from a business perspective. Current Unilever CEO, Alan Jope, in an interview with Professor Ranjay

Gulati of the Harvard Business School, stated that purpose-driven, sustainable-living brands represented 60% of the company's revenue and were growing three times faster than the rest of the portfolio. Two other benefits of sustainable business mentioned were a saving of 1.2 billion euros through sustainable sourcing and being a magnet for talent acquisition (Gulati, 2022).

A specific example of linking brands to SDGs are Unilever's Dove skin care and cleansing products and Domestos, a cleaning agent and disinfectant. The Dove Self-Esteem Project partners with UN Women to help 10 million young people gain self-esteem and body confidence, to advance gender equality (SDG 5). Domestos supports UNICEF's efforts to combat unsafe sanitation and improve hygiene (SDG 6). In 10 years, the partnership has helped 28 million people gain access to safe toilets (Unilever.com, n.d.).

Song et al. (2022) further noted that companies reporting progress tended to focus most heavily on SDG 8 (Decent Work and Economic Growth) and SDG 13 (Climate Action), and that the corporations in the information technology sector were the most engaged with the SDGs. Also, it was noted that SDG 2 (Zero Hunger) and SDG 14 (Life below Water) received the least attention.

Global Reporting Initiative (GRI)

The UN Global Compact, discussed earlier, is a list of 10 principles that signatory companies agree to support. They also agree to advance the 2030 Agenda for Sustainable Development and the SDGs. In 2010, the UN Global Compact recommended the GRI Standards as the reporting framework for companies to communicate progress against the SDGs (sustaincase.co, 2023).

The Global Reporting Initiative (GRI) is a nonprofit foundation headquartered in the Netherlands. GRI created a reporting system that covers corporate economic, environmental, and social performance indicators. The GRI Reporting Standards and system provide organizations with a common language to communicate their environmental and societal impacts and allow organizations to embed the SDGs into their existing business and reporting processes. It focuses on economic performance, including direct and indirect economic impact and procurement practices; environmental aspects, including such items as materials, energy and water usage, biodiversity, emissions, and waste; and social elements, which include subcategories of labor practices and decent work, human rights, and social and product responsibility. There are three sets of standards: Universal Standards applicable to all organizations; Sector Standards for reporting sector-specific impacts; and Topic Standards for reporting on specific topics. A complete listing of the guidelines and detailed explanations of all the categories can be found on the GRI's website (GRI, 2023a).

GRI Standards are used by more than 10,000 organizations in over 100 countries and "as confirmed by 2022 research from KPMG, the GRI Standards remain the most widely used sustainability reporting standards globally" (GRI, 2023b). The KPMG study contained an analysis of sustainability and Environmental, Social, and Governance (ESG) reports and websites for 5,800 companies in 58 countries, territories, and jurisdictions. The complete report, *Big Shifts, Small Steps, Survey of Sustainability Reporting 2022*, can be found on its website (KPMG, 2022).

S&P Dow Jones Indices

Sustainability, its definition, management guidelines to promote it, and outcomes are no longer the concern only of international, quasi-governmental organizations or NGOs, but are now also the concern of some private investment companies such as S&P Global (formerly McGraw-Hill Financials). This publisher is a provider of credit ratings, benchmarks, and indices (e.g., S&P 500 and the Dow Jones Industrial Average) in the global capital and commodity markets. One of its divisions, the Dow Jones Sustainability Indices, tracks the stock performance of the world's leading companies using environmental, social, and governance criteria. These data serve as benchmarks for investors who integrate sustainability considerations into their portfolios and provide a platform for companies who want to adopt sustainable best practices.

Each year approximately 4,500 of the world's largest companies in terms of free-float market capitalization listed in the S&P Global Broad Market Index (BMI) are invited to participate. They are sent the Corporate Sustainability Assessment (CSA) to complete regarding their sustainability efforts, which are then evaluated according to specified criteria, scored, and verified. The top companies in each sector are then included in the indices. The Dow Jones Indices also contain ethical exclusion subindices for investors who wish to limit their exposure to controversial activities such as Armaments & Firearms, Alcohol, Tobacco, Gambling, and Adult Entertainment (Dow Jones Indices, 2023).

Unlike the UN Global Compact or the GSI, the DJSI considers financial materiality. It identifies the sustainability factors that drive business value and that have an impact on the long-term valuation assumptions used in financial analysis and focuses on their impact. Each industry is assessed differently according to its specific value drivers.

Recalling the earlier discussion of Unilever, in 2022 it was the only company awarded the S&P Global Gold Class distinction in the Personal Products industry, meaning its ESG score was within 1% of the industry's top-performing company's score. In 2023, while still among the leaders, it had slipped to the Silver Class level being one of four in the top 5% with LG H&H Co. from the Republic of Korea being the only Gold Class honoree. The 2023 complete scores can be found under Further Resources at the end of the chapter.

Greenwashing and Bluewashing

It would be naïve not to acknowledge that some companies can be hypocritical in their support of sustainability and social responsibility in the areas covered by the Global Compact and SDGs. Do companies participate in the Global Compact simply to bolster their image? Yes, **greenwashing** is alive and well, along with its newer companion term, **bluewashing**, referring to organizations' deceptive or exaggerated claims regarding their social and community practices.

Endorsing ESG principles is easy to do, but this act alone does not mean that a company is committed to advancing them. Earth.org is a not-for-profit environmental organization engaging in climate communications and raising awareness about biodiversity loss and the deterioration of natural ecosystems worldwide (earth.org, 2023). It has published a list of 10 companies that have been caught greenwashing.

Reflection Exercise 11.2: Greenwashing Awareness

Go to https://earth.org/greenwashing-companies-corporations/ to see the list of 10 companies that have been caught greenwashing.

Questions:

1. Which, if any, of these companies' products do you currently use?
2. Will you continue to use them? Why or why not?
3. Are you likely to follow any of the suggested action steps listed at the end of the article? If so, which ones?

The Relationship between ESG and Financial Performance

Does sustainability pay? This is an important question given that corporations and investors are paying more attention to ESG factors, and there now exist several sources of ESG ratings in addition to the DJSI. Another useful source for corporate sustainability ESG research, ratings and investing is Morningstar/Sustainalytics (https://www.sustainalytics.com/about-us).

What do all the available data and research say about the relationship between ESG and corporate financial performance? How do a strong ESG focus and excellent execution create value in ways that impact financial performance? Researchers have identified five pathways to value creation (Henisz et al., 2019).

1. **Top-line growth.** This pathway can open new markets and attract new customers looking for more sustainable products. Unilever's Sunlight dishwashing product, which uses less water than its other brands, outpaced category growth [eco-friendly dishwashing detergents] by more than 20% in several water-scarce markets.
2. **Cost reduction.** This pathway includes lower energy and water usage.
3. **Reduced regulatory and legal interventions.** In addition to reducing costs from potential unfavorable government actions, firms may become eligible for government subsidies.
4. **Increased productivity.** It is possible to attract qualified, motivated employees seeking purpose in their careers and to increase job satisfaction and motivation of existing employees.
5. **Investment and asset optimization.** Firms can allocate capital to higher-returning, long-term, sustainable plants and equipment and avoid write-downs in projects and equipment that may be vulnerable to environmental degradation issues.

Although these benefits may be attainable, it is important to realize that they will not happen automatically. Investments in ESG should be consistent with a firm's strategy. Developing a robust net positive program also will most likely necessitate a reevaluation of the firm's existing strategic alignment and require a realignment of its systems and/or structures as explained in Chapter 9.

There is evidence that there is a financial benefit. Early meta-analysis studies concluded that there was a positive association between corporate social performance and corporate financial performance. However, the results also suggested that this outperformance occurs only in the long term (Dixon-Fowler et al., 2013; Margolis & Elfenbein, 2008; Orlitzky et al., 2003).

A study with a very different design compared 90 high-sustainability firms with a matched set of low-sustainability ones (Eccles et al., 2014). This study examined the financial performance of these firms over an 18-year period and found that "high sustainability companies significantly outperform[ed] their counterparts over the long term, both in terms of stock market and accounting performance" (Eccles et al., 2014, p. 2835). Additionally, the authors discovered some of the practices that most likely contributed to this better performance. High-sustainability companies were more likely to:

- have boards of directors that were formally responsible for sustainability.
- form a separate board committee for sustainability.
- link executive compensation to sustainability metrics.
- be owned by proportionately more long-term investors.
- measure information related to key stakeholders such as employees, customers, and suppliers.
- measure and disclose relatively more nonfinancial data.

The above studies were conducted before 2015. A more recent meta-analysis of more than 1,000 studies was done by researchers from the NYU/Stern Center for Sustainable Business and Rockefeller Asset Management (Whelan et al., 2020). They found a "positive relationship between ESG and financial performance for 58% of the 'corporate' studies focused on operational metrics such as ROE, ROA, or stock price; 13% showed neutral impact; 21% mixed results (the same study finding a positive, neutral or negative results); and only 8% showed a negative relationship" (Whelan et al., 2020, p. 25). Some of the report's key takeaways included:

- Financial performance improves over the long term.
- Sustainability initiatives at corporations appear to drive financial performance due to improved risk management and innovation.
- Managing for a low-carbon future appears to improve financial performance.

All the studies referred to better performance by sustainable companies in the *long term*.

Bansal and DesJardine (2014) thus argue that time is central to the notion of sustainability, and that managing intertemporal trade-offs in strategic decision-making is critical for sustainable businesses. Recalling the UN's 1987 definition of development as that which "meets the needs of current generations without compromising the ability of future generations to meet their own needs, (World Commission on Environment and Development (1987), first paragraph)," Bansal and DesJardine translate this to the corporate level of analysis as "business sustainability can be defined as the ability of firms to respond to their short-term financial needs without compromising their (or others') ability to meet their future needs" (Bansal & DesJardine, 2014, p. 70). They observe that,

Firms must choose between investing less for smaller profits sooner and investing more for greater profits later (Laverty, 1996). These same principles apply to the trade-off between exploitation and exploration (March, 1991). Firms profit from exploitation by marketing and selling current products and services, but must also invest in exploration activities, such as research and development, to secure a future pipeline of products and services. (Bansal & DesJardine, 2014, p. 70)

Short-term thinking is contrary to sustainable, long-term thinking. This temporal dichotomy is one of the significant management paradoxes that global leaders must navigate.

Creating Sustainable Value

Arguments about the role of sustainability, corporate citizenship, creating shared value, or other terminology for ESG initiatives often tend to pit business against society and moral actions against profitable ones. Positioning shareholders against other stakeholders creates a false dichotomy. Shareholders are a subset of stakeholders, and management should be trying to do the best they can for all groups. The Sustainable Value Framework (Figure 11.4) illustrates the four possible outcomes of the shareholder/stakeholder paradox followed by examples of companies in the four quadrants.

Quadrant 1: Worthington Industries. Sustainable (both win, upper right). This is the quadrant managers of sustainable businesses are aiming for. *Investor's Business Daily*'s 100 Best ESG Companies for 2022 (IBD, 2022) ranked Worthington Industries as the #1 ESG company based on the Dow Jones ESG rating of 2,208 public companies combined with IBD's composite rating. Its ESG score was 75.8. Scores over 70 are considered excellent and indicate the company is following best practices in all ESG areas and has no significant internal or external problems (Krychiw, 2023). The IBD Composite Rating looks at the company's financial metrics such as earnings growth, profit margins, and share price. The Composite Rating overweights the stock's earnings per share (EPS) and relative price strength against other stocks. Worthington's three-year EPS growth rate was 61% and its return on equity (ROE) was 26%. Worthington is one of the largest processors of flat rolled steel in the United States. It also makes pressure cylinders for gases such as oxygen, refrigerants, and other industrial gases as well as retail products like propane tanks. It plans to split into two businesses: its steel processing business and consumer products, and its building products and sustainable energy solutions businesses.

Stakeholder value	+	2 Unsustainable (shareholders lose value and other stakeholders benefit)	1 Sustainable (both win)
	−	3 Unsustainable (both lose value)	4 Unsustainable (shareholders benefit and other stakeholders lose value)
		− Shareholder value +	

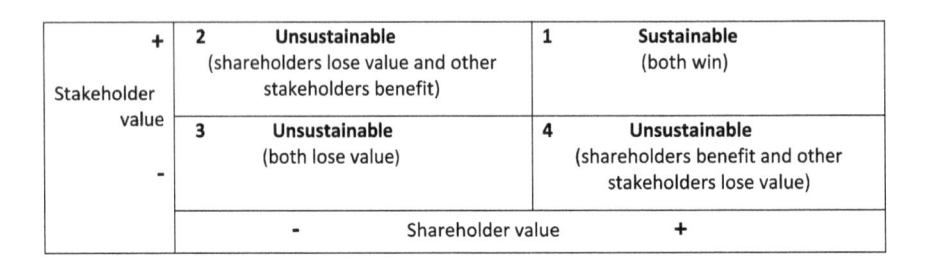

Figure 11.4 Sustainable value framework. Adapted from Lazlo (2008).

Other companies that make up the top five on IBD's top 100 list include J.B. Hunt Transportation, Texas Instruments, Verisk Analytics, and Apple.

Quadrant 2: Mattel. Unsustainable (shareholders lose value and other stakeholders benefit, upper left). Visible examples of this quadrant tend to be associated with boycotts of products. Although sales may dip slightly, most boycotts do not affect sales or shareholders in the long term (Diermeier, 2012). An interesting example to illustrate this category was toy manufacturer Mattel in 2007. A lack of attention to its suppliers' practices in China created the need for a large recall, due to lead paint being used and small strong magnets in the products that could be unsafe for children. It later emerged that most of the product recalls (17.4 million of the 19.6 million recalled toys) were due to the Mattel design flaw of the magnets, not the Chinese suppliers (Blanchard, 2007).

As suppliers of Mattel, the Chinese firms received value from the Mattel business, and customers may have benefited from lower prices on toys made in China. But the result of Mattel not coordinating its global supply chain effectively ultimately took value from the Mattel shareholders. From May 1, 2007, before the recall, until a year later, Mattel's share price declined by 34.4%. Meanwhile, its major competitor, Hasbro, gained 11% in the same period. Mattel apologized publicly for their errors and focused on fixing their supply chain; the company recovered all the value of its share drop by the end of 2010.

In the decade 2013–2023, Mattel only experienced 2% annualized growth including seven fiscal years of negative growth, and its stock price dramatically underperformed the S&P 500 (Welbeck Ash Research, 2023). However, in August 2023 it was anticipating a major improvement due to the *Barbie* movie.

Quadrant 3: BP. Both lose (unsustainable, lower left). A high-profile example in this quadrant is British Petroleum (BP) and the Deepwater Horizon explosion and oil spill in the Gulf of Mexico on April 20, 2010, the worst environmental disaster in US history. Beaches, fisheries, and wetlands were damaged, and thousands of people's livelihoods were affected.

BP shareholders at the time lost a lot of value. Between January 4 and April 19, 2010, BP's share price, adjusted for dividends and splits, fluctuated between US$53.43 and $54.14 with average sales volumes ranging from 4.5 to 10.5 million shares. From April 26 to June 21, 2010, the adjusted share price ranged from a high of $47.15 down to $24.84 on average volumes of sales of 37.5 to 147.2 million shares. For the period from June 26, 2010 to December 31, 2012, share prices stabilized in a range of $26.98–$45.94. Seven years later, by the end of 2017, BP shares had still not recovered their pre–Deepwater Horizon price. Its shares recovered in 2018 and 2019 but then followed oil price declines during the COVID-19 pandemic. In December 2020, BP share price recovered to $20.52 (Pistilli, 2021).

BP paid over US$60 billion in criminal and civil penalties, natural resource damages, economic claims, and cleanup costs (Uhlmann, 2020). "At the time of the spill it was worth $180 billion ... and few other companies could afford the costs BP incurred" (Uhlmann, 2020).

Who else lost? Just about everyone except maybe the lawyers involved in the case. Eleven workers lost their lives as a result of the explosion. In January 2013, a federal judge approved the agreement between the Justice Department and BP in which it pleaded guilty to 14 criminal charges and paid a fine of US$4 billion (Krauss, 2013). Although this agreement settled the criminal case for BP, in 2022 the company still faced numerous lawsuits. In addition to the monetary costs, two BP officials were charged with manslaughter and a former VP was charged with obstruction of Congress and making false statements.

The company suffered long-term damage to its reputation and since 2000 has spent US$500 million on brand enhancement (McGuire et al., 2022). It changed its logo and rebranded its slogan as "Beyond Petroleum," a move many observers considered to be greenwashing. By 2022, BP abandoned the new slogan and went back to focusing on petroleum.

Quadrant 4: BP again. Unsustainable (shareholders benefit and other stakeholders lose value). In August 2022, BP recorded its second-highest quarterly profits in history from strong refinery profits and high energy prices. Simultaneously, it was accused of "unfettered profiteering" as it increased its payments to shareholders (The Guardian, 2022). Six months later, it announced that it was reducing its plans to cut emissions from 35–40% that it had announced in 2020 in compliance with the 2015 Paris climate accord down to 20–30%.

This is a company once praised for detailing its energy transition plan and one that had been considered a pioneer in climate action by some. It had "pledged to transform itself by halting oil and gas exploration in new countries, slashing oil and gas production, and boosting capital spending on low-carbon energy" (Halper & Gregg, 2023, 9th paragraph). Now it appears to be reneging on those pledges.

Does BP truly belong in Quadrant 4 or is its leadership engaging in temporal, paradoxical management as discussed in the next section? Time will tell if our placement of it there is temporary as it transitions to a more sustainable future.

The Sustainable Development Paradox: Navigating Competing Demands of Shareholders and Stakeholders

How can executives guide their companies to that upper right quadrant of value creation for both shareholders and stakeholder? Sustainability and sustainable transformation have been described as a "wicked problem" (Starik & Kanashiro, 2013), characterized by multiple stakeholders, disputed values, complex interconnectedness, foggy problem definition, limited or contested knowledge, and ongoing change (McMillan & Overall, 2016). Binary, either-or thinking mindsets and approaches tend to oversimplify the complexity surrounding sustainability issues. To address these often seemingly intractable challenges, we previously introduced paradoxical "both-and thinking" as an aspect of mindful global leadership in Chapter 2. The both-and thinking perspective advanced in the paradoxical thinking literature is a frame of reference well suited to addressing challenges that persist over time; where different objectives interact in complex ways; and where short-term, trade-off thinking is incapable of producing desired, sustainable outcomes. Sustainable development is a paradox in which the interconnected variety of competing demands must be considered simultaneously and navigated.

Organizational sustainability requires the integration of environmental, social, and economic outcomes (Benkert, 2021). Recall that the UN World Commission on Environment and Development in 1987 defined sustainable development as "development that meets the needs of the present without compromising the ability of future generations to meet their own needs" (World Commission on Environment and Development, 1987). This is often framed in an organizational context in Elkington's terms as a simultaneous consideration of "people, planet and profit" or the "triple bottom line." It confronts corporate decision-makers with the short-term/long-term, stakeholder/shareholder problem.

Leading and managing sustainability is a question of addressing sustainability in the plural, *sustainabilities*, in that multiple aspects of sustainability are interconnected in a myriad of ways. A plurality of competing agendas can appear and present competing demands. Advancement of one dimension of sustainability may create both negative as well as positive synergies in other dimensions (Gao & Bansal, 2013; Hahn et al., 2018; Jay et al., 2017). For instance, advancement of environmental concerns may jeopardize profitability, yet may also facilitate growth and opportunities for innovation in products and services.

With the 17 UN SDGs, no single corporate or organizational actor is likely to be able to pursue all at the same time, and an individual SDG may at times be at odds with other SDGs. For example, working to preserve "Life below water" (SDG 14) may be detrimental to achieving "No poverty" (SDG 1), when jobs and livelihood in the fishing industry disappear. "Decent work and economic growth" (SDG 8) similarly may hamper efforts to take "climate action" (SDG 13). Of course, there can also be positive synergies between the goals – both globally considering the whole planet as well as locally in the individual corporation. Creation of win-win solutions between a diversity of sustainability objectives is an ideal and a stretch goal that often is difficult to achieve in practice. Consequently, it makes sense to explore dimensions of sustainability together to capture interactive effects as well as side effects and to manage sustainability in business as a dynamic, ongoing balancing act.

Navigating Sustainability Paradoxes
Choosing your battles and avoiding overpromising are central to navigating sustainability paradoxes. There are several critical skills needed to navigate paradoxes (Nielsen et al., 2023). These include:

- **Reflection** or the ability to see things from many angles.
- **Courage** to use the paradox constructively to challenge the organization to develop and to do things differently than expected by other people.
- **Communication** or the ability to address many different sides of the paradox and strike a balance in one's communication without favoring one perspective over another.

Consider, for instance, Orsted, a multinational Danish energy supplier with a mission and vision to create "a world that runs entirely on green energy" (Ørsted, n.d., first paragraph), 2023). In 2023, Orsted was named one of the world's most sustainable companies and the world's most sustainable electricity company in Corporate Knights' Global 100 index. Although Orsted's sustainability agenda is predominantly focused on one dimension of sustainability, namely taking climate action through renewable energy supply solutions, and within that overall frame focusing on the environmental dimension of sustainability, they face competing demands between different aspects of their green mission. Green conflicts could take the form of competing demands between establishing offshore wind farms (thus increasing renewable energy resources, which is good for the climate) while at the same time protecting vulnerable natural habitats and biodiversity in the areas where sea windmill parks are placed. In response to such paradoxical tension, Orsted has established a partnership between companies, authorities, and other stakeholders of the vision of a CO_2-neutral energy system while also working toward nature protection and restoration.

Let's return to BP. Its 2022 Sustainability Report proclaims BP is aiming to be a net-zero company by 2050 or sooner. This goal would seem to conflict with its actions discussed earlier when it recently said it was reducing its carbon emission goals while simultaneously rewarding shareholders, landing it in Quadrant 4 of the Sustainable value framework in Figure 11.4. According to CEO Bernard Looney, in the three years since 2019, BP has increased its investment in transition growth engines – bioenergy, convenience stores, EV charging, hydrogen and renewables – from

3% to 30% of BP's total capital investment; and in February 2023 it decided to invest an additional US$8 billion by 2030 into its transition strategy (BP, 2022).

This could be an example of navigating the stakeholder/shareholder paradox by satisfying investors in the short term and investing long term in innovation and sustainable activities. It will, however, require courage to balance the competing demands as it continues to navigate the paradox, and exceptional communication efforts by BP's management to pull it off.

Forming partnerships is an important pathway for navigating sustainability paradoxes, which BP's report indicates that it has done. This is particularly important in volatile times (e.g., due to COVID-19 or the war in Ukraine) when initial assumptions and evaluations may change quickly as new information comes to light or stakeholders voice concerns previously not considered. Responding to concerns of some actors may well give rise to unintended or negative consequences with others. Global managers need courage and corporations need resilience in organizational processes to allow them to aim at moving targets without being paralyzed by complexity.

Conclusion: Getting Everything Right at the Same Time?

Involving and communicating with internal and external stakeholders are important aspects of navigating paradoxes associated with sustainable transformation. This itself is a field of paradoxical tensions. On the one hand, companies see the need to openly communicate their sustainability missions and visions in response to increased societal expectations, but on the other hand they fear that initiatives may be labeled as greenwashing on social media platforms (Uldam, 2018). The Volkswagen emission scandal was a telling example of a corporation managing impressions rather than actual emissions by marketing its products as sustainable when the reality was different (Gaim et al., 2021). Even companies where no criminal activity has taken place can quickly find themselves in the middle of a controversy as consumers question the reality of sustainability claims, regardless of whether the criticisms have merit or not.

Corporations need to communicate sustainability visions to mobilize and engage external and internal stakeholders but may feel the need to downplay activities or not communicate aspirations at all out of fear of a negative backlash. These are typically stretch goals, the results of which will materialize sometime in the future. In the short term, the company is open to criticism of shallow marketing and deception. But not having the courage to face criticism could be a bigger risk, as critical stakeholders may be disillusioned and disengage from advancing sustainable transformation. Communication of paradoxical "both-and" messages may be construed as inaccurate, ambiguous, or an expression of ambivalence that may have negative impacts (Rothman & Wiesenfeld, 2007). At the same time, ambiguity can foster a capacity for change and innovation while silence and inaction may hamper the transformative potential of paradoxes.

Christensen, Morsing, and Thyssen (2013) use the term "aspirational talk" to describe communicating stretch goals with the specific purpose of instigating action. This idea of aspirational talk is a well-suited point of reference for collaborative communication on sustainability paradoxes. Sustainability initiatives are likely to be contested with opposing considerations and complex interconnections, which will make communication of unilaterally "good" decisions of sustainability concerns extremely rare if not nonexistent. Consequently, researchers of sustainable competency development suggest viewing change activities as being aimed at the advancement of a "culture of critical commitment." This means trying to foster enough engagement to make a behavioral difference, yet at the same time facilitating critical reflexivity to enable change agents to learn and adapt from the experience instead of mindlessly sticking to plans or rules. They need to keep options open and calibrate to novel situations, contexts, or knowledge (Sterling & Gray-Donald, 2007).

Current and future global leaders in the public and private sectors will need to be aspirational and to have the courage and skills to lead their organizations and the world to create a sustainable future.

Further Resources

Nielsen, R. K., Bévort, F., Henriksen, T. D., Hjalager, A.-M., & Lyndgaard, D. B. (2023). *Navigating leadership paradox: Engaging paradoxical thinking in practice.* De Gruyter.

Nielsen, R. K., & Lyndgaard, D. B. (2018). *Grasping global leadership: Tools for next practice.* Confederation of Danish Industry, Global Leadership Academy.

Polman, P., & Winston, A. (2021). *Net positive: How courageous companies thrive by giving more than they take.* Harvard Business Review Press.

Savitz, A., & Weber, K. (2013). *Talent, transformation, and the triple bottom line: How companies can leverage human resources for sustainable growth.* Jossey-Bass.

For more information on the global frameworks we reviewed, we suggest you go directly to their sources. All four sites have extensive research published, case examples, and best practice reports:

- UN Global Compact: https://www.unglobalcompact.org/
- Global Reporting Initiative: https://www.globalreporting.org/
- Dow Jones Sustainability Indices: http://www.sustainability-indices.com/
- S&P Global ranking: https://www.spglobal.com/esg/csa/yearbook/2023/ranking/

Bibliography

Bansal, P., & DesJardine, M. R. (2014). Business sustainability: It is about time. *Strategic Organization, 12*(1). *12*(1), 70-78.

Benkert, J. (2021). Reframing business sustainability decision-making with value-focussed thinking. *Journal of Business Ethics, 174*(2). 441-456.

Blackwell, K. (2014, July 31). *Milton Friedman's property rights legacy*. Forbes. Retrieved April 8, 2024, from https://www.forbes.com/sites/realspin/2014/07/31/milton-friedmans-property-rights-legacy/

Blanchard, B. (2007, September 21). *Mattel apologizes to China for toy recalls*. Reuters. Retrieved April 2018 from https://www.reuters.com/article/us-china-safety-mattel/mattel-apologizes-to-china-for-toy-recalls-idUSPEK10394020070921

Bowen, H. R. (1953). *Social responsibilities of the businessman*. Harper & Row.

British Petroleum. (2022). *BP sustainability report 2022*. Retrieved August 21, 2023, from https://www.bp.com/content/dam/bp/business-sites/en/global/corporate/pdfs/sustainability/group-reports/bp-sustainability-report-2022.pdf

Business Roundtable. (2019). *Business Roundtable redefines the purpose of a corporation to promote an economy that serves all Americans*. Retrieved July 17, 2023, from https://www.businessroundtable.org/business-roundtable-redefines-the-purpose-of-a-corporation-to-promote-an-economy-that-serves-all-americans

Carroll, A. B. (1979). A three dimensional model of corporate performance. *Academy of Management Review, 4*(4), 497–505.

Carson, R. (2002). *Silent spring*. Houghton Mifflin Harcourt.

Christensen, L. T., Morsing, M., & Thyssen, O. (2013). CSR as aspirational talk. *Organization, 20*(3). https://doi.org/10.1177/1350508413478310.

Collins, J. C., & Porras, J. I. (1994). *Built to last: Successful habits of visionary companies*. Harper Business.

Diermeier, D. (2012). When do company boycotts work? *Harvard Business Review, 90*(7–8). Retrieved April 8, 2024, from https://hbr.org/2012/08/when-do-company-boycotts-work

Dixon-Fowler, H. R., Slater, D. J., Johnson, J. L., Elstrand, A. E., & Romi, A. M. (2013). Beyond "does it pay to be green?" A meta-analysis of moderators of the CEP-CFP relationship. *Journal of Business Ethics, 112*(2), 353–366.

Dow Jones Indices. (2023). Retrieved July 21, 2023, from https://www.spglobal.com/spdji/en/documents/methodologies/methodology-dj-sustainability-indices.pdf

Earth.org. (2023). Retrieved August 17, 2023, from https://earth.org/editorial-guide/

Eccles, E. G, Ioannis, I., & Serafeim G. (2014). The impact of corporate sustainability on organizational processes and performance. *Management Science, 60*(11), 2835–2857.

Elkington, J. (1997). *Cannibals with forks: The triple bottom line of 21st century business*. Capstone.

Financial Times. (2021). Retrieved August 17, 2023, from https://ig.ft.com/sites/business-book-award/books/2021/longlist/net-positive-by-paul-polman-and-andrew-winston/

Financial Times. (n.d.). *BP draws line under Gulf spill costs*. Financial Times. Retrieved February 2018 from https://www.ft.com/content/ff2d8bcc-49e9-11e6-8d68-72e9211e86ab

Freeman, E. R., Wicks, A. C., & Parmar, B. (2004). Stakeholder theory and "the corporate objective revisited". *Organizational Science, 15*(3), 364–369.

Freeman, R. E. (2010). *Strategic management: A stakeholder approach*. Cambridge University Press.

Friedman, M. (1970, September 13). *The social responsibility of business is to increase its profits.* The New York Times Magazine, SM Section, 17.

Gaim, M., Clegg, S., & Cunha, M. P. E. (2021). Managing impressions rather than emissions: Volkswagen and the false mastery of paradox. *Organization Studies, 42*(6), 949–970.

Gao, J., & Bansal, P. (2013). Instrumental and integrative logics in business sustainability. *Journal of Business Ethics, 112*(2), 241–255.

Gibson, W. (1999). *Future has arrived.* Quote Investigator. Retrieved August 21, 2023, from https://quoteinvestigator.com/2012/01/24/future-has-arrived/

Global Reporting. (2018). *About GRI.* GRI. Retrieved February 2018 from https://www.globalreporting.org/Information/about-gri/Pages/default.aspx

GRI. (2023a). https://www.globalreporting.org/standards

GRI. (2023b). https://www.globalreporting.org/about-gri/

Guardian. (2022). *BP accused of "unfettered profiteering" as profits triple; company failures surge – business live.* Retrieved August 20, 2023, from https://www.theguardian.com/business/live/2022/aug/02/bp-profits-oil-gas-energy-bills-price-cap-cost-of-living-business-live

Gulati, R., Deep Purpose. (2022, October 24). https://www.hbs.edu/news/podcasts/deep-purpose/Pages/podcast-details.aspx?episode=5040524540

Hahn, T., Figge, F., Pinkse, J. et al. (2018). A paradox perspective on corporate sustainability: Descriptive, instrumental, and normative aspects. *Journal of Business Ethics, 148.* https://doi.org/10.1007/s10551-017-3587-2.

Halper, E., & Gregg, A. (2023). *BP dials back climate pledge amid soaring oil profits.* https://www.washingtonpost.com/business/2023/02/07/bp-climate-emissions-oil-profits/

Henisz, W., Koller, T., & Nuttall, R. (2019, November). Five ways that ESG creates value. *McKinsey Quarterly,* 1–12.

IBD. (2022). *Top 100 ESG stocks.* Investors.com. Retrieved August 20, 2023, from https://www.investors.com/news/esg-companies list top 100 esg-stocks-2022/

Jay, J., Soderstrom, S., & Grant, G. (2017). Navigating the paradoxes of sustainability. In W. K. Smith et al. (Eds.), *The Oxford handbook of organizational paradox.* Oxford Handbooks (online ed.), https://doi.org/10.1093/oxfordhb/9780198754428.013.18.

Johnston, P., Everard, M., Santillo, D., & Robèrt, K. (2007). Reclaiming the definition of sustainability. *Environmental Science and Pollution Research International, 14,* 60–66.

KPMG. (2022). *Global survey of sustainability reporting, 2022.* Retrieved August 18, 2023, from https://assets.kpmg.com/content/dam/kpmg/se/pdf/komm/2022/Global-Survey-of-Sustainability-Reporting-2022.pdf

Krauss, C. (2013, January 29). *Judge Accepts BP's $4 Billion Criminal Settlement Over Gulf Oil Spill.* The New York Times, Section B, 3.

Krychiw, J. (2023). *ESG scores: Why they matter?* https://esg.conservice.com/esg-scores-why-they-matter/#:~:text=What%20is%20a%20good%20ESG,than%2070%20is%20considered%20excellent

Laszlo, C. (2008). Sustainable value. *Problems of Sustainable Development, 3*(2), 25–29.

Laverty, K. J. (1996). Economic "short-termism": The debate, the unresolved issues, and the implications for management practice and research. *Academy of Management Review, 21*(3), 825–860.

Le, T. (2022). *4 Key Takeaways from Unilever's path toward net positive.* Alltech.com. Retrieved August 10, 2023, from https://www.alltech.com/

blog/4-key-takeaways-unilevers-path-toward-net-positive

Levitt, T. (1958). The dangers of social responsibility. *Harvard Business Review*, 36, 41–50.

Lewis, S. (2010, October 26). *Learning from BP's "sustainable" self-portraits: From "integrated spin" to integrated reporting*. Retrieved February 2013 from Corporate Disclosure Alert. http://corporatedisclosurealert.blogspot.com/2010/10/from-integrated-spin-to-integrated.html

March, J. G. (1991). Exploration and exploitation in organizational learning. *Organization Science*, 2(1), 71–87. Special Issue: Organizational Learning: Papers in Honor of (and by) James G. March.

Margolis, J. D., & Elfenbein, H. A. (2008). Do well by doing good? Don't count on it. *Harvard Business Review*.

McGuire, W., Holtmaat, E. A., & Prakesh, A. (2022). *Penalties for industrial accidents: The impact of the Deepwater Horizon accident on BP's reputation and stock market returns*. Retrieved August 1, 2023, from https://www.ncbi.nlm.nih.gov/pmc/articles/PMC9200171/

McMillan, C., & Overall, J. (2016). Wicked problems: Turning strategic management upside down. *Journal of Business Strategy*, 37(1), 34–43.

Nader, R. (1966). *Unsafe at any speed: The designed-in dangers of the American automobile*. Pocket Books Publishing.

Nielsen, R. K., Bevort, F., Henriksen, T. D., Hjalager, A. M., & Lyndgaard, D. B. (2023). *Navigating leadership paradox: Engaging paradoxical thinking in practice*. De Gruyter.

Orlitzky, M., Schmidt, F., & Rynes, S. (2003). Corporate social and financial performance: A meta-analysis. *Organizational Studies*, 24(3), 423.

Ørsted. (n.d.). *Our vision is to create a world that runs entirely on green energy*. Retrieved March 29, 2024 from https://orsted.com/en/who-we-are/our-purpose/our-vision-and-values

Pearson, M., Rithmire, M., & Tsai, K. (2021). Party-state capitalism in China. *Current History*, 120(827), 207–213.

PEW Research Center. (2021). *Gen Z, Millennials Stand Out for Climate Change Activism, Social Media Engagement with Issue*. Retrieved August 19, 2023, from https://www.pewresearch.org/science/2021/05/26/gen-z-millennials-stand-out-for-climate-change-activism-social-media-engagement-with-issue/

Pistilli, M. (2021). *What was the BP stock price before the Deepwater Horizon spill?* Investing News Network. Retrieved August 20, 2023, from https://investingnews.com/daily/resource-investing/energy-investing/oil-and-gas-investing/bp-oil-stock-price-before-spill/

Polman, P., & Winston, A. (2021). *Net positive: How courageous companies thrive by giving more than they take*. Harvard Business Review Press.

Ramseur, J. L., & Haggerty, C. L. (2015, April 17). *Deepwater Horizon Oil Spill: Recent Activities and Ongoing Developments*. Congressional Research Service. Retrieved on March 29, 2024, from https://crsreports.congress.gov/product/pdf/R/R42942.

Rothman, N. B., & Wiesenfeld, B. M. (2007). The social consequences of expressing emotional ambivalence in groups and teams. In E. A. Mannix, M. A. Neale, & C. P. Anderson (Eds.), *Affect and groups* (Research on Managing Groups and Teams, Vol. 10, pp. 275–308). Emerald Group Publishing Limited. https://doi.org/10.1016/S1534-0856(07)10011-6.

Savitz, A. (2006). *The triple bottom line*. Jossey-Bass Publishers.

Savitz, A., & Weber, K. (2013). *Talent, transformation, and the triple bottom line: How companies can leverage human resources for sustainable growth*. Jossey-Bass.

Skapinker, M. (2018, December 11). *Unilever's Paul Polman was a standout CEO of the past decade*. Financial Times. Retrieved March 24, 2023, from https://www.ft.com/content/e7040df4-fa19-11e8-8b7c-6fa24bd5409c

Song, L., Zhan, X., Zhang, H., Liu, J., & Zheng, C. (2022). *How much is global business sectors contributing to sustainable development goals?* Science Direct. Retrieved July 16, 2023, from https://www.sciencedirect.com/science/article/pii/S2772737822000074

Spector, B. (2008). Business responsibilities in a divided world: The Cold War roots of the corporate social responsibility movement. *Enterprise and Society, 9*(2), 314–336.

Spector, B. (2013). *Implementing organizational change: Theory into practice* (3rd Ed.). Pearson.

Starik, M., & Kanashiro, P. (2013). Toward a theory of sustainability management: Uncovering and integrating the nearly obvious. *Organization and Environment, 26*(1), 26(1), 7-30.

Sterling, S., & Gray-Donald, J. (2007). Editorial. *International Journal of Innovation and Sustainable Development*, Special issue: Sustainability and education: Towards a culture of critical commitment, 2(3/4), 241–248.

Sustaincase.com. (2023). *UN Global Compact recommends the GRI standards for sustainability reporting*. Retrieved August 12, 2023, from https://sustaincase.com/un-global-compact-recommends-the-gri-standards-for-sustainabilityreporting

Uhlmann, D. (2020, April 23). *BP paid a steep price for the Gulf oil spill but for the US a decade later, it's business as usual*. The Conversation. Retrieved July 31, 2023, from https://theconversation.com/bp-paid-a-steep-price-for-the-gulf-oil-spill-but-for-the-us-a-decade-later-its-business-as-usual-136905

Uldam, J. (2018). Social media visibility: Challenges to activism. *Media, Culture & Society, 40*(1), 41–58.

Unilever.com. (n.d.). *Sustainable development goals*. Retrieved August 15, 2023, from https://www.unilever.com/planet-and-society/sustainability-reporting-centre/sustainable-development-goals/

United Nations. (2023). *SDG Global Business Forum – media advisory*. Retrieved July 14, 2023, from https://unglobalcompact.org/news/5102-07-13-2023

United Nations. (2023). *Transparency builds trust*. Retrieved July 14, 2023, from https://unglobalcompact.org/participation/report

United Nations. (2023). *The Ten Principles of the UN Global Compact*. Retrieved March 29, 2024 from https://www.unglobalcompact.org/what-is-gc/mission/principles

UN Statistics Division. (2023). *Sounding the alarm: SDG progress at the midpoint*. Retrieved August 17, 2023, from https://unstats.un.org/sdgs/report/2023/progress-midpoint/

Welbeck Ash Research, Seeking Alpha. (2023). *Mattel: Struggling financials but some scope for optimism*. Retrieved August 1, 2023, from https://seekingalpha.com/article/4613630-mattel-struggling-financials-but-some-scope-for-optimism

World Commission on Environment and Development. (1987). *Towards Sustainable Development, No. A/42/427*. Our Common Future: Report of the World Commission on Environment and Development, UN Documents. Retrieved March 29, 2024, from http://www.un-documents.net/ocf-02.htm

World Economic Forum. (2021). *What is stakeholder capitalism?* Retrieved August 22, 2023, from https://www.weforum.org/agenda/2021/01/klaus-schwab-on-what-is-stakeholder-capitalism-history-relevance/

12 Competing with Integrity and Ethical Decision-Making

> One of the truest tests of integrity is its blunt refusal to be compromised.
> Chinua Achebe, Nigerian author and poet (1930–2013)

Key Learning Objectives

At the end of this chapter, students will be able to:

- Recognize the distinction between integrity and ethics.
- Differentiate between ethical and legal behavior.
- Compare major ethical frameworks.
- Develop a personal set of guidelines to deal with ethical dilemmas.

Overview: Competing with Integrity

Ethics and personal **ethical behavior** do not always receive the attention that they deserve in business courses, so we focus on personal integrity here and how ethical considerations may arise in your career.

The objective is to challenge you to consider your responsibilities as a business leader more broadly than simply from financial, market, or legal perspectives. There can also be human, social, or legal consequences from your decisions. The human and social impact of decisions should be considered at the time these decisions are being made. And it is not just the consequences to some faceless group of people in some distant country that you need to consider. There can be personal consequences from your decisions as well.

Table 12.1 Global mindset framework applied to personal integrity

	Individual/Personal	Organizational
Self	Clarify and understand my beliefs about ethical behavior.	Clarify and understand my organization's approach to corporate social responsibility and sustainability.
Other	Clarify and understand other beliefs about ethical behavior in the context of other cultures and principal theories of moral philosophy.	Clarify and understand other corporate approaches to social responsibility and sustainability in the context of other industries, other cultures, and principal codes of conduct.
Choice	Belief in and commitment to a set of ethical principles.	Belief in and commitment to an approach to social responsibility and corporate sustainability.

In Chapter 2, we presented the four domains of the global mindset framework: individual and organizational; self and other. In Chapter 11, we discussed corporate responsibility and sustainability at the organizational level as shown in Table 12.1. Now we will cover ethical issues at the individual/personal level as indicated.

Personal Integrity

What is integrity? Professor Glenn Rowe from the Ivey Business School describes integrity as "consistency among what you believe in your heart; think in your head; what you say with your mouth; and what you do – your behavior and actions" (Rowe, 2012). Integrity also is commonly defined as doing the right thing, even when no one is watching.

Acting with integrity is the same as acting ethically, but the word "integrity" does not have the negative connotation, the moralizing tone, or the sense of naïveté that the word "ethics" carries for some people. According to De George, in order to act with integrity you must behave according to your own highest norms of behavior as well as according to ethical and moral norms of society (De George, 1993).

Competing with integrity means that corporate executives should compete in a way that is consistent with their own highest values and norms of behavior. Although these values and norms are self-imposed and self-accepted, they cannot be simply arbitrary and self-serving; but neither is there a requirement to be perfect.

The least clear aspect of managerial responsibility may be in the domain of ethics, which is the "moral thinking and analysis by corporate decision makers regarding the motives and consequences of their decisions and actions" (Amba-Rao, 1993, p. 555). Ethics is the study of morals and systems of morality, or principles of conduct. The study of ethics is concerned with the right or wrong and the "should" or "should not" of human decisions and actions. This does not mean that all questions of right and wrong are ethical issues, however. There is right and wrong associated with rules of etiquette that vary from culture to culture – for example, in which hand to hold your knife and fork, or in the use of language and rules of grammar. Holding a fork in the wrong hand or speaking ungrammatically does not constitute unethical behavior.

The ethical or moral frame of reference, in contrast, is concerned with human behavior in society and with the relationships, duties, and obligations between people, groups, and organizations. It is concerned with the human consequences associated with decisions and actions, consequences not fully addressed in the pursuit of profit, more sophisticated technology, or larger market share. In this concern for human outcomes, an ethical frame of reference differs from other perspectives, such as financial, marketing, accounting, or legal. An ethical perspective requires that you extend consideration beyond your own self-interest (or that of your company) to consider the interests of a wider community of stakeholders, including employees, customers, suppliers, the public, and even foreign governments. It also advocates behaving according to what would be considered "better" or "higher" standards of conduct, not necessarily the minimum acceptable by law.

Ethical decisions do not necessarily arise separately from finance, marketing, or production decisions, because problems in the real world do not come with neat labels attached: here is a finance problem; here is a marketing problem; and now, an ethical problem. Managers may categorize issues by functional area or break up a complex problem into components, such as those mentioned. Usually, policy issues and decisions are multifaceted and simultaneously may have several components. They also may have ethical dimensions that managers should consider. However, in addressing a typical complex problem, the ethical dimension may often be overlooked.

If situations did come with labels, people could apply the techniques and concepts they had learned, such as net present value to a financial problem or market segmentation to a marketing problem. What would happen if a problem labeled "ethical dilemma" arrived? A manager might be in a quandary, lacking a way of analyzing, let alone resolving, it.

The decision-making tools for this type of situation probably would be absent. Business schools, traditionally, did not emphasize the teaching of ethics as rigorously as they did the teaching of finance, marketing, or operations. Nor were students trained to think about ethical issues in the same way that they were trained to think about the frameworks and techniques for functional areas of specialization.

However, after numerous scandals in the United States (e.g., Enron, Wells Fargo, Theranos, WeWork, Paycheck Protection Program fraud associated with the COVID-19 outbreak) and in Europe (e.g., Parmalat's fraud and bankruptcy in Italy, Barclay's Libor manipulation in the United Kingdom, Volkswagen's Dieselgate, Siemens' bribery and Wirecard's *fraudulent* financial reporting in Germany, Danske Bank and Nordea's money laundering scandal in Denmark), this is changing, as business schools place greater emphasis on managerial integrity.

Ethical versus Legal Behavior

A question always arises as to the distinction between legal and ethical behavior. If one acts in accordance with laws, is that not sufficient? However, society relies on more than laws to function effectively in many spheres of endeavor. And not all of society's norms regarding moral behavior have been codified into law, and laws can be slow to change. There can, therefore, be many instances of questionable behavior that are not illegal. Acting legally is the minimum required behavior for executives.

Henderson provided a useful way to think about the relationship between ethical and legal actions (Henderson, 1982). He created a matrix based on whether an action was legal or illegal and ethical or unethical, similar to that shown in Table 12.2. Assuming that executives want to act legally and ethically (quadrant 4) and avoid making decisions (or acting in ways) that are illegal and unethical (quadrant 2), the decisions that create dilemmas are the ones that fall into quadrants 1 and 3.

Consider the decision of a chemical company manager who refuses to promote a pregnant woman to an area of the company where she would be exposed to toxic chemicals that could harm her child. In the United States, pregnancy discrimination is against the law. The Equal Employment Opportunity Commission

Table 12.2 **Framework for classifying behavior**

	Illegal	Legal
Ethical	1 Illegal & Ethical	4 Legal & Ethical
Unethical	2 Illegal & Unethical	3 Legal & Unethical

(EEOC) enforces three federal laws that protect job applicants and employees who are pregnant (EEOC, 2023). The manager probably would be acting ethically, but illegally. Perhaps the problem could be solved by delaying the promotion, if possible. This simple example illustrates a decision that can be ethical but not legal; there also may be solutions that allow a win–win outcome in which the decision is legal and ethical because of the way it is made.

In quadrant 3, a classic example was the marketing of infant formula in developing countries. In 1998, an estimated 590,000 infants worldwide acquired HIV from their mothers through breastfeeding, 90% of whom were in Africa (DeKock et al, 2000). Infant formula was a possible solution. However, many countries had poor sanitation, polluted water, and high illiteracy rates that prevented parents from reading the infant formula directions. Over a period of time, hundreds of thousands of babies perished, and the use of infant formula was blamed for it. Although marketing infant formula was not illegal, the United Nations criticized companies for unethical marketing given the local conditions. UNICEF claimed that formula milk sold through "aggressive and unethical" marketing practices also led to stunted growth of children in Southeast Asia (Choe, 2012).

Although the marketing of formula milk became a very visible issue in the early 2000s with the HIV epidemic, the controversy continues today. A multi-country study of the marketing of formula milk by the World Health Organization and UNICEF states:

The International Code of Marketing of Breast-milk Substitutes is a landmark public health agreement passed by the World Health Assembly in 1981. Yet exploitative marketing practices continue in defiance of the Code. Digital media have been used to further amplify the reach and impact of marketing of formula milk. Even during the Covid-19 pandemic, companies continue to prey on parents' fears to increase sales of milk formula ... Formula milk companies distort science and medicine to legitimize their claims and push their product. They make false and incomplete scientific claims and position formula as close to, equivalent or superior to breast milk despite growing evidence [to the contrary]. (World Health Organization, 2022)

Ignoring human rights in global supply chains or manufacturing and selling cigarettes that kill through normal use may be other examples of legal but unethical behavior. In 2008, the deregulation of the banking industry in the United States and the excesses that developed in subprime mortgage lending led to a global financial crisis. Subprime mortgage lending is not illegal, but it became predatory and unethical when mortgage brokers targeted the elderly or low-income people who would never be able to repay their mortgages or borrowers who did not understand the transactions. Employing child labor in some countries might be legal but in many countries would be considered unethical. Other situations that may be legal but considered by some to be unethical include the unequal treatment of women in some countries; laws prohibiting assisted suicide for terminally ill people; or prohibiting the use of medical marijuana by people with epilepsy or multiple sclerosis.

It should be recognized that not all laws are ethical. A classic example is apartheid in South Africa, which was legal but clearly not moral. This historical example raises the question about whose laws and values should be followed when conflicts arise. These are questions each person and company need to answer for themselves. The challenge is to find ways of operating that are consistent with local laws *and* high standards of conduct as we understand them. This goal is attainable with thorough analysis and carefully considered action. In those situations where a win–win outcome is not possible, there is always the option of choosing not to operate in that environment.

The decision to walk away and lose business may seem naïve, but we have met and interviewed executives of very successful companies that have done just that. One CEO described how his company turned down a large contract in an African country because there was no way to avoid paying a bribe to a government official. Another explained that, in his experience, if a company developed a reputation for acting ethically, usually it was not subjected to unethical demands. Each person also has to make their own decision and live with the consequences of their actions.

Integrity issues arise in many areas of a business: the type of products produced, marketing and advertising practices, business conduct in countries where physical security is a problem, requests for illegal payments to secure contracts or sales, and protection payments to prevent damage to plants and equipment or injury to employees. Some products are controversial in themselves, such as tobacco, and some are controversial even within a country, such as the abortion pill in the United States, since they facilitate behavior that some people would consider unethical or immoral. Other products, such as jeans or rugs, may not be as controversial per se, but their production may raise ethical questions.

The United Nations Global Compact 2021–2023, discussed in detail in Chapter 11, is a set of principles covering the areas of human rights, labor, environment, and anti-corruption that 18,000 companies and 3,800 non-business organizations in 160 countries have endorsed. These principles provide a framework of ethically responsible business practices and corporate sustainability that

> starts with a company's value system and a principles-based approach to doing business … Responsible businesses embody the same values and principles wherever they have a presence and know that good practices in one area do not offset harm in another (United Nations, n.d.).

The following sections provide some examples from the areas covered by the UN Global Compact, across different industries.

Human Rights and Labor

Potential ethical and/or legal issues may arise in managing supply chains when products are purchased from manufacturers or contractors that, for example, maintain poor working conditions, use child labor or prison/forced labor, or damage the environment. One of the most widely reported and egregious examples was the 2013 collapse of the Rana Plaza in Bangladesh, an eight-story building that housed five garment factories. The collapse killed more than 1,100 people and injured more than 2,500 (International Labour Organization, 2023). By way of contrast, Gildan Activewear of Montreal acquired a factory in the same area in 2015 but added fire escapes, an elevator, and a water treatment system. An inspection by a US-based firm led to the structures being reinforced at a cost of close to $1 million.

Global Empathy with Bangladesh

Global Empathy

I walk down Oxford Street
all the way to Bangladesh
Five T-shirts for £6
how can that be?
My thoughts are distracted by a sign across the street
flogging the same shirts for £5
That's less than dirt cheap
and my should-self lost out again
Your new T-shirt may be comfortable to sweat in
but consider what other salty toil
tainted this fabric before you?

Karsten Jonsen

Global Empathy, from *Time for Amanda* by Dr. K. van Zanten Jonsen

Monitoring a company's supply chain for potential abuses and taking action to correct them are increasingly being recognized as a management responsibility for the contracting company and have become a serious concern for corporations. In the following, we will look at a few industries in greater detail.

Automobiles

Around 2021, momentum grew to adopt electric vehicles, pushed by competitive manufacturers such as Tesla and encouraged by incentives such as federal and state tax credits; California's executive order and the European Parliament's requirement state that all new cars sold, respectively, in California and the EU by 2035 be fully electric or plug-in electric.

Auto manufacturers scrambled to develop battery-manufacturing capability and to source the new metals needed to produce them. The headline of an article in the *Washington Post* summarized a problem they faced: "EV supply chains have a human rights problem. Can tech fix it?" (Washington Post, 2022).

Consumers, regulators, and investors all wanted to know where the metals come from in order to support their sustainability claims and qualify for tax credits under laws such as the Inflation Reduction Act of 2022 in the United States and the EU's battery passport. Companies were concerned that some suppliers of sustainable cobalt may be including some extracted with child labor, or that nickel supplies may have been smuggled out of Russia in violation of sanctions. To address these concerns, automakers started developing methods and programs to track the origins of materials, including stops at intermediaries en route to factories. They contracted with consulting companies that provide supply chain traceability solutions in preparation for the EU Battery Regulation and Battery Passport. They utilized QR codes, satellites, and blockchain technology. Blockchain is a series of highly encrypted data records transmitted and stored over a large network of computers. It replaces traditional paper bills of lading and permits (among other things) and facilitates payment processing, locating items, and tracing products' stops in the supply chain from origin to destination (Sarathy, 2022).

Clothing

Levi Strauss and Company (LS & Co.) stopped purchasing from subcontractors in Myanmar and China because of practices such as using child and prison labor to manufacture products. In 1991, the company developed a set of Global Sourcing and Operating Guidelines (GSOG) to (a) improve the lives of workers by establishing standards addressing workplace issues for its partners and subcontractors, and (b) aid in the selection of countries for sourcing products. It also contains a Country Assessment Guide to evaluate country level issues such the legal system, human rights environment, and the political, economic, and social environment. It was the first apparel company to establish a comprehensive ethical code of conduct for manufacturing and finishing contractors. The company's terms of engagement (TOE) were aimed at its business partners and primarily based on the United Nations Universal Declaration of Human Rights. Since then, the GSOG has been expanded and modified based on feedback from nongovernmental organizations (NGOs). It addresses ethical standards, legal requirements, environmental requirements, and community involvement, and specifically the issues of child labor, forced labor, disciplinary practices, working hours, wages and benefits, freedom of association, discrimination, and health and safety (Levi Strauss & Co., personal communication).

The original TOE were based on a philosophy of compliance and "do no harm," but in 2012 the company decided that compliance, monitoring, and reporting progress were not sufficient to really make a difference in the lives of the suppliers' workers and their communities, so the company pioneered a development-oriented approach, the *Worker Well-being* initiative. This focused on financial empowerment; health and family well-being; and equality and acceptance. In 2020, it had reached 195,000 workers in 118 factories in 16 countries. The goal is to reach 300,000 workers by 2025 (Levi Strauss & Co., 2021).

In 2020, the company received the *Financial Times* Boldness in Business award in the category of corporate responsibility and environment. As it continues to look toward the future, Jeffrey Hogue, Chief Sustainability Officer, stated in the 2020 Sustainability Report that the company has a strong emphasis on **circularity,** or designing products to eliminate waste and recapture waste as a resource to manufacture new materials and products (Environmental Protection Agency, 2021).

Rugs

In the 1980s, the International Labor Organization (ILO), the US Department of Labor, and human rights groups drew attention to the illegal use of child labor in the hand-woven rug industry. In 1995, RUGMARK began functioning based on discussions with a coalition of NGOs, businesses, government entities, and multilateral groups, such as UNICEF, to combat child labor. The first carpets bearing the RUGMARK label were exported from India at the beginning of 1995, mainly to Germany. Later, countries promoting the RUGMARK label grew to include England, the United States, Canada, and Nepal. It now has 300 licensees in India. In 2009, the RUGMARK Foundation rebranded its commercial focus as GoodWeave International with more than 170 brand partners in 17 countries while it continued its social welfare mission (The Ruggist, 2009).

What is a company's responsibility in ensuring that its suppliers are not using child labor? Some people would argue that children are better suited to making rugs because they are more dexterous than adults, and that their families, who need the money, would be worse off if the children were not working. Opponents, however, point out that many of the children were found to be victims of debt bondage or forced labor, practices banned by the United Nations and condemned as modern forms of slavery.

Is participating in GoodWeave the only way to counter child labor? Is it ever acceptable to use child labor? Ethical issues, by definition, are never simple. The issue about manufacturing rugs is not as simple as "do not use child labor." We spoke at length with a small business owner who exports rugs from Pakistan and Afghanistan. She visits her manufacturers regularly and encourages community development around the making of rugs. There were many girls as young as eight years who were working in her craft shops:

If I did not hire these girls, they would not be in school. They would be in the fields. Their life expectancy would be shorter; they would be working alone. In the workshop, they sit together with women of three or more generations, they learn a skill, and they learn about their culture. Because they are in my workshop, I can provide good meals and people and materials to provide at least some education and social support for them. Am I doing the right thing? According to the press and many consumers, definitely not! But I do believe that, in this case, hiring these girls and trying to provide a better environment for them is the right thing.

These are the types of situations you are likely to encounter as a global leader and the types of decisions you may be called on to make.

Food

Haribo, the German maker of the popular gummy candies, was the focus of a German broadcasting network documentary in 2017 that accused it of being "unknowingly complicit in both modern-day slave labor and animal abuse" (Fantozzi, 2017). Workers on plantations in Brazil from where its carnauba wax came were subject to cruel and inhumane treatment. The company reported that it had looked into these allegations and found no evidence that it or its wax suppliers used forced labor. It also said that it helped start *The Initiative for Responsible Carnauba* to improve social and biodiversity conditions in carnauba wax sourcing areas, and that it now uses only beeswax.

In 2015, a class action lawsuit was filed against Nestlé in California for allegedly using fish caught by enslaved workers in its cat food. Nestlé commissioned an independent study by Verité, a "global, independent, non-profit organization that conducts research, advocacy, consulting, training, and assessments with a vision that people worldwide work under safe, fair, and legal conditions" (Verite, n.d.). The company focused on the issues of child labor, forced labor, human trafficking, and gender discrimination. Nestlé publicly announced the results of the study that found slavery and forced labor existed in its seafood supply chain, and committed itself to eliminating such labor forms from its sourcing network.

By 2020, more than 99% of the seafood Nestlé sourced from Thailand was traceable to fish farms or specific vessels. Nestlé partnered with the Thai government to support vessel audits and educate Thai fishers on workers' rights. Additionally, all their suppliers who sourced seafood from Thailand incorporated Nestlé's Responsible Sourcing Standard requirements in their policies and included them in relationships with their own suppliers (Nestlé, 2020).

Blockchain technology is being used in the retail sector as well as in the industrial sector to alleviate some of the above concerns. Walmart, for example, partnered with IBM to create a food traceability system. In 2017, it also partnered with other large food retailers to increase food traceability. It claims to be the first to trace shrimp exports from farms to international retailers (Walmart, 2021).

Bribery, Corruption, and Protection Money

Lafarge Cement is perhaps an extreme example of a company's executives putting profit over principle and people. In October 2022, the French company pleaded guilty in a New York federal court to providing material support in 2013–2014 to terrorist organizations ISIS and the al Nusrah Front, affiliated with al Qaeda. The company agreed to pay $778 million and serve three years of probation (United States Department of Justice, 2022).

The executives allegedly negotiated a revenue-sharing agreement with ISIS to protect its plant in Syria and to block competitors from importing cement from Turkey. Deputy Attorney General Lisa Monaco stated that "Lafarge hid the arrangement through fake contracts, phony invoices, corrupt intermediaries and off-system emails" (Engineering News-Record, 2022). She also said that "today's guilty pleas to terrorism charges by multinational construction conglomerate Lafarge SA and its Syrian subsidiary reflect corporate crime that reached a new low and a very dark place" (Wall Street Journal, 2022).

The US Department of Justice's legal proceedings continued the company's legal problems. In France, Lafarge had been accused of aiding and abetting crimes against humanity. In May 2022, the Paris Appeals Court upheld the indictment for complicity in human rights violations. Eight former executives, including two former CEOs, were indicted on charges of financing terrorism (New York Times, 2022). In the lawsuit, former Syrian employees claimed they were pressured to continue working even though the civil war was rapidly approaching their area.

More common ethical and legal dilemmas that executives may encounter are requests for bribes or offers of "kickbacks" – illegal payments to a person approving contracts or large projects.

The US Department of Justice charged the science, technology, and engineering company Kellogg Brown & Root (KBR) with paying $182 million to secure a $6 billion construction contract for a liquefied natural gas plant in Nigeria. The company pleaded guilty and paid $402 million in fines, while the CEO was sentenced to 2.5 years in prison (New York Times, 2008).

A culture of bribery also developed in Siemens over the years. It appeared to be a way of doing business until March 24, 1999, when German tax law changed. Under the previous tax law, deductions of "bribes were disallowed only if either the briber or the recipient had been subject to criminal penalties or criminal proceedings which were discontinued on the basis of a discretionary decision by the prosecution" (U.S. Department of State Archive, n.d., 20th paragraph). Peter Solmessen, who was a board member and general counsel of Siemens, explained, "It was largely a failure of leadership. It seems employees believed that they had to pay bribes in order to get business" (Solmessen, 2012). In 2007, a new CEO, Peter Löscher, was hired and quickly moved to change the culture. Within months he replaced "80% of the top level of executives, 70% of the next level down, and 40% of the level below that" (Löscher, 2012).

Siemens eventually pleaded guilty to violating the Foreign Corrupt Practices Act (FCPA) and agreed to a fine of US$1.6 billion to American and European authorities for bribes and kickbacks for identity cards in Argentina, transportation projects in Venezuela, and a cell phone network in Bangladesh.

Unfortunately, some executives apparently did not learn from others' mistakes and have committed similar transgressions. In 2010, the British arms, security, and aerospace company BAE Systems pleaded guilty to making false statements about its accounting practices in a corruption and bribery scandal related to arms deals in Saudi Arabia and Africa.

In 2012, Walmart was involved in a bribery scandal in Mexico. An executive of the company in Mexico allegedly paid US$52,000 to have a zoning map redrawn of the area around the Teotihuacan pyramids so that it could build a store where one would not previously have been permitted, and this, apparently, was not the first instance of such behavior (New York Times, 2012).

In 2013, a former program manager for the US Army Corps of Engineers was sentenced to 19 years in prison on charges that he led a ring of corrupt public officials and government contractors in a bribery and kickback scheme that stole more than US$30 million through inflated and fictitious invoices. Fifteen people and one company were charged (Federal Bureau of Investigation, 2013).

In 2017, Deutsche Bank was fined US$7.2 billion for misleading investors back in 2008 about the "toxic" mortgage-backed securities it was selling and then another US$41 million for failing to maintain adequate controls against a Russian money-laundering scheme.

However, not all legal or ethical lapses involve bribery. Between 2011 and 2016, Wells Fargo employees, driven by fear of losing their jobs and the company's evaluation and reward systems, created over 1.5 million fake customer accounts. In 2015, VW was found to have created cheating software to circumvent emissions checks in the United States and Europe. And in 2017, Uber revealed that a year earlier it had paid hackers $100,000 to remain silent about the theft of personal data on 57 million customers.

The ubiquitous occurrence of bribery has led to efforts to curtail it. In addition to the UN's Global Compact, other examples include the OECD's Anti-Bribery Convention, the UK's Bribery Act 2010, and the Foreign Corrupt Practices Act (FCPA) in the United States.

The Foreign Corrupt Practices Act

In 1977, the United States Congress passed into law the Foreign Corrupt Practices Act (FCPA) in response to investigations that discovered that over 400 US companies had made questionable or illegal payments to foreign government officials, politicians, and political parties for a range of reasons. Twenty years later, the United States and 33 other countries signed the OECD Anti-Bribery Convention (officially Convention on Combating Bribery of Foreign Public Officials in International Business Transactions).

Under the FCPA, it is illegal for a US citizen, or a foreign company with securities listed in the United States, to make a payment to a foreign official to obtain or retain business or direct business to any person or company. Since 1998, the rules also apply to foreign firms and persons while in the United States.

Specifically, the law prohibits,

any offer, payment, promise to pay, or authorization of the payment of money or anything of value to any person, while knowing that all or a portion of such money or thing of value will be offered, given or promised, directly or indirectly, to a foreign official to influence the foreign official in his or her official capacity, induce the foreign official to do or omit to do an act in violation of his or her lawful duty, or to secure any improper advantage in order to assist in obtaining or retaining business for or with, or directing business to, any person. (United States Department of Justice, n.d.)

The FCPA does contain an exception for "facilitating or expediting payments" for "routine governmental actions" such as processing permits, licenses, work orders, or visas. These are situations where an official does not have the discretionary power to award business or ignore violations of law or regulations.

The law requires companies whose securities are listed in the United States to make and keep records that accurately reflect the transactions of the corporation and to maintain an adequate system of internal accounting controls. Companies that have been found to violate the Act tend to plead guilty to accounting lapses and pay a fine rather than pleading guilty to bribery. In addition to criminal and civil penalties, they may be barred from doing business with the federal government. Debarment from public procurement is being used as a weapon to combat bribery, and numerous countries besides the United States have adopted it.

Bribery and corruption are global problems that are not limited to public officials in a few developing countries. Executives of global corporations headquartered in developed countries are affected, and some have been implicated in scandals and sentenced to jail. Global executives should not be smug about assuming that the locus of the problem is elsewhere – as the old saying goes, "It takes two to tango."

Transparency International

Transparency International (TI) (www.transparency.org) is a NGO that has been established to combat the problem of bribery and corruption. Since 1993, when it was founded, TI has become the leading NGO combating national and international corruption. TI has developed chapters in more than 100 countries and works with numerous intergovernmental organizations like the OECD, World Bank, the Organization of American States (OAS), and the European Union to develop and monitor anti-corruption legislation and treaties. It analyzes corruption by measuring its occurrence through surveys, and it has created resources and tools used by people around the world in the fight against corruption.

These tools include the Corruption Perceptions Index (https://www.transparency.org/en/cpi/2022), Global Corruption Barometer (a worldwide public opinion survey on corruption), and an Anti-Corruption Knowledge Hub, an online tool where TI presents its research and knowledge as, for example, a series of topic guides and country-specific research. The 2022 **Corruption Perception Index** ranks 180 countries by their perceived levels of public-sector corruption as determined by expert assessments, opinion surveys, and 13 different data sources from reputable, independent institutions that capture perceptions of corruption by experts and businesspeople within the previous 2 years. The score ranges between 100 (least corrupt) and 0 (most corrupt). The 10 countries that scored the highest (least corrupt) on the 2022 Index were Denmark, Finland, New Zealand, Norway, Singapore, Sweden, Switzerland, the Netherlands, Germany, and Ireland. Canada was 14th, the United Kingdom was 18th, and the United States was 24th. Two-thirds of the countries had scores of lower than 50, indicating serious corruption problems. The five countries that scored the lowest (most corrupt) were Somalia, Syria, South Sudan, Venezuela, and Yemen.

Other Examples of Ethical Dilemmas

Not all ethical dilemmas fall into the categories established by the UN Global Compact.

Employee Security

Situations in which the physical security of employees could be a problem may present ethical issues for managers. Consider a situation, known to the authors, in which British expatriate women working in the Middle East training center of a North American–based bank found themselves. They were en route to conduct a training program in Lagos, Nigeria, and were supposed to be met by one of the bank's local staff who would assist them through difficulties in customs at the airport. When the local staff member failed to appear, the women felt forced to pay bribes to bring legitimate training materials and equipment into the country. Soon after paying the money, their taxi was stopped at the darkened perimeter of the airport and uniformed men pointed guns at them. The women were subject to a shakedown again and felt very vulnerable, particularly with no foreign currency left. After repeatedly showing their documents and denying that they were violating any laws, they were finally permitted to pass.

What responsibility did the local management bear for this security lapse? And what was the ethical responsibility of the experienced managers for whom the women worked who sent them into such a situation so ill-prepared? What is a manager's responsibility regarding the implementation of his or her decisions, particularly when the specific action has to be taken by another person? Years later, one of the current authors conducted a training program in a different African country for a European-based company and learned that travel to and in Lagos for its executives remained a security priority. This company developed elaborate safety procedures for its executives traveling there. The January 2023 Travel Advisory from the US Department of State stated, "Reconsider travel to Nigeria due to crime, terrorism, civil unrest, kidnapping, and maritime crime" (U.S. Department of State, 2023).

In recent years, the world is often perceived to have become a more dangerous place, and situations in which physical security is a managerial concern are becoming more common for global companies.

Many companies currently operate in countries where personal security concerns, political violence, or terrorism may be issues. In 2008, a sophisticated, large-scale terrorist attack took place in Mumbai, India, that left 175 people dead, including 29 foreign nationals. A terrorist group, Deccan Mujahideen, claimed responsibility for the attack. Its members had received training from Lashkar-e-Taiba, a group fighting to bring independence to Muslims in the Indian Kashmir. News reports at the time suggested that they were apparently searching for and targeting foreigners, although many more Indians died in the attack than foreigners. *The Telegraph* reported that this "terrorist attack nearly wiped-out top management at Unilever." The European CEO and the CEO-elect of Unilever along with the entire board of the Indian subsidiary were dining at the Taj Mahal Palace hotel in Mumbai at the time (Hope, 2009). Unilever's Paul Polman, portrayed in Chapter 11, was one of the attendees.

In January 2013, terrorists seized an Algerian gas field for 4 days until the Algerian army liberated it and killed more than 30 terrorists. In the process, however, the terrorists killed more than 20 hostages from numerous countries. In 2015, terrorists killed 12 people in Paris in an attack on the offices of Charlie Hebdo, a satirical newspaper.

It may be tempting to say that the examples above come from industries that you won't be working in or occurred in countries where you won't be working. However, you do not need to be working for a global engineering company, a global oil company, or other natural resource industry companies in remote and difficult areas to face these issues. You could be a banking or consumer goods executive or a consultant managing a project in Lagos, Mumbai, Madrid, or Paris, or you might only be visiting these cities on business.

Global leaders need to learn to live and work in a world of uncertainty and risk. The more you learn about other countries, the better you understand the risks involved. Familiarity with and understanding of a country provide the necessary perspective for accurately assessing investment risks, determining acceptable levels of risk, and managing those risks. To put it in colloquial terms, "basing global investment decisions on economic data without understanding the political context is like basing nutrition decisions on calorie counts without examining the list of ingredients" (Bremmer, 2005).

Companies need to have strategic and tactical plans for managing risks. Large companies can develop risk specialists to contribute to informed decision-making, and smaller firms can access consultants for specific decisions. All companies are advised to listen to expatriates and locals working in the field when they provide systematic assessments of their environments, usually required periodically by the home office. Individual managers can add to the quality of their own decision-making by reading broadly, by understanding the history of regions in which they operate, and by seeking (and paying attention to) information from international field personnel.

An Emerging Concern: Artificial Intelligence's Use by Global Leaders

The use of artificial intelligence (AI) in global leadership can have significant consequences, both positive and negative. Here are some key considerations:

1. Data-driven decision-making: AI can process vast amounts of data and generate insights that can aid global leaders in making more informed decisions. It can analyze complex patterns and correlations, identify trends, and provide predictive analytics. This can enhance efficiency, accuracy, and effectiveness in decision-making processes.
2. Improved policy formulation: AI can assist leaders in analyzing and understanding complex policy issues by quickly processing and synthesizing large amounts of information. It can help identify potential impacts, assess risks, and propose evidence-based solutions, thus aiding in the formulation of more effective policies.
3. Enhanced efficiency and productivity: AI technologies, such as automation and machine learning, can streamline administrative tasks, optimize processes, and increase overall efficiency. This can free up time for leaders to focus on more strategic and high-value activities.
4. Economic and societal implications: The widespread adoption of AI in global leadership can have significant economic and societal consequences. It may lead to job displacement in certain industries as automation replaces repetitive or routine tasks. However, it can also create new job opportunities and foster innovation in AI-related fields. Global leaders must consider the potential impacts on employment, income distribution, and skills development.
5. Ethical and fairness concerns: AI algorithms and decision-making systems can introduce biases and unfairness, as they are trained on historical data that may reflect societal prejudices or inequalities. Leaders need to ensure transparency, accountability, and fairness in AI systems to avoid perpetuating discrimination or bias in decision-making processes.

6. Security and privacy risks: The use of AI in global leadership raises concerns about data security and privacy. AI systems rely on vast amounts of data, and if not properly protected, sensitive information can be compromised. Leaders must prioritize cybersecurity measures to safeguard critical data and protect against potential threats.
7. Human–AI collaboration: The integration of AI into global leadership requires a careful balance between human judgment and AI-driven insights. Leaders need to understand the limitations of AI systems and use them as tools to augment human decision-making rather than replace it. Effective human–AI collaboration can leverage the strengths of both to achieve optimal outcomes.
8. Global governance and regulation: The widespread adoption of AI in global leadership necessitates international cooperation and the development of regulations and frameworks to address ethical, legal, and societal implications. Leaders must work together to establish standards, guidelines, and policies that ensure responsible and beneficial use of AI technologies.

It is important for global leaders to be mindful of these consequences and proactively address the challenges associated with the use of AI to maximize the benefits and mitigate potential risks.

Consequences of the Use of Artificial Intelligence in Global Leadership

The previous subsection was written entirely by the artificially intelligent language model Chat-GPT in response to the authors' prompt: "What are the consequences of the use of artificial intelligence in global leadership?" We submitted its response to a plagiarism checker to make sure it was not plagiarized before publishing it. Chat-GPT, fluent in both computer and human languages, is but one example of the AI tools that have become available in recent years. AI can be defined as "artificial tools that can automatically accumulate experience (i.e., make sense of objective environments) and constantly learn from past experience to perform cognitive tasks" (Pan & Froese, 2023, p. 100924).

Generative AI, large language models such as Chat-GPT, or machine learning are all technologies that are central to the so-called fourth industrial revolution. No aspect of work life will be immune from generative AI changes: "We used to believe that 'thinking work' was insulated from mechanization. However, what machines have wrought on 'doing work' for the last 300 years they will do to 'thinking work' in the next 50" (Phan et al., 2017, p. 253).

New technology may provide new solutions but also has the potential to disrupt markets, work processes, and relationships. The utopian, fourth industrial revolution view envisions AI benefiting the world by spurring innovation, advancing medical and scientific knowledge, increasing productivity, and driving economic growth. Alternatively, the dystopian scenario envisions job displacement through automation, increased unemployment, income disparity and social unrest, and government surveillance systems. The reality is not likely to be one of these extremes, but it is important to question how AI should be used responsibly by global leaders.

Regulation, responsible development, and use of AI have become a focus of attention of individual companies, national governments, and supranational organizations. Some developers of AI even suggested in early 2023 that giant AI experiments be put on hold temporarily to take a timeout to think, since *"advanced AI could represent a profound change in the history of life on Earth and should be planned for and managed with commensurate care and resources"* (Future of Life, Institute, 2023, first paragraph).

In the absence of legislation, several supranational bodies (e.g., OECD, UN, UNESCO, and the European Commission) have formulated ethical guidelines for the responsible, human-centric, and trustworthy use of AI. In 2017, a conference was held at the Asilomar Conference Grounds in California to discuss how to avoid a negative impact of AI on society. The conference was attended by leading academics, researchers, entrepreneurs, and thought leaders. Some of the important AI principles emerging from this conference include (Future of Life Institute, 2017):

- Research Goal: The development of AI should be beneficial to all humans and the environment.
- Safety: AI systems should be designed and operated in a way that minimizes the risk of unintended harm to humans.
- Transparency: The design, development, and deployment of AI systems should be transparent, and AI systems should be able to explain their decisions and actions to humans.
- Privacy: AI systems should be designed to protect personal privacy and data security.
- Fairness: It should be ensured that AI is designed and operated fairly, without bias or discrimination.
- Human Control: Humans should be able to control AI systems and prevent them from causing harm.
- Shared Benefit: AI should benefit society as a whole, not just a small group of individuals or organizations.
- Responsibility: Those responsible for developing and deploying AI systems should be accountable for their impact on society.

The full list of the Asilomar AI Principles is available at the "Future of Life" website.

Aspects of management and leadership can be automated, but mindful global leaders should use these technologies for productive and ethical purposes.

Responding to Ethical Problems

How might managers respond when they encounter ethical problems such as the examples that we have described or work in countries where corruption is rampant and where they may encounter requests for bribes? One of the first things they may do is avoid the ethical dilemma through the process of rationalization. They may focus on some other aspect of the problem. For instance, they may transform the ethical problem into a legal or accounting problem. The reasoning seems to be that so long as one is behaving legally or, for example, in accordance with accepted accounting practices, nothing else is required. As we said earlier, compliance with laws and professional regulations is a minimum requirement for responsible managers.

Another avoidance behavior is to see the problem as only one small piece of a larger puzzle and to assume that someone higher up in the organization must be looking after any unusual aspects, such as ethical considerations. Alternatively, the decision-maker might try to make it someone else's problem – perhaps a customer, supplier, or person in higher authority – with the comment: "I was following my boss's orders" or "They were my customer's instructions." However, when a customer asks for a falsified invoice on imported goods for his or her records, with the difference deposited in a foreign bank, and someone provides this "service," it is clearly not only the customer's behavior that is questionable.

Rationalizing one's behavior by transforming an ethical problem into another type of problem, assuming responsibility for only one specific, technical component of the issue, or claiming that it is someone else's problem gives one the feeling of being absolved of culpability by putting the burden of responsibility on another person or department.

Who is responsible for ensuring that managers act ethically? We believe that corporations have a responsibility to make clear to their employees what sort of behavior is expected of them. This means that executives in headquarters have a responsibility not just for their own behavior but also for providing guidance to subordinates. Many companies have corporate codes to do just this. However, global executives need to consider carefully whether their codes of conduct are effective. Donaldson found that effective codes of conduct meet three criteria (Donaldson, 2000):

1. Senior management must be committed to ethical behavior and the codes of conduct, and the codes must affect "everyday decisions and actions."
2. External or "imposed" codes are not generally effective. Companies must develop their own and take ownership of their codes.
3. Various important stakeholders (employees, customers, suppliers, or NGOs) must be involved in shaping the development and implementation of the codes.

Although a company has a responsibility to outline what behavior it expects from an employee, the person on the spot facing the decision is ultimately responsible for their own behavior, with or without guidance from headquarters. In the cases that you will study in this book, you will be asked to develop your own stance on the issues. Think carefully about the problems to develop reasoned positions. You may find yourself in a similar situation someday and will have to make a critical decision. We hope that, by working through the decisions in these cases now, you will be better able to deal with similar decisions later.

As we personally encountered ethical dilemmas or talked with others who had experienced them, we wrote cases and developed a managerial framework for thinking about and analyzing the problems to guide ourselves and to teach our classes. We make no claim that the framework presented in the following section is a complete or definitive treatment of the topic of ethics. We do think it provides a practical and managerial way to think about the topic.

Ethical Frameworks

Moral philosophers have developed theories for thinking about moral issues and for analyzing ethical problems, but these generally have not been included in international business curricula. There are various approaches for analyzing ethical problems, and there are conflicting positions and prescriptions among them. We have observed that people advocate actions representing the major theories but without understanding the foundations or the strengths and weaknesses of their positions. Consider the following discussion:

Joe: "If we don't pay what he is asking, we will lose the contract and people back home will lose jobs. Is that ethical when people can't feed their families?"

Jan: "I don't care. What you are suggesting is absolutely wrong."

Max: "Now hold on, it doesn't seem to be against the rules there. It is a different culture. Everyone is doing it. They need the extra money to support their families. Besides, we should not impose our system of morality on other cultures."

You may have heard or taken part in similar exchanges. The people in the conversation above may not realize it, but they are engaged in a discussion of moral philosophy. Often, it is this type of discussion that tends to excite emotions and generate heated arguments, rather than provide insight or a thoughtful course of action.

In the brief exchange above, one sees elements of utilitarianism, Kant's categorical imperative, and cultural relativism. These are commonly invoked frameworks, which is why they were chosen here. Each represents a different ethical map and moral calculus. Since you may likely take part in similar discussions (or arguments) during your career, knowledge of these three frameworks will be useful. The intent is to help you link everyday reasoning and the positions you might espouse to the ethical frameworks underlying them.

The main categories of ethical theories can be divided into **consequential** (or **teleological**) theories, which focus on the consequences, outcomes, or results of decisions and behavior; **rule-based** (or **deontological**) theories, which focus on moral obligations, duties, and rights; and **cultural** theories, which emphasize cultural differences in standards of behavior. Understanding the differences will help you develop your own perspective and position on competing with integrity. It will also help you recognize and counter some of the assumptions underlying arguments for actions and decisions that may be unethical or illegal. Each of these theories is briefly discussed in turn next.

Consequential Theories

Consequential theories focus on the goals, end results, and/or consequences of decisions and actions. They are concerned with doing the maximum amount of "good" and the minimum amount of "harm." Utilitarianism is the most widely used example of this type of moral framework. It argues for doing the best for the greatest number of people or acting in a way that provides more net utility than an alternative act. It is essentially an economic cost–benefit approach to ethical decision-making. If the benefits outweigh the costs, then that course of action is indicated.

The limitations of this approach are that it is difficult or impossible to identify and account for all the costs and benefits, and, since people have different utility curves, it is difficult to decide whose curve should be used. In real life, how do you compute this utility curve? Finally, to weigh the costs and benefits, one often relies on quantitative data, usually economic data, and many important variables that should be considered are not quantifiable and, therefore, tend to be ignored.

Rule-Based Theories

Rule-based theories include both absolute (or universal) and conditional theories. The emphasis of these theories is on duty, obligations, and rights. For example, if an employee follows orders or performs a certain task, management has an obligation to ensure that the task is not illegal or harmful to that person's health. People in power have a responsibility to protect the rights of the less powerful. These theories are concerned with the universal "shoulds" and "oughts" of human existence – the rules that guide all people's decision-making and behavior wherever they are.

One of the best-known absolute theories is the categorical imperative of the German philosopher Immanuel Kant. Whereas utilitarianism takes a group or societal perspective, the categorical imperative has a more individualistic focus: individuals should be treated with respect and dignity as an end in itself; they should not be used simply as a means to an end. Harm should not be done to a person even if the ultimate end is good. The criteria should be applied consistently to everyone. One of the questions to ask is: If I were in the other person's (or group's or organization's) position, would I be willing for them to make the same decision that I am going to make, for the same reasons?

The "Trolley Problem" is a classic thought experiment in moral philosophy contrasting potential actions illustrating the consequential and rules-based perspectives. It is thought to have been created by an English philosopher Philippa Foot (Brandeis, n.d.).

Reflection Question 12.1: The Trolley Problem

A runaway trolley is heading down the tracks toward five workers who will all be killed if the trolley proceeds on its present course. You are standing next to a large switch that can divert the trolley onto a different track. The only way to save the lives of the five workers is to divert the trolley onto another track that only has one worker on it. If you divert the trolley onto the other track, this one worker will die, but the other five workers will be saved.

1. How would the decision differ between a consequential and rules-based perspective?
2. What would you personally do, and why?

A variation on absolute theories is fundamentalism. In this case, the rules may come from a book like the Bible, Koran, or Torah. In these systems, one is dealing with a revealed, authoritative, divine wisdom. Difficult questions arise when considering which book or prophet to follow and whose interpretation of the chosen book to use. Priests, ministers, mullahs, or rabbis who may reflect the views of an elite segment of society, or possibly an isolated group, usually interpret the books. There can be conflicting interpretations within the same religion as well. The interpretations may be inconsistent with current social and environmental circumstances, as well as with the beliefs of large segments of a society. The rules that people follow can also be secular as well as religious.

One shortcoming of these types of deontological prescriptions is that they allow you to claim that you are not responsible for your own behavior: "I was just following orders" is a common excuse. The result may be the same – you do not have to think for yourself or make a moral judgment, but rather you can avoid it by claiming to be following a higher authority.

Cultural Theories

Although the two former perspectives may be self-sufficient within a single, cultural context, decision-makers often run into ethical dilemmas when traversing between contexts and associated cultures. With cultural theories, local standards prevail. Cultural relativism is interpreted to mean that there is no single right way; in other words, people should not impose their values and standards on others. The reasoning behind the argument is usually that we should behave as the locals behave: "When in Rome, do as the Romans do." One problem, however, comes from the fact that the local people we are encouraged to emulate may not necessarily be exemplary. In your own culture, you know that people exhibit different standards of behavior. Does that mean we should advocate that businesspeople coming to the United States act like the people at Wells Fargo, for example, just because those people were Americans? Or should expatriate managers working in Germany follow the example set by VW executives because they were German? Adopting this philosophy also can encourage denial of accountability and the avoidance of moral choice. Using arguments based on this philosophy, the morality of bribes or actions of repressive regimes, for example, do not have to be examined very closely.

The three theories described above, and their key tenets, are summarized in Figure 12.1.

A perspective that provides useful insight into cultural relativism is the process of intellectual and ethical development (Perry, 1970). Although Perry's ideas

Ethical Theory

Consequential
- Concerned with consequences, goals, outcomes
- Concerned with doing the maximum good and minimum harm
- Cost-benefit approach

Rule-based
- Emphasis on duty, moral obligation
- Concerned with "ought's"

Absolute (Universal)

Conditional (not discussed)

Cultural
- Emphasizes different standards of conduct
- Espouses observing local standards

Decision-Making Tenets

Utilitarianism
- Do the best for the most
- Produce the most net utility

Categorical imperative (Kant)
- Respect for individuals – treat as ends, not means to ends
- If you were in the other person's situation, would you want the same decision made?
- Apply criteria consistently

Fundamentalism
- From a book
- Revealed wisdom
- One authority

Cultural relativism
- No one authority
- Local standards prevail

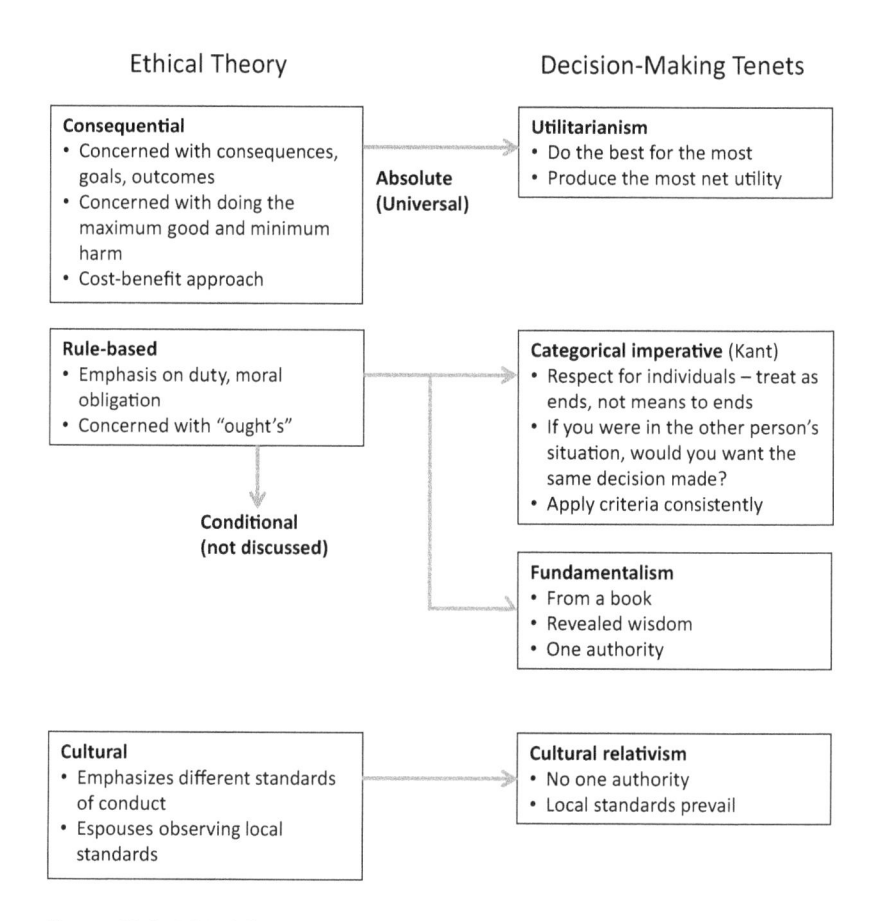

Figure 12.1 Ethical frameworks.

reflect a cultural bias toward individualism and were derived from a narrow part of the US population, understanding the three major progressive stages of perspective-taking (out of nine in total) is illuminating. The first stage is **dualism**, in which a bipolar structure of the world is assumed or taken for granted. According to this perspective, there is a clear right and wrong, good and bad, us and them. These positions are defined from one's own perspective based on membership of a group and belief in or adherence to a common set of traditional beliefs.

The next stage, posited by Perry as a more developed perspective, is **relativism**, in which the dualistic worldview is moderated by an understanding of the importance of context, which helps a person see that knowledge and values are dependent on local situations. As we have seen through earlier parts of this book, different people in different parts of the world think and believe differently, and a relativistic mode of making ethical judgments recognizes this fact. As originally observed by the French mathematician, philosopher, and inventor Blaise Pascal, "Truth on this side of the Pyrénées is error on the other" (Pascal, 1669-1670; translation by the authors).

In Perry's scheme, the third stage of development is **commitment in relativism,** in which a person understands the relativistic nature of the world but makes a commitment to a set of values, beliefs, and a way of behaving within this expanded worldview. The goal is to arrive at the point where you assume responsibility for your own actions and decisions based on careful consideration and the application of the essential tools of moral reasoning: deliberation and justification. Perry suggests that progression to this stage is not automatic or guaranteed, and that people may become "delayed" in their development or even "stuck" in the earlier stages.

Our inclusion of Perry's ideas is meant to encourage self-awareness and recognition that simple, **cultural relativism** is not the highest end point of moral development. Underlying our perspective throughout this book are (1) the assumption that you are interested in developing a relativistic understanding of the world and (2) encouragement for you to decide about your own commitments within this relativistic framework.

Universalism, Relativism, and the "Asian Values" Debate

The previous brief discussion of different theories in moral philosophy provides a context for understanding the underlying ethical positions of what has been termed the "Asian values" debate. This was a 1990s political ideology that went dormant but reappeared in 2017. At one level, it is the age-old debate in moral philosophy about universalism versus relativism. Is there a universal set of rules that should be followed, or are morals and ethics relative dependent on the culture? Are one culture's beliefs, values, and practices superior and preferable to those of another? Whose laws, values, or ethics should be followed if and when a disagreement develops, a different course of action is proposed, or a conflict arises? This theoretical debate became more tangible when it turned into an international debate about human rights and economic growth. The rise of China as an economic power moving to become the world's largest economy has brought it back into relevance in the 21st century.

In 1948, the United Nations adopted the Universal Declaration of Human Rights (UDHR). Since that time, there have been discussions and disagreements over which of the human rights specified in its 30 Articles are universal and which are culturally influenced. China, long criticized by "the West" for human rights violations, issued a White Paper on Human Rights in China in November 1991. Although it supported the development of the international human rights regime, China argued that human rights were a matter of domestic jurisdiction.

In 1993, the Bangkok Declaration was signed by more than 30 Asian and Middle Eastern countries. It presented the view that the UDHR embodied statements of Western values and were at odds with "Asian values" and not applicable to Asia.

Singapore's first Prime Minister Lee Kuan Yew alleged in 1994 that the imposition of Western values is a form of **cultural imperialism**, stating: "It is not my business to tell people what's wrong with their system. It is my business to tell people not to foist their system indiscriminately on societies in which it will not work" (Zakaria, 1994). In this interview, he described some of the differentiators that he saw between East and West:

The fundamental difference between Western concepts of society and government and East Asian concepts – when I say East Asians, I mean Korea, Japan, China, Vietnam, as distinct from Southeast Asia, which is a mix between the Sinic and the Indian, though Indian culture also emphasizes similar values – is that Eastern societies believe that the individual exists in the context of his family. He is not pristine and separate. The family is part of the extended family, and then friends and the wider society. (Zakaria, 1994, p. 113)

Although he admired parts of the American system, he was critical of other parts:

As an East Asian looking at America, I find attractive and unattractive features. I like, for example, the free, easy and open relations between people regardless of social status, ethnicity or religion ... a certain openness in argument about what is good or bad for society; the accountability of public officials; none of the secrecy and terror that's part and parcel of communist government.

But as a total system, I find parts of it totally unacceptable: guns, drugs, violent crime, vagrancy, unbecoming behavior in public – in sum the breakdown of civil society. The expansion of the right of the individual to behave or misbehave as he pleases has come at the expense of orderly society. In the East, the main object is to have a well-ordered society so that everybody can have maximum enjoyment of his freedoms. This freedom can only exist in an ordered state and not in a natural state of contention and anarchy. (Zakaria, 1994, p. 111)

In 1996, at the 29th International General Meeting of the Pacific Basin Economic Council, Dr. Mahathir Mohamad, Prime Minister of Malaysia, continued to defend the prioritization of local cultural norms when he said that there was a belief among many in the West that their values and beliefs were universal; that too much democracy could lead to violence, instability, and anarchy; and that the West was using ideals such as democracy and human rights as tools to recolonize parts of Asia.

In the remarks of Lee and Mohamad one can see the primary values that are in conflict in this debate.

- The East values community and family (interdependence or collectivism) while the West values the individual and independence. In the East, responsibility toward family and community takes precedence over individual interests and privileges. In the East, people have duties and obligations while in the West they have rights.
- The East values order and harmony, which is reflected in respect for age, leaders, persons of authority, hierarchy, and institutions. The West values personal freedom, individual initiative, and competition, which is reflected in democracy, the rights of individuals, and capitalism.
- The West believes in universalism while the East practices particularism. Universalism emphasizes rules, laws, and generalizations while particularism emphasizes exceptions, circumstances, and relations. Particularism is often expressed in the East in practices like *guanxi* (the use of interpersonal relationships) in China, which also can be interpreted by some from a Western perspective as corruption or bribery.

Not all Asian political leaders and academics see "Asian values" as different from, and an alternative to, Western cultural beliefs. Asia is not a monolithic, homogeneous area. Critics dismiss the idea that a common set of distinctively Asian principles exists, given Asia's immense cultural, religious, and political diversity. There are regional differences between East, Southeast, and South Asia, and cultures within these regions have highly varying historical and religious backgrounds including Hindu, Muslim, Confucian, Shinto, and Buddhist traditions.

Nobel Laureate Amartya Sen disagreed with the proponents of "Asian values" and with those who believe that human rights are an artifact solely of Western culture. He disputed the "grand contrast" between Asian and Western values: "The so-called Asian values that are invoked to justify authoritarianism are not especially Asian in any significant sense … The people whose rights are being disputed are Asians … " (Sen, 1997, p. 30).

Echoing Sen, critics argue the debate is not so much about cultural values but about maintaining political power and an excuse for autocratic governments to suppress individual rights and dissidents. In May 2017, at a conference at the University of the Philippines, the keynote speaker was Judge Raul C. Pangalangan of the International Criminal Court, who expressed surprise at the longevity of this 1990s political ideology. He noted that variations of this theme were used by authoritarian regimes to support the way they governed and to denounce Western detractors for their criticism and interference.

Some events give credence to Sen's and Pangalangan's observations that political regimes use "Asian values" to counter Western criticism.

In November 2017, Justin Trudeau, Prime Minister of Canada, criticized Philippine President Rodrigo Duterte's record on human rights and his war on drugs in which, by some estimates, extrajudicial killings have claimed 7,000 victims (CBC News, 2017). Duterte told Trudeau, "It angers me when you are a foreigner you do not know exactly what is happening in this country."

An article in the *Manilla Times* commented,

Those who thought that the Asian values debate died with Lee Kuan Yew should think again. The old debate is coming back in a different form courtesy of [Duterte's] drug war and the wide-ranging quarrel over "human rights" that it has provoked. (Makabenta, 2017)

That same year, China's head of the Publicity Department of the Chinese Communist Party said,

Western countries are trying to push their culture and political values onto others, seducing them into abandoning their own … There are especially some Western countries who use their technological advantages and dominance of discourse that they have accumulated over a long period to peddle so-called "universal values." (Reuters, 2017)

Observers continually dismiss the Asian values debate as no longer relevant, but it repeatedly reappears. Consider the joint statement by Russia and China at the opening of the Beijing Olympics in 2022:

There is no one-size-fits-all template to guide countries in establishing democracy. A nation can choose such forms and methods of implementing democracy that would best suit its particular state, based on its social and political system, its historical background, traditions and unique cultural characteristics. It is only up to the people of the country to decide whether their State is a democratic one. (Office of the President of Russia, 2022)

Some academics have argued that "academic moral theory is useless," and the "Asian values" debate tends to lend credence to that view, since it does not lead to actionable decision criteria without embracing the beliefs of one side or the other (Peerenboom, 2003). There does not seem to be any way to cut through the arguments to find the "truth." One is left with having either to impose one's beliefs and values on the other through coercion or by the conflicting parties agreeing to disagree.

It is important for managers to be able to recognize the basis for their moral and ethical decisions and to be aware, for example, if they are shifting from one theory to another as a way of avoiding tough decisions. Global executives must make decisions and take action, and they do not have the luxury of simply debating the issue. How do they decide? How does he or she choose among mutually conflicting moral theories? Integrative Social Contracts Theory may help in finding a path forward.

Integrative Social Contracts Theory: A Way to Avoid Ethical Paralysis?

Integrative Social Contracts Theory (ISCT), developed by Donaldson and Dunfee (1999), is one approach for resolving conflicting ethical viewpoints. ISCT can be a useful tool when making decisions and determining a course of action. However, before showing how to apply this theory, it is helpful to put it in context with the theories previously discussed. On a continuum with extreme relativism at one end and extreme universalism at the other end, ISCT is a pluralistic theory and probably closer to the relativism end of the continuum as shown and described in Figure 12.2.

ISCT essentially posits that local communities and cultures can determine ethical norms for members of that society, but that these norms must be based on the rights of individual members to exercise "voice" and "exit." To be legitimate, these

Theory	Position
Extreme relativism	No ethical view, regardless of source or basis, is better than any other.
Cultural relativism	No ethical view held by one culture is better than any other view held by another culture.
ISCT (Pluralism)	There exist a broad range of ethical viewpoints that may be chosen by communities and cultures. The possibility exists that conflicting ethical positions in different communities are equally valid. There are, however, circumstances in which the viewpoint of a particular culture will be invalid due to either a universally binding moral precept or the priority of the view of another culture or community.
Modified universalism	There exists a set of precepts expressible in many different ethical languages that reflects universally binding moral precepts and that captures many issues of global ethical significance. These precepts rule out the possibility of two conflicting ethical positions in different cultures being equally valid.
Extreme universalism	There exists a single set of precepts expressed only in a single ethical language that reflects universally binding moral precepts and that captures all issues of global ethical significance. These precepts rule out the possibility of two conflicting ethical positions in different cultures being equally valid.

Figure 12.2 Integrative Social Contracts Theory in context.
(Thomas Donaldson and Thomas W. Dunfee, *Ties That Bind*, Harvard Business Review Press, Boston, MA; 1999; p. 23.)

local norms or principles must be compatible with macro-level norms, "hypernorms," which are universal precepts. If there is a conflict, the hypernorms take priority.

The challenge, therefore, is to know if a principle has hypernorm status. Donaldson and Dunfee offer 11 types of evidence that support the existence of hypernorm status. The more types of supportive evidence, the stronger the case for hypernorm status of a particular principle.

1. Widespread consensus that the principle is universal.
2. Component of well-known global industry standards.
3. Supported by prominent NGOs such as the International Labor Organization or Transparency International.
4. Supported by regional governmental organizations such as the EU, OECD, or OAS.
5. Consistently referred to as a global ethical standard by the global media.
6. Known to be consistent with precepts of major religions.
7. Supported by global business organizations such as the International Chamber of Commerce or the Caux Round Table.
8. Known to be consistent with the precepts of major philosophies.
9. Generally supported by a relevant international community of professionals such as accountants or engineers.
10. Known to be consistent with the findings of universal human values.
11. Supported by the laws of many different nations.

One such set of hypernorms would be the Universal Declaration of Human Rights, which can be found on the United Nation's website.

Competing with Integrity: Some Guidelines to Consider

Managers have multiple objectives that they must consider because they are embedded in a complex network of relationships. The interests, goals, and values of the various actors in any situation can potentially conflict. In Chapter 9, we described Paula Caligiuri's (2012) concept of **cultural agility** as it applied to strategy implementation. Recall that cultural agility is a mindful, context-aware managerial repertoire comprised of three behavioral responses:

- **Cultural minimization.** Some higher-order organizational, professional, or societal considerations such as hypernorms supersede local cultural norms and

override them. Possible examples include health and safety, quality, codes of conduct, and ethics. These might be considered imperatives by the organization.
- **Cultural adaptation.** Management style and/or decisions are adjusted to fit the local cultural norms. Possible examples include marketing messages or some HR policies.
- **Cultural integration.** This could be compromise, combining practices or finding a "third way."

Cultural agility is a critical skill for global managers that is applicable to cross-cultural personal interactions, strategy execution, and, most definitely, ethical decision-making. Even working in a new cultural context, these mindful leaders "know what's going on" and "can read the situation." They have developed the requisite behavioral repertoire to meet the moment. Caligiuri states, "Global professionals often need to operate with cultural minimization, working to override any cultural differences and ensure a common standard or outcome" (Caligiuri, 2012, p. 48). Similarly, Molinsky's (2013) concept of **global dexterity** describes the challenge of successfully adapting to foreign contexts without losing yourself in the process as "fitting in" without "giving in."

Identifying the interests, goals, and values of the various actors in your organization's network helps in structuring an analysis. To assist in analysis and promote rational discussion of ethical dilemmas, a series of diagnostic questions and some recommendations are presented next that we hope can serve as a guide for you in the future.

Prepare for Ethical Dilemmas

1. Develop relationships, but with care.

To the extent possible, enter strong, trust-based relationships with customers and suppliers. These relationships will allow you to assess the impact of "requests," and you will be less likely to be pushed into behaviors that you believe are unethical or irresponsible. Enter dependent relationships with care. If you increase dependency on a particular customer or supplier, be certain about the relationship and make certain you retain enough power to maintain your standards. Don't wait until you are in a crisis situation to reach out to important industry, community, regulatory, and possibly religious groups in a country. Build relationships and social capital with multiple stakeholders as early as possible to enhance your reputation and develop support in order to increase your leverage that will empower you to follow your own standards if the need arises.

2. Get the best information possible.

Take the time to get the facts, all of them. Avoid fuzzy thinking. Avoid using or being swayed by hearsay or unsubstantiated assertions. These are statements that have no specifics to go with them: "Everybody is doing it"; "We'll lose business if we don't do it"; "It's a normal practice." Unsubstantiated assertions like these, parading as analysis, are often "red flags" that should push you to seek more details.

Identify the Impact on Stakeholders

3. Identify all stakeholders.

Remember that a company has multiple groups of stakeholders: shareholders, home country government, host country governments, customers, suppliers, employees, and unions. There are probably others that could be added to that list, but the point is to comprehensively identify the stakeholders and their interests. It can be easy to ignore some of them, particularly when they may be thousands of miles away and not able to stand up for their interests and rights. Ethical managers do not avoid them or pretend that they do not exist.

4. Assess your responsibilities and obligations to these stakeholders.

Identify the responsibilities that your organization may have to external stakeholders as well as internal stakeholders. Be clear about your responsibilities and obligations to these groups. For example, a decision about whether to shut down operations in a country may involve both external and internal ethical issues.

Take the situation of an insurance company with which one of the authors and his colleague were involved. The company was selling life insurance in Uganda during a period of civil war. Years earlier, the company's operation was nationalized and now was having its ownership restored. The branch in Uganda was not profitable, and a financial analysis showed that it should be shut down.

From a profit-and-loss perspective, the decision may have been easy to make. But what were the company's responsibilities to the managers who ran the company in their interest after it had been nationalized and who were concerned about possible violence to field personnel and to themselves if the company closed its operations? And what were its obligations to its policyholders? The issue may not be whether the company should shut down, but how it should handle its responsibilities, obligations, and commitments to its employees, customers, and shareholders during the process of shutting down.

Assess and Select Options

5. Identify a broad range of options.

Some options will jump up immediately, such as "pay the bribe" or "don't pay the bribe." Are there options that have not been identified? In trying to identify possible action, avoid characterizing decisions using false dichotomies – either/or characterizations. Alternatives and options do not have to be win/lose positions. For example, the statement "We need to pay the bribe or lose the business" portrays the situation as win/lose, but it may not be. These positions often develop because the initial analysis was not as complete as it could have been. This mind-set can limit the action possibilities open to the manager. Strive for a win/win situation. Is there a way to solve the problem that satisfies all parties and allows you to fulfill your obligations – in other words, can you find ways to expand the pie rather than dividing it?

6. Analyze the assumptions behind the options.

What assumptions are being made? What ethical framework is being invoked? Whose utility is being maximized? Whose values are being used? Consider multiple (including opposing) viewpoints and examine them carefully. Weigh the costs and benefits to all stakeholders.

7. Select an option and develop an action plan.

If you have followed the steps above, you will be in a better position to develop an action plan. Some decision criteria to consider include: do the best for all involved stakeholders; fulfill obligations; observe laws and contracts; do not use deception; and avoid knowingly doing harm (physical, psychological, economic, or social).

Consider Your Own Position Carefully

In conducting objective, arm's-length analyses, it is easy to take ourselves – the ones who make the decisions – out of the picture. Remember that there can be personal consequences associated with your decision. People have lost their jobs because someone higher in the organization needed a scapegoat, and others have gone to jail for the actions someone else committed. Don't just think about the decision from your role as a manager. Consider your roles as community leader, spouse, parent, or global citizen. Ask yourself if you will be acting in accordance with your own highest set of values and norms. Certainly, look after the interests of your company in your role as manager, but also look after your own interests. You may be the only one that does!

8. Make decisions that are your responsibility.

   Do not avoid making ethical decisions on issues that are your responsibility by passing the responsibility on to someone else or waiting until the problem passes.

9. Don't let people put the weight on your shoulders for illegal or unethical decisions.

   Do not accept responsibility for decisions that are not your responsibility. Some people will try to find a scapegoat to make a particularly difficult, possibly illegal or unethical decision. Do not let them use you. How do you protect yourself? You can ask for the decision or directive in writing or suggest an open meeting with other people present to discuss it.

10. Do not use "culture" as an excuse for improper actions.

    Just because the local company does not treat its toxic waste properly does not mean that it is acting as a role model for that culture. Beware of confusing culture and an individual's personality and character. If a person is asking for something that is illegal or unethical, that tells you something about that person's character, not necessarily about his or her culture.

11. Act in accordance with your own values.

    Consider the "billboard" or the "light-of-day" tests. When you drive to work in the morning, would you be happy to see your decision or action prominently announced on a large billboard for everyone to read? Or, in today's virtual, remote work, and social media environment, would you like your decisions and actions to be posted for everyone to see and discuss? Alternatively, would you be willing to discuss your actions in a meeting where you would be subject to questions and scrutiny? Could you justify them? Would your actions look as reasonable in the open, in the light of day, as they might have looked when the decision was made behind closed doors?

Conclusion: A Final Word

As you progress through your career as a global leader, we encourage you to maintain high standards. We suggest that you follow an adage that we have modified: "When in Rome, don't do as the Romans do, but rather do as the *better* Romans do."

Ask yourself, and answer honestly, if you are behaving according to your highest values and expectations of yourself. Are you happy with your answer? If not, you know what to do!

Reflection Question 12.2: Revisiting an Ethical Problem

Take a few minutes to think about an ethical dilemma you may have faced in your (work) life and write down a few sentences about this situation to use as your point of departure answering the following questions:

1. What happened?
2. Why did this situation present you with an ethical dilemma?
3. How did facing this ethical dilemma make you feel?
4. What did you do, or maybe did not do, to resolve the situation?

Based on your description of this ethical dilemma, try to view this experience in the light of the types of logics and different approaches to ethical decision-making presented in this chapter. In the light of the discussion of ethical decision-making, do you notice something new about your chosen ethical dilemma?

Further Resources

The Caux Round Table (CRT) is an international network of principled business leaders working to promote a moral capitalism. The CRT Principles apply fundamental ethical norms to business decision-making. The statement is taken from "About CRT," https://www.cauxroundtable.org/, accessed September 10, 2022.

Singer, P. (2011). *Practical ethics* (3rd Ed.). Cambridge University Press.
An influential book on ethics in an international context is Singer's 2002 book, *One World: The Ethics of Globalization* (Yale University Press).
Donaldson and Dunfee's 1999 book, *Ties That Bind: A Social Contracts Approach to Business Ethics* (Harvard Business Review), explains the role of social contracts. We would like to thank Sheila Puffer and Dan McCarthy of Northeastern University for introducing us to this perspective.
Badaracco Jr., J. L. (2016). *Defining moments: When managers must choose between right and right*. Harvard Business Review Press.
Cho, J., Morris, M. W., & Dow, B. (2018). How do the Romans feel when visitors "do as the Romans do"? Diversity ideologies and trust in evaluations of cultural accommodation. *Academy of Management Discoveries*, 4(1), 11–31.
Winston, A. S. (2021). *Net positive: How courageous companies thrive by giving more than they take*. Harvard Business Review Press.

Bibliography

Alderman, L. (2022, May 18). *Lafarge human rights violations.* New York Times. Retrieved October 23, 2022, from https://www.nytimes.com/2022/05/18/business/lafarge-human-rights-violations.html?searchResultPosition=5

Amba-Rao, S. (1993). Multinational corporate social responsibility, ethics, interactions and third world governments: An agenda for the 1990's. *Journal of Business Ethics, 12,* 555.

Barstow, D., & Xanic von Bertrab, A. (2012, December 18). *How Wal-Mart used payoffs to get its way in Mexico.* New York Times. Retrieved August 25, 2023, from https://www.nytimes.com/2012/12/18/business/walmart-bribes-teotihuacan.html

Beaver, W. (1995, March–April). Levi's is Leaving China. *Business Horizons,* 35–40.

Brandeis University. (n.d.). *The Trolley Problem.* Retrieved September 15, 2023, from https://people.brandeis.edu/~teuber/Trolley_Problem-PHIL_1A.pdf

Bremmer, I. (2005). *Managing risk in an unstable world.* Harvard Business Review. Retrieved August 25, 2023, from https://hbr.org/2005/06/managing-risk-in-an-unstable-world

Caligiuri, P. (2012). *Cultural agility: Building a pipeline of successful global professionals.* Jossey-Bass.

Cassel, D. (1995). Corporate initiatives: A second human rights revolution. *Fordham International Law Journal, 19*(5), Article 10.

CBC News. (2017, November 14). *Duterte tells leaders to "lay off" after Trudeau raises human rights in Philippines.* CBC News. Retrieved March 29, 2024, from https://www.cbc.ca/news/politics/duterte-trudeau-drugs-human-rights-1.4401848

China White Paper. (n.d.). *International human rights activists.* Retrieved from http://www.china.org.cn/e-white/7/7-L.htm

Choe, K. (2012, May 11). *Infant formula contributes to malnourishment – UNICEF.* Newshub. Retrieved September 2022 from http://www.newshub.co.nz/world/infant-formula-contributes-to-malnourishment-unicef-2012110608

Christie, M. (2009, October 16). *Au revoir RugMark ... Hello GoodWeave!* The Ruggist. Retrieved August 22, 2022, from https://theruggist.com/2009/10/au-revoir-rugmark-hello-goodweave.html

Cohen, E. (2012, September 20). *Banning child labor: The symptom or the cause?* CSRwire Talkback. Retrieved November 2017 from http://www.csrwire.com/blog/posts/547-banning-child-labor-the-symptom-or-the-cause

Cousineau, S. (2013, May 1). Gildan's balancing act in Bangladesh, Sophie Cousineau. *The Globe and Mail.*

De George, R. (1993). *Competing with integrity in international business.* Oxford University Press.

DeKock, K. M., Fowler, M. G., Mercier, E., de Vincenzi, I., Saba, J., Hoff, E., et al. (2000). Prevention of mother-to-child HIV transmission in resource poor countries. *Journal of American Medical Association, 283,* 1175–1182.

Donaldson, T. (2000, October 6). *The promise of corporate codes of conduct.* Human Rights Dialogue. Retrieved September 2022 from https://www.carnegiecouncil.org/publications/archive/dialogue/2_04/articles/896

Donaldson, T., & Dunfee, T. (1999). *Ties that bind.* Harvard Business School Press.

Drohan, M. (1994, February 14). To bribe or not to bribe. *The Global and Mail,* p. B7.

Equal Employment Opportunity Commission. (2023). Retrieved August 26, 2023, from https://www.eeoc.gov/pregnancy-discrimnation#:~:text=The%20EEOC%20enforces%20three%20federal,sex%20 discrimination%2C%20including%20 pregnancy%20discrimination

Environmental Protection Agency. (2021, November 29). *What is a circular economy?* Retrieved August 22, 2022, from https://www.epa.gov/recyclingstrategy/what-circular-economy

Fanelli, J., & Ramey, C. (2022, October 18). *French cement firm Lafarge pleads guilty to conspiring to support Islamic State.* Wall Street Journal. Retrieved October 18, 2022, from https://www.wsj.com/articles/french-cement-firm-lafarge-pleads-guilty-to-conspiring-to-support-islamic-state-11666110832?mod=Searchresults_pos1&page=1

Fantozzi, J. (2017, October 26). *A new documentary claims Haribo gummy bears are made using slave labour in Brazil.* Business Insider. Retrieved September 2022 from http://www.businessinsider.com/investigation-into-haribo-alleges-slave-labor-2017-10

Federal Bureau of Investigation. (2013). *Former U.S. Army Corps of Engineers manager sentenced to more than 19 years in prison in $30 million bribery and kickback scheme.* Retrieved August 23, 2022, from https://archives.fbi.gov/archives/washingtondc/press-releases/2013/former-u.s.-army-corps-of-engineers-manager-sentenced-to-more-than-19-years-in-prison-in-30-million-bribery-and-kickback-scheme

Fragile States Index. (n.d.). *Fund for Peace.* Retrieved September 2022 from https://fragilestatesindex.org/

Future of Life Institute. (2017). *Asilomar AI Principles.* Retrieved April 8, 2024, from https://futureoflife.org/open-letter/ai-principles/

Future of Life Institute. (2023, March 22). *Pause Giant AI Experiments: An Open Letter.* Retrieved March 29, 2024, from https://futureoflife.org/open-letter/pause-giant-ai-experiments/

GoodWeave. (n.d.). *Standards development.* Retrieved September 2022 from http://goodweave.org/proven-approach/standard/development/

Helper, E. (2022, October 20). Washington Post. Retrieved October 23, 2022, from https://www.washingtonpost.com/business/2022/10/20/ev-supply-cchain-battcry-tracking/

Henderson, V. (1982). The ethical side of enterprise. *Sloan Management Review, 23,* 37–47.

Hope, C. (2009, November 26). *How Mumbai terrorist attacks nearly wiped out top management at Unilever.* The Telegraph. Retrieved September 2022 from https://www.telegraph.co.uk/news/worldnews/asia/india/6645178/Revealed-how-Mumbai-terrorist-attacks-nearly-wiped-out-top-management-at-Unilever.html

International Labour Organization. (n.d.). *Consumer search: Rana Plaza.* Retrieved May 26, 2023, from https://www.ilo.org/Search5/search.do?sitelang=en&locale=en_EN&consumercode=ILOHQ_STELLENT_PUBLIC&searchWhat=rana+plaza&searchLanguage=en

Krauss, C. (2008, September 3). *Former KBR executive pleads guilty to bribery.* New York Times. Retrieved August 23, 2022, from https://www.nytimes.com/2008/09/04/business/04bribe.html

Leggate, J. (2022, October 18). *Lafarge agrees to pay US$778 million in fines over Islamic State payments.* Engineering News-Record. Retrieved October 23, 2022, from https://www.enr.com/articles/55089-lafarge-agrees-to-pay-us-778-m-in-fines-over-islamic-state-payments

Levi Strauss & Co. (2021). *Sustainability.* Retrieved September 2022 from Sustainability Guidebook: https://www.levistrauss.com/sustainability-report/

Levi Strauss & Co. (n.d.). *Worker well-being.* Retrieved August 22, 2022, from https://www.levistrauss.com/how-we-do-business/worker-well-being

Löscher, P. (2012). *The CEO of Siemens on using a scandal to drive change.* Harvard Business Review. Retrieved August 25,

2023, from https://hbr.org/2012/11/the-ceo-of-siemens-on-using-a-scandal-to-drive-change

Makabenta, Y. (2017, May 13). *Dopey drug war recalls Asian values debate*. The Manila Times. Retrieved November 2017 from http://www.manilatimes.net/dopey-drug-war-recalls-asian-values-debate/326982/

Molinsky, A. (2013). *Cultural dexterity*. Harvard Business Review Press.

Moore, E. (2012, June 8). *Civets, Brics and the Next 11*. Financial Times. Retrieved November 2017 from https://www.ft.com/content/c14730ae-aff3-11e1-ad0b-00144feabdc0

Nestlé. (2020). *Responsible sourcing of seafood at Nestlé: 2020 Thailand Action Plan progress*. Retrieved June 24, 2023, from https://www.nestle.com/sites/default/files/2021-03/nestle-responsible-sourcing-seafood-progress-report-2020.pdf

Office of the President of Russia. (2022, February 4). *Joint statement of the Russian Federation and the People's Republic of China on the international relations entering a new era and the global sustainable development*. Retrieved August 24, 2022, from http://en.kremlin.ru/supplement/5770

Pan, Y., & Froese, F. J. (2023). An interdisciplinary review of AI and HRM: Challenges and future directions. *Human Resource Management Review*, *33*(1), 100924.

Pascal, B. (1669–1670). *Misère* no. 9 / 24. Accessed April 8, 2024, from http://www.penseesdepascal.fr/Misere/Misere9-moderne.php.

Peerenboom, R. (2003). *Beyond Universalism and Relativism: The evolving debates about "Values in Asia"*. Journals. Retrieved on March 29, 2024, from https://journals.iupui.edu/index.php/iiclr/article/view/17786/17969

Perry, Jr., W. (1970). *Forms of intellectual and ethical development in the college years: A scheme*. Holt, Reinhart & Winston.

Phan, P. , Wright, M. , & Lee, S. H. (2017). Of robots, artificial intelligence, and work. *Academy of Management Perspectives*, *31*(4), 253–255.

Reuters. (2017, November 16). *China minister warns against seduction of values by Western nations*. Retrieved August 24, 2022, from https://www.reuters.com/article/us-china-politics-culture/china-minister-warns-against-seduction-of-values-by-western-nations-idUSKBN1DH0AU

Rivers, M. (2022, April 25). *Sweet and squishy as ever, the gummy universe keeps expanding*. New York Times. Retrieved August 23, 2022, from https://www.nytimes.com/2022/04/25/dining/haribo-gummy-bear.html

Rowe, G. (2012). *Statement made in class during International Week of the EMBA at IPADE*. Mexico City.

Sarathy, R. (2022). *Enterprise strategy for blockchain: Lessons in disruption from fintech, supply chains, and consumer industries*. The MIT Press.

Sen, A. (1997, May 25). *Human rights and Asian values*. Carnegie Council. Retrieved March 29, 2024 from https://www.carnegiecouncil.org/publications/archive/morgenthau/254

Solmessen, P. (2012, May 1). *Siemens changes its culture: No more bribes*. (NPR interview, S. Inskeep, Interviewer.) Retrieved April 8, 2024, from https://www.npr.org/2012/05/01/151745671/companies-can-recovery-from-bribery-scandals

The United States Department of Justice. (2022). Lafarge Pleads Guilty to Conspiring to Provide Material Support to Foreign Terrorist Organizations. Retrieved June 23, 2023, from https://www.justice.gov/usao-edny/pr/lafarge-pleads-guilty-conspiring-provide-material-support-foreign-terrorist

The United States Department of Justice. (n.d.). *Foreign Corrupt Practices Act*. Retrieved September 2022 from https://www.justice.gov/criminal-fraud/foreign-corrupt-practices-act

Transparency International. (2022). *Corruptions Perceptions Index.* Retrieved September 2022 from https://www.transparency.org/en/cpi/2021

Transparency International. (n.d.). Retrieved from https://www.transparency.org/research

United Nations. (n.d.). *The Ten Principles of the UN Global Compact.* Retrieved September 20, 2023, from https://www.unglobalcompact.org/what-is-gc/mission/principles

US Department of State. (2023). *Nigeria travel advisory.* Retrieved August 31, 2023, from https://travel.state.gov/content/travel/en/traveladvisories/traveladvisories/nigeria-travel-advisory.html

US Department of State. (n.d.). Battling International Bribery. Released by the Bureau of Economic and Business Affairs Washington, DC, July 1999. Retrieved August 25, 2023, from https://1997-2001.state.gov/issues/economic/chapter4.html

Verite. (n.d.). *About.* Retrieved November 2017 from https://www.verite.org/about/

Walmart. (2021). *Blockchain in the food supply chain.* Retrieved August 25, 2023, from https://tech.walmart.com/content/walmart-global-tech/en_us/news/articles/blockchain-in-the-food-supply-chain.html

World Health Organization and the United Nations Children's Fund (UNICEF). (2022). *How the marketing of formula milk influences our decisions on infant feeding.* World Health Organization (WHO). Retrieved August 21, 2022, from https://www.unicef.org/media/115916/file/Multi-country%20study%20examining%20the%20impact%20of%20BMS%20marketing%20on%20infant%20feeding%20decisions%20and%20practices,%20UNICEF,%20WHO%202022.pdf

Zakaria, F. (1994). Culture is destiny: A Conversation with Lee Kuan Yew. *Foreign Affairs, 73*(2), 109–126.

Decision-Making Cases

IVEY | Publishing

CASE IV-1: GETYOURGUIDE: MANAGING A SUDDEN SHOCK TO BUSINESS GROWTH[1]

W32660

Sabrina Goestl and Vanessa C. Hasse wrote this case solely to provide material for class discussion. The authors do not intend to illustrate either effective or ineffective handling of a managerial situation. The authors may have disguised certain names and other identifying information to protect confidentiality.

This publication may not be transmitted, photocopied, digitized, or otherwise reproduced in any form or by any means without the permission of the copyright holder. Reproduction of this material is not covered under authorization by any reproduction rights organization. To order copies or request permission to reproduce materials, contact Ivey Publishing, Ivey Business School, Western University, London, Ontario, Canada, N6G 0N1; (t) 519.661.3208; (e) cases@ivey.ca; www.iveypublishing.ca. Our goal is to publish materials of the highest quality; submit any errata to publishcases@ivey.ca. i1v2e5y5pubs

Copyright © 2023, Ivey Business School Foundation

Version: 2023–09-07

In late March 2020, Johannes Reck, co-founder of the German online travel experience provider GetYourGuide, had to inform his employees that his company's revenues had plummeted to zero within the past few weeks.[2]

Just a few weeks earlier, Asian governments had reported the first cases of people infected with a novel coronavirus.[3] Reck's initial reaction, similar to that of many, was: "Well, we've already had the terrorist attacks in Paris, I already know [how to navigate a] crisis, it's no problem, we'll manage."[4] Contrary to this optimistic early assessment, however, the pandemic spread across the globe, and governments all over the world reacted with border closures, quarantine and mask mandates, social distancing requirements, and complete lockdowns of any "non-essential" activities.[5]

For GetYourGuide, these developments came as an abrupt shock after years of steady growth and bright prospects for the future. Over the previous ten years, the business had developed from a simple idea formed by a group of friends in a student dormitory into a market-leading company in the travel experience industry with a valuation of over $1 billion[6] and more than 600 employees in fifteen global offices.[7]

---

[1] This case has been written on the basis of published sources only. Consequently, the interpretation and perspectives presented in this case are not necessarily those of GetYourGuide or any of their employees.
[2] Marcel Rosenbach, "Stunde null," *Der Spiegel*, September 19, 2020, 74–75.
[3] Caroline Kantis, Samantha Kiernan, Jason Socrates Bardi, Lillian Posner, and Isabella Turilli, "Updated: Timeline of the Coronavirus," ThinkGlobalHealth, accessed September 30, 2022, https://www.thinkglobalhealth.org/article/updated-timeline-coronavirus.
[4] Beat Balzli, "GetYourGuide-Chef Reck: 'Wir werden von TripAdvisor und Tui kopiert,'" Wirtschafts-Woche Chefgespräch, August 27, 2021, https://www.wiwo.de/podcast/chefgespraech/podcast-chefgespraech-getyourguide-chef-reck-wir-werden-von-tripadvisor-und-tui-kopiert/27552384.html.
[5] Kantis et al., "Updated: Timeline of the Coronavirus."
[6] All $ amounts are in US dollars unless otherwise stated.
[7] Miriam Schröder, "Neues Einhorn aus Berlin: GetYourGuide sammelt fast eine halbe Milliarde Dollar ein," *Handelsblatt*, May 16, 2019, https://www.handelsblatt.com/unternehmen/dienstleister/spektakulaere-finanzierungsrunde-neues-einhorn-aus-berlin-getyourguide-sammelt-fast-eine-halbe-milliarde-dollar-ein/24349544.html; "GetYourGuide Press Center," GetYourGuide, accessed version from October 5, 2019, through WayBack Machine, https://web.archive.org/web/20191005111257/ https://press.getyourguide.com/.

By March 2020, all this suddenly seemed to be in jeopardy. GetYourGuide was hit like a tidal wave by the COVID-19 pandemic and the restrictive measures that were imposed in its wake. The pandemic had not only stopped current bookings of tours and activities but also triggered a massive wave of cancellations and refund requests for previously booked experiences.[8] To satisfy the urgent need for cash when there was almost no revenue, GetYourGuide investors demanded aggressive cost savings.[9]

What were GetYourGuide's options for handling the cancellations and issuing refunds while ensuring that their employees were safe during this global health emergency? How could the company satisfy investor demands for drastic cost reductions without endangering the business's long-term competitiveness? And what could the company learn from this crisis to build resilience and be better prepared for future shocks? GetYourGuide needed a plan to navigate effectively through this uncertain time.

The Global Travel Experience Industry in 2019

The global tourism sector included five distinct industry groups: transportation, accommodation, food and beverage, experiences/attractions, and travel services. The latter referred to providers that sold tourism-related products or services to customers on behalf of suppliers.[10] Put together, these industry groups had a substantive share in the worldwide economy. In 2019, travel and tourism accounted for more than 10 percent of the global gross domestic product (GDP), with a total GDP contribution of $9.63 trillion. This figure had gradually increased over the previous decade, up from a contribution of $5.8 trillion in 2009.[11] The sector employed 334 million people globally in 2019. Most of them worked in the Asia Pacific region (184.3 million), Europe (37.9 million), North America (26.2 million), and Africa (25.1 million).[12] International tourist arrivals worldwide grew by 4 percent in 2019 to reach $1.5 billion. This growth was led by the Middle East (+8 percent), followed by the Asia Pacific Region (+5 percent), Europe and Africa (both +4 percent), and the Americas (+2 percent).[13] International tourists accounted for 28 percent ($1.9 trillion) of global travel and tourism spending in 2019. The remaining 72 percent were spent by domestic travelers who explored their own respective countries.[14]

Attractions and activities, increasingly branded as "experiences," formed one of the five industries in the tourism sector. There were different categories of tourist attractions: heritage attractions (e.g., museums, art galleries, nature parks, botanical gardens), entertainment attractions (e.g., arcades, amusement parks, water parks), recreational attractions (e.g., golf courses, skiing facilities), commercial attractions (e.g., souvenir shops, craft stores), and industrial attractions (e.g., wineries, fish hatcheries, factories).[15]

For all these experiences, the economic value typically resided in tourists paying for access (i.e., entry tickets) and for additional services, such as guided tours. The value of

---

[8] Johannes Reck, "Our Hybrid Approach to Work," GetYourGuide, July 21, 2021, https://inside.getyourguide.com/blog/2021/7/16/our-hybrid-approach-to-work.
[9] Balzli, "GetYourGuide-Chef Reck."
[10] "Tourism Facts," Tourism HR Canada, accessed October 3, 2022, https://tourismhr.ca/labour-market-information/tourism-facts/.
[11] "Travel & Tourism: Economic Impact 2022," World Travel and Tourism Council, April 22, 2022, https://wttc.org/Portals/0/Documents/EIR/EIR2022%20Global%20Infographics%20Page%201.pdf?ver=2022-04-25-102003-887
[12] "Economic Impact Reports," World Travel and Tourism Council, accessed June 30, 2023, https://wttc.org/Research/Economic-Impact.
[13] "UNWTO World Tourism Barometer and Statistical Annex," UNWTO World Tourism Organization, January 2020, https://www.e-unwto.org/doi/epdf/10.18111/wtobarometereng.2020.18.1.1?role=tab.
[14] "Travel & Tourism: Economic Impact 2022," World Travel and Tourism Council.
[15] Stephen Boyd, "Cultural and Heritage Tourism in Canada: Opportunities, Principles and Challenges," *Tourism and Hospitality Research* 3, no. 3 (February 2002): 211–33.

the global tours and experiences market was estimated to be between $150 billion and $200 billion, growing at about 9 percent a year.[16] Traditionally, the two most important sales channels for tours and tickets had been local ticket offices and phone calls to the operators. In recent years, however, purchasing experiences online had grown in popularity, with 28 percent of US travelers reporting that they booked their tours and tickets on the Internet (see Exhibit 1).

Online buyers typically had two options: They could either buy the ticket directly from the operator's website or leverage a digital distributor, also called an online travel agency (OTA), which resold the experience on behalf of the operator. Since OTAs offered tickets from a variety of suppliers, they often carried a greater selection of activities and allowed for better price transparency than the operators. For frequent OTA bookers, an account with an agency also eliminated the need to re-enter credit card information or other details on the operator's website.[17] From an experience provider's viewpoint, OTAs represented a convenient opportunity to reach a large audience, given that the majority of tour operators worldwide were small resource-constrained suppliers with fewer than 5,000 customers annually.[18] OTAs received a commission fee for each booking, typically around 15 to 30 percent of the price.[19]

Historically, OTAs did not always focus on reselling experiences. The more traditional offerings mainly concerned transportation (especially flights) and accommodation. It was not until the late 2000s that founders started to identify this market gap, and a growing number of digital experience distributors emerged (see Exhibit 2). One of the earliest entrants was Civitatis, which was founded in 2008 and focused on Spanish-language activities.[20] A few years later US-based Peek (founded in 2012) and Hong Kong-based Klook (founded in 2014) emerged, both of which had since raised hundreds of millions of dollars in funding. Similar start-ups had expanded throughout the years, with some being driven out of the market by more successful competitors, and others thriving by offering specific niche experiences.[21]

Faced with this host of new entrants into the online travel market, established brands tried to keep up by building specialized offerings and acquiring competitors. In 2014, TripAdvisor acquired the largest online tours and activities agency at the time, Viator, for approximately $200 million.[22] In 2015, Expedia launched a new offering called "Things to Do," allowing customers to book a complete vacation package on the Expedia website, including flights, accommodation, and activities.[23] In 2016, Airbnb followed suit by launching its "Trips" feature, which combined the company's traditional accommodation offerings with

---

[16] "Tours and Travel Activities Report 2019," TourScanner, October 31, 2019, updated March 15, 2023, https://tourscanner.com/blog/tours-and-travelactivities-report-2019/.

[17] Jenna Blumenfeld, "Attractions Travelers: Do They Book Through OTAs or Direct?" Arival, February 25, 2020, https://arival.travel/attractions-travelers-do-they-book-through-otas-or-direct/.

[18] Rosie Spinks, "Someone Should Tell Airbnb that Travelers Don't Like Booking Tours Online," Quartz, March 7, 2018, https://qz.com/quartzy/1222596/airbnb-experiences-wants-travelers-to-book-tours-online-but-do-travelers-want-to/.

[19] David Easton, "OTA Comission [sic] Rates: The Complete Guide to OTA Fees," Hotel Price Reporter, October 22, 2020, https://www.hotelpricereporter.com/blog/ota-rate/.

[20] "Civitatis," Crunchbase, June 29, 2023, https://www.crunchbase.com/organization/civitatis.

[21] "Peek," Crunchbase, June 29, 2023, https://www.crunchbase.com/organization/peek-com; "Klook," Crunchbase, June 29, 2023, https://www.crunchbase.com/organization/klook.

[22] Sean O'Neil, "TripAdvisor Acquires Viator, the Tours and Activities Agency, for $200M," PhocusWire, July 24, 2014, https://www.phocuswire.com/TripAdvisor-acquires-Viator-the-tours-and-activities-agency-for-200M.

[23] "Create Complete Travel Itinerary with Expedia's 'Things to Do'," WebInTravel, May 18, 2015, https://www.webintravel.com/create-complete-travel-itinerary-with-expedias-things-to-do/.

additional categories of "Places" (guidebooks, meet-ups, and audio walks) and "Experiences" (activities). The latter category focused primarily on offering unique activities that were designed and led by local experts. Examples included salsa dancing lessons in Panama and samurai swordplay workshops in Japan.[24]

The competitive landscape in the travel experience industry was constantly evolving since the basic value proposition was easy to copy, and the fundamental technology requirements included only a website and a booking tool. This made the market attractive for new entrants, including tech giants such as Google – a company that had continuously expanded their travel offerings over the past few years and had already started offering sophisticated trip-planning features (including tours and activities) through their Google Travel and Google Maps apps.[25]

GetYourGuide and Their Founders

Reck was a millennial (Generation Y) from a family with generations of university law degree holders. Given his father's position as a politician within the German Christian Democratic Union party and later in the top-level management of a leading telecommunications company, Reck had early opportunities to meet influential figures such as German chancellors and high-level executives.[26] After graduating from high school, Reck considered following his family's tradition by pursuing a law degree, but he soon realized that his passion lay with brain research and chose to study biochemistry at the Swiss Federal Institute of Technology (ETH).[27]

During his studies, Reck became close friends with fellow students Tao Tao, Martin Sieber, and Tobias Rein. With Tao, he enrolled in ETH's Model United Nations student club, which involved attending a conference in Tao's hometown of Beijing in 2007. Reck happened to land in Beijing a day earlier than his friend. Unable to read any of the Chinese signs or communicate with locals, Reck barely made his way to the hotel.[28] Exploring the city or going sightseeing was practically impossible. Only after Tao arrived and acted as a local tour guide was Reck able to appreciate Beijing's beauty. He recalled Tao remarking: "Suddenly everyone was nicer, the food was twice as good, and everything cost half as much."[29]

Inspired by this experience, the friends returned home and sought to create something that would make travel experiences more enjoyable for people around the world. They drafted their first business plan during the Venturelab course at ETH – and with that, the idea for GetYourGuide was born.[30]

---

[24] "Airbnb Expands Beyond the Home with the Launch of Trips," Airbnb, November 17, 2016, https://news.airbnb.com/airbnb-expands-beyond-the-home-with-the-launch-of-trips.

[25] Dennis Schaal, "Google Travel is Now One Step Closer to One-Stop Shopping," Skift, May 14, 2019, https://skift.com/2019/05/14/google-travel-looks-more-like-an-online-travel-agency-by-putting-all-the-pieces-together/.

[26] Balzli, "GetYourGuide-Chef Reck."

[27] Carina Kontio, "GetYourGuide-Gründer: 'Ich sehe es als meinen Hauptjob an, Topleute zu halten,'" Handelsblatt, August 20, 2020, https://www.handelsblatt.com/unternehmen/management/vordenker/vordenker-johannes-reck-getyourguide-gruender-ich-sehe-es-als-meinen-hauptjob-an-topleute-zu-halten/26065460.html.

[28] Lars Spannagel, "Start-up GetYourGuide: Zwei Berliner revolutionieren, wie wir reisen," Tagesspiegel, June 12, 2019, https://www.tagesspiegel.de/gesellschaft/zwei-berliner-revolutionieren-wie-wir-reisen-5021134.html.

[29] Joseph Heaven, "Zurich One of Europe's Best-Kept Tech Secrets, Says GetYourGuide CEO Reck," April 9, 2019, https://www.venturelab.swiss/Zurich-One-of-Europes-BestKept-Tech-Secrets-Says-GetYourGuide-CEO-Reck.

[30] Isabelle Mitchell, "World Shaper of Tomorrow: GetYourGuide Leads the Travel Industry into the Future," Top 100 Swiss Startups, March 17, 2021, https://www.top100startups.swiss/World-shaper-of-tomorrow-GetYourGuide-leads-the-travel-industry-into-the-future; "Aus Liebe zum Entdecken," GetYourGuide, accessed October 3, 2022, https://www.getyourguide.de/about/?visitor-id=78WU2JKHYQEPMICZ2QUBJQTAMSI51B2T&locale_autoredirect_optout=true.

Business Model Development and Growth

Initially, GetYourGuide was conceptualized as a peer-to-peer platform for students. When planning a vacation, users could search for local peers willing to give them a tour.[31] However, in its first 18 months, only 200 students signed up to the platform and a total of four bookings were completed – three of which came from Reck's mother. As Reck put it, "We failed miserably!"[32]

The turning point came when a Swiss rafting company requested to be listed on the platform in exchange for several hundred Swiss Francs.[33] Reselling experiences from professional tour providers for a fee was something the founders had not previously thought about. "That was the moment that opened our eyes to the real market opportunity: [to connect] tour operators and activity providers [...] with travellers," Reck recalled.[34] In 2009, Reck, Tao, Sieber, and Rein officially founded GetYourGuide[35] as a business-to-consumer (B2C) marketplace for travel experiences, designed to generate revenue by charging a commission fee from tour suppliers.[36]

Over the years that followed, the founders were busy building a catalogue of travel experiences, establishing the new company headquarters in Berlin (the German start-up hub), and attracting customers to the website. All these activities were expensive, and capital was scarce during these early stages. Tao later reflected: "The first sponsors were our families. Back then, we paid ourselves a salary that corresponded to 40 percent of the minimum wage in Switzerland."[37] During this time, the founders also handled all customer calls themselves, which allowed them to gain crucial insights about the importance of truly making the customer happy.[38] As Reck emphasized,

> Customer satisfaction and retention [is] really like the key metric that you should be looking for [...]. The key thing that you need to figure out first is actually, "Is that product that I built something that sticks, right? Is it something that consumers need – where you have a product–market fit, and where people actually come back to?"[39]

Reck further noted that GetYourGuide never rushed to obtain funding or accelerate growth:

> That's a mistake that I see with a lot of start-ups: They are too concerned with, like, venture funding and [...] growing instead of [...] product–market fit. [...] We really built this business, you know, with a great degree of consideration. [...] Because we were so constrained, we constantly needed to iterate and innovate, you know, at much greater velocity and on a shoestring, so with very little budget, and, you know, that actually led us then to find the right growth model for the company that was investible.[40]

And the investments came. In 2013, GetYourGuide managed to raise their first large series A funding at a value of $14 million; they had several other successful funding rounds in the following years (see Exhibit 3).[41] With a subsequent $484 million

---

[31] Heaven, "Zurich."
[32] Invisible Media, "Johannes Reck (GetYourGuide) Teaches How to Grow and Scale Fast," McKinsey & Company Experience Studio, July 4, 2019, YouTube video, 18:51, https://www.youtube.com/watch?v=3MsBDCZRNAA.
[33] Heaven, "Zurich."
[34] Heaven, "Zurich."
[35] "Our Journey So Far," GetYourGuide, June 29, 2023, https://www.getyourguide.com/about/.
[36] Rasso Knoller, "Zeig mir deine Welt," Forum, October 19, 2018, https://magazin-forum.de/de/node/11508.
[37] Knoller, "Zeig mir deine Welt,"
[38] Johannes Reck, "Why Trump's Tweets Push your Startup," March 4, 2020, in Bits & Pretzels, editor-in-chief Britta Weddeling, podcast, MP3 audio, 40:46, https://www.bitsandpretzels.com/posts/how-trumps-tweets-help-european-startups.
[39] Invisible Media, "Grow and Scale Fast."
[40] Invisible Media, "Grow and Scale Fast."
[41] "GetYourGuide," Crunchbase, accessed October 3, 2022, https://www.crunchbase.com/organization/getyourguide/ company_financials.

series E funding in May 2019, GetYourGuide officially became a "unicorn," a term investors use for the rare type of start-up companies that are valued at over $1 billion.[42]

Supported by this success, Reck and his team continued to look for innovations to further expand their business model. The company gleaned insights for best practices from consumer data to make experiences even more enjoyable. The funding also allowed them to launch their own travel experience offerings in 2018, which became the successful GetYourGuide Originals feature.[43] As Reck noted, "We've had tremendous success, we have an average score of 4.8 [out of a 5-point rating system] compared to 4.4 for the other marketplace activities." Originals also had a 40 percent higher repeat rate than other experiences offered on the platform.[44]

Vision and Values

When asked about where he saw GetYourGuide in ten years, Reck staked out an ambitious vision for the company:

> I see GetYourGuide as the travel companion and also as the everyday companion as far as the topic of experiences is concerned. [...] That we will more or less become the Netflix of the real world – if you want to have fun, if you want to be entertained, if you want great activities, then it has to be available personalized for you directly on your smartphone.[45]

To achieve this vision, GetYourGuide created a company culture shaped by five core values: "Clarity" referred to clear, open, and concise communication ("We do more and talk less"). "Commitment" acknowledged that it took hard work, initiative, and grit to achieve great success every day ("We collaborate to succeed as a team"). "Learning" was defined as an openness to risk taking and a continuous push to move outside the comfort zone ("We love challenging and difficult situations"). "Positivity" was based on encouraging a light-hearted way of dealing with every situation ("Positive actions come from positive thoughts"). "Passion" focused on being driven to create the best possible customer experience ("We constantly strive to offer our customers exceptional experiences alongside delightful service").[46]

This value-based company culture was reflected in all of GetYourGuide's processes, especially in the onboarding experience of new employees. Incoming employees – whether in Germany, Switzerland, or any other location – participated in a training program at the headquarters in Berlin to familiarize themselves with the company's strong culture.[47]

Leadership and Structure

As CEO, Reck led the company from its headquarters in Berlin. He was motivated by a continuous drive to make a change in the industry:

> Building a company is actually not about the funding round at all. Our biggest successes have been about how we've changed the market and how we've had an impact on customers.[48]

---

[42] Schröder, "Neues Einhorn aus Berlin."
[43] Ingrid Lunden, "GetYourGuide Widens its Horizons, Will Expand its Originals Short Tours into Day Trips and More," TechCrunch, December 12, 2019, https://techcrunch.com/2019/12/12/getyourguide-widens-its-horizons-will-expand-its-originals-short-tours-into-day-trips-and-more/; Balzli, "GetYourGuide-Chef Reck."
[44] Lunden, "GetYourGuide Widens its Horizons."
[45] Sebastian Matthes, "Getyourguide-Gründer Reck: 'Google behindert Innovationen,'" *Handelsblatt Disrupt* (translated using DeepL translator), April 9, 2021, https://www.handelsblatt.com/audio/disrupt-podcast/handelsblatt-disrupt-getyourguide-gruender-reck-google-behindert-innovationen/27080562.html.
[46] "GetYourGuide's Core Values," GetYourGuide, accessed version from November 12, 2020, through WayBack Machine, https://web.archive.org/web/20201112040719/https:/inside.getyourguide.com/blog/2017/9/19/getyourguides-core-values.
[47] Invisible Media, "Grow and Scale Fast."
[48] Reck, "Why Trump's Tweets Push your Startup."

What gets me up in the morning is the next feature that we're launching and the new product line that we're going into. This is where I can see that impact in real time with customers around the world.[49]

As a leader, Reck placed great focus on transparency and participation from all employees. Everyone in the company – from first-year customer service agent to CEO – was given full access to all company data. Reck believed that having well-informed employees was crucial for fostering new ideas:

One of the best growth hacks is [to] actually just walk through [your own] company and talk to a random amount of people and just ask them "Hey, how should we grow, you know? What's a good idea [...]? What is something we should be testing today?" [...] We've had some of our best ideas from those types of sessions.[50]

Co-founder Tao was also part of the executive team, leading the company's business operations in the role of chief operating officer. Five additional executives completed GetYourGuide's Berlin-based leadership team (see Exhibit 4).[51]

Apart from the headquarters in Berlin, GetYourGuide's second largest location was in the company's founding city of Zurich. Zurich was GetYourGuide's engineering hub under the lead of co-founder and principal engineer Rein. Reck noted that this location was a strategic choice:

Switzerland is absolutely the first choice in Europe as a tech location, especially for highly qualified employees. Our history and close ties with ETH are important. It's great that Zalando and Google are also expanding further in Zurich. We want to play a part in this![52]

Over the years, an additional fifteen global sales offices were opened in destinations with high traction from customers and local suppliers.[53] On-the-ground marketing and sales employees ensured successful growth across these locations, including in Madrid, Sydney, and Cape Town.[54]

By the beginning of 2020, GetYourGuide had grown into a truly global company with more than 600 employees worldwide. Customers could select from over 55,000 experiences, ranging from trying out paddle boards for under $5 to traditional city tours and entry tickets for around $20–$100, and several-thousand-dollar experiences, such as a private sunset marriage proposal arrangement in Dubai's Burj Khalifa, the tallest building in the world. Since the company's beginnings, over 30 million tours and tickets had been booked through GetYourGuide, which made them the global market leader in experience bookings.[55] Monthly growth numbers were beyond 100 percent.[56] Given this track record, the company expected 2020 to become yet another record year.[57]

Then, on January 27, 2020, the first COVID-19 case was confirmed in Germany.[58]

---

[49] Mitchell, "World Shaper of Tomorrow."
[50] Invisible Media, "Grow and Scale Fast."
[51] "Executive Team," GetYourGuide, accessed version from October 12, 2019, through WayBack Machine, https://web.archive.org/web/20191012115246/https://press.getyourguide.com/executive-team.
[52] David Torcasso, "Es wäre doch bescheuert, in der Schweiz Stellen zu kürzen," *Handelszeitung* (translated using DeepL translator), November 5, 2020, https://www.handelszeitung.ch/unternehmen/es-ware-doch-bescheuert-in-der-schweiz-stellen-zu-kurzen.
[53] "GetYourGuide Press Center," GetYourGuide, accessed October 3, 2022, https://press.getyourguide.com.
[54] "Jahresabschluss zum Geschäftsjahr vom 01.01.2020 bis zum 31.12.2020," GetYourGuide Deutschland GmbH, May 5, 2022.
[55] "GetYourGuide Press Center," GetYourGuide.
[56] Jan Guldner, "Corona trifft GetYourGuide hart: '2020 existiert für uns nicht,'" *WirtschaftsWoche*, May 15, 2020, https://www.wiwo.de/erfolg/gruender/corona-trifft-getyourguide-hart-2020-existiert-fuer-uns-nicht/25833368.html.
[57] Rosenbach, "Stunde null."
[58] "Germany's COVID Timeline: From First Case to 100,000 Dead," *AP News*, November 25, 2021, https://apnews.com/article/coronavirus-pandemic-health-europe-epidemics-berlin-b61de99739774c1f52b4ba6860054d6d.

Emergence of the COVID-19 Pandemic

After starting with a few initial cases in Asia, the COVID-19 virus was spreading rapidly by the beginning of 2020. Country after country announced their first confirmed cases and deaths associated with the virus. By late February 2020, COVID-19 had fully arrived in Europe and the Americas. To slow the spread of the disease, governments took drastic actions: borders were closed; COVID-19 patients were isolated in quarantine; events and activities were cancelled; hotels and restaurants were shut down; social distancing guidelines were enforced; and many countries even went into full lockdowns, prohibiting citizens from leaving their houses without urgent reason.[59]

The travel sector was one of the most severely impacted by the pandemic as COVID-19 brought years of continuous growth to an abrupt halt. In March 2020, global international tourist arrivals were down 65 percent from 2019 levels, and they were expected to drop even further with more nations closing their borders.[60] For GetYourGuide, bookings halved from forecast levels in the beginning of March and practically vanished by the end of the month. The company had started the year with record booking numbers, and suddenly their revenue stream had dropped to almost zero.[61] At the same time, customers started to cancel pre-booked experiences and demanded reimbursements, since the company had previously instituted a generous refund warranty.[62] Reck reflected on this period as the most stressful one of his life[63]:

We needed lots of cash, had a lot more work than usual, and no revenue.

In a matter of days, we needed to take care of thousands of affected customers, enable mass cancellations for future bookings, build a plan to reduce our cost base, and last but not least ensure that our team was safe in what was a very turbulent and dynamic situation.[64]

GetYourGuide investors got worried.[65] They approached Reck to demand quick and drastic cost-saving measures:

The investors came in [...] and of course they said, "Look! In America, every retail and travel company is cutting 25 or 30 or 40 percent of their staff." There was a period where it felt like I couldn't lay off enough people [in the eyes of the investors]. At the time, I resisted this and said, "Look, let's see what happens first."[66]

The German government tried to mitigate the negative consequences of the pandemic restrictions on companies. On March 22, 2020, they launched a package of support measures to aid liquidity and solvency, including an economic stabilization fund, special loan programs, and tax deferral options. In addition, they simplified access to short-time work allowance, which is a common measure to prevent unemployment in Germany. It is usually used for periods of low workloads during which private sector employees accept a reduction in working time and pay, and the state makes up for part of the lost salaries after confirming the work reduction.[67]

Such government measures, however, were not enough to alleviate all concerns. The travel and tourism sector's future looked

---

[59] Kantis et al., "Updated: Timeline of the Coronavirus."
[60] "International Tourism and COVID-19," United Nations World Tourism Organization, accessed October 3, 2022, https://www.unwto.org/tourism-data/international-tourism-and-covid-19.
[61] Douglas Busvine, "German Travel Tech Start-ups Hunker Down for 'Nuclear Winter,'" Reuters, March 16, 2020, https://www.reuters.com/article/us-health-coronavirus-europe-travel-idINKBN21320N.
[62] Rosenbach, "Stunde null."
[63] Balzli, "GetYourGuide-Chef Reck."
[64] Reck, "Our Hybrid Approach to Work."
[65] Rosenbach, "Stunde null."
[66] Balzli, "GetYourGuide-Chef Reck."
[67] "'Was wir jetzt brauchen, ist Solidarität,'" German Government, accessed March 25, 2020, via WayBack Machine, https://web.archive.org/web/20200928194415/https://www.bundesregierung.de/breg-de/themen/coronavirus/olaf-scholz-bundestag-1734726.

highly uncertain and bleak, and Reck said that the industry was estimated to lose $50 billion per month due to the COVID-19 pandemic.[68] Reck even likened the threat to a "nuclear winter":

> In the next couple of weeks I think we'll all just go into hibernation mode. [...] Just survival over the next 12-24 months, by any travel company, will be a massive competitive advantage.[69]

Responding to the Crisis

The most immediate cause for worry was the safety of GetYourGuide's employees. COVID-19 first and foremost posed a health emergency. Having employees come to the office and work in proximity to one another would not only constitute a health risk for them but likely also put unnecessary strain on the health care systems of the countries in which GetYourGuide operated. Letting everyone work from home, however, also came with challenges. GetYourGuide needed to ensure that employees across all locations had the necessary equipment to work remotely, such as additional screens, video conferencing software, and appropriate chairs and desks. In addition, the company's culture thrived on spontaneous personal interactions in the office. Would it be possible to uphold the team spirit and motivation throughout this highly stressful period without any face-to-face conversations? How could GetYourGuide ensure that everyone was coping but also performing well?

Another pressing challenge was the massive wave of cancellations and refund claims flowing into the company. It seemed impossible to respond to each customer email or phone call individually.[70] Reck and his team needed a quick way to handle the claims. A possible solution was to develop a software program that would take care of the cancellations and refunds automatically, but could GetYourGuide develop one fast enough? And would it allow for appropriate customer service, given that a core company value was the passion for creating the best possible customer experience?

With near-zero revenue and growing pressure from investors, GetYourGuide also urgently needed a comprehensive cost savings plan. Would Reck have to give in to investors' demands and let go of some of his employees? If yes, how big of a cut would he have to make? And which employees would have to go? Reck was scared that mass layoffs might not only hurt the affected staff but also destroy what he had worked so hard for over the previous ten years.[71] Were there any alternatives?

Another expense that could potentially be reduced was the leasing costs for the company's office space. GetYourGuide had recently signed a ten-year lease for their new headquarters location, a historic former electrical substation in Berlin's trendy and affluent Prenzlauer Berg neighborhood. The extensively redesigned place had capacity for over 800 employees.[72] Subleasing parts of this space to other companies could reduce some of the cost. However, it was unclear whether anyone would want to rent additional office space while social distancing and remote working were encouraged. Reck also needed to consider what the medium-term working model at GetYourGuide should look like. Would everyone come back to the office after the pandemic, or would remote work play a bigger role in the company's future? And

---

[68] Johannes Reck (@JohannesReck), "The global tourism industry is estimated to lose up to $50bn per month due to Corona. Where others see a wall, I see tremendous opportunity. Now is the time to stand strong," Twitter, March 4, 2020, 12:51 p.m., https://twitter.com/JohannesReck/status/1235170949953196037.

[69] Busvine, "German Travel Tech Startups."

[70] Rosenbach, "Stunde null."

[71] Rosenbach, "Stunde null."

[72] Dominik Bath, "GetYourGuide plant neuen Campus in Berlin," Berliner Morgenpost, September 3, 2018, https://www.morgenpost.de/bezirke/pankow/article215240895/Get-your-Guide-plant-neuen-Campus-in-Berlin.html.

what did "after the pandemic" even mean? In a few weeks? Months? Years?

Even if GetYourGuide made it through this crisis, strategizing for the longer-term future was not trivial either. Competition in the travel experience industry was fierce, with US travel giants like TripAdvisor and Google quickly catching up to GetYourGuide and copying their business model.[73] Reck was especially concerned about a potentially unfair competitive advantage Google had, claiming the US corporation used not only the advertising revenues but also information from their business customers (such as GetYourGuide) to build up their own travel services:

> Google steals content and data from its partners in the travel market to compete with them. [...] In the medium term, the threat from Google is more existential for us than that from COVID.[74]

Would GetYourGuide be able to keep pace with such strong overseas competitors while also dealing with local challenges in Germany, including demographic change, a regulatory structure that was at times innovation averse, and a shortage of skilled workers?[75] Reck considered the latter issue especially critical:

> In Germany, there's no way around it, we have to take care of skilled migration and finally address this issue in a meaningful way. That's interwoven with the tech industry because our biggest problem is the shortage of skilled workers.[76]

Climate change was another issue to think about, considering that travel was one of the most problematic "environmental sins."[77] To address this problem, GetYourGuide needed to promote a more climate-friendly way of traveling.

As Reck opened the staff meeting at the end of March 2020, his company, grown from humble beginnings in a student apartment into a $1 billion unicorn start-up, faced immense uncertainty and challenges. Which solutions could he and his team devise for the short term, medium term, and long term to not only ensure GetYourGuide's survival but actually see the business emerge from the crisis stronger and thrive in the future? Or were the pandemic-related challenges simply too many, forcing Reck to give up his dream and exit or even close GetYourGuide? After all, in addition to all the difficulties Reck faced in steering GetYourGuide through this crisis, he was also needed elsewhere. Reck's wife was pregnant, and they were expecting their first child to arrive at any moment.[78]

---

[73] Balzli, "GetYourGuide-Chef Reck."
[74] Rosenbach, "Stunde null."
[75] Balzli, "GetYourGuide-Chef Reck."
[76] Balzli, "GetYourGuide-Chef Reck."
[77] Antje Blinda, Dinah Deckstein, Claus Hecking, Alexander Kühn, and Martin U. Müller, "Luxus Urlaub," *Der Spiegel*, July 17, 2021, 56-61.
[78] Rosenbach, "Stunde null."

EXHIBIT 1: Most Popular Sales Channels for Tours and Tickets among US Travelers in 2019

Channel	Percentage
Online	28%
Ticket office at attraction	26%
Over the phone	22%
Hotel front desk or concierge	16%
Multi-attraction pass	7%

Source: Created by authors using Anne Failing and Douglas Quinby, "How Visitor Attractions Can Adapt to the New Traveler Path to Purchase," Arival, August 31, 2021, https://arival.travel/wp-content/uploads/2021/08/Arivals-Attractions-Revisited-Aug-21.pdf.

EXHIBIT 2: Overview of Main GetYourGuide Competitors

Competitor	Founding/Launch Year	Headquarters	Total Funding Amount in US$ Millions	Strategic Focus
Civitatis	2008	Madrid, Spain	110	Spanish-speaking activities
TourRadar	2010	Vienna, Austria	67	Multi-day tours
Peek	2012	San Francisco, CA, United States	120	Software solutions (e.g., inventory management, dynamic pricing, marketing analytics)
Klook	2014	Hong Kong, China	722	Experiences which encourage spontaneity with on-the-go booking and QR-code features
Viator (by TripAdvisor)	Founded 1995 Acquired by TripAdvisor 2014	Miami Beach, FL, United States	N/A	Curated experiences with quality and value guarantee
Expedia "Things to Do"	2015	Seattle, WA, United States	N/A	Holistic travel experiences (flights, accommodation, and activities)
Airbnb "Experiences"	2016	San Francisco, CA, United States	N/A	Unique experiences designed by local experts

Notes: "QR" stands for "quick response;" Civitatis' total funding amount of €100 million was converted to US$ using the historic currency conversion rate from March 31, 2020.

Source: Created by authors using Crunchbase, "Details of Companies Similar to GetYourGuide," Crunchbase Companies, accessed July 12, 2022; "Create Complete Travel Itinerary with Expedia's 'Things to Do,'" WebInTravel, May 18, 2015, https://www.webin travel.com/create-complete-travel-itinerary-with-expedias-things-to-do/; "Airbnb Expands Beyond the Home with the Launch of Trips," Airbnb, November 17, 2016, https://news.airbnb.com/airbnb-expands-beyond-the-home-with-the-launch-of-trips/.

EXHIBIT 3: Overview of GetYourGuide Funding Rounds

Date Announced	Name	# of Investors	Money Raised (US$ Millions)	Lead Investor(s)
Jan 7, 2013	Series A – GetYourGuide	2	14	Highland Europe, Spark Capital
Jan 30, 2014	Series A – GetYourGuide	5	4.5	Fritz Demopoulos, Kees Koolen
Jul 31, 2014	Series B – GetYourGuide	3	25	Highland Capital Partners, Spark Capital
Nov 13, 2015	Series C – GetYourGuide	8	50	Kohlberg Kravis Roberts
Nov 2, 2017	Series D – GetYourGuide	7	75	Battery Ventures
Feb 27, 2019	Secondary Market – GetYourGuide	1	N/A	Swisscanto Private Equity
May 16, 2019	Series E – GetYourGuide	6	484	SoftBank Vision Fund

Source: Created by authors using Crunchbase, "GetYourGuide Funding Rounds," accessed July 12, 2022, https://www.crunchbase.com/organization/getyourguide/company_financials.

EXHIBIT 4: GetYourGuide Leadership Team

Johannes Reck — CEO & Co-founder

Tao Tao — COO & Co-founder
Former leader of the company functions Business Development, Supply, and Customer Service at GetYourGuide

Udi Nir — Chief Technology Officer
Former VP of Engineering and Chief Technology Officer of online marketplaces, retailers, and communication platforms, including eBay, Instacart, ModCloth, and Threadsy

Nils Chrestin — Chief Financial Officer
Former Group CFO of online fashion site Global Fashion Group, and investment professional at Morgan Stanley

Email Martinsek — Chief Marketing Officer
Former Director of product at travel booking platform Hotwire, and consultant at Accenture

Eva Glanzer — Chief People Officer
Former Head of HR, HR manager, and recruiting and development manager at online marketplace and software companies, including DaWanda, alfabet AG and Zanox

Ameet Ranadive — Chief Product Officer
Former Product Director at Instagram, VP of Revenue Product at Twitter, co-founder of startup Dasient, strategy consultant at McKinsey and engineer at Hewlett-Packard

Source: Created by authors using "Executive Team," GetYourGuide, accessed version from October 12, 2019, through WayBack Machine, https://web.archive.org/web/20191012115246/https://press.getyourguide.com/executive-team.

CASE IV-2: GHANA INVESTMENT FUND LIMITED: ETHICAL ISSUES

Darrold Cordes and Won-Yong Oh wrote this case solely to provide material for class discussion. The authors do not intend to illustrate either effective or ineffective handling of a managerial situation. The authors may have disguised certain names and other identifying information to protect confidentiality.

This publication may not be transmitted, photocopied, digitized, or otherwise reproduced in any form or by any means without the permission of the copyright holder. Reproduction of this material is not covered under authorization by any reproduction rights organization. To order copies or request permission to reproduce materials, contact Ivey Publishing, Ivey Business School, Western University, London, Ontario, Canada, N6G 0N1; (t) 519.661.3208; (e) cases@ivey.ca; www.iveycases.com. Our goal is to publish materials of the highest quality; submit any errata to publishcases@ivey.ca. i1v2e5y5pubs

Copyright © 2019, Ivey Business School Foundation

Version: 2019-10-22

On September 29, 2017, Richard Dawson, the chief executive officer of RenY Corporation (RenY) based in Hong Kong, was onboard a flight from Accra, Ghana, to his home in Las Vegas. Dawson had just spent two challenging weeks establishing the Ghana Investment Fund Limited (GIF), which aimed to invest in the entrepreneurial ideas of university graduates in Ghana. The establishment of GIF went smoothly in the hands of Derik Badu, a graduate from the University of Ghana, and Charles Kweku, a business consultant who had previously worked in the United Kingdom for several years, and Dawson had come to know them both well. For GIF to operate in Ghana as a foreign-owned entity, it had to be registered at the Registrar General's department. To bid for government contracts, GIF had to be registered at the Ministry for Works and Housing (MWH). This process was proceeding smoothly until Dawson was confronted with a dilemma he could not immediately resolve: he had just learned that the awarding of major government contracts in Ghana lacked transparency, and that successful outcomes may require inducement payments that Dawson believed to be unethical.

Background

Country Overview: Ghana

Ghana, a country in West Africa, was a former British colony that gained independence in 1957. The country had retained many of the former institutions of government including the parliamentary system, legal system, and many government structures. According to the World Factbook Ghana 2017:[1]

- In 2016, Ghana had a population of 28,206,728 with a real gross domestic product (GDP) of approximately $46 billion.[2]
- Ghana had an abundance of natural resources, but agriculture made up about 20 percent of its GDP and more than 50 percent of its workforce.
- Gold and cocoa were the major exports.
- The full exploitation of recently discovered offshore oil reserves had been mitigated by declines in the world prices for oil and gas.

[1] "The World Factbook: Ghana," Central Intelligence Agency, July 18, 2018, updated October 1, 2019, accessed April 10, 2019, www.cia.gov/library/publications/resources/the-world-factbook/geos/gh.html.
[2] All $ amounts are in US dollars unless otherwise specified.

- Following a period of sustained growth, Ghana was experiencing the effects of a depreciating currency, as well as large budget and current-account deficits.
- The austerity programs accompanying an International Monetary Fund (IMF) loan in 2015 had focused attention on decreasing inefficiencies in the public sector, eliminating subsidies, and increasing tax revenues.[3]

Company Background: RenY Corporation (RenY)

RenY was established by Dawson in Hong Kong in 2010 as a management consulting and corporate advisory entity, with clients in the United States, China, and Australia. The company consulted on oil, gas, and commercial property development projects in China, and also provided a range of expert services related to small public company restructuring and raising capital from private investors in Australia. RenY was positioned to take advantage of the attractive corporate and tax environment in Hong Kong, its efficient banking system, and excellent foreign exchange provisions, as it was on the doorstep of the highly industrialized Guangdong province of Southern China. RenY had been contracted to undertake preliminary investigations into opportunities in Ghana for importing and wholesaling a range of seafood and other related products manufactured in China. RenY was also contracted by clients in the United States to assess markets in West Africa for sugar, rice, cooking oil, and other food products to be imported from Asia and South America. Dawson had traveled to Ghana many times since 2011 to develop a comprehensive understanding of the business and political environment and to learn about the public infrastructure needed to more fully inform RenY's clients.

RenY Corporation in Ghana

During these visits, Dawson observed the lack of public infrastructure, inadequate public health services, poor education facilities and programs (especially in rural areas), and increased urban stress due to economically inspired migration from rural areas to the cities by young people. The delivery of health, education, energy, transport, telecommunication services, and programs to stimulate jobs and economic growth was exacerbated by corruption at every level of government, by the legal systems, and by hegemonic political and business groups.

Foreign investment failed to produce transformational change in the region under the United Nations Millennium Development Goals[4] and the United Nations Economic Commission for Africa (UNECA) objectives.[5] The UNECA Sustainable Development Report on Africa Managing Land-Based Resources for Sustainable Development (2011) stated that sustainable development

> calls for integrating economic growth, social development and environmental management as interdependent, mutually supportive and reinforcing pillars of long-term development. It calls for participatory and multi-stakeholder approaches to dealing with development issues, involving a wide range of actors – government, private sector, civil society organizations, institutions of higher learning, and research and development partners.[6]

---

[3] "IMF Survey: Ghana Gets $918 Million IMF Loan to Back Growth, Jobs Plan," International Monetary Fund, April 3, 2015, accessed April 10, 2019, www.imf.org/en/News/Articles/2015/09/28/04/53/socar040315a.

[4] United Nations, *The Millennium Development Goals Report 2015*, accessed April 10, 2019, www.un.org/millenniumgoals/2015_MDG_Report/pdf/MDG%202015%20rev%20(July%201).pdf.

[5] United Nations Economic Commission for Africa," *MDG Report 2015: Lessons Learned in Implementing the MDGS, Summary*," September 2015, accessed April 10, 2019, www.uneca.org/sites/default/files/PublicationFiles/mdg-report-2015_eng_summary_rev2sept15.pdf.

[6] "Sustainable Development Report on Africa I: Managing Land-Based Resources for Sustainable Development," United Nations Economic Commission for Africa, January 2011, accessed April 10, 2019, http://repository.uneca.org/handle/10855/14946.

In 2013, Dr. Daniel Twerefou at the University of Ghana produced a report on West Africa for the UNECA in which he noted that

> economic growth within the subregion has been driven more by donor inflows rather than domestic savings ... [and] FDI [foreign direct investment] failed to generate the employment needed to increase incomes and reduce poverty in the subregion. This was mainly because it focused more on capital-intensive extractive industries/sectors, especially the exploitation of mineral resources without value addition to these resources.[7]

The World Investment Report 2015 stated that West African FDI was focused on projects that had low job creation, such as telecommunications, mining, retail, and financial services.[8] Health concerns such as the Ebola crisis had resulted in a significant drop in FDI in West Africa since early 2014.[9] Twerefou also noted that

> most countries in the sub-region are not undergoing the structural transformation needed to improve the quality of life of the people and ensure sustainable development. The shrinking of the agricultural sector's contribution to GDP, accompanied by a decrease, or at best, a stagnation of the manufacturing sector, suggests a pseudo-transformational process whose overall impact on growth and poverty should be properly assessed.[10]

On the long flight home, Dawson reflected on his long career as a manufacturer of information technology and in service delivery of information systems. He had expertise in small business start-ups, business restructuring, and capital funding. He was convinced that graduates from Ghana's many tertiary institutions could be agents for transformational change if they were provided with the right business stimuli, mentoring, and collaborative support. Dawson was aware of the plight of these graduates who, after having satisfied their national service obligations, were unlikely to gain employment in their fields of expertise. Dawson believed he could muster the resources needed to stimulate economic growth in Ghana through graduate-led small business development, and he was motivated to commit to this goal despite the ethical dilemma he now faced. He saw this as a large profitable opportunity for RenY, which could also address low-income deprivation in the region and reach many of the United Nations Sustainable Development Goals (see Exhibit 1).

Vision for Transformational Change
Research

Dawson had been given anecdotal information on the potential number of Ghana's graduates who were unemployed – between 200,000 and 400,000 graduates were not employed or were employed in areas not aligned with their professional expertise. One report suggested that one million graduates could be unemployed, but this number could not be verified. These numbers were derived from news media reports and from the membership of the Graduates Ghana (GaG) and Entrepreneurs Ghana (ENG) groups – two

---

[7] Daniel Kwabena Twerefou, "Report on Sustainable Development Goals for the West Africa Subregion: Summary," United Nations Economic and Social Council, October 23, 2013, accessed April 10, 2019, www.uneca.org/sites/default/files/uploaded-documents/SDG/2013/sdg2013_draft-sdgs-report-west-africa_en.pdf.

[8] United Nations Conference on Trade and Development: UNCTAD, World Investment Report 2015: Reforming International Investment Governance, accessed April 10, 2019, https://unctad.org/en/PublicationsLibrary/wir2015_en.pdf.

[9] "The Economic Impact of the 2014 Ebola Epidemic: Short and Medium Term Estimates for West Africa," The World Bank, October 8, 2014, accessed April 10, 2019, www.worldbank.org/en/region/afr/publication/the-economic-impact-of-the-2014-ebola-epidemic-short-and-medium-term-estimates-for-west-africa.

[10] Twerefou, op. cit.

student and youth advocacy groups seeking to provide better career paths for graduates and vocationally trained youth.

During the first half of 2017, Dawson commissioned a study to try to determine a more accurate measure of the number of unemployed graduates, their interest in entrepreneurial pursuits, and their business interests. He engaged with both ENG and GaG in an Internet and social-media campaign to invite graduates to register their interests and ideas for development. This led to the construction of several websites and social-media profiles that focused attention on a registration website. Social-media campaigns targeted graduates who listed one of three universities in their social-media profiles. In the space of about three weeks, more than 9,000 likes were recorded along with almost 2,000 graduates submitting detailed ideas about what they would like to do if they were funded. Analysis of the registrations indicated that approximately 500,000 of Ghana's graduates were unemployed or not employed in areas they were trained for. The business proposals covered a wide range of ideas in agribusiness, construction, manufacturing, retail, and services. This highly encouraging outcome reinforced Dawson's belief that he could access a considerable pool of intellectual capital vital to his ideas for business development.

Electronic Commerce

Dawson was impressed with the degree of interconnectedness of graduates discovered during the research. Internet access and social media had great reach into communities across all regions of Ghana. Further, he observed that mobile payments were expanding rapidly as an alternative to traditional banking facilities. With mobile payments, people were able to transfer small amounts of money to each other and to pay merchant accounts via their mobile phones. Cash could be collected at locations designated by the telecommunications carrier. These transactions were convenient and cost less than traditional bank services.

This information inspired Dawson to consider electronic commerce (e-commerce) as a platform for enabling graduate-led businesses to gain access to local, national, and global markets for the sale of goods and services. This could lead to the disintermediation of agents that typically extracted most of the value from the supply chains and could also allow graduate-led businesses to access these markets by dealing directly or through collaborative portals. Dawson had a strong background in information technology and felt confident that e-commerce delivery platforms could be built and proliferated at reasonably low costs. He could see many small businesses, each with its own professional e-commerce website, reaching out to markets everywhere. Coupled with proven social-media skills, all the basic ingredients for market research and market reach were in place.

Financial Capital

Dawson needed to find methods to raise money to cover start-up and initial operating costs of the graduate-led businesses. Could these projects be funded the traditional way? Typically, start-ups were funded through the entrepreneur's own funds, and family and friends. Analysis of the submissions by graduates during the research phase indicated that $3,000 to $10,000 covered most of the start-up capital estimated by the graduates for their ideas. The initial idea trialed by Dawson was to crowd-fund the capital needed for each project through donations. A donor website was set up and several projects listed for funding. Graduates could use social media to channel their connections to their online profiles and encourage them to contribute. However, this plan failed because the donor website was not promoted through radio and television exposure, and the graduates themselves were unable to muster the support of their immediate circle of family and friends to the extent that was hoped.

Dawson realized that a different approach was needed to escalate the project's visibility to get independent coverage from national and international media outlets. He subsequently decided to fund the initial stages from his own resources and then work to engage other private sector investors over time.

Mentoring and Collaboration

Dawson realized that the graduate-led projects could not be supported in isolation. Providing mentoring to help the graduates formulate and operationalize their business ideas had many benefits. Mentors would be drawn initially from a handful of motivated and successful businesspeople who could share their time among several graduate-led projects.

The idea was to seed the first few projects with these mentors who would then develop graduates to become mentors for new graduate projects over time. The mentoring would take place using electronic media and face-to-face meetings. This approach would also assist in the development of collaborative groups in similar industry sectors. ENG and GaG would play an important role in facilitating collaboration through special events, industry seminars, social-media promotions, and competitions. They would also act as advocates for graduates to gain exposure to, and benefit from, government and business initiatives – through support programs, contracts, and employment.

The Next Stage

Dawson had mustered the ingredients for what he believed would make this a successful venture. His research had shown that many graduates were eager to start and that e-commerce could deliver many benefits and increased market scope. He also knew that the financial capital was adequate to get multiple projects underway simultaneously while building the supporting infrastructure for a much larger expedited rollout in the future.

He was also confident that he had the resources on the ground to build this project as a Ghanaian-inspired initiative with genuine indigenous roots. The success of this undertaking could lead to economic, social, and environmental growth in many low-income communities and aligned with the objectives of the United Nations Sustainable Development Goals (see Exhibit 1); this plan would also be a for-profit undertaking for GIF and for each of the graduate-led projects.

The next stage was the "doing," but as Dawson sat through the last part of his flight, he reflected further on the challenges that were ahead of him.

Dilemma

The meetings in Ghana with officials at the Registrar General's Office went well, and GIF was subsequently registered as a foreign-owned entity with little difficulty. Similarly, the process at the Ministry for Works and Housing also proceeded with no apparent difficulties, and the license to bid as a contractor for government contracts was issued. With all the proper paperwork in hand, the trio of Dawson, Badu, and Kweku proceeded to a meeting at Stanbic Bank for the account opening.

Dawson wanted a US$ foreign currency account and a local Ghanaian cedi account so that foreign remittances could be held as hard currency and local payments could be processed efficiently. Dawson was aware of certain foreign-exchange restrictions that imposed limits on the repatriation of funds and on the amount of foreign currency cash that could be withdrawn, but he felt he could work within these restrictions initially, so the accounts were duly opened.

Dawson, Badu, and Kweku then returned for a celebratory dinner at the hotel where Dawson was staying. At this dinner, Kweku dropped a bombshell. He said, "You must realize, Mr. Dawson, that the contractor's license is not really worth anything. We are unlikely to get any government contracts under that license." Dawson was astonished and said, "But we went through the process and we paid the fees and got the license. What more should we have done?"

Kweku was experienced in representing international clients in infrastructure and resource projects in Ghana, and he was well qualified to address this question. He replied,

> Mr. Dawson, there is a way of doing business here that is a little different to what is publicly announced. You must understand that large government contracts in Ghana attract interested groups from China, India, Turkey, and elsewhere. They each have their own way of doing business, and it is not exactly what you would like to hear. They come in with large pockets of cash, and they ask to see what contracts are available and they pay for the right to win contracts of their choice. We have not done that. We have followed the letter of the law, and you wanted that from the outset. The reality is different.

Dawson looked at Kweku; he could tell that this was how it worked. "Why didn't you tell me that from the beginning?" Dawson inquired. Kweku replied, "It is not in the national interest for me to be discussing such things so openly, and I did not want to allow this knowledge to impact on your judgment of how to organize in Ghana. We have worked within the law, and it was my obligation to help you with that." Kweku went on to explain the different levels of contractor licensing and the process for getting favorable treatment in government contracts. Kweku finished by saying, "If you want to bid for certain projects you must play by these rules, otherwise the rule of the purse will defeat you."

Dawson retired to his hotel room to prepare for his departure the following day. He was troubled by what he had just been told because certain infrastructure projects such as community housing, renewable energy, water supply, and sanitation aligned well with his plan for mobilizing coalitions of graduates and industry expertise to bid for and deliver on these contracts. This was a major setback – how could he condone unethical institutional practices while insisting and supporting the ethical development of graduate-led businesses?

Compliance with the law of the land and cultural norms was essential for the success of these businesses; to do otherwise would lead to the proliferation of corrupt and unethical business practices resulting in loss of reputation for the fledgling Ghanaian businesses. This weighed heavily on Dawson's mind during his journey home to Las Vegas.

Decision

Dawson wondered if the contract award process was indicative of the operations of other government agencies and whether or not he and his team could work within an overall environment that might have entrenched unethical practices and corrupt motives (see Exhibit 2).

RenY was subject to the laws of Hong Kong. Under the Prevention of Bribery Ordinance (see Exhibit 3), bribery was unlawful in the public and private sectors within Hong Kong, but it did not explicitly prohibit bribery elsewhere. Dawson was an Australian citizen living as a permanent resident (i.e., a Green Card holder) in the United States, and he had just formed a new company that would undertake research across Sub-Saharan Africa. Was he subject to the Foreign Corrupt Practices Act (see Exhibit 4) in the United States, which prohibits the bribery of government officials anywhere outside of the United States? Was he also subject to any other similar ordinance in Australia?

Dawson was also concerned about the reputation of Ghana and other West African countries with respect to money laundering, and wondered if there was any risk of being inadvertently caught up in investigations caused by the movement of funds related to his business objectives. He also recalled that in 2015 the Judicial Council of Ghana suspended 22 circuit court judges and magistrates and placed 12 high court judges under investigation for alleged bribery.[11]

---

[11] "22 Judges Suspended," Joyonline, September 9, 2015, accessed April 10, 2019, www.myjoyonline.com/news/2015/september-9th/breaking-22-judges-suspended.php.

A pattern was emerging in Dawson's mind – Ghana's government institutions could not be trusted and the enforcement of the rule of law was not assured (see Exhibit 5). Dawson had also experienced bank fraud relating to a wire transfer from Hong Kong to a purportedly reputable bank in Ghana. The wire transfer was redirected to another account, and the Ghanaian bank sent fraudulent responses to inquiries from Dawson's bank in Hong Kong. The Economic and Organized Crime Office in Ghana seemed powerless to intervene; officials connected to the Presidency of Ghana had to take action to resolve the matter.

Dawson was enthusiastic about his ideas for engaging Ghana's graduates in sustainable development projects in communities across the nation. Ghana was a peaceful country without internal violence since its independence from Britain in 1957.[12] Its electoral processes had generally been conducted transparently without evidence of fraud. The country had made significant improvements in the reduction of poverty and had met the United Nations Millennial Development Goal of a 50 percent reduction in poverty by 2015.[13] Initiatives in education had reduced illiteracy rates, and increased food nutrition had reduced developmental health issues in children.

Dawson had spent the best part of the previous five years cultivating contacts and researching business opportunities in West Africa. Against this backdrop of challenges and opportunities Dawson had to decide – was this investment going to result in nothing, or was there a way to move forward?

[12] Muhammad Dan Suleiman, "Global Insecurity and Local Conflicts in Ghana," *Peace Review: A Journal of Social Justice* 29, no. 3, (2017): 315–324, doi: 10.1080/10402659.2017.1344759.

[13] UN Communications Group (UNCG) and CSO Platform on SDGs, *The Sustainable Development Goals (SDGs) in Ghana: Why They Matter & How We Can Help*, November 2017, accessed April 10, 2019, www.undp.org/content/dam/unct/ghana/docs/SDGs/UNCT-GH-SDGs-in-Ghana-Avocacy-Messages-2017.pdf.

EXHIBIT 1: United Nations Sustainable Development Goals

Goal #	Outcomes	Goal #	Outcomes
1	No poverty	10	Reduced inequalities
2	Zero hunger	11	Sustainable cities and communities
3	Good health and wellbeing	12	Responsible production and consumption
4	Quality education	13	Climate action
5	Gender equality	14	Life below water
6	Clean water and sanitation	15	Life on land
7	Affordable and clean energy	16	Peace, justice, and strong institutions
8	Decent work and economic growth	17	Partnerships for the goals
9	Industry, innovation, and infrastructure		

Source: "Do You Know all 17 SDGS?," YouTube video, 1:24, posted by United Nations, April 20, 2018, accessed April 10, 2019, https://youtu.be/0XTBYMfZyrM.

EXHIBIT 2: Corruption Perceptions Index (partial)

Rank	Score	Country
1	88	Denmark
13	77	Australia
14	76	Hong Kong
22	71	United States of America
78	41	Ghana
180	10	Somalia

Source: "Corruption Perceptions Index 2018," Transparency International, accessed April 11, 2019, www.transparency.org/cpi2018.

EXHIBIT 3: Hong Kong Prevention of Bribery Ordinance (POBO)

Hong Kong's Prevention of Bribery Ordinance (POBO) does not criminalize the payment of bribes to foreign government officials. Hong Kong's companies are also not liable. Outside of Hong Kong, directors and employees may have criminal liability in jurisdictions where the bribery of public officials is an offence.

Source: "Cap. 201 Prevention of Bribery Ordinance," Hong Kong e-Legislation, November 7, 2018, accessed April 10, 2019, www.elegislation.gov.hk/hk/cap201.

EXHIBIT 4: United States Foreign Corrupt Practices Act (FCPA)

The Foreign Corrupt Practices Act of 1977, as amended, 15 U.S.C. §§ 78dd-1, et seq. ("FCPA"), was enacted for the purpose of making it unlawful for certain classes of persons and entities to make payments to foreign government officials to assist in obtaining or retaining business. Specifically, the anti-bribery provisions of the FCPA prohibit the willful use of the mails or any means of instrumentality of interstate commerce corruptly in furtherance of any offer, payment, promise to pay, or authorization of the payment of money or anything of value to any person, while knowing that all or a portion of such money or thing of value will be offered, given or promised, directly or indirectly, to a foreign official to influence the foreign official in his or her official capacity, induce the foreign official to do or omit to do an act in violation of his or her lawful duty, or to secure any improper advantage in order to assist in obtaining or retaining business for or with, or directing business to, any person. Since 1977, the anti-bribery provisions of the FCPA have applied to all U.S. persons and certain foreign issuers of securities. With the enactment of certain amendments in 1998, the anti-bribery provisions of the FCPA now also apply to foreign firms and persons who cause, directly or through agents, an act in furtherance of such a corrupt payment to take place within the territory of the United States. The FCPA also requires companies whose securities are listed in the United States to meet its accounting provisions. See 15 U.S.C. § 78 m. These accounting provisions, which were designed to operate in tandem with the anti-bribery provisions of the FCPA, require corporations covered by the provisions to (a) make and keep books and records that accurately and fairly reflect the transactions of the corporation and (b) devise and maintain an adequate system of internal accounting controls.

Source: "Foreign Corrupt Practices Act," The United States Department of Justice, February 3, 2017, accessed April 10, 2019, www.justice.gov/criminal-fraud/foreign-corrupt-practices-act.

EXHIBIT 5: Ghana Criminal Offences Act (GCOA)

Despite corruption levels in Ghana being low compared to other African countries, rampant corruption, weak rule of law and an under-regulated property rights system are significant impediments to business confidence. Low-level government employees may ask for a "dash" (tip) in return for facilitating license and permit applications, and companies applying for licenses and permits are frequently confronted with demands for facilitation payments. Companies also contend with high corruption risks when dealing with Ghana's public procurement system. While there is no singular piece of legislation to tackle corruption, the Ghana Criminal Offices Act (GCOA) criminalizes corruption in the form of active and passive bribery, extortion, wilful exploitation of public office, use of public office for private gain, and bribery of foreign public officials. Moreover, corruption is deemed illegal, and both agent and principal are liable, regardless of nationality. Corruption under section 239 of the GCOA is defined as "corruption of a public officer," and subsequent clauses define various forms of corruption, including bribery and extortion. This definition does not include corporate or private bribery offences, and bribery between citizens is not outlawed.

Source: Kaunain Rahman, "Overview of Corruption and Anti-Corruption in Ghana," U4 Anti-Corruption Resource Centre, 2018, accessed April 10, 2019, www.u4.no/publications/overview-of-corruption-and-anti-corruption-in-ghana-2018-update.

Index

Locators in **bold** refer to tables and those in *italics* to figures, though these are not separately indexed where they appear concurrently with main text.

absolute theories (ethics), 467–468
accommodation
   American-Japanese partnership example, 339
   developing a global mindset, 37–39
   extent to which cultural accommodation is appreciated, 146
   see also adaptation
acculturative stress, 229–232
acquisitions, 287–294
action-orientation, cultural differences, 156, *160*–161
adaptation
   culture shock on international assignments, 229–232
   difference between multiculturalism and polyculturalism, 146
   organizational alignment, 338, 476
   overseas effectiveness, 221–222
   training and preparation for international assignments, 227–229
   "who should adapt?", 174–175
   see also Map-Bridge-Integrate framework
administrative systems, cultural context, 315–317
Age of Agile, 349
agile mindset, 349
agriculture, rice-growing and wheat-growing cultures, 62–63
alignment *see* organizational alignment
alliances
   choice of partner, 292–294
   cultural adaptation, 339
   cultural integration, 340
   cultural minimization, 339
   joint ventures, 290
   Tiffany-Swatch case study, 389–400
Amazon
   aligning strategy, 326–327
   book retail industry, 322–323
   launch in India, 296

ambition, 70, 303
amplification, decision-making, 213–214
anti-corruption measures, 427, 455–459
anticipatory stage (change), 350
Apple, 356
appraisal processes, 334–335
Argentina, McDonald's case study, 83–*90*
Arla Foods
   cartoon crisis, 90–98
   mission statement, 99
artificial intelligence (AI), 461–464
Ashby, W. R., 213
Ashby's Law of Requisite Variety, 213
"Asian values" debate, 470–474
aspirational talk, 440
assimilation, 37–39
assumptions, cultural influence on, 67–68, 70–71
automobile industry
   change and design thinking, 351
   human rights and labor, 452

banking industry, 2008 financial crisis, 449–450
Barnes & Noble Booksellers, 322–323
behaviors
   aspirational talk, 440
   change and design thinking, 352–365
   cultural influence, 72, 73–74
   destroyer dynamic, 169–170
   India-US cultural clashes, 246–247
   integrity and ethics, 446–448, 464–465, 476–*479*
   leading organizational change, 360–**363**
   see also organizational cultures
Beiersdorf case study, 373–388
Belt and Road Initiative (BRI), 11–12
best product (BP) competition, 321
bias, talent management, 222–223
biculturalism, 75–77
big, hairy, audacious goals (BHAGs), *425*
Blockbuster, 323

Index 507

blockchain technology, 455
bluewashing, 431
   see also sustainable organizations
Bond, M., 121–122
book retail industry, 322–323
born global businesses, 295–296
BP (British Petroleum), 435–436, 438–439
brainstorming, 166, 409
Brexit, 9
bribery, 455–459
brick-and-click model, 25
bridging
   cross-cultural communication, 152–*153*
   decentering, 154–158
   engaging, 153–154
   physical bridge building case study, 149–150
   recentering, 158–162
   see also Map-Bridge-Integrate framework
business models, 322–323
business process outsourcing (BPO), 241–242
business responsibility
   see corporate social responsibility; responsible businesses
Business-to-Business (B2B), 296–297
business trips
   see international assignments

C-suite recruitment, 224
Cabletronica, 371–372
Caligiuri, Paula, 339
Canadian International Development Agency (CIDA), 228
capital management case study, 240–*249*
capitalism
   shareholder, 419–420
   stakeholder, 421–424
   state, 420
careers
   see talent management
cartography in culture, 137–145
   see also mapping cultures
categorical imperative, 467
category width, 25–26
cause-effect relations, 17–18
Centers of Excellence (CoE), *302*
centralized hubs, 280
   see also organizational structures
certainty orientation, cultural differences, 135–137, **141**, 159

change agents, 358, 360–**363**, **364**–365
   see also global organizational change
Chat-GPT, 462
Chile, Global Multi-Products (GMP) case study, 312–314, 332, 335
China
   Belt and Road Initiative (BRI), 11–12
   rice-growing and wheat-growing cultures, 62–63
choke points, 12–13
circularity, sustainable organizations, 453
climate change, 420–421
clothing industry, 452–453
cognition
   cultural influences, 68–69
   mapping cultures, **139**, 144
cognitive dissonance, 38, 70
cognitive skills, 214–215
cohesion
   lateral collaboration, 303
   team effectiveness, 193
collaborative connectivity, 207–208, 440
collaborative leadership, 21–22
collectivist cultures
   comparison of India and America, 246–247
   evaluation and reward systems, 335
   interdependent orientation, 128–130, **141**, 156
command and control, 21–22
Commercial Cold Storage and Logistics (CCS Logistics), 402–414
common ground
   equalizing value, 170–172
   recentering, 159
common reality, 158–162
common rules of interaction, 158–162, *165*–166
communication
   aspirational talk, 440
   direct vs indirect, 132–135, **141**
   global organizational change, 362–**363**
   see also cross-cultural communication; interpersonal skills; technology-mediated interaction
communication skills
   see interpersonal skills; talent management
Communities of Practice (CoP), 302
community responsibility, 426
competences
   global leadership, 40–47
   organizational change, 359–360
   skills required from contemporary global leaders, 13

competitive strategy framework, 318-319
complex adaptive system, globalization as, 16-17
complex interdependence, 329-330, **331**
complexity of globalization, 15-19
    elimination vs. amplification, 213-214
    impact on leaders, 21-22
    talent management, 212-213
    teams across global companies, 181-182
computer chips market, 12-13
conflict resolution, 165, 195, 330-332
    see also disagreements
connective leadership, 20-21
connectivity, 207
consequential theories (ethics), 466
conservation, World Wide Fund for Nature (WWF), 205-206
consumer protection, 426
consumerism, McDonald's around the world, 66
context
    see primacy of context
context sensitivity, 26
    see also mindfulness; primacy of context
coordinated federation, 279
corporate social responsibility
    definitions, 418
    evolution of corporate social responsibility and sustainability, 418-421
    frameworks for, 425-426
    global mindset, **418**
    Global Reporting Initiative, 429-430
    greenwashing and bluewashing, 431
    purpose of business models, 417
    relationship between ESG and financial performance, 431-439
    S & P Dow Jones Indices, 430-431
    stakeholder theory, 421-424
    sustainability paradoxes, 439-440
    UN Global Compact, 426-429
corporate sustainability, 418
corruption/anti-corruption measures, 427, 455-459
cost center managers, 335-336
cost leadership (competitive strategy framework), 318-319
cost value, 298-299
Covid-19 pandemic, 11
    economic nationalism, 12-13
    GetYourGuide case study, 485-496
    impact on culture and values, 74-75
    international assignments, 217

crises response case studies
    see Arla Foods; McDonald's Argentina case study; Steelworks' Xiamen plant case study
crisis stage (change), 351, 354-357
    see also conflict resolution; disagreements
cross-cultural communication
    bridging, 152-153
    culturally diverse teams, 197-199
    decentering, 154-158
    destroying value, 168-170
    engaging, 153-154
    equalizing value, 170-172
    integrating, 162-168
    recentering, 158-162
    Uwa Ode case study, 258-264
    via technology, 172-**174**, **177**
CSR
    see corporate social responsibility
cultural accommodation
    American-Japanese partnership example, 339
    developing a global mindset, 37-39
    extent to which cultural accommodation is appreciated, 146
    see also adaptation
cultural adaptation
    see adaptation
cultural agility, 339, 475-476
cultural differences
    "Asian values" debate, 471-474
    within countries, **138**
    direct vs indirect communication, 132-135, **141**
    egalitarian vs status orientation, 130-132, **141**
    independent vs. interdependent orientation, 128-130, **141**
    knowledge about, 36
    organizational structures, 333
    perceptions, 68-71
    risk vs. certainty, 135-137, **141**
    task vs relationship orientation, 126-128, **141**
    see also international assignments
cultural imperialism, 471-474
cultural integration, 340, 476
    see also integrating component, Map-Bridge-Integrate framework
cultural minimization, 339, 475-476
cultural relativism, 466, 468-**474**
cultural theories (ethics), 468-470
culturally diverse teams, 197-199
    see also cross-cultural communication

Index 509

culture
    around administrative and management systems, 315–317
    cartography in, 137–145
    definition, 59–60
    dynamics influences of, 73–77
    effect on individuals and interactions, 67–72
    evolution and persistence, 62–63
    groups of people, 60–61
    influence on strategy, 324–326
    in international management, 58–59, 77–79
    Map-Bridge-Integrate framework, 120, 145–146
    mapping cultures, 120–122
    observing, 63–67
    organizational alignment, 336–340
culture shock, 229–232
    coping techniques, 231–232
    return shock, 232–234
Cushy Armchair (CA) case study, 371–372
customer bonding, 321
customer-centric organizations
    delta model (strategy), 320–322
    Galbraith's approach, 319–320
    industry trends, 324
cybersecurity, 462

data-driven decision-making, 461
data security/privacy, 462
decentering, cross-cultural communication, 154–158
decentralized federation, 280
decision-making
    amplification, 213–214
    assumption-based thinking, 67–68
    complexity, 213–214
    cultural decentering example, 155–157
    digital transformations, 299
    egalitarian vs status orientation, 130–132, 156
    global-local pressures, 276–279
    integrity and ethics, 446–448, 476–*479*
    organizing for digital transformations, 299
    strategy and alignment, 318
    team effectiveness, 191
    use of AI, 461
Delta Beverages case study, 265–270
delta model (strategy), 320–322
design thinking, organizational change, 352–365, 367
destroying value, 168–170, 171

differentiation (competitive strategy framework), 318–319
digital nomads, 216–218
    see also international assignments
digital transformations, organizing for, 298–299
Diglot Capital Management (DCM) case study, 240–*249*
dilemmas, 50
    see also paradox thinking
direct communication
    anticipating and resolving disagreements, 165
    cultural differences, 132–135, **141**, *161*
disagreements
    anticipating and resolving, 165
    "Asian values" debate, 470–474
    conflict resolution, 165, 195, 330–332
    continuous learning, **175**–176
    destroyer dynamic, 168–170
    ethical dilemmas, 476–*479*
    faultlines in diverse teams, 198–199
    Integrative Social Contracts Theory, 474–475
    tasks-people-structure triangle, 330–332
    team effectiveness, 193, 194
discipline
    individual contribution to the team, 191
    virtual teams, 200–201
diversity
    see culturally diverse teams
divisional structures, 282–287
    see also multinational enterprises (MNEs)
divisions of labor, 333
    see also organizational structures
Dow Jones Indices, 430–431
dualism, 469
duty of care, 225–227
DVD technology, 323

E = f (PAIS) equation, 221–222
ecological fallacy, 137–138
economic nationalism, 9, 12–13
efficiency
    and culture, 59–60, 72
    destroyer dynamic, 169
    mapping cultures, 144
    skills required from contemporary global leaders, 13
egalitarian orientation, cultural differences, 130–132, **141**, 156
elimination of input variety, 213–214

Elkington, John, 421
emergent outcomes, 16–17
empathy
   and decentering, 154–158
   design thinking, 353, 360
   team effectiveness, 193
employee performance
   appraisals and rewards, 334–335
   fostering organizational cultures, 336–337
   top management support during organizational change, 357–358
   when facing organizational change, 359–360, 363
employee security, 459–461
Employer of Record (EOR) services
   industry overview, 100–101
   Oyster HR case study, 103–113
   recent trends and the Covid-19 pandemic, 101–103
employment practices/policies, 425–426, 427, 451–455
empowerment, to participate, 163–164, 168
engaging, cross-cultural communication, 153–154
Enterprise Resource Planning (ERP) systems, 150–152
the environment
   see primacy of context
environmental issues
   1960s/70s environmentalism, 419–420
   climate change, 420–421
   environmental protection frameworks, 426, 427
   generational differences, 74–75
   greenwashing and bluewashing, 431
   relationship between ESG and financial performance, 431–439
   sustainable development, 418, 421
   sustainable leadership, 29
   World Wide Fund for Nature (WWF), 205–206
   see also sustainable organizations
Equal Employment Opportunity Commission (EEOC), 448–449
equalizing value, 170–172, 198
equity joint ventures, 289–294
escalation of commitment, 356–357
ESG (environmental, social, and governance), 421, 431–439
   see also corporate social responsibility
ethics, 418, 446–448
   artificial intelligence (AI), 461–464
   bribery, corruption, and protection money, 455–459
   corporate sustainability frameworks, 425–426
   employee security, 459–461
   ethical versus legal behavior, 448–451
   frameworks and theories, 465–475
   Ghana Investment Fund (GIF), 497–505
   guidelines to consider, 475–480
   net positive companies, 424–425
   personal responsibilities and consequences, 445
   purpose of business, 417, 422–423
   responding to ethical problems, 464–465
   use of AI, 461
   see also corporate social responsibility; integrity
ethnocentric errors, 70
evaluation, organizational structure, 335–336
excessive persistence, 356–357
executing strategy
   see strategy
executing, team effectiveness, 191
expatriate attrition, 233–234
expatriate relocations, 218–219
   destinations, 215–222
   female expatriates, 223
   returning home, 233–234
   selection criteria, 221, 266–270
experience value, 298–299

facilitative leadership, 21–22
fast execution, 299
Fearon, D. S., 117–118
feedback, and globalization, 16–17
financial performance, relationship with ESG, 431–439
flexpatriates, 216–218
   see also international assignments
flux, 18
Flynn, Peter, 274–275
focus (competitive strategy framework), 318–319
food industry, human rights and labor, 454–455
Foreign Corrupt Practices Act (FCPA), 457–458
formal positions of authority, 19–20
Foster, Charles, case study, 237–239
free-market capitalism, 419–420
Freeman, R. Edward, 421–424
Friedman, Milton, 419–420
Fukuyama, Francis, 8
Fund for Peace, 224
fundamentalism, 468

Galbraith, J. R., 319–320
gender, women as global leaders, 222–223

General Agreement on Tariffs and Trade (GATT), 8
generational differences
    attitudes to environment and sustainability, 420–421
    cultural change, 74–75
geographically distributed teams, 196–197, 199–204
    see also remote working
GetYourGuide, 485–496
Ghana Investment Fund (GIF), 497–505
Gibson, William, 421
global business knowledge, 40
Global Compact, 426–429
global companies
    complexity, 15–19
    coordination of teams across, 181–182, 204–207
    future of global work, 304
    meaning of, 14–15
    small enterprises, 294–298
Global Competencies Inventory (GCI), 45
global dexterity, 476
global financial crisis (2008), 17, 449–450
global integration, 276–281
    see also integrating component, Map-Bridge-Integrate framework
global key account manager (KAM) role, 300–301
global leadership
    see leadership; mindful global leadership
global learning, 278
global-local paradox, 48, 52–53
    matrix organizations, 283–287
    strategy, 276–281, 305
global mindset, 15, 33–35
    components and domains, 35–37
    as criteria for international assignment selection, 221
    definition, 33–34
    developing through learning, 37–39
    developing your own, 39–40
    integrity, 446
    responsible businesses, **418**
Global Multi-Products (GMP), Chile, 312–314, 332, 335
global organizational change, 344–345
    Beiersdorf case study, 380–381
    design thinking, 352–365, 367
    IBM case study, 345–348
    initiating change and adopting new behavior, 360–**363**
    mindset-centered approach, 349
    organization renewal, **365**–366
    readiness for, 354–357
    reasons for change, 348, 362
    reinforcing the change, **364**–365
    three types of change, 350–352
    top management support, 357–358
global orientation, 280
Global Reporting Initiative (GRI), 429–430
Global Rescue, 225–226
global Small- to Medium-Sized Enterprises (SMEs), 296–297
Global Sourcing and Operating Guidelines (GSOG), 452–453
globalization
    complexity of, 15–19
    concerns over, 9
    phases of, 8, 10
    "then" and "now", 7–9
GLOBE project (Global Leadership and Organizational Behavior Effectiveness), 122
GlobeSmart dimensions, 126–137
Google Translate, 173–**174**
greenwashing, 431, 439
    see also sustainable organizations
grocery home-delivery services, 24–25

Hall, E. T., 121
Hax, A., 320–322
health inspection case study, McDonald's, 83–*90*
Hofstede, G., 36, 121–122
House, R. J., 122
human literacy, 214–215
    see also interpersonal skills
human resources
    see professional development; talent management
human rights, 426, 427, 449–450, 451–455
hyperawareness, 299
hypernorms, 474–475

IBM
    agile mindset, 349
    global organizational change, 345–348
    less formal collaboration, 302
ideas, building on, 165–166
identity
    cultural influence, 60, 72
    destroyer dynamic, 169

identity (*cont.*)
   equalizing value, 171
   mapping cultures, 144–145
   multiculturalism, 75–77
   team effectiveness, 193
immigration, concerns over, 9
incremental leadership, 20–21
independent orientation, cultural differences, 128–130, **141**, 165–166
India
   business process outsourcing (BPO) sector, 241–242
   Delta Beverages case study, 265–270
   Diglot Capital Management (DCM) case study, 240–249
   launch of Amazon in, 296
   religious diversity, 243, 245
   superstitions in, 243–244
indirect communication, 132–135, **141**, 161
   anticipating and resolving disagreements, 165
individual growth
   effective teams, 184
   international assignments, 215–222
   see also talent management
individualistic cultures
   categorical imperative, 467
   comparison of India and America, 246–247
   conflict resolution, 331–332
   evaluation and reward systems, 335
   independent orientation, 128–130, **141**, 165–166
infant formula case study, 449
informal positions of leadership, 19–20
Information Technology (IT) systems, implementing in a global organization, 150–152
   see also technology-mediated interaction
informed decision-making, 299
inorganic growth, 287–288
inpatriate assignments, 219–220
institutional culture
   see organizational cultures
institutions, 315–316
integrated network model, 280–281
integrating component, Map-Bridge-Integrate framework, 162–168, *163*
integrative leadership, 20–21
Integrative Social Contracts Theory (ISCT), 474–**475**
integrity, 446–448
   artificial intelligence (AI), 461–464
   bribery, corruption, and protection money, 455–459
   employee security, 459–461

ethical frameworks, 465–475
ethical versus legal behavior, 448–451
global mindset, 446
guidelines to consider, 475–480
human rights and labor, 451–455
personal responsibilities and consequences, 445
responding to ethical problems, 464–465
inter-organizational interfaces, 293
interdependence
   conflict resolution, 330–332
   and globalization, 16–17
   tasks-people-structure triangle, 328–330, 331
interdependent orientation, cultural differences, 128–130, **141**, 156
internal team climate, 190, 193–197
   see also teams
international acquisitions, 287–294
international assignments, 215–222
   adaptation and culture shock, 229–232
   destinations, 215–222
   duty of care, 225–227
   flexpatriates, 216–218
   returning home, 233–234
   selection criteria, 221, 266–270
   Uwa Ode case study, 258–264
   women as global leaders, 222–223
international management, culture in, 58–59, 77–79
   see also mindful global leadership
international orientation, 279
International SOS, 226
international trade, 8
Internet of Things (IoT), 12–13
interpersonal interaction
   cartography in culture, 137–145
   effectiveness in, 117–120
   GlobeSmart dimensions, 126–137
   mapping cultures, 120–122
interpersonal skills, 42
   bridging differences, 152–153
   building relationships remotely, 201
   conflict resolution, 331–332
   skills-building, 214–215
   team effectiveness, 190–195
   see also communication; talent management
intersectionality, 75–77
investment center managers, 335–336
ISIS (terrorist organization), 455–456
Italy, integrating example, 167
Ivey Management Services, 237–239

Jamous, Tony, 295
Japan
    American-Japanese partnership example, 339
    as interdependent culture, 128–129
    recentering example, 159–161
    status orientation, 164
joint ventures, 290
    choice of partner, 292–294
    cultural adaptation, 339
    cultural integration, 340
    cultural minimization, 339
    Tiffany-Swatch case study, 389–400

Kahneman, D., 67–68
Kant, Immanuel, 467
knowledge
    about other organizations, 36–37
    about own organization, 36
    of cultural differences, 36
    global business knowledge, 40
    lateral collaboration, 303
    mapping cultures, 145–146
    of self, 35
    tacit, 219
Kolb, David A., 207
Kozai Group, 45

labor practices, 427, 451–455
language
    Google Translate, 173–**174**
    impact of language differences, **176**
    as part of culture, 63–64
    technology-mediated interaction, **177**
lateral collaboration, 300–303
leadership
    competences, 40–47
    crisis at Steelworks' Xiamen plant case study, 250–257
    joint ventures, 293
    lateral collaboration, 302
    leading people across boundaries, 19–22
    vs. management, 19–20
    mindfulness, 22–23
    organizational change, 360–**363**
    organizing for digital transformations, 299
    paradox thinking, 47–54
    skills required from contemporary global leaders, 13
    in smaller global businesses, 297–298
    typology of, 20–21
    women as global leaders, 222–223
    see also mindful global leadership
learning
    active, 39–40
    alliances and joint ventures, 293–294
    balancing globalization and localization, 278
    developing a global mindset, 37–39
    for development and effectiveness, **175**–176
    a global mindset, 37–39
    skill-building, 214–215
    team effectiveness, 192–193
legal issues
    bribery, corruption, and protection money, 455–459
    employment practices/policies, 451–455
    ethical versus legal behavior, 448–451
    human rights and labor, 451–455
Levitt, Theodore, 419
local markets
    extent to which cultural accommodation is appreciated, 146
    global integration versus local responsiveness, 276–281
    global-local paradox, 48, 52–53
long-term focus, 49, 433–434
long-term project teams, 180
loose cultures, 73–74
low context cultures, 133–134, 331–332

machine learning, 461–464
Mahmood, Tan Sri Dr. Jemilah, 75–77
Malaysian culture, 75–77
management style
    cultural adaptation, 476
    making organizational changes, 338, 355
    mapping cultures, 155–157
    see also leadership
management systems, cultural context, 315–317
management teams, 180
    see also top management
management, vs. leadership, 19–20
Map-Bridge-Integrate framework, 120, 145–146, 166
    bridging component, 152–**153**
    destroying value, 168–170
    equalizing value, 170–**172**
    implementing IT systems in a global organization, *150*–152
    integrating component, 162–168

Map-Bridge-Integrate framework (*cont.*)
  mapping component, 120–122
  who should adapt?, 174–175
mapping cultures, 120–122
  cartography in culture, 137–145
  comparison of tools, 123–125
  GlobeSmart dimensions, 126–137
  Map-Bridge-Integrate framework, 120, 145–146
  stereotyping, 137–139
matrix organizations, 283–287, 306
Mattel, 435
MBI
  see Map-Bridge-Integrate framework
McDonald's
  cultural differences, 66
  health inspection in Argentina case study, 83–90
  withdrawal from Russia, 10–11
media attention
  Arla Foods and the cartoon crisis, 90–98
  Ghana Investment Fund, 500–501
  greenwashing and bluewashing, 431, 439
  McDonald's case study, 88–90
  Tiffany-Swatch case study, 397
media richness, 202–203
  see also technology-mediated interaction
meetings
  cultural differences in approach to, 158–159
  empowering participation, 163–164, 168
  heartbeat meetings, 203–204
  integrating, 167
Mexican banking system, 339
Microsoft, 356
mindful global leadership, 22–23
  building relationships, 201
  change and design thinking, 352–365
  competences, 40–47
  executing strategy, 326–327
  global mindset, 33–40
  interpersonal interaction, 117–120
  paradox thinking, 47–54
  pathways to, 54–55
  talent management, 212–213
mindfulness
  continuous learning, 175–176
  cultivating, 28
  definition, 22–23, 28
  destroyer dynamic, 169–170
  elements of, 25–27
  in global business, 23–25

  in leadership, 22–23
  mapping cultures, 120–122
  practical approach to, 27–28
  team effectiveness, 192–193
mindset-centered approach
  agile mindset, 349
  three types of change, 350–352
  see also global mindset
Mittelstand, 297
morality, 446–448
  see also ethics; integrity
motivation
  appraisals and rewards, 334–335
  to communicate cross-culturally, 153–154
  facing organizational change, 359–360
movie rental business, 323
multi-domestic orientation, 280
multiculturalism
  as applicable to all, 75–77
  culturally diverse team performance, 197–199
  difference between multiculturalism and polyculturalism, 146
  empowering participation, 163–164
  recentering, 159–161
  Uwa Ode case study, 259–260, 261–263
  see also cross-cultural communication
multinational enterprises (MNEs), 273–274
  acquisitions and alliances, 287–294
  balancing globalization and localization, 278
  generic MNE orientations, 279–281
  global organizing, 281
  lateral collaboration, 300–303
  multi-divisional structures, 282–287
  primacy of context, 274–276, 304–305
  supply-chain activities, 286–287

Napoleon Bonaparte, 22–23
national cultures, 60–61
  interaction with organizational culture, 78
  within-country diversity, 138
  see also cultural differences
The National Intelligence Council, 13–14
neoliberalism, 11
Nestlé, 454–455
net positive companies, 424–425
  see also corporate social responsibility
Netflix, 323
the Netherlands, TJX's launch in, 325–326
Nigeria, Uwa Ode case study, 258–264

Nivea, expanding the global reach of, 373–388
non-equity alliances, 289–294
non linear trajectories, 350

online grocery home-delivery, 24–25
online retail, 352
operational leadership, 20–21
organization design, 274
organizational alignment, 311
    critical role of systems, 333–340
    within the environmental context, 310–312, 314–317
    executing strategy, 317–327
    Global Multi-Products (GMP) in Chile, 312–314
    in practice, 340–342
    tasks-people-structure triangle, 327–333
organizational change
    see global organizational change
organizational cultures, 61
    accepting change, 348, 365–366
    interaction with national culture, 78
    supporting performance, 336–337
organizational level, 273–274
organizational structures
    acquisitions and alliances, 287–294
    Beiersdorf case study, 374–376
    cultural influences, 333
    emerging ways of organizing, 298–303
    generic MNE orientations, 279–281
    global organizing in MNEs, 281
    matrix structure, 283–287, 306
    multi-divisional structures, 282–287
    primacy of context, 274–276, 304–305
    supply-chain activities, 286–287
    T-shaped structures, 285–286
    tasks-people-structure triangle, 327–333, 340–342
outsourcing, 241–242
overseas effectiveness, 221–222
Oyster HR case study, 100, 103–113

paradox thinking, 47–54
    production-commercial paradox, 49
    short- and long-term paradox, 49
    stability-change paradox, 354–355
    sustainability paradoxes, 436–440
    see also global-local paradox
participation
    empowerment, 163–164, 168
    global organizational change, 363

partner selection process, 292–294
    see also joint ventures
pension plan example, 186–188, 189, 194–195
Perceive-Interpret-Evaluate (PIE) framework, 68–69, 72, 155
perceptions
    cultural differences, 68–71
    global leadership competences, **43**, 44
performance appraisal, 334–335
Perry, Jr, W., 468–470
personal integrity
    see integrity
personal protective equipment (PPE), Covid-19 pandemic, 12–13
personal responsibilities, 445
    see also ethics; integrity
perspective-taking, 25–26
    see also mindfulness
PESTEL (political, economic, social, technological, environmental, and legal) influences, 315
Peter Flynn Company, 274–275
PIE
    see Perceive-Interpret-Evaluate (PIE) framework
planning
    global organizational change, 353
    international assignments, 227–229
    team effectiveness, 191
    virtual teams, 200–201
platform value, 298–299
platforms, born global businesses, 295–296
polyculturalism
    cultural accommodation, 146
    difference between multiculturalism and polyculturalism, 146
pooled interdependence, 328–329, 331
populist politics, 9
Porter, Michael, 318–319
power
    authority and flexibility, 283–287
    egalitarian vs status orientation, 130–132, 141, 156
pragmatic cultures, 156
Prahalad, C. K., 15
premature abandonment, 356–357
primacy of context
    Global Multi-Products (GMP) case study, 312
    mindfulness, 26
    organizational alignment, 310–312, 314–317
    strategy, 274–276, 304–305, **326**
    sustainable leadership, 29

problems, 50
　see also paradox thinking
process orientation, 27, 291–292
　see also mindfulness
product-centric organizations, 319–320
product quality
　see quality
production-commercial paradox, 49
production teams, 180
professional development
　see individual growth; talent management
profit center managers, 335–336
profitability, relationship between ESG and financial performance, 431–439
project management, 187–188, 191
protection money, 455–459
psychological safety, 193, 194
purchasing power parity (PPP), 66
purpose of business
　ethics and the global mindset, 418
　major models of, 417

quality
　production-commercial paradox, 49
　responsible businesses, 419

rationalization, and ethics, 464–465
reactive stage (change), 351
realism, 11
recentering, cross-cultural communication, 158–162
reciprocal interdependence, 329–330, 331
reciprocity, 195
recruitment
　for C-suite, 224
　international assignment selection, 221, 266–270
　selection and development, 332
redundancy case study, Oyster, 100, 103–113
redundancy, developing resilience, 13
relationship management
　global leadership competences, 43, 44
　in strategy and international joint ventures, 292–293
　see also interpersonal skills
relationship orientation, cultural differences, 126–128, 141
relativism, 469–470
　see also cultural relativism

religious diversity, India, 243, 245
religious freedoms, Arla Foods and the cartoon crisis, 90–98
remote working
　Covid-19 pandemic, 74–75
　cross-cultural communication, 172–174
　digital nomads, 218
　teams working virtually, 199–204
RenY Corporation, 497–505
research and development (R&D), Beiersdorf case study, 377–378
resilience, 13
responsibility centers, 335–336
responsible businesses
　bribery, corruption, and protection money, 455–459
　employment practices/policies, 425–426, 427, 451–455
　evolution of corporate social responsibility and sustainability, 418–421
　frameworks for, 425–426
　global mindset, 418
　Global Reporting Initiative, 429–430
　greenwashing and bluewashing, 431
　integrity and ethics, 446–448, 464–465, 476–479
　major models of, 417
　net positive companies, 424–425
　purpose of business, 417, 422–423
　relationship between ESG and financial performance, 431–439
　S & P Dow Jones Indices, 430–431
　stakeholder theory, 421–424
　sustainability paradoxes, 436–440
　UN Global Compact, 426–429
restructuring project, Beiersdorf case study, 380–381
return on investment (ROI), 219
returning home, international assignments, 233–234
rewarding employees, 334–335
risk, ethical dilemmas, 460–461
risk orientation, cultural differences, 135–137, 141
roadmap, global organizational change, 362–363
Ropes, Charles A., 274
rugs industry, 453–454
rule-based theories, 467–468
Russia, invasion of Ukraine, 10–11

Index

S & P Dow Jones Indices, 430–**431**
safety
    employee security, 459–461
    human rights and labor, 451–455
    international assignments, 225–227
    psychological, 193, 194
sailing teams example, 181–183, 192–193
Sarbanes-Oxley Act, 335
Scandinavian cultures, decentering example, 155–157
scheduling
    across time zones, 181, 200, 218
    heartbeat meetings, 203–204
    making organizational changes, 355–356
schemas, 37
Schultz, M., 78
Sears, 326–327
self knowledge, 35
self-management, **43**, 44–45
senior management
    see mindful global leadership; top management
sequential interdependence, 329, 331
service teams, 180
shareholder capitalism, 419–420
short-term focus, 49, 433–434
short-term response teams, 180
Siemens, 456
simple interdependence, 328–329, 331
Singapore, crisis at Steelworks' Xiamen plant case study, 250–257
situational readiness, 222
skills-building, 214–215
    see also learning; talent management
slack, developing resilience, 13
small enterprises, and strategy, 294–298
Small- to Medium-Sized Enterprises (SMEs), 296–297
small win theory, **364**–365
social identity, from culture, 60
social perception, 68–71
socio-technical systems, organizations as, 311
soft skills, 214–215
    see also talent management
Spain
    integrating, 167
    SME case study, 297–298
stability-change paradox, 354–355
    see also global organizational change
stakeholder theory/stakeholder capitalism, 421–424

standardization, 277
Stanford Design School, 352–353
state capitalism, 420
status orientation, cultural differences, 130–132, 141
    building on ideas, 165–166
    empowering participation, 164
Steelworks' Xiamen plant case study, 250–257
stereotyping cultures, 137–139, **139**–140
strategic alliances, 289–294
strategy, 273–274
    acquisitions and alliances, 287–294
    cultural influences, 324–326
    emerging ways of organizing, 298–303
    future of global work, 304
    global business of small enterprises, 294–298
    global integration versus local responsiveness, 276–281, 305
    Global Multi-Products case study, 312–314
    global organizing in MNEs, 281
    multi-divisional structures, 282–287
    organizational alignment, 317–327, 340–342
    primacy of context, 274–276, 304–305, **326**
    tasks-people-structure triangle, 327–333
stretch goals, 21–22
strong cultures, 73–74
sub-cultures, 61
subprime mortgage crash, 17
superstitions, in the Indian workplace, 243–244
supply chains
    choke points, 12–13
    human rights and labor, 451–455
    strategic orientation and alignment, 286–287
sustainability, 418
sustainable development, 418, 421
Sustainable Development Goals (SDGs), 425, 427–429, 437–438
sustainable leadership, 29
sustainable organizations
    circularity, 453
    definitions, 418
    evolution of corporate social responsibility and sustainability, 418–421
    frameworks for, 425–426
    global mindset, **418**
    Global Reporting Initiative (GRI), 429–430
    greenwashing and bluewashing, 431
    net positive companies, 424–425
    purpose of business, 417, 422–423

sustainable organizations (*cont.*)
    relationship between ESG and financial performance, 431–439
    S & P Dow Jones Indices, 430–431
    stakeholder theory, 421–424
    sustainability paradoxes, 436–440
    UN Global Compact, 126–129
    World Wide Fund for Nature (WWF), 205–206
Sustainable Value Framework, 434–436
Swatch Group, alliance with Tiffany, 389–400, 401
system lock-in (SLI) competition, 321–322
systems
    cultural context, 315–317
    global leadership competences, 42
    organizational alignment, 333–340
    organizations as socio-technical systems, 311

T-shaped structures, 285–286
tacit knowledge, 219
TACK framework, 302–303
talent management, 211–216
    C-suite recruitment, 224
    international assignments, 215–222
    international assignments – adaptation and culture shock, 229–232
    international assignments – destinations, 224–225
    international assignments – duty of care, 225–227
    international assignments – returning home, 233–234
    international assignments – training and preparation, 227–229
    mindful global leadership, 212–213
    selection and development, 332
    skill-building, 214–215
    talent-supply gap, 212
    tasks-people-structure triangle, 327–333
    women as global leaders, 222–223
task deliverables, teams working toward, 184
task orientation, cultural differences, 126–128, 141
tasks-people-structure triangle, 327–333, 340–342
Tata group, 288
team growth, 184
teams
    as the basic unit of work and collaboration, 179–180
    coordination across global organizations, 181–182, 204–207
    cultural diversity, 197–199
    design and structure, 185–190
    getting the team basics right, 181–182, 197
    independent vs. interdependent orientation, 128–130
    internal team climate, 190, 193–197
    lateral collaboration, 300
    operations and processes, 190–193, 195–197
    outcomes and goals, 183–185
    remote working, 199–204
    types, 180
technological change
    in market context, 274–276
    organizing for digital transformations, 298–299
technological skills, 215
technology-mediated interaction
    across different language, 177
    choice of technology and performance, 202–203
    Covid-19 pandemic, 74–75
    cross-cultural communication, 172–174
    digital nomads, 218
    implementing IT systems in a global organization, 150–152
    teams working virtually, 199–204
teleological theories (ethics), 466
terrorism, 455–456, 460
Tesco, brick-and-click model, 25
Tiffany, alliance with Swatch, 389–400
tight cultures, 73–74
time zone scheduling, 181, 200, 218
Ting-Toomey, S., 331–332
TJX Companies, 325–326
top management
    Beiersdorf case study, 381
    making organizational changes, 357–358, **363**
    Steelworks' Xiamen plant case study, 252, 255–256
    Swatch case study, 393
    women as global leaders, 222–223
    see also mindful global leadership
total customer solutions (TCS) competition, 321
tracking, team effectiveness, 191
trade
    and globalization, 8
    liberalization across borders, 9
training
    focus of skills-building efforts, 214–215
    international assignments, 227–229
    see also learning

translation, technology-mediated, 173–174, 177
transnational orientation, 280–281
Transparency International, 458–459
triple bottom line, 421
　see also corporate social responsibility
trolley problem (ethics), 467
Trump, Donald, 9
trustworthiness
　TACK framework, 302–303
　team effectiveness, 193–194
　see also integrity

Ukraine, invasion by Russia, 10–11
UN Global Compact, 426–429
uncertainty
　ethical dilemmas, 460–461
　non linear trajectories, 350
　risk orientation, 135–137, 141
Unilever, 424–425
United Kingdom
　recentering example, 159–161
　TJX's launch in, 325–326
United States
　American-Japanese partnership example, 339
　cultural clashes case study, 246–247
　Diglot Capital Management (DCM) case study, 240–249
　recentering example, 159–161
Universal Declaration of Human Rights (UDHR), 470–471
universal theories (ethics), 467–468, 470–474
Uruguay, recentering example, 159–161
utilitarianism, 466

Vaill, P., 117–118
values
　see ethics; integrity; Sustainable Value Framework
variety in global companies
　Ashby's Law of Requisite Variety, 213
　complexity of globalization, 17
video conferencing, 202–203
　see also remote working
virtual teams, 199–204
　see also remote working
volatile, uncertain, complex, and ambiguous (VUCA), 16
VUCA (volatile, uncertain, complex, and ambiguous), 16–17, 276, 349, 365

Walmart, 24, 456
weak cultures, 73–74
Webvan, 24–25
Wells Fargo, 457
Western values, 471–474
"wicked problems", 436–437
Wilde, D., 320–322
women as global leaders, 222–223
work-life balance, 74–75, 218
World Economic Forum (WEF)
　global companies, 14–15
　international trade, 8
　phases of globalization, 8, 10
World Wide Fund for Nature (WWF), 205–206
Worthington Industries, 434

Zappos, 336